D1068364

Longmans' Linguistics Library

In Memory of J. R. Firth

Also in Longmans' Linguistics Library

The Linguistic Sciences and Language Teaching
M. A. K. HALLIDAY, ANGUS McINTOSH AND PETER STREVENS

General Linguistics. An Introductory Survey
R. H. ROBINS

A Linguistic Study of the English Verb
F. R. PALMER

What *is* Language? A New Approach to Linguistic Description
ROBERT M. W. DIXON

IN MEMORY OF

J. R. FIRTH

Edited by

C. E. BAZELL J. C. CATFORD
M. A. K. HALLIDAY R. H. ROBINS

LONGMANS

LONGMANS, GREEN AND CO LTD
48 Grosvenor Street, London W1

Associated companies, branches and representatives throughout the world

First published 1966

Made and printed in Great Britain by
William Clowes and Sons, Limited
London and Beccles

Preface

Professor John Rupert Firth died suddenly on 14th December, 1960, only four years after his retirement from the Chair of General Linguistics in the University of London. It is an irony of history that his death should have occurred just on the eve of an unprecedented expansion of general linguistic studies in this country, an expansion largely due to his untiring efforts and devotion to his subject during his professional life.

Firth's career in linguistics in Great Britain dates from 1928, when, on his return from India, he was appointed to the Department of Phonetics in University College London. In 1938 he moved to the School of Oriental and African Studies, and in 1944 he was appointed to the Chair of General Linguistics, the first chair of that title in this country. His standing in the subject, and his position in the university, enabled him to establish general linguistics as an academic discipline in its own right, accepted among university studies in Great Britain as it had already been accepted in the inter-war years in the United States, through the work of such scholars as Boas, Sapir and Bloomfield. His success can be measured by considering the present position. There are now some ten professors of linguistics, and as many departments of linguistic studies, in British universities; this does not include those whose titles relate to such older established fields as comparative philology, phonetics, and the study of particular languages, and work in general linguistics goes on in several universities under different titles or within other departments. This is by no means the end of the expansion; indeed, its limits are now more likely to be set by the insufficiency of trained personnel than by lack of interest in the subject on the part of universities.

This interest is in great part the result of Firth's enthusiasm and of his wide-ranging coverage of his subject, both in lectures and publications. At least three dominant strands can be traced in his work: his attention to the history of linguistics and its growth in and through the cultural environment of successive generations in India, western antiquity, and modern Europe; the contextual theory of language, whereby meaning, interpreted as function in context, was made the centre of his analysis both of linguistic form and of linguistic function; and prosodic phonology, the first reaction against what appeared at the time as the excessive rigidity of the phoneme theory of the 1940s, encased within the dogmas of separation of levels and biuniqueness of transcription.

Firth as a teacher and colleague was unmatched, and all those who studied under his direction or worked with him owe to him many original insights into the working of language in human society and into the place of linguistics within the sciences of man. He was not, however, it must be admitted, the clearest of writers, and one regrets the absence of a major book from him setting out in full and in detail his standpoint and his methods. He lives best in the work of those whom he inspired and stimulated, and the present volume, dedicated to his memory, is intended as a tribute to him from some of those who, as pupils, colleagues, or associates, at some time fell under his influence.

No directives were given on the subjects to be selected by the authors, but the editors hope that the scope of the topics and languages covered will give some idea of the wide field of linguistic interest that Firth both exhibited himself and fostered in others.

C.E.B.
J.C.C.
M.A.K.H.
R.H.R.

Contents

CONTENTS

Bibliography

THE WRITINGS OF J. R. FIRTH

1929 *Pioneers: Being selected prose for language study*, compiled and edited with notes, glossary and exercises by J.R.Firth and M.G.Singh; pp. ix, 259. London.

1930 *Speech*; pp. 80. London: Benn's Sixpenny Library, No. 121.

1933 Notes on the Transcription of Burmese, *BSOS* 7.137–140.

1934 Linguistics and the Functional Point of View, *English studies* 16.2–8.

The principles of Phonetic Notation in Descriptive Grammar, *Congrès international des sciences anthropologiques et ethnologiques: Compte rendu de la première session* [*à*] *Londres* 325–328.

Sectional Proceedings of the International Congress of Anthropological and Ethnological Sciences, First Session (in) London: Section H, Languages and Writing, *Man* 34.150–152.

A Short Outline of Tamil Pronunciation, appendix xxxiv to A.H.Arden, *A progressive grammar of Tamil.* Madras.

The Word 'Phoneme' *Maître phonétique* 46.44–46.

1935 The Technique of Semantics, *TPS* 36–72.

The Use and Distribution of Certain English Sounds: Phonetics from a Functional Point of View, *English studies* 17.2–12.

1936 Alphabets and Phonology in India and Burma, *BSOS* 8.517–546.

Phonological Features of Some Indian Languages, *Proceedings of the Second International Congress of Phonetic Sciences* [*held at*] *London* [*in*] *1935* 176–182. Cambridge.

1937 The Structure of the Chinese Monosyllable in a Hunanese Dialect (Changsha) [with B.B.Rogers], *BSOS* 8. 1055–1074.

The tongues of men; pp. vii, 160. London.

1938 A Practical Script for India, *Indian listener* 3.356–357.

1939 Specimen: Kashmiri, *Maître phonétique* 68.67–68.

1941 Speech in Fellowship and Community, *The new era in home and school* 22.185–189.

1942 Alphabets for Indian Languages, in Daniel Jones, *The problem of a national script for India* 12–17. Hertford.

1944 Introduction [on pronunciation and the alphabet], in A. H. Harley, *Colloquial Hindustani* ix–xxx. London.

1945 Wartime Experiences in Linguistic Training, *Modern languages* 26.38–45.

1946 The English School of Phonetics, *TPS* 92–132.

1947 The Place of the Spoken Language and the Use of Technical Aids in Language Teaching, *Proceedings of the Sir William Jones Bicentenary Conference* [*held at*] *Oxford* [*in*] *1946* 30–33, 59. London.

1948 The Semantics of Linguistic Science, *Lingua* 1.393–404.
Sounds and Prosodies, *TPS* 127–152.
Word Palatograms and Articulation, *BSOAS* 12.857–864.

1949 Atlantic Linguistics, *Archivum linguisticum* 1.95–116.

1950 Improved Techniques in Palatography and Kymography [with H. J. F. Adam], *BSOAS*, 13.771–774.
Introduction [on spelling and pronunciation], in T. Grahame Bailey, *Teach yourself Hindustani* xi–xli. London.
Personality and Language in Society, *Sociological review* 42.37–52.

1951 General Linguistics and Descriptive Grammar, *TPS* 69–87.
Modes of Meaning, *Essays and studies of the English Association* NS 4. 118–149.

1955 Joseph Wright the Scholar, *Transactions of the Yorkshire Dialect Society* 9.55.22–33.
Structural Linguistics, *TPS* 83–103.

1956 Indian Languages, *Encyclopædia Britannica* s.v.
Introduction [on spelling and pronunciation], in T. Grahame Bailey, *Teach yourself Urdu* xi–xxxix. London.
Linguistic Analysis and Translation, in *For Roman Jakobson: Essays on the occasion of his sixtieth birthday* 133–139. The Hague.
Philology in the Philological Society, *TPS* 1–25.
Plenary Session 1, Linguistics and the Problem of Meaning, Report; Preliminary Remarks on the Report; Comment at the End of the First Session; Concluding Remarks at the End of

the Second Session, *Proceedings of the Seventh International Congress of Linguists* [*held at*] *London* [*in*] *1952* 6–9, 181–185, 202, 230–233. London.

1957 Applications of General Linguistics, *TPS* 1–14.

Ethnographic Analysis and Language with Reference to Malinowski's Views, in R. W. Firth (ed.), *Man and culture: An evaluation of the work of Bronislaw Malinowski* 93–118. London.

Hindustani Language, *Encyclopædia Britannica* s.v.

Papers in linguistics 1934–1951; pp. xii, 233. London.

Phonetic Observations on Gujarati, *BSOAS* 20.231–241.

A Synopsis of Linguistic Theory 1930–1955, in *Studies in linguistic analysis* (special volume of the Philological Society) 1–32. Oxford.

1959 The Treatment of Language in General Linguistics, *Medical press* 242. 146–147.

Linguistics in the Laboratory, *Zeitschrift für Phonetik und allgemeine Sprachwissenschaft* 12. 27–35.

This Bibliography was first published in the *Bulletin of the School of Oriental and African Studies* 24. 417–8 (1961).

Mutation in 'Spoken North Welsh'

K. H. ALBROW

During the time he spent in Edinburgh a year or so before his death, Professor Firth remarked of a seminar of T. Hill—'Rewriting other people's grammars'—that he highly approved of the procedure. It is also by no means unknown that he highly approved of Henry Sweet. It is the object of what follows to combine these two elements, in the sense that what follows is in part a re-writing (though in part a re-investigation) of part of the phonology of the 'Spoken North Welsh' of Sweet's Philological Society paper of that name. It could even be said that it is intended as the *writing* of the phonology of one feature of this speech (if such a statement does not seem too presumptuous in face of the work of such a linguist as Sweet), since no phonological statement is alluded to as such in Sweet's paper, and certainly of course none in the prosodic, polysystemic, grammatical sense that Firth held so strongly to be necessary, and of which this is intended as a tributory example—it is to be hoped a fitting one.

By chance a North Welsh speaker, F. Roberts, has been on the staff of Edinburgh University for the last two years, and has been known to me for about eighteen months. While not coming from Gwynant itself (the area of Sweet's investigation), he does in fact come from only about twenty miles away, from Abersoch, on the coast. While not professing to be an expert on Welsh, and disclaiming all intention to set myself up as one, I have long been interested in this language and the Celtic languages in general and therefore took the opportunity of hearing for myself many of the features referred to by Sweet (not apparently much affected by the distance of twenty miles and eighty-odd years), and at the same time considered the application of the Firthian type of phonological statement particularly to the so-called mutations at word junctions in relation to the grammar of (North) Welsh as far as I am acquainted with it. This article is an attempt at such a statement.

The data of the Welsh of this area is somewhat different from the data of standard literary Welsh, whether orthographic or spoken.

F. Roberts is in the habit of speaking standard Welsh with a Northern accent as his Welsh koine except at home; but confirms Sweet's findings in regard to these differences for his home speech. These differences will be mentioned in their place.

There is no need to explain what is meant by the term mutation. A brief outline of the phonetics of the various mutations will be given in general terms first, using exemplary items for each type of initial affected. At word initial position varying phonetic features occur in relation to various structures both nominal and verbal in the Welsh of this district as elsewhere. The distribution of some of these features can be illustrated from the noun only, in structure with the preceding possessive pronouns və 'my', i 'his', i 'her' and, for 'radical' forms, the noun in isolation, e.g.:

pɛn	*head*	taːd	*father*	kaːθ	*cat*
və mɦɛn	*my head*	və nɦaːd	*my father*	və ŋɦaːθ	*my cat*
i bɛn	*his head*	i daːd	*his father*	i gaːθ	*his cat*
i fɛn	*her head*	i θaːd	*her father*	i χaːθ	*her cat*

braud	*brother*	duːrn	*fist*	gɛnɛθ	*girl*
və mraud	*my brother*	və nuːrn	*my fist*	və ŋɛnɛθ	*my girl*
i vraud	*his brother*	i ðuːrn	*his fist*	i ɛnɛθ	*his girl*
i braud	*her brother*	i duːrn	*her fist*	i gɛnɛθ	*her girl*

mam	*mother*	nain	*grandmother*
və mam	*my mother*	və nain	*my grandmother*
i vam	*his mother*	i nain	*his grandmother*
i mɦam	*her mother*	i nɦain	*her grandmother*

ɬɔŋ	*ship*	rɦɔːð	*gift*
və ɬɔŋ	*my ship*	və rɦɔːð	*my gift*
i lɔŋ	*his ship*	i rɔːð	*his gift*
i ɬɔŋ	*her ship*	i rɦɔːð	*her gift*

lamp	*lamp*	rɨban	*ribbon*
və lamp	*my lamp*	və rɨban	*my ribbon*
i lamp	*his lamp*	i rɨban	*his ribbon*
i lɦamp	*her lamp*	i rɦɨban	*her ribbon*

vinɛgr	*vinegar*
və vinɛgr	*my vinegar*
i vinɛgr	*his vinegar*
i vɦinɛgr	*her vinegar*

jaiθ	*language*	wats	*watch*
və jaiθ	*my language*	və wats	*my watch*
i jaiθ	*his language*	i wats	*his watch*
i ɦjaiθ	*her language*	i ɦwats	*her watch*

avaɫ	*apple*
və avaɫ	*my apple*
i avaɫ	*his apple*
i ɦavaɫ	*her apple*

It is customary to speak of four mutations over-all in relation to the variations of word-initial consonants which occur, but to find all four of them only under [p] [t] and [k], since the consonants after [i] 'her' for [b, d, g] are phonetically the same as those in the group with noun only, and for [m, n] the same after [və] 'my'. For [ɬ], [rɦ], [l], [r], [v], [j], [w] and vowel there are also less variations in these structures, and for other consonants none. These last will not be said to enter into mutation, but it seems more profitable for the others, even including [n], [ɬ], [rɦ], etc., to postulate entry into mutation at all points; even where exponents of some phonological terms set up to handle the mutations are the same for more than one structure. This is the first point.

The type of phonological analysis proposed here is of course in terms of 'sounds and prosodies'. A phonemic account of the phenomenon under discussion would be in terms of change of initial consonant of a particular word, so that 'the word "head"' for instance would appear as say pen, mhen, ben, or fen, according to context. Further, braud 'brother' for example would have the same initial consonant as the above-mentioned ben of i ben '*his* head', and so on. This is of course one approach, and the relationship pen/ben on the one hand and braud/vraud on the other can be handled separately under some sort of morphophonemic statement. The analysis proposed here expressly by-passes the phonemic type of statement and relates sound (through phonetics) to grammatical structure (in this case pronoun-noun or noun), making the statement in such terms incidentally that the phonematic unity of the word (noun) under consideration is preserved, the variations at the phonetic level being handled prosodically. The advantage of this type of phonological analysis has been pointed out before,[1] together with the advantage for linguistic statement of the ability to stress the permanent in the varying structures, generalizing, as Firth expressed it, above the phonematic level prosodically the phonetic features associated with these structures. Statement follows.

1. *Plosive words*

It is clear from a comparison of [pɛn] with [və mɦɛn], [i bɛn], [i fɛn]; [taːd] with [və nɦaːd], etc. and [kaːθ] with [və ŋɦaːθ] etc., that each set has a common feature,[2] namely labiality, dentality and velarity. It is also clear that [pɛn], [və mɦɛn], [i bɛn], [i fɛn] are related to each other as plosive, nasal, plosive with voice, and fricative, and that there is a comparable relationship between other initials in plosive words (and also, as maintained below, between other initials in non-plosive words too). It is further clear from a comparison of [pɛn] with [braud], [və mɦɛn] with [və mraud] etc. that these are opposed at all points, either as 'aspirated' to 'unaspirated', or as plosive to fricative. This is true for dental and velar places of articulation too, except that with velar initials the opposition with [i] 'his' is phonetic plosive—zero ([i ɛnɛθ]), not plosive—fricative. This will not affect the phonological parallelism, however.

These, then, are the phonetic details with which I am concerned in these forms. If now a four-term junction system is set up for these forms (again, this system will be shown to be applicable to non-plosive words as well) as R (radical), N, S, H, to handle the structural relation in noun and pronoun-noun structures, and a two-term system, as h, h̄, to handle the oppositions [pɛn]/[braud] etc., [taːd]/[duːrn] etc., the various types of junction feature can be generalized as below:

^{Rh}pɛn	^{Rh}taːd	^{Rh}kaːθ
və ^{Nh} ,,	və ^{Nh} ,,	və ^{Nh} ,,
i ^{Sh} ,,	i ^{Sh} ,,	i ^{Sh} ,,
i ^{Hh} ,,	i ^{Hh} ,,	i ^{Hh} ,,
'*brawd*'	'*dwrn*'	'*geneth*'
$^{\mathrm{R\bar{h}}}$praud	$^{\mathrm{R\bar{h}}}$tuːrn	$^{\mathrm{R\bar{h}}}$kɛnɛθ
və $^{\mathrm{N\bar{h}}}$,,	və $^{\mathrm{N\bar{h}}}$,,	və $^{\mathrm{N\bar{h}}}$,,
i $^{\mathrm{S\bar{h}}}$,,	i $^{\mathrm{S\bar{h}}}$,,	i $^{\mathrm{S\bar{h}}}$,,
(= [i vraud])	(= [i ðuːrn])	(= [i ɛnɛθ])
i $^{\mathrm{H\bar{h}}}$,,	i $^{\mathrm{H\bar{h}}}$,,	i $^{\mathrm{H\bar{h}}}$,,
(= [i braud])	(= [i duːrn])	(= [i gɛnɛθ])

It is to be noted in the case of h̄ words that [b], [d] and [g] of [i braud], [i duːrn], [i gɛnɛθ] are regarded as H (traditionally 'aspirate') mutations of $^{\bar{h}}$p/t/k, even though phonetically comparable to the R forms with these initials. This preserves the parallelism with h initials—and in any case the stops are almost certainly only comparable, not absolutely identical, in the two different environments.

2. *Nasal words*

Similar considerations apply here, and it is possible to generalize in precisely comparable terms, the types of junction-feature being generalized as below again (all nasal words are h̄):

$^{R\bar{h}}$mam	$^{R\bar{h}}$nain
və $^{N\bar{h}}$,,	və $^{N\bar{h}}$,,
i $^{S\bar{h}}$,, (= [i vam])	i $^{S\bar{h}}$,, (= [i nain])
i $^{H\bar{h}}$,, [3](= [i mɦam])	i $^{H\bar{h}}$,, [3](= [i nɦain])

It is to be noted once again that the same (or comparable!) phonetic elements, [m], [n] are analysed as phonologically different in relation to the structures in which they occur. Incidentally, no velar initial occurs with nasality.

3. *Liquid words*

Again similar considerations apply, junction features being generalized as below (liquid words occur with both h and h̄)

'llong'	'rhôdd'
^{Rh}ləŋ	^{Rh}rɔːð
və ^{Nh} ,,	və ^{Nh} ,,
i ^{Sh} ,, (= [i ləŋ])	i ^{Sh} ,, (= [i rɔːð])
i ^{Hh} ,, (= [i ɬəŋ])	i ^{Hh} ,, (= [i rɦɔːð])
'lamp'	'ruban'
$^{R\bar{h}}$lamp	$^{R\bar{h}}$rɨban
və $^{N\bar{h}}$,,	və $^{N\bar{h}}$,,
i $^{S\bar{h}}$,, (= [i lamp])	i $^{S\bar{h}}$,, (= [i rɨban])
i $^{H\bar{h}}$,, [4](= [i lɦamp])	i $^{H\bar{h}}$,, [4](= [i rɦɨban])

Once again it is to be noted that the same junction prosodies have been used at the same points, even when the phonetic exponents are not the most obvious. This has been done in the interests of the most general uniformity. It is not then difficult to accept that e.g. the exponent of l and r with N is oral, not nasal, or that the exponent of S is voiced in each case. This simply becomes a fact about liquid initials and S. It may be noted that all h̄ liquid words are foreign in origin.

4. *Fricative words*

Similar considerations apply here again, the phonetics of words like the following being exactly parallel to that of h̄ liquid initials. Only h̄ words occur here, since h fricative words do not mutate (e.g. 'ffenestr'). Features are as below:

Rh̄vinɛgr
və Nh̄ „
i Sh̄ „ (= [i vinɛgr])
i Hh̄ „ [4](= [i vɦinɛgr])

(Again the word is of foreign origin.)

5. *Vocalic words*

These are again comparable to the preceding types of word. Their features may be generalized as below:

Rh̄jaiθ	Rh̄aval	Rh̄wats
və Nh̄ „	və Nh̄ „	və Nh̄ „
i Sh̄ „ (= [i jaiθ])	i Sh̄ „ (= [i avaɬ])	i Sh̄ „ (= [i wats])
i Hh̄ „ [5](= [i ɦjaiθ])	i Hh̄ „ (= [i ɦavaɬ])	i Hh̄ „ [5](= [i ɦwats])

Note: From another point of view, [jaiθ] is y, [avaɬ] ə and [wats] w prosodic within vocalic words. This does not concern us here, but is the reason why they are grouped together. This is convenient because phonetically they are parallel particularly in the 3rd person feminine structure, differing on the whole at this point from the preceding types. It is interesting to note once again that h̄ liquid, fricative and now w vowel words are all of foreign origin; their phonetic exponents in mutation follow the pattern of the native (h̄) n-nasal words.

Thus h, ḣ are associated with word beginning throughout; R, N, S, H with noun, first person pronoun-noun, third masculine pronoun-noun, third feminine pronoun-noun structures respectively. Exponents of h are all voiceless or aspirated, except with S, when exponents are voiced (see S). Exponents of h̄ are all voiced.

Exponents of R are in keeping with the nature of initial C or V. Exponents of N are nasality with plosive and nasal initials, orality with all others. Exponents of S are voice with h words, friction with orality with h̄ plosives, m and fricatives, in keeping with the nature of initial C or V with h̄ nasals, liquids and vowels. Exponents of H are friction with orality with h plosives, plosivity with h̄ plosives, voicelessness or aspiration with h liquids and vowels, aspiration with h̄ nasals, liquids, fricatives and vowels.

Consonants are p, t, k, m, n, l, r, v.

As stated at the beginning I am not an expert in Welsh, and it is realized that this is not the whole story. Rather these few structures have been selected to illustrate an approach in linguistic analysis. The resultant statement is designed to emphasize the patterning behind the variations in the exponents of the structures and systems set up. As stated, verbal and other grammatical structures show similar phonological structures and systems, though these are not mentioned here.

It may be worth pointing out that under this statement there is no phonological correspondence between e.g. the [f]s of [i fɛn] 'her head' and say [i fɛnɛstr] 'her window', the first being ^{Hh}p—and the second ^{h}f, or more probably ^{h}v (since the [v] of [vinɛgr] has already been called $^{(\bar{h})}$v rather than f). ([fɛnɛstr] is of course unmutated). It may also be worth pointing out that Welsh orthography can be said to be similarly 'prosodic' at this point (though not everywhere), writing 'ei *ph*en', for the first, 'ei *ff*enestr' for the second. This seems to me to be sound linguistics, whatever the historical reason for this spelling, since though phonetically the same they have quite different statuses in the language. Such prosodic, polysystemic features of orthography are more common I think than is sometimes admitted, and the Firthian approach not so strange as is sometimes suggested. Be that as it may, this is certainly how I see this approach applied to the Welsh data here selected. Though the statement here might appear somewhat extreme in certain respects, it is I think in general such as would be associated with the name of J.R.Firth in British linguistics.

Notes

[1] R.K.Sprigg: "Junction in Spoken Burmese," *Studies in Linguistic Analysis.* (Special Volume of the Philological Society, Oxford, 1957) pp. 104–138.

[2] See the article by T.Hill in this volume.

[3] These are the forms which deviate from literary Welsh.

[4] Again forms which deviate from literary Welsh.

[5] Again forms which deviate from literary Welsh.

A Problem of Greek Accentuation

W. S. ALLEN

The term 'prosody' is one which appears with a characteristic function and frequency in the writings of J. R. Firth;[1] and whilst it there acquires a breadth of meaning more akin to its Alexandrian than to its recently familiar usage, Firth was also well aware of its classical source as referring to the tonal accent of ancient Greek (*προσῳδία*). A consideration of certain details of the Greek tonal system is therefore perhaps appropriate to this volume.

The problem concerns the significance of the 'grave' accent-mark as it is found in our current texts. So far as the spoken language was concerned, the Greeks themselves distinguished a high tone which they term *ὀξύς* ('sharp', 'acute') and a low tone which they termed *βαρύς* ('heavy', 'grave'). The high tone was the culminative accentual feature in the sense of occurring once and only once in every full word, and as such was sometimes referred to as the *κύριος τόνος*, 'tone proper', whereas the low tone was termed *συλλαβικός*, i.e. 'inherent in the syllable'.

The use of accent-marks is not a feature of our earliest records; it may well have arisen partly as a result of a decline in the oral tradition of epic poetry (so that Greek speakers themselves required guidance in the pronunciation of unfamiliar forms), and partly from the needs of teaching Greek as a foreign language. The traditional accent-marks seem in fact to have been invented at Alexandria around 200 B.C. At first, to judge from papyri, they were used sporadically and mostly to resolve ambiguities; but subsequent extensions and modifications in their use led eventually to the system as we now know it.[2]

In one of the early transitional systems the practice was to indicate every tone by its appropriate symbol (e.g. *Θὲόδὼρὸς*); in the papyri we also find a system which marks grave accents only where they precede an acute (e.g. *φὶλὴσὶστέφανον*), and in some cases an expected final acute accent-mark may be omitted (e.g. *πὰγκρὰτης*). Such systems were clearly uneconomical, and were later replaced by the current (Byzantine) system whereby only high tones are indicated (with the acute mark or, if the high tone is on the first mora[3] of a long vowel or a diphthong, with the circumflex); where, however, an acute mark might be expected on a *final* syllable, it is replaced by a grave—except in the case of interrogatives or when followed by an enclitic or a pause (thus e.g. ἀγαθός τε, ἔστιν ἀγαθός· but ἀγαθὸς ταμίας). This is in fact the only circumstance in which the grave mark is used.

It is clear that the exceptions (where the final acute mark, and presumably high tone, are preserved) are inherently special cases; pre-pausal environment and interrogation are liable to involve special features of clause or sentence intonation; and since an enclitic in Greek forms a single accentual unit with the preceding full word, the syllable in question is not final. The problem is presented by those cases where the final is in fact marked grave—the so-called 'enclinomena'.

There have been various hypotheses about the accentual nature of such final syllables.[4] It has been held that the grave mark has no special significance and that they carried a normal high tone; that the tonal accent was replaced by a stress; or that the high tone was reduced to an intermediate level; and many scholars have accepted what appears to be suggested by the marking[5] (as also by some of the grammarians' statements, though these are less precise than we could wish), that there was a complete neutralization of the accentual opposition in favour of the low tone.[6]

There seems little to support the first two views; the fact that in Modern Greek such syllables bear a stress accent no less than those marked acute or circumflex, is not necessarily relevant, since it could well be explained as a generalization of the pre-pausal forms. The choice, then, lies between a lowered variant of the high tone,[7] and a low tone. The former receives some support from the music of the Delphic hymn-fragments, in which the grave-marked syllables are almost never set to a lower note than any other syllable in the word, nor, on the other hand, to a higher note than the first syllable or the high-toned syllable of the following word.[8] The musical treatment could admittedly represent an artificial compromise in the direction of the pre-pausal form;[9] but we shall provisionally adopt the interpretation which it seems to support, viz. that the syllables marked grave bore a lowered variant of the high tone rather than an actual low tone. As between the two possible interpretations this requires the more complex explanatory hypothesis, which we shall now attempt to provide.

The Greek accent is traditionally conceived as consisting essentially of the culminative high tone, the remainder of the word having automatically low tones and so being structurally irrelevant. But in the closely related Vedic system we know that in addition the pre-tonic syllable carried a specially low variant of the low tone, and the post-tonic syllable carried a high-to-low glide variant;[10] in fact in the *RigVeda* it is the pre- and post-tonics that are marked, the high tone itself being unmarked (thus e.g. *agnínā* appears as *a̲gninā̀*).

So far as the post-tonic glide is concerned, there is evidence that a similar phenomenon occurred in Greek; for in the musical fragments, 'when a long unaccented vowel was sung on two notes, there was a tendency . . . in the case of those following an accented syllable to make the first the higher'.[11] Moreover, in Greek as well as Vedic, when a syllable contained a long vowel or a diphthong, i.e. a two-mora nucleus, the high tone and the falling glide could both occur within that one syllable, and this complex received special notice by the Greek writers; it is in fact such syllables which are marked with the 'circumflex' sign.

In Aristotle's enumeration of the Greek tones,[12] the 'complex tone' appears not to be specially mentioned; this would be understandable in so far as it was simply a combination of the high tone with a variant of the low. What Aristotle, and several other writers, do, however, mention is an otherwise unidentified μέσος, 'middle' tone. Grammont may be right in identifying this with the glide which formed the second part of the complex;[13] but it might also refer to the glide on the syllable following a high tone;[14] and it is not impossible that the term might in fact have included the 'complex tone' as a whole,[15] which from a phonetic point of view was probably similar to the glide on a long vowel or diphthong in the syllable following a high tone. The Indians in fact use the same term '*svarita*' (and the written texts use the same symbol) for both the comparable phenomena in Vedic;[16] the Delphic hymns also show a similar treatment of both.

One might therefore envisage the Greek accent as comprising not simply the high tone but a more extended 'contonation' (to use a Firthian term)[17] including both the high tone and the following fall; we have seen that a syllable marked with the circumflex did in fact contain this combination within itself.[18] The importance of the falling glide as an integral part of the accent is further indicated by the rule of enclisis whereby a high tone may not be immediately followed by another high tone[19] (thus e.g. ἄνθρωποί τινες, δῶρόν ἐστιν, but μεγάλοι τινές, *not* μεγάλοί τινες). For an accentuation such as the latter would deprive the full word *μεγάλοι* of the falling glide which is part of its characteristic accent—and full words normally preserve their accent in enclisis.

The full operation of such an accentual system is dependent upon conditions which do in fact prevail in Vedic and may well be Indo-European. In Vedic the elements of the 'contonation' may extend across word-boundaries; thus in a sequence such as *rayím aśnavat póṣam* the pre- and post-tonic elements are distributed as follows (as shown by the *RV* markings): *r̲ayim àśnava̲t poṣàm.* Here the initial syllable of the second (unaccented) word carries the post-tonic glide from the high-toned final of the first, and its final syllable carries the pre-tonic low for the high-toned initial of the third. But in Greek the word developed a more autonomous phonological status than in Vedic,[20] involving a clearer demarcation between 'close' and 'open' juncture (in the sense of generally typifying transitions respectively within and across word-boundaries);[21] the effect of consonant-groups on quantity, for example, shows marked differences in the two cases.[22] There was no need in Greek (as there was in Vedic) of a special '*pada*' (word-isolate) tradition[23] in order to ensure correct word-division in the transmission of oral texts.

There was an exception to this autonomy in the case of enclitics—which formed a phonological unity with the preceding full word; so that in a sequence such as *ἀγαθός ἐστιν* the first syllable of the enclitic *ἐστιν* could in fact carry the post-tonic falling glide. But an accentuation *ἀγαθός βασιλεύς* would involve the glide being carried by the initial syllable of a following full word, i.e. the extension of the terminal part of the contonation across a word-boundary. This, we propose, would have been contrary to Greek junctural principles (being characteristic of close and not open juncture), and it is here that the original 'contonational' system, as preserved in Vedic, would have broken down in Greek. On the assumption that a high tone could not be followed by a low without a transitional glide, the situation could be resolved only by a lowering of the final high tone and/or a raising of the initial low to the extent that left the initial no lower than the final; the conditions requiring a falling glide would thus be removed.

One point, however, would still require explanation. If the second word begins with a high tone, it is not immediately clear why a high-toned final should be lowered (e.g. *ἀγαθὸς ἄνθρωπος* or *καλὸν δῶρον*)—for no fall in pitch would be involved in any case. This difficulty could be met only by assuming that, except in post-pausal position, a high tone required a lower pitch to precede it. This, as we have seen, is suggested by the marking system (as also by contemporary phonetic statements) of the *RV*; it is further indicated by the tonal sandhi of the *Śatapatha-Brāhmaṇa*, whereby a high tone followed by a high tone is reduced to a low.[24] This could be an original IE feature, and so inherited by Greek; it would, however, imply that Greek had here maintained a pre-tonic feature across the word-boundary, whereas it had eschewed this post-tonically. It was in fact Meillet's opinion that the Greek lowering of final high tones originated in just this environment, and was only subsequently transferred by analogy to the environment before low-toned initials.[25]

The above hypotheses are of some complexity, but this seems inevitable if one accepts the evidence of the musical inscriptions at its face value, and declines to follow Meillet in postulating an analogical extension. If, however, one minimizes the musical evidence, and assumes a complete neutralization in final position, a considerably less complex hypothesis can be made. One would assume simply that a high tone cannot occur without a following falling glide; and that consequently, when such a glide is precluded, viz. after a word-boundary, so also is the high tone. Such a hypothesis would be simpler than Meillet's in this case, since it would not involve any analogical assumptions.

An explanation not unlike this was offered as long ago as 1876 (as Tronskij has recently noted[26]) by the Slavist L. Masing,[27] who suggested that the sequences of syllables preceding and following a high tone in Greek carried respectively a rising and a falling 'Stimmbewegung', and that these movements were delimited by the word-boundaries. Thus a final high tone would be impossible before another full word, since it would imply an immediately following falling pattern, whereas the following word would in fact begin with either a rising pattern or another high tone.

Finally it may be mentioned that the 'contonational' view of the Greek accent here proposed incidentally provides the possibility of a very simple statement regarding the limits of recessive accentuation in Attic. The traditional statements of this are more than a little involved: e.g. 'The acute may stand on any of the last three syllables, the circumflex only on the last or last but one. But the acute cannot stand on the last but two, nor the circumflex on the last but one, unless the vowel of the last is short'.[28]

A considerable simplification is possible by introducing the concept of the *mora*—resulting in Jakobson's formulation:[29] 'The span between the accented and the final mora cannot exceed one syllable'. By introducing the further concept of a *contonation* which includes the post-tonic falling glide, one may reduce the statement to an even more concise and perhaps more rational form,[30] viz.: 'Not more than one mora may follow the contonation'.

Notes

1 See especially J.R. Firth, 'Sounds and Prosodies', *TPS* 1948, pp. 127 ff.

2 For a concise summary of the various systems see E. Sclwyzer, *Griechische Grammatik* I (Beck, München, 1938/53/59), pp. 373 ff.

3 On the mora concept see especially R. Jakobson, 'Die Betonung und ihre Rolle in der Wort- und Syntagmaphonologie', *TCLP* IV (1931), pp. 164 ff.

4 See e.g. I. M. Tronskij, *Drevnegrečeskoe udarenie* (Akad. Nauk, Moscow–Leningrad, 1962), p. 75.

5 In some early papyri such syllables are in fact left unmarked (cf. E. H. Sturtevant, *Pronunciation of Greek and Latin*2 (Ling. Soc. of America, Philadelphia, 1940), p. 100); and in the current system the grave could simply have the function of showing the *potentially* tonic nature of the syllable.

6 E.g. J. Vendryes, *Traité d'accentuation grecque* (Klincksieck, Paris, 1938), pp. 39 ff. Cf. R. Jakobson, *Selected Writings* I (Mouton, 's Gravenhage, 1962), p. 264 ('On Ancient Greek Prosody', = 'Z zagadnień prozodji starogreckiej', in *Z zagadnień poetyki: Prace ofiarowane K. Wóycickiemu*, Wilno, 1937).

7 The fact that some papyri mark, and some grammarians appear to prescribe, an acute accent, is no argument against its being a lowered variant of that accent (cf. Sturtevant, loc. cit.).

8 Cf. J. Wackernagel, *Rheinisches Museum* 51 (1896), p. 305; R. P. Winnington-Ingram, *Symbolae Osloenses* 31 (1955), pp. 66 f. This does not, however, mean that we should equate this variant with the 'middle accent' of the grammarians (cf. Sturtevant, loc. cit.).

9 Cf. Vendryes, op. cit., pp. 41 f; A. Meillet, *MSL* 20 (1918), p. 167.

10 Cf. W. S. Allen, *Phonetics in Ancient India* (O.U.P., London, 1953/61), pp. 87 ff.

11 R. L. Turner, *CR*. xxix (1915), p. 196.

12 *Poet*. 1456 b; cf. *Rhet*. 1403 b.

13 *Phonétique du grec ancien* (I.A.C., Lyon, 1948), p. 388.

14 Cf. F. Blass, *Pronunciation of Ancient Greek*, trsl. Purton (Cambridge, 1890), p. 133.

15 Cf. H. M. Hoenigswald, 'Media, Neutrum und Zirkumflex', *Festschrift A. Debrunner* (Francke, Bern, 1954), pp. 209 ff; Vendryes, op. cit., p. 44. A scholium on Dionysius Thrax (ed. Hilgard: Teubner, Leipzig, 1901, p. 136.18) does in fact make this identification.

16 In some Vedic texts an 'independent *svarita*', i.e. complex tone (but regularly indicated by the grave-sign), becomes 'dependent' by generating an acute on the preceding syllable; thus the contraction of *evá* + *etád* gives *evàitád*, whence (in the ŚatapathaBrāhmaṇa) *évaitád*. This would be parallel to the development in Attic Greek known as 'Vendryes' Law', whereby e.g. ἑτοῖμος becomes ἕτοιμος.

17 Cf. A. E. Sharp, 'A tonal analysis of the disyllabic noun in the Machame dialect of Chaga', *BSOAS* xvi.1 (1954), p. 164.

[18] Cf. also J. Kuryłowicz, *L'accentuation des langues indo-européennes*[2] (Polska Akad. Nauk, Wrocław, 1958), p. 107.

[19] On the doubtful exception of 'synenclisis' (sequence of enclitics) see e.g. Vendryes, op. cit., pp. 87 ff.

[20] Note particularly the tendency to generalize a single morphophonological variant—e.g. the loss of final stops in all environments (probably originating in prepausal position: the original distribution is preserved only in οὐκ and ἐκ, which are closely connected with the following word).

[21] Cf. the discussions of the scholia on Dionysius (e.g. p. 156 Hilgard); also H. Ehrlich, *KZ* xxxix (1906), pp. 583 f. (from which it appears that whilst a final consonant was in open juncture with an initial vowel, the consonant before an elided vowel was in close juncture with the initial).

[22] See e.g. P. Maas, *Greek Metre*, trsl. Lloyd-Jones (Oxford, 1962), p. 77.

[23] Cf. Allen, op. cit., pp. 19 f. (the Atharvaveda-Prātiśākhya, iv. 107, comments: 'The study of the word-isolates is designed to teach the beginnings and ends of words, and their correct form, tone and meaning').

[24] Cf. J. Wackernagel, *Altindische Grammatik* I (Vandenhoeck & Ruprecht, Göttingen, 1896), § 252.

[25] *MSL* 13 (1905), pp. 245 ff.

[26] Op. cit., p. 76.

[27] *Die Hauptformen des serbisch-chorwatischen Accents* (*Mém. de l'Acad. Imp. des Sciences de St. Pétersbourg*, ser. 7, vol. xxiii, no. 5), pp. 36 ff.

[28] E. A. Sonnenschein, *Greek Grammar*[13] (Kegan Paul, London, 1929), p. 132.

[29] *Selected Writings* I, p. 263.

[30] Outwardly more rational in so far as it does not make reference to syllabic criteria in an otherwise mora-based system. The syllabic element has admittedly been included in the definition of the 'contonation'; but as a result of our associating it with the post-tonic glide, it is possible to relegate it to phonetic rather than phonological status—by making the phonetically plausible assumption that in Greek a fall automatically terminates at the end, and never in the middle, of a syllabic nucleus; and that this is the reason for the accentual equivalence of e.g. φέρομεν and φέρωμεν.

The Verb in Spoken Tamil

R. E. ASHER

This paper is an examination of the verbal forms of colloquial Tamil and a classification of verbs on the basis of certain phonological features of the 'stem', both phonematic and prosodic. The relevant phonematic units, with few exceptions, are those in 'stem' final position. The relevant prosodies are those of the syllable structure of the 'stem' and those relating to features of junction of 'stem' and suffix. Details of the phonological analysis are given only when relevant to a discussion of the morphology.

A complete paradigm of all the possible forms of a given Tamil verb would number well over a hundred items, if one takes into account 'positive' and 'negative' forms, 'simple' tenses and 'compound' tenses, 'finite' and 'non-finite' forms. It is, however, accepted, that most of these can be predicted if one knows only a few of the positive, finite forms. In fact the analysis presented here would seem to show that, once a division into two classes is made, it is sufficient to know the phonological shape of the stem in order to be able to predict any verbal form. Accordingly the forms examined here are restricted to positive, finite, simple tense forms.

Forms cited are from the speech of Mr. Rama Subbiah, a first generation Malayan immigrant from the Trichinopoly district of South India. They have, however, been checked against material gathered in the field in 1955–56 from a number of speakers in the North Arcot District and in Madras. Those in the latter group included both residents of the city of long standing and speakers whose homes, like Rama Subbiah's, were in the central districts of Madras State. The forms will be found to be representative of the speech of large numbers of people in the central and north-eastern parts of the Tamil-speaking region of India. Nevertheless it is not considered by the present writer that there is adequate evidence at this stage to allow us to speak of the existence of 'Standard Colloquial Tamil'.[1]

A further note is necessary on what is meant by 'spoken' Tamil. The utterances of educated Tamilians may readily be divided into 'reading style' and 'colloquial style'. The former is the language of formal written prose or that used, in the majority of cases, in public speaking, broadcasting, classroom teaching and so on. The latter is the language of ordinary conversation. These two styles would appear to require separate statements at all levels—phonetic, phonological, grammatical or lexical. Until recent years most analyses of Tamil have, be it tacitly or explicitly, dealt with the 'reading style'.[2] So, too, have teaching courses and grammars, including one called *Spoken Tamil.*[3] In the present paper 'spoken Tamil' is to be taken as referring exclusively to the colloquial style.

The transcription used, which has much in common with the conventions of the Tamil writing system,[4] whilst not being intended to represent a symbolization of a statement of the phonology, will make it clear to a reader with a knowledge of Tamil, that the phonological analysis does not take into account words of foreign origin. The reasons are twofold. Firstly it is accepted here, as Professor Firth suggested in a number of contexts,[5] that loanwords in Tamil are best handled at the phonological level as belonging to separate systems from that profitably set up for native words. Secondly, loans, common enough among nouns, are extremely rare among verbs. An overall phonemic statement for Tamil would give a very false picture of the structure of the verb.[6]

A few notes on the general interpretation of the transcription follow.[7] Where necessary, more precise values will be stated in I.P.A. terms and bracketed.

1. **y** (not **j**) is used for the palatal semi-vowel.
2. **v** is a labio-dental frictionless continuant.
3. 'Plosive' symbols: **k, c, ṭ, t, p**. Double letters, which occur medially, represent a 'tense' voiceless plosive—not necessarily 'doubled' in impressionistic phonetic terms; **-cc-** is an affricate. Single letters in word initial position represent a voiceless plosive (in the case of **c**, [s] or [tʃ]). Medially, between vowels or between a vowel and **r** or **n**, they are realized as a voiced plosive or as a voiced or voiceless fricative, i.e. they have the feature of 'laxness' as opposed to the 'tenseness' associated with their pronunciation when double. In homorganic nasal/plosive complexes a voiced plosive is implied (in the case of **c**, [dʒ]). **t** is dental.
4. When other consonants—nasals, laterals, semi-vowels—occur as geminates, the implication at the phonetic level will be that of greater duration than in the case of single consonants.

5. **r** is a tapped alveolar consonant. In the consonant groups **ɳr, lr** and **ɭr** there is a cessation of nasality or of laterality before the onset of the **r**. A narrow phonetic transcription would therefore be [ɳɖr], [ldr] and [ɭɖr].

6. **ɽ** is a retroflex voiced frictionless continuant.

7. Final nasal consonants in the transcription imply not consonant articulation, but nasalization of the vowel of the last syllable. They are an indication, too, of the prosodies of juncture.[8]

8. For other consonants the conventions of the I.P.A. will be an adequate guide. The full list of consonant symbols used is: **k, c, ʈ, t, p, ŋ, ɲ, ɳ, n, m, y, v, r, l, ɭ, ɽ.**

9. Vowels. Five short and five long: **i, ii, e, ee, a, aa, o, oo, u, uu. u** in word-final position does not have the feature of lip-rounding. Syllables containing what is phonetically a front-closing diphthong will have a vowel symbol followed by **y**.

A discussion of the verb or verbal piece in Tamil cannot avoid consideration of the pronominals, and a brief account of these will be given first. Nouns and pronominals are sub-classes of the category of nominals. Pronominals are further sub-divided into (1) demonstrative pronouns and (2) pronouns of the first and second person.

1. Demonstrative pronouns fall into the further category of 'deictics'. 'Deictics' form a three-term system, the exponents of which are initial **i-, a-, e-** in a number of groups of three words, the words of each group being identical apart from this initial vowel. Examples are: **ippa** 'now', **appa** 'then', **eppa** 'when'; **iŋke** 'here', **aŋke** 'there', **eŋke** 'where'.[9] Similarly among the pronominals: **ivan** 'he' ('this man'), **avan** 'he' ('that man'), **evan** 'who' ('which man'). For the sake of economy the convention of citing only the second term of the three, when discussing nominal/verbal concord, will be followed in giving examples of pronominal forms. Thus we have **avan, ava, avaru, avaŋka, atu.**

2. **naan, namma, naaŋka, nii, niiŋka.**

The pronominals are regularly colligated with verbal forms in two-word noun + verb complexes as follows:

naan	**naʈakkaran**
namma	**naʈakkaroom**
naaŋka	**naʈakkaroom**
nii	**naʈakkare**
niiŋka	**naʈakkariiŋka**
avan	**naʈakkaraan**

ava	**naṭakkaraa**
avaru	**naṭakkaraaru**
avaŋka	**naṭakkaraaŋka**
atu	**naṭakkutu**

There are thus nine verbal forms.[10] Eight of these are regularly colligated with eight of the pronominal forms in complementary distribution. The ninth is colligated with either **namma** or **naaŋka**, but with no other.

As for nouns in general, the category of singular/plural is established for pronouns. The exponent of plurality is **-CCa**, where CC is a homorganic nasal + plosive or a long nasal. A further category of person is set up. Formal justification is found in the phonematic shape of the first syllable of pronominal forms. The various terms of these categories are named for the purpose of reference: 'first person singular', 'first person plural (inclusive)',[11] 'first person plural (exclusive)', 'second person singular', 'second person plural', 'third person singular (masculine)', 'third person singular (feminine)', 'third person singular (honorific)', 'third person plural (masculine and feminine)', and 'third person neuter'. It should be noted that the correspondence between grammatical number and the notion of 'oneness' or 'plurality' is not one-to-one. For example, **avaŋka vantaaŋka** 'they came' may also mean 'he' (or 'she') 'came'—with respect for the person spoken of being implied.

Positive finite verb forms in Tamil are susceptible in most instances to ready segmentation into three parts, namely 'stem' (here **naṭa** 'walk'), 'tense infix' (here **-kkar-**) and 'personal ending'. Personal endings are the same for all tenses of all verbs, with the exception of the third person neuter.[12] It is because of the frequency of the possibility of segmentation of this sort that Tamil has been classified as an 'agglutinative' language.

Juncture prosodies are set up for the pronominals and for the personal endings as outlined in the following table. C and V represent the generalized phonematic elements[13] and small superscript letters the prosodies.

	Pronominals		*Personal endings*	
1st pers. sing.	**naan**	CVV^n	**-an**	$-V^n$
1st pers. pl. (incl.)	**namma**	$CVCCV^r$	**-oom** (incl. and excl.)	$-VV^n$
1st pers. pl. (excl.)	**naaŋka**	$CVVCCV^r$		
2nd pers. sing.	**nii**	CVV^y	**-e**	$-V^y$
2nd pers. pl.	**niiŋka**	$CVVCCV^r$	**-iiŋka**	$-VVCCV^r$
3rd pers. sing. (masc.)	**avan**	VCV^n	**-aan**	$-VV^n$
3rd pers. sing. (fem.)	**ava**	VCV^r	**-aa**	$-VV^r$

	Pronominals		*Personal endings*	
3rd pers. sing. (hon.)	**avaru**	$VCVC^{w}$	**-aaru**	$-VVC^{w}$
3rd pers. pl. (m./f.)	**avaŋka**	$VCVCCV^{r}$	**-aaŋka**	$-VVCCV^{r}$
3rd pers. neuter	**atu**	VC^{w}	**-utu**	$-VC^{w}$

Phonetic exponents are different in different environments. The two environments to be considered are (1) word final position, (2) when there follows one of a small number of separable suffixes which are non-free forms and all of which have vowel initial. An example is the interrogative particle **-aa**. In general terms:

In environment (1) —^{n} implies a nasalized vowel, —^{r} phonetic zero, —^{w} a back vowel, —^{y} a front vowel.

In environment (2) —^{n} implies a vowel (not significantly nasalized) + nasal consonant (**n** where the preceding vowel is **a** or **aa**, **m** where the preceding vowel is **oo**), —^{r} a retroflex lateral, —^{w} phonetic zero, —^{y} a palatal semi-vowel.[14]

This, in I.P.A. terms, means:

Pronominals		*Personal endings*	
Environment 1	Environment 2	Environment 1	Environment 2
[nɑ̃ː]	[nɑːnɑː]	[-ɛ̃ː]	[-ənɑː]
[nɐmmə]	[nɐmməɭɑː] }	[-õː]	[-oːmɑː]
[nɑːŋgə]	[nɑːŋgəɭɑː] }		
[niː]	[niːjɑː]	[-æ]	[-ejɑː]
[niːŋgə]	[niːŋgəɭɑː]	[-iːŋgə]	[-iːŋgəɭɑː]
[avɛ̃]	[avənɑː]	[-ɑ̃ː]	[-ɑːnɑː]
[avə]	[avəɭɑː]	[-ɑː]	[-ɑːɭɑː]
[avərɯ]	[avərɑː]	[-ɑːrɯ]	[-ɑːrɑː]
[avəŋgə]	[avəŋgəɭɑː]	[-ɑːŋgə]	[-ɑːŋgəɭɑː]
[aðɯ]	[aðɑː]	[-uðɯ]	[-uðɑː]

The grouping of verbal forms in three paradigms for each verb permits the setting up of the three-term category of tense ('past', 'present', 'future'). The phonetic exponents of a given tense are not precisely the same for each verb. They can, nevertheless, be described in general terms as:

1. Present: 'tense' velar plosive articulation + vocalic[15] + **r**; *or* **r** ~ vocalic + **r** (~ 'lax' velar articulation + vocalic + **r**, in a few very rare cases).

2. Future: 'tense' labial plosive articulation; *or* 'lax' labio-dental articulation.

3. Past: non-velar, non-labial articulation. There is a greater range of possibilities here than in the case of the other two tenses, though all fall within the group of tongue-tip or -blade articulations. **r**, one exponent of present tense, is, however, excluded.[16]

That there are, as noted in the preceding paragraph, two possibilities of consonant articulation ('tense' or 'lax') in the segment of a verbal form that is the exponent of grammatical tense allows the division of verbs into two classes. These will be called Class I and Class II. Class I has 'tense' velar plosive articulation as a marker of present tense and 'tense' bilabial plosive articulation as a marker of future tense. Class II does not have this phonetic feature of 'tenseness' in the corresponding segment. Whilst there is thus a regular correspondence between the markers of present and future tenses, there is no such correlation between the structure of the past tense and that of the other two tenses. It can, however, be shown that within each of the two classes, I and II, there is a correlation between the form of the past tense and the phonological structure of the verbal stem: that is to say that very few verbs need to be considered 'irregular'. Features to be taken into account are the prosodies of syllabic structure and of stem final, and the phonematic units occurring in final position (and, very occasionally, those of the penultimate segment).

CLASS I ('tense' plosive articulation in past and future forms)

(a) *y-prosodic.* All stems have V in final position. In this position a three-term system of phonematic units is set up: ι ϵ α.[17] In this group, ϵ is always accompanied by the prosody of vowel length. ι and α are always short. Possibilities, in terms of generalized phonological structure, are:

(i) Final ι: $VC\iota^y$, $CVC\iota^y$, $CVCC\iota^y$, $CVVC\iota^y$, $VVCVCC\iota^y$, $VCCVC\iota^y$.
(ii) Final ϵ: $C\epsilon\epsilon^y$.
(iii) Final α: $C\alpha^y$, $VC\alpha^y$, $CVC\alpha^y$.

These are exemplified in the table which follows. The order of items is: phonological structure of stem, singular imperative,[18] past tense, present tense, future tense, 'meaning'.

$VC\iota^y$	**aṭi**	**aṭiccan**	**aṭikkiran**	**aṭippan**	'strike'
$CVC\iota^y$	**piṭi**	**piṭiccan**	**piṭikkiran**	**piṭippan**	'grasp'
$CVCC\iota^y$		**manniccan**	**mannikkiran**	**mannippan**	'excuse'[19]

CVVCι^{y}	**vaaci**	**vaaciccan**	**vaacikkiran**	**vaacippan**	'read'
VVCVCCι^{y}	**aarampi**	**aarampiccan**	**aarampikkiran**	**aarampippan**	'begin'
VCCVCι^{y}	**endiri**	**endiriccan**	**endirikkiran**	**endirippan**	'rise'
C$\epsilon\epsilon^{y}$	**teey**	**teeccan**	**teeykkiran**	**teeyppan**	'rub'
Cα^{y}	**tay**	**taccan**	**taykkiran**	**tayppan**	'sew'
VCα^{y}	**uṭe**	**uṭaccan**	**uṭaykkiran**	**uṭayppan**	'break'
CVCα^{y}	**paṭe**	**paṭaccan**	**paṭaykkiran**	**paṭayppan**	'offer in homage'

The phonetic exponents of y-prosody are therefore:

(i) With final -ι: a close front vowel in stem final position of all forms, a close front vowel in the syllable showing present tense[20] (the **-kk-** of this morphological segment is also somewhat fronted), a palatal feature in the consonants of the marker of past tense.

(ii) With final -ϵ: a front closing diphthong in the stem except in past tense forms, palatal features in markers of present and past tense (cf. (i)).

(iii) With final -α: the imperative form has as stem final a closing diphthong moving from [a] to [i] in the case of monosyllabic roots and a half-open front vowel in other cases. Other features are as for (ii).

(b) *w-prosodic.* All stems are again stated as having V in final position, and a three-term system is set up: ι ϵ α. Generalized possibilities are:

(i) Final ι: C$\iota\iota^{w}$, VCι^{w}, CVCι^{w}.
(ii) Final ϵ: C$\epsilon\epsilon^{w}$.
(iii) Final α: VCα^{w}, CVCα^{w}.

Examples are:

C$\iota\iota^{w}$		**puuttutu**	**puukkutu**	**puukkum**	'blossom'[21]
VCι^{w}	**aru**	**aruttan**	**arukkaran**	**aruppan**	'cut'
CVCι^{w}	**kuṭu**	**kuṭuttan**	**kuṭukkaran**	**kuṭuppan**	'give'
C$\epsilon\epsilon^{w}$	**keeḷu**	**keeṭṭan**	**keekkaran**	**keeppan**	'ask'
VCα^{w}	**aḷa**	**aḷantan**	**aḷakkaran**	**aḷappan**	'measure'
CVCα^{w}	**naṭa**	**naṭantan**	**naṭakkaran**	**naṭappan**	'walk'

The phonetic exponents of w-prosody are absence of palatal features where they were stated to be present in consonant or vowel articulations of verbal forms with y junction prosody. Thus, for example, the marker of present tense here (**-kkar-**) has a central vowel. It will be noted that within this w-prosodic group there are certain differences, particularly as regards the past tense forms. There is a correlation between these differences and differences in the phonematic unit in stem final position. In addition to what has been said about this group of verbs in general we are thus able to state that

(i) where we have $-\iota\iota^{w}$ or $-\iota^{w}$, the imperative form will end in a close back vowel and the past tense marker will be **-tt-**.

(ii) where we have $-\epsilon\epsilon^{w}$, the imperative will have **-ee-** followed by **-ḷu** and the past tense marker will be **-ṭṭ-**, these two forms having the common feature of retroflexion.[22]

(iii) where we have $-\alpha^{w}$, the imperative will end in a rather open central vowel and the past tense marker will be **-nt-**.[23]

CLASS II ('lax' articulation in past and future forms)

(a) *y-prosodic.* All stems end in V. The phonematic units in this position (as for I^{y} and I^{w}) form a three-term system: ι ϵ α. Generalized possibilities are:

(i) Final ι: $C\iota\iota^{y}$, $VC\iota^{y}$, $CVC\iota^{y}$.
(ii) Final ϵ: $C\epsilon^{y}$, $C\epsilon\epsilon^{y}$.
(iii) Final α: $C\alpha^{y}$, $C\alpha\alpha^{y}$, $VC\alpha^{y}$, $CVC\alpha^{y}$.

Examples:

$C\iota\iota^{y}$		**tiiɲcutu**	**tiiyutu**		'be burnt'
$VC\iota^{y}$	**eri**	**eriɲcan**	**eriyaran**	**erivan**	'throw'
$CVC\iota^{y}$	**kuni**	**kuniɲcan**	**kuniyaran**	**kunivan**	'bend down'
$C\epsilon^{y}$	**cey**	**ceɲcan**	**ceyran**	**ceyvan**	'do'
$C\epsilon\epsilon^{y}$		**meeɲcutu**	**meeyutu**	**meeyum**	'graze'
$C\alpha^{y}$		**vaɲcaan**	**vayraan**		'abuse'
$C\alpha\alpha^{y}$	**paay**	**paaɲcutu**	**paayutu**	**paayum**	'jump'
$VC\alpha^{y}$		**uṭaɲcutu**	**uṭayutu**	**uṭayum**	'break'
$CVC\alpha^{y}$		**nuḷaɲcan**	**nuḷayaran**	**nuḷayvan**	'enter'[24]

A statement of the phonetic exponents of y-prosody is as for verbs of group I^{y}, except that by definition the marker of present tense for verbs of group II^{y} does not contain the element of 'tense' velar plosion (which, in verbs of group I^{y}, is of a somewhat fronted quality). It is to be further noted that, though sharing the palatal feature with verbs of group I^{y}, the past tense marker of verbs of group II^{y} is **-ɲc-** (not **-cc-**).

(b) *w-prosodic.* With one exception,[25] all stems are stated to end in C.[26] The statement of the classification of verbs in this group is considerably more complex than that of the verbs of any of the preceding groups, I^{y}, I^{w} and II^{y}. It is necessary to set up a four-term system for the exponents of past tense: **-t-**, **-nt-**, **-ʈ-**, and **-ən-**. These can be correlated with the phonological structure of the stem, though more needs to be said about this structure than was found necessary in describing the two-term system of exponents of past tense for verbs of group I^{w}. Once again, all verbs in this w-prosodic group show an absence of palatal features in the segments that mark tense. There follows an account of the members of the four-term system of verbs of this group.

(i) Verbs having past tense in **-t-** are those which have stem final in **ɼ** preceded by a short non-front vowel. Examples are few and are limited to two syllabic structures:

Vɼ^{w}	**aɼu**	**aɼutan**	**aɼukaran**	**aɼuvan**	'weep'[27]
CVɼ^{w}		**toɼutaan**	**toɼukaraan**	**toɼuvaan**	'worship'

(ii) Verbs having past tense in **-nt-** are those which have stem final in **ɼ** preceded by a short front or a long open vowel, or stem final in **r** preceded by one of the syllabic structures CV-, CVV-, CVCV-, VCCVV-.

Examples are again found to be relatively few in number:

Vɼ^{w}		**eɼunt-**[28]			'rise'
CVɼ^{w}		**viɼuntan**	**viɼukaran**		'fall'
CVVɼ^{w}		**vaaɼntan**	**vaaɭran**	**vaaɼuvan**	'live'[29]
CVr^{w}	**vaa**	**vantan**	**varran**	**varuvan**	'come'
CVVr^{w}		**ceentan**	**ceerran**	**ceeruvan**	'arrive at'
CVCVr^{w}		**vaɭantan**	**vaɭarran**	**vaɭaruvaan**	'grow up'
VCCVVr^{w}	**ukkaaru**	**ukkaantan**	**ukkaarran**	**ukkaaruvan**	'sit down'

The exponents of **-r**^{w} vary in accordance with the structure of the stem and the tense. In all cases the exponent is zero in the past tense forms, **-r-** in the present and **-ru-** in the future tense. In imperative forms there is consonantal zero and a lengthening of the stem vowel in the case of monosyllables having short V, and **-ru** in all other cases.

(iii) Verbs having **-ʈ-** as marker of past tense are those which have stem final in **ʈ** preceded by a short vowel (or by long **oo**, itself preceded by a consonant[30]).

Examples:

CVʈ^{w}	**viʈu**	**viʈʈan**	**viʈran**	**viʈuvan**	'leave'
Cooʈ^{w}	**pooʈu**	**pooʈʈan**	**pooʈran**	**pooʈuvan**	'put'
CVVCCVʈ^{w}	**kuupp(i)ʈu**	**kuupp(i)ʈʈan**	**kuuppiʈran**	**kuuppiʈuvan**	'call'[31]
CVCVCCVʈ^{w}	**purappaʈu**	**purappaʈʈan**	**purappaʈran**	**purappaʈuvan**	'set out'

(iv) Verbs having past tense in **-ən-** include all combinations of stem finals and syllabic structures not stated for (i), (ii) or (iii), and in addition a **-ṭ** final stem with the structure CVCVṭ.[32] The phonematic unit ə in the past tense marker is realized as a central vowel or as zero depending on the nature of the final consonant of the stem.

Examples:

Vṉṉ^{w}	**eṉṉu**	**eṉṉnan**[33]	**eṉran**	**eṉṉuvan**	'count'
VVr^{w}	**eeru**	**eernan**	**eerran**	**eeruvan**	'climb'
VVṭ^{w}	**ooṭu**	**ooṭnan**	**ooṭran**	**ooṭuvan**	'run'
VVṭṭ^{w}	**ooṭṭu**	**ooṭṭnan**	**ooṭṭran**	**ooṭṭuvan**	'drive'
VVtt^{w}	**eettu**	**eettanan**	**eettaran**	**eettuvan**	'light (a lamp)'
CVŋk^{w}	**taŋku**	**taŋnan**	**taŋkaran**	**taŋkuvan**	'stay'
CVṭṭ^{w}	**veṭṭu**	**veṭṭnan**	**veṭṭran**	**veṭṭuvan**	'cut'
CVṉṉ^{w}	**paṉṉu**	**paṉṉnan**	**paṉran**	**paṉṉuvan**	'make'
CVll^{w}	**collu**	**connan**	**colran**	**colluvan**	'say'
CVmp^{w}	**nampu**	**namnan**	**namparan**	**nampuvan**	'trust'
CVVc^{w}	**peecu**	**peecnan**	**peecran**	**peecuvan**	'speak'
CVVṭ^{w}	**paaṭu**	**paaṭnan**	**paaṭran**	**paaṭuvan**	'sing'
CVVkk^{w}	**tuukku**	**tuukkanan**	**tuukkaran**	**tuukkuvan**	'lift'
CVVŋk^{w}	**vaaŋku**	**vaaŋnan**	**vaaŋkaran**	**vaaŋkuvan**	'buy'
CVVṭṭ^{w}	**kaaṭṭu**	**kaaṭṭnan**	**kaaṭṭran**	**kaaṭṭuvan**	'show'
CVVtt^{w}	**maattu**	**maattanan**	**maattaran**	**maattuvan**	'change'
CVVnt^{w}	**niintu**	**niintanan**	**niintaran**	**niintuvan**	'swim'
VCVt^{w}	**eṛutu**	**eṛutanan**	**eṛutaran**	**eṛutuvan**	'write'
VCVkk^{w}	**erakku**	**erakkanan**	**erakkaran**	**erakkuvan**	'take down'
VCVŋk^{w}	**eraŋku**	**eraŋnan**	**eraŋkaran**	**eraŋkuvan**	'descend'
CVCVṭ^{w}	**tiruṭu**	**tiruṭnan**	**tiruṭran**	**tiruṭuvan**	'steal'
CVCVv^{w}	**kaṛuvu**	**kaṛuvanan**	**kaṛuvaran**	**kaṛuvuvan**	'wash'
CVCVtt^{w}	**niruttu**	**niruttanan**	**niruttaran**	**niruttuvan**	'stop'
CVCVCVVṭ^{w}	**veḷayaaṭu**	**veḷayaaṭnan**	**veḷayaaṭran**	**veḷayaaṭuvan**	'play'
Coo^{w}	**poo**	**poonan**	**pooran**	**poovan**	'go'

As the examples show, the phonetic exponent of past tense is [ən] when the stem final is a dental consonant, a voiceless velar plosive (**-kk**) or **-v**. In all other cases it is [n]. It is to be further noted that stem final **-ŋk** is regularly realized as [ŋ] in the past tense, and stem final **-mp** as [m].[34]

THIRD PERSON NEUTER FORMS

As has already been stated, these do not fall into the same simple pattern as other forms, which may be readily divided into three segments attributable to stem, tense marker and personal ending, the latter being the same for a given person/number, whatever the tense. A few examples will show that none of this is wholly true for the third person neuter.

	Past	*Present*	*Future*
1st pers. sing.	**kuḷiccan**	**kuḷikkiran**	**kuḷippan**
3rd pers. neuter	**kuḷiccutu**	**kuḷikkutu**	**kuḷikkum** [kuḷikkũ]
1st pers. sing.	**kuṭuttan**	**kuṭukkaran**	**kuṭuppan**
3rd pers. neuter	**kuṭuttuccu**	**kuṭukkutu**	**kuṭukkum**
1st pers. sing.	**eriɲcan**	**eriyaran**	**erivan**
3rd pers. neuter	**eriɲcutu** **eriɲcuccu**	**eriyutu**	**eriyum**
1st pers. sing.	**viṭṭan**	**viṭran**	**viṭuvan**
3rd pers. neuter	**viṭṭutu** **viṭṭuccu**	**viṭutu**	**viṭum**
1st pers. sing.	**vantan**	**varran**	**varuvan**
3rd pers. neuter	**vantuccu** **vantutu**	**varutu**	**varum**

Thus the personal ending that is colligated with the pronominal **atu** is, in past tense forms, **-utu** ~ **-uccu**. These forms are sometimes in free variation. In other cases only one of the two is possible.[35] In the present tense of verbs of Class I the ending **-utu** is combined with the 'tense' velar plosion associated with the present tense of verbs of this class, but without the **Vr** which forms part of this tense marker in forms colligated with any other pronominal. For the present tense of Class II verbs the sequence is stem + zero + **-utu**. The case of the future tense form is less straightforward still. The distribution of the two possibilities is clear: **-kkum** is found immediately after the stem in verbs of Class I, and **-um** in verbs of Class II. Further segmentation on the basis of comparison with other forms is, however, not possible. The most convenient concept for dealing with this would seem to be that of 'portmanteau morph'.[36] The **-kk-** segments for this person in both present and future forms are distinctly fronted when the stem is of the y-prosody type.

TRANSITIVE/INTRANSITIVE

The contrast at the phonetic level between 'tense' plosion and 'lax' consonant articulation sometimes has the function of differentiating between members of pairs of words which are semantically linked and which apart from this feature are structurally identical. The focus of the contrast may be at either of two points:

1. Stems of identical phonematic and prosodic structure may be

found in Classes I and II. E.g. **uṭ**α^{y} 'break'. A syntactic statement will analyse such verbs in Class I as 'transitive' and in Class II as 'intransitive'. There is, nevertheless, by no means a complete correlation between Class I and 'transitivity' and Class II and 'intransitivity'.

2. Members of certain pairs of stems belonging to the same sub-class (II^{w} (iv)) differ only in the nature of the final consonant of the stem. E.g. **ooṭ**^{w} 'run', **ooṭṭ**^{w} 'drive'; **eraŋk**^{w} 'go down', **erakk**^{w} 'take down'; **tirump**^{w} 'turn round', **tirupp**^{w} 'give back'. In such cases 'tense' plosion (symbolized by a double consonant) again correlates with 'transitivity'.

NOTE ON COMPARISON OF SPOKEN AND WRITTEN FORMS

The verbal forms of written Tamil are usually divided in European grammars of the language into seven classes on the basis of the consonants occurring (in terms of spelling) in the suffixes marking tense.[37] The classification is:

Verb class	*Present*	*Future*	*Past*
I	**kiṟ**[38]	**v**	**t ~ ṭ ~ ṟ**
II	**kiṟ**	**v**	**nt**
III	**kiṟ**	**v**	**iṉ**
IV	**kiṟ**	**v**	**ṭṭ ~ ṟṟ ~ kk**[39]
V	**kiṟ**	**p**	**ṭ ~ ṟ**
VI	**kkiṟ**	**pp**	**tt**
VII	**kkiṟ**	**pp**	**nt**

My group I^{y} includes verbs from Class VI, I^{w}(i) from VI, I^{w} (ii) from V, I^{w} (iii) from VII, II^{y} from II, II^{w} (i) from I, II^{w} (ii) from II, II^{w} (iii) from IV, II^{w} (iv) from III.

Notes

1 On this subject see Kamil Zvelebil, 'On Finite Verb Terminations in Colloquial Tamil', *Archiv Orientální*, 31 (1963), pp. 109–118.

2 For a discussion of certain features of the colloquial language, see Zvelebil, loc. cit., and a series of articles, 'Dialects of Tamil', *Archiv Orientální*, 27 (1959), pp. 272–317 and 572–603, and 28 (1960), pp. 220–224 and 414–456. See also M. Shanmugam Pillai, 'Tamil—Literary and Colloquial', *IJAL*, Vol. 26, No. 3 (1960), Part III, pp. 27–42.

3 A. C. Clayton, *An Introduction to Spoken Tamil* (4th ed., Madras, 1949). Another similarly misleading title is A. M. Мерварт, *Грамматика Тамильского Разговорного Языка* (Leningrad, 1929).

4 On the use of this type of transcription for the purpose of identifying forms in a grammatical description, cf. F. R. Palmer, 'The "Broken Plurals" of Tigrinya', *BSOAS*, XVII, 3 (1955), p. 548, n. 5.

[5] See, for example, 'Sounds and Prosodies', *Papers in Linguistics 1934–1951* (London, 1957), p. 121, n. 1. For an example of such a polysystemic approach, see Eugenie J.A. Henderson, 'The Phonology of Loanwords in some South-East Asian Languages', *TPS*, 1951, pp. 131–158.

[6] An overall analysis of one sort of Tamil is given by Murray Fowler, 'The Segmental Phonemes of Sanskritized Tamil', *Lg.*, XXX (1954), pp. 360–367. The place of loanwords in a phonological analysis of Tamil is discussed in some detail by Gordon H. Fairbanks, 'Frequency and Phonemics', *Indian Linguistics*, XVII (1957), [For the year 1955–56], pp. 105–113.

[7] The best detailed account of the sounds of Tamil is contained in J.R. Firth's 'A Short Outline of Tamil Pronunciation', published as an Appendix to the revised edition of A.H. Arden, *A Progressive Grammar of Common Tamil* (Madras, 1934) (though Firth preferred not to have it reproduced in later editions of the Grammar). This 'Outline' is concerned mainly with the 'reading style', but most of what it has to say about details of pronunciation is valid for the spoken language. Nothing, however, is said about the nasalized vowels that occur in word-final position in the 'colloquial style', since the corresponding articulation in the 'reading style' is of a nasal consonant.

[8] See below, pp. 18–19.

[9] For a fuller list see G.U. Pope, *A Handbook of the Ordinary Dialect of the Tamil Language* (7th ed., Oxford University Press, 1911), pp. 32–33.

[10] For most other speakers there is an additional form not recognized by Rama Subbiah, namely a 'third person neuter plural'. This would add to the paradigm **atuŋka naṭakkutuŋka**. The appropriate entry in the table on pp. 18–19 would then be: **atuŋka** VCVCCV^{r} **-utuŋka** -VCVCC^{r}. [Since this article was completed, Dr. Subbiah would appear to have accepted that this 'neuter plural' form does occur in his speech, at least occasionally. See his *A Syntactic Study of Spoken Tamil*; Thesis submitted for the Ph.D. degree of the University of London, 1965, p. 31.]

[11] Where R.S. has **namma** for this pronominal form, others among my informants have **nampa**. For their speech the statement of the nature of the exponent of plurality in the pronominal system (p. 18) would exclude the phrase 'or a long nasal'.

[12] See below, pp. 24–25.

[13] Cf. F.R. Palmer, 'The Verb in Bilin', *BSOAS*, XIX, 1 (1957), p. 134, for a similar approach.

[14] The usefulness of this type of treatment of 'linking sounds' is suggested by Firth, 'Sounds and Prosodies', *Papers*, pp. 131–132.

[15] The quality of the vowel in this syllable (front close, or central) is one of the phonetic exponents of the stem-final prosodies (y or w) that are set up. See below, p. 20.

[16] It must be admitted here that the juxtaposition of the two words *tense*, one referring to a grammatical category and the other to a phonetic feature, is awkward. They will be distinguished in the body of this paper by the use of the word in single quotation marks to refer to the phonetic feature that is opposed to 'lax' and the use of the word without quotation marks to refer to the grammatical category.

[17] It must be stressed that these symbols carry no implication of frontness or backness, but merely symbolize degrees of openness.

[18] Dictionary entries for verbs are usually in the form of the singular imperative. In discussions of the written language it is often stated that the singular imperative of

Tamil verbs is 'the same as' the 'root' or 'stem'. No such view is accepted in this paper. The 'stem' is an abstraction set up to facilitate statements about the relationship between different parts of the verb.

19 Gaps, as here, will sometimes occur in the lists of examples. This means that no such form occurs in the speech of my informant, though it does not necessarily mean in all cases that it is impossible for all speakers. Where possible, examples are given in the first person singular form. If this has not been found to occur, the third person singular (masculine) is given. If examples are found of neither, the third person neuter (the only form for some verbs) is given.

20 A case of 'vowel harmony', a feature particularly susceptible to prosodic-type analysis. Cf. Firth, 'Sounds and Prosodies', *Papers*, pp. 130 and 134. For detailed application of Firth's theory to the analysis of 'vowel harmony' see F.R. Palmer, '"Openness" in Tigre: A Problem in Prosodic Statement', *BSOAS*, XVIII, 3 (1956), pp. 561–577, and Natalie Waterson, 'Some Aspects of the Phonology of the Nominal Forms of the Turkish Word', ibid., pp. 578–591.

21 Third person neuter forms. See above, note 19.

22 The verb listed (**keeḷu**) is in fact the only example of group I^w (ii). The fact that it enables us to show symmetric grouping within I^y and I^w is perhaps sufficient justification for setting up a separate sub-class, rather than speaking of **keeḷu** simply as an 'exception'.

23 One verb not accounted for in the statement of possibilities for verbs of Class I is **iru** 'be', which by virtue of its having 'tense' plosive articulation in the markers of present and future tense and its having **-nt-** as marker of past tense, would seem to come near to fitting in group I^w (iii). However, the problem of the final vowel of the stem and differences that are found in the present tense forms (a common first person singular form, for example, is **naan irukkan**) suggest that in this case at least it is more economical to speak of an 'irregular' verb.

24 My other informants have **ɼ** here where R.S. has **ḷ**. In other cases the two sounds are for him in free variation. In yet other cases he agrees with my other informants in having only **ɼ**. This is not the place to ask why such a complex situation exists, though one might note that some dialects, in both the reading and the colloquial style, have only **ḷ** where others have either **ḷ** or **ɼ**, depending on the lexical item.

25 **poo** 'go'.

26 An alternative, as the material presented will suggest, would have been to treat all as having V in stem final position, with this phonematic unit forming a 'one-term system' and having as its exponent, depending on the environment, a close back vowel, a central vowel, or zero. It has seemed more appropriate to treat these phonetic features as exponents of the w-prosody.

27 For all (C)V$ɼ^w$ stems in this class R.S. has **-kar-** [ɣər] as marker of present tense, whereas no other w-prosody verbs of Class II have velar articulation in this segment. The fact that the consonant is a 'lax' one, however, means that this does not need to be treated as an 'irregular' feature. My other informants have **aɼaran** etc. here.

28 No personal ending is given here, since the only forms found to occur are compound past tense forms. The restricted scatter of this verb and of **toɼu** in sub-class (i) suggest the alternative solution of stating them to be 'exceptions'. (i) would then be said to include verbs of the structure V$ɼ^w$ and (ii) verbs of the structure CV$ɼ^w$. In this paper the choice has been made to reduce the number of 'exceptions' to a minimum even at the cost of a slightly more complex statement.

[29] Though the present tense (except for the third person neuter **vaaɽutu**) has ɭ where the other tenses have ɽ, the sounds are not in free variation here. See above, note 27.

[30] This awkward supplementary statement is made necessary by the need for a formula that will cover the otherwise exceptional **pooʈ-**.

[31] It is a feature of polysyllabic stems of this structure that the phonetic realization of the phonematic unit *i* is zero in certain contexts. It continues to have as an exponent the voicing of single following ʈ, which, it will be remembered, was stated as being voiced in intervocalic position (see above, p. 16).

[32] This statement is again one made to cover a single item which would otherwise be an 'exception'. Cf. notes 28 and 30 above.

[33] The consonant cluster in this past tense form has very little movement forward from the retroflex towards the alveolar position. It is, however, noticeably longer in duration than the 'double' nasal of imperative and future tense forms.

[34] Sometimes varying with [mb] in slower speech for R.S., and always [mb] for some speakers. Some speakers also have [ŋg] where R.S. has [ŋ] in past tense forms.

[35] The distribution of these forms is not entirely clear, though there would appear to be a tendency towards correlation with certain types of stem. Once more (cf. note 24) it is not the purpose of this paper to say *why* such variation exists, but it is to be noted that for some speakers only **-utu** is possible and for others only **-uccu**. For speakers who use a 'third person neuter plural' form (see above, note 10) verbs having past tense neuter singular ending **-uccu** will have the possibility of neuter plural ending **-uccuŋka.** In the case of the future tense the verb form will be the same for neuter plural as for neuter singular.

[36] See Charles F. Hockett, 'Problems of Morphemic Analysis', *Lg.*, 23 (1947), p. 333. See also J. R. Firth, 'A Synopsis of Linguistic Theory, 1930–1955', *Studies in Linguistic Analysis* (Special Volume of the Philological Society, Oxford, 1957), p. 14, where he speaks of 'cumulative' exponents of more than one grammatical category.

[37] See A.H.Arden, *A Progressive Grammar of Common Tamil* (5th ed., Madras 1954), pp. 144–149, and Preface to *A Dictionary, Tamil and English. Based on J.P. Fabricius's 'Malabar-English Dictionary'* (3rd ed., Tranquebar, 1933). The University of Madras *Tamil Lexicon* (1924–36) has 13 classes, the result of having separate classes for each of the variant past tense forms of I and IV. It has been shown that by such devices as the establishment of a 'morpheme{*X*} meaning perhaps "transitive of preceding verb stem" and phonemically zero' the number of these classes necessary for a description of the verb in written Tamil can be reduced to three. See Leigh Lisker, 'Tamil Verb Classification', *JAOS*, 71 (1951), pp. 111–114.

[38] As far as possible the same symbols are used in this transliteration of the letters of the Tamil script as are used above for a transcription of spoken forms. Exceptions result from the recognition by the script of two 'n' (which are in complementary distribution) and two 'r' (which in intervocalic position are not distinguished at the phonetic level by speakers from most areas. Double **r̲r̲** is phonetically [ttr]. **r** does not occur doubled).

[39] In 'process' terminology, these suffixes are the result of the doubling of the last consonant of the stem.

Some Prosodic Features in Terena

JOHN T. BENDOR-SAMUEL

1. INTRODUCTION

Professor J.R.Firth reacted against the apparent emphasis of many linguistic treatises upon segmentation. His own interest lay especially in features which characterize stretches of speech and which can be stated for more than one segment. Thus, in handling phonological description, he developed the concept of the prosodic feature in contradistinction to the phonematic unit.[1]

This article will attempt to describe certain prosodic features which may be set up in stating the phonological structure of Terena.[2] Other apsects of Terena phonology will be mentioned but only in so far as this is necessary to an understanding of the prosodic features which are being presented.

A prosodic feature or prosody may be defined as a phonological category whose phonetic exponents either extend over more than one place in the phonological structure or have implications for more than one place.[3] In Terena prosodies may extend over or have implications for various stretches of speech corresponding to the syllable, phonological word, phonological phrase, phonological clause and phonological sentence. These prosodies will, therefore, be presented grouped according to their domain of relevance, namely syllable, phonological word, etc.

The terms phonological word, phonological phrase, phonological clause and phonological sentence are used for units in the hierarchy set up to handle the phonological description of the language[4] and must be kept distinct from the terms of the grammatical system. There is, naturally, a good deal of congruence between the phonological word and the grammatical word, and between the phonological phrase and the grammatical phrase, etc. It is for this reason that similar words are used but these sets of terms must not be assumed to be identically congruent. It lies outside the scope of this paper[5] to state the congruences between the grammatical and phonological description though occasionally reference may be made to this. Since this article is concerned solely with phonological structure it seems redundant to repeat 'phonological' before every use of the terms word, phrase, clause and sentence. It will, therefore, be assumed that these terms are units in the phonological hierarchy unless it is stated otherwise.

2. SYLLABLE PROSODIES

In structure syllables consist of phonematic units[6] and prosodic features. Every syllable irrespective of its phonematic structuring has one prosodic feature stated for the syllable. There are three syllable prosodies: palatalization, backness and the absence of palatalization and backness. These are termed the i-prosody, u-prosody and ə-prosody respectively. These prosodies form a mutually exclusive closed system.

The phonetic exponents of the i-prosody are as follows:

1. Palatalization of the initial C unit of the syllable, together with
2. Fronting of the initial articulation of the V unit functioning as nucleus of the syllable.

The phonetic exponents of the u-prosody are as follows:

The backing of all front vowels to a back position.

The phonetic exponents of the ə-prosody are the absence of the phonetic features described for the other syllable prosodies.

Examples[7]

ʃàne	'people'	^{i}SA^{ə}NE[8]	íhyi	'pepper'	^{ə}I ^{i}HI
isáne	'field'	^{ə}I^{ə}SA ^{ə}NE	ɲìu	'mosquito'	^{i}NI ^{ə}U
hyiʃòe	'dress'	^{i}HI ^{i}SO^{ə}E	ɨ́hɨkaʃo	'he taught'	^{u}I ^{u}HI^{ə}KA ^{i}SO
ɨ̀hɨ	'tail'	^{u}I ^{u}HI			

3. WORD PROSODIES

In structure words consist of syllables and prosodic features. Every word, irrespective of its syllabic structuring, has one prosody stated for the word. There are three word prosodies: nasalization, yodization and the absence of nasalization and yodization. These are termed the n-prosody, y-prosody and z-prosody.

All words marked by the n-prosody are found to correspond to grammatical words which are marked by the grammatical category of first person. All words marked by the y-prosody are found to correspond to grammatical words which are marked by the grammatical category second person.

The phonetic exponents of the n-prosody are as follows:

1. Lowering of the velum throughout the word until the first stop or fricative, the nasalization continuing through the initial part of the articulation of that stop or fricative, together with

2. Continued vibration of the vocal cords after the velum is raised during the articulation of the first stop or fricative, together with

3. Narrowing of the opening between the alveolar ridge and tongue with grooving of the tongue producing increased friction when H is the first fricative.

The phonetic exponents of the y-prosody are as follows:

1. In the case of words other than certain two-syllable words, a fronting and raising of the first vowel except that when that vowel is I the second vowel is fronted and raised and if that vowel is I, the third vowel is fronted and raised and so on through the word until the first vowel which is not I. In words having a vowel cluster for the first and second syllable, if the first vowel is I or E, the feature of fronting and raising extends to both vowels. This same feature extends for all syllables of words in which all the vowels are E. All examples found have been nouns, and almost all have had two syllables. With some speakers the feature of fronting and raising also extends through the first two syllables when these are both U but this pattern is found much less frequently. Or

2. In the case of two-syllable words which
(a) have as first vowel U, O or A and
(b) have type B stress on the first syllable, this fronting and raising is only partial for the first syllable and results in a vowel cluster consisting of the fronted and raised vowel followed by the unfronted and non-raised vowel. In such circumstances type A stress on the second vowel is found.

The phonetic exponents of the z-prosody are the absence of all the phonetic features listed above for the other two word prosodies.

Examples[9]

nő^{ŋ}gone	‘my need’	^{Nə}NO^{ə}KO^{ə}NE	^{n}dùti	‘my head’	^{Nə}TU^{ə}TI
nékone	‘your need’	^{Yə}NO^{ə}KO^{ə}NE	tiúti	‘your head’	^{Yə}TU^{ə}TI
nókone	‘his need’	^{Zə}NO^{ə}KO^{ə}NE	tùti	‘his head’	^{Zə}TU^{ə}TI
^{m}bìho	‘I went’	^{Nə}PI^{ə}HO	^{n}ʒìʃo	‘my dress’	^{Ni}HI^{i}SO
pìhe	‘you went’	^{Yu}PI^{ə}HO	ì^{n}za	‘my name’	^{Nə}I^{ə}HA
pìho	‘he went’	^{Zə}PI^{ə}HO	ì^{n}zo	‘I hoed’	^{Nə}I^{ə}SO

4. PHRASE PROSODIES

In structure phonological phrases consist of words and phrase prosodic features. Every phrase, irrespective of its word structuring, is marked by the prosody of stress. Stress is both a phonological and grammatical feature of Terena.[10] All words except particles may be stressed on two different syllables and the selection of one of these two syllables in any one utterance frequently has syntactic implications.

In simple phrases[11] the stress prosody has two points of focus: a major and a minor focal point. The major focal point is always the last word in the phrase. The minor focal point when it occurs, marks the first word of the phonological phrase. Stress focusing on the final word of the phrase is termed full stress, and stress focusing on the non-final word of the phrase is termed secondary stress. Every phrase is marked by the sub-feature of full stress irrespective of its word structuring, but the sub-feature of secondary stress is found only when the phrase consists of more than one word. In this way the prosodic feature of stress is handled as a feature running through the phrase, having one or two points of focus—like a wave with a major crest and a minor crest—the major point of focus being termed full stress and the minor point of focus being termed secondary stress.

The sub-feature of full stress has various phonetic exponents, all of which extend over one word. For this reason the sub-feature is described in terms of the word. These exponents are loudness, length and pitch and may be stated as follows:

1. The utterance of one syllable of a word with greater loudness and articulatory force than other syllables of that word. When this syllable consists of a single V nucleus, this feature usually begins with the C margin of the preceding syllable but reaches its peak on the single V nucleus, together with

2. Length focusing on the C immediately following the nucleus of the syllable marked by loudness; or, if that syllable is the third syllable of the word and followed by a V syllable, on the V nucleus of the syllable marked by loudness if that vowel is more open than the following vowel, or otherwise on that second vowel, together with

3. A higher pitch on the syllable marked by greater loudness than on the preceding and following syllables. It should be noted, however, that when a phonological phrase occurs in final position in a phonological clause, the pitch pattern of the clause is determined by the tune accompanying that clause. Quite often that tune differs in some respect from the normal pitch pattern of the phrase.

Full stress with these phonetic exponents is termed type A stress. There is generally a contrast in the placement of stress in that stress of type A falls on one or other of two given syllables, but when in certain definite limited circumstances this contrast of placement is inoperative, another set of phonetic exponents is found. Thus a contrast which is vital to the grammatical system of the language is maintained.

This second set of phonetic exponents is as follows:

1. Loudness as described above, together with
2. Length focusing on the V which is the nucleus of the syllable marked by greater loudness, together with
3. A low falling pitch on that syllable.

When full stress has this set of phonetic exponents it is termed type B stress.

Full stress always falls on one of the first three syllables of the word. Two syllables of every word may be so marked, so only one of these two stressable syllables will be stressed at any one utterance. Which these two stressable syllables are, is an arbitrary feature of the language. There is no way of predicting this except on the basis of stress classes of the word stems and roots. In general the stress pattern of any word is determined by its root.

The sub-feature of secondary stress always falls on the first syllable of the phonological phrase irrespective of the stress pattern that that particular word may have when it is marked by full stress. The phonetic exponent of secondary stress is the utterance of the first syllable of the word with greater loudness and articulatory force than other syllables of that word. The features of length and pitch which have already been presented as exponents of full stress are not found.

Though it is convenient to state the exponents of the two sub-features of the stress prosody in terms of the word there are definite advantages in regarding stress as a phrase rather than as a word feature. If stress is handled at the word level rather than the phrase level statements about the fusion or loss of stress have to be made in order to account for the features termed secondary stress in this analysis.

Examples[12]

'yara yóti	'this night'
'haˀi tikóti	'fruit'
'ako énʒa	'I don't know'
óvoku	'his house'
pìho	'he went'

5. CLAUSE PROSODIES

In structure, clauses consist of phrases and clause prosodic features. Every clause, irrespective of its phrase structuring, is marked by a prosody of intonation.

Whenever any stretch of speech which corresponds to the phonological clause is heard, variations of pitch over the clause are noticed. These variations are limited in number. These pitch patterns are said to accompany the clause rather than some lower element of the phonological hierarchy since they correspond to features generally regarded as intonation. Intonation is here treated as a prosodic feature because its phonetic exponents are stated for the clause as a whole rather than for some one segment of the clause and because it delimits one clause from another.

To handle the various pitch patterns observed at the phonetic level a number of intonation patterns are set up. Every clause is marked by one or other of these intonation patterns of which there are five.

Within each intonation pattern there are variations of pitch determined by the occurrence of the prosodic feature of stress. The intonation patterns, however, account for the changes of pitch over the clause as a whole. Furthermore the pitch features of the intonation patterns override the normal pitch determined by stress features when these are different.

Since the description of these five intonation patterns [13] would exceed the limits of this article an example of a clause marked by the three most frequently occurring tunes is given below.

ˈkahyaˀa ʃúpu

tune one: ‘he wanted mandioca.’

tune two: ‘he wanted mandioca . . .’

tune three: ‘did he want mandioca?’

6. SENTENCE PROSODIES

In structure, sentences consist of clauses and sentence prosodic features. Though the beginning and end of a phonological sentence coincide with the beginning and end of a phonological clause, a phonological sentence often consists of more than one clause. The phonological sentence corresponds to a stretch of speech which begins and ends with a pause.[14] This pause may therefore be said to be one of two exponents of the sentence prosody. Even though it does not extend over more than one place in the sentence it has definite implications for the whole sentence since it delineates the sentence.

The sentence prosody has a second exponent of voicelessness. The final syllable of a sentence is often partially or completely voiceless. This feature is to some extent idiolectal and tends to occur more frequently in certain types of speech, e.g. narrative. However, it is sufficiently widespread to be noted. When the last syllable of the sentence is -ti this voicelessness is especially noticeable.

Certain pitch features also serve to delineate the phonological sentence. When the sentence consists of two or more clauses marked by tunes 1 or 2, at times the pitch drops slightly over the whole phonological sentence. Furthermore the end of the sentence always coincides with the end of the clause and in the case of tune 1 in particular the clause final pitch fall marks the end of a phonological sentence. This suggests the possibility of an alternative analysis combining the levels here treated separately as clause and sentence.

Example[15]

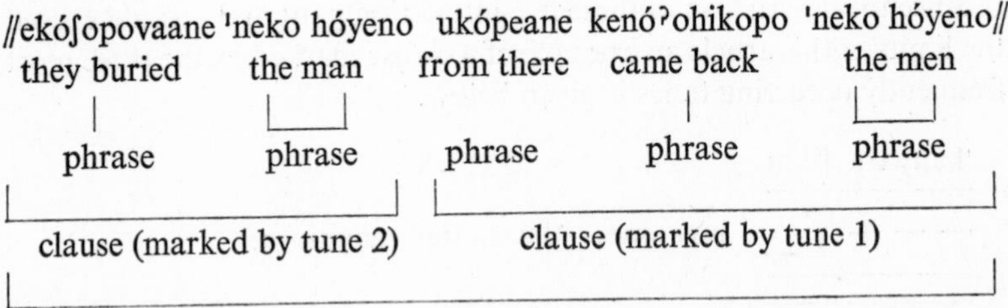

One phonological sentence consisting of two phonological clauses and corresponding to two grammatical sentences.

7. PHONOLOGICAL SYSTEM

In this article the phonological analysis of Terena has been presented as an interlocking hierarchy of levels of statement. Sentences consist of clauses, clauses of phrases, phrases of words, words of syllables and syllables of phonematic units. Conversely phonematic units function in syllables, syllables in words, words in phrases and phrases in clauses and clauses in sentences. A unit at a given level consists of elements from the next lowest level and operates in turn as an element at the next highest level.

Syllables consist not only of phonematic units, however, but also of prosodic features. So it is with words and phrases: there are syntagmatic features termed prosodies which mark the particular unit. It is, for instance, insufficient to describe the phonological clause merely in terms of phonological phrases of which it is composed, without also describing the pitch features which mark the clause.

The overall phonological system may be schematized as follows:

	Units	*Elements*	*Syntagmatic Features*
LEVELS	the phonological sentence	one or more clause	sentence prosody of voicelessness and pause
	the phonological clause	one or more phrase	one of five intonation patterns
	the phonological phrase	one or more word	prosody of stress
	the phonological word	one or more syllable	N- Y- or Z-prosody
	the phonological syllable	one or more phonematic unit	i- u- or ə-prosody
	the phonematic unit		

Such a description of the phonology of Terena may be paralleled by a grammatical statement[16] completely independent but equally hierarchical, postulating a series of levels with units at a given level consisting of elements from the level next below together with certain syntagmatic features. In each case, too, the unit may be said to function as an element at the next highest level. In the grammatical description, as in the phonological, it is not sufficient to speak of units as comprising a structure consisting of elements arranged in place since there are also syntagmatic features whose domain of relevance extends beyond any of the elements of the structure. These syntagmatic features are very varied. They include relationships within a structure e.g. one element presupposing another and not vice versa, or features normally handled as agreement and concord.

Such descriptions whether of phonological or of grammatical structures may surely claim to avoid some of the limitations of linear beads-on-a-string segmentation by attempting to give due attention to features which extend over longer stretches of speech.

Notes

1 See J.R. Firth, 'Sounds and Prosodies', *TPS* 1948, pp. 127–152.

2 Terena is an Arawak language found in south-west Mato Grosso, Brazil, and spoken by approximately 5,000 people. Material for this paper was gathered during 1959 and 1960 while residing at Chacara União near Miranda, Mato Grosso, with my wife and two colleagues of the Summer Institute of Linguistics, Miss Muriel Perkins and Miss Muriel Ekdahl. This work was carried out under the auspices of the National Museum of Brazil. In addition to the help given me by my colleagues I wish to acknowledge the patient assistance of many of the residents of Chacara União.

3 Cf. R.H. Robins, 'Some Aspects of Prosodic Analysis', Proceedings of the University of Durham Philosophical Society, Volume 1, Series B (Arts) No. 1, 1957.

4 See Section 7 of this paper.

5 It is hoped to publish a full description of the phonological and grammatical structure of Terena which is at present in MS.

6 Phonematic units are further divided into C and V units. In Terena there are twelve C units (P T K ʔ M N H S L R V and Y) and five V units (I E A O U). The terms Phonematic Unit and Phoneme should not be confused. For a phonemic analysis of Terena see my 'Some Problems of Segmentation in the Phonological Analysis of Terena', *Word* 16. 3 (1960), pp. 348–355.

7 These examples are written in a phonetic transcription except that phonetic features associated with type A stress are symbolized by ′, with type B stress by ‵, and with secondary stress by ˈ. See Section 4 for details. The phonological symbolization will generally be limited to the symbolizing of those aspects of the analysis which are being presented in the particular section concerned.

8 Raised $^{i\ ə\ u}$ before the syllable symbolize the respective syllable prosodies.

9 Raised $^{N\ Y\ Z}$ before the word symbolize the respective word prosodies.

10 A full description of the stress system of the language is given in my 'Stress in Terena', *TPS* 1962, pp. 105–123.

11 A complex phrase is set up in addition to the simple phrase. Complex phrases occur infrequently, averaging 3% of phrases in the material examined. The structure of the complex phrase and the stress features which mark it are described in my 'Stress in Terena'. The patterns and exponents of stress with the complex phrase confirm the validity of analysing stress at the phrase rather than at the word level but as they parallel very closely the system described here for the simple phrase the details are not repeated.

12 Full stress is symbolized by ′ (type A), ‵ (type B), and secondary stress by ˈ.

13 A full description of these intonation patterns is in MS form as part of an overall description of Terena phonology and grammar.

[14] Pause may occur at other points than the end of the phonological sentence. Speakers may be interrupted or pause for breath. In such cases the feature of voicelessness is not present. Furthermore such pauses do not correlate with phonological clause boundaries and the intonation features associated with the clause are not found.

[15] Double bars indicate pause.

[16] See my 'A Structure-function description of Terena phrases', *JCLA* 8.2 (1963).

Notes on the Semantics of Linguistic Description

G. L. BURSILL-HALL

Modern linguists have for the most part a regrettable tendency to ignore the long history of their science or else to dismiss the efforts of their predecessors condescendingly as of little or no value except in so far as they might be of purely historical interest. Apart from anything else, the study of the history of linguistics is very revealing in terms of changing intellectual trends and attitudes of mind towards the subject-matter of linguistics. It is a source of great intellectual interest to see how scholars of other generations thought about the problem of linguistic description. It is for instance important to see how they sought by means of their technical vocabulary and very specific techniques to make statements, which to their eyes were rigorous statements, about the facts of language.[1]

The late J. R. Firth was one linguist who was very much aware of the long line of the history of grammatical description;[2] he taught that statements about the different stages in the history of linguistic description must be made in terms of and with reference to the particular context of situation, i.e. the intellectual atmosphere in which the theory was engendered in the same way that statements about a living language text must be made in terms of its own context of situation. Here too, the history of linguistics has much to teach us, since linguistic description relies to some extent at least on technical terminology taken from everyday language and it is revealing to study the efforts of other linguists to produce a satisfactory language of linguistic description. Firth was himself very conscious of the inadequacy of everyday language as a second-order language, and pointed to the necessity for modern linguistics to reconsider and tighten a great many of its key terms.[3]

The object of this paper is to suggest the necessity for the technical language of linguistic description to be seen in the light of the intellectual forces which created it; at the same time, within such a technical language certain terms and processes will reveal very clearly the epistemological standpoint of the creators of this metalanguage. The Modistae are an excellent example of the necessarily close ties between linguistic description and its formative influences. They were a group of grammarians in the thirteenth and fourteenth centuries producing theories of grammar which reflect a remarkable degree of sophistication and are worthy representatives of the golden age of mediaeval scholasticism.

1. It is dangerous and quite erroneous to classify the whole of a grammatical theory in terms of certain features used in the description of some categories. The Modistae, it is true, established the declinable partes orationis on the basis of concepts borrowed from the philosophy of reality, but not all their terms and grammatical features were so described.[4] The important thing to remember is that a terminology is necessitated by a system of thought[5] and that starting from their epistemological premise, there is an obvious degree of inevitability about Modistic terminology. If we are to dismiss the grammatical theories of the Modistae, as indeed we must, it is because we must reject the whole system of thought behind their theorizings. In so doing, we are responding to Firth's demand[6] that systems of linguistic thought with their terminologies all make their contributions to the semantics of linguistic science.

It is equally important, as again Firth[7] pointed out, to apply the techniques of semantics to an examination of the technical language of linguistic or grammatical science. One of the problems in examining a body of linguistic doctrine, no matter how coherent it may have been at the time when it was actively practised, is that it is often extremely difficult to sense the exact use of the technical terms of such a metalanguage; it becomes even more difficult when certain key terms are extensively used and probably in more than one sense. The difficulty is further increased when the terms in question have been taken from one discipline and applied without overt explanation, though by no means indiscriminately, to another discipline. Halliday has referred to the different relations of the participants to the writer of a text in the linguistic situation;[8] we are faced here with two sets of relations, i.e. the mediaeval student of grammar and the modern student of linguistics. Yet a further complication arises in terms of the interpretation of the author's intent in making certain assertions and using certain technical terms. Halliday points out[9] that once a text has been committed to paper the creative effect of the writer derives from the relationships established between the 'text' and the reader, but this is precisely what we have to avoid in the critical examination of a grammatical theory, especially one which was produced centuries ago; there must be no question of phatic communion, but we must seek instead for the intent of the author in using his technical terms.

Once more we are back to Firth's dictum, that the terminology is necessitated by a system of thought, and yet how is the scholar to establish the intent of the author when he is allowed only the bare bones of the text and when he is perforce unaware of any of the constituents of the context of situation? How is the scholar to unravel the meanings of this technical vocabulary when he is faced with apparent confusion and redundancy of usage? One way of unraveling the enigma is by applying what can be called the 'collocation test'.[10] Robins has rightly pointed out[11] that collocation is not an operative level of analysis with all words, but what becomes clear from an examination of any Modistic text is that the collocations of these technical terms represent ordered series of words; Firth points out that the[12] setting up of words in ordered series constitutes a very important procedure in linguistic analysis and the argument here is that this constitutes an equally important part of the examination of the language of linguistic description. One of the problems in the creation of a technical language for linguistic description is the avoidance of association of the term with its meaning in everyday language; this can be turned to the advantage of the analyst when he comes to examine another grammarian's technical language. Meaning by collocation implies by definition that there will be no resorting to shifted terms; the use by the Modistae of their technical vocabulary can be explained and understood by an examination of the narrow and extended collocations of these terms.[13]

The Modistae were more than superficially influenced by contemporary intellectual trends; they applied to their theories of grammar not only the technical language of mediaeval metaphysics and logic but also the constructs and concepts of this philosophy. Despite the fact that the Modistae insisted on the necessary separation of grammar and logic,[14] it was inevitable from the very fact that they were both logicians and grammarians that there would be a considerable degree of cross-fertilization of these disciplines.

Mediaeval metaphysics had taught the intimacy between the reality of things and their conceptualization by the mind; thus grammar became the study of the formulation of these concepts. The Modistae retained the system of word-classes such as it had been evolved by Donatus and Priscian and sought to reframe their definitions of these word-classes in the light of the trends of mediaeval metaphysics. The partes orationis were established as the correlates of reality; two primary elements had been established within the world of things, i.e. permanence (*habitus*) and becoming (*fieri*), and the grammarian adopted these as a means of establishing the essential difference between the *nomen* and *pronomen*, and *verbum* and *participium*, the former expressing permanence and stability and the latter the concept of becoming. By this means, the system of word-classes of Latin was divided, in terms of the use of metaphysical criteria into those word-classes which embodied substance (*ens*), those which embody movement and becoming (*esse*), and a third group which are responsible for the 'disposal' (*disponere*) of the *ens* or *esse*.

The Modistae, however, resorted to the terminology of mediaeval hylomorphic theory for a method and appropriate technical terms to distinguish the noun and pronoun and the verb and participle. There is no need to dwell on the use of the distinction between matter and form, act and potentiality by the mediaeval philosophers in their assertions about substances, but these contrasts devised by the philosopher were introduced into grammatical parlance in order to establish the difference between the noun and pronoun as well as between the verb and participle. It must not be imagined that the Modistae were so naïve as to equate matter (*materia*) as a terminological device with prime matter (*materia prima*) as a metaphysical concept. The linguist, as Firth pointed out,[15] is always faced with the problem of using an inadequate vehicle, viz. language, to talk about itself. It is by no means unreasonable to expect that the Modistae, having embarked on the logicization of the semi-formal grammatical categories of Priscian should, in order to be consistent, continue to use the technical terminology of logic.[16]

2. The techniques of linguistic description employed by the Modistae have been described in detail elsewhere;[17] it is enough to state here that Modistic grammatical theory rested on the study of words and their properties as the signs of things which are capable of functional signification. This signification is stated grammatically by means of the partes orationis which combine the understanding of the thing, its expression, and the signifying of the thing, but the real grammatical tool was the analysis of the pars orationis into its modes of signifying divided into essential and accidental modes.

There was complete inter-dependence in this theory between the structure of reality and the operations of the mind; the partes orationis became therefore the linguistic formulation of these concepts. The establishing of the modes of signifying (*modi significandi*) was the crucial stage in Modistic grammatical procedure; prior to the level of the mode of signifying, we can say that whether we are dealing with the sequences of *vox*, *signum* and *dictio* or of *modus essendi* and *modus intelligendi*, everything was pre-linguistic. With the establishment of the modes of signifying we are linguistic and *potentially* grammatic, and here we encounter the first real intrusion of non-linguistic terminology into the analysis of a word-class. The Modistae, although sparing in their actual use of substantia and accidentia as technical terms, were clearly inspired by the dichotomy expressed in Aristotle's Categories and divided the modes of signifying into substantial and accidental;[18] it should also be mentioned that one of the Modistae, i.e. Siger de Courtrai, also makes use of this distinction analogically[19] to distinguish substantive and adjective and noun (*nomen*) and verb (*verbum*).

The distinction between substance and accident entails the distinction of act and potentiality which carries with it the distinction of matter and form. It does not come within the purview of this paper to examine the philosophical implications of these terms; it is sufficient to say that these terms were used by the Modistae as part of their descriptive scheme, though this does not necessarily mean that they always carried with them their metaphysical connotations.[20]

Part of the Modistic scheme derives from the progression of *modus essendi*, *modus intelligendi*, *modus significandi*, and *modus consignificandi*; each mode carries with it the potentiality of a higher mode, i.e. the *modus essendi* carries with it the *ratio intelligendi*, the *modus intelligendi* implies the *ratio significandi*, and the *modus significandi* the *ratio consignificandi*, and it is not until the stage of *modus consignificandi*, which is the realization of the *ratio consignificandi*, that the pars orationis can become functional, i.e. can have any syntactic function.[21]. Quite clearly then, the contrast of *modus* and *ratio* can be considered a binary opposition which functioned linguistically in the same way as the metaphysical contrast of act (*actus*) and potentiality (*potentia*).

The Modistae also made extensive use of the materia-forma contrast to set up a number of binary oppositions at various levels as well as stages of analysis. This contrast serves, for instance, to distinguish in the first place the declinable from the indeclinable partes orationis, and within the first group, the noun is distinguished from the pronoun and the verb from the participle by means of the matter-form contrast. This contrast is also used to distinguish a *dictio* and pars orationis, i.e. they both have *vox* in common which can be said to constitute their prime matter; the *dictio* is signifiable, i.e. it has the potentiality of signifying (*ratio significandi*), whereas the pars orationis is consignifiable, i.e. it possesses the potentiality of consignifying (*ratio consignificandi*),[22] which is another way of saying that it is capable of functioning syntactically.

The declinable partes orationis, i.e. *nomen* and *pronomen, verbum* and *participium*, were established as correlatives of things in the world of external reality; to be more exact, the *nomen* and *pronomen* represent stability and permanence while the *verbum* and *participium* represent becoming.[23] The *nomen* and *pronomen* share the essence of the *modus entis*, the *verbum* and *participium* the *modus esse*, whereas the indeclinable partes orationis represent together the *modus disponibilis*.[24] The contrast of matter and form is then used to distinguish the *nomen* and *pronomen*, and the *verbum* and *participium*. The noun and pronoun, for instance, signify substance; this they have in common and it thus constitutes their general feature, or if we are going to keep more closely to their terminology, this represents the material member of the contrast. The distinction between the *nomen* and *pronomen* is thus a 'formal' one in that both signify by means of the mode of essence or substance (*modus entis*); the *nomen*, however, possesses form in that it signifies quality, whereas the *pronomen* is merely capable of being determined by form, i.e. this does not mean that there is so much absence of form but rather that it is immanent.[25] The feature of form was used to mark the different types of *nomen*, but the *pronomen* possesses different values (of the same *pronomen*) but not different types.

Similarly, the *verbum* and *participium* possess the same matter or general feature, that of the mode of becoming (*modus esse*) and these two partes orationis are then distinguished by means of their 'form'. The verb and participle are rendered discrete by means of the formal distinction of separation (*distantia*) which is a feature of the verb but not of the participle;[26] this is in fact syntactic criteria, though the Modistae stated it in metaphysical terms and certainly had no such formal (in the modern structural sense of the term) usage in mind.

The contrast of matter and form, in fact, colours the whole of the technical language of the Modistae; the various modes of being, understanding, and signifying (*modus essendi, intelligendi*, and *significandi*) were distinguished within each other by means of this contrast, but more important still, this distinction was used within the modes of signifying in order to represent features common to more than one pars orationis in contrast to those which are peculiar to one pars. The essential mode of signifying (*modus significandi essentialis*) of any pars orationis is divided into general and specific;[27] the general represents *materia* while the specific represents *forma*,[28] and so we find in the description of these declinable partes orationis a close inter-play of the binary contrasts of matter and form and act and potentiality. Much has been already made of the fact that the noun and pronoun, for instance, have the same matter, but not the same form: Siger de Courtrai stated, in order to mark the contrast linguistically, that matter is '*ens*' but only in potentiality, not in act.[29] Thus matter is only informable, so that by virtue of act, the formal distinction is achieved which renders the pars in question discrete from all the other partes orationis.

3. There is one problem which is always present in formulating a linguistic theory, i.e. that of a technical terminology; certain words acquire a specific technical value when used in a specific context, even though they may possess a variety of meanings in everyday language. In dealing with matters of modern technical terminology of linguistics, the problem is not as acute as when we come to examine the technical language of linguistic theorists of some period long in the past. All sorts of complications arise; the mere fact of the passage of time has obviously altered the function of terms which were used, e.g. by the Modistae and which are still used; an excellent example is that of '*demonstratio*' which was used by the Modistae in a very different sense from that of the accepted use of today.[30] Additional complications result from the fact that in this instance the Modistae were by no means 'pure' grammarians but were at the same time logicians and philosophers; although they insisted on the severe separation of their subject-matter, there is quite clearly a great cross-fertilization of technical terms between these sister disciplines.

A further complication arises from the very fact of time; the Modistae used certain terms with great frequency and others occur either very infrequently or else in very easily definable contexts. It is the former that present difficulties to the student of Modistic grammatical theories. The modern student is as much a participant in the context of situation as were the students of the Modistae, but because the circumstances of the situation are different and because of many obscurities within the context, these terms are often very difficult and sometimes almost impossible to interpret. In order to understand these terms, the modern scholar has to resort to the linguistic device of meaning by collocation; the great advantage of this method of course is that linguistic methods and devices are being used to establish the meaning of these linguistic terms.[31]

The value of the collocation test can perhaps be best seen by a brief examination of the meaning, i.e. function of three technical terms, *ratio*, *modus*, and *consignificatio*. The first two occur with great frequency and present a problem to the unsuspecting student when he first approaches his text; the last term is a most important one, since the function of consignification was as a necessary link between the word-class and its syntactic role.

The term '*ratio*' occurs with great frequency in two basic types of collocation; elsewhere it may be used without any specific technical usage. The Modistae used '*ratio*' as a technical term within the metalanguage and at the syntactic stage of linguistic discourse; the use of the term within the metalanguage also involves its use in the description of the word-classes, so that there is a real degree of similarity in its use at the word-class and syntactic stages. In such collocations it is used to express the capability of doing something[32] and appears to have been used as the grammatical device of expressing *potentia* just as *modus* expresses *actus* grammatically, so that *ratio* is to *forma* and *potentia* as *modus* is to *materia* and *actus*. In collocation with terms such as *principium*, *terminus*, *suppositum*, *oppositum*, which are vital terms in the Modistic scheme of syntactic descriptions, *ratio* expresses the idea of potential syntactic function, e.g. Thomas of Erfurt suggested[33] that word-order was a relevant factor in case-theory and therefore implies, by means of the collocations *ratio principii*, *ratio termini*, that a case-form can acquire a different value by virtue of its word-order. Much the same type of quasi-formal analysis can be made of the relationships in an SP construction.

Interesting collocations are those of *ratio* and *consignificare*; elsewhere, *consignificare* is used to imply connotation or secondary meaning, but in collocation with *ratio*, it clearly indicates syntactic meaning or function. A pars orationis is such by means of its modes of signifying (*modi significandi*) but it is functionally useless until it can consignify or combine syntactically with another pars orationis.[34] Thus, the Modistae used the collocation '*ratio consignificandi*' to express the capability (*potentia*) of a pars orationis to combine meaningfully, i.e. functionally, with another pars orationis (which obviously had its own *ratio consignificandi*) to form a construction, which they did by means of their modes of consignifying (*modi consignificandi*).

Elsewhere, ratio is used in its everyday sense[35] and the collocation test becomes the only effective means of differentiating between its use as a technical term and its use in its everyday sense.

4. *Conclusion:* There are at least two factors which have to be considered in the examination of the technical language of any particular linguistic theory, and it should be possible to state these in appropriate terms taken from current linguistic terminology. The current intellectual trend serves to set the context of situation which provides the type of language to be used and creates the general, all-embracing tone of the technical language; this is a statement couched in everyday language implying that the epistemological background of the theorist will colour the whole tenor of his technical discourse as well as supplying a whole series of technical terms and processes. The meaning, i.e. functional use of the analyst's technical terms can and should be displayed by means of the descriptive process of collocation; this is not by any means the only way of establishing the 'meaning' of a technical term but there is one positive value to the application of the collocational test. In the description of natural languages, collocation is a means of stating part of the meaning of a word without having to resort to shifted terms and the same can be said of the analysis of the meanings of terms within the technical language of linguistics.

This last device may perhaps not be so very necessary for the modern analyst considering the technical language of contemporary analytical techniques, though this is not to dismiss its usefulness in the case of an obscure term in some modern theory or other. In the case of a theory, drawn up in terms of an intellectual background and concomitant technical terminology more remote in time and entirely different in its general nature, it may well be the only satisfactory guide to the meaning of these *termini technici.* This is certainly true of the metalanguage of the Modistae; it cannot be expected that the student of past theories of grammar will be immediately conversant with the intellectual trends current at the time these theories were formulated, but the collocation test will provide him with a linguistic means of working out in linguistic terms the meaning of their technical language.

It is important to recognize that just as the concept of context of situation and of collocation are vital parts of the analytical process of the linguistic description of a 'text', so too the student of the history of linguistic theory should apply these devices to the analysis and description of the theory under description, i.e. the same analytical processes can be applied to a metalanguage just as they can be to a natural language.

References

The texts used in this study are:

(1) Siger de Courtrai, *Summa Modorum Significandi*, ed. G. Wallerand (Les Œuvres de Siger de Courtrai, Les Philosophes belges, Vol. 8). Louvain, 1913.
(2) Thomas of Erfurt, *Grammatica Speculativa.* M. Doyon, Québec, 1962.
(3) Martin of Dacia, *Tractatus de Modis Significandi*, ed. H. Roos (Corpus Philosophorum Danicorum Medii Aevii, Vol. 2.). Copenhagen, 1961.

Notes

1 It would be wrong and misleading to say that scholars of previous eras were all linguistically naïve; they were for the most part aware of the differences between the technical use of terms especially in a restricted language and their use in everyday language.

2 J.R. Firth, 'The Semantics of Linguistic Science', *Papers in Linguistics*, p. 139.

3 J.R. Firth, op. cit., pp. 140–141.

4 Their definition of the *nomen substantivum* is much more of a functional definition than a metaphysical or logical one, e.g. Thomas of Erfurt, #10.5: modus significandi per modum per se stantis sumitur a proprietate ipsius essentiae determinatae; et hic modus constituit nomen substantivum.

5 J.R. Firth, op. cit., p. 140.

6 J.R. Firth, op. cit., p. 141.

7 J.R. Firth, op. cit., p. 141.

8 M.A.K. Halliday, *The Language of the Chinese Secret History of the Mongols*, Oxford (1959), p. 14.

9 M.A.K. Halliday, loc. cit.

10 J.R. Firth, 'Modes of Meaning', *Papers in Linguistics*, pp. 190–215.

J.R. Firth, 'A Synopsis of Linguistic Theory', *Studies in Linguistic Analysis*, pp. 11–13.

11 R.H. Robins, 'General Linguistics in Great Britain 1930–1960', *Trends in Modern Linguistics*, p. 24.

12 J.R. Firth, 'General Linguistics and Descriptive Grammar', *Papers in Linguistics*, p. 228.

13 These assertions of the validity of the collocation test in no way clash with Halliday's argument, cf. M.A.K. Halliday, 'Categories of the Theory of Grammar', *Word* 17 (1961), p. 249; in this instance, we are not dealing with categories within a linguistic theory which must be mutually defining but with the functions of certain technical terms. In so far then that collocation can be considered a part of lexicography, definition in the lexicographical sense is permissible; we are in fact faced with a narrower definition than lexicography would normally provide and which is forced upon us by the very nature of the context of situation, i.e. we are concerned with the

mutual prehensibility of these terms within the restricted language of Modistic theory, cf. J.R.Firth, 'Synopsis', p. 2.

[14] Siger de Courtrai, p. 135: sicut logica defendit animam nostram a falso in speculativis et a malo in practicis, sic grammatica defendit virtutem nostram interpretativam ab expressione conceptus mentis incongrua in omnibus scientiis.

[15] J.R.Firth, 'The Semantics of Linguistic Science', p. 140.

[16] Modern linguistic theorists have also advocated the use of technical terminology borrowed from other disciplines, in particular, logic, cf. the work of Professor Y.Bar-Hillel.

[17] G.L.Bursill-Hall, *The Doctrine of Partes Orationis in the Speculative Grammars of the Modistae* (unpublished Ph.D. Thesis, University of London), 1959.

G.L.Bursill-Hall, 'Mediaeval grammatical theories', *Canadian Journal of Linguistics* 9 (1963), pp. 39–54.

[18] F.P.Dinneen, S.J., *An Introduction to General Linguistics* (pre-publication edition), Washington, D.C., 1964, p. 19.

[19] Siger de Courtrai, p. 140: nomen dignius est verbo quia substantia dignior est accidente.

[20] The weakness of the Modistic scheme is in fact that these terms are used almost always with either a semantic or philosophic flavour but rarely in a purely formal sense.

[21] Siger de Courtrai, p. 95: modus consignificandi per quem pars est pars praesupponit rationem significandi, vocem et significatum.

[22] Martin of Dacia, #4: dictio est vox habens rationem significandi aliquid.

Thomas of Erfurt, #4: rationem consignificandi, quae vocatur modus significandi activus, per quam vox significans fit consignum, vel consignificans; et sic formaliter est pars orationis.

[23] Martin of Dacia, #16: modus significandi essentialis generalis nominis est modus significandi per modum habitus et quietis.

Martin of Dacia, #19: modus significandi pronominis est modus significandi per modum habitus et quietis.

Martin of Dacia, #20: modus significandi essentialis generalis verbi est modus significandi per modum fieri distantis a substantia.

Martin of Dacia, #24: modus significandi essentialis generalis participii est modus significandi per modum fieri indistantis a substantia.

[24] This contrast reveals the curious strength and weakness of Modistic method. There is a remarkable degree of consistency on criteria which modern linguists would find unacceptable, but when we come to the indeclinable partes orationis, it is as if the Modistae were compelled to resort to much more formal criteria, since it is quite clear that these partes orationis cannot obviously be stated in terms of the correlates of reality, cf. Siger de Courtrai, p. 153: partes indeclinabiles trahunt sua significata ab adiunctis, dicendum quod habent significata et modos significandi secundum se licet varientur secundum adiuncta, quod convenit, quia omnes per modum disponentis significant et disposito variatur secundum variationem disponibilis.

[25] Thomas of Erfurt, #97: illud, quod sic est indeterminatum, quod non excludit, nec includit formam, nec formae determinationem, non est privativum; et sic se habet modus significandi pronominis, qui est modus indeterminati de se, determinabilis tamen.

[26] Thomas of Erfurt, #25.1: modus significandi essentialis generalissimus verbi est

modus significandi rem per modum esse, et distantis a substantia . . . uterque modus, scilicet esse, et distantis, sit forma verbi absolute sumpti, tamen comparando verbum ad participium, modus esse habet rationem materiae, respectu verbi, quia facit verbum cum participio convenire; sed facere convenire, est proprietas materiae: modus autem distantis habet rationem formae, quia facit verbum ab omnibus aliis distare et differe.

[27] Siger de Courtrai, p. 95: modorum significandi essentialium alius generalis, alius specialis seu specificus.

[28] The general mode of the noun and pronoun is the modus entis, cf. Thomas of Erfurt, #23: modus entis habet rationem materiae; the special mode of the noun is the modus determinatae apprehensionis, cf. Thomas of Erfurt, #23: modus determinatae apprehensionis habet rationem formae.

[29] Siger de Courtrai, p. 125: materia est ens in potentia et non in actu.

[30] *Demonstratio* to the Modistae expressed the property of certainty and presence, cf. Thomas of Erfurt, #100: pronomen demonstrativum significat rem sub ratione vel proprietate praesentiae seu notitiae primae.

[31] Cf. J.R. Firth, 'Synopsis', p. 11.

[32] Thomas of Erfurt, #4: pars est pars secundum se per hanc rationem significandi, seu modum significandi activum, tanquam per principium formale . . . rationem consignificandi, quae vocatur modus significandi activus, per quam vox significans fit consignum, vel consignificans; et sic formaliter est pars orationis.

[33] Thomas of Erfurt, #88: genitivus est modus significandi rem in ratione principii, vel termini differenter, proprietate.

Thomas of Erfurt, #85: casus est modus significandi accidentalis nominis, mediante quo nomen proprietatem principii, vel termini consignificat.

[34] Siger de Courtrai, p. 95: modus consignificandi per quem pars est pars praesupponit rationem significandi, vocem et significatum.

Thomas of Erfurt, #4: sed est pars relata ad aliam per eamdem rationem consignificandi activam.

[35] Siger de Courtrai, p. 130: si ista oratio est congrua: 'amo est verbum', aut hoc est ratione significati, aut ratione modi significandi, aut ratione vocis.

Number in Rarotongan Maori

J. E. BUSE

This paper examines the interlocking number systems, grammatical and lexical, which emerge from an analysis of Rarotongan utterances. These systems relate ultimately—and in different ways—to the activity of counting and the resultant concepts of singularity, duality, plurality, paucality and multiplicity. The analysis is based on a corpus of material elicited from native speakers in the Pacific and an informant in London during the preparation of a Rarotongan dictionary and grammar.

Rarotongan Maori is spoken on the island of Rarotonga in the Southern Cooks and is readily understood by speakers of other dialects in the Group. It is closely related to neighbouring East Polynesian languages, especially the Tuamotu dialects and Tahitian, and to New Zealand Maori; it is less closely related to Tongan, Niuean, Samoan and Ellice; less closely again to (Bauan) Fijian; and ultimately to other members of the Malayo-Polynesian family. As the language is little known, we give first a few brief notes on its phonology and grammar.

A (segmental) phonemic analysis shows a nine-term consonant system:

/*p*/	/*t*/	/*k*/	/ʻ/[ʔ]
/*m*/	/*n*/	/*ng*/[ŋ]	
/*v*/			
	/*r*/		

and the usual Polynesian five-term vowel system:

/*i*/				/*u*/
	/*e*/		/*o*/	
		/*a*/		

plus, since each vowel may be contrastively long or short, a length phoneme: /¯/

Minimal pairs for the consonants are: *pā*[1] 'wall', *tā* 'hit', *kā* 'burn', ʻ*ā* 'four', *mā* 'clean', *nā* 'by', *ngā* dual particle, *vā* 'gap', *rā* 'sun', and (contrast with zero) *ā* 'belonging to'; for long vowels: *kī* 'full', *kē* 'different', *kā* 'burn', *kō* 'poke', *kū* 'golden carp'; for contrastive length: *pa'i* 'taro bed', *pa'ī* 'ship'; *kekē* 'foreign', *kēkē* 'armpit'; *tane* 'a skin disease', *tāne* 'male'; *toto* 'blood', *totō* 'drag'; *paku* 'dandruff', *pakū* 'thump'. Consonant clusters do not occur in careful speech, but vowel clusters are common. Syllable structures are statable as V or CV. Because V.V (e.g. *oi*), CV.V (*koi*) and CV.CV (*koki*) structures take about the same utterance time as V̄ (*ō*) and CV̄ (*kō*) structures, and cause similar morphophonemic changes in a preceding word, it is convenient to regard the latter as phonologically dissyllabic (i.e. as V.V and CV.V), although this does not match the syllable as defined phonetically by (say) sonority peaks.

Rarotongan words comprise two basic groups: (1) full-words, a large open class of 'content forms', occurring in the nuclear position in the phrase and bearing the main phrasal stress; (2) particles and clitics, closed groups of free or piece-bound monomorphemic 'function forms', which occur either before or after full-words in sequentially-defined classes that always maintain strict order relative to one another within the phrase. Full-words consist of a single free morpheme (occasionally two morphemes in close juncture) with or without one or more of the following affixes:

(i) a reduplication morpheme, of which two types predominate: (a) partial reduplication, characterized by repetition of the first syllable(s) of the base form, e.g. *'eke*: *'e'eke*, *roa*: *roroa*, *kī*: *kikī*; (b) full reduplication, characterized by repetition of the whole base form, e.g. *'eke*: *'eke'eke*, *roa*: *roaroa*; *kī*: *kīkī*.

(ii) a stem-forming prefix (e.g. *ma-* ~ *mā-*, *tī-*): *ma-'iti*, *mā-'iti'iti*, *tī-poki(poki)*.

(iii) a causative prefix (*'aka-* or *tā-*) added either direct to the root (*'aka-'eke('eke)*, *tā-poki(poki)*) or to the stem (*'aka-mā-'iti'iti*, *tā-tī-pokipoki*). Occasionally both causative prefixes may be present, in which event *'aka-* normally precedes *tā-*, e.g. *'aka-tā-'ipa'ipa*.

(iv) a suffix, either (a) passive (e.g. *-a*, *-ia*), cf.

kua 'oe (au) i te vaka	'(I) paddled the canoe'
kua 'oe-a (e au) te vaka	'the canoe was paddled (by me)'

or (b) nominalizing (e.g. *-manga*, *-tanga*), cf. *tanu* 'bury', *tanu-manga* 'burial-place, tomb'. A full-word such as *'aka-tā-tī-pokipoki-a* exhibits the maximum morphological complexity, containing a fully-reduplicated root (*pokipoki*), a stem-forming prefix (*tī-*), both causative prefixes

(ʻ*aka-*, *tā-*), and a passive suffix (*-a*). Passive suffixation sometimes produces morphophonemic change in the root, e.g. *popoki*: *pōki-a, pā*: *pa-ia.*

Syntactic analysis yields fifteen form-classes:[2]

Pre- or inter-phrasal:	conjunctions
Intra-phrasal:	
pre-nuclear (particles):	prepositions
	determinatives
	number particles
	tense particles
nuclear (full-words):	verbs
	statives
	nouns
	negatives
post-nuclear (particles or clitics):	adverbial particles
	passive clitic
	nominalizing clitic
	direction particles
	location particles
	modifying particles

The ten intra-phrasal classes of particles and clitics occur in the sequence listed above. With the sole exception of the modifying particles only one member of each of these classes can be present in a given phrase, though not all classes need be represented. Of the four pre-nuclear classes, prepositions, determinatives and number particles are mutually exclusive with (do not occur in the same phrase as) the tense particles. The nuclear position in the phrase is occupied by full-words, either singly or in clusters of up to (at least) five. When only one full-word appears certain colligational constraints operate between it and the pre-nuclear particles and post-nuclear clitics.

These constraints may be used to divide full-words into the four sub-classes of verb, stative, noun and negative. *Verbs* colligate with all pre-nuclear and all post-nuclear classes. *Statives* colligate with all pre-nuclear classes and all post-nuclear classes except the passive clitic. *Nouns* colligate with all pre-nuclear classes except the tense particles and with all post-nuclear classes except the passive and nominalizing clitics. *Negatives* (there are only four: *kāre* 'not', ʻ*auraka,* ʻ*aua,* ʻ*eia*ʻ*a,* 'don't') colligate with none of the pre-nuclear classes, but with all of the post-nuclear classes except the clitics. The following table summarizes the colligability of each of the four full-word classes with each of the pre-nuclear and post-nuclear classes. A plus-sign indicates potential colligability, a minus sign indicates non-colligability. It will be observed that the four post-nuclear particles can occur with each of the full-word classes.

		FULL-WORD CLASSES			
		verbs	statives	nouns	negatives
PRE-NUCLEAR	prepositions	+	+	+	–
	determinatives	+	+	+	–
	number particles	+	+	+	–
	tense particles	+	+	–	–
POST-NUCLEAR	adverbial particles	+	+	+	+
	passive clitic	+	–	–	–
	nominalizing clitic	+	+	–	–
	direction particles	+	+	+	+
	location particles	+	+	+	+
	modifying particles	+	+	+	+

Verbs, statives and nouns can occur in mixed clusters in the nuclear position; negatives usually occur only alone. There is very little constraint[3] on the distribution of full-words within clusters, but the latter may be classified as verbal, statival or nominal clusters according as the whole complex exhibits the colligational restraints of (respectively) a single verb, stative or noun. In clusters the first immediate constituent constitutes the head, the second the attribute:

va'ine mānea 'beautiful woman, woman of beauty'
woman beauty

mānea va'ine 'feminine beauty, beauty of woman'
beauty woman

pa'ī aua'i 'steam-ship'
ship smoke

aua'i pa'ī 'smoke from a ship'
smoke ship

pū aua'i 'smoke-stack, chimney, funnel'
stack smoke

pū aua'i pa'ī 'ship's funnel'
stack smoke ship

pa'ī pū aua'i 'ship with funnel'
ship stack smoke

pa'ī pū aua'i roroa 'ship with long funnels'
ship stack smoke long

The above are all nominal clusters.

The phrase as a phonological unit may be defined by juncture phenomena, but this does not altogether correspond with the compositional phrase, a syntactic unit defined and delimited by markers. Phrases are classed as verbal if they commence with a tense particle; as nominal if they commence with a preposition, determinative or number particle; as negatival if they commence with a negative.

The method used here to classify full-words differs from that commonly adopted for other Polynesian languages.[4] Full-words have been grouped to yield classes with a mutually-exclusive membership (no form appears in more than one class), although three of the classes, nouns, statives and verbs, show considerable overlap in their functional range.[5] Nouns have the most limited distribution, being barred from the verbal phrase except as elements in verbal or statival clusters. Statives have a wider functional range: besides sharing the distributional potentialities of nouns, they also occur nuclearly in the verbal phrase and colligate with the nominalizing clitic. Verbs have the widest range: they have all the distributional potentialities of statives, plus the possibility of appearing with the passive clitic.

An alternative analysis,[6] instead of making the *total* distributional range the determining factor in classification, might prefer to assign the same form to different classes whenever it appeared in a different syntactic function, thus tying class to function on a one-to-one basis. This is the method commonly used in describing Polynesian languages. If such an analysis assigned what is here classed as a noun (e.g. *vaka* 'canoe') to let us say Class A when it occurred with a preposition, determinative or number particle (*tōna vaka* 'his canoe'), then it would assign what is here classed as a stative (e.g. *mānea* 'beautiful') to Class A when it appeared with a preposition, determinative or number particle (*tōna mānea* 'her beauty'), but to a second class (Class B) when it appeared with a tense particle (*ka mānea ʻa-ia* ʻshe will be beautifulʼ). It would assign what is here classed as a verb (e.g. *ʻaere* ʻgoʼ) to Classes A and B when its distribution overlapped that of the statives (*tāna ʻaere* ʻhis goingʼ, *ka ʻaere ʻa-ia* ʻhe will goʼ), but perhaps to a third class (Class C) when it occurred with the passive clitic (*ka ʻaere-ʻia te motu* ʻthe island will be visitedʼ).

The classification adopted here (exclusive class membership, overlapping functional ranges) is preferred to the commoner method (overlapping class membership, exclusive functional ranges) mainly because it seems to give a better match with morphological and semantic classes. For instance, what are here classed as nouns do not normally—there are a few exceptions—exhibit reduplication, and are usually concrete. Statives, on the other hand, often show both types of reduplication. The semantic value of these morphological changes remains constant whether the stative is used in a verbal or nominal phrase. Compare the diminutive component carried by full reduplication in the verbal phrase *kua anuanu* (*te vai*) ʻ(the water) has cooled off a bitʼ and the nominal phrase *te anuanu* (*o te vai*) ʻthe coolness (of the water)ʼ as against the base form in *kua anu* (*te vai*) ʻ(the water) has gone coldʼ and *te anu* (*o te vai*) ʻthe coldness (of the water)ʼ. Statives are usually abstract, denoting qualities, states and conditions, e.g. colour words, size and shape terms. Verbs, syntactically distinguished from statives by their colligability with the passive clitic, also form a morphological class by virtue of their colligability with the passive suffix, a privilege not shared by nouns and statives. Verbs and statives enter into different relations with nominal phrases: for instance, after verbs a nominal phrase introduced by the preposition *i* marks the goal of the action; after statives it marks the cause of the condition. Compare the verb *pēʻi* ʻthrowʼ and the stative *puta* ʻwound(ed)ʼ in the identical frames:

kua pēʻi au i te toka ʻI threw the stoneʼ
kua puta au i te toka ʻI was wounded by the stoneʼ.

That this is not merely a notional distinction conditioned by English ideas of transitivity can be demonstrated by the different transformational potentialities of the two sentences. For example, the first sentence has a subject-emphasizing variant:

nā-ku i pēʻi te toka ʻit was me that threw the stoneʼ

but this is impossible with the second sentence:

*(*nā-ku i puta te toka*).[7]

There is perhaps no reason to expect the membership of syntactic classes to correspond with that of morphological or semantic classes (though partial correspondences are often to be noted), and certainly no justification for allowing semantic groupings to bias formal statement. Nevertheless, when there are genuinely alternative methods of syntactic classification, there may be a case for adopting the one which gives maximum correspondence with classes set up by different criteria at other levels.

Members of the following form-classes may expone[8] number: determinatives, number particles, nouns (including the sub-class of pronouns), statives (including the sub-class of numerals) and verbs.

Determinatives as number exponents. The only determinatives concerned here are *te* ~ *t-* and absence. Compare the following:

te vaka	'the canoe' or 'the canoes'
tōku vaka	'my canoe' or 'my canoes'
ōku vaka	'my few canoes'

te and *t-* are in complementary distribution: *t-* appears before the possessive morphemes *ō*, *ā*, *a-*, and the locative morpheme *ē*, when these forms appear in determinatival complexes (see below); *te* appears in all other positions.[9] Neither *te* nor *t-* carries number, but the absence of *t-* marks the following noun, stative or verb as paucal. We have, therefore, a number distinction between a specific paucal and a general term.

Constructions such as *tōku vaka* 'my canoe(s)' are four-unit structures: (1) the determinative, *t-* 'the', (2) the possession morpheme, *ō* 'of', (3) the possessor, *-ku* 'me', (4) the possessed, *vaka* 'canoe(s)'. Filling Place 1 in the structure is a commutation of *t-* and absence,[10] the latter marking the possessed as paucal:

1	2	3	4	
t-	*ō*	*-ku*	*vaka*	'my canoe(s)'
	ō	*-ku*	*vaka*	'my few canoes'

Filling Place 2 in the structure is a four-term system of (i) *ō*, indicating that the possessor (in Place 3) stands in a subordinate or inalienable relationship to the possessed (in Place 4); (ii) *ā*, indicating that the possessor stands in a dominant or alienable relationship to the possessed; (iii) *a-*, indicating that the possessor stands in a neutral relationship, i.e. neither specifically subordinate nor specifically dominant, to the possessed—this morpheme neutralizes the subordinate : dominant opposition exponed by *ō* : *ā*; (iv) *ē*, indicating that the Place 3 form is spatially or numerically related to the Place 4 form. For example:

1	2	3	4	
t-	*ō*	*-ku*	*tūtū*	'my photo' (photo of me)—subordinate
t-	*ā*	*-ku*	*tūtū*	'my photo' (I took or own it)—dominant
t-	*a-*	*-ku*	*tūtū*	'my photo'—neutral
t-	*ē*	*-rā*	*tūtū*	'that photo there'—spatial
	ē	*toru*	*tūtū*	'three photos'—numerical

Filling Place 3 in the structure may be a personal pronoun, a deictic pronoun (*-ia* 'here by me', *-nā* 'there by you', *-rā* 'yonder') or a numeral. There are constraints between the forms in Places 2 and 3: *ō* and *ā* colligate with all pronouns except the three deictics; *a-* with singular personal pronouns only; *ē* only with deictics and numerals. The Place 1 terms (*t-*, absence) colligate with all four Place 2 terms and with all Place 3 terms except the numerals above 'one', which colligate in this construction only with absence. Two forms, *taua* 'the (one(s) in question)' and *tō* 'your (neutral possession)' contain a portmanteau, the second morphs, *aua* and *ō*, filling Places 2 and 3 in the structure:

1	2 3	4	
t-	*aua*	*tūtū*	'the photo(s) we're discussing'
t-	*ō*	*tūtū*	'your photo(s)'—neutral possession.

Short nominal phrases may appear downgraded in Place 3:

1	2	3	4	
t-	*ā*	*te ariki*	*kai*	'the chief's food'
t-	*ē*	*-rā atu*	*vaka*	'the next canoe along'
t-	*ō*	*nana'i i te pōpongi*	*varaoa*	'yesterday morning's bread'

Filling Place 4 in the structure may be a noun (e.g. *puaka* 'pig') or nominal cluster, a stative (e.g. *mānea* 'beautiful') or statival cluster, or a verb (e.g. *'aere* 'go') or verbal cluster:

1	2	3	4	
	ā	*-'au*	*puaka*	'your few pigs'
t-	*ō*	*-na*	*mānea*	'her beauty'
t-	*ā*	*-ku*	*'aere*	'my going, my journey'

It is convenient to refer to the complex of forms occupying Places 1, 2, and 3 as determinativals, since the whole complex commutes with other determinatives which are monomorphemic free forms. Determinativals may be sub-classed as possessives (when *ō*, *ā*, or *a-* stands in Place 2) or demonstratives (when *ē* stands in Place 2).

Rarotongan determinativals exhibit one or two similarities with the semantically similar English determiners (Hill's Group V):[11] in each language possessives and demonstratives belong to one positional class (i.e. are mutually exclusive within the phrase) and precede the nominal head. Rarotongan determinativals and English determiners both signal a two-term number distinction, but whereas all Rarotongan determinativals may expone number, it is exponed in the English class only by the demonstratives (*this*, *these; that*, *those*). In any case, the distinction is different in nature: in Rarotongan there is a contrast between a specific paucal (*ērā vaka* 'the few canoes over there') and a general term (*tērā vaka* 'the canoe(s) over there'); in English there is a contradictory opposition between singular and plural (*that canoe*, *those canoes*), use of the demonstrative compelling the statement of number. In Rarotongan, use of the *t-* form makes no statement of number and the speaker is under no grammatical constraint to use the specific paucal form when only a few things are involved, unless a numeral above 'one' appears in Place 3. (There may, of course, be social constraint, as when speaking modestly of the number of one's own possessions.)

Number particles as number exponents. Rarotongan has two number particles: *ngā*, marking the following full-word as dual, and *au*, marking it as multiple:

tāna ngā puaka	'his couple of pigs'
tāna au puaka	'his many pigs'

The number particle need not, however, be present:

tāna puaka	'his pig(s)'

There is, therefore, in the particle position a three-term contrast between a specific dual (*ngā*), a specific multiple (*au*), and a general term (absence).[12] The only constraint between the determinatival system (*t-*: absence) and the number particle system (*ngā*: *au*: absence) is that determinative absence and the multiple number particle are mutually exclusive (i.e. **āna au puaka* is inadmissible).

Nouns as number exponents. The great majority of nouns carry no formal mark of number. The few that do form two groups. Group 1 (all with human referents, often kinship terms) lengthens a stem vowel to form a specific plural:

va'ine	'woman, women'	*vā'ine*	'women'
tangata	'man, men'	*tāngata*	'men'
tua'ine	'a man's sister(s)'	*tuā'ine*	'a man's sisters'

The distinction here is between a general term (short root vowel) and a specific plural (long root vowel). Group 2 forms a plural by full reduplication:

ava	'reef-channel(s)'	*avaava*	'small reef-channels'
miro	'garfish'	*miromiro*	'some small garfish'
potonga	'hunk(s)'	*potopotonga*	'little lumps, gobbets'

The contrast again is between a general term and a specific plural, but with these nouns reduplication exponesa diminutive component as well as simple plurality. One noun, *tamaiti* 'child', is used with singular reference only; the stative *tamariki* 'children, be a child' serves as a plural: *tāna tamariki* 'his children'. This appears to the only example of singular : plural opposition.

A sub-class of nouns, personal pronouns, expone a three-term number system of singular: dual: plural. The pronouns are given below in the forms in which they appear when standing as subject to a verbal phrase:

	FIRST		SECOND	THIRD
SINGULAR	*au*		*koe*	*ia*
	INCLUSIVE	EXCLUSIVE		
DUAL	*tā-ua*	*mā-ua*	*kō-rua*	*rā-ua*
PLURAL	*tā-tou*	*mā-tou*	*kō-tou*	*rā-tou*

The dual and plural forms all contain two morphemes: (1) a four-term person system of *tā-* (inclusive), *mā-* (exclusive), *kō-* (second), *rā-* (third); (2) a two-term number system of *-ua* ~ *-rua* (dual), *-tou* (plural). The singular forms are portmanteaus, exponing both person and singular number. There is partial resumptive constraint between pronouns and the other number systems. Thus a nominal phrase containing a paucal determinatival must be resumed by a dual or plural pronoun; a nominal phrase containing a dual number particle is normally resumed by a dual pronoun, a phrase with a multiple particle by a plural pronoun, etc. There is also resumptive constraint between pronouns and a few collective nouns, e.g. *pea* ‘pair’ and *puke* ‘a couple’ must be resumed by a dual pronoun, *aronga* ‘group’ and *ānana* ‘herd, band’ by a plural pronoun. Similarly one name must be resumed by a singular pronoun, two names by a dual pronoun, etc.

kua ‘oro te au va‘ine ki uta ē kua ngaro rātou
.... *te ngā va‘ine* .... *rāua*
.... *‘a Tangaroa* .... *‘a ia*
.... *‘a Tā ē Pā* .... *rāua*
.... *te ānana keiā* .... *rātou*

the (many) women ran inland and they (plural) became lost
the (two) women .... they (dual) ....
Tangaroa .... he ....
Tā and Pā .... they (dual) ....
the band of robbers .... they (plural) ....

Numerals as number exponents. Rarotongan numerals are a sub-class of statives, distinguished by their potentiality of being prefixed by *toko-*, indicating that human beings are being counted, and by *taki-*, indicating that the numeral is being used distributively:

ko ‘ai te toko-rima? ‘who is the fifth (person)?’
ka taki-rima mē tu‘a ‘share them out in fives’

The numerals run from ‘one’ to ‘nine’: *ta‘i* ‘one’, *rua* ‘two’, *toru* ‘three’, *‘ā* ‘four’, *rima* ‘five’ (also ‘hand’), *ono* ‘six’, *‘itu* ‘seven’, *varu* ‘eight’, *iva* ‘nine’. The other terms in the count-system are mainly nouns (*nga‘uru* ‘a ten’, *tekau* ‘a score’). The larger numbers are mostly borrowed from English (*‘ānere* < ‘hundred’, *tauatini* < ‘thousand’). Numerals, of course, make an explicit lexical statement of number, but constraint is mostly of the resumptive type:

toko-rua tangata ..... *rāua* ‘two men ..... they (dual)’
toko-toru tangata ..... *rātou* ‘three men ..... they (plural)’

Numerals above ‘one’ appear only in paucal determinativals, i.e. only *ē rua tangata* ‘two men’ is permissible, not **tē rua tangata*; *ta‘i* may, however, appear with both *t-* and absence:

tēta‘i tangata ‘a certain man, certain men’
ēta‘i tangata ‘some (few) men’

Naturally there is also constraint with the number particle system, e.g. *ngā tangata toko-rua* 'two men' is permissible, but not **te au tangata toko-rua*.

Reduplication as a number exponent. In the great majority of verbs and statives, partial reduplication carries a complex of meanings. Some or all of the following components are usually present: (1) intensive action: *kua tupu te rākau* 'the plant(s) grew', *kua tutupu te rākau* 'the plant(s) grew rapidly (or luxuriantly)', 'the plant(s) grew and grew'; *kua piri te pā* 'the door is shut', *kua pipiri te pā* 'the door is jammed'; (2) completed and maintained action: *kumu* 'squeeze', *kukumu* 'hold the fist clenched'; (3) plural action: *kua 'oki te tangata* 'the man (men) returned', *kua 'o'oki te tangata* 'the men returned'; (4) reciprocal action: *kua 'ongi 'a Tere iāia* 'Tere kissed her', *kua 'o'ongi rāua* 'they kissed one another'.

Full reduplication carries the following meanings: (1) frequentative action: *kua tuputupu mai te kao* 'the buds are coming out (here and there, a few on each tree)'; (2) progressive or gradual action: *kua tuku rātou i te kupenga* 'they lowered the net', *kua tukutuku rātou i te kupenga* 'they paid out the net'; diminutive action, weakened state: *kua miri 'a Mere i tōna mokotua* 'Mere rubbed his back', *kua mirimiri 'a Mere i te punua kiore* 'Mere fondled (stroked gently) the kitten'. Again, more than one of these components may be present: compare the diminutive–frequentative complex in the following: *kua mātipi 'a Tere i te taro*, 'Tere sliced the taro', *kua mātipitipi 'a Tere i te pēni*, 'Tere sharpened the pencil' (using a knife with repeated small slicing movements); *kua kanapa te uira* 'the lightning flashed', *kua kānapanapa te tai* 'the sea sparkled'.

As a rule there is little to be gained by attempting to isolate number from the other components in these forms, especially as there is rarely any constraint between subject and verb or verb and object in the reduplicated forms. Nevertheless, a few statives do form specific plurals by partial reduplication and in these cases only the plurality component is present: *te rākau roa* 'the long stick(s)', *te rākau roroa* 'the long sticks'; *kua ma'ata te puaka* 'the pig(s) has (have) got big', *kua mama'ata te puaka* 'the pigs have got big'. Other examples are *kino*: *kikino* 'bad', *meitaki*: *memeitaki* 'good'. The unreduplicated forms may be used whether the referent is one object or several, but the reduplicated forms only with a plural referent.

A handful of forms show a third type of reduplication, double reduplication. This consists of double repetition of the first syllable of the base form, with lengthening of the first syllable of the reduplicated form:

base form	partial rdpl.	full rdpl.	double rdpl.
moe (sleep)	*momoe*	*moemoe*	*mōmomoe*
moto (punch)	*momoto*	*motomoto*	*mōmomoto*
no'o (stay)	*nono'o*	*no'ono'o*	*nōnono'o*
'oro (run)	*'o'oro*	*'oro'oro*	*'ō'o'oro*

Doubly-reduplicated forms are very rarely heard, but older speakers appear to use these forms only with a dual subject or occasionally with a plural subject with the implication of paired action, e.g. *'ārāvei 'iōra rātou ē mōmomoto atūra* 'then they all came together and started fighting (one with another)'. Double reduplication is never used if the subject has a singular referent. Younger speakers hardly ever use the doubly-reduplicated forms, but substitute the partially-reduplicated forms, which also carry the components of intensive or maintained action. It seems likely that double reduplication represents an old dual or reciprocal, now obsolescent.

Leaving aside these obsolescent doubly-reduplicated forms, the following are the main number systems that have been noted:

(1) a two-term system of paucal : general, exponed in the determinatival by absence: *t-*, (*āna puaka* 'his few pigs', *tāna puaka* 'his pig(s)');
(2) a three-term system of dual : multiple : general, exponed in the number particles by *ngā* : *au* : absence;
(3) a two-term system of plural : general, exponed (i) in a few nouns by lengthening of the stem vowel (*vā'ine* : *va'ine*, *tangata* : *tāngata*); (ii) in a few nouns by full reduplication (*avaava* : *ava*, *potopotonga* : *potonga*), but here a diminutive component is also present; (iii) in a few statives by partial reduplication (*roroa* : *roa*, *memeitaki* : *meitaki*). In most partially reduplicated forms, however, the number component is combined with components of intensity and maintained action;
(4) a three-term system of singular : dual : plural, exponed by personal pronouns (e.g. *koe* : *kōrua* : *kōtou*);
(5) a multi-term numeral system.

Characteristic of the first three systems is the lack of a specific singular and the appearance of what is here called a general term. This means that the Rarotongan speaker is not compelled to make a statement of number as are speakers of languages where the category is exponed by a contradictory opposition (e.g. *this* : *these*). Though there is partial constraint between these systems, e.g. the paucal determinatival and the multiple number particle are mutually exclusive, the speaker is always free to use the general term, regardless of any specific number statement in the other two systems.

It is the interlocking of the different systems, e.g. the resumption of a nominal phrase containing a dual number particle by a dual personal pronoun, which justifies setting up number as a generic category in Rarotongan, though descriptive analysis must, of course, separate the individual systems on a formal basis.

Notes

1 Rarotongan forms are cited in the normal orthography, except that /¯/ and /ʻ/ are marked wherever they occur. Rarotongans usually write them—if at all— only where confusion might arise between minimal pairs. A hyphen is occasionally used to draw attention to a morpheme boundary.

2 Rarotongan word-classes are examined in more detail in J.E.Buse, 'The Structure of the Rarotongan Verbal Piece', *BSOAS* xxvi.1 (1963), and in 'The Structure of Rarotongan Nominal Pieces', *BSOAS* xxvi.2 (1963). The terminology used here differs slightly, but the analysis is basically the same.

3 I.e. the constraint is insufficiently generalizable for inclusion in the 'grammar'—there is, of course, more particularized or 'lexical' constraint.

4 See, however, Bruce Biggs, 'The Structure of New Zealand Maori', *Anthropological Linguistics*, iii.3 (1961), esp. pp. 23–27 and 37–38.

5 See the table on p. 55.

6 Different methods of classification in cases of this type are outlined in C.E. Bazell, *Linguistic Typology* (O.U.P. 1958), p. 7 et seq.

7 See further in J.E.Buse, 'Rarotongan Sentence Structures', *BSOAS* xxvi.3 (1963), p. 635 et seq.

8 The verb 'expone' is used throughout to avoid such circumlocutions as 'serve as the exponent of' (a category).

9 Compare: *te vaka ō-ku* 'the canoe(s) of mine' with: *t-ō-ku vaka* 'my canoe(s)', the *t-* alternant appearing when the possessive complex (*ō-ku* 'of me') is intercalated before *vaka*, the head of the construction.

10 'Absence' is used here instead of 'zero' because although the absence of *t-* is relevant to the statement of number it has no overt allomorph, i.e. there is contrast but no alternation. Cf. W. Haas, 'Zero in Linguistic Description'. *Studies in Linguistic Analysis* (Oxford, 1957), esp. pp. 41–49.

11 Archibald A.Hill, *Introduction to Linguistic Structures* (New York 1958), p. 176 et seq.

12 Absence is here grammatically as well as semantically relevant, e.g. *te vaʻine* 'the woman, women' could be resumed by any personal pronoun, but *te au vaʻine* 'the many women' only by a plural pronoun. Cf. J.Carnochan, 'The Category of Number in Igbo Grammar', *Afr. L. S.*, iii (1962), p. 115.

Some Modes of Anglo-Saxon Meaning

MARJORIE DAUNT

I. The Spectrum of Meaning

In his *Modes of Meaning*[1] (1951), J. R. Firth described a scheme of approach to 'meaning' in language 'other than or rather including sense'. This scheme he called the 'Spectrum of Meaning'. Two quotations from his essay explain his theory:

> 'Having made the first abstraction by suitably isolating a piece of "text" or part of the social process of speaking for a listener or of writing for a reader, the suggested procedure for dealing with meaning is its dispersion into modes, rather like the dispersion of light of mixed wavelengths into a spectrum.'
>
> 'To make statements of meaning in terms of linguistics, we may accept the language event as a whole and then deal with it at various levels, sometimes in a descending order, beginning with social context and proceeding through syntax and vocabulary to phonology and even phonetics, and at other times in the opposite order.'

Firth's order of approach is:

(a) the verbal process in the context of situation;
(b) the technique of syntax—concerned with the word process in the sentence;
(c) phonology (which) states the phonematic and prosodic processes within the word and sentence, regarding them as a mode of meaning;
(d) phonetics which links all this with the processes and features of utterance. 'Surely it is part of the meaning of an American to sound like one.'

J. R. Firth often urged me to apply this scheme, as far as was possible to Anglo-Saxon, and especially to Anglo-Saxon poetry, since that was in many ways more 'native' than much of the later prose. This I am now attempting to do, but the difficulties have been great. When Firth applied his spectrum to Swinburne, no one else had ever looked at Swinburne from that point of view, but Anglo-Saxon poetry has been analysed and examined in thousands of books, articles and theses on most of the levels of the spectrum so that a complete spectrum approach would repeat much that is now knowledge taken for granted. After much testing, comparing, counting statistics, sifting, discarding and formulating, I can only offer results as pioneer findings, some as experiments which might be profitably developed.

Firth had many advantages in applying his spectrum. He could assume for his material, especially for Swinburne, a pronunciation and basic syntax reasonably like his own educated modern English. Swinburne was not obliged to work in any traditional poetic convention so that his mannerisms were free and his own; also Firth could supply the collocations implicit in many words and phrases from his own lifelong, linguistic experience. His 'silly ass, young ass', etc., trail clouds of context behind them. How different is the case when we turn to Anglo-Saxon poetry. The poet's personal art has to be disentangled from the centuries-old poetic tradition in which he had been trained. This can only be done by patient extraction of features of style common to the majority of Anglo-Saxon poems and then a proportion of usage must be established to show idiosyncrasy of any one poet. Then when something has been found which seems individual it can only be claimed tentatively on account of the lost poems. Who can be sure that *beadu-leoma*, 'the flame of battle', one of the very finest kennings for the sword, now found only in *Beowulf* did not also occur in *Ingeld*?

The present investigation has been partly based on the first hundred lines of *Beowulf*, *Andreas*, *Elene* and *Guþlac I* (11. 30–130).

Results have of course been tested elsewhere. Statistics have been summarized but the full counts are available. The findings might be grouped 'useful', 'hopeful' and 'possible'.

II. The Useful Findings

These, as might be expected, lie largely on the contextual and collocational levels, which in Anglo-Saxon cannot be entirely divorced. Collocation has to be established and this can only be done by collecting contexts. The collocations of Anglo-Saxon poetry are of two kinds, either single words with other word or words, or what are often called 'compounds' which are so variable and flexible that it seems reasonable to regard them as a form of free collocation.

Professor R. Quirk has recently published a paper on the literary collocations of alliterating groups[2] and this is most interesting, but there is a wide field to explore in simpler and less literary words, such as *god* 'good', *murnan, wadan, eadig.*[3]

Murnan works with *mod* in various syntactic groupings, *murnan on mode, murnende mod,* etc., and is always deeply serious and sad, but when *murnan* is collocated with *ne,* or *ne þearf* the overtones are satiric. Grendel *ne mearn* at the slaughter he inflicted on the Danes, far from it indeed.

Wadan has overtones of the cleaving of water; it is used for ships, for swords going through flesh and, more important, through *blood.* Then it is collocated with warriors walking purposefully, in fact striding, and even of Grendel striding along. The long stride is only one stage away from our sense of 'wading'. In this sense *wadan* is never used of women. In later prose it is used figuratively of plunging mentally into depths of thought. The verbal collocations are revealing: *þurh, ofer, on* ('in').

All these collocations add to the flavour of Anglo-Saxon poetry and many more words should be tested on the collocation level. Most important among those I have tested is *god* 'good'. As Hamlet rightly said 'thinking makes it so' and, in *Beowulf, god* is charged with pre-Christian heroic values.

God is collocated with *cyning,* and is used only for the 'great' kings Hroþgar (and Hroþulf), Hygelac, Onela and Ongenþeow, and Scyld; in the case of the last-named, his *god* quality is explained in the preceding lines. He snatched away the mead-benches of his enemies and terrified them. The hero Beowulf is, of course, *se goda* and Æschere is *ær-god.*

God is also collocated with ship, sword, hawk, and *þara goda* of which Grendel is ignorant, is generally accepted as referring to 'the gentle art of swordsmanship'. The word also appears in contexts denoting manly physical prowess, such as the collocation with *guþrinc.* Beowulf is frequently *god* in this sense and Wiglaf, in his taunting of the cowards, says his lord needs *godra guþrinca.* Such brave warriors won the hoard which the last survivor put in the dragon's cave. In the 'ugly duckling' version of Beowulf's youth, the Geatas thought that he was not *god,* but an *æþeling unfrom.* A very significant collocation comes in the polite remark of the Danish coast-warden to Beowulf and his men that it must happen to *god-fremmendra swylcum* that they return safely. This refers to their obvious fighting qualities, *god* is something you *do.*

A step away from this leads to the other qualities a noble heroic warrior should possess, chief among which comes open-handedness, largesse. Beowulf and Hroþgar are both *gum-cystum god*, and *gode* (Instrumental), as a means by which a young man may gather followers round him, is paralleled by *fromum feohgiftum*. It is violence and meanness that keeps Heremod from ever being *god*, in spite of his splendid fighting prowess. The queen, Wealhþeow, is famous for behaving as a queen should, *gode mære*, and she looks in vain for nobility of spirit, *gode*, from Hroþulf. Beowulf as king:

Swa bealdode bearn Ecgþeowes
guma guðum cuð, godum dædum
dreah æfter dome nealles druncne slog
heord-geneatas; næs him hreoh sefa

In polite address it has overtones of courteous behaviour. Beowulf says to the coast-warden 'Be so *god* as to advise us', very much as we should today. When he later asks to approach Hroþgar, *swa godne*, it is almost the equivalent of 'His Highness' or 'Excellency'.

A little ambiguously Hroþgar is *frod and god*, evidently a traditional rhyming phrase which seems to combine qualities of head and heart. It appears elsewhere. Occasionally, *gode* is what is given, 'gift' or 'goods'.

Nowhere in *Beowulf* does *god* have the overtones of personal morality, as opposed to social, which the word 'good' has today. The old values died hard. 'Good knights' in the Middle Ages were often far from 'good'. And we still use the word with ships, horses, swords (if any), knives, but noticeably *never* with bombs or rockets.

A man can be 'good' at games still or a 'good man in a team', 'a good craftsman', 'a good soldier', but *not* 'a good shop-keeper' or even 'merchant' or 'wholesaler'.

It is a surprise to find when we turn to the three more definitely Christian poems *Andreas*, *Elene* and *Guþlac I* that the word *god* scarcely appears and then not in the heroic sense. Andreas is considered to be strongly influenced by *Beowulf*, but is not in this use; *godne* is found twice referring to God and God's kindness. As a noun it comes twice in the phrase *gode orfeorme* 'lacking prosperity' (or happiness), once it is plainly 'needs, or means of living'.

Elene has only three instances of *god*; *god-dend* 'benefactors, givers of money', obviously a faint echo of the past, and equally obviously avoiding *god fremmende*, *frodra ond godra*, the traditional phrase is used, and *goda geasne* 'destitute of all good things' is said by Satan.

Guþlac is once *god*, but since he is *Cristes cempa* and *eadig oretta*, this looks like a bridge from the heroic to the Christian outlook.

I have dealt with *god* at some length because it looks as if the collocations of many quite simple words might reveal a determination on the part of the strongly Christian poets to avoid words which could rouse the older pre-Christian ideals, which were certainly strong enough to live for centuries, and instead to give Christian value to words which had been comparatively harmless. This conversion is plain in the case of *eadig*.

In *Beowulf* this word always refers to material possessions, the *eadig* man leaves land and possessions to his heirs.

The compounds of *eadig* which are really collocations, are *ceap-*, *dom-*, *efen-*, *hreþ-*, *hwæt-*, *sige-*, *sigor-*, *tir-*, all either indicating possessions or the victory which brings them, and the glory they brought. It was not a very difficult transition from treasure on earth to treasure in Heaven, and it was made.

Elene is *seo eadige* = *beata* and *eadige* are the blessed souls in Heaven.

Two more words the collocations of which changed from very high to low are *beot* and *gilp*, the vow to undertake some brave deed and the proper and natural triumph when it is achieved. There would be no need to dwell on these words, about which much has been written, if several distinguished recent editors[4] did not put 'boast' as the *first* meaning in their *Beowulf* vocabularies. The word does not occur in *Beowulf* in any collocation which could suggest the overtones of modern 'boast'. The *gilp-cwide* of Beowulf pleased the Queen. The collocations are *æfnan*, *gelæstan*, *ne aleogan* when the undertaking is carried out, *ne þearf* when it fails.

Beowulf sadly *beot-wordum spræc niehstan siþe*; the operative word here is *niehstan*.

Only two instances are less clearly praiseworthy. The Heaþobeard warrior, who egged on the young man to kill the Dane wearing the treasures which his dead Heaþobeard father had lost at the Danish invasion, was angry because the Dane had a right to *gilp*, however tactless it might be. The father had been killed in battle, not murdered; *morþor*, the word used here, means any killing disapproved of, not 'murder' in the modern sense. Again *Unferþ* is henceforth to be more silent about *gilp-spræce* of warlike deeds presumably his own, or does it mean doubting Beowulf's? As far as the poem tells *Unferþ* has never made a *gilp*.[5]

In *Andreas*, *beot* is entirely avoided and *gilp* appears only once referring to the courage of Andreas but put, significantly, into the mouths of his enemies.

Neither *beot* nor *gilp* is to be found in *Elene* which is not surprising since they are not words for a woman.

In *Guþlac*, who in his younger years might have uttered both, only *gilp* appears twice and the collocations are bad; *gilp* against the power of God will fail, and arrogance grows through *idel gilp*. A glance at the dictionary will show that the words become more and more 'boastful' in the mouths of the homilists, as indeed they must if humility is to be preached. In short *beot* and *gilp* were correct behaviour for a pre-Christian warrior. Till the artificial Code of Chivalry came into fashion, whether the clergy approved or not, the warrior could say what he meant to attempt, achieve it, and say he had done it. I can only beg the editors to remove 'boast' from *Beowulf* editions.

In the second group of loose-compound collocations there are many which are clearly in the poetical vocabulary

e.g. *heoro-*,[6] *hild-*, *beadu-*

Here the poet's idiosyncrasies are easier to find.

In *Beowulf*, only, appear:

heoro-weallende, *heoro-wearh*, *heoro-serce*,
heoro-hociht, *heoro-drync*, *heoro-dreor;*

heoru 'sword' brings 'blood' with it, or 'sharpness' or 'danger.'

Hygelac died *heoro-dryncum*, i.e. the swords drinking his blood. If the *Beowulf* poet invented this collocation it shows how fine his imagination was. He uses several other *heoro-* collocations from the common stock.

Andreas has only *heoru-dolg* 'sword wound'. *Elene* has *heoro-dreorig* (also in *Beowulf*) a good collocation 'dripping with fresh shed blood', *heoro-grim* and *heoro-cumbol*, all of which are found elsewhere; *Guþlac* has none. In the case of *beadu-* *Beowulf* has seven forms not found elsewhere but these are mostly solid words for swords and armour, with the exception of *beadu-leoma*, already mentioned, which is highly picturesque if we remember that when the Saxons had swords they fought sabre.

Andreas has only two unimaginative *beadu-* words which are unique and *Elene* has *beadu-þreat* as a sole instance, which again is practical rather than imaginative. The same exciting art in the *Beowulf* poet shows in the collocations of *hild*—twenty-seven in all. Of these ten are only in this poem and two at least of the unique ones are of fine quality; *hilde-leoma* is the same as *beadu-leoma* and shows how persistently the idea haunted the verse, and *hilde-gicel* 'battle-icicle' describes how the sword melted in Beowulf's hand when the poisonous blood of Grendel's mother was on it.

Andreas has ten *hild-* word groups and of these *hilde-þrymm*, *hild-stapa*, *hild-bedd* are individual, but not highly imaginative.

Still among the 'useful' results of examination by spectrum is one from the phonetic level. If the metrical stresses are looked at from this angle it will be found that in all four poems a large majority are strongly voiced. It is a phonetic commonplace that a vowel or consonant is longer before a voiced consonant than before a breath one; e.g. *bead* is longer than *beat*, *send* than *sent*. Anglo-Saxon *wid-* would be longer than *wit-* and more voiced.

These frequencies can be tested by a count based on what we do know about Anglo-Saxon consonants. In the first twenty-one lines of the four poems the proportions of stressed syllables are:

Beowulf	Breath	19	Voice	65
Andreas		27		55
Elene		30		54
Guþlac		17		63

These results may be compared with stressed syllables in later prose passages of equal length where, of course, we can only stress from sense:

Ælfred's *Orosius*[7]	Breath	39	Voice	55
The Voyage of Ohthere[8]		30		61
The Voyage of Wulfstan[9]		30		71
The Parker Chronicle[10] (896)		44		62

This preponderance of voice in some poems is important for realization of the sound of the lines. It is part of the 'meaning' of *Beowulf*, possibly to be more musical than *Elene*, and of the 'meaning' of *Guþlac* to be as musical in this respect as *Beowulf*.

The last twenty lines of *Beowulf* show the same Breath-Voice proportions, 19–61, but *Andreas*, ll. 1429–1459, has Breath-Voice = 32–124 which is nearer to Beowulf, but *Elene*, ll. 1147–1167, still has a more prose-like frequency Breath-Voice, 32–52.

The same preference for Voice shows in the use of double consonants. We know that double consonants were 'long', e.g. *cwelan* and *cwellan* were different words. These long consonants might hold the line up, particularly if they were Breath Sounds. In the first hundred lines of our four test-poems, taking only main stresses, the double consonants are:

Beowulf	Breath 6	Voice 16
Andreas	5	14
Elene	4	9
Guþlac	9	19

The significance of all these statistics from the 'meaning' point of view is that voiced consonants are much better to sing, or intone, through, and carry further when spoken. Anyone who has learnt singing from a competent singing master will remember hours of practice at 'singing consonant' exercises. Is it impossible that *Scops* trained in a long tradition of oral, and *not* impromptu, poetry had evolved a 'sound voice technique' and that any good poet understood this?

III. The Hopeful Findings

These are for the most part on the phonological[11] level. The 'metre' of *Beowulf* and other Anglo-Saxon poems has been examined for about 150 years and recently classified exhaustively by A. J. Bliss[12] and his patient and useful work deserves the gratitude of all Anglo-Saxonists.

For me the most valuable part of the work is Chapter Seventeen ('Towards an Interpretation'), where Bliss strongly opposes the views of Heusler and Pope, the latter of whom always seems to me to be making up a pleasant artificial game, and ignoring the conditions of life, purpose and heredity of the Anglo-Saxon poems. Especially good is the passage:

> 'It must be regretfully admitted that we know nothing at all of Anglo-Saxon music, and the only contemporary music of which we have any detailed knowledge, the Gregorian chant, is certainly not isochronous; its rhythm is variable, and is entirely dependent on the natural prose rhythm of the words sung; any such arbitrary lengthening of words and syllables as is required by the chronometric theory is quite alien to its nature. It is still possible of course that Anglo-Saxon music was entirely different from the Gregorian chant, and was, in fact, isochronous, but we are certainly not entitled to assume it, still less to base an elaborate theory on the assumption.'

There are some other points to be considered in this connection, what J. R. Firth would call the Context of Situation. When *Beowulf* was composed there was no existing English prose and the present almost devout, and often blinkered, approach to 'poetry' could not have existed either.

The distinction was alliterative verse for the generally non-reading public, Latin prose for the intellectuals. The plain aim of most Anglo-Saxon verse was instruction, the audience must understand and if possible memorize what they heard. This verse method lasted for centuries. If these poems were 'sung' in the hall, after food, to men who had been out on strenuous exercise all day, they *must* have kept the rhythm and pattern of the spoken language,[12] or the *Scop* would have been drowned by snores. It is dangerous to compare Anglo-Saxon verse with any modern verse pattern, unless perhaps blank verse. Too much importance is given to 'half-lines', not that they do not exist but the pause (if any) is a breath-pause, not an artistic device. The *Scop* might be a young man with good lungs, capable of 'singing' two lines, or an older man who needed to 'sneak' breath.

cf. *Nu her þara banena byre nat-hwylces*
frætwum hremig on flet gæþ (Beo. 2053–2054)

Here the 'caesura' of l. 2053 is the very slightest possibility for a breath, the real breath pause is at the end of the line and in the middle of the next line, l. 2054a stands out emphasized, while 2054b is not really important since *her* has already said it.

The whole question of prosody should be considered not only in lines but in *sense-groups*. (Who would suggest that Shakespeare's verse was ever mouthed out in half-line units?) The basic rhythm of the poet is not in the line only, but runs on. This is what Sievers was reaching for in his last years when he denounced his 'types' and tried to discover a basic personal rhythm for each poet. I believe he was inspired to do this by hearing an opera singer singing long passages, the words of which in Germany have to be heard.

The 'spectrum' led me to examine the sense-groups however they are punctuated in printed editions. The first fifty-two lines of *Beowulf*, grouped by sense and classed as ABCDE half-lines for convenience, run:

CCDACA / CAAEABA / BAEADCAA / C / BAACA /
ECAA / CAE / A–D–AE / CADCCAACA / EAA /
BCAC / ACABBDDA / BAAE / BAACA / BCA /
DAACA / BACBA / AACAAD / ADAACA / BE /
AADAB /

Here are 21 Sense-Groups and of these 6 end with the sequence ACA, ACA comes at the beginning of one group and the middle of another;

E ends 3 groups and each seems to want an emphasis. Space will not allow me to go further here, but *Andreas* ll. 1–50 are useful for contrast:

ACAEA / BDBABDA / AADCABCDC /
BBAAA / BAABDAA / BCA / AAAAA /
BABCBDAA / CCDADAA / AAEBDADA /
AAADBDA / AACDBCA / CBACCEEACE /
AAA / CDC / BACADBA /

Here the noticeable features are AAA three times and AAAAA in one group; naturally the As tend to be of different kinds according to Bliss's classification. It would be interesting to analyse further the variations of repeated types here, and elsewhere. This section, however, is only the 'hopefuls'. This is a prosodic meaning, which might help to answer the question 'Why, from reading only, are we sure Cynewulf did not compose *Beowulf*?'

Then idiosyncrasy in alliteration comes in here. A simple count shows one poem to have more instances of the alliteration on one sound than another, though the poetic vocabulary must have been much the same for all. In the first hundred lines of the four poems the top five sounds in frequency are:

Beowulf	vowel 16, F 13, H 13, W 10, L 9
Andreas	H 16, vowel 14, M 13, W 11, F 8
Elene	W 15, H 15, vowel 13, C 8, R 7
Guþlac	vowel 16, H 16, W 12, M 9, G 9

These counts may have been made in some cases, as Kent did for *Elene*, but even he only said 'vowel alliteration was very frequent', and I have not seen final statistics of preference.

IV. The Possible Findings

Under this heading come some odd pieces of linguistic information shown up by the spectrum which might be enlarged into further aspects of 'meaning'.

All four poems have a tendency to run alliterating lines in groups, and *Beowulf* tends to have longer groups.

e.g. *Beowulf* (1–100)	vowel FW (7–9) F vowel W (21–23, 91–93)
	GF vowel (13–15, 20–22) F vowel G (45–47)
	vowel G F (71–73)
	F vowel H (55–57, 76–78)

Is there a phonetic relationship of labial and velar here?

Later in *Beowulf* (1251–) the patterning is most marked:

vowel G vowel	(1252–54)
H S H	(1288–90)
vowel F vowel	(1292–94)
S vowel S vowel	(1311–13)
vowel R vowel	(1324–26)
H vowel vowel H	(1327–30)
F N F	(1339–61)
vowel H vowel	(1371–73)
F S F	(1378–80)

In *Elene* (1–100) WH comes 6 times, once combined into WH WH:

WH WH	(17–20)
W vowel H	(63–65) and
WH vowel	(72–75)

and two long groups SWH vowel S vowel W (72–77) and
vowel H W S H vowel (82–87)

Similar groups and sequences are to be found in *Andreas* and *Guþlac I.* There is a tendency towards certain groups GW, GH or WF and pairs of alliterating lines are fairly frequent. The frequency of any of these features might be a 'meaning'.

A second 'possibility' is the further exploration of the Anglian origin of *Beowulf* and the others on the phonetic level. The Anglian origin is invoked by editors to make *hean huses* a 'complete' half-line or to explain *sendan* in Grendel's behaviour. But we do know a few phonetic facts about Anglian and one is that where West Saxon had [æ:] Anglian had [æ:] and [e:] resulting from difference of origin.

A line like:

leode gelæstan lof-dædum sceal (Beo. 24)

would in Anglian have [e:] in *dædum* and so show a pleasant variation of vowel comparable to Chaucer's delightful:

Whan Zefirus eek with his swete breeth

If established Anglian characteristics are replaced in *Beowulf* interesting results appear. I am not suggesting that we ought to go back. If King Alfred passed the West Saxon version as he may have done, it is good enough for me.

A small last point is one that I have not seen noticed, that is the alliterative 'pick-up'. Fairly often the last non-alliterating stress of a line alliterates with the line below, or, occasionally, above:

e.g. *þæt hine on ylde eft gewunigen*
wil-gesiþas þonne wig cume (Beo. 22–23)

This could be accidental, but it could also be a sense junction or emphasis.

Sometimes the non-alliterating stresses of two lines pair in alliteration.

In *Beowulf* (1–100) pick-up alliteration comes 8 times and 'pairs' 5 times.

In the first hundred lines *Andreas* has 9 'pick-ups', *Elene* 12, *Guþlac I* 7. Interpretation of these phenomena, if any is possible, will require detailed examination of the sense of each passage but interpretation is not in the terms of my commission, so here they remain 'prosodic meaning'.[13]

V. Conclusion

It will be obvious to anyone who has troubled to read as far as this, that the syntactic level has been entirely neglected. I can only apologize. The problem of sorting out poetic syntactic features from those of genuine native (not translated), and much later prose, and then again comparing poet with poet, has proved too great for this first effort. Much has been written on the syntax of *Beowulf* but only detailed comparison of poetic usage would establish what was peculiar to that poet. It might be a special construction (cf. *Leng hu geornor*, which is only in *Guþlac I*) or it might be a larger proportion, or smaller, of some construction found elsewhere. The syntactic level has not been explored under the spectrum and so yields no 'meaning' here.

Some of the findings above, especially the collocation ones, might help in dating a poem, as either pre-Christian or borderline. As unfortunately we have so little possible borderline poetry surviving, we can only say that the *Beowulf* poet's free use of the heroic vocabulary is intentional, jam to cover the medicine he means the hearers to take.

Once more I must emphasize what I said in the beginning. This whole article is an experiment; its results are given tentatively as an offering in memory of the man who changed all my work in mid-career by his teaching, and made me see that 'language' was life and not 'letters'. I am quite sure that if J.R.Firth could read this article he would say 'That's all wrong', and at once show me what I ought to have done.

Notes

[1] J.R.Firth, 'Modes of Meaning' (1951), in *Papers in Linguistics 1934–1951* (London, 1957).

[2] R.Quirk, 'Poetic Language and Old English Metre', in *Early English and Norse Studies* (A. H. Smith Festschrift, London, 1963).

[3] Other words which have been collocated for this paper are *scriþan, ellen, þringan, halig, bregdan.*

[4] Klaeber, and Wrenn.

[5] Gustav Hübener in a series of articles from 1926 onwards put forward a very interesting and valuable theory of the origin of the folk-tales of the Beowulf-Grendel type. He connected them in the far past with the medicine-man of the tribe whose duty it was to exorcize the fear of the tribe. If he failed a stranger had to come in. Many of the problems of *Beowulf* are cleared by this theory which has been undeservedly neglected and which I hope to write up again. Unferþ could have some past achievements, but not against Grendel. Hübener never suggested that the *Beowulf* poet realised the origins of the story. Chambers always said 'It is folk-lore'. So it is, but folk-lore has roots.

[6] C.J.E.Ball has doubted whether *heoro* was a very free collocation as it so seldom appears alone. It *does* appear alone, however.

[7] [8] [9] [10] All these passages are from Sweet, *An Anglo-Saxon Reader* (Oxford, 1876/1950).

[11] It is difficult to know *where* to place this metrical finding. 'Prosodic' in Firth's terminology hardly applies. 'Phonological' seems to me stretch this far, in view of his definition of phonology.

[12] Sievers in his *Schallanalyse*, as is well known, was trying to trace individuality of the author's basic rhythm in the stream of poetry (or prose). He was led to this by hearing an opera-singer singing his rôle, we are told. How far Sievers was successful is hard now to assess.

[13] C.J.E.Ball pointed out to me that W.Perrett had referred to 'pick-up' alliteration in the *Hildebrandslied*, in *M.L.R.* vol. 31, p. 535, where he says that 'it can hardly be fortuitous'. This led me to Willy Krogmann's edition, *Das Hildebrandslied*, Philologische Studien und Quellen 1959, where he has built a critical text on just this 'pick-up' technique (cf. Einleitung S.19 ff.), referring to Perrett. This opens an exciting field of research. It might even prove to be a means of dating. R.W.Chambers, *Introduction to Beowulf*, p. 316, shows a genealogy where names fall into pick-up verse. He calls it 'very old'.

On Contextual Meaning

JEFFREY ELLIS

It is generally recognized that one of Firth's decisive contributions to linguistic theory[1] was the concept of 'context of situation'.[2] It is also widely recognized that he left this concept in many ways unelaborated.[3] In developing linguistic theory further on the basis of his methodological framework of levels of linguistic analysis[4] we are left with the formidable task of establishing categories, as powerful and as general as possible, to relate the level of form with that of situation.

The present paper is a very tentative venture in ventilating some of the problems involved in arriving at a programme for research into this complex subject.[5]

It is not, nor does it include, an account of Firth's thought on the subject, which it takes for granted,[6] still less of other thought on the same basis.[7] It also presupposes M.A.K.Halliday's classification and terminology of the levels of linguistic analysis and other theoretical categories and scales.[8]

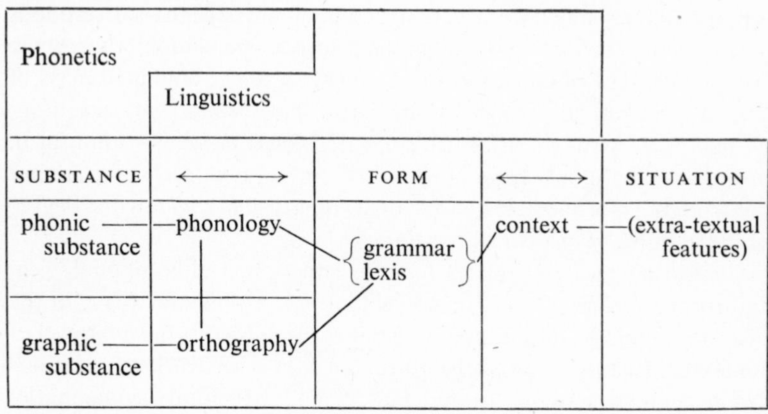

This classification of levels is represented by the diagram showing the levels of substance, form and situation and interlevels of phonology/

graphology and context, and the 'demilevels' of grammar and lexis and 'alternative levels' and 'alterinterlevels' of phonetics and graphics, phonology and graphology.[9]

Within this scheme of levels, meaning is seen as a relation between items at the various levels.

The *phonological* (or *graphological*) meaning of an item such as a term in a phonological system is its relation to other phonological items, its place in the total phonological system concerned; thus, for example, the items which may be identified by some of their phonetic features, the initial written as *p* in English and that written as *p* in German, have not the same phonological meaning since they have a different place in a different system (similarly, and more obviously, the graphological items Roman *p* and Cyrillic *p* (or Greek *ρ*)).

Similarly the *formal* meaning of a formal item or category, either grammatical or lexical, is its relation to other formal items or categories. For example, the nominative in Greek, in a five-term system of cases, has a different formal meaning from the nominative in Latin, in a six-term system.[10]

Both phonological and formal meaning correspond to the information of information theory in being dependent on, and quantifiable in terms of, the number of oppositions in the given system.

But *formal* items also have a *contextual* meaning. (The fact that we do not speak in the other direction of a phonological meaning of formal items (but rather of the phonological exponence of formal distinctions) is part of the asymmetry of levels-structure of language that corresponds to its function as relating (through the complex articulation of form) the finite material of phonic or graphic substance to the unlimited mass of situation.[11] Nor do *phonological* items have *contextual* meaning; *phonaesthetic* items (to use Firth's term[12]) would be items within form, distinguished not only from units on the normal rank-scale of grammar but from the morpheme-or-above items of lexis, *inter alia* by the degree of indeterminacy of their patternings.)

Contextual meaning relates form to situation. Unlike phonological and formal meaning, then, it is a relation not *within* a level (or, in the case of phonology, interlevel), but *between* levels (*across* the interlevel of context)—it can of course be formulated as a network of relations *within* context, systemic (paradigmatic) and structural (syntagmatic) ones of the formal meaning type, but what is important is that this network is determined, not within the level (or interlevel) as formal meaning is, but by the joint action of formal distinctions (independently established in the statement by formal analysis) and the situational differentiations to which they relate.

All formal items have contextual meaning, both grammatical items and lexical items.[13] Whether we speak of *grammatical contextual* meaning and *lexical contextual* meaning may depend on our conception of the inner structure of the interlevel of context in its relation to form and to situation (cf. n. 9), but in any case when we speak of grammatical meaning and lexical meaning *tout court* the reference will be to formal meaning.

Situation is extra-linguistic; as a general category, unlike context, it is the same for all languages. (There is no such thing as grammatical situation or lexical situation, and context is differentiated, differently for different languages, as to these demilevels only by the differentiation at the formal end.[14]) What differs for different languages is the selection of situational features made by the different systems of contextual meaning.[15]

Contextual meaning is either potential or instantial (or, less unambiguously, 'potential' or 'actual'[16]). (Some kinds of *formal* meaning (syntagmatic[17]) too are either potential or instantial, e.g. in lexis collocability (probability of collocations derived from instances)—instantial collocating.) The potential contextual meaning of a formal item is the range of possible contextual meanings of that item considered in abstraction from any text; its instantial contextual meaning is the actual meaning in a given instance of occurrence in a given place in a given text with a given situation.

Between these extremes we might recognize a cline[18] of potentiality/instantiality, and associate with it (in some relation of interdependence to be theoretically specified) the scale of delicacy of focus to be discussed below. The distinction between context and situation themselves might then be regarded as an indelicate extraction from a cline (that would run from most potential 'context' of the language's items to the unique actual 'situation' of utterance), which might correlate with the possible (non-dichotomous) distinctions mentioned in n. 9. However, while more delicate theory (or 'metatheory') might locate a number of nodal points on this cline by some kind of statistical operation on cases of application of the scales,[19] for present purposes a simple dichotomy will be assumed of 'context' and 'situation', to be taken as data (of method) for the practical purposes of expository contextualization here envisaged, with delicacy of focus and other possible scales reserved for subsequent, here summary, treatment.

The unit of form related (or of formal relation) to *situation* is the utterance (instantial meaning). On this basis, and on the basis of the formal categories of a given language, will be abstracted the categories of context of the given language (potential meaning). The unit of form related (of formal relation) to *context* is the potential[20] utterance, so that the minimum unit is the sentence. Thus the theoretical means of arriving at the contextualization of items less than the sentence (e.g. the tense of verbs) will be by comparison of sentences and their situations and hence contexts differing in one item. This does not deny the possibility of *statement* of context of items at all ranks;[21] on the contrary, it gives it foundation.

In order to analyse the specific situations related to whole utterances and to complement the categories of form in establishing the distinctions of context necessary for a given language, the following components of situation seem to be among those necessary. These situational components, and any additional or more delicate divisions that may be made, are general, applying as abstract categories to extra-linguistic situations whatever language is involved in the speech event; the features of context on the other hand that will be referred to cases of them, and therefore the selection made from them, will differ from language to language. They are here expounded as applying to spoken and non-literary (and non-fictional) utterances; the application to written, and any kind of literary, texts will require further development.[22]

By *immediate situation* is meant everything relevant other than included under other heads (such as *participants*), in the place and at the time of the speech event.

By *wider situation* is meant everything relevant in the universe at any time. (Since linguistics is concerned with the use of natural languages, 'relevance' will be interpreted in the light of what is specific to a given culture and its language, just as for immediate situation it will be judged by what distinguishes one situation and its utterances from another, and what is trivial because common to all human communication (or to whatever division of it is assumed as already described before a particular study) will be passed over in silence.)

For example, the immediate situation of the utterance 'How do you do' could be said to be one of introduction, and the wider situation to involve a community assuming certain courtesies.

By *features of participants*, or simply *participants*, are meant relevant features, both 'immediate' and 'wider', of anyone in the immediate situation, *performer* (e.g. speaker) or *addressee* (e.g. hearer), who actively determines the utterance, or is relevantly affected by it. (A person who introduces two others is *not necessarily* a participant in the situation of the consequent utterance 'How do you do' (but is in any case a feature of the wider situation, as participant in an antecedent utterance).)

For example the participants in 'How do you do' may be characterized (immediate features) as newly met, those in 'How are we feeling today, Mrs. Smith?' (wider features, yielding an immediate relationship) as doctor (or nurse) and patient.

By *register-range* is meant the total repertory of registers of the performer, his idiolect classified from a register point of view (both placed among other idiolects and itself subdivided).

By *register*[23] itself, a linguistic, not situational category, is meant a division of idiolect, or of what is common to idiolects, distinguished by formal (and possibly substantial) features and correlated with types of situation of utterance (these distinguished by such components as those here enumerated). It is a paradigmatic term; the corresponding syntagmatic one is *register-features* of the utterance.

Register is a subdivision of *language-variety*,[24] distinguished from *local* or *social variety* by varying with immediate features of the situation of utterance, whereas local or social characterize a participant as wider features—in so far as linguistic material ascribable to local or social origin is used in correlation with immediate features, it has become register. Register-range, as total idiolect (and a 'wider feature'), is in any case locally and socially conditioned; as a particular case, bilinguals (e.g. many Welshmen) have a register-range drawing on different tongues.[25]

By *register-choice* is meant the particular register out of the performer's range to which the utterance may be assigned (irrespective of how deliberate or unconscious the selection may have been), the specificness of the assignment depending on the delicacy of the analysis, and the analysis resting in the first place on linguistic features but in the statement correlating with situational ones.

For example, the register-range of 'How do you do' may be characterized as normal (educated), the register-choice as that of conversation (as to role), of greeting (as to field (and role—restricted variety)), formal (as to the formality scale), spoken colloquy (as to mode); the register-range of 'How are we today, Mrs. Smith?' as that of a performer who is *inter alia* a doctor (or nurse), the register-choice as that of medical consultation (as to field), conversation (as to role), informal (as to the formality scale), spoken colloquy (as to mode), possibly (as to residual register-choice) introducing or disposing of some attitude such as encouragement.

By *thesis*[26] is meant the event, process, action, state of affairs, etc., to which the utterance refers.[27] Its relation to the immediate situation of utterance is infinitely variable, unlike that of animal communication.[28] (Hence the importance of complementing Firth's emphasis on immediate situation with adequate analysis of reference.) Its relation to situation and contextual meaning in general is that it is the situational component providing the instantial meaning corresponding to *potential reference*, which is the *referential* component (or band(s) in the spectrum) of potential *contextual* meaning, as thesis is the *referential* part of *situation.* As contextual meaning relates form to situation, referential contextual meaning relates form to thesis.

For example, the potential reference of 'How are we (doing)?' is a question as to the present condition (or successfulness) of the performer and/or one or more addressees and possibly one or more third persons, the instantial thesis (in the doctor-patient situation taken as example) is a question as to the present condition of the specific addressee.

This formulation[29] of thesis and reference includes the component 'question as to': the categories statement, question, etc., as contextual items, corresponding to situational relations between participants and thesis-elements, are among the more general referential elements to be ascribed to any thesis[30] but are nonetheless contextual and referential, and should not be conflated either with formal elements (like interrogative clause-structure) or with non-referential elements of situation like attitudes (on the cline or spectrum referential/non-referential they are clearly far enough apart).

Another subdivision of the referential of a similar order of generality is *context of mention*, the situational component determining (and recognizable by) the formal division of the sentence, or other part of the utterance, into *given* and *new* (also *contrast*), and underlying also the formal category of *topic* (which is a form of *cohesion*).[31] Given-new and topic have a correlation, which may be complex; given-new tends to be more obvious (more immediately analysable) in spoken utterances with exponent in intonation, topic (more highly organized) in written texts (towards the beginning of the cline of mode in n. 24). *A topic* is a piece of text (it may be the whole) with continuity of linking of sentences by pronominal or any other form of pointing back (or forward). A *topic unit* is a piece with one given linking, that is one situational item (thesis-element) to which the contextual meaning of the linking formal items refers.

For example, the following[32] constitutes a topic, the spans covered by all occurrences of each numbered item constitute topic units, and given and new (the latter subsuming contrast) are noted.

Lavoisier: The phlogiston theory (1) was very complicated (1, 2) and therefore it is a pity (*new*) that it was rejected. (1, 2 *given.*)
Boyle: Why? We want simple (3) theories not (*new: contrast*) complicated (2) ones. (2 *given*, 3 *new.*)
L.: No, a complex theory (2) will afford far more mental stimulation (4) (*new*) then a simple one (3). (2, 3 *given*, 4 *new.*)
B.: But a simple theory (3) enables one to predict (*new*, 5) better and . . . (3 *given*, 5 *new.*)
L.: O.K., but mental stimulation (4) is more important (*new*) than ability to predict (5). (4 *given*, 5 *given.*)
B.: In any case I don't (*new*: *contrast*) think that the phlogiston theory (1) was at all complicated (1, 2). (1, 2 *given.*)

(1. phlogiston theory complicated; 2. complicated theories; 3. simple theories; 4. mental stimulation; 5. prediction.)

By *tone*, *etc.*, is meant the non-referential part of contextual meaning, as differentiated by Ogden and Richards into tone, intention and feeling (distinguished by relation to performer and/or addressee). This is a linguistic category, a feature of an utterance, the situational correlates being attitudes in the participants, themselves determined by situation and previous utterances.

For example, in 'How are we?' with instantial second person reference not in medical situation, the tone, etc., may be patronizing and/or jocular.

Referential and non-referential is an independent dimension of classification of contextual meaning, applying for example equally to grammatical and to lexical contextual meaning.

The distinction between referential and non-referential, at least in application to specific items, may be regarded as another extraction from a cline. A simple dichotomy would have to admit a great variety of borderline cases.[33]

The *analysis* of thesis, and reference generally, and its *presentation*, faces (besides the general difficulty of delicacy of focus—see below) the difficulty of finding a formulation that will represent adequately the referential meaning (at whatever delicacy of focus) in its relevant entirety and articulation, but without the non-referential meaning with which it is bound up in any natural language.[34] To attempt to disentangle the two may appear to do violence to the facts of the linguistic data, and this is one of the many reasons why the analysis of contextual meaning can never attain the rigour of that of form and formal meaning. But this is in no way a reason for not making the attempt—*all* linguistic analysis, in the measure that it *lacks delicacy*, is an over-simplification.

A possible method, given appropriate resources of elaboration, would be to apply, by generalization, transference, and extension in delicacy (where required), the kind of *notation* used in symbolic logic.[35] (Such notation would not in principle be confined only to this part (referential) of contextual description, but by convention a given body of it (that in fact with the greatest ramifications) could be so restricted.)

For example, the potential reference of 'How are we?' could be represented as '?(deg. H) 1/2(2) (3(3)) (tR = present)', where H = health (for tR see below), an instantial thesis as '?(deg.H) 2 (tθ ⊃ tS)' (for tθ ⊃ tS see below).[36]

As instantial/potential has been seen to be an extraction from a cline, so thesis/reference notations belong to places on a cline or scale of delicacy of notation.[37]

For example, a more delicate notation of 'How are we now?' in a given situation could be '?(deg.H) 2(= Pt, 1 = Dc) (tθ ⊃ tS & > tTr)', where (very much *ad hoc*) Pt = (the given) patient, Dc = doctor, Tr = a certain treatment (for > see below), a less delicate of certain aspects of it '?(x) 2 (tR = y)', where x = some specified relation, y = some specified time.

This scale of delicacy of *notation* should be clearly distinguished from other scales of delicacy.[38]

In addition to other dimensions of analysis that include a general scale of delicacy, analysis of reference, and possibly of other kinds of contextual meaning, will involve a special scale which is a kind of delicacy (though not necessarily delicacy of analysis) and may be regarded metaphorically as a kind of focus.[39]

Consider an example, say that of n. 33 above, 'He grabbed the best chair' and 'He plumped himself in the best chair': can these two utterances be said to have the same reference? (Or take R. Queneau's *Exercices de style*, or its English translation,[40] or both together: have they *all* the same reference?) Much argument will surely be saved if instead of answering simply either yes or no we say that it depends on the delicacy of focus.

The potential references are different but overlapping, inasmuch as the instantial thesis may or may not be the same (he may (for example[41]) have *both* seized the chair with his hands *and* sat down heavily in it). If it *is* the same, the relation of each utterance to it is different (precisely because the potential references are different), but at one point on the scale of delicacy of focus the 'reference' can be said to be the same.

While the two references have each potentially too delicate a focus to be always the same, 'He took the best chair', which has a necessarily less delicate focus than either, represents the point, or section of the scale, within which they do coincide, just as 'He took a chair' would for 'He took the best chair' and 'He took an armchair'.

While in utterances with common referential situation (a possible 'same' instantial thesis) with different degrees of delicacy of focus (e.g. 'He took a chair' and 'He took an armchair') these are realized as different contextual features (which are realized as different formal features), delicacy of focus itself is situational (or along the situation/context cline), whereas delicacy of notation is a delicacy of analysis in either context or situation. Thus delicacy of notation (a relation between notation and contextual meaning) and delicacy of focus (a relation between contextual meaning and thesis or between contextual meanings) may be varied together or independently.

Contextual meaning characterizes formal items or categories. While formal items or categories are identified by formal oppositions, contextual meaning is identified by their relation to situation, and potential contextual meaning by an accumulation of instantial contextual meanings. A single formal item or category in one formal environment ('co-text') may have a different potential contextual meaning from that in another formal environment, e.g. the difference between the English Past tense in most occurrences ('System 1') and in certain bound clauses with 'sequence of tenses' ('System 2'), e.g. 'he said he was sorry', 'if you went there, you would . . .' or (in an extended sense of 'sequence of tenses') 'it's time you did . . .'

Grammatical formal categories like the Past tense may be designated, in many cases traditionally,[42] by a label derived from the contextual meaning; in cases like the English Past (or, e.g., Singular), where there is a 'minority' contextual meaning like the System 2 meaning of the Past (or the generic meaning of the Singular), the 'majority' meaning is represented by the label. There may be cases where evidence is lacking that the 'label' meaning is the majority one,[43] e.g., some would argue, of the English Present.[44]

The designation of grammatical categories can be kept a separate matter from the investigation of their actual contextual meanings, provided one is clear on the scope of terms used,[45] and then the traditional designations generally retained; and if one is considering revising these designations at all, a thorough investigation of the contextual meanings and their statistics, and their interrelations in the total system of the language, is called for first.[46]

With these terminological provisos, an example of contextualization of formal items may be taken from tense (a formal category), System 1 in English (a formally stateable restriction), in its reference to time (a situational element).

There are in English (System 1) three elements of structure of tense (formally stateable) at each of a number of places in the structure of the verbal group, namely Past, Present, Future (designations of formal items, supported by tradition and by considerations of interrelation and systemic economy).

In order to state the situational analysis of the formal category tense in any language that has it (cf. n. 46; tense being understood as a certain kind of formal category (in the system of the verbal group) with a certain kind of temporal contextual meaning), two temporal situational components are needed, time of immediate situation of speaking (tS) and time of thesis ($t\theta$) (other kinds of temporal categories (formal oppositions with certain temporal contextual meanings) would need *t* of appropriate elements,[47] e.g. aspect in Slavonic languages (or Greek, etc.) needs π (pragma, the 'event, etc.' part of the thesis represented by the lexical verb part of the utterance), to relate t.fin. π (fin. = termination) to $t\theta$).[48]

Thus the situational relation $t\theta < tS$ ($<$ = a lesser time than, before) yields the contextual meaning tR = past (R = reference, potential contextual meaning corresponding to thesis); $t\theta > tS$: tR = future; $t\theta = tS$ (where $=$ is a relation other than exclusively before or after, including $\supset$ (includes) and $\gtrless$ (before *and* after)[49]): tR = present (i.e. non-(exclusively) past/future).

In many languages, e.g. Russian, these relations alone are represented by tense. In others, e.g. Latin, French, a further relation must be introduced between $t\theta$ and $t\theta_2$, where θ_2 is a 'secondary thesis' with time distinct from that of the thesis as a whole, e.g. Pluperfect: $t\theta < tS$, $t\theta_2 < t\theta$; tR = past in past.

In English, further relations still, with certain restrictions on combination, up to a probable maximum (in informal registers) of θ_5,[50] must be introduced to contextualize possible places in the tense structure of the verbal group, e.g. 'They'll have been going to have been building a National Theatre for ten years now!': $t\theta > tS$, $t\theta_2 < t\theta$, $t\theta_3 > t\theta_2$, $t\theta_4 < t\theta_3$, $t\theta_5 \subset t\theta_4$.[51]

Reference has been made, in describing categories of English, to parallel and contrasting contextualizations in other languages. Context studies and comparative descriptive linguistics are in fact intertwined in more than one way. Situational theory demands the widest study, descriptive and comparative, of the most varied languages (cf. n. 15). Comparative description itself depends on identifiable situation as *tertium quid comparationis* for comparability of form (both as to contextual meaning and, ultimately, formal meaning). And to say for example that a text and its translation have (ideally) the same instantial contextual meaning while having (not only different instantial formal meanings but) different potential meanings[52] is only one instance of possible insights exchangeable between the two bodies of theory.

In the considerable work yet to be done on contextual meaning, as on comparative descriptive linguistics and other branches within general comparative linguistics, this mutual dependence will figure with growing prominence.

Notes

[1] Cf. e.g. R.H.Robins, 'John Rupert Firth' (obituary), *Language* 37 (1961), pp. 191–200, p. 194.

[2] The term context *of* situation is not used below, distinction being made between context *and* situation; the composite term could be reserved for the sense given it in D.MacAulay's 'Notes on some noun-initial mutations in a dialect of Scottish Gaelic', *Scottish Gaelic Studies* 9 (1962) pp. 146–175, of the whole event, comprising both speech event and its situation, represented by the diagram of levels referred to below.

[3] Robins, p. 195.

[4] See M.A.K.Halliday's 'Categories of the theory of grammar', *Word* 17 (1961), pp. 241–292 (also Robert M.W.Dixon's 'A Logical statement of grammatical theory (as contained in Halliday's "Categories of the theory of grammar")', *Language* 39, (1963)).

[5] Thanks are due to my colleagues with whom I have discussed the subject, especially to Robert M.W.Dixon, M.A.K. Halliday, R.Hasan, T.Hill, Professor Angus McIntosh, J.McH.Sinclair, and J.N.Ure, and to J.C.Catford and H.D.Berg and all who took part in the discussion on Theory of Context and Situation at the Spring Conference of the Linguistics Association (Great Britain) and the Hull Linguistic Circle at Hull, May, 1962. Cf. also Dixon's *Linguistic Science and Logic* (Janua Linguarum 28, The Hague, 1963).

[6] Firth's own formulations had a certain emphasis, valuable as a corrective to the

excessively referential conception of extra-linguistic components which previously predominated. For the pre-Firthian history of the concept of context of situation itself (Wegener, Malinowski, Gardiner, etc., with the concept not yet integrated into linguistics as an abstract level) see Firth's paper in Raymond Firth (ed.), *Man and Culture* (London, 1957) pp. 93–118.

[7] E.g., F.R.Palmer, 'Linguistic hierarchy', *Lingua* 7 (1958), pp. 225–241 (cf. *Archivum Linguisticum* 13, pp. 37, n. 1, 42, n. 4); T.F.Mitchell, 'The Language of buying and selling in Cyrenaica: a situational statement', *Hesperis* 1957, pp. 31–71; B.Kachru, 'An Analysis of some features of Indian English: a study in linguistic method', Ph.D. thesis, Edinburgh, 1961; M.A.K.Halliday, Angus McIntosh and Peter Strevens, *The Linguistic Sciences and Language Teaching* (London, 1965).

[8] See n. 4; the concept of delicacy (integrated by Halliday into his scales) is McIntosh's, as is that of potential and instantial meaning introduced below (n. 16). (On scales cf. also n. 38 below.)

[9] It has been suggested in discussion (cf. n. 5) that a more delicate division would break down the dichotomy between context and situation with one or more additional divisions on one or both sides of the present dividing-line; but there is no agreement on the details of this.

[10] On further discussion of such examples, in relation to kinds of meaning, cf. Ellis, 'General linguistics and comparative philology', *Lingua* 7 (1958), pp. 134–174, p. 168, n. 128, and references there, also C.E.Bazell, *Archivum Linguisticum* 1, p. 7. Note that the name *nominative* itself here belongs to the category of contextual designation of formal oppositions (cf. n. 43 below).

[11] There is not space here to develop this fundamental theoretical (linguistic and linguistic-philosophical) notion and the unsolved problems involved; for some brief discussion cf. *Zeichen und System der Sprache* (Berlin, 1961–62), especially Vol. 1, pp. 47–50, Vol. 2, p. 44 (and to references there add H.J.Uldall, *Outline of Glossematics*, Part 1 (Copenhagen, 1957), pp. 26–27).

[12] Cf. Ellis 'On comparative descriptive linguistics', *Studia in honorem S.Mladenov* (Sofia, 1957), pp. 555–565, p. 558, n. 2. Also E.Nida, 'A System for the description of semantic elements', *Word* 7 (1951), pp. 1–14, p. 6.

[13] This needs stating to counter the widespread conflation of 'semantic' and lexical (and of 'formal' and grammatical). Also the notion that *all* items of either kind, and not only ones distinctive of language-varieties, have a 'contextual function' is implicitly contradicted not only by Palmer, op. cit. in n. 7, but even (by default: 'contextual features of the variety' only, not also item) in the exposition of Halliday-type (or at least, (explicitly)-influenced) theoretical framework in P.D.Strevens' inaugural lecture 'The Study of the present-day English language' (Leeds, 1962); the notion is of course bound up with the recognition of referential as well as non-referential contextual meaning to be discussed below.

[14] We may note that if we do then distinguish within the interlevel of context (relating form and situation) grammatical context (relating grammar and situation) and lexical context (relating lexis and situation), these are 'demiinterlevels', not 'alter-interlevels' as in the other interlevel, phonology/graphology (where the direction of relevant determination is 'inwards'—cf. on the essential 'asymmetry' of language at n. 11 above).

[15] Dixon's 'Descriptive Logic', op. cit. in n. 5, Chap. 3, 4, (n. 103) emphasizes the need for one logic per language, and certainly a general 'logic' of situation must be

(*inter alia*) approached through an accumulation of particular language, and particular-comparative (context and situation), studies. Cf. below (n. 46) on comparison and designation, etc. (On the Whorfian position cf. 'On comparative descriptive linguistics', p. 516, n. 6.)

16 Angus McIntosh, '"Graphology" and meaning', *Archivum Linguisticum* 13, pp. 107–120, pp. 112 ff.

17 What might appear to be instantially differentiated paradigmatic formal meaning of a *formal item* is in fact the assignment of an expression (sequence of phonological or graphological items) to exponence of different formal items. Or, in a case like Gaelic *tha*, forming sometimes a system with *is* (which has contextual meaning of 'permanent being'), but not when followed by *a(g)* plus verbal noun, the formal item (identifiable morphologically, as having past *bha*, etc.) must be regarded as exponent of terms in two different (formal) systems (one with contextual meaning of 'being', and (partial exponent of term in) one of 'tense'), not one 'potential' system. (It still of course has a unitary potential *contextual* meaning of 'temporary being'.)

18 'Categories of the theory of grammar', pp. 248–249.

19 Cf. the reference above to problems of interaction of theory and research. We need a theory in order to programme computer examination of large bodies of text (or, as here, of theoretical operations on the results of the first examination); we also need such examination in order to develop the theory further, especially in the less advanced sections like lexis or context.

20 Assuming that we can leave aside, though their analysis will be interesting, exceptional cases where the utterance appears to be less than a sentence in being part of something itself a sentence which is divided between two speakers, e.g. 'You finished before —' '— John did'.

21 For *rank* see 'Categories', pp. 250–254.

22 For a more delicate classification than 'spoken' and 'written' see below, n. 24, on *mode*. Cf. also n. 27.

23 Cf. *Archivum Linguisticum* 13, pp. 41–42.

24 The following is a provisional framework of classification of varieties (for more delicate filling in), with situational correlates:

Varieties distinguishing one idiolect (and possibly one period of idiolectal biography) from another, on scales of: *local variety* ('dialect' in various senses (whether tongue or something less than a tongue), 'accent' (substantial, whatever else))—local origin of performer (or of components of his language); *social variety* ('social dialect', interpenetrating with local variety, e.g. 'local dialect', 'degree of accent', 'koine', 'substandard', 'standard', 'R.P.')—status-cum-(social) origin of performer.

Varieties within idiolect (at a given time), *registers*, on scales of: *field*—subject-matter (province of *reference*); *role*-variety—social, etc., role of performance (conversation, literature, etc.) (including varieties *restricted* in formal resources like that of military commands); *formality*—(personal) relation between *participants* (cf. M. Joos's frozen-formal-consultative-casual-intimate (*The Five Clocks*, Bloomington, 1962)); *mode*—medium of utterance and degree of feedback from addressee(s) (e.g. 'written' (as used indelicately earlier in this paper), tape-recorded, broadcast, televised, epistolary, telephonic, note-passing, normal oral colloquy).

The above situational correlates will distinguish one utterance or text from another; but the varieties may also co-occur within one text: (e.g. in ancient drama) local (Greek dialects) and social (Sanskrit and Prakrits) varieties; in conversational utterances, field and formality, and (in anecdote) role; in literature, field, role (e.g. narrative, dialogue) and mode, and (in dialogue) formality; in non-literary writing, field. There appears to occur also, *within* a text only, a *residual* register-choice (using material of the text-distinguishing registers just as registers generally may use that of local or social variety) marking transitions within the text or utterance in the performer's attitude (related to *tone*, *etc*., below), answering (more or less) to '(individual) style' as traditionally understood. (These syntagmatic transitions may (as a performer feels his linguistic way in partially new situations) ultimately result in paradigmatic shifts in the register-range.)

(The above attempts to provide a comprehensive terminology to include distinctions propounded by some of those acknowledged in n. 5, especially Catford, Halliday, Hill, Sinclair and Ure.)

25 Cf. T. Hill, 'Institutional linguistics', *Orbis* 7 (1958), pp. 441–455, especially pp. 441–444 for definition of *tongue*, including *dialect* (in a strict sense) as opposed to accent.

We may note that possession of a second tongue not shared with, or even at all comprehensible to, all one's co-participants may react on the attitudes of the immediate situation; this will be covered as a situational component under the headings of register-range and register-choice.

26 Sometimes termed 'situation referred to', but risk of confusion with situation of utterance demands a quite distinct term.

27 The term *refer* (*reference*, *referential*) has acquired associations of philosophical controversies (not to mention the 'referent' of some schools of semantics) better avoided, but no alternative term seems available; it must be understood strictly as a technical term of contextual and situational linguistics. In this sense, then, 'reference' is irrespective of *truth*, and unicorns can be 'referred to' as much as lions. Indeed, the distinction between truth and falsehood is hardly material to contextual study as such, that between either and fiction being much more important. In both error or unintended falsehood and intentional lying, as much as in truth, the performer intends the addressee to fit the thesis into the universe of his ordinary experience (referentially, as distinct from any literary allusions, etc., in presentation); in fiction, on the contrary (where 'the poet lieth not, for he affirmeth nothing'), the thesis creates a secondary universe (in some complex relation, referentially and non-referentially, to the primary universe), which is one reason for the greater complexity needed in the contextual analysis of literary utterance (cf. n. 22).

(For analysis of this kind of meaning see now also the work of J. Lyons and of G. N. Leech.)

28 Cf. C. F. Hockett, *A Course on modern linguistics* (New York, 1958), Chapter 64; even if some animal communication, such as that of bees, may be said to differentiate thesis from immediate situation, the variability of the relation is strictly limited.

29 or paraphrase; cf. below on the problem of making formulation more rigorous (and variable in delicacy) by symbolic notation.

30 N. I. Fel'dman, *Voprosy Yazykoznaniya* 1954, pp. 121, 122, 126, classifies such general elements as 'logical content', distinct from 'material content' (the rest of reference) as well as from 'expressive content' (non-referential meaning). (Cf. n. 15.) It is with shifts in logical content in this sense that some transformations of transformational grammar correlate. (This note was written in 1961–2, before the explicit development of the 'semantic component' of generative grammar.)

[31] On context of mention cf. 'On comparative descriptive linguistics', p. 561, nn. 3, 4; on cohesion see M. A. K. Halliday, 'The Linguistic study of literary texts', in *Proceedings of the 9th International Congress of Linguists*, C. C. Bowley, 'Cohesion and the paragraph: a textual analysis', unpublished General Linguistics Diploma dissertation, Edinburgh, 1962.

[32] Test text devised by Robert M. W. Dixon.

[33] E.g., in utterances like 'He grabbed the best chair' or 'plumped himself in the best chair', while there might be general agreement that the contextual meaning of 'best' is (predominantly) referential, there might not be about an element of the (instantial) contextual meaning of 'grabbed' and 'plumped' and their collocation with 'best' (the formal element collocation contributing its potential contextual meaning to the determination of the instantial contextual meaning of the utterance).

[34] No implication is intended that artificial languages may escape this constraint—in fact the restricted 'languages' in international use can be shown to bear marks of their origin, usually 'Standard Average European', e.g. the position of '=' in the symbolization of mathematical propositions, and it would be surprising if tone, etc., did not to some reduced extent come too—but they nonetheless serve their referential purposes more efficiently than natural language without them, and it may not be too much to hope for the same of the sort of notation envisaged below.

[35] Cf. H. Freudenthal, *LinCos* (*Design of a language for cosmic intercourse*), Part 1 (Amsterdam, 1960), for an attempt to apply such notation to the full range of situations of natural languages, but (since its object is differently conceived) without the linguistic analysis of each (or even any) language that would be indispensable for context-theory purposes; a complementary approach might be to apply the techniques of linear analysis used for corresponding *texts* in comparative descriptive linguistics (Ellis, 'On comparative descriptive linguistics'; M. A. K. Halliday, 'Linguistics and machine translation' (*Zeitschrift für Phonetik*, 1962) to correspondences of *text* and '*situation*' (i.e. conveniently simple (relatively) pictorial notation of situation) in the more elaborate kind of pictorial manuals of language instruction (than the 'rough' sort to which Firth apparently referred in 'Personality and language in society', *The Sociological Review*, Vol. 42, pp. 37–52, p. 43), such as *English through pictures* (I. A. Richards and C. M. Gibson, New York, 1945, etc.). (Cf. I. A. Richards and C. Gibson, 'Mechanical Aids in Language Teaching' (*English Language Teaching*, Vol. XII (1957), pp. 3–9), pp. 7–8: 'The collaboration between pictures and co-varying sentences can be extremely intimate. Both are symbols jointly referring to or mediating something else—a fictitious *situation*. The more we imaginatively reflect upon the relations between the three (*Meaning of Meaning* fashion), the more intricate they will seem to become. Sometimes the sentence will be about the picture—but at the same time it will also be about what the picture is of. And, again, at the same time the picture will be about the sentence: telling us what it says.')

[36] The placing of elements in what appears to be the Carnapian sequence of relation—term(s) in relation (or to be a Celtic clause-structure, contrasting with the order mentioned in n. 34 and used here within the time (*t*)- notation) is provisional; conventions of abbreviation, punctuation, spacing, etc., etc., are even more tentative.

[37] Such recognition of relativity in thesis and its description not only distinguishes the notation itself from Real Character (or other notions of an international ideography), or from 'the artificial language' for machine-translation, but should defend context and situation as a worthwhile study from C. E. Bazell's (in itself quite true)

argument in *Linguistic Form* (Istanbul, 1953) against 'content'-studies that the meaning of words can be stated only in or as words, and go some way towards meeting Robins' (p. 195) 'external world, wherein linguistics can scarcely claim the ability to compass the relevant environment' (cf. above at n. 11). It also seeks to avoid the question of 'ultimate reality' (cf. Dixon, op. cit. in n. 5, Chap. 1).

38 The original *scales* of Halliday's 'Categories' were propounded within the (descriptive) demilevel of *grammar*, with the scale of *exponence* linking to other levels, the scale of *rank* (cf. n. 21 above) also in phonology, and *delicacy* also in lexis. Quite independent scales of delicacy are required both in *comparative* linguistics and for the description of contextual meaning.

39 For this and other images cf. the reference to 'On comparative descriptive linguistics' in n. 52 below.

40 R. Queneau, *Exercises de style* (Paris, 1947); trsl. B. Wright (London, 1959).

41 This is an indelicate way of anticipating the scientific linguistic (probabilistic, statistical) finding that in some situations (distinguished by particular elements) either utterance could and would be used (by one or more performers), in others only one or the other.

42 Alternative sources of designation include: from formal meaning (e.g. subjunctive, Slavonic 'attributive' adjective), numerical (e.g. 'zweiter Kasus', 'Partizip II', but more often used for morphological classes of exponents, e.g. First Aorist, Class IV strong verb), morphological (e.g. strong (adjective), Slavonic 'long' adjective), or by exemplificatory exponent (e.g. Wemfall, Hebrew pa^{c}al).

43 Or even, in some traditional designations, where the label has only an indirect relation to the contextual meaning if any, e.g., whether the whole case-system (and not just vocative, locative, etc.) can be credited with contextual meanings or not, and whatever number of contextual or formal meanings, say in Latin, the nominative and accusative have, the majority one at least of the nominative is not 'naming', and 'accusative' has to be translated back into Greek to make sense.

44 The status of the English Future is a more complex problem, on the formal side research being needed *inter alia* into actual current person-number usage of *will*, *shall*, and *'ll* (e.g., for comparison with System 2 Past, *if you will* (e.g. *be so kind . . .*) seems not to commute with *if we shall*), but on the contextual it seems clear that the majority meaning (of either *shall* or *will*) is 'future'.

45 Certain conventions could be adopted (cf. Gabelentz's German (e.g. Hauptwort) and Latin (e.g. Substantivum) terms for Classical Chinese 'parts of speech' (formal items) and 'syntactical uses' (formal environments and/or grammatical contextual meanings)), such as writing with capital initials the designations that otherwise might be taken as describing contextual meanings themselves (e.g. Past/past).

46 Similarly while the traditional use of the same designation (e.g. 'nominative') for different languages is procedurally irrelevant to the analysis and description of the contextual meanings of any one language (cf. among others the references in n. 10), it is not irrelevant to the question of designation (nor is inter-language investigation irrelevant to the development of descriptive situational theory, cf. n. 15 and below).

47 Not to mention categories of the verbal group, associated formally with tense (and aspect), e.g. in Turkish and Bulgarian, that involve e.g. whether θ itself $=$ S (as indeed languages like English involve whether θ $=$ utterance in the 'minority' case of contextual meaning of formal item Present simple in verbs like 'swear': 'I (hereby) swear', 'I (do) declare').

48 Cf. *Archivum Linguisticum* 13, p. 46, pp. 210–212.

49 There seems to be, and surely is, a difference between generalizing from different contextual meanings to the extent of losing any content in the designation, e.g. conflating Past in Systems 1 and 2 as 'remote', and generalizing from e.g. $\supset$ and $\gtrless$ in such a way as to fit 'Present' into one system (System 1) with Past and Future. (Cf. n. 17.)

50 This is one way in which θ_2 differs from π (another is that π enters also into contextualization of *Aktionsarten* (cf. *Archivum Linguisticum* 13, pp. 46–47) (e.g. π determinate = fin. π indeterminate)); in languages like Bulgarian, moreover, t. fin. π enters into relations also with θ_2 itself, etc.

51 Since θ_{n+1} '=' θ_n would contradict the need for θ_{n+1} (and this is needed only for *t*), the situational statement of the contextual meaning 'present in' must differ from the = of simple 'present'.

52 Cf. the formulation at pp. 563–564 of 'On comparative descriptive linguistics'.

The Meaning of Pali in Tikopia[1]

RAYMOND FIRTH

This essay is written in commemoration of J. R. Firth, with whom, though we were not genealogically related, I felt a kinship of the spirit. His continued efforts to bring linguistics and social anthropology together, his intellectual robustness in attacking broad problems, as well as our personal friendship, meant that for me he was the linguist above all to whom I could turn for aid on questions of handling language material. I regret only that we did not collaborate more closely, and especially that a joint study we had once lightly planned, using his linguistic skills on my Tikopia texts, never did eventuate. This essay, then, is the product of a social anthropologist alone, lacking in technique of analysis and language of statement, as J. R. Firth himself observed of Malinowski (1957, p. 110).

The specific problem with which I am concerned here is the definition of a Tikopia word used fairly commonly to describe the actions of an individual in certain social situations. The questions which arise in the establishment of the meaning of the word are: exactly in what kinds of circumstances is it used; is the word applicable to all circumstances of the given order or only to some; what is the relation of this word to other words which seem to be similar in some aspects?

In the sociological sphere I think I can answer these questions reasonably well. But I have also a more general problem. Modern social anthropologists expect to acquire fluency in the vernacular of the people among whom they work, and to collect most of their material by such means. They do not use interpreters. But this means that they are their own interpreters, with all the responsibility that this task entails. The very great advance in systematic methods of accumulation of field data and in the sophistication of theoretical analysis has tended to obscure the gravity of the linguistic and semantic issues involved. It has come to be a matter of faith that the anthropologist speaks and understands the vernacular well enough to provide an interpretation which can be trusted as an indication of what the people themselves do and think.

Yet often such interpretation rests on assertion, not proof, as far as the linguistic data are concerned.

The problem is illustrated by S. F. Nadel's description of the Nupe concept of *Sokó* (1954, pp. 10 *et seq.*). This word Nadel first translates as God-the-Sky, since the same word also denotes the sky in the visible, physical sense; but then he goes on to use the name 'God' in brief. Nadel states that God is sometimes said to dwell in the sky, but that like other assertions about the nature of the supreme deity this is sometimes contradicted; the commonest and most emphasized statement is that God is far away. Yet in a different, more mystic sense he is present, always and everywhere, although hidden, invisible. God 'clearly' has awareness, intellect and some of the sensitivity of man, for he is appealed to in ordinary language. But he is not personified more concretely, and indeed no one knows if he is like man or not. Now throughout this description Nadel writes of 'he'. But in a footnote he explains that in Nupe personal pronouns have no gender and do not distinguish between animate and inanimate objects. He adds that 'for purely practical reasons' he has continued to employ the personal pronoun (for *Sokó*) in the (English) masculine form. But if then, as seems equally appropriate, we should substitute the pronoun 'it' for 'he' in the above description, a very different much less anthropomorphic idea of a pervasive Sky entity could be built up!

In his account of Nuer religion (1956) Evans-Pritchard largely avoids this particular difficulty of anthropomorphization by rarely using the personal pronoun, but by writing only of 'God', 'Spirit' (though see, e.g. pp. 1, 118). He stresses in various ways that the different kinds of spirits—of the sky, of the home, of a totem, etc.—whether named or not, are simply 'refractions' at different levels, of the supreme entity—different sorts of manifestations of Spirit; though 'God is also experienced unrefracted at all levels, down to the individual' (p. 121). Yet the *linguistic* evidence for such statements of identity and experience is sparse. One example cited of how the diverse spiritual figures of Nuer thought are to be regarded as social refractions of the idea of God is a ceremony for cleansing from homicide, in which representatives of the two parties each address spirits by different category-titles, speaking over an ox tethered for sacrifice. Evans-Pritchard states that although the invocations were made to different titles they were all made over the same victim, and this same victim was offered up by all the parties concerned. 'This appears to me to be *proof* (my italics) that the sacrifice was made to one and the same being' (p. 110). This is a plausible interpretation.

But on this evidence alone one is not entitled to exclude the possibility that the sacrifice was in fact regarded as *shared* by the distinct spirits belonging to the two sides, and that these spirits were not necessarily regarded as identical. Again, Evans-Pritchard clearly distinguishes the ghost (*joagh*) of a dead person from the soul (*tie*) of the living, and these from Spirit of an external kind (*kwoth*). But the identification of *kwoth* is not completely clear. Evans-Pritchard states that in its verbal form *kwoth* suggests both the intangible quality of air and the breathing or blowing out of air. It connotes violent breathing out of air in contrast to ordinary breathing, and it describes such actions as blowing on the embers of a fire, snorting and the hooting by steam pressure of a river steamer. 'As a noun, however, *kwoth* means only Spirit...' (1956, p. 1). But I find it odd that a verb which describes the actions of violent blowing has no corresponding substantival usage, especially since we are told that the Nuer liken God to wind (p. 4). Can *kwoth* not mean air in violent motion?

Problems of interpretation of religious ideas of other peoples are difficult, and in such anthropological analyses lack of space may hinder any very elaborate linguistic treatment. We may therefore have to be content for the most part with assertion rather than demonstration. But the problem should not be overlooked.

For much of the description of everyday activities, the 'small change' of anthropological studies, these questions of interpretation are not of much significance. One can accept the author's generalizations as being backed by unmentioned empirical observations. But when it is a question of a term with a great deal of abstract connotation, a term the meaning of which is perhaps critical for a whole phase of analysis, then it is different. What is needed here is some demonstration of a systematic kind as to what degree of linguistic coverage has been obtained, the basis on which plausible alternatives of meaning have been excluded. Linguist and anthropologist alike have a right to know that the statements about meaning which appear on the surface of the exposition have beneath them a solid sub-stratum of vernacular textual formulations and supporting evidence in observation of behaviour.

I do not claim that my own handling of linguistic material has been very different from that of other British social anthropologists. But I have long felt the need for some serious consideration by myself and others of the quality of the linguistic evidence which I, as an anthropologist, use as a basis for my interpretations.[2] The present article is offered as a sample of this evidence to show both the strength and weakness of what I believe to be current anthropological practice.

The first question is how far in his interpretation of the meaning of an exotic word does the anthropologist rely on his written records and how far on memory? My written evidence for my interpretation of *pali* is given by entries in my field notebooks, supplemented for general context by records from my field diary. My first record was made about a month after I arrived in Tikopia. It was:

> '*Mako* held nearly every night in Ravenga. *E pali* in *fasi nei* on account of Noakena.'

There are three points to note about this. First, though by this time I was using Tikopia vernacular exclusively for communication, I was *recording* in a mixture of Tikopia and English. Mentally I was translating and abstracting some phrases, leaving others in the textual form in which I heard them, and commingling my own comments with the recorded speech. (Apart from this, I was also taking down texts of dictated kind.) Secondly, as a working anthropologist I was more concerned to make a sociological record than a lexicographical one; Tikopia terms often appeared in use in my notebooks, as component parts of statements or descriptions, before I attempted to give precision to their meaning in the form of a specific translation. Thirdly, the statements here given embodying the term *pali* were not part of a *linguistic* discussion, but referred to a set of observed *social* events at the time. *Mako* was dancing; Ravenga was the district on the other side of the island from which I was living; *fasi nei* was 'this side'—where I was living; and Noakena was the son of a friend of mine, and grandson of the local chief. This boy had been lost at sea some months before. The community was in varying degree of mourning for him, and the statement means that whereas the people on the other side of the island were dancing freely, those on the side where Noakena had lived were not.

A few days later occurs my second entry:

> '*E pali* for Mairunga, *tuatina* of dead child of Pa Motuangi, to take part in dance at Ravenga (or any dance).'

Here the reason for a man not taking part in dancing was that he was a mother's brother (*tuatina*) of a dead child.

Several clues to the meaning of *pali* emerge from these statements. It is a condition or state applying to a person; it applies because of a particular relation—including a kinship relation—to another person;

it has something to do with reaction to a death; it is restrictive, being negative for dancing; it has some degree of localization.

But an anthropologist does not necessarily record in vernacular text all that he overhears or discusses. He lives through many situations, observing, reacting, memorizing, classifying and interpreting his experiences, which may emerge only much later in recorded form. My next entry embodying the word *pali* was nine months later. It arose again from events concerned with the death of Noakena. Preparations were being made for an elaborate funeral ceremony in which his grave-clothes would be formally buried (not his body, which had never been found). The ceremony was to last several days, and would include a dance of farewell to the dead boy, performed by his father, grandfather and other close patrilineal kinsmen. The occasion was one of high emotional tension, spread throughout the lineage (cf. Firth, 1951, pp. 61–72). His father, Pa Rangifuri, had described to me a dream he had had about his son, and then gave me the text of a dance song which would probably be performed on the occasion. In it occurred the expression, '*E kua fakaevaeva*'—'Oh, (we) have been made to rise'. In explanation of this Pa Rangifuri said:

'*Kita nokopali, ka tera ku fakaeva ki runga.*'

'We continued to be *pali*, but now have risen up above.' My explanatory comment in my notebook was 'Person who was barred from dancing, now prohibition removed, his body rises up light.' (The general connotation of *eva* is rising lightly, gently, floating up.)

The meaning of *pali* emerges a little further from this. It is not a momentary condition, but one which may have continuity; yet it can be temporary, not permanent. It is associated with the idea of (sitting or lying) *down*, in contrast to that of *rising up* to dance. Moreover, its antithesis to dancing is such that the act of dancing is in effect a signal of the end of being *pali*. There is also the implication that whereas dancing is a state of lightness, *pali* is the opposite. *Pali*, then, can be translated as mourning restriction.

From my first field expedition I have very few texts in which the word *pali* appears. To the field anthropologist, meaning is conveyed by a combination of observation of verbal and non-verbal behaviour with explanation by informants; it is often further strengthened by personal participation in events, in which understanding is tested by the reactions of others to the anthropologist's behaviour. He acts out his concept of what a word means, and if he is wrong he expects that the inappropriateness of his actions in a particular context will be made clear by himself or by others. When, therefore, early in my first Tikopia expedition, I thought I had attained a sociological understanding of *pali* sufficient to allow me to interpret statements made about it, and situations in which it was operative, I made no further specific inquiry about it or record of it in linguistic terms. It was easy enough for me to follow the explanation of why a person in mourning could not dance, or adopt an attitude of respect and sympathy when I found that someone was described as *pali*. Reviewing my knowledge of *pali* and of mourning generally in the context of the happenings in the Tikopia society, I was able to follow through the social condition of people such as Pa Rangifuri who had suffered family loss, from the time when they remained in deepest seclusion in their houses, restricted in the food they ate, in their movements abroad, the songs they sang, to the time when, restored to full social life, they could dance once again and were no longer *pali*.

On my second expedition to Tikopia I started from this standpoint. Deaths from epidemic disease were frequent during my stay, and I noted occasionally some incident which seemed to define the *pali* condition more precisely. Was *pali* an individual or a group restriction? Most references I had to *pali* referred to men. What about women? It appeared that they too were *pali*, but did they cease to be so at the same time as their husbands?—not necessarily. I recorded a case of a man whose son died. He was *pali*, but after a fairly short time he 'rose' to dance in a festival, partly no doubt because of the urging of the leaders of the community that dancing should be continued even at this time of general mourning, to keep up the spirits of the people (Firth, 1959, pp. 97–99). But his wife still remained *pali*, at her own wish. This condition then was not automatic, but rested to some extent on personal decision and initiative. It also was not of the all-or-none category; it allowed of modification according to circumstances. I had found in my first expedition that mourning applied to absence as well as to death. I now found this confirmed. Members of one village community stopped dancing and regarded themselves as *pali* because of the departure abroad of two of their prominent men. But it was pointed out to me that their period of abstention would not be long, because they were mourning not death but absence, and it would depend on their leaders when they would begin dancing again.

Pali clearly referred to abstention from dancing; but did it include singing? As I came over the lake one evening in a canoe, the young man who was paddling me was singing a hymn—though he had not then become a Christian. I said to him, 'Sing us a dance song!' He replied, 'I am *pali*'. I said, 'Sing us a dirge then!' So he complied. For a *pali* person to sing then was quite permissible, but it should be a serious song, not a frivolous one.

I discussed with one of the leaders mentioned above the question of period in the removal of the ban on dancing. He explained, '*E roa ki te pali o fenua vare*, 'It is long for the *pali* of common people', but on the death of a chief it is said '*ke lolo fakaariki—sise e nofo roa*', meaning 'let the ban be after the manner of chiefs—not sitting long'. In other words, the mourning of commoners can be prolonged but not that of chiefs. And if a chief dies, people decorate themselves quite soon after and stand up to dance. This was exemplified by the statement that if a chief dies the sacred dances of the religious cycle of the Work of the Gods (Firth, 1940b, Chaps. VIII, IX) are not abandoned, but take place as usual, maybe almost at once. The sociological significance of this is that a Tikopia chief is a symbol of the community integration. He should not be for long out of social circulation. If his kin die, his formal mourning should be short; if he himself should die, his successor should soon be free to carry on the community's affairs.

Other points about *pali* for which I have no direct textual evidence are the following: when a person is ill or injured or exiled, his immediate kin are not *pali*. They do not necessarily dance or otherwise appear in public, but this is regarded as an ordinary response to emotion and, when a person is sick, to the dictates of service. It is not a convention with any specific binding force. The term *pali* then does not include all conscientious behaviour but only such as is regarded as obligatory by social convention. Incidentally, a person is spoken of or speaks of himself as *pali* with no embarrassment.

In the Tikopia textual statement quoted above the term *lolo* was used as an alternative to *pali*. It was treated as a synonym. '*Lolo—te rua o te taranga e pali i te matenga ne fai*'; '*Lolo* is a duplicate of the speech "is *pali*," from a death that occurred.'

It is convenient at this point to consider some aspects of the linguistic status of the word *pali*. The discussion of *lolo* and *pali*, in the context of the funerals that were taking place daily, led me to try and establish *pali* a little more firmly in its phonemic and linguistic context. With the help of the same man whom I have quoted above as informant, I listed the distribution of *p–l–* word forms and their meaning. The results are set out in the Table.

FINAL VOWEL	FIRST VOWEL				
	A	E	I	O	U
A	PALA damp	PELA mud	(PILA) —	POLA hide	PULA stare PULAPULA speak weightily
E	(PALE) —	PELE many	(PILE) —	/POLE/ Proper name from abroad (Vanikoro)	PULE cowrie shell
I	PALI under taboo of mourning	(PELI) —	PILI lay above	/POLI/ Proper name of legendary ancestor	(PULI) —
O	(PALO) —	PELO egg yolk	/PILO/ Proper name of an alien resident (Maori)	(POLO) —	(PULO) —
U	/PALU/ Proper name no other meaning known	(PELU) —	(PILU) —	(POLU) POLULU animal species	/PULU/ Proper name of a god

(—) Form absent. / / Proper name, no ordinary word form.

Anthropologists may not be impressed by this exercise, feeling that it adds little or nothing to one's understanding of the term *pali.* But this systematic survey of simple phonetic combinations allowed me to see that there was no set of other words closely allied to *pali* in form and meaning, which I had so far overlooked.

It will be noted that not all vowel combinations are used semantically, and that of the fifteen so used five are proper names. Three of these are said to be of foreign origin, one is the name of a legendary ancestor and the fifth is that of a feared god. Of the combinations used as ordinary meaningful words, most have some associations of an unpleasing character (to Tikopia as well as to us): damp; mud; hiding; staring; a breaking egg showing the yolk. *Lolo* offers fewer combinations.[3] But as regards vowel distribution, *lili* does not occur as a separate word, nor do any of the mixed vowel combinations *lale*, *lelo*, etc. *Lala* and *lele* are rather improper words for hymen and clitoris respectively, and *lulu*, occurring in ancient song, is said to describe the penetration of the female by the male organ (Firth, 1940b, p. 268). The word *polulu* is the name of a low-grade animal (? a millipede) which in a mythological story tried to hinder the operations of a culture hero.[4]

In syntax, as will have been inferred already from my textual evidence, *pali* can be used either as an adjunct, following a noun, or with a verbal particle, or as a substantive with a specificatory article.[5]

In Tikopia speech, *pali* is differentiated from a range of other terms applying to restraint or restriction, such as *mono*, block, obstruct; *noa*, tie, shackle; *pi*, obstruct; *puke*, grasp, restrain. Some of these, such as *mono* or *pi*, can be used abstractly as well as concretely. *Pali*, therefore, applies to a specific kind of restriction.

To sum up, *pali* is a word applied to persons, signifying that they are in a condition of restriction, such restriction relating especially to dancing. The restriction is an aspect of mourning, and arises from a death or prolonged absence. It applies primarily to kin, but may be extended by analogy to the followers of a chief. The restriction is temporary, not permanent, and is greater for commoners than for chiefs. It is a social convention regarded as obligatory, but it is not automatic in that while socially validated, personal decision is involved as to when it shall be terminated. Moreover, while socially and personally the restrictive behaviour is regarded as appropriate, it is not enjoyed by the person concerned, but is regarded as burdensome.

But there are still two sociological problems to consider: how is the *pali* condition ended? How does *pali* stand in regard to the general body of mourning restrictions—are there various other kinds of abstentions in such circumstances?

These two questions may be pursued together for a while by considering the mourning history of a particular man mentioned earlier, Pa Rangifuri, which extended for about a year. When I arrived he was in deep mourning for his lost son. I noted that he always stayed in his house, except for brief periods in the early morning and evening, when he went down to the seashore to bathe, etc. When I visited him he told me that owing to affection for his son he could eat only breadfruit, papaya and spinach; his staple food in fact was breadfruit, which was cooked only by his wife. At this same time food was plentiful in the island, and at Pa Rangifuri's own house I was given an elaborate taro pudding made with a kind of baked desiccated coconut, a special delicacy—the food of chiefs, he called it—made by my host himself. In other words, the bereaved father was not lacking in food of fine quality; he was practising a voluntary abstention in conformity to his emotions and the rule of his society.

In conformity with general practice when a chief's heir dies, a restriction had been put by the boy's grandfather on sea-fishing from canoes on that side of the island, and on taking coconuts from orchards in that area. A fortnight after I arrived, and several months after the boy's death, a ceremonial lifting of restriction from the coconut palms for a time took place (6th August 1928), allowing the people at large to improve the quality of their food. A week later (13th August) the taboo on canoe fishing for flying-fish was lifted by the chief, and from then on crews went out by torchlight every night. But the bereaved father was not among them, nor were any of his close patrilineal kin.

A fortnight later (30th August) an old woman died in a village close by that in which Pa Rangifuri lived. He attended the funeral, but returned to his house to sleep; he did not take a very active part. A week later (8th September) another old woman died, this time on the other side of the island. Pa Rangifuri told me that he could not go to this funeral, owing to the loss of his son; he had gone to the earlier one, but that had been on his own side of the island. (But his brothers went, so the family was represented.) Mourning etiquette thus had its space correlates as well as its time correlates. By this time Pa Rangifuri was moving abroad locally rather more freely; for example he was visiting my house by day. A week later (16th September) he attended another funeral on his own side of the island, and played a very active part; as a member of the 'parental group' of the deceased he received a large basket of food, which he reciprocated with fishhooks and other goods—enlisting my aid thereto! But he still refused (24th September) to travel with the mourning party to another village down the coast on the same side of the island, saying again that this was on account of his son. By this time Pa Rangifuri was taking up his ordinary pursuits again; he occupied himself outside his house in the cool of the evening by carving out a small wooden bowl. About this same time (27th September) one of his kin from a nearby village came to his house with a basket of fine food for him to eat—'being mindful of him'. They wailed together for the dead boy, then Pa Rangifuri ate of the food. A few days later (1st October) Pa Rangifuri and his cousin were heard wailing. They were going out fishing together for the first time since the deaths of their sons, and they were purging their grief in the customary manner. This was only about six weeks after the cousin's bereavement, but his son had been only an infant and not the chief's heir. It was a grand occasion, with a local fleet of seventeen canoes, and other fleets from nearby villages; two of the chief's canoes had been relashed and refurbished.

The next morning Pa Rangifuri went out fishing with his remaining son; he was now fully integrated again into ordinary economic life. But he was not yet fully integrated into social life. In particular, he was not yet dancing. This took another three months. As time went on, he occupied himself in fishing, in net-making and canoe building, going about openly in daylight in the normal way. But in the middle of December there was a ceremony to relieve the chief and his family from their mourning obligations. Necklets of frangipani flowers were hung upon them and they came to listen to the chanting of dance songs, since a dance was planned for the following day. Pa Rangifuri alone refrained from these celebrations, and the day before they occurred people arrived at his house to wail with him. The next day there was dancing in the village until nightfall. The chief emerged from his seclusion and danced, and Pa Rangifuri's own remaining son danced, but he himself stayed unseen in his own house.

A fortnight later there was a great dance festival in which both sides of the island were concerned, but from it Pa Rangifuri was absent. Not until early January was his mourning laid down. His 'opposite number' on the other side of the island, the eldest son of the premier chief, came over to anoint Pa Rangifuri with crimson turmeric pigment (a symbol of all social or ritual celebration) and so end his mourning. The next day (9th January) there was a dance festival in Ravenga on the other side of the island. The visitor of the night before returned and hung on Pa Rangifuri's neck a frangipani necklet, the symbol of decoration for a dance. Pa Rangifuri then attended the dance. Late in the morning his sponsor came up to him, put a leaf dance-ornament in his belt, gave him a calico kilt and insisted that he put them on. He then provided him with a dance bat and they went out together to participate. Pa Rangifuri took part quite enthusiastically, though he looked a little shy at first. At the conclusion of the dance he shouted out a formula, as a ceremonial announcement of his release from his mourning. It was a notable occasion, and he slept that night in the house of the local chief, that is, away from his own side of the island.

About ten days later the sequel in relieving Pa Rangifuri from his *pali* obligations took place when a presentation of bark-cloth and food was made to him from the family of the leading chief on the other side of the island. This meant that he was now free to eat of any food that he wished, and should not regard himself as bound by mourning requirements from this time. Now he was fully absorbed into all the major social events of the island, including dancing. He still, however, had one final stage to pass through before his mourning obligations were relieved. This was the burial of his son's grave-clothes—the formal interment of the boy's social personality. This took place in June 1929, as mentioned earlier, and restored for a brief period Pa Rangifuri to a *pali* condition, which, however, was soon lifted. That Pa Rangifuri was not completely satisfied to dance in the festival before all the rites for his son had been accomplished was clear from what he said to me later. He explained why he had not taken part in the dancing on an earlier night; he had been requested by his father to do so, but refused. He had danced for the great festival only at the insistence of the premier chief, but for ordinary affairs he had been still preserving some remnants of his mourning. He said that he would not have allowed any member of his own district to come and anoint him with turmeric; if they had come he would have killed them. Hence, he implied, when this was known his equivalent in rank from the other side of the island (who was also a representative of his mother's clan) came and he could not refuse. (Here is an instance of the subtle blending of personal feeling and response to social dictate which is characteristic of many Tikopia affairs. There was no way of knowing whether Pa Rangifuri would have persisted in his intransigent attitude, because the solution followed a well-established Tikopia pattern.)

I did not witness these immediate ceremonies over Pa Rangifuri because I was busy elsewhere, but I was told about them by participants. From their statements and analogous accounts the procedure is as follows: lifting of mourning usually occurs when a dance festival is projected. Representatives of the mourner's mother's family then go with turmeric to anoint him. Protestations of unwillingness to be relieved are common. If it is a person's father or son that has died, then conventionally, I was told, a man may run away and hide, the implication being that he does not wish his mourning to be lifted. In this case the visitor with the turmeric will not trouble to search for him, but will smear the turmeric on the housepost as a substitute. On his return the mourner sees the turmeric on the post and wails, from his affection for the dead and as a sign that he is abandoning his mourning. If, however, the mourning is not for a very close relative, such as a mother-in-law, then a mourner does not trouble to hide. But if the mourner does not try and hide he may still attempt to restrain the visitor from applying the turmeric, and at the moment when it is applied will hide his face and begin to wail a dirge in which other members of the family will probably join. Later, the mother's family representatives make a presentation of barkcloth and food to the mourner and his family, who reciprocate with sinnet cord, a wooden bowl or a paddle. The whole operation is termed *furunga kere*, cleansing the soil. The idea apparently is that the application of turmeric, associated with dancing, cleanses the mourner's body from the funeral taint.

Considerable figurative usage is involved in this whole situation. A family which has lost a member may go out of mourning *seriatim*, and by degrees. At the first major dance festival after the bereavement of Pa Rangifuri, his father the chief and two of his brothers emerged to dance on the first day. Another brother went to the festival but did not dance. He was said to 'sit' (*nofo*) only, but in fact as well as sitting and watching he worked hard at food preparations. On the following day he too 'stood up' (*tu*) and danced. Two other brothers were walking about publicly but did not go to the dance, while Pa Rangifuri, as father of the deceased boy, still remained in his house. The terms *nofo* ('sitting') and *tu* ('standing') have a technical significance, distinguishing a person in half-mourning and 'out of mourning' respectively as far as dancing is concerned, while *pali* indicates a person who is still in full mourning.

What has been said so far about the context of *pali* behaviour refers mainly to restraint upon public appearance and especially upon dancing. The concept involves essentially restriction of bodily movement, of which movement abroad outside one's house and dancing are most outstanding examples. But Tikopia mourning custom involves also other types of behaviour. No special clothing is worn analogous to the wearing of black in Western mourning—though it would be regarded as odd to put on new clothing, and close kin of the deceased may wear round their necks articles worn by the dead person. But Tikopia mourning is characterised by restrictions in regard to food. Are these food restrictions part of the *pali* concept or not? This is not clear from the textual evidence which I have on record. What I have in my notebooks is a brief statement about food abstention at mourning, to which the term *tapu* is applied. It is necessary then to examine the relation between these two terms very closely.

Statements in my notebooks from my early days in Tikopia show that a principal mourner is expected to refrain from all 'good food'—large fish, pudding with coconut cream, taro, yam, etc. Only 'bad food' such as papaya, breadfruit and spinach are allowed, as also *fukao* and other wild berries which are not highly esteemed in the ordinary way. It was my understanding that these food abstentions which a father or other close kinsman adopts immediately on a person's death were also regarded as coming under the *pali* head, since they form part of the general scheme of restrictive obligations regarded socially as obligatory upon every principal mourner.[6] It would be tempting to assert merely that this is so, but I must admit that I can find no statement in my field notebooks which would give precise evidence for this assertion. Here is an area in which my interpretation depends upon my general understanding of usage and not upon any verifiable textual records. This being so, some further analysis can be made.

Food abstentions in connection with mourning can be seen by an anthropologist to be of two kinds, though they shade into one another, and the Tikopia may not distinguish between them very clearly. One kind of food restriction begins the moment mourning begins and continues together with the other kinds of restrictions upon public appearance and dancing. But when the period of *pali* has ended, and the erstwhile mourner has now begun to dance again and take full part in public life, he may still practise some food restrictions. These are of a more personal order. He keeps them not primarily because society regards it as obligatory upon him to do so, but because he regards it as consonant with either his dignity or his affection to maintain some austerity in memory of his dead kinsman.

I have records of such abstentions from my early period in Tikopia. In 1928 my next-door neighbour described to me how, if he wished, taro could be taboo to him, and that this was according to a person's choice. Such an abstention might be relieved by a kinsman who might prepare a meal including the rejected foodstuff and bring it as a gift. In stock phraseology the visitor would say, 'Brother, long has been your dwelling away from this food. I am going to present to you fish and other food.' The mourner replies, 'What are you doing? Let me abide longer.' The visitor answers, 'Oh, take it up, long has been your dwelling for your parent.' The mourner and his visitor will then wail together and then eat.

The word which I have translated taboo is *tapu* in the original ('*kuou ka fifia ka tapu te taro*'—I shall wish that taro shall be taboo.) The same term is used in Tikopia, as elsewhere in Polynesia, for a very wide range of restrictive behaviour—in regard to the names of affinal kin, imparting of esoteric information, sacred rites of the Work of the Gods, conduct in temples, touching the head of a father or of a chief, use of coconuts from orchards, relashing a bonito hook, etc.[7]

In each of these contexts some kind of restrictions of behaviour exist. In general it may be said that whereas *pali* is a form of social restriction, *tapu* involves ritual restriction. In other words, the sanctions for maintenance of *pali* behaviour are disapproval, whereas the sanctions for maintenance of *tapu* behaviour are supernatural punishment. But this description is too simple as far as *tapu* is concerned. In Tikopia the term *tapu* is by no means always associated with ritual actions nor with the sanction of fear of supernatural punishment on breach. The term may be used in everyday life to refer to a simple prohibition with the sanction for breach of an essentially human kind. The young child of an informant one day was about to touch the anthropologist's notebook. The father said to him '*Tapu*', and then he said to me, 'Say (to him) it is taboo' (*muna atu e tapu*). Here there was no suggestion of trying to frighten the child by a threat of the supernatural. If the child had persisted nothing more than a smack would have resulted.

It is in this non-ritual sense that the Tikopia use the term *tapu* to apply to mourning restrictions about food. Such mourning restrictions are fairly common, as indicated by the question often asked of a person who has recently been attending a funeral, 'Are you tabooed to anything (*koke e tapu ki anea*)?' meaning—is there any particular food which the person is barred from eating?

On my first expedition to Tikopia I recorded some of these personal food taboos. My attention was drawn to them emphatically again on my second expedition by a curious incident. It was the time of great food shortage and the Government administrative officer who was visiting Tikopia at the time conceived the excellent idea of trying to introduce the Tikopia to a wider range of vegetable foodstuffs than they were in the habit of using—certain fern shoots, etc. With some samples of these foods were cooked a large fish known as *pāra*, caught by trolling from the administrator's vessel as it circumnavigated the island. On board were a Tikopia chief and several of his close kin, also men of rank, and the administrator invited them to partake of a meal as a demonstration. A few ate the fish and vegetables, but most passed them politely over and consumed tea and biscuits. When later I enquired about this, it appeared that one man abstained from shyness, another being old, because of lack of teeth, and another, the chief, gave as an excuse that he was seasick. But some men said that the fish was taboo to them. In this case the men concerned were keeping the mourning restriction for their late chief, who had died a number of years before. The normal food taboos for a dead chief, they said, included flying-fish, Spanish mackerel, bonito and shark, but if the dead chief had been an expert fisherman, then a wider range of foods, including the most important reef fish and fish secured out at sea, were also treated as taboo. I asked, if a fisherman practising such taboos pulled up such a fish, would he keep it or throw it back? The answer was that he would pull it up and take it to his chief who might eat it or, if it was taboo to him also, hand it on to someone else. These food restrictions are not only applicable to men. Wives follow their husbands in such matters, and even children may up set their own food taboos. 'If a child is knowledgeable he will make his taboo. But another child may not know about taboos.'

These individually created taboos are like the *pali* restrictions about dancing, expected to last for only a limited period. In the same way they can be lifted by the formal action of another person—it would be regarded as improper for a man simply to drop his food taboo. One man explained to me about the fish, 'This is a custom of this land. I too used to be taboo in respect of it. Today I have been fed, I have eaten of it. A man who is dwelling (in seclusion) because of his parents, (restricted) from fish and good food, does not eat at his wish; he is fed by his kinsfolk, by another man.' The ceremonial 'feeding' process may take place between husband and wife. A wife follows her husband's food taboo for one of his kin 'because his lips have eaten only husks. He has eaten poor food.' In other words, she undertakes his taboos from sympathy. Sometimes then a man will 'feed' his wife in order to relieve her of the obligation. But sometimes a wife may insist on maintaining a taboo when it is lifted from her husband by another 'feeder'. She says, 'You eat, you are a man, and the taboo will dwell with me.' Her idea is that she is a woman and it is right that 'her throat should have the husks' because as a woman she pays respect to her husband, who has to carry on his daily work. Later on such a husband will 'feed' his wife and lift the taboo, seeing that she has continued the obligation on their behalf. When a woman marries, if both she and her husband have been practising food taboos, she will adopt his as well. But in such a case her husband's kin are sympathetic towards her. When she has kept their taboo for some time they say, 'Let us go and prepare food to feed our married woman.' Sometimes, especially if the dead person was his father, a man refuses to have his mourning lifted. The reason is that he thinks of his father and himself eating of that food together in past time—as we might say, it sticks in his throat.

The significance of eating as an antithesis to mourning comes out very clearly from such instances. Very commonly in most societies not-eating is a sign of *personal* stress. The Tikopia have to some degree reversed the proposition, and with them *social* stress is manifested in a more formal way by not eating. When a chief has gone on a voyage, for the first day or two it is the custom in Tikopia for no oven to be lit in any of the cookhouses of his clansfolk. Only children, from whom social obligations are still regarded as not fully onerous, eat; no adults eat. So, conversely, the ending of social stress is signalized by not only the formal presentation of food to the person affected, but by the actual feeding of him by his visitor. He is coaxed to take food. Morsels are specifically put before him with the injunction, 'Eat'. In this way he is made to feel that the abandonment of his obligation is not a matter of his own wish but the wish of others. The system is built on responsibility for decision to abandon mourning being taken by someone else. The system works well so long as the rules are generally understood and followed, so long as other persons have a sense of obligation which makes them take responsibility and look after the welfare of the person in mourning.

This Tikopia material on food *tapu* makes it clear that some of the generalizations which have been made about the concept of taboo are not necessarily universal, if *tapu* is always translated as taboo. Steiner (1956), following Ernest Crawley (1902, pp. 6 *et passim*), has argued that taboo is an element of all those situations in which attitudes to values are expressed in terms of danger behaviour, and the narrowing down of localization of danger is a major function of taboo. The mourning restrictions on food described as *tapu* by the Tikopia do not seem to involve a concept of danger for the person observing them or for others. They are personally created and socially removed; there is no ritual sanction involved. It may be thought that the Tikopia believe that if the mourner does not keep food taboos the spirit of the dead person will be angry and wreak vengeance. Of such belief I have no evidence. The whole context in which these taboos operate is one of a sense of obligation to kin, not danger from kin or for kin.

These food taboos can now be related to the notion of *pali*. Between *pali* and *tapu* in Tikopia there is a clear semantic overlap in that both deal with restrictions on behaviour. *Pali* exclusively and *tapu* in part refers to mourning behaviour. *Pali* apparently and *tapu* certainly can include restrictions upon food. Where does the difference lie? The exact degree of coincidence and difference I cannot specify as I have no textual record, nor do I remember having specifically questioned any Tikopia on the matter. But it is clear that the meaning of *tapu* covers a much wider range of circumstances than that of *pali*, and that in this wider range are many circumstances in which the restraint is regarded as ritual as well as social. Where an overlap occurs in respect of food restrictions, I infer that *pali* applies to those food restrictions which are part of the general mourning situation following immediately on the death of a kinsman, and which are regarded as socially obligatory. *Tapu*, on the other hand, seems to apply to those food restrictions which continue after the period of *pali* is ended and which, though socially approved, are not obligatory but are primarily at the initiative of the person concerned.

A few general observations may be made from all this analysis. The social anthropologist and the linguist operate with linguistic material at different levels. The social anthropologist is concerned with generalizations about human behaviour in a social context, not primarily with generalizations about verbal behaviour. The kind of sociological analysis of his field material which a modern social anthropologist undertakes is normally convincing enough to his colleagues at the level at which he operates. It is understood to rest not only upon his linguistic records in his notebooks, but also upon a mass of experience of both verbal and non-verbal behaviour of the people he has studied, going far beyond the data comprised in his records. On the other hand, the linguistic part of his records, when closely examined, may turn out to be imprecise.

For interpretation of concepts in the vernacular it is necessary for the anthropologist to go beyond his notebook records. The scale of his theoretical problem and the range of his observations are such that he cannot give adequate contextualization (in writing or by tape records) of every word needed in his exposition. Memory of his own repeated experiences must supply some of the clues. But this has its hazards. Memory involves selection of experience. Choice must often be made among alternative attributions, where a slight alteration in the criteria used may make a big difference in the ultimate meaning. In my own work I have been often conscious of the delicacy of discrimination needed to avoid plumping for the easier attribution of meaning, the one that fits best a particular theoretical view or line of exposition. Great care is necessary then lest the social anthropologist or his readers mistake for evidence of meaning what may be in some cases only affirmation.

BIBLIOGRAPHY

Capell, A. (1962) 'Oceanic Linguistics Today', *Current Anthropology* Vol. III, pp. 371–396.

Crawley, E. (1902) *The Mystic Rose*, London.

Durrad, W. J. (1927) *Journal of the Polynesian Society* Vol. XXXVI, p. 12.

Elbert, S. H. (1953) 'Internal Relationships of the Polynesian Languages and Dialects', *Southwestern Journal of Anthropology* Vol. IX, pp. 147–173.

Evans-Pritchard, E.E. (1956) *Nuer Religion*, Oxford.

Firth, J.R. (1957) 'Ethnographic Analysis and Language with Reference to Malinowski's Views' in *Man and Culture* (ed. Raymond Firth), pp. 93–118, London.

Firth, Raymond (1936) *We, The Tikopia: A Sociological Analysis of Kinship in Primitive Polynesia*, London.

—— (1939) *Primitive Polynesian Economy*, London.

—— (1940a) 'The Analysis of Mana: An Empirical Approach', *Journal of the Polynesian Society* Vol. XLIX, pp. 483–510.

—— (1940b) *Work of the Gods*, 2 vols. (London School of Economics Monographs in Social Anthropology, Nos. 1 and 2).

—— (1951) *Elements of Social Organization*, London.

—— (1959) *Social Change in Tikopia*, London.

—— (1963) 'L and R in Tikopia Language', *Oceanic Linguistics* Vol. II, pp. 49–61.

Nadel, S.F. (1954) *Nupe Religion*, London.

Steiner, F. (1956) *Taboo*, London.

Notes

[1] I am much indebted for helpful comment and criticism on a draft of this paper to my colleagues in the University of London, Professor E. J. A. Henderson, Mr. G. B. Milner and Professor R.H. Robins of the School of Oriental and African Studies; and to my graduate seminar in social anthropology at the London School of Economics. I am also grateful for facilities in the preparation of this article to a personal research grant from the Behavioral Sciences Division of the Ford Foundation.

[2] Cf. my article on 'The Analysis of *Mana*: An Empirical Approach'. (Firth, 1940a.)

[3] A phonetic question arises in regard to the use of l. Radcliffe-Brown used to state that *l* and *r* are mutually exclusive in Polynesian languages (v. also Elbert, 1953, p. 153; Capell, 1962, p. 380). While in general this seems so, it does not hold for Tikopia, where many l-words and some l/r pairs of words exist, with quite different semantic use. Parallel to the p-l- and l-l- series are sets of p-r- and r-r- words, some with the same vowel combinations, but others different. There is no word *pari* to correspond to *pali*, but there is a word *roro* (coconut cream) to correspond to *lolo*.

What is interesting is the relative fewness of the l-words as against comparable r-words in the vocabulary, thus making all such l-words liable to stand out in use. Moreover, the series in -r- display overall a much wider semantic range than words in -l- of similar structures (v. Firth, 1963, p. 49).

I owe the following note to Mr. G. B. Milner. 'The word *pali* is of interest from a comparative point of view. It occurs widely in Eastern Polynesian in the sense of cliff, etc., while in Samoan I have recorded it in the form *laupali*, a word "not in polite usage" meaning vulva. What is even more important is that Tikopian *pali* is probably a cognate of a word found in many Indonesian languages which have become known to ethnographers because they generally connote a restriction of some kind. The only article I know which discusses this is an old one (1893) in the *Bijdragen T.L.V.* (V-8) by Kern. "Woordverwisseling in het Galelareesch" (pp. 120–128). Galela appears to be one of the non-Austronesian languages of Northern Halmahera but Kern evidently regards the Galela word *saäli* as cognate with *pali* in Dayak, *fady* in Malagasy and Malay *pamali* (now written *pĕmali*). Possibly also with Mota *qualiga* (presumably Mota *q* is to be pronounced *kpw*). In all those instances the root denotes a restriction of some kind, Mota, Malagasy and Galela being grouped by Kern on the grounds that in all three languages a word-taboo or restriction of some kind is involved.'

In the light of this, it is interesting to note also that P. Favre, *Dictionnaire Malais-Français*, Vienna, 1875, p. 111, gives the meaning of *pĕmali*, as *illicite*, *défendu*. R. J. Wilkinson, *A Malay-English Dictionary*, Mytilene, 1932, translates *pĕmali* as taboo, and adds 'etymologically from *pali*, of which *pantang* was the courtly and is now the commoner form'. He points out that in some contexts *pantang* means taboo at certain times only—e.g. birth-taboos; whereas *pĕmali* means taboo at all times—e.g. a boy may never touch a rotten egg. In his *Malay-English Dictionary* (Singapore, 1903), the meaning of *pĕmali* is given as forbidden; tabooed; a prohibition.

[4] It may not be far-fetched then to regard *pali* and *lolo*, the obligations of which are regarded as onerous, as having sets of phonetic associations of a depressing, somewhat restrictive, character. In general, it could be said that the p-r- and r-r- series involve words of more positive status than do the p-l- and l-l- series.

[5] A correction is necessary to the original recording of my second statement given above (p. 99). '*E pali* for Mairunga . . .' was not a precise rendering of Tikopia usage, which states that a person is *pali*, not that it is *pali* for him to do something.

[6] The term *pali* occurs in a Tikopia Vocabulary compiled mainly from material collected by Rev. W. J. Durrad of the Melanesian Mission, edited by Herbert W. Williams, *Journal of the Polynesian Society*, Vol. 36, 1927, p. 12. The meaning there is given as an intransitive verb, fast, which indicates that Durrad, who saw many funerals, regarded the restrictions as applying to food.

[7] Space forbids citation of the considerable textual evidence I possess. For discussion of the term in various aspects, see Firth 1936, pp. 182–186 *et seq.*; 1939, pp. 201–212; 1940, pp. 182–186; 1959, *passim.*

Linguistic Relevance

W. HAAS

1. LINGUISTIC ANALYSIS

Linguistics shares its subject-matter with many other disciplines. Psychology, acoustics, physiology, logic, anthropology, literary criticism have all their accounts to give of human speech. What one discipline regards as complex and problematic, and therefore in need of analysis, another accepts as simple, 'given', intuitively clear. This is what distinguishes and connects them. I shall be concerned to ask about linguistics in particular, to what sort of analytic discipline it, and it alone, subjects the facts of human speech?

The reason why we have to ask about analytic methods, is simply that there is no such thing as exhaustive analysis. There is no complete description. To describe is to select; and in any descriptive effort, if it is part of a theoretical discipline, selection is determined by something more definite than just 'interest'. *General principles of relevance* determine (i) what to fasten upon as problematic 'fact', and (ii) what to select as the kind of simple 'data' to which those problematic facts will be reduced. In trying to state explicitly, what the principles are, by which a linguistic analysis proceeds, when picking out what *it* regards as complex and problematic or, on the other hand, as simple and basically significant in the unending and infinitely varied 'flow' of human speech, we are in fact exploring the foundations of this particular 'discipline'. We are trying to elicit from an ancient practice what may be regarded as the general theoretical frame of its descriptive and explanatory work. Clearer awareness of the implicit principles may be expected to increase their power—and, incidentally, to enable us more effectively to relate linguistic studies to the work of those other disciplines which, in their different ways, cover the same field.

1.1 Aims and Assumptions

To the linguist, fundamentally the most puzzling characteristic of language is its enormous productivity—that obvious ability we have, every one of us, of always adding something new to an infinite variety of utterances; of saying what has never been said before, and understanding what we have never heard before. To explain how this is possible, is the root-problem of linguistic analysis. It is of course immediately clear that there are, and must be, certain partial similarities between the new utterances and the old—certain regularities in those operations of saying and understanding: what is novel must be assumed to arise from a new but regular combination of old parts. The first task, then, of linguistic description—somewhat analogous to the chemist's attempt to 'explain' the puzzling variety of material things—may be said to be a reductive one: the task, namely, of reducing the practically infinite variety of utterances to a relatively few recurrent relations of a relatively few recurrent elements. So much seems to be obvious and uncontroversial. But much that is less obvious seems to follow from having located the problem and determined the task in this way.

Something about the objects to be described and analysed must be taken for granted; and the question is, how much. One may ask, for instance, whether it would be profitable to apply linguistic methods to arbitrary stretches of speech, i.e. to nothing more than certain events of acoustic disturbance. We seem to require more, as a basis for linguistic operations: nothing less, in fact, than that succession of different *significant utterances* which is our problem. They are the objects of our analysis. Precisely as the chemist is not concerned to verify the perceived variety of material things (including the instruments of his laboratory), so the linguist simply observes the various meaningful utterances and knows of their distinct existence, without feeling obliged to explain how he knows it. Neither the chemist's nor the linguist's presupposition is beyond question. But the question is asked by other disciplines—by psychologists, anthropologists, philosophers. The linguist (and, *mutatis mutandis*, the chemist) asks about the *internal structure* of his 'facts', always taking for granted that he can observe and roughly distinguish them.

J. R. Firth refers here to a 'basic postulate', which he calls 'the implication of utterance'. 'Language text', he says, 'must be attributed to participants in some context of situation', before it can be analysed.[1] The various global forms and meanings of the pieces of text, which are subjected to linguistic analysis, are regarded as 'given' by the linguist, though they are capable of being 'established' and 'explained' by anthropological inquiries—that is, by a study of speakers and listeners in 'contexts of situation'. This tells us something about the relation between the linguistic and the social studies of human speech. 'Context of situation', says Firth, 'makes sure of the sociological component' of linguistic descriptions. It 'is a convenient abstraction at the social level of analysis, and forms the basis of the hierarchy of techniques', which are employed by linguistic analysis proper.[2]

L. Bloomfield was equally explicit on what he called 'the fundamental assumption of linguistics'. 'We must assume', he said, 'that in every speech-community some utterances are alike (or partly alike) in form and meaning'.[3] This is the basis of linguistic analysis. Bloomfield, however, made it unnecessarily difficult for himself, and his followers, to feel at ease with this fundamental assumption. In Bloomfieldian linguistics, likeness of meaning becomes a source of trouble. It is formulated in such a way as to allow mysterious 'elements' of meaning ('sememes') to attach themselves to the clear-cut formal elements of any given utterance. As a result, an unmanageable crowd of elusive extra-lingual entities intrudes, in haphazard fashion, into the very fabric of linguistic analysis; whereas for Firth, situational context, lying itself safely *outside* the utterance, provides all we need to presuppose in order to describe the significant functions and elements within.

It is on account of that 'semantic' function of any described utterance —a function in 'contexts of situation'—that Firth regarded the whole of linguistic description, from syntax to phonetics, as a statement of various 'modes of meaning'. The unfortunate idiosyncrasy of this special terminology—which confined the term 'semantic' to an anthropological study, while ascribing 'meaning' to everything that is linguistically relevant, whether it be a sentence or a word or a mere sound—seems to have been seriously misleading.[4] It suggested a highly eccentric and esoteric theory, precisely at the point at which Firth in fact affirmed what is generally acknowledged to be the fundamental presupposition of linguistic studies. Indeed, he succeeded, where others had failed— namely, in admitting extra-lingual presuppositions, without allowing them to disrupt the proper autonomy of linguistic studies. Extra-lingual 'context of situation', which replaces all those sporadically intrusive 'semantic entities', was simply thought of as infusing every linguistic element with *relevance*, or, as Firth put it, with some 'mode of meaning'.[5]

Yet, whatever the difference between Firth and Bloomfield, they were agreed on one important point—namely, that the objects of linguistic analysis are not just physical objects, not arbitrarily selected 'stretches of speech'. Such, they were sure, would not offer them enough information for their reductive task. 'As long as we pay no attention to meanings', says Bloomfield, 'we cannot decide whether two uttered forms are "the same" or "different".'[6] To be able to decide so much as this, we need to assume that some of those physical 'stretches' make sense, and that they make different kinds of sense (though full information as to what specific sense any utterance makes will not need to be presupposed as given).[7] Meaningful utterances, then, many and various, are the objects of linguistic inquiry. The linguist's concern is with their internal constitution, the question being how to reduce them to recurrent elements in recurrent relations.

1.2 Metalinguistics

If there were no *general* statements to be made about the reductive work of linguistic analysis, if we could do no more than refer to various skills, guesses and inarticulate intuitions, then, indeed, we could not speak of either a *discipline* of linguistic analysis or a *theory* of linguistic description. We should have to admit that linguistics has not emerged yet from the uncertainty of an inspired art or craft.

This may have to be especially stressed today, when linguists are invited once more to accept miscellaneous skills and guesses as sufficient for linguistic analysis, and to satisfy their theoretical ambition outside linguistics. Everybody is entitled to change his occupation. But having done so, he must not pretend to be continuing with his old job. A theory like 'Generative Grammar', which refers to the logical properties of various given grammars, rather than directly to the empirical properties of human speech, is not a linguistic theory about speech, any more than a logical theory about the statements of various kinds of physics could be regarded as a physical theory about the material world. One may wonder, how scientists in other fields would react, if it were suggested to them that they should change their approach in the way currently proposed for linguistics. Would anybody accept a 'generative meteorology' to replace the present search for effective methods and theories in this particular field? Would it not be ludicrous to suggest that a rigorous logical theory, *not* about the weather but about the very imperfect understanding we have of it, i.e. a theory about any such *statements* as might be derived from sundry methodological hints, hunches and guesses about the weather, could qualify as meteorological theory? In a similar way, should we not deceive ourselves, if we thought that by formalizing and logically evaluating various intuitive statements about language we could provide ourselves with a linguistic theory? A linguistic theory is a tool for the handling of speech-material, a tool for arriving at systematic statements about languages. Any further handling of such statements is a task of what might be described as metalinguistic theory, a branch of applied logic. Meta-linguistics may be of considerable use for the testing of linguistic descriptions, and of the theories behind them. A theory such as that of Generative Grammar will help us to keep our tools in order. It raises many highly interesting, even linguistically interesting, questions. But though it might usefully tell us which of two bad grammars is the worse, it cannot tell us how to obtain a third which is better. For its statements are about grammars, never directly about languages.[8]

The last forty years have seen the gradual evolution of a working theory of linguistic description.

2. LINGUISTIC STRUCTURE

To try to account for the many and various meaningful utterances in terms of 'recurrent elements in recurrent relations' is not to set ourselves two tasks—(i) to find the elements, and (ii) to establish the relations. We cannot do the one without the other. This is why linguistic theory is a theory of linguistic *structure*, and modern linguistics is known as 'structural linguistics'. What is essential about linguistic elements (and more important than their intrinsic properties) is the fact that they are terms in a systematic network of mutual relations, terms in a structure. This, again, is familiar. But again, some of the consequences are not.

2.1 Distribution and Domain

The task of discovering the significant elements and relations is of course critically determined by the kind of fundamental presupposition we choose to adopt with regard to our analysandum. If what we accept as 'given' for our analysis were to be mere stretches of speech, then any relations that could be established within such stretches would turn out to be basically physical relations, i.e. relations of co-occurrence ('distribution'), and the elements would be just smaller stretches ('segments') and physical properties of such.

For instance, from the sentence immediately preceding, we might select the stretch [kłˈprə], in order to test it for significant relations of co-occurrence. We should then find that it occurs not only in the environment [ˈfizi–pətiˑzəf], but also in others such as [ˈmjuːzi–didʒi],

[ˈmedi-bləm], [ˈtæ-fitəbli], etc.; and we shall also find that this distribution of [kɫˈprɔ] is not significantly paralleled by the distribution of any other segment. By saying that the distribution of a particular segment has no significant parallels we should mean then that there are no *general* distributional statements that can be made about this segment (or its environment).

The question is, whether it is in fact possible adequately to analyse utterances in this way. Z. S. Harris claims that a language *can* be described completely 'in terms of a distributional structure, i.e. in terms of the occurrence of parts (ultimately sounds) relative to other parts', i.e. purely as a physical phenomenon. 'Distributional statements', he says, 'can cover all the material of a language, without requiring support from other types of information'.[9] If this is so, then we should have to admit that the structure of a language consists in physical relations, and descriptive linguistics would be, fundamentally, a branch of physics.

This would be a tremendous achievement; and it would clearly be absurd of us to raise objections in defence of alleged non-physical characteristics of language, if we could be shown that a physical description of it is both feasible and adequate. But this, it seems to me, has not been shown. The cited assertion is a profession of faith—a faith in alleged possibilities of the future, rather than a statement of actual achievement. Harris's achievements in the field of Linguistic Analysis are of course such that it would be foolish to try to belittle them and presumptuous to praise them; but his 'methods' do in fact require 'support from other [and non-physical] types of information'. They would be seriously misrepresented, if they were described as purely 'distributional'. They are *not* concerned *exclusively* with the relation of stretches of speech (ultimately sounds) to one another. The 'distributions' we are referred to do not consist simply in relations of parts to other parts, of segments or features to arbitrary environments. Part-part relations in the proposed analysis obtain almost invariably *within determinate significant units*, ultimately within meaningful utterances. This is true of the way in which Harris (and almost any other linguist) identifies his phonological elements as just those 'parts' which are capable of distinguishing *significant utterances*. It is true again of the way in which morphological elements are established by criteria of distributional patterning; when the distributional parallels between 'larger stretches', so called, are regarded as relevant, if, and only if, they allow us to make general structural statements *about significant utterances*.[10] And it is also true of that subsidiary procedure, by which Harris establishes tentative morphemic boundaries (in order to avoid the impossible task of having to test all possible segments); for this procedure requires us to count the number of *different significant utterances* that can be obtained by 'completing' given stretches of speech.[11]

It is, in fact, this indispensable condition of meaningful utterance that has been lamented recently as the defeat of *mechanical* discovery-procedures. Defeat it is, if, as Harris seems to have done, we really aim at such procedures. If analytic operations were really to be restricted to producing relations of co-occurrence, i.e. mechanical relations among sundry segments of speech, then, indeed, we could not succeed with the primary reductive work of linguistic analysis. To speculate whether we might succeed sometime in the future is of little use so long as we are unable to suggest, even vaguely, *how we might* succeed.

Those who knew J. R. Firth remember his frequent strictures upon the preoccupation of some linguists with questions of 'procedure'. What he had in mind, and what he opposed, was the kind of ambition which is frequently voiced (though it is not realized) in Harris's 'Methods'—a search for a mechanical 'schedule of procedure', which ignores the 'sociological component' of linguistic studies and denies the 'implication of significant utterance'. Yet Firth was not opposed to methodological inquiries. He was clearly concerned with the operational foundations of linguistic theory. What was wanted, here, he would call '*techniques*', rather than 'procedures'. 'The Technique of Semantics' was the title of one of his earlier and most significant contributions to linguistic analysis.

The most general statements we can make about languages are derived from just those techniques or operations of analysis to which language-material has proved to be responsive. The operations performed by one observer must be repeatable and controllable by others. Mechanical aids are always welcome; but this is no reason why the linguist should be required to replace himself by a machine.

The linguist's operations of analysis, including those proposed by Harris, have never been mechanical. This is reflected in the general restriction which has to be put upon any part-part relations which are established among elements of speech: they carry the implication of part-whole relations. (Aspiration is an allophonic feature of English 'stops', when the latter are *word*-initial; ignore word-boundaries, and aspiration is distinctive.[12] English *-ly* is an adverbial suffix, if the *word* of which it is part has adverbial function in its *phrase*, etc., etc.) Parts, simple or co-occurrent, are always part of significant units; and every such unit, as a whole, is assumed to be given independently, i.e. it cannot, itself, be adequately defined in terms of its parts.[13] This fundamental prerequisite of linguistic analysis has not remained entirely unrecognized even among the advocates of purely distributional methods, though recognition has generally been confined to footnotes, and has failed to affect the statement of method in the main text. Harris, for instance, tells us explicitly: 'An important factor in the compact statement of relation among elements is *the specification of the domain over which the relation occurs*.'[14] But if we admit that distributional relations are subject to such limitations, shall we not have to accept a notion of linguistic structure which it is impossible to represent in *purely* distributional terms?

In the following I shall attempt to determine more precisely, within what kind of general relational framework it is that we establish the structure of a language, and what kinds of linguistic value appear in such a framework.

2.2 The Basic Operations

The kind of order which we are able to extract from the speech of a community when we establish its 'language', is determined by the analytic operations which we choose, and are able, to perform upon its given utterances. These operations provide, in fact, an ostensive definition of the basic structural relations.

Fundamentally, the operations of linguistic analysis are just two: (a) cutting (segmentation) and (b) replacement (substitution). The first gives us 'segments' (e.g. sounds or words or phrases), each occupying a discrete stretch of time; the second yields either segments or mere features of such (e.g. voicing or stress-patterns or pitch-contours or order). Segmentation of an utterance yields elements *in sequence*. Replacement of part of a given utterance (segment or feature) by part of another yields elements which are characterized as alternative values for the same function.[15] All the various more specific operations of linguistic analysis (such as overlapping segmentation, minimal replacement, permutation, simultaneous replacement of discontinuous parts, omission, i.e. replacement by 'nil', expansion, i.e. replacement of 'nil', etc.) seem to be special cases of those two basic types of operation. If this is so, then it should be possible to explain the general features of linguistic structure by exposing more fully the kinds of relation which are established by performing those basic operations.

We note immediately that, unless we impose some special restrictions on it, there can be no special linguistic significance in mere segmentation. Here, we generate relations of linear sequence; and such, though supremely convenient, are not of specifically linguistic interest.[16] They merely exhibit the trivial truth that speaking takes time. An utterance may be segmented in an infinite number of ways, and theoretically the segments may be of any size. What is linguistically relevant is not this physical operation of cutting itself, but the decision *where* to make the cuts. And this decision will depend, fundamentally, on that other operation, replacement, carried out under certain restrictions. It is a special type of substitutability that yields relevant information about segments as well as features.

It is not surprising that considerations of linguistic relevance require us to rely primarily on operations of replacement (substitution). For, (i) replacement operations involve the recognition of different utterances as partially similar (e.g. *pin*, *tin*, *bin*, etc., as similar with regard to . . . *in*) —which serves the reductive purpose of linguistic analysis; and (ii) such operations indicate the points at which there obtains freedom of choice in the construction of utterances—a freedom which characterizes human speech distinctively as a non-automatic, voluntary, continually creative activity. The task of Linguistic Analysis is to state the limits of this freedom of choice, i.e. the range of available elements, and the dependencies which circumscribe their substitutabilities.

Operations of substitution apply to 'specified domains'. It follows that elements picked out by replacement (say, *boy* in *The boys went home*, as being replaceable by *girl*, *dog*, etc.) are not found in any *mere* environment, but always in the *complementary* environment of a specified unit-frame (such as the sentence-frame *The . . . went home.*). For, the critical operation is not mere substitution but always *contrastive* substitution, in Trubetzkoy's terminology—'opposition', in Hjelmslev's —'commutation'. Thus, a uniform technique of comparison yields distinct units of a specified type—the type being determined by the 'frame' (or 'function').

2.3 The Basic Relations

In order to state, more exactly, how this technique gives rise to a general relational framework of linguistic elements, we shall best describe it in terms borrowed from the logician. We shall say that contrastive substitution applies to a *function*; 'function' to mean the kind of incomplete expression which may be obtained from a definite significant unit (a sentence, phrase, or word), when some part (segment or feature) of it is replaced by a 'variable' (marked by dots '. . .' or, say, 'X'), while the rest, which determines the function and the range of the variable, is left 'constant'. Thus, *The . . . s went home* would be called a 'sentence function'. We may say then that *The boys went home, The girls went home*, etc., are different values of the same sentence function; that *boy*, *girl*, etc., are different values of its variable, that they 'share', 'satisfy', 'fulfil' or 'fill' the same function, that they are 'values *for*' it. We shall also say, with a slight but innocuous abbreviation, that the sentence *The boys went home* is a function of *boy* (instead of saying that it is a value of a function of *boy*). The 'range' of the variable is what is usually described by linguists as a 'substitution-class' or 'paradigm'.

Every contrastive (commutable) element appears, then, in a network of relations. It (e.g. *boy*) stands in

(a) *syntagmatic* relations to a certain environment (e.g. to *the*, *went*, *home*);
(b) *paradigmatic* relations to all other elements which are capable of satisfying the same function (e.g. to *girl*, *dog*, *traveller*, etc.); and
(c) *functional* relations to units of higher level (such as the sentence *The boys went home*).

The last of these three types of relation, it will be noticed, is usually passed over in silence—perhaps because it implies the first two. But it needs mentioning, because it is not implied by them. (Note, for example, that *boy*, above, stands in syntagmatic relation also to the environment /ə . . . wen/, where it would be replaceable by, say, *strapping* in *A strapping wench.*)[17] To mention functional relations is to acknowledge explicitly that substitution, being contrastive, has been applied to significant units of utterance, not to arbitrary portions of speech.

The syntagmatic and paradigmatic relations of an element are distributional; i.e. they are relations of it, as part, *to other parts on the same level*; its functional relations are relations of it, as part, *to whole units of higher level.*

We could say that, in this way, every complex utterance is represented as the value of a number of functions—as a product of syntagmatically connected choices from various paradigms.

To give a structural description of linguistic elements is to describe them in terms of those three relations. We shall describe most linguistic elements in two ways: each, except the simplest, as *function* (or rather, a value of functions) of simpler elements; and again, each, except the most complex, as *component value* (*with* others, and *in contrast* to others) *for* functions of higher level.[18]

Thus, what Harris claims to be true of every linguistic element, namely, that it is identified (a) 'relatively to the other elements at *its* level', and (b) 'in terms of particular elements at a *lower* level',[19] would appear to be true only of the most complex, that is, sentences which, in fact, are only marginally 'elements' of grammar. The description of phonetic elements requires reference to the higher-level grammatical elements which they constitute (generally, word-functions and phrase-functions), and the description of these, in turn, requires reference to the sentences of which they are part. Acquaintance with (a) their distribution and (b) their internal composition is not enough. This is why it has proved impossible strictly to adhere to a 'schedule of procedure', by which the analysis of a language would begin with the simplest elements and gradually build up ever more complex ones. We cannot proceed 'from sound to sentence'. It is not surprising that even those linguists who profess adherence to a purely distributional theory of analysis find it necessary to refer to significant units of higher level at every stage of their procedure. If such reference is presented as just a 'heuristic device', which does not affect the theory, then so much the worse for the theory. An inescapable 'heuristic device', which enters our linguistic reasoning at every point, *ought* to be incorporated in the theory. The result of doing just this would be entirely desirable.

The terms 'function' and 'structure' (which in current linguistic discussion appear so often as mere words of fashion) will then be clearly defined, and seen to be closely connected. The notion of *linguistic function*—very much akin to the logician's—will be derived from the basic operation of contrastive substitution; and the same operation will give rise to the three basic relations of *linguistic structure*: syntagmatic, paradigmatic, and functional. It is in terms of function and structure, as here defined, that we are able to state with sufficient precision, what is meant by a portion or feature of speech being *linguistically relevant*.

3. *LINGUISTIC VALUES*

3.1 Variancy and Constancy in Linguistic Functions

When an utterance is viewed as value of a function (e.g. *The boys went home*, as value of the function *The . . . s went home*), some part of it (e.g. *boy*) is viewed as 'variant' (value of a variable) relatively to the rest, which is being taken as 'constant'. One and the same utterance may be viewed as value of a number of different functions (e.g. *The boys went home* is also a value of the functions . . . *boys went home*, *The boys . . . home*, etc.). Let us call these 'the functions of the utterance'. The same part (e.g. *boy*) may thus appear in two roles, either that of variant (as in *The . . . s went home*) or that of constant (as in *The boys . . . home*). Corresponding to these two functional roles, we are able to distinguish *two basic types of linguistic relevance*: these may be distinguished respectively as *diacritical power* and *determinant power*.

This is not to say that the mere performance of either of those two roles by some part of an utterance could, in itself, be sufficient reason for assigning linguistic value to that part. It is only under certain conditions that paradigmatic variancy and syntagmatic constancy are found to endow 'parts' with diacritical or determinant power. But if the conditions of 'being linguistically relevant' *can* be stated in this way, i.e. as specific restrictions upon the two complementary roles, which any feature or segment of speech may fill in utterance-functions, then we should be within reach of a systematic and exhaustive account of linguistic values.

3.2 Diacritical Power

The conditions under which paradigmatic variation is linguistically significant are familiar. They are implicit in the very notions of linguistic function and structure (cf. 2.2, 2.3 above). A variant (replaceable) part of an utterance is relevant, if it is regularly 'contrastive' (commutable) in some functions, i.e. if, in some cases, the replacement of the part (by another or by nil) is regularly correlated with a difference of meaning or structure between the resulting function-values. The variation is then described, in familiar terminology, as 'not free', and the variant feature or segment as 'distinctive'. We may say that it has *diacritical power*, this being one type of linguistic value—a value which implies functional variancy.

A segment or feature, which is established as commutable (contrastive) in some functions, is generally recognized as 'distinctive' also in other functions, in which it may not be commutable (e.g. /b/ is a distinctive phonological element of *botany* no less than of *bin*; /e/ in /ekoˈnomiks/ is a different phoneme from /i/ in /ikoˈnomiks/; and *s* is a distinctive grammatical element of *two cats*.)[20] But an element which occurs only very rarely in minimal contrast to others will of course be only marginally distinctive.

Diacritical power is generally accepted as a sufficient condition for selecting a segment or feature as *phonologically* relevant. It is clearly not a sufficient condition of *grammatical* relevance. But it is not without importance for the discrimination of grammatical elements. The overwhelming majority of such elements, i.e. all those which are said to 'have meaning', have also diacritical power. In fact, within a sentence of normal length, the elements actually exerting diacritical power are pre-eminently grammatical; there are generally very few minimal phonological replacements that yield viable alternative sentences. (*The toy/bear/boy-s went home* seem to exhaust such alternatives in our example.) The morphemic analysis of a sentence will normally be characterized as a division of it into such smaller units as will permit the maximum overall number of contrasts, i.e. the widest range of alternative sentences. There are good reasons for saying, as we commonly do say, that we 'choose our words' when speaking, rather than that we choose sounds. Such procedures as have been proposed for 'establishing' morphemes rely heavily on diacritical power (or, as Harris called it somewhat misleadingly, 'distributional independence'[21]). There seems to be no doubt, then, that for the vast majority of grammatical elements, diacritical power is a necessary (though not a sufficient) condition of their relevance.

There is much difference of opinion on points of detail (on problems of identifying elements, phonetic and grammatical, on the neutralization of contrasts in certain conditions, on zero-elements, etc.); but diacritical power seems to be very generally accepted as at least one criterion of linguistic relevance, on the phonological as well as the grammatical level of linguistic description.[22]

There is far less agreement about criteria of relevance for elements which are *not* distinctive.

3.3 Determinant Power

3.3.1 Relevance without contrast. It is generally recognized today that, in describing the structure of utterances, we have to take account of some highly significant elements whose diacritical power is nil or practically nil. Familiar examples are syllables, the fixed lexical accent of some languages, vowel-harmony, the German glottal stop, all of them part of phonological description. The times are past, when students of phonology were inclined to look upon everything in speech that was 'non-distinctive' as 'redundant'—times not very long ago, when Firth warned us that 'a paradigmatic technique of oppositions . . . has reached, even overstepped, its limits', and asked that 'paradigmatic systems' be supplemented and corrected by the study of what he called 'syntagmatic prosodies'.[23] But the general criteria of 'syntagmatic relevance', and especially their relation to 'diacritical power', seem to have remained a source of puzzlement and confusion.

Symptomatic of the prevailing confusion is the fact that 'syntagmatic relevance', so called, has commonly been treated as if it were a purely phonological problem. Firth, it is true, declared that his own emphasis on 'the phonetics and phonology of synthesis' (rather than of 'paradigmatic differentiation') accorded well with 'the view that syntax is the dominant discipline in grammar';[24] but, surprisingly enough, he never pursued the analogy, obvious though it was that there are important grammatical elements which contract no contrasts or do so only very rarely. Examples are numerous—the 'cases' of nouns in many languages, derivational suffixes such as the English adverbial *-ly*, or the nominal *-ness*, words such as *to* (in *I want to go*), and many more. Of such grammatical elements, it is always difficult or impossible to say 'what they mean'. It is generally said that they have 'no referential meaning' but have something else—namely, 'functional' or 'structural' meaning. What that is, exactly, we are not told, and, of course, we are used to vagueness in statements about meaning. But what we do know about these elements is that they are without, or practically without, diacritical power. This suggests an analogy to phonological analysis, and it seems reasonable to suppose that in pursuing this analogy we may gain insight into some very general properties of linguistic structure.

The situation seems to be analogous on both levels of analysis. When, on the *grammatical* level, we have obtained all the distinctive elements (i.e. all those parts of utterances which would generally be described as 'having meaning'), we are left with a residue of important non-distinctive or practically non-distinctive elements—in the same way as, on the *phonological* level of analysis, when we have accounted for all the distinctive phonemic and prosodic elements (i.e. all the segments and features that would commonly be said to 'distinguish meanings'), we are left with a residue of non-distinctive or practically non-distinctive elements, some of which, so far from being discountable as just 'conditioned', must be recognized as highly significant constituents of the given phonological structure.

When we examine such residual non-distinctive elements, we soon discover that the kind of role they have in utterances is *not incompatible* with diacritical power; that, in fact, that kind of role can be, and often is, performed by elements which, in addition, have distinctive value. The distinction we shall have to make, then, is *not* between two kinds of *element*, but between two kinds of *value*. These are merely more easily *seen* to be different, whenever an element happens to display either to the exclusion of the other.

It is not without interest to review some attempts that have been made to distinguish and connect the two kinds of linguistic relevance. Since the more explicit of these attempts have been confined to phonology, in discussions of so-called 'phonological markers', I shall consider these (3.3.2), before returning to the general problem (3.4).

3.3.2 Phonological Markers. Any discussion of these must refer to Trubetzkoy. He spoke of certain sounds as 'signals' marking grammatical units. They did so, either by merely indicating how many such units there are in an utterance ('culminative function'), or by indicating this as well as marking the boundaries between the units ('delimitative function'). He regarded both these functions as 'auxiliary' beside the central and indispensable 'distinctive function'.[25] But in his treatment of *Grenzsignale* (boundary-signals), he emphasizes that their particular role is as much 'part of linguistic form as are syntactic rules of word-order or concord'.[26] 'They might be compared', he says, 'with traffic signals in the streets. Until recently there were no such signals even in large cities, simply because we could get along without them: we only needed to be more careful and more attentive. This is the reason, too, why they are not to be found on every street-corner, but only on *some*. In the same way, signals of linguistic boundaries do not occur in all the pertinent places, but just here and there. There is, however, this difference, that whereas traffic signals are always found on the 'particularly dangerous' crossroads, the distribution of linguistic boundary-signals in most languages appears to be quite haphazard—a difference which must be due to the fact that while a traffic system is artifically designed and rationally controlled, a language is organically formed and developed. Nevertheless, there is, psychologically, this similarity between linguistic boundary-signals and traffic signals, that both permit an occasional relaxation of our attention.'[27]

Trubetzkoy's chapter on 'delimitative function' is a model of linguistic investigation. Though, as the last completed chapter of an uncompleted book, it leaves much unexplored, its lucidity in what it does explore stands in remarkable contrast to a great deal of subsequent confusion. Let us note three of these later confusions, which Trubetzkoy's treatment of the subject might easily have helped to guard us against.

Firstly, the confusion of 'value' and 'element'. In dealing with boundary-signals, 'phonematic' as well as 'aphonematic', Trubetzkoy made clear that he was concerned with a kind of linguistic value (or, as he called it, 'function') which, though different from 'diacritical power', could yet join it in the same element. One of his examples is the breathed vowel-onset ('spiritus asper') of ancient Greek which, while being itself a phoneme (ὧς : ὦς, ἕξ : ἔξ etc.), also signalled the beginning of a word. In other cases, the boundary-signal may be represented by an allophone, that is, a non-distinctive conditioned element, such as the 'glottal stop' of certain German vowels, which marks the beginning of a morpheme, or by a regular word-accent.[28] Similarly Firth says of the even more varied non-distinctive values which he calls 'prosodic', that 'almost any type of "sound" may have prosodic function, and the same "sound" may have to be noticed both as a [phonematic] consonant or vowel unit and as a prosody'.[29] Here we have just what has been frequently overlooked.[30]

A. A. Hill, for instance, in a recent study devoted largely to Firth's work, quotes the statement just cited; but though he finds it 'extremely suggestive', he sets out to 'accommodate' Firth's prosodies, i.e. to equate them with 'American phonemes', segmental and suprasegmental, with phonotactic rules, suprasegmental morphemes, and, when nothing else will do, with purely phonetic elements—all this in the belief that such accommodation of the *elements* would be roughly equivalent to Firth's account of their specific *values*.[31] Again and again, he seems to forget that the elements concerned, having always been in those different niches, were not meant by Firth to be dislodged when he asked us to view them also and mainly as performing 'prosodic functions'. If we viewed them as being *just* in those many and various places and sets, where Hill's criteria of relevance would leave them, we should of course have to agree, and say with Hill that we 'can find little that clearly unites these items into a single group'. The question, whether linguistic description demands something like Trubetzkoy's 'boundary-signals' and Firth's 'prosodies', is *not* a question, primarily, of 'accommodating all elements'; we do not ask here, primarily, whether or not 'prosodies' add to our inventory. The question is rather, whether descriptions of this kind are required for giving an adequate account of the functions and values of the elements we have. To say to someone who is pointing out the determinant power of certain phonological elements that you can do without it, simply because those elements will get noticed by 'the same investigative techniques which have been used with conventional phonemes',[32] is like saying to someone who is trying to explain the special role of traffic signals that there is no need, because no doubt the objects he is referring to will be noticed anyway as so many different colours of street lighting.[33]

Such misinterpretations, however, are by no means entirely, or even to any great extent, the interpreter's fault. It is true, as Hill points out, that 'Firth has not given a clear and inclusive definition of *prosodies*'. We are not told, in general terms, what exactly to understand by 'prosodic function' (that non-diacritical value which for Firth need not be 'delimitative'); and, more especially, we are not told what the relation is between these two kinds of value, the distinctive and the prosodic. Worse than that—what is, in fact, a relation of different but compatible values has often been seriously *mis*represented—though again, neither by Trubetzkoy nor by Firth. The misrepresentation of that relation seems to be due, largely, to another confusion, beside that of 'value' and 'element'.

Secondly, then, *the confusion of linguistic value with mode of manifestation.* Firth's term 'prosodies' seems to have been misleading in this respect.[34] It is clear from Firth's examples that his 'prosodies', which may include phonemes like English /h/ or /ŋ/ or non-distinctive segments like the German 'glottal stop', are *not* in any way confined to 'suprasegmentals' or 'prosodemes'. The same is true of Trubetzkoy's *Grenzsignale.* These values, like the distinctive, may be exhibited in all possible ways: by segments or features (uni- or multi-segmental), or even by mere relations of order among features or segments. Trubetzkoy cites ordered sequences, such as *consonant* +/*h*/ or *nasal* + *liquid*, which are signals of morphemic boundaries in German. He calls them 'group-signals'; Firth's term for them (e.g. for z + ʃ in *has she*) is 'junctions'. It is clearly wrong, then, to suppose that all elements to which one would ascribe Firth's or Trubetzkoy's non-diacritical kind of relevance, are characterized by some particular mode of phonetic manifestation: though it is true that prosodic contours (in the usual sense of 'prosodic') and phonotactic order are prominent among the forms of such elements.

The prevalence of non-segmental modes of manifestation has led some linguists to misinterpret Firth's 'prosodies' as just 'suprasegmental' and 'phonotactic', though Firth's own examples and the most cursory look at Trubetzkoy's last chapter should have warned them against such a mistake.[35] It is serious, because it disposes of what is an important distinction of *linguistic values* as just a difference in *phonetic appearance.* This misinterpretation is easily dealt with. It just says what is wrong. More difficult are others which do not err so much in saying what is wrong, as in failing to say what is right. These are:—

Thirdly, theories which make a vacuous distinction. I am referring to the distinction of 'opposition' and 'contrast', as applied to Trubetzkoy's diacritical and delimitative values ('functions').[36] According to Martinet, the difference between the two types of value is simply that an element of 'distinctive function' contrasts with such others as can take its place in the utterance, while an element of 'delimitative function' contrasts with its neighbours. The difference of values is founded in two kinds of discreteness: paradigmatic (which Martinet calls 'opposition') and syntagmatic (for which he reserves the term 'contrast').[37]

This seems persuasive for a number of reasons. There is, in the first place, the familiarity of the general scheme of paradigm and syntagma, which is here used for distinguishing two general types of linguistic value. Secondly, the notion of syntagmatic contrast appears to be especially suited for describing the prosodic contours and phonotactic junctions which are so prominent among elements of 'delimitative' value. (Though Martinet himself is quite explicit on the existence of 'autres moyens démarcatifs',[38] the notion of syntagmatic contrast must have recommended itself originally for the treatment of contours and junctions.[39]) And there is, thirdly, room here for the plain truth of Trubetzkoy's treatment of the matter. We may continue to hold, as Martinet does: (a) that elements may be phonologically relevant not only on account of being 'distinctive', but also on account of being 'markers' of successive grammatical units; (b) that the same element may be relevant on both accounts; though also (c) that for an element to have delimitative value, no 'opposition' to it is required. But if Trubetzkoy's account of 'markers' is found to be compatible with Martinet's 'syntagmatic contrast', the reason is simply that nothing is added to it. For, what, precisely, does it mean to require of a marker that it should 'contrast' with its neighbours? To say of some part of a syntagma that it contrasts with the rest of it—i.e. that it differs from, and co-occurs with, other parts—is surely no more than to say that it is part of a syntagma, a tautology which must be true of any part of any given expression, whether it be distinctive or a marker or plain irrelevant. Syntagmatic contrast can contribute nothing towards explaining the relation between our two kinds of linguistic value. We are liable, here, to be misled by a specious analogy between two kinds of 'contrast'. Paradigmatic contrast ('opposition') is certainly a significant fact: it is a prerequisite of choice, and of distinctive value. But syntagmatic contrast is only a prerequisite of 'being a part'; it can lend no support to any specific kind of linguistic relevance.[40]

3.4 The two types of value distinguished

To seek clarity here is no mere pedantry. As long as the distinction between the fundamental types of linguistic value remains misdrawn, the connection of them will remain unintelligible, and our conception of the structure of language will continue to lack coherence. We might find it puzzling at first that an important distinction, the need for which is generally accepted, should have eluded so many attempts to say, precisely, how to draw it; but the puzzle dissolves, when we discover that the persistent failure is due to that very common and radical defect of linguistic theory which we have already had occasion to mention—namely, a fragmentary notion of linguistic structure. If the structural relations of linguistic elements are taken to be just paradigmatic and syntagmatic, it being forgotten or ignored that these distributional relations are always contained within the domains of determinate functions, then we shall necessarily have deprived ourselves of the possibility of clearly distinguishing and connecting what are, in fact, two kinds of functional value; we shall have to be content to keep them apart by a mere negation—namely, as 'distinctive' and 'non-distinctive' respectively. Their difference and their connection cannot be stated adequately except *in terms of the properties of a linguistic function.* It is paradigmatic *variancy* that supports the one type of value, and relative syntagmatic *constancy* that supports the other.

To illustrate briefly, and with reference to familiar phonological facts: If we have fixed upon word-functions to provide us with phonemic oppositions (i.e. with paradigms of distinctive sounds and of distinctive features), then any relatively constant element of these same word-functions, such as a regular 'word-accent', will be important. It will be important, not because it or the words are 'syntagmatically contrastive' (which can mean no more than that they occur), but because of the *relative constancy* with which that accent *determines* a certain type of functions, namely, word-functions, thus *marking* the values of these as 'words'.

The connection is clear: variancy and relative constancy in linguistic functions are complementary. And the difference too is clear, as we find that each supports its own kind of linguistic value. Neither is, by itself, a sufficient condition of relevance; to be linguistically relevant, each requires a regular correlation with its function-values: paradigmatic variancy to be correlated with a *difference*, in meaning or structure, between the resulting function-values; and relative syntagmatic constancy to be correlated with a *general type* of the different function-values. Any *variant* segment or feature which fulfils its condition of relevance is said to have *diacritical power*, and to be '*distinctive*' of *specific* function-values. Any *relatively constant* segment or feature which fulfils its own (altogether different) condition of relevance may be said to have *determinant power*, and to be a *marker* of a *type* of function-values.

What precisely is meant, here, by a 'general type' of function or function-values? This question is analogous to asking about logical or mathematical functions, what *kinds* of such are to be regarded as formally significant. The logician refers to certain 'formal constants'—the copula, the logical connectives 'and', 'or', 'greater than', etc.; these formal constants are markers of logically significant functions. The reason why the functions are significant is of course found, not in the markers themselves but in what they mark—i.e. in the fundamental types of proposition of which they are invariant components. Similarly in linguistic analysis. The first question to be asked about the significance of markers must be about the things they mark: What are the fundamental types of construction? A type of construction may be expressed as a type of function. It is exemplified by certain combinations of variant elements; and it may be marked by some few components which remain constant with regard to these variants.

We are not here examining *what* types of construction are worth establishing. We merely note that, in establishing such types, we are liable to operate with two kinds of linguistic value: on the one hand, necessarily, with a large number of distinctive variants and, on the other, very frequently, with a few relatively constant markers.

A type of function may be generally significant for either or both of two reasons:

(i) It may be required for stating *regularities in the distribution of lower-rank units* entering it as variants. For example, in order to state regularities in the combination of phonemes, we generally have to view them as variant constituents of syllables; the syllable is then a significant type of linguistic function, and any relatively constant component of it has importance as a phonological marker.

(ii) It may be required for stating *regular structures of higher-rank units*, into which its own values enter as variants: for example, there are regularities of sentential structure which can only be stated in terms of the distribution of 'phrases', and which could not be stated adequately in terms of the morphemes or words which enter into the phrase-functions; hence the importance of certain types of phrase, and of their markers.

The significance of markers, we may say briefly, is that they mark *structural regularities* of the language, these being either *internal* to the units marked, or *external* to them, or both.

4. MARKERS AND DISTINCTIVE ELEMENTS

We may try to survey actual occurrences of distinctive and determinant units, i.e. consider the interplay, in given utterances, between elements of choice and elements of constraint.

4.1 Boundary-Signals, Prosodies, Markers

We should now be clear that, even within the confines of phonology, Trubetzkoy's culminative and delimitative 'functions' are no more than special cases of non-distinctive relevance. This is what Firth had wished to make clear when he introduced his 'prosodies'; they are, in fact, phonetic elements of determinant power. Some prosodies are boundary-signals, but many are not. In the main, Firth seems to have added two further kinds of phonological determinant:

(i) markers of *phonological units of higher rank* (of syllables, stress-groups, tone-groups, etc.) and
(ii) markers of *grammatical categories.*

The facts to which he drew attention are still grossly neglected. And the reason seems to be still that intrinsically incomplete notion of indeterminate distribution, and of undetermined paradigms. The only way of describing those facts adequately is to subject them to 'a different set of abstractions from those appropriate to phonematic structure'. It is important, then, to consider what difference it makes, when we do *not* insist here on the contrastive kind of relevance that appears to 'a paradigmatic technique of oppositions'.[41]

(i) Phonological units higher in rank than the phoneme have of course always been recognized; it has even been acknowledged at times that what is generally a sequence of phonemes, such as a syllable or an 'accentual group', is *immediately perceived* as a simple unit, i.e. somehow perceived to stand out as relatively constant and recurrent, over and above the variant elements within the unit.[42] We seem to perceive directly that *pit* exemplifies the same phonological function as *sock*, *full*, *mat*, etc., but not the same function as is exemplified by *spit* or *split* or *pity*; and such direct perception points to the presence of markers. But the attempt to identify such markers (e.g. prominence-patterns of syllables, or accentual contours) has always been frustrated by that insistent prejudice which forbids us to recognize a non-distinctive element as phonologically relevant. As a rule, we are then invited to hunt for exceptional and even sporadic contrasts, in order to 'establish' the marker—that is, an element whose sole or primary significance it is, precisely, *not* to be contrastive itself but to determine a regular framework for *other* elements to contrast in.[43] When this attempt fails, when the markers of syllables, stress-groups, tone-groups, etc., fail to be found in any but the most freakish contrasts, then we may be told, that these units are to be established by purely distributional ('phonotactic') criteria. But in this way no justice will be done to their markers, i.e. to our immediate perception of just those determinant elements which mark the given distributional domain, the phonological structure of which may then be grossly distorted.[44] Firthian 'prosodies' have room for phonotactic considerations; indeed, they imply such. But a description purely in terms of phonotactic relations is frequently not adequate, where a description in terms of prosodies would be.

(ii) There is, secondly—and perhaps even more significantly—the use of phonological elements as markers of *grammatical categories*. Again, we find that many of these 'prosodies' have had their true importance overlooked, simply because one was content to note some very marginal diacritical power, which they might happen to have in addition to their primary determinant power.

To give just one example: Any phonological description of German will tell us that the accentual patterns of certain verbal compounds may be distinctive; there are a few such contrasts as ˈ*übersetzen*—*überˈsetzen* ('to ferry over'—'to translate'), ˈ*wiederholen*—*wiederˈholen* ('to fetch back'—'to repeat'). This is certainly worth stating. But to suggest that such a statement comes anywhere near to exhausting the phonological relevance of those accentual patterns would be quite erroneous. If we attend to the *determinant* power of these patterns, we find their importance extending far beyond their few and rare contrasts: they mark an indefinitely large number of verbal constructions and idioms as 'separable' and 'inseparable', respectively. Even with regard to accentually contrasted words such as ˈ*übersetzen* and *überˈsetzen*, it is important to note that the difference between them has a much wider significance than that of distinguishing two lexical units. By its accent, one is *marked* as transformable into *ˈsetzeˈüber*, *ˈübergesetzt*, *ˈüberzusetzen*, and the other as transformable into *überˈsetze*, *überˈsetzt*, *zu überˈsetzen*. What is significant, here, is the fact that *ˈübersetzen* is marked as belonging to a very large class of verbs and verbal phrases (most of which do not admit of accentual opposition): *ˈabgeben*, *ˈaufsuchen*, *entˈgegenkommen*, *zuˈGrunde gehen*, etc.; while *überˈsetzen* is marked as belonging to another large class: *beˈsetzen*, *verˈgehen*, *entˈkommen*, *zerˈbrechen*, etc. We take notice of these accentual patterns, not so much on account of the few cases in which they are distinctive, as on account of the great regularity with which they mark important grammatical categories.[45]

This extension of the notion of markers which we owe to Firth is bound greatly to enrich phonological description. It will at the same time establish closer links—links without confusion—between phonology and grammar.[46]

Yet, even with this, we have not made full use of the notion of markers. There is a last step of generalization which we seem ready to take, as we realize their general structural significance and see more clearly how they are related to the distinctive elements of utterances. There is no reason why we should find markers only among phonological elements; they are found equally on the level of grammatical analysis, where, as they combine with 'signs', and may even themselves be 'signs', their principal role is to signal significant types of grammatical construction.

All those inflectional suffixes whose diacritical power is generally 'neutralized', and whose 'meaning' is accordingly utterly elusive, are significant, mainly or exclusively, as markers of constructions. Again, derivational suffixes, such as English *-ly*, *-ish*, *-ness*, *-ize*, which contract contrasts very rarely, and are aptly described as 'adverbial', 'adjectival', 'nominal', 'verbal', etc., are mainly or exclusively markers of grammatical categories.[47] Prepositions and conjunctions, though they frequently occur in contrastive positions, and are semantically significant, are yet at least equally important as markers of syntactical constructions. Again, this is familiar. But once more, no justice can be done to the familiar facts, as long as we insist on forcing all grammatical units into the same mode of linguistic relevance.[48] It is, in fact, the task of syntactical inquiries to state how elements occurring in two *different* modes of relevance interact in the sentence: i.e. broadly, how freedom of choice is confined within fixed and, frequently, marked ranges.[49]

4.2 Markers and Categories

Any structural regularity pertaining to the values of a certain type of function can be stated as a regular restriction upon successive paradigms—a restriction upon their ranges and upon the succession of their members. (We can, for instance, state it as a regular characteristic of the English syllable that its onset admits of no more than three phonemes, and that of these the first must be /s/, the second /p/ or /t/ or /k/ and the third /r/, /l/, /j/ or /w/.) This is to say that variants enter the function in accordance with a few general patterns; and any marker, in 'determining' such a function, determines the positions of the variants and the ranges of their paradigms. It is possible then to represent a type of function by listing such permissible patterns, i.e. listing a few ordered sequences of syntagmatic categories ('position-classes'). (This is, in fact, the usual way of describing the syllables of a language; we list the permissible sequences of phoneme-categories—say, of 'vowels' and 'consonants': V, CV, CCV, VC, VCC, CVC, etc. Similarly, we should normally describe a general type of grammatical function by listing the permissible sequences of grammatical categories—for example, listing for the English noun-phrase, something like DN, DAN, DMAN, etc., with the appropriate bracketing.[50]) This is just current practice; yet the role of markers in such descriptions does not seem to have been made sufficiently clear.

Linguists have tended to underrate the significance of markers. They have done so in the belief that the occurrence of markers was generally redundant. This seems to be true, for instance, of Trubetzkoy's boundary-signals. But—as Trubetzkoy realized—redundancy in the marker of a general structure is something very different from redundancy in an individual distinctive element.

What, exactly, is it, for a determinant element to be 'redundant'? We may regard the marker of a function as *wholly* 'redundant', if the classes of distinctive elements entering the function under its syntagmatic categories do not overlap with classes of elements entering other types of function under different categories; i.e., putting it in Firthian terms: if the syntagmatic categories of the marked function do not share any of their 'exponents' with different categories of other functions. In that case, *no explicit* marker can ever be required for determining the permissible patterns. For, if every distinctive element that can enter the function belongs to one and only one category, its mere occurrence *implicitly* marks the pattern. For example, if of the different phoneme-categories (onset, peak, coda, etc.) which represent syllable patterns, no two are ever exemplified by the same phoneme, then all syllable-patterns are marked implicitly by the mere sequence of phonemes. (And sequence in itself is no marker but a universal constant of speech.)

As a rule, however, paradigms under different syntagmatic categories will share some of their members. The marker of the function will then be 'redundant', only when the function is exemplified by 'unshared' exponents of its categories (e.g. an English 'noun' by *food, door, ear*); on the other hand, the marker will be required for determining the function, when it is exemplified by 'shared' exponents of its categories (e.g. an English 'noun' by *drink, table, hand*).

A syntagmatic category may be marked by nothing more than *order with regard to some other category*. Frequently, the latter will then need to be *implicitly marked*. It may be the case, for instance, that no exponent of a syllable-peak is identical with any exponent of the margins, while onset-paradigms overlap with coda-paradigms. In that case, onset and coda are explicitly marked by order, i.e. as being, respectively, before and after the implicitly marked exponent of the 'peak'. The situation is similar, when we find syntactical categories to be determined by 'characteristic environments' or 'critical frames'. The relative constant of the function ('the frame') consists of exponents which mark their category implicitly, and other categories are determined with reference to that 'constant'. The technique of analysis which is here appropriate, is familiar.[51] Having chosen, say, *the* or *my* as the relative constant of a phrase-function (*the* —) or (*my* —), we proceed to define the category of distinctive lexical variants in the marked position as 'noun'. The 'constant' of the function, while implicitly marking its own category ('determiner'), is at the same time, in antecedent position, an explicit marker of the 'noun-phrase'.[52]

It is instructive to view these familiar techniques of analysis as operations with constants and variants in linguistic functions. In this way, we seem to be able to dispel the obscurity, which has always surrounded the decisive initial step of choosing the 'critical frames'. This kind of choice, which so far has appeared to be little more than a precarious and arbitrary trick—a hunch to be justified 'by results'—becomes accountable and informative in itself, when we recognise it as an operation with determinant and distinctive values. It is only important, here, to remember that both kinds of value may be present in the same element: linguistic functions are frequently determined by markers of distinctive value.

4.3 Markers of Distinctive Value (*Parameters*)

Consider, for instance, markers contrasting in a paradigmatic set such as *the*, *a*, *my*, *your*, *every*, etc., in, say, (— *boy asked for you*). It can hardly be maintained that the meanings which are exhibited in the contrasts of such a paradigm are necessarily different in kind from meanings exhibited in other contrasts (e.g. that the semantic contrast between *my* and *your* is essentially different from the contrast between *asked for* and *looked for*, or that the contrast between, say, the substitution-markers *he* and *she* is essentially different from the contrast between *boy* and *girl*). This is of course the old problem of so-called 'empty words' which are not really empty.[53] A morpheme is not either 'full' or 'empty', nor is it more or less full (or empty). Of each of two different and compatible types of morphemic value—one, primary, the other, secondary—it may have more or less; it may 'have meaning' as well as mark a grammatical construction.

More to the point is the suggestion that paradigms of markers, as distinct from other paradigms, represent *closed sets of relatively few and frequent elements*.[54] This seems to be true of all distinctive markers, and even specifically true of them. While there may be closed sets of relatively few elements, which are not markers, there are probably no sets of distinctive elements both few *and* very frequent, which are yet not markers.

These properties of markers' paradigms are not just incidental; they are derivable from the special role of markers in utterances. The frequency of the contrasting elements in these paradigms derives obviously from their being markers of general types of function; and their restricted number derives partly from their frequency,[55] and partly from their being implicit markers of their own grammatical category. For, clearly, the relatively most frequent elements cannot be many; and a class of elements, each of which implicitly marks the type of class it belongs to, must be capable of being *given by enumeration*. This is why of all the properties mentioned by Fries as characteristic of 'function words', the most important is the fact that 'in order to respond to certain structural signals *one must know these words as items*'.[56] Expressing this limitation in linguistic rather than psychological terms, we say that distinctive markers contrast in sets which are given by enumeration of their members. This does not require us to be content with enumeration as a definition of their class. On the contrary, having with their help determined the grammatical category of other and open sets, we then return to the determinant elements and redefine their class 'abstractly', i.e. by its relation to those other sets.[57] This redefinition then gives us a 'grammatical class' in the proper sense, i.e. 'not a *list of* formal items but an *abstraction from* them'.[58]

The *relation* between (a) the distinctive markers and (b) the distinctive variants of a linguistic function may be explained in terms closely analogous to those in which we should explain the role of two kinds of variable in mathematical formulae (such as $ax + by = c$). Distinctive markers are values of 'constant' variables (such as a, b, and c in such formulae); distinctive variants are values of the 'variable' variables (such as x and y). More acceptably, we may name the first kind of variables 'parameters' (or 'coefficients'), and the second the 'unknown'. Lewis Carroll's 'Jabberwocky' gives us formulae consisting of 'known' grammatical (and phonological) markers that act as parameters for the 'unknown' variables, which are indicated by 'nonsense'. (It is on account of those parameters that the verse is characterized as English nonsense.) Here is the basis of that psychological requirement of having to 'know' the marker as an individual item. It is taken to be 'constant' or 'known' (whether as a single item or an alternation of such), *while* we consider the variancy of values of x and y, and the relations between these. Such diacritical power as the individual marker might have is disregarded in considering it *as a marker*. In other words, and more informatively: we investigate the range and relations of the 'unknown' values only *after* the markers' parameters are supposed to have been determined. This is, in fact, the normal sequence in our technique of analysis. Yet, having determined the grammatical properties of the variables, we then turn back and, regarding the markers now as 'unknown', we define or redefine the parameters.

The linguist, then, no less than the mathematician, has found it perfectly feasible, and extremely useful, to operate with two kinds of variable, one of them treated as constant with regard to the other. It is by tracing out this interplay between determinant power and diacritical power that he arrives at general statements about the working structure of a language.

4.4 The Organization of Verbal Behaviour

It is not surprising that the structural organization of human speech should be described in terms of two kinds of functional value.

It seems firstly to be true of *any organization*—biological, social, or linguistic—that there are primarily two ways in which a part of it may be especially relevant:

(i) by its having diacritical power, i.e. by the difference made to some larger whole of which it is part, by the fact that it *is* a part of it, or that *it* is the part; and/or

(ii) by its having determinant power, i.e. by its determining the range, within which *other* elements may make their distinctive contributions,

For an element to have diacritical power, it must be capable of being significantly replaced in, or chosen for, its position. For an element to have determinant power, *other* elements must be capable of being significantly replaced in, or chosen for, *their* positions. It is clear then that one element may combine both powers. But we find, as a rule, that, for reasons of economy, the two powers are unevenly distributed: diacritical power being more characteristic of some elements, and determinant power of others, the former being by far the more numerous

There appear to be, secondly, *particular* reasons why the elements of a *language* should, in their co-operative occurrences, exhibit these two powers. To be continually productive of ever new 'acts of speech', a language must admit of individual choice; but for such acts to be shared (by a community and, indeed, by successive periods in an individual's life), choice must be contained within the limits of fixed ranges and patterns. Distinctive value reflects the freedom of choice we have in speaking a language; determinant value reflects the constraints to which we submit. It is the task of Linguistic Analysis to state the extent of that freedom, and the nature of those constraints.

Notes

1 *Papers in Linguistics 1934–1951*. 'General Linguistics and Descriptive Grammar', p. 220.

2 Op. cit. 'Personality and Language in Society', p. 182 f.

3 *Language*, pp. 78, 144. The words in parenthesis 'or partly alike' appear in Bloomfield's 'A Set of Postulates for the Science of Language', *Lg* 2 (1926). They could be omitted later by interpreting 'utterance' to mean 'any portion of speech', whether a complete 'act of speech' or less.

4 E.g. 'The Technique of Semantics', op. cit. pp. 26 ff.

5 It was precisely the disruptive force of Bloomfield's theory of meaning that induced some of his followers to try to *eliminate* reference to meaning from linguistic description, i.e. to try to make linguistics a physical science.

6 Op. cit., p. 77.

7 Cp. also Hockett, *A Course in Modern Linguistics* (New York, 1959) p. 134.

8 I am referring here to 'Generative Grammar', not necessarily to 'Transformational Grammar'. It is unfortunate that the two terms are sometimes used interchangeably (for instance, in Gleason's *Introduction to Descriptive Linguistics*, 2nd edition, ch. 12). This is confusing, because (i) generative grammar may, but need not, make use of transformations, and (ii) transformational comparisons of linguistic structures may be used within linguistic analysis proper, and outside any formal generative framework (for example, by Harris, 'Discourse Analysis', *Lg* 28 (1952), 'Co-occurrence and transformation in linguistic structure', *Lg* 33 (1957)).

9 'Distributional Structure', 146 f., *Word* 10 (1954).

10 See especially *Structural Linguistics*, ch. 12.

11 'From Phoneme to Morpheme', *Lg* 31 (1955).

12 E.g. in the example cited by D. Jones, /plʌmpaiz/ *versus* /plʌmphaiz/.

13 This was never forgotten by the pioneers of modern linguistics. Trubetzkoy speaks of 'Rahmeneinheiten' (e.g. *Grundzüge der Phonologie*, p. 225). Firth introduces his discussion of 'Sounds and Prosodies' by saying: 'Words will be my principal isolates' (*Essays*, p. 122). Sapir and Bloomfield always took an appropriate 'frame' of distributional relations for granted.

14 *Structural Linguistics*, p. 369, fn. 11 (my italics). Similarly, in 'Distributional Structure' (section 3.5), where Harris finds that he ought to be content with having 'domains' determined by just trial and error. In fact, since the number of possible trials would be practically infinite, he tacitly accepts the domain of significant utterance.

15 What is meant, here, by 'function' and 'value for a function' will be defined more precisely later (see § 2.3 below).

16 Cp. Firth, *Papers*, p. 147.

17 It would of course be wrong to say that *boy* 'contrasts' here with *strapping*, the reason being that /ə . . . wen/ is no linguistic function, so that *boy* can have no functional relation to /əboiwen/, such as it has to /ðəboiwent/.

18 I do not propose, here, to pursue the question of defining linguistic units. This has been attempted elsewhere (*TPS*, 1954) with a paper that, more recently, has found a welcome echo in E. Benveniste's contribution to the IXth International Congress of Linguists.

19 Z. S. Harris, *Structural Linguistics*, p. 370 (my italics).

20 The conditions in which it is possible to recognize a distinctive element in redundant position, will of course differ according to whether the element is phonological or grammatical. The question, however, in either case will be whether the rest of the structure *admits* the element concerned, even though it does not require it.

21 *Structural Linguistics*, ch. 12.

22 Such objections to it as were made recently by N. Chomsky (*Semantic Considerations in Grammar*, 1955) seem to proceed from two misunderstandings: (i) interpretation of the required 'regular correlation' (between variant elements and function-values) as logical implication or even equivalence, and (ii) extension of the required commutability from some functions to all. What Chomsky has proved is, simply, that neither of these misinterpretations can be maintained.

23 *Sounds and Prosodies*, *TPS* 1941, reprinted in *Papers in Linguistics 1934–1951* (pp.137, 133).

24 Ibid., p. 138.

25 *Grundzüge der Phonologie*, pp. 29 f., 241–261. (Trubetzkoy's 'function' evidently corresponds to my 'functional value'.)

26 Ibid., p. 255.

27 Ibid., p. 242.

28 *Grundzüge*, pp. 243–245 (referring also to Firth's early observations on Tamil).

29 *Papers*, p. 131.

30 Even in *Preliminaries to Speech-Analysis* by Jakobson, Fant and Halle, there is a section (1.5) entitled 'The distinctive features compared to the other sound features' (these others being called 'configurational'), which certainly implies that we are dealing here with a distinction of *elements*. It is only confusing, though correct, when this implication is then contradicted by a footnote which says that 'in certain cases single distinctive features can assume an additional configurational *function*'.

31 'Suprasegmentals, Prosodies, Prosodemes', *Lg* 37 (1961), pp. 464–467.

32 Ibid., p. 462, and passim.

33 Professor Hill's own considerable contributions to the description of prosodic markers (*Introduction to Linguistic Structures*, pp. 181 f., 193 f., 259 f., 353 f.) do in fact demand liberation from the techniques of a purely phonemic analysis.

34 It is remarkable that Jakobson's term 'configurational' (*Preliminaries*, 1.5) is misleading in the same way, though without having misled its author.

35 An informative account of Firthian 'prosodic analysis' appeared recently in R. H. Robins' *General Linguistics: An Introductory Survey* (London, 1964), section 4.4.

36 I am here using the term 'delimitative function' in the wider sense, in which it may be taken to include the weaker 'culminative function'.

37 This is how one would be inclined to interpret Martinet's statements in *Éléments de Linguistique Générale* (§ 1.20, 3.1, 3.33, 3.36), though a certain vagueness about ascribing 'contrastive function' to elements ('lorsqu'ils contribuent à faciliter, pour l'auditeur, l'analyse de l'énoncé en unités successives') would also admit of another interpretation (*see* note 40, below).

38 *Éléments*, § 3.37.

39 Jakobson applies it, more appropriately, *only* to the analysis of prosodic contours (*Fundamentals*, 3.4). It should be noted, however, (i) that syntagmatic contrast, so applied, involves the use of categories (such as 'pitch', 'stress', etc.) as dimensions which determine *in what respect* the successive elements contrast (*cf. Preliminaries*, § 1.4), and (ii) that, contrary to what is often asserted (e.g. in *Preliminaries*, § 1.4), even a determinate syntagmatic contrast within a phonological contour is very different from a paradigmatic opposition in that it *need not confer relevance* on the contrasting bits of the contour. We may prefer to leave it unanalysed, and regard the whole of the internally contrastive contour as a single element, either a distinctive prosodeme or a Firthian marker.

40 There may be an alternative interpretation of Martinet's attempt to distinguish 'distinctive' and 'delimitative' values in terms of 'opposition' and 'contrast'. While 'opposition' refers to the substitution of phonological as well as grammatical elements, 'contrast' might be intended to refer to successive *grammatical* elements only. However, it is true of a grammatical element as much as of a phonological one that to

describe it as 'syntagmatically contrastive' is to say no more about it than that it occurs in a syntagma. In either case 'contrast' is an idle term. It has been called in to establish some kind of intelligible relation between two kinds of phonological value; and all it can do is to please our aesthetic sense with some kind of specious symmetry.

[41] *Papers*, p. 136 f.

[42] For instance, by Martinet, *Éléments*, § 3.34.

[43] See, for instance, the cursory treatment of syllables under the heading 'prosodic distinctive features' (!) in Jakobson–Fant–Halle, *Preliminaries*, § 1.4, citing a single syllabic/non-syllabic contrast from Old Czech as a kind of admission-ticket to the phonological inventory. Similarly, the English syllable is sometimes treated as if its structural significance were all founded in sporadic syllabic/non-syllabic contrasts such as that between *lightning* and *light(e)ning*.

[44] If, for instance, we fail to take account of the determinant power of syllable-markers, we shall be led to establish contrasts, say, between /o/ and /p/ in 'chaos' /keios/ and 'capes' /keips/, or between /ə/ and /n/ in 'tower' /tauə/ and 'town' /taun/. For, as Martinet has pointed out (*Éléments*, 3.21), we should not be able to exclude such 'pairings' by referring to a difference in syllabic structure, if that structure itself is to be defined exclusively in terms of the distribution of phonemes. For analogous cases in grammar, see below, n. 47.

[45] Work done at the London School of Oriental and African Studies suggests that such markers have frequently been overlooked, simply because nobody has looked for them. For references, see the Bibliography in Firth's *Papers in Linguistics 1934–1951*.

It is unfortunate that an understandable emphasis on this neglected aspect of phonology has often given the impression of a conflict between Firthian 'prosodic' analysis, on the one hand, and phonemic analysis, on the other, when in fact the two are not only compatible but complementary.

[46] We may further add those phonological markers which are correlated with 'characteristic contexts of experience and situation'—e.g. significant alliterations such as *stand, still, stare, stick, stack* ... or *sweep, swipe, swoop*—which Firth described as fulfilling a 'phonaesthetic function' (*Papers*, pp. 38 f., 194 et passim).

[47] Frequently, what appears to be a minimal contrast is nothing of the sort. E.g. substitution of NIL for *-ly* in *He looked quickly/He looked quick* is not really contrastive; it does not operate upon any one constant function. The function which is satisfied by *quickly* is different from the one satisfied by *quick*; the ambiguous *looked* represents different morphemes, and fills different structural positions, in those two occurrences. Similarly, *to* and *a* do not contrast in *I want ... drink.*

[48] Cf. C. E. Bazell, 'On the Problem of the Morpheme', *Word* 18 (1962), p. 137. It is certainly true, as Bazell has shown convincingly, that not all morphemes 'have meaning'. Those, however, which have not, depend for their relevance on those which have. It is conceivable that all the morphemes of a language should be significant, but inconceivable that all should be non-significant markers.

[49] It is worth noting, here, that linguists with educational interests have generally been more perceptive in this respect than have been those concerned with linguistic theory. See, especially, C.C. Fries, *The Structure of English*.

[50] where D = determiner, N = noun, A = adjective, M = modifier.

[51] Cp. Z.S. Harris, *Structural Linguistics*, chs. 15, 16; C.C. Fries, *The Structure of English*, pp. 89, 62, and passim.

[52] The importance of a marker will of course be the greater, the more frequently it is required for determining its functions. But its importance will also depend on a number of other factors—mainly, on the structural significance of the type of function marked, and on the regularity, with which it is marked. Criteria for the *grading* of determinant values require a good deal of further investigation, as do, in fact, also those for the grading of diacritical values.

[53] Cp. O. Jespersen, *The Essentials of English Grammar*, § 36.6 et passim.

[54] Cp. Fries, op. cit., p. 104 f.

[55] This is why their set could also be regarded as 'closed' in the sense that a fairly limited corpus of utterances will give us all of its members, and that the set will be 'identical in any corpus of the language' (cp. Z. S. Harris, *Structural Linguistics*, 15.5 n. 20).

[56] C. C. Fries, op. cit., p. 106.

[57] The two definitions need not define the same set. The enumerated set of elements of unique membership may be a subset of the abstractly defined class. The abstract class of 'determiners' in English seems to be an example. The enumeration of markers includes only *the*, *a/an*, *every*, *my*, *our*, *your*, *his*, *her*, *their*; while the other elements of the class (*each*, *some*, *this*, *one*, *two*, etc.) are markers only indirectly, i.e. in so far as each would be capable of being replaced in a function by some element of the enumerated set. They are clearly not so replaceable in all their functions.

[58] M. A. K. Halliday, 'Categories of the Theory of Grammar', *Word* 17 (1961), p. 264. The distinction I am trying to make between two kinds of paradigm (though it extends to phonology) appears to have some affinity with Halliday's distinction between 'grammar' and 'lexis'. Halliday stresses the difference between 'closed' and 'open sets'—a distinction which, though not incidental, is in itself not decisive. There may be closed sets without any significant determinant power. Moreover, it should be made clear that the systems of 'grammar' and 'lexis' cannot be regarded as mutually exclusive, or even overlapping, with regard to the *elements* comprised in them. *Every* lexical element enters into grammatical relations; but most of them do so merely as illustrative symbols (i.e. as member of a class), and only some enter *per se* (i.e. as individual item).

The obscurity of Halliday's distinction between 'grammar' and 'lexis' seems to be due to a confusion and conflation of two very different distinctions—on the one hand, that between parameters and 'unknown' variables, and, on the other, that between grammar and semantics (in C. E. Bazell's terminology, between 'grammatical constraints' and 'semantic restraints': cf. 'Three misconceptions of grammaticalness', *Georgetown University Monograph Series on Languages and Linguistics*, No. 17 (1964), ed. C. I. J. M. Stuart). The two distinctions cannot be made to cut along the same line; and the reason is, precisely, that grammatical markers may be distinctive.

Lexis as a Linguistic Level

M. A. K. HALLIDAY

At a time when few linguists, other than lexicographers themselves, devoted much attention to the study of lexis, and outlines of linguistics often contained little reference to dictionaries or to other methods in lexicology, J. R. Firth repeatedly stressed the importace of lexical studies in descriptive linguistics.[1] He did not accept the equation of 'lexical' with 'semantic',[2] and he showed that it was both possible and useful to make formal statements about lexical items and their relations. For this purpose Firth regarded the statement of collocation as the most fruitful approach, and he sometimes referred, within the framework of his general views on the levels of linguistic analysis, to the 'collocational level'.[3]

The aim of this paper is to consider briefly the nature of lexical patterns in language, and to suggest that it may be helpful to devise methods appropriate to the description of these patterns in the light of a lexical theory that will be complementary to, but not part of, grammatical theory. In other words, the suggestion is that lexis may be usefully thought of (a) as within linguistic form, and thus standing in the same relation to (lexical) semantics as does grammar to (grammatical) semantics, and (b) as not within grammar, lexical patterns thus being treated as different in kind, and not merely in delicacy, from grammatical patterns. This view is perhaps implicit in Firth's recognition of a 'collocational level'.[4]

One of the major preoccupations of grammatical theory in present-day linguistics is the extension of grammatical description to a degree of delicacy greater than has hitherto been attained, and it is rightly claimed as a virtue of contemporary models that they permit more delicate statements to be made without excessive increase in complexity. A grammar is expected to explain, for example, the likeness and unlikeness between *this brush won't polish* and *this floor won't polish*, the three-way ambiguity of *John made Mary a good friend*, and the non-acceptability of *beautiful hair was had by Mary* beside the acceptability of *the last word was had by*

Mary. Such explanations require the recognition of distinctions which, as is well known, begin to cut across each other at a relatively early stage in delicacy, and the model has to accommodate cross-classification of this kind. The form of statement adopted (and the terminology) will of course depend on the model; but it is generally agreed that all such patterns need to be accounted for.[5]

As part of the process of accounting for these distinctions the grammar attempts, both progressively and simultaneously, to reduce the very large classes of formal items, at the rank at which they can be most usefully abstracted (for the most part generally as words, but this is merely a definition truth from which we learn what 'word' means), into very small sub-classes. No grammar has, it is believed, achieved the degree of delicacy required for the reduction of all such items to one-member classes, although provided the model can effectively handle cross-classification it is by no means absurd to set this as the eventual aim: that is, a unique description for each item by its assignment to a 'microclass', which represents its value as the product of the intersection of a large number of classificatory dimensions.

If we take into account the amount of information which, although it is still far from having been provided for any language, contemporary grammatical models can reasonably claim to aim at providing, there would seem to be two possible evaluations of it. One is that, when the most delicate distinctions and restrictions in grammar have been explained, all formal linguistic patterns will have been accounted for; what is left can only be accounted for in semantic terms. The second is that there will still remain patterns which can be accounted for in formal linguistic terms but whose nature is such that they are best regarded as non-grammatical, in that they cut across the type of relation that is characteristic of grammatical patterning.

The particular model of grammar that is selected may suggest, but does not fully determine, which of these two views is adopted operationally. For example, a model which distinguishes sharply between the grammar of a language and the use of the grammar, regarding corpus-based statistical statements as proper only to the latter, and therefore as outside the range of validity of a descriptive statement, is less easily compatible with the second view than is a model which does not make this distinction and which allows statistical statements a place in linguistic description; nevertheless it is not wholly incompatible with it.[6] Lexical statements, or 'rules', need not be statistical, or even corpus-based, provided that their range of validity is defined in some other way, as by the introduction of a category of 'lexicalness' to parallel that of grammaticalness.

One may validly ask whether there are general grounds, independent of any given model, for supplementing the grammar by formal statements of lexical relations, at least (given that the aim of linguistics is to account for as much of language as possible) until these are shown to be unnecessary. It may be a long time before it can be decided whether they are necessary or not, in the sense of finding out whether all that is explained lexically could also have been incorporated in the grammar; there still remains the question whether or not it could have been explained more simply in the grammar. The question is not whether formal lexical statements can be made; they are already made in dictionaries, although at a low level of generality, in the form of citations. The question of interest to linguists is how the patterns represented by such citations are to be stated with a sufficient degree of abstraction, and whether this can best be achieved within or outside the framework of the grammar.

Let us consider an example. The sentence *he put forward a strong argument for it* is acceptable in English; *strong* is a member of that set of items which can be juxtaposed with *argument*, a set which also includes *powerful. Strong* does not always stand in this same relation to *powerful*: *he drives a strong car* is, at least relatively, unacceptable, as is *this tea's too powerful.* To put it another way, *a strong car* and *powerful tea* will either be rejected as ungrammatical (or unlexical) or shown to be in some sort of marked contrast with *a powerful car* and *strong tea*; in either case the paradigmatic relation of *strong* to *powerful* is not a constant but depends on the syntagmatic relation into which each enters, here with *argument*, *car* or *tea*.

Grammatically, unless these are regarded as different structures, which seems unlikely, they will be accounted for in a way which, whatever the particular form of statement the model employs, will amount to saying that, first, *strong* and *powerful* are members of a class that enters into a certain structural relation with a class of which *argument* is a member; second, *powerful* (but not *strong*) is a member of a class entering into this relation with a class of which *car* is a member; and third, *strong* (but not *powerful*) is a member of a class entering into this relation with a class of which *tea* is a member. It would be hoped that such classes would reappear elsewhere in the grammar defined on other criteria. *Argument*, *car* and *tea* will, for example, already have been distinguished on other grounds on the lines of 'abstract', 'concrete inanimate' and 'mass'; but these groupings are not applicable here, since we can have *a strong table* and *powerful whisky*, while *a strong device* is at least questionable.

The same *patterns* do reappear: *he argued strongly, I don't deny the strength of his argument, his argument was strengthened by other factors. Strongly* and *strength* are paralleled by *powerfully* and *power, strengthened* by *made more powerful.* The same restrictions have to be stated, to account for *the power* (but not *the strength*) *of his car* and *the strength* (but not *the power*) *of her tea.* But these involve different structures; elsewhere in the grammar *strong, strongly, strength* and *strengthened* have been recognized as different items and assigned to different classes, so that *the strong of his argument* has been excluded on equal terms with *the strong of his car. Strong* and *powerful,* on the other hand, have been assigned to the same class, so that we should expect to find *a powerful car* paralleled by *a strong car.* The classes set up to account for the patterns under discussion either will cut across the primary dimension of grammatical classification or will need to be restated for each primary class.

But the added complexity involved in either of these solutions does not seem to be matched by a gain in descriptive power, since for the patterns in question the differences of (primary) class and of structure are irrelevant. *Strong, strongly, strength* and *strengthened* can all be regarded for this present purpose as the same item; and *a strong argument, he argued strongly, the strength of his argument* and *his argument was strengthened* all as instances of one and the same syntagmatic relation. What is abstracted is an item *strong,* having the scatter *strong, strongly, strength, strengthened,* which collocates with items *argue* (*argument*) and *tea*; and an item *power* (*powerful, powerfully*) which collocates with *argue* and *car.* It can be predicted that, if *a high-powered car* is acceptable, this will be matched by *a high-powered argument* but not by *high-powered tea.* It might also be predicted, though with less assurance, that *a weak argument* and *weak tea* are acceptable, but that *a weak car* is not.

As far as the collocational relation of *strong* and *argue* is concerned, it is not merely the particular grammatical relation into which these items enter that is irrelevant; it may also be irrelevant whether they enter into any grammatical relation with each other or not. They may be in different sentences, for example: *I wasn't altogether convinced by his argument. He had some strong points but they could all be met.* Clearly there are limits of relevance to be set to a collocational span of this kind; but the question here is whether such limits can usefully be defined grammatically, and it is not easy to see how they can.

The items *strong* and *power* will enter into the same set as defined by their occurrence in collocation with *argue*; but they will also enter into different sets as defined by other collocations. There is of course no procedural priority as between the identification of the items and the identification of the paradigmatic and syntagmatic relations into which they enter: 'item', 'set' and 'collocation' are mutually defining. But they are definable without reference to grammatical restrictions; or, if that is begging the question, without reference to restrictions stated elsewhere in the grammar. This is not to say that there is no interrelation between structural and collocational patterns, as indeed there certainly is; but if, as is suggested, their interdependence can be regarded as mutual rather than as one-way, it will be more clearly displayed by a form of statement which first shows grammatical and lexical restrictions separately and then brings them together.[7] If therefore one speaks of a lexical level, there is no question of asserting the 'independence' of such a level, whatever this might mean; what is implied is the internal consistency of the statements and their referability to a stated model.

Possible methods of lexical analysis, and the form likely to be taken by statements at this level, are the subject of another paper, by J. McH. Sinclair, appearing in the present volume.[8] Here I wish to consider merely some of the properties of this type of pattern in language, and some of the problems of accounting for it. Clearly lexical patterns are referable in the first place to the two basic axes, the syntagmatic and the paradigmatic. One way of handling grammatical relations on these two axes is by reference to the theoretical categories of 'structure' and 'system', with the 'class' definable as that which enters into the relations so defined. In lexis these concepts need to be modified, and distinct categories are needed for which therefore different terms are desirable.

First, in place of the highly abstract relation of structure, in which the value of an element depends on complex factors in no sense reducible to simple sequence, lexis seems to require the recognition merely of linear co-occurrence together with some measure of significant proximity, either a scale or at least a cut-off point. It is this syntagmatic relation which is referred to as 'collocation'. The implication that degree of proximity is here the only variable does not of course imply how this is to be measured; moreover it clearly relates only to statements internal to the lexical level: in lexicogrammatical statements collocational restrictions intersect with structural ones. Similarly in place of the 'system' which, with its known and stated set of terms in choice relation, lends itself to a deterministic model, lexis requires the open-ended 'set' assignment to which is best regarded as probabilistic. Thus while a model which is only deterministic can explain so much of the grammar of a language that its added power makes it entirely appropriate for certain of the purposes of a descriptive grammar, it is doubtful whether such a model would give any real insight into lexis. Collocational and lexical set are mutually defining as are structure and system: the set is the grouping of members with like privilege of occurrence in collocation.

Second, in grammar a 'bridge' category is required between element of structure and term in system on the one hand and formal item on the other; this is the class. (This specific formulation refers to the 'scale-and-category' version of a system-structure model; but it is probably true that all models make use of a category analogous to what I am here calling the 'class'.) In lexis no such intermediate category is required: the item is directly referable to the categories of collocation and set. This is simply another way of saying that in lexis we are concerned with a very simple set of relations into which enter a large number of items, which must therefore be differentiated qua items, whereas in grammar we are concerned with very complex and variable relations in which the primary differentiation is among the relations themselves: it is only secondarily that we differentiate among the items, and we begin by 'abstracting out' this difference. In other words there is a definable sense in which 'more abstraction' is involved in grammar than is possible in lexis.

Third, the lexical item is not necessarily coextensive on either axis with the item, or rather with any of the items, identified and accounted for in the grammar. For example, on the paradigmatic axis, in *she made up her face* one can identify a lexical item *make* up_1 whose scatter and collocational range are also illustrated in *your complexion needs a different makeup*. This contrasts with the lexical item *make* up_2 in *she made up her team* and *your committee needs a different makeup*. That the distinction is necessary is shown by the ambiguity of *she made up the cast*, *she was responsible for the makeup of the cast*. Grammatically, the primary distinction is that between *made up* and *makeup*; this distinction of course involves a great many factors, but it also relates to many other items which are distinguishable, by class membership, in the same way. If the grammar is at the same time to handle the distinction between *make* up_1 and *make* up_2 it must recognize a new and independent dimension of class membership on the basis of relations to which the previous dimension is irrelevant. Any one example can of course be handled by *ad hoc* grammatical devices: here for instance the potentialities of *make* up_2 in intransitive structures are more restricted. But such clearly grammatical distinctions, even when present, are so restricted in their range of validity that the generalizing power of a grammatical model is of little value as compared with the cost, in increased complexity, of the cross-classifications involved.

It may be worth citing a further example of a similar kind. We can distinguish grammatically, but not lexically, between *they want the pilot to take off* (= 'so that they can take off') and (='they desire him to do so'): these are not necessarily distinguished by intonation, although the unmarked tone selections are different. On the other hand it is easier to distinguish lexically than grammatically between *he took two days off* (='he did not work') and (='he reduced the time available'). In *the takeoff of the president* (='his becoming airborne') and (='the imitation of the president') the distinction can usefully be made both in grammar and in lexis.

On the syntagmatic axis, it may be useful to recognize a lexical item which has no defined status in the grammar and is not identified as morpheme, word or group. For example, in *he let me in the other day for a lot of extra work*, one could handle *let in for* as a single discontinuous item in the grammar; but this complexity is avoided if one is prepared to recognize a lexical item *let in for* without demanding that it should carry any grammatical status. Similarly the ambiguity in *he came out with a beautiful model* may be explained, instead of by giving two different grammatical descriptions, by identifying two distinct lexical items, *come* and *come out with* (and of course two different lexical items *model*).

It is not suggested of course that such non-coextensiveness between the items of grammar and those of lexis is the norm, but merely that for certain purposes it is useful to have a descriptive model of language that allows for it. At the same time the above considerations suggest that the lexical component requires not, as it were, a second 'runthrough' of the model designed for the grammar but rather a specifically lexical model with distinct, though analogous, categories and forms of statement.

Nor is it suggested that the set of patterns recognized as language form is neatly divided into two types, the grammatical and the lexical. A model for the description of language form may recognize only one kind of pattern and attempt to subsume all formal relations within it:

some grammatical models, as has been noted, envisage that it is the grammar's task to distinguish *strong* from *powerful* as well as to distinguish *a* from *the* and 'past' from 'present'; while a lexicographical model in which *a* and *the*, as well as *strong* and *powerful*, are entered in the dictionary and described by means of citations could be regarded as in a similar way attempting to subsume grammar under lexis. Even where the model recognizes two distinct kinds of pattern, these still represent different properties of the total phenomenon of language, not properties of different parts of the phenomenon; all formal items enter into patterns of both kinds. They are grammatical items when described grammatically, as entering (via classes) into closed systems and ordered structures, and lexical items when described lexically, as entering into open sets and linear collocations. So in *a strong cup of tea* the grammar recognizes (leaving aside its higher rank status, for example as a single formal item expounding the unit 'group') five items of rank 'word' assignable to classes, which in turn expound elements in structures and terms in systems; and the lexis recognizes potentially five lexical items assignable to sets.

But, to take a further step, the formal items themselves vary in respect of which of the two kinds of pattern, the grammatical or the lexical, is more significant for the explanation of restrictions on their occurrence qua items. The items *a* and *of* are structurally restricted, and are uniquely specified by the grammar in a very few steps in delicacy; collocationally on the other hand they are largely unrestricted. For the item *strong*, however, the grammar can specify uniquely a class (sub-class of the 'adjective') of which it is a member, but not the item itself within this class; it has no structural restrictions to distinguish it from other members of the class (and if the members of its 'scatter' *strong*, *strength*, etc., turn out to operate collocationally as a single item then this conflated item is not even specifiable qua class member); collocationally, however, it is restricted, and it is this which allows its specification as a unique item. There might then appear to be a scale on which items could be ranged from 'most grammatical' to 'most lexical', the position of an item on the scale correlating with its overall frequency ranking. But these are three distinct variables, and there is no reason to assume a correlation of 'most grammatical' with either 'least lexical' or 'most frequent'. The 'most grammatical' item is one which is optimally specifiable grammatically: this can be thought of as 'reducible to a one-member class by the minimum number of steps in delicacy'. Such an item may or may not be 'least lexical' in the sense that there is no collocational environment in which its probability of occurrence deviates significantly from its unconditioned probability.

In a lexical analysis it is the lexical restriction which is under focus: the extent to which an item is specified by its collocational environment. This therefore takes into account the frequency of the item in a stated environment relative to its total frequency of occurrence. While *a* and *of* are unlikely to occur in any collocationally generalizable environment with a probability significantly different from their overall unconditioned probabilities, there will be environments such that *strong* occurs with a probability greater than chance. This can be regarded, in turn, as the ability of *strong* to 'predict' its own environment. As extreme cases, *fro* and *spick* may never occur except in environments including respectively *to* and *span* (the fact that *to and fro* accounts for only a tiny proportion of the occurrences of *to*, while *spick and span* may account for all occurrences of this item *span*, is immaterial to the specification of *fro* and *spick*); here it is likely that, for this very reason, *to and fro* and *spick and span* are to be regarded as single lexical items.

It is the similarity of their collocational restriction which enables us to consider grouping lexical items into lexical sets. The criterion for the definition of the lexical set is thus the syntactic (downward) criterion of potentiality of occurrence. Just as the grammatical system (of classes, including one-item classes) is defined by reference to structure, so the lexical set (of items) can be defined by reference to collocation. Since *all* items *can* be described lexically, the relation of collocation could be regarded as being, like that of structure, chain-exhausting, and a lexical analysis programme might well begin by treating it in this way; but this is not a necessary condition of collocation, and if closed-system items turn out, as may be predicted, to be collocationally neutral these items could at some stage be eliminated by a 'deletion-list' provided either by cross-reference to the grammar or, better, as a result of the lexical analysis itself. Once such 'fully grammatical' items are deleted, collocation is no longer a chain-exhausting relation.

Moreover while grammatical structures are hierarchically ordered, so that one can recognize a scale of 'rank' each of whose members is a chain-exhausting unit (text items being then fully accounted for in sentence structure and again in clause structure and so on), it does not seem useful to postulate such an ordered hierarchy for lexis. Lexical items may indeed enter into a sort of rank relation: it is likely, for example, that on collocational criteria we would want to regard *stone*, *grindstone* and *nose to the grindstone* each as a separate lexical item, and though triads of this kind may be rare it looks as though we need the categories of 'simple' and 'compound', and perhaps also 'phrasal', lexical item, in addition to 'collocational span', as units for a lexical description. Since the only 'structural' relation in lexis is one of simple co-occurrence, these represent a single serial relation: the item *stone* enters (say) into the collocation *grindstone*, which then does not itself collocate exactly like the sum of its parts but enters as an item into (say) the collocation *nose to the grindstone*, which likewise does not collocate like the sum of its parts but enters as an item into (say) the collocation *he's too lazy to keep his nose to the grindstone*. The first stage of such compounding yields a morphological (upward) grouping of items, the 'lexical series' which, like its analogue in grammar, may or may not coincide with the syntactic grouping recognized as a 'set': *oaktree ashtree planetree beechtree* presumably do operate in the same set, while *inkstand bandstand hallstand grandstand* almost certainly do not. The 'series' is formed of compound items having one constituent item in common; this item, here *tree* and *stand*, is the 'morphologically unmarked' member of the series and, likewise, if the series forms a set it may or may not be the 'syntactically unmarked' member of the set. Equivalence or non-equivalence between series and set is an interesting feature of lexical typology: one would predict that in Chinese, for example, practically all such series do form sets (with an unmarked member), whereas in Malay and English they very often do not.

The lexical item itself is of course the 'type' in a type-token (item-occurrence) relation, and this relation is again best regarded as specific to lexis. The type-token relation can be made dependent on class membership: just as in grammar two occurrences assigned to different primary classes, such as *ride* (verb) and *ride* (noun), can be regarded as different (grammatical) items, so in lexis two occurrences assigned to different primary sets can be regarded as different lexical items. This can then be used to define homonymity: if the two occurrences of *model* in the example above are shown to differ according to criteria which would assign them to different sets then they represent two homonymous items. It is not to be assumed, of course, that grammatically distinguished items such as *ride* (verb) and *ride* (noun) may not also operate as distinct lexical items, as indeed they may; merely that *if* they turn out to belong to the same set they will on that criterion be said to constitute a single lexical item, as also will *strong*, *strength*, *strongly* and *strengthen*, and perhaps also (if they can be suitably delimited) non-cognate 'scatters' such as *town* and *urban*. This would provide a basis for deciding how many lexical items are represented by 'expressions' such as *form*, *stand* and *term*.

If we say that the criterion for the assignment of items to sets is collocational, this means to say that items showing a certain degree of likeness in their collocational patterning are assigned to the same set. This 'likeness' may be thought of in the following terms. If we consider *n* occurrences of a given (potential) item, calling this item the 'node', and examine its 'collocates' up to *m* places on either side, giving a 'span' of 2*m*, the 2*mn* occurrences of collocates will show a certain frequency distribution. For example, if for 2,000 occurrences of *sun* we list the three preceding and three following lexical items, the 12,000 occurrences of its collocates might show a distribution beginning with *bright*, *hot*, *shine*, *light*, *lie*, *come out* and ending with a large number of items each occurring only once. The same number of occurrences of *moon* might show *bright*, *full*, *new*, *light*, *night*, *shine* as the most frequent collocates.

On the basis of their high probability of occurrence (relative to their overall frequency) in collocation with the single item *sun*, the items *bright*, *hot*, *shine*, *light*, *lie*, *come out* constitute a weak provisional set; this resembles the weak provisional class recognizable in the grammar on the basis of a single 'item-bound' substitution frame—although in lexis it is *relatively* less weak because of the lower ceiling of generality: lexis is more item-bound than grammar. If we intersect these with the high frequency collocates of *moon* we get a set, whose members include *bright*, *shine* and *light*, with slightly greater generality. That is to say, *bright*, *shine* and *light* are being grouped together because they display a similar potentiality of occurrence, this being now defined as potentiality of occurrence in the environment of *sun* and in that of *moon*. The process can be repeated with each item in turn taken as the node; that is, as the environment for the occurrence of other items. The set will finally be delimited, on the basis of an appropriate measure of likeness, in such a way that its members are those items showing likeness in their total patterning in respect of all those environments in which they occur with significant frequency.

This is of course very much oversimplified; it is an outline of a suggested approach, not of a method of analysis. As Sinclair has shown, however, methods of analysis can be developed along these lines. Many other factors are involved, such as the length of the span, the significance of distance from the node and of relative position in sequence, the possibility of multiple nodes and the like. One point should be mentioned here: this is the importance of undertaking lexicogrammatical as well as lexical analysis. It is not known how far collocational patterns are dependent on the structural relations into which the items enter. For example, if *a cosy discussion* is unlikely, by comparison with *a cosy chat* and a *friendly discussion*, is it the simple co-occurrence of the two items that is unlikely, or their occurrence in this particular structure? All that has been said above has implied an approach in which grammatical relations are not taken into account, and reasons have been given for the suggestion that certain aspects of linguistic patterning will only emerge from a study of this kind. But it is essential also to examine collocational patterns in their grammatical environments, and to compare the descriptions given by the two methods, lexical and lexicogrammatical. This then avoids prejudging the answer to the question whether or not, and if so to what extent, the notion of 'lexicalness', as distinct from 'lexicogrammaticalness', is a meaningful one.[9]

An investigation on the lines suggested requires the study of very large samples of text. The occurrence of an item in a collocational environment can only be discussed in terms of probability; and, although cut-off points will need to be determined for the purpose of presenting the results, the interest lies in the degree of 'lexicalness' of different collocations (of items and of sets), all of which are clearly regarded as 'lexical'. Moreover the native speaker's knowledge of his language will not take the form of his accepting or rejecting a given collocation: he will react to something as more acceptable or less acceptable on a scale of acceptability. Likely collocations could be elicited by an inquiry in which the subject was asked to list the twenty lexical items which he would most expect to find in collocation with a given node;[10] but the number of such studies that would be required to cover even the most frequent lexical items in the language is very large indeed. Textually, some twenty million running words, or 1,500–2,000 hours of conversation, would perhaps provide enough occurrences to yield interesting results. The difficulty is that, since lexical patterns are of low generality, they appear only as properties of very large samples; and small-scale studies, though useful for testing methods, give little indication of the nature of the final results.

It is hard to see, however, how the results could fail to be of interest and significance for linguistic studies. Their contribution to our knowledge of language in general, and of one language in particular, may perhaps be discussed in relation to the use of the term 'semantics'. If lexis is equated with semantics, the implication is that lexical patterns can only be described either externally (that is, as relations between language and non-language, whether approached denotatively or contextually) or lexicogrammatically (that is, in dependence on grammatical patterns). This restriction leaves two gaps in our understanding of language: the internal relations of lexis, and the external relations of grammar—that is, lexis (lexical form), and grammatical semantics. But linguistics is concerned with relations of both types, both internal (formal, within language) and external (contextual or 'semantic', between language and non-language); and all linguistic items and categories, whether operating in closed contrasts, like *the* and *a*, or 'past' and 'present', or in open ones, like *strong* and *powerful*, enter into both. Moreover, as Firth stressed, both these types of relation are 'meaningful': it is part of the meaning of 'past' that it contrasts with 'present', and it is part of the meaning of *strong* that it collocates with *tea*. The fact that the labels for grammatical categories are chosen on semantic grounds should not be taken to imply that they represent an adequate substitute for grammatical semantics; but equally the existence of traditional methods in lexical semantics does not mean that lexical items display no internal, formal patterns of their own.

A thesaurus of English based on formal criteria, giving collocationally defined lexical sets with citations to indicate the defining environments, would be a valuable complement to Roget's brilliant work of intuitive semantic classification in which lexical items are arranged 'according to the *ideas* which they express'.[11] But even such a thing as a table of the most frequent collocates of specific items, with information about their probabilities, unconditioned and lexically and grammatically conditioned, would be of considerable value for those applications of linguistics in which the interest lies not only in what the native speaker knows about his language but also in what he does with it. These include studies of register and of literary style, of children's language, the language of aphasics and many others. In literary studies in particular such concepts as the ability of a lexical item to 'predict' its own environment, and the cohesive power of lexical relations, are of great potential interest.[12] Lexical information is also relevant to foreign language teaching; many errors are best explained collocationally, and items can be first introduced in their habitual environments.[13] A further possible field of application is information retrieval: one research group in this field is at present undertaking a collocational analysis of the language of scientific abstracts.[14]

Only a detailed study of the facts, such as that now being undertaken by Sinclair (the principles and methods worked out by him are described in the paper already referred to in the present volume), can show in what ways and to what extent the introduction of formal criteria into the study of lexis, as implied by the recognition of a 'lexical level', are of value to any particular applications of linguistics. But there seem to be adequate reasons for expecting the results to be interesting; and if they are, this is yet another indication of the great insight into the nature of language that is so characteristic of J.R. Firth's contribution to linguistic studies.

Notes

[1] See especially 'The Technique of Semantics', *TPS* 1935 (reprinted in J.R. Firth, *Papers in linguistics 1934–1951*, London, Oxford U.P., 1957).

[2] 'Modes of meaning', *Essays and Studies* (*The English Association*), *1951* (in *Papers in linguistics 1934–1951*; pp. 195–196): 'It must be pointed out that meaning by collocation is not at all the same thing as contextual meaning, which is the functional relation of the sentence to the processes of a context of situation in the context of culture. . . . Meaning by collocation is an abstraction at the syntagmatic level and is not directly concerned with the conceptual or idea approach to the meaning of words'. Compare also 'The Use and distribution of certain English sounds', *English Studies* 17.1 (1935) (in *Papers in linguistics 1934–1951;* p. 37), in reference to 'lexical substitution-counters' (lexical items): 'This (sc. the lexical) function should not be misnamed *semantic*'.

[3] See 'A Synopsis of linguistic theory', *Studies in linguistic analysis* (Special Volume of the Philological Society), Oxford, Blackwell (1957), p. 12. In the present paper 'lexical level' has been used in preference to 'collocational level' in order to suggest greater generality and parallelism with the grammatical level.

[4] It is also stated explicitly by Firth in 'A Synopsis of linguistic theory', p. 12: 'Collocations of a given word are statements of the habitual or customary places of that word in collocational order but not in any other contextual order and emphatically not in any grammatical order'. Note that here 'order' refers to the 'mutual expectancy' of syntagmatically related categories, such as elements of structure in grammar or phonology, and *not* to linear sequence: cf. ibid., pp. 5, 17 and my 'Categories of the theory of grammar', *Word* 17.3 (1961), pp. 254–255.

[5] That is, that distinctions are made which involve the recognition of more finely differentiated syntagmatic relations in the grammar, and that these in turn define further sub-classes on various dimensions within previously defined classes.

[6] The place of collocational restrictions in a transformational grammar is considered by P.H. Matthews in 'Transformational grammar' (review article), *ArchL* 13.2 (1961).

[7] For a discussion of the relation between grammatical and lexical patterns see Angus McIntosh, 'Patterns and ranges', *Lg* 37.3 (1961).

[8] See J. McH. Sinclair, 'Beginning the study of lexis', *passim.*

[9] The implication is, in effect, that 'wellformedness' is best regarded as 'lexicogrammaticalness', and that a departure from wellformedness may be ungrammatical, unlexical or unlexicogrammatical. That the last two are distinct is suggested by

such examples as *sandy hair*, *sandy gold* and *sandy desk: sandy desk* is unlexical, in that this collocation is unlikely to occur in any grammatical environment, whereas *sandy gold* is merely unlexicogrammatical: there is nothing improbable about *golden sand*. An analogous distinction is observable in clichés: in *shabby treatment* the mutual expectancy is purely lexical, and is paralleled in *they treated him shabbily*, *a shabby way to treat him* and so on, whereas the collocation *faint praise* is restricted to this structure, in the sense that it will not occur with similar probability under other grammatical conditions.

[10] Compare the methods used to assess the *disponibilité* of lexical items in the development of 'Français Fondamental': see G. Gougenheim, R. Michea, P. Rivenc and A. Sauvageot, *L'élaboration du français élémentaire*, Paris, Didier (1956).

[11] P. M. Roget, *Thesaurus of English words and phrases* (1936 ed.), London, Longmans (1960), p. xiii.

[12] Cf. J. R. Firth, 'Modes of meaning'.

[13] The following text examples may be cited in this connection: festive animals, circumspect beasts, attired with culture, funny art, barren meadows, merry admiration, the situation of my stockings was a nightmare, lying astray, fashionable airliner, modern cosy flights, economical experience, delightfully stressed, serious stupid people, shining values, a wobbly burden, light possibility, luxurious man, whose skin was bleeding, driving a bicycle, old and disturbed bits of brick wall, a comprehensive traffic jam, her throat became sad, my head is puzzled, people touched with assurance, thoughts are under a strain, a sheer new super car.

[14] This research is being undertaken by Dr. A. R. Meetham and Dr. P. K. T. Vaswani at the National Physical Laboratory, Teddington, Middlesex.

Towards a Prosodic Statement of Vietnamese Syllable Structure

EUGÉNIE J. A. HENDERSON

The beginnings of my professional association with Professor J. R. Firth were coeval with those of my working acquaintance with the Vietnamese language, and the interaction between the two over the years was such as to suggest Vietnamese phonology as a fitting theme for a paper in the present volume.

When I made my first attempts at a phonetic description of Northern Vietnamese twenty years ago the prevailing tendency might fairly be said to be to use 'one magic phoneme principle within a monosystemic hypothesis'.[1] Such an approach produces 'phonemic solutions' that are in many ways unsatisfactory as statements of phonological function, whatever their merits from other points of view. There are aspects of Vietnamese pronunciation and of the distribution of Vietnamese sounds that are a challenge to phonetician and phonologist alike, as is witnessed by the variety in the phonetic descriptions and phonemic solutions that have been offered so far. Certain peculiarities of pronunciation and apparent disparities in distribution are so regular that it is clear that they should properly be viewed as systematic rather than accidental,[2] as integral parts of a coherent whole rather than as irrelevant oddities. The ideal phonological statement would be one in which these 'apparently eccentric features take a normal place',[3] one that would not so much solve the apparent problems as provide a framework within which they were found no longer to exist.[4] In the quest for such a statement I have found the outlook and techniques advocated by Firth both provocative and illuminating. It is the aim of this paper, not to provide a definitive phonological statement of Vietnamese syllable structure, for which much further work would be required,[5] but to demonstrate some of the lines of approach suggested by prosodic analysis to specific phonological problems, many of which have close parallels in others of the vast range of languages in the Sino–Tibetan linguistic area. An attempt has been made to break free from some of the limitations imposed by more conventional analytical procedures, following Firth's teaching that 'no analysis or mode of analysis is the only one accurate or sacrosanct, but any account of the language, in any terms, is an adequate statement and analysis, provided that, and to the extent to which, it comprehensively and economically explains what is heard (and read) in the language, and "renews connection" with further experience of it',[6] and that 'under otherwise equal circumstances one will prefer that theory, which covers a larger field of phenomena, or which from some points of view appears to be . . . clearer'.[7]

Phonic Data

The phonic data which will be referred to in subsequent sections of this article are set out in the tables on pp. 168–173. These tables display the syllables attested by my informants for Northern and Southern Vietnamese, Northern Vietnamese (NV) being for the purpose of this paper defined as the educated speech of Hanoi, and Southern Vietnamese (SV) as the educated speech of Saigon.[8] The Northern material is set out on the left-hand page and the corresponding Southern material on the right-hand page.

The consonant letters in the Vietnamese system of spelling that may occur at the beginning of syllables appear horizontally in alphabetical order numbered from 2 to 24, absence of an initial consonant letter being numbered 1. Below each letter appears a symbol or symbols representing its pronunciation in general phonetic terms. It should be noted that 'c' and 'k', 'g' and 'gh', 'ng' and 'ngh', are pairs of orthographic variants, the first form in each case being that found before the letters 'a', 'o' and 'u' and the second that found before the letters 'i', 'y' and 'e'. Since there is no difference in pronunciation corresponding to the variation in spelling, each pair heads a single column, thus: c, k; g(h); ng(h).

In my material as originally recorded, the complexes of vowel and consonant letters and tone-marks that may follow the initial consonant letters appear vertically in alphabetical order, and in the appropriate place at the intersection of vertical column and horizontal line a tick marks every attested occurrence of the syllable concerned, special marks being added where the occurrence was limited to (a) words of known and relatively recent foreign borrowing; (b) exclamations or onomatopes; (c) bound forms restricted to compounds or reduplicative formations; and (d) forms about which the informant was doubtful, or which he recognized as being in free variation with some other form. Considerations of space make it necessary in the present paper to include only the sequence of vowel and consonant letters of the final complexes, without tone-marks, and to reserve all other comments for the main text of the article. In the tables as here presented the finals without tone-marks appear vertically in alphabetical order numbered from 1 to 163. Such pairs of orthographic variants as 'i' and 'y', 'uinh' and 'uynh', 'uit' and 'uyt' are grouped together as one final. When examining the recorded occurrences of 'qu' it must be borne in mind that this is the orthographic representation of initial 'c' or 'k' with a following labial semivowel, and the finals with which it occurs should be compared with those spelt 'oa', 'ua', etc. Such finals are, for convenience, recorded twice, once in strict alphabetical order, i.e. 'qua' appears at the intersection point of 'qu' and 'a', and a second time, in round brackets, in the relevant column from the phonetic point of view, i.e. at the intersection point of 'qu' and 'oa'. Forms such as 'quy', 'quyên', etc., are recorded both at the intersection point of 'qu' and 'i, y', 'iên', etc., and, in round brackets, in the relevant phonetic section, i.e. with finals 141 to 145. Forms such as 'giên', 'giêng' appear only in the relevant phonetic section, i.e. with finals 47 to 53, not under the 'ê' spellings which might be misleading, since NV **z**, SV **j** > 'gi' never occur before the vowel **e**.[9]

To the right of each orthographic final appears in brackets the maximum number of tones theoretically possible for a syllable with such a final, and to the right of that again a phonetic rendering of its pronunciation, without tonal indications. For syllables ending with a continuant the maximum number of tonal possibilities is 6 for NV, 5 for SV, while for both dialects the maximum for syllables ending with a stop is 2. At the intersection of vertical column and horizontal line is shown the number of tones upon which a given syllable is found: thus, the number 3 at the intersection point of column 12 and line 31 in the NV table means that a syllable spelt 'men' is recorded as occurring on 3 tones out of a theoretical maximum of 6.

The system of phonetic transcription used is based upon that of the International Phonetic Alphabet and is in the main self-explanatory, but the following points should be noted:

Initial Consonants **ɓ-** snd **ɗ-** are glottalized, but not implosive; **ɗ-** is alveolar in NV, post-alveolar and retroflex in SV. **th-** and **t-** are dental. NV **z** and **s** are alveolar. SV **ʃ** is slightly retroflex with narrowing in the alveolar or post-alveolar region; SV **s(j)** is a fronter, non-retroflex fricative, sometimes palatalized so that a light palatal off-glide is heard. SV **(b)j** is a laxly articulated bilabial plosive followed by a palatal fricative. In connected speech frequently the fricative only is pronounced. (ˀ) indicates that a glottal plosive may occur at the beginning of the syllables so marked. **l-** and **n-** are alveolar in NV, post-alveolar and slightly retroflex in SV in most contexts. In **ɲ-** the sides of the front of the tongue are raised and approach each other in the palato-alveolar area, sometimes meeting in the middle so that palatograms may show a wipe right across the palate. NV **ch**, which is lightly aspirated, is similarly articulated, but palatograms never show a wipe right across the palate. Palatograms of SV **c**, which is unaspirated, show post-alveolar narrowing caused by the raising of the sides of the tongue, and sometimes show a wipe right across the palate in this area. SV **tɹ** is a retroflex affricate, **ɹ** a post-alveolar fricative, SV **j** < 'gi' has strong friction in adagio speech, **j** < 'd' is always frictionless.

Final Consonants **-p**, **-t**, and **-k** are unexploded. NV **-t** and **-n** are alveolar, the contact for **-n** being commonly rather further back than for initial **n-**. -k̹ and -ŋ̹ are fronted velars.[10] SV **-t** is alveolar or post-alveolar and retroflex. SV **-n** is post-alveolar and markedly retroflex. SV **-k** is further back than NV **-k**, frequently uvular. -k͡p and -ŋ͡m indicate simultaneous velar and bilabial articulations.

Vowels. All Vietnamese vowels vary considerably as to the degree of opening according to the tone of the syllable in which they occur. In the tables the pronunciation indicated is based upon that appropriate to the 'bằng' and 'sắc' tones, i.e. the closest of the variants. There is also variation in the degree of centralization and diphthongization correlated with consonantal articulations in the syllable and sometimes with tone. An attempt is made to indicate this in the phonetic transcription where it appears relevant to the phonolgical analysis. **ï**, **ë**, and **ɛ̈** are centralized vowels, slightly fronter than **ɨ**, **ə**, and **ɐ**. NV **ɯ** and **ɤ** are generally fronter than SV **ɯ** and **ɤ** and somewhat closer in most contexts. NV **ə** is between SV **ɨ** and **ə**. SV **a** is very front, NV **a** is central. SV **ʌ** is a half-open back unrounded vowel.

When the material was being collected, dictionaries were sometimes referred to and the informant's reaction to forms recorded there sometimes sought. The aim, however, in compiling the lists was to record only those forms known to and used by the informant himself. As

Emeneau has pointed out,[11] dictionaries are of limited use for this purpose as most of them contain many highly literary Sinicized forms unfamiliar even to educated speakers of the language. In my experience, they also appear sometimes to contain forms which can only be accounted for as dialectal mis-spellings.[12] Examination of the pronunciation columns in the tables will show how readily such mis-spellings can arise. SV does not distinguish in pronunciation finals ending in 'n' and 'ng', 't' and 'c', except after 'ô' and 'o', and SV speakers are in consequence frequently uncertain as to their spelling. My Southern informant when called upon to record the incidence or absence of the relevant finals, felt obliged in most cases to treat them as single forms except in the case of 'ươc' and 'ươt', about the spelling of which he appeared to have no doubts. Conversely, NV does not distinguish initial 'tr' and 'ch', or initial 'd', 'r', and 'gi' in colloquial style, and so mis-spellings sometimes arise. Orthographic forms which were readily recognized by my informants as 'mis-spellings' such as 'hoéc' for 'hoét', 'khuyếc' for 'khuyết', etc., have been omitted in the tables, and the syllables entered under the regular spellings.[13] Similarly, orthographic sequences which were immediately rejected as non-occurrent such as 'ei', 'ou', 'iei', etc., are not included, but others which were accepted as possible forms by my informants, but which turned out upon investigation to be non-occurrent, such as '-uôp', '-ơc', '-ơng', are included.

It is not claimed that the syllable count itself is exhaustive or without error but it is believed that it reflects a fair picture of the points at issue. The tables derive in the main from a single informant for each dialect, though the pronunciation of the Northern dialect has been checked with upwards of half a dozen other speakers, and that of the Southern with two or three. The Northern material was worked over more thoroughly and for a longer period of time than the Southern material and is for this reason likely to be more reliable. The Southern material is incomplete[14] but is included as displaying some interesting points of difference to the Northern material, which, while often posing new problems for solution, sometimes suggest helpful lines of approach to those of the sister dialect. In pronouncing syllables in isolation, my Southern informant sometimes produced pronunciations which did not, so far as my observations went, occur in more natural speech. Such forms, which are suspected to be spelling pronunciations only, are enclosed in round brackets in the tables after what is believed to be his natural pronunciation.

TABLE A

NORTHERN

Spelling	Pron:	1	2	3	4	5	6	7	8	9	10	11	12	13	14	15	16	17	18	19	20	21	22	23
Spelling			b	c, k	ch	d	đ	g(h)	gi	h	kh	l	m	n	ng(h)	nh	ph	qu	r	s	t	th	tr	v
	Pron:	(ʔ)	ɓ	k	ch	z	ɗ	ɣ	z	h	x	l	m	n	ŋ	ɲ	f	kw	z	s	t	th	ch	v
1 a	(6) a	4	4	4	4	5	5	4	6	4	3	6	6	6	4	5	4	4	6	5	6	3	5	5
2 ac	(2) a : k	1	2	1	2	1	1	2	2	2	2	2	2	2	1	2	1	2	2	2	2	2	2	2
3 ach	(2) ɛ̈iķ	1	2	2	1	0	0	1	0	2	1	2	2	1	2	2	1	2	2	2	2	2	2	2
4 ai	(6) a: i	3	4	5	4	6	5	4	4	6	4	5	6	5	6	6	3	5	4	5	5	5	4	6
5 am	(6) a: m	2	1	3	2	1	4	0	3	4	3	5	1	4	0	4	2	0	5	3	4	4	4	0
6 an	(6) a: n	2	5	5	3	2	4	2	5	5	2	3	5	5	3	4	5	4	5	5	5	3	6	5
7 ang	(6) a: ŋ	1	3	5	2	4	5	3	4	6	1	6	6	5	4	4	3	6	5	4	5	2	5	6
8 anh	(6) ɛ̈iŋ	3	3	5	4	2	4	2	2	5	3	6	6	4	3	3	2	4	4	4	5	5	4	2
9 ao	(6) a: u	3	6	5	5	4	5	3	3	5	5	6	4	5	4	5	3	3	6	5	5	5	5	2
10 ap	(2) a: p	1	0	1	1	0	1	0	1	1	2	2	0	2	1	2	2	0	2	2	2	2	1	0
11 at	(2) a: t	0	2	1	2	2	0	1	1	2	1	2	2	2	2	2	2	2	2	2	2	0	2	2
12 au	(6) au	0	0	2	2	1	2	1	2	2	1	4	3	1	3	3	1	3	4	2	3	2	3	0
13 ay	(6) ai	1	1	4	5	6	5	4	2	2	2	4	4	6	3	4	3	3	6	3	3	4	2	3
14 ăc	(2) ak	0	1	2	1	2	2	1	1	1	1	2	1	1	1	1	1	2	2	2	2	1	2	0
15 ăm	(6) am	1	3	3	3	2	5	3	2	3	2	4	3	3	3	5	0	3	4	3	3	3	3	1
16 ăn	(6) an	1	2	3	4	4	2	2	2	3	3	5	5	4	3	5	1	4	4	4	3	5	2	3
17 ăng	(6) aŋ	1	0	2	4	2	4	2	1	3	4	5	3	4	1	5	2	6	3	3	3	4	6	6
18 ăp	(2) ap	0	0	2	2	0	1	2	0	0	1	2	2	1	0	1	0	2	1	1	1	1	1	2
19 ăt	(2) at	0	0	1	2	1	2	2	2	1	1	2	2	0	2	2	1	2	0	2	1	1	2	2
20 âc	(2) ək	0	2	0	0	0	0	1	1	0	1	1	1	1	0	1	0	1	1	0	1	0	0	2
21 âm	(6) əm	4	4	5	4	3	5	4	3	5	3	5	6	4	6	5	1	0	5	5	4	6	5	3
22 ân	(6) ən	3	4	5	3	4	2	2	2	2	0	6	6	3	5	3	6	6	4	3	6	4	6	6
23 âng	(6) əŋ	0	1	2	1	1	1	1	1	2	0	3	2	4	1	1	1	1	1	2	3	0	1	3
24 âp	(2) əp	1	0	2	2	1	1	2	2	1	1	2	1	1	1	2	2	0	2	2	2	2	2	2
25 ât	(2) ət	0	2	2	2	1	2	1	0	1	2	2	2	0	2	2	2	2	1	0	2	2	2	2
26 âu	(6) əu	2	4	5	4	4	5	2	3	5	3	4	6	4	5	5	2	1	3	4	5	3	5	3
27 ây	(6) əi	1	5	4	4	5	6	5	4	0	0	5	4	4	4	5	0	5	3	5	3	3	2	6
28 e	(6) ɛ, ɛə	2	6	4	5	2	3	4	2	3	5	6	6	2	3	6	2	5	5	4	3	4	3	5
29 ec	(2) ɛk	0	0	1	0	0	0	0	0	0	0	1	1	0	0	0	0	0	0	0	0	0	0	0
30 em	(6) ɛm	1	0	4	1	1	2	1	1	1	1	4	2	2	0	4	0	0	1	1	2	2	0	0
31 en	(6) ɛn	1	2	3	3	0	2	1	0	3	2	4	3	1	2	1	2	3	3	4	1	2	0	5
32 eng	(6) ɛŋ	0	0	2	0	0	0	0	0	0	0	1	0	0	0	0	0	0	0	0	0	0	0	0
33 eo	(6) ɛu	3	2	5	4	1	4	1	2	4	2	6	5	3	4	5	2	5	3	4	2	3	4	2
34 ep	(2) ɛp	1	1	2	1	2	1	1	1	1	1	2	1	2	0	0	1	1	1	0	0	1	0	0
35 et	(2) ɛt	0	1	1	2	0	1	1	0	1	1	2	2	2	1	1	2	2	1	2	2	1	1	2
36 ê	(6) e	2	4	5	3	4	6	3	0	3	3	5	3	5	3	3	3	2	4	2	6	5	5	4
37 êch	(2) ëiķ	1	1	1	2	1	1	2	0	0	0	2	1	0	2	0	2	1	1	0	1	1	2	2
38 êm	(6) em	1	0	1	2	3	3	0	0	1	0	0	1	3	0	0	0	0	0	0	1	2	4	0
39 ên	(6) en	0	3	0	0	2	2	0	0	0	2	3	3	4	0	1	1	1	3	3	1	0	2	1
40 ênh	(6) ëiŋ	0	2	1	1	1	1	2	0	1	3	4	2	1	2	0	1	0	2	3	1	0	0	4
41 êp	(2) ep	1	1	0	0	0	0	0	0	0	0	1	0	1	0	0	0	0	1	1	0	2	0	0
42 êt	(2) et	0	0	1	2	1	0	0	0	2	0	2	1	1	0	0	2	2	2	2	1	1	0	2
43 êu	(6) eu	0	1	1	0	1	1	0	0	0	2	0	1	2	2	2	4	0	3	0	0	2	0	4
44 i, y	(6) i	4	5	5	5	6	2	2	3	3	4	3	6	5	5	6	5	6	6	6	6	5	6	6
45 ia	(6) iə	1	2	2	2	3	4	0	0	1	2	2	2	2	1	0	1	0	5	2	3	2	0	1
46 ich	(2) ïiķ	2	1	2	1	2	2	0	0	0	1	1	2	2	1	1	2	0	1	1	2	2	1	0
47 iêc	(2) iək	0	0	0	1	2	1	1	1	0	0	1	0	0	0	1	0	0	2	1	2	1	0	1
48 iêm	(6) iəm	3	0	5	2	3	3	0	1	3	3	6	0	3	2	2	0	0	0	1	5	3	0	0
49 iên	(6) iən	2	4	3	2	3	4	1	1	5	3	5	4	2	4	2	4	4	3	2	6	4	2	5
50 iêng	(6) iəŋ	1	1	4	1	1	1	0	3	0	1	4	4	1	1	0	0	0	2	2	1	2	0	3
51 iêp	(2) iəp	0	0	2	1	1	1	0	0	2	1	2	0	0	0	0	0	0	1	0	1	2	1	0
52 iêt	(2) iət	1	2	2	1	1	0	0	2	0	1	1	1	2	1	1	1	2	2	1	2	2	2	2
53 iêu	(6) iəu	3	1	5	3	3	5	0	1	3	2	5	4	1	1	3	2	0	5	1	4	5	2	0
54 im	(6) im	2	0	2	3	3	0	1	0	1	0	2	2	0	0	1	1	2	3	1	5	1	2	1
55 in	(6) in	3	0	3	1	1	0	0	1	1	1	0	3	1	1	3	0	0	3	1	2	2	1	3
56 inh	(6) ïiŋ	4	3	3	5	2	5	1	0	2	1	6	2	3	2	0	2	2	3	4	6	5	6	3

STATEMENT OF VIETNAMESE SYLLABLE STRUCTURE

SOUTHERN

	1	2	3	4	5	6	7	8	9	10	11	12	13	14	15	16	17	18	19	20	21	22	23	24
		b	c, k	ch	d	đ	g(h)	gi	h	kh	l	m	n	ng(h)	nh	ph	qu	r	s	t	th	tr	v	x
Pron:	(ʔ)	ɓ	k	c	j	ɗ	ɣ	j	h	x	l	m	n	ŋ	ɲ	ph	kw	ɹ	ʃ	t	th	tɹ	(b)j	s(j)
(5) a	5	5	5	5	3	5	5	5	5	4	5	5	4	4	4	3	5	5	5	5	4	4	5	5
(2) a : k	2	2	2	2	1	2	2	1	2	2	2	2	2	2	2	2	2	2	2	2	2	2	2	2
(2) ɐt	2	2	2	2	2	2	1	0	2	1	2	2	1	1	0	2	1	2	2	2	2	2	2	2
(5) a: i	4	5	5	5	5	5	4	4	5	3	5	5	5	5	5	3	3	4	4	5	4	4	4	3
(5) a: m	2	1	4	2	1	4	0	3	5	3	5	1	2	1	4	2	0	2	5	4	4	3	1	4
(5) a: ŋ	3	5	5	5	2	5	4	5	5	4	5	5	5	3	5	4	3	5	5	5	3	5	5	3
(5) a: ŋ								as for an																
(5) ɐn	3	5	5	5	3	4	4	2	5	2	5	5	2	3	3	2	3	5	5	4	5	3	4	2
(5) a: u	4	5	5	4	3	5	3	3	5	4	5	5	5	4	5	3	2	4	5	5	5	5	1	4
(2) a: p	2	0	2	1	0	2	0	1	2	2	2	1	2	1	1	1	0	2	1	2	1	0	0	2
(2) a: k								as for ac																
(5) a: u								as for ao																
(5) a: i								as for ai																
(2) ak	1	2	2	2	2	2	2	2	1	1	2	2	2	2	2	1	2	2	2	2	1	2	2	2
(5) am	3	5	5	5	5	5	5	1	2	1	5	2	4	5	3	0	0	4	5	4	5	4	1	2
(5) aŋ	1	4	5	4	3	4	4	2	4	5	5	5	4	3	5	2	5	4	4	5	5	3	5	4
(5) aŋ								as for ăn																
(2) ap	1	2	2	2	2	2	2	2	2	1	2	2	2	1	2	1	0	2	2	2	2	1	2	2
(2) ak								as for ăc																
(2) ʌk	1	2	2	2	2	2	1	2	1	1	2	2	1	2	2	2	2	2	2					
(5) am, ʌm	4	5	5	5	5	5	5	0	2	1	5	3	2	5	4	1	1	5	5					
(5) ʌŋ	3	5	5	5	3	1	2	1	2	3	5	4	2	4	4	5	3	4	3					
(5) ʌŋ								as for ân																
(2) ap, ʌp								as for ăp																
(2) ʌk								as for âc																
(5) au	3	4	5	3	5	5	1	1	2	2	4	5	4	3	3	1	1	2	2					
(5) ɨi	2	5	4	3	3	5	4	4	1	2	5	4	2	3	3	1	2	3	3					
(5) ɛ	2	5	5	4	3	4	5	0	5	4	5	5	3	3	5	3	0	4	4	4	4	4	4	4
(2) ɛək	1	1	1	1	0	1	1	0	1	1	1	1	0	1	1	1	0	1	1	1	1	1	1	1
(5) ɛm	2	0	3	3	1	1	4	0	2	0	5	2	2	0	3	0	0	1	0	2	1	0	0	2
(5) ɛəŋ	1	5	5	3	0	3	3	0	3	1	3	2	1	2	1	2	0	4	2	1	2	2	4	3
(5) ɛəŋ								as for en																
(5) ɛu	3	3	4	4	1	4	0	1	3	1	4	4	3	1	3	2	0	2	1	4	2	4	1	4
(2) ɛp	2	2	2	1	2	1	2	0	2	1	2	2	2	1	2	1	0	0	0	1	2	0	0	1
(2) ɛək								as for ec																
(5) e, ei	3	5	5	5	3	5	2	0	3	2	4	3	2	3	2	3	2	4	1	4	5	4	3	5
(2) ɨt, ət	1	2	1	2	1	0	0	0	2	0	1	1	0	0	0	1	2	0	2	1	1	1	1	2
(5) em	2	0	1	1	0	3	0	0	0	0	0	1	3	0	0	0	0	1	0	1	2	0	0	0
(5) ən	1	5	1	1	0	2	1	0	2	0	4	5	4	2	2	1	2	2	2	1	0	2	2	2
(5) ɨn, ən								as for ên																
(2) ep	0	1	0	0	0	0	0	0	0	0	0	0	1	0	0	0	0	1	0	0	0	0	0	2
(2) ət								as for êch																
(5) eu	0	3	1	0	2	2	0	0	2	2	3	1	2	3	1	0	1	2	0	0	1	1	0	0
(5) i, ɪi	4	5	5	5	5	3	3	1	3	4	4	5	3	4	5	4	5	4	3	5	5	5	5	5
(5) iə	1	3	4	5	1	4	0	0	1	2	4	3	2	1	0	1	0	3	0	3	3	1	1	3
(2) ɨt	2	2	2	2	1	2	1	0	1	2	1	2	2	1	1	1	2	2	0	2	2	2	2	2
(2) iək	1	2	2	1	2	1	0	2	0	2	2	2	0	1	2	0	0	2	1	2	2	1	2	1
(5) im	4	1	5	4	3	3	2	0	2	2	5	2	2	3	2	1	0	1	0	4	2	1	1	1
(5) iəŋ	2	5	5	4	4	5	0	3	5	3	5	5	3	4	2	3	2	2	2	5	5	4	4	1
(5) iəŋ								as for iên																
(2) ip	0	2	2	1	1	1	1	0	2	1	1	1	0	1	2	0	0	1	0	2	2	1	0	1
(2) iək								as for iêc (except after qu.)									2							
(5) iu	3	2	5	5	5	5	1	0	4	3	5	3	2	1	4	2	0	5	1	5	5	4	1	4
(5) im								as for iêm																
(5) ɨn	3	5	4	4	3	5	0	1	4	2	5	5	3	3	4	2	0	4	3	5	5	4	5	5
(5) ɨn								as for in (except after qu.)									2							

TABLE A *cont'd*

NORTHERN

Spelling	Pron:	1	2	3	4	5	6	7	8	9	10	11	12	13	14	15	16	17	18	19	20	21	22	23
Spelling			b	c, k	ch	d	đ	g(h)	gi	h	kh	l	m	n	ng(h)	nh	ph	qu	r	s	t	th	tr	v
	Pron:	(ʔ)	ɓ	k	ch	z	ɗ	ɣ	z	h	x	l	m	n	ŋ	ɲ	f	kw	z	s	t	th	ch	v
57 ip	(2) ip	0	1	2	0	2	0	0	0	1	0	1	0	1	0	2	0	0	0	0	0	1	0	0
58 it	(2) it	2	2	2	1	2	2	1	0	1	1	0	2	2	0	0	0	2	2	2	2	2	0	1
59 iu	(6) iu	1	1	2	3	3	1	0	3	1	2	3	1	3	0	1	0	1	3	0	3	2	0	1
60 o	(6) ɔ, ɔə	3	5	5	3	4	5	3	4	3	3	4	6	6	6	4	3	0	6	4	3	5	5	6
61 oa	(6) wa	2	0	0	0	1	2	1	0	5	3	4	0	1	4	2	0	(4)	0	0	5	5	0	0
62 oac	(2) wa:k	2	0	0	1	0	1	0	0	1	1	0	0	0	2	0	0	(2)	0	0	2	0	0	0
63 oach	(2) wĕiķ	0	0	0	0	0	0	0	0	1	0	0	0	0	0	0	0	(2)	0	0	0	0	0	0
64 oai	(6) wa:i	3	0	0	2	0	2	0	0	3	2	2	0	0	5	1	0	(5)	0	1	2	3	0	0
65 oam	(6) wa : m	0	0	0	0	0	0	0	0	0	0	0	0	0	1	0	0	0	0	0	0	0	0	0
66 oan	(6) wa:n	3	0	0	0	0	5	0	0	5	3	4	0	1	2	0	0	(4)	0	2	3	4	1	0
67 oang	(6) wa:ŋ	0	0	0	3	0	1	0	0	4	5	5	0	0	1	2	0	(6)	0	0	2	2	3	0
68 oanh	(6) wĕiŋ	1	0	0	0	0	0	0	0	3	2	0	0	0	0	0	0	(4)	0	0	0	0	0	0
69 oao	(6) wa:u	0	0	0	0	0	0	0	0	0	0	0	0	0	1	0	0	(3)	0	0	0	0	0	0
70 oap	(2) wa:p	1	0	0	0	0	0	0	0	0	0	0	0	0	0	0	0	0	0	0	0	0	0	0
71 oat	(2) wa:t	0	0	0	0	0	1	0	0	1	1	2	0	0	1	0	0	(2)	0	1	1	2	1	0
72 oau	(6) wau	0	0	0	0	0	0	0	0	0	0	0	0	0	0	0	0	(3)	0	0	0	0	0	0
73 oay	(6) wai	0	0	0	0	0	0	0	0	0	0	0	0	0	2	0	0	(4)	0	0	0	0	0	0
74 oăc	(2) wak	0	0	0	0	0	0	0	0	1	0	0	0	0	1	0	0	(2)	0	0	0	0	0	0
75 oăm	(6) wam	1	0	0	0	0	0	0	0	0	1	0	0	0	0	0	0	(3)	0	0	0	0	0	0
76 oăn	(6) wan	0	0	0	0	0	0	0	0	0	2	0	0	0	0	0	0	(4)	0	0	0	1	0	0
77 oăng	(6) waŋ	0	0	0	0	0	0	0	0	0	1	0	0	0	0	0	0	(6)	0	0	0	1	0	0
78 oăp	(2) wap	0	0	0	0	0	0	0	0	0	0	0	0	0	0	0	0	(2)	0	0	0	0	0	0
79 oăt	(2) wat	1	0	0	0	0	0	0	0	0	0	0	0	0	1	0	0	(2)	0	0	0	1	1	0
80 oc	(2) auk͡p	2	2	0	2	2	1	1	1	2	1	2	2	2	2	2	1	0	2	2	2	2	2	1
81 oe	(6) wɛ	2	0	0	0	0	0	0	0	3	3	4	0	0	2	1	0	(5)	0	0	4	0	0	0
82 oem	(6) wɛm	0	0	0	0	0	0	0	0	0	0	0	0	0	0	0	0	0	0	0	0	0	0	0
83 oen	(6) wɛn	0	0	0	0	0	0	0	0	1	1	0	0	0	1	1	0	(3)	0	0	0	0	0	0
84 oeo	(6) wɛu	0	0	0	0	0	0	0	0	0	1	0	0	0	3	0	0	(5)	0	0	0	0	0	0
85 oep	(2) wɛp	0	0	0	0	0	0	0	0	0	0	0	0	0	0	0	0	(1)	0	0	0	0	0	0
86 oet	(2) wɛt	0	0	0	0	0	0	0	0	1	1	0	0	0	0	0	0	(2)	0	0	1	0	0	0
87 oi	(6) ɔi	3	1	5	4	2	2	3	3	3	2	5	5	3	3	2	0	0	6	5	3	3	4	3
88 om	(6) ɔm	2	1	1	1	3	2	1	0	4	2	6	4	1	2	4	0	0	6	3	3	3	4	1
89 on	(6) ɔn	1	3	2	2	3	2	2	1	3	1	4	5	4	4	4	0	0	4	2	3	3	3	4
90 ong	(6) auŋ͡m	3	2	4	5	3	4	1	2	5	2	5	5	4	3	4	4	0	5	5	3	3	6	4
91 oong	(6) ɔŋ	0	1	0	0	0	0	0	0	0	0	0	0	0	0	0	0	0	0	0	0	0	0	0
92 op	(2) ɔp	2	1	1	1	0	0	1	0	2	0	1	1	1	1	1	0	0	0	0	2	2	0	0
93 ot	(2) ɔt	2	1	1	1	0	0	2	1	1	0	2	2	0	2	2	1	0	2	2	1	2	2	2
94 ô	(6) o	4	5	5	1	2	6	1	3	5	3	6	5	5	4	4	3	0	6	6	4	4	4	5
95 ôc	(2) əuk͡p	2	1	2	1	2	2	1	1	2	0	2	2	1	1	0	0	0	2	0	2	2	1	1
96 ôi	(6) oi	4	4	4	4	4	6	2	3	5	2	5	4	6	2	2	3	0	5	3	4	3	5	2
97 ôm	(6) om	2	0	2	2	0	1	2	0	2	0	4	1	3	1	2	1	0	1	1	1	0	1	0
98 ôn	(6) on	3	4	3	3	3	4	0	0	3	2	5	2	1	5	3	1	0	3	1	4	4	3	1
99 ông	(6) əuŋ͡m	2	5	5	4	2	4	2	3	3	3	4	6	4	3	4	4	0	6	4	3	2	4	3
100 ôp	(2) op	2	2	1	1	0	1	1	0	2	0	2	0	2	0	1	1	0	1	1	2	1	0	0
101 ôt	(2) ot	2	1	2	2	2	2	1	0	2	0	2	2	2	2	2	0	0	2	2	2	1	0	0
102 ơ	(6) ɤ	5	5	4	5	4	3	2	2	4	1	6	6	5	4	6	3	3	6	6	4	6	6	6
103 ơc	(2)	0	0	0	0	0	0	0	0	0	0	0	0	0	0	0	0	0	0	0	0	0	0	0
104 ơi	(6) ɤi	4	4	4	1	2	2	2	2	4	3	4	3	2	4	1	3	0	5	2	2	5	3	4
105 ơm	(6) ɤm	1	3	1	2	1	2	2	0	1	1	5	1	2	1	2	1	0	2	1	1	2	4	0
106 ơn	(6) ɤn	2	2	1	2	4	3	0	1	3	1	4	4	0	1	6	0	0	3	4	1	3	6	2
107 ơng	(6)	0	0	0	0	0	0	0	0	0	0	0	0	0	0	0	0	0	0	0	0	0	0	0
108 ơp	(2) ɤp	0	1	0	1	1	1	0	0	2	1	2	1	1	2	1	0	0	1	0	1	0	2	0
109 ơt	(2) ɤt	2	1	1	1	0	1	2	1	1	0	2	2	1	1	2	1	0	1	2	0	2	2	2
110 ơu	(6) ɤu	0	0	0	0	0	0	0	0	0	0	0	0	1	0	0	0	0	0	0	0	0	0	0
111 u	(6) u	4	3	6	3	3	3	1	0	4	3	5	6	2	5	4	6	0	6	5	5	5	4	5
112 ua	(6) uə	5	3	2	3	3	3	0	1	1	1	4	3	3	0	1	0	0	4	2	3	3	0	2

B *cont'd*

SOUTHERN

		1	2	3	4	5	6	7	8	9	10	11	12	13	14	15	16	17	18	19	20	21	22	23	24
ng			b	c, k	ch	d	đ	g(h)	gi	h	kh	l	m	n	ng(h)	nh	ph	qu	r	s	t	th	tr	v	x
	Pron.	(ʔ)	ɓ	k	c	j	ɗ	ɣ	j	h	x	l	m	n	ŋ	ɲ	ph	kw	ɹ	ʃ	t	th	tɹ	(b)j	s(j)
	(2) ip								as for iêp																
	(2) ɨt								as for ich																
	(5) iu								as for iêu									2							
	(5) ɔ	2	5	5	3	3	5	3	4	3	4	5	5	5	5	3	3	0	3	4	3	4	4	4	4
a	(5) wa	1	0	0	2	2	3	1	0	5	3	4	2	1	3	1	0	(5)	0	1	4	3	0	0	4
ac	(2) wa:k	0	0	0	0	1	1	0	0	2	1	2	0	0	1	0	0	(2)	0	1	2	2	0	0	1
ach	(2) wat	0	0	0	0	0	0	0	0	2	1	0	0	0	0	0	0	(1)	0	0	0	0	0	0	0
ai	(5) wa:i	2	0	0	0	0	3	0	0	4	2	2	0	0	3	1	0	(3)	0	1	0	1	0	0	3
am	(5)	0	0	0	0	0	0	0	0	0	0	0	0	0	0	0	0	0	0	0	0	0	0	0	0
an	(5) wa:ŋ	2	0	0	2	2	5	0	0	5	3	5	0	1	1	1	0	(3)	0	1	4	4	0	0	1
ang	(5) wa:ŋ								as for oan																
anh	(5) wɐn	1	0	0	0	1	0	0	0	3	2	0	0	0	1	0	0	(3)	0	0	0	0	0	0	0
ao	(5)	0	0	0	0	0	0	0	0	0	0	0	0	0	0	0	0	(2)	0	0	0	0	0	0	0
ap	(2) wa:p	2	0	0	0	0	0	0	0	0	0	0	0	0	0	0	0	0	0	0	0	0	0	0	0
at	(2) wa:k								as for oac																
au	(5)								as for oao																
ay	(5) wa:i								as for oai																
ic	(2) wak	0	0	0	1	0	0	0	0	2	1	0	0	0	1	0	0	(2)	0	0	0	1	0	0	0
im	(5) wəm	0	0	0	0	0	0	0	0	0	0	0	0	0	0	0	0	0	0	0	0	0	0	0	0
in	(5) waŋ	0	0	0	0	0	0	0	0	1	2	0	0	0	0	0	0	(5)	0	0	0	1	0	0	0
ing	(5) waŋ								as for oăn																
ip	(2)	0	0	0	0	0	0	0	0	0	0	0	0	0	0	0	0	0	0	0	0	0	0	0	0
it	(2) wak								as for oăc																
	(2) aukp͡	2	2	2	2	1	1	2	1	2	1	2	2	1	2	2	1	0	2	2	2	2	2	1	3
	(5) (w)ɛ	1	0	0	1	2	1	0	0	2	3	3	0	0	1	0	0	0	0	0	0	0	0	0	0
m	(5)	0	0	0	0	0	0	0	0	0	0	0	0	0	0	0	0	0	0	0	0	0	0	0	0
n	(5) wɛəŋ	0	0	0	1	0	0	0	0	1	1	0	0	0	0	0	0	0	0	0	0	0	0	0	0
o	(5) wɛu	0	0	0	0	0	0	0	0	0	0	0	0	0	0	0	0	0	0	0	0	0	0	0	0
p	(2) wɛp	0	0	0	0	0	0	0	0	0	0	0	0	0	0	0	0	0	0	0	0	0	0	0	0
t	(2) wɛək	0	0	0	0	0	0	0	0	2	1	1	0	0	0	0	0	0	0	0	1	0	0	0	0
	(5) əi	4	1	3	5	0	3	3	1	1	2	5	4	2	3	2	0	0	2	3	1	1	2	3	1
n	(5) əm	1	1	1	3	2	2	1	0	1	3	5	1	2	0	0	0	0	1	1	2	0	1	0	2
	(5) əŋ	2	5	3	3	2	3	2	1	2	1	5	5	3	3	2	0	0	2	1	1	4	2	1	0
g	(5) auŋ͡m	2	4	5	3	2	2	2	3	4	0	5	5	2	3	2	4	0	3	1	2	3	4	4	2
ng	(5) əŋ͡m	0	1	0	0	0	0	0	0	0	0	1	0	0	0	0	0	0	0	0	1	0	0	0	0
	(2) əp	1	2	1	1	0	0	2	0	1	0	0	2	1	0	0	0	0	0	0	1	0	0	0	2
	(2) ək	1	2	2	2	0	2	2	1	1	1	2	2	0	2	2	0	0	1	2	1	2	2	0	2
	(5) o, ou	4	5	5	2	2	4	1	1	5	3	4	4	3	3	3	3	0	4	3	4	3	2	4	2
	(2) aukp͡	1	2	2	1	1	2	2	1	2	1	1	2	1	1	1	0	0	1	0	2	1	1	0	1
	(5) oi	3	3	5	1	2	5	3	0	5	2	5	4	5	2	2	1	0	3	1	3	3	5	2	2
n	(5) om	2	2	3	3	0	2	1	0	0	0	0	1	0	0	0	0	0	1	0	1	0	1	0	0
	(5) oŋ	3	5	3	2	1	3	0	0	2	2	2	2	2	2	0	1	0	3	2	3	2	2	0	1
g	(5) auŋ͡m	3	4	5	4	2	4	3	3	3	2	3	5	4	4	3	2	0	3	3	3	3	5	1	1
	(2) op	0	2	2	0	0	2	0	0	2	1	2	2	1	2	0	0	0	0	0	1	0	0	0	2
	(2) ok	1	1	2	2	2	2	0	0	2	0	2	2	1	1	2	0	0	2	2	2	1	1	0	0
	(5) ɤ, ʌɤ	5	5	4	5	4	5	1	3	4	3	4	5	4	4	5	3	3	3	5	4	5	5	5	2
	(2)	0	0	0	0	0	0	0	0	0	0	0	0	0	0	0	0	0	0	0	0	0	0	0	0
	(5) ɤi	1	4	4	1	0	2	1	3	3	4	3	2	4	1	1	1	0	2	2					
n	(5) ɤm	0	3	2	3	0	3	0	0	0	0	1	2	1	0	0	0	0	1	2	1	1	0	0	1
	(5) ɤŋ	2	2	2	3	1	2	1	1	3	1	4	3	0	0	1	0	0	3	2	3	0	4	0	0
g	(5)	0	0	0	0	0	0	0	0	0	0	0	0	0	0	0	0	0	0	0	0	0	0	0	0
	(2) ɤp	0	2	0	2	0	2	0	0	2	1	2	0	2	0	2	0	0	0	0	0	0	0	0	2
	(2) ɤk	2	1	1	1	0	1	1	0	2	0	1	0	0	2	2	1	0	1	2	0	1	2	2	1
	(5)	0	0	0	0	0	0	0	0	0	0	0	0	0	0	0	0	0	0	0	0	0	0	0	0
	(5) u, ʊu	5	3	5	3	5	5	2	0	5	5	4	5	2	2	2	5	0	4	5	5	5	4	4	3
	(5) uə																								

TABLE A *cont'd*

NORTHERN

Spelling	Pron:	1	2	3	4	5	6	7	8	9	10	11	12	13	14	15	16	17	18	19	20	21	22	23
Spelling			b	c, k	ch	d	đ	g(h)	gi	h	kh	l	m	n	ng(h)	nh	ph	qu	r	s	t	th	tr	v
	Pron:	(ʔ)	ɓ	k	ch	z	ɗ	ɣ	z	h	x	l	m	n	ŋ	ɲ	f	kw	z	s	t	th	ch	v
113 uâc	(2) wək	0	0	0	0	0	0	0	0	0	0	0	0	0	0	0	0	(1)	0	0	0	0	0	0
114 uâm	(6) wəm	0	0	0	0	0	0	0	0	0	0	0	0	0	0	0	0	0	0	0	0	0	0	0
115 uân	(6) wən	1	0	0	1	0	0	0	0	2	2	2	0	0	0	3	0	(6)	0	0	3	4	1	0
116 uâng	(6) wəŋ	0	0	0	0	0	0	0	0	0	1	0	0	0	0	0	0	(1)	0	0	0	0	0	0
117 uâp	(2) wəp	0	0	0	0	0	0	0	0	0	0	0	0	0	0	0	0	0	0	0	0	0	0	0
118 uât	(2) wət	1	0	0	0	0	0	0	0	0	1	1	0	0	0	0	0	(2)	0	1	1	1	2	0
119 uâu	(6) wəu	0	0	0	0	0	0	0	0	0	0	0	0	0	0	0	0	(1)	0	0	0	0	0	0
120 uây	(6) wəi	0	0	0	0	0	0	0	0	0	2	0	0	0	0	0	0	(5)	0	0	0	0	0	0
121 uc	(2) uk	2	1	2	2	0	2	1	1	2	1	2	2	2	2	2	2	0	2	2	2	2	2	1
122 uê	(6) ɥe	2	0	0	0	0	0	0	0	4	1	0	0	0	1	2	0	(2)	0	0	2	2	0	0
123 uêch	(2) ɥëiķ	0	0	0	0	0	0	0	0	0	1	0	0	0	1	0	0	(1)	0	0	2	0	0	0
124 uênh	(6) ɥëiŋ	0	0	0	0	0	0	0	0	0	4	0	0	0	0	0	0	(0)	0	0	0	0	0	0
125 ui	(6) ui	5	3	4	3	0	3	1	2	2	1	5	5	3	2	2	3	0	4	3	4	5	2	2
126 uinh, uynh	(6) ɥïiŋ	1	0	0	0	0	0	0	0	2	2	0	0	0	0	0	0	(2)	0	0	0	0	0	0
127 uit, uyt	(2) ɥit	0	0	0	0	0	0	0	0	1	0	0	0	0	1	0	0	(2)	0	0	0	0	0	0
128 um	(6) um	5	1	3	4	0	1	0	2	2	2	5	0	1	2	1	0	0	4	4	4	3	3	1
129 un	(6) un	3	3	2	3	0	2	0	2	2	0	6	4	1	3	2	3	0	4	3	1	3	2	2
130 ung	(6) uŋ	3	2	5	5	0	4	0	0	4	4	6	2	3	1	5	5	0	6	5	4	6	6	4
131 uôc	(2) uək	0	1	2	0	0	1	2	0	0	0	2	0	1	0	1	0	1	1	0	0	2	0	0
132 uôi	(6) uəi	0	3	2	3	1	3	0	0	0	0	1	4	2	2	0	0	0	4	1	1	0	0	0
133 uôm	(6) uəm	0	1	0	1	0	0	0	0	0	0	2	1	1	0	3	0	0	1	0	1	0	0	0
134 uôn	(6) uən	1	2	2	1	0	0	0	0	0	1	2	3	0	1	0	0	0	0	1	1	2	0	0
135 uông	(6) uəŋ	2	2	2	3	2	1	1	0	2	2	3	4	1	0	0	1	0	3	2	2	2	2	1
136 uôp	(2) uəp	0	0	0	0	0	0	0	0	0	0	0	0	0	0	0	0	0	0	0	0	0	0	0
137 uôt	(2) uət	0	1	0	2	1	1	1	0	0	0	2	1	2	0	1	0	0	2	1	2	1	0	2
138 uơ	(6) wɤ	0	0	0	0	0	0	0	0	1	0	0	0	0	0	0	0	(3)	0	0	0	1	0	0
139 up	(2) up	2	1	2	2	0	0	0	1	2	0	1	2	1	2	0	2	0	0	1	0	0	0	0
140 ut	(2) ut	2	1	2	2	0	2	0	0	2	0	2	2	1	2	2	1	0	2	2	1	2	2	2
141 uy	(6) ɥi	3	0	0	1	2	0	0	0	3	1	2	0	0	3	1	0	(6)	0	2	5	4	3	0
142 uya	(6) ɥiə	0	0	0	0	0	0	0	0	0	1	0	0	0	0	0	0	0	0	0	0	0	0	0
143 uyên	(6) ɥiən	1	0	0	5	1	0	0	0	4	3	2	0	0	4	2	0	(4)	0	2	4	2	2	0
144 uyêt	(2) ɥiət	0	0	0	0	1	0	0	0	2	1	0	0	0	0	0	0	(2)	0	0	2	1	0	0
145 uyu	(6) ɥiu	0	0	0	0	0	0	0	0	0	1	0	0	0	0	0	0	0	0	0	0	0	0	0
146 ư	(6) ɯ	3	1	6	4	5	0	0	2	3	3	6	1	2	4	4	0	0	0	5	5	5	5	0
147 ưa	(6) ɯə	2	5	5	5	4	2	1	2	2	1	5	4	4	4	1	0	0	6	5	1	4	1	4
148 ưc	(2) ɯk	2	2	2	2	2	2	0	0	2	0	1	2	2	1	1	1	0	2	2	2	2	0	2
149 ưi	(6) ɯi	0	0	1	1	0	0	1	0	0	0	0	0	0	1	0	0	0	0	0	0	0	0	0
150 ưm	(6)	0	0	0	0	0	0	0	0	0	0	0	0	0	0	0	0	0	0	0	0	0	0	0
151 ưn	(6) ɯn	0	2	0	0	0	0	0	0	0	0	0	0	0	0	0	0	0	0	0	0	0	0	0
152 ưng	(6) ɯŋ	3	2	3	4	3	3	1	0	4	1	6	2	4	4	3	2	0	4	4	6	3	4	4
153 ươc	(2) ɯək	1	1	1	1	1	1	0	0	0	1	1	0	2	2	1	1	0	1	0	2	2	1	1
154 ươi	(6) ɯəi	1	1	3	1	1	0	0	0	0	1	4	2	0	2	2	0	0	6	2	2	0	0	0
155 ươm	(6) ɯəm	3	3	1	0	0	1	3	0	2	1	2	1	2	0	0	0	0	2	0	3	0	0	0
156 ươn	(6) ɯən	2	0	0	0	0	0	0	0	1	0	3	2	0	0	0	2	0	2	2	0	0	1	3
157 ương	(6) ɯəŋ	1	1	4	4	3	3	2	3	4	1	5	2	2	3	4	5	0	3	3	5	5	5	4
158 ươp	(2) ɯəp	1	0	1	0	0	0	0	0	0	0	0	2	1	0	0	0	0	0	0	0	0	0	0
159 ươt	(2) ɯət	1	0	0	1	0	0	0	0	0	1	2	1	0	0	0	0	0	1	1	0	2	1	1
160 ươu	(6) ɯəu*	0	1	0	0	0	0	0	0	1	1	1	1	0	0	0	1	0	1	0	1	0	0	0
161 ưp	(2)	0	0	0	0	0	0	0	0	0	0	0	0	0	0	0	0	0	0	0	0	0	0	0
162 ưt	(2) ɯt	0	1	1	0	2	1	0	2	0	0	1	1	1	0	2	1	0	2	2	0	0	0	1
163 ưu	(6) ɯu	1	0	5	0	0	0	0	0	3	1	3	1	1	1	0	1	0	0	2	2	0	2	0

* Pronounced iəu by many speakers, but not by my two principal informants.

ε B *cont'd*

SOUTHERN

		1	2	3	4	5	6	7	8	9	10	11	12	13	14	15	16	17	18	19	20	21	22	23	24
ng			b	c, k	ch	d	đ	g(h)	gi	h	kh	l	m	n	ng(h)	nh	ph	qu	r	s	t	th	tr	v	x
	Pron.:	(ʔ)	ɓ	k	c	j	ɗ	ɣ	j	h	x	l	m	n	ŋ	ɲ	ph	kw	ɹ	ʃ	t	th	tɹ	(b)j	s(j)
âc	(2) wək	1	0	0	0	0	0	0	0	0	1	1	0	0	0	0	0	(2)	0	0	1	1	1	0	1
âm	(5) wəm	0	0	0	0	0	0	0	0	0	0	0	0	0	1	0	0	(1)	0	0	0	0	0	0	0
ân	(5) wiŋ	1	1	0	1	0	0	0	0	2	1	2	0	0	0	2	0	(3)	0	0	3	4	1	0	1
âng	(5) wiŋ								as for uân																
âp	(2)	0	0	0	0	0	0	0	0	0	0	0	0	0	0	0	0	0	0	0	0	0	0	0	0
ât	(2) wək								as for uâc																
âu	(5)	0	0	0	0	0	0	0	0	0	0	0	0	0	0	0	0	0	0	0	0	0	0	0	0
ây	(5) wii	0	0	0	0	0	0	0	0	0	2	0	0	0	0	0	0	(2)	0	0	0	0	0	0	0
c	(2) uk	2	2	2	2	2	2	2	2	2	1	2	1	2	2	2	2	0	2	2	2	2	2	2	2
ê	(5) we	2	0	0	0	1	0	0	0	4	1	0	0	0	1	2	0	(2)	0	0	2	2	0	0	2
êch	(2) wit	0	0	0	0	0	0	0	0	0	1	0	0	0	2	0	0	(2)	0	0	0	0	0	0	0
ênh	(5) wən, win	0	0	0	0	0	0	0	0	0	0	0	0	0	1	0	0	0	0	0	0	0	0	0	0
i	(5) ui	3	5	5	4	4	5	2	0	2	1	5	5	3	3	3	3	0	4	2	4	4	3	2	5
inh, ynh	(5) win	1	0	0	0	0	0	0	0	2	2	0	0	0	0	0	0	(2)	0	0	0	0	0	0	0
it, yt	(2) wit	1	0	0	0	0	0	0	0	1	0	0	0	0	2	0	0	(2)	0	1	0	0	0	0	1
m	(5) um	3	4	4	4	3	2	0	1	1	1	3	1	2	0	2	0	0	2	2	4	2	3	0	2
n	(5) uŋ	3	5	5	3	5	4	0	2	3	2	5	4	3	3	3	4	0	2	3	5	5	4	4	1
ng	(5) uŋ								as for un																
ôc	(2) uək																								
ôi	(5) ui								as for ui																
ôm	(5) uəm																								
ôn	(5) uəŋ																								
ông	(5) uəŋ																								
ôp	(2)	0	0	0	0	0	0	0	0	0	0	0	0	0	0	0	0	0	0	0	0	0	0	0	0
ôt	(2) uək																								
ơ	(5) wɤ	4	0	0	0	0	0	0	0	0	0	0	0	0	0	0	0	(3)	0	0	0	0	0	0	0
p	(2) up	2	2	2	1	0	0	0	1	2	0	0	1	1	0	0	0	0	0	1	1	0	0	0	2
t	(2) uk								as for uc																
y	(5) wi	3	0	0	1	1	0	0	0	3	2	2	0	0	2	1	0	(5)	1	5	3	3	0	1	5
ya	(5) iə	0	0	0	0	0	0	0	0	0	1	0	0	0	0	0	0	0	0	0	0	0	0	0	0
yên	(5) wiəŋ	2	0	0	5	1	0	0	0	4	3	2	0	0	3	0	0	(2)	0	0	4	2	2	0	2
yət	(2) wiək	0	0	0	0	1	0	0	0	2	1	0	0	0	1	0	0	(2)	0	0	2	1	0	0	0
yu	(5) iu	0	0	0	0	0	0	0	0	0	0	0	0	0	0	0	0	(2)	0	0	0	0	0	0	0
	(5) ɯ, ɣɯ	3	2	5	4	3	2	0	1	4	2	3	0	2	4	3	0	0	0	4	5	5	5	0	3
a	(5) ɯə	2	4	4	4	5	2	0	3	1	1	4	3	1	4	1	0	0	2	2	4	2	1	2	1
c	(2) ɯk	1	1	1	1	1	1	0	1	0	0	1	1	1	0	1	1	0	1	1	1	1	1	1	1
i	(5) ɯi	0	3	4	1	1	0	1	0	1	2	3	1	0	3	0	1	0	2	2	2	0	0	0	1
m	(5)	0	0	0	0	0	0	0	0	0	0	0	0	0	0	0	0	0	0	0	0	0	0	0	0
n	(5) ɯŋ	3	3	2	5	4	3	1	0	4	1	3	2	4	2	2	1	0	3	4	4	2	3	3	4
ng	(5) ɯŋ								as for ưn																
ơc	(2) ɯək	1	2	1	2	1	2	0	0	1	0	2	0	1	2	0	1	0	1	0	2	2	1	0	2
ơi	(5) ɯi								as for ưi																
ơm	(5) ɯəm	1	3	1	0	0	1	0	0	1	0	2	0	0	0	0	0	0	2	0	1	0	0	0	0
ơn	(5) ɯəŋ	2	2	3	3	4	2	2	3	4	1	4	4	2	2	3	3	0	4	4	5	4	5	4	4
ơng	(5) ɯəŋ								as for ươn																
ơp	(2) ɯp	1	0	1	0	0	0	0	0	0	0	0	1	1	0	0	0	0	0	0	1	0	0	0	0
ơt	(2) ɯək	1	0	0	0	1	0	0	0	0	1	2	2	0	0	0	0	0	1	1	0	1	0	1	0
ơu	(5) ɯu	1	3	5	0	0	0	0	0	3	2	2	2	0	1	0	0	0	1	2	2	0	1	0	0
p	(2)	0	0	0	0	0	0	0	0	0	0	0	0	0	0	0	0	0	0	0	0	0	0	0	0
t	(2) ɯk								as for ưc																
u	(5) ɯu								as for ươu																

The Problems

Below are listed the principal problems raised for the phonologist by the material summarized in the preceding section:

1. The numerical disparity between the consonants found in syllable initial position and those found in syllable final position, and the relations between them.[16]

2. (i) The seemingly irregular patterning of initial unaspirated plosives whereby, though **t** and **ɗ** both occur, the voiced bilabial has no voiceless congener, and the voiceless velar no voiced congener; (ii) the phonological significance of the fact that **ɓ** and **ɗ** are glottalized rather than plain voiced plosives; and (iii) the absence of a corresponding velar glottalized plosive.[17]

3. The uneven distribution of initial consonants before a following bilabial semivowel. (See finals 61–79, 81–86, 113–120, 122–124, 126–127, 138, 141–145.)[18]

4. The relative infrequence of such initials as 'gi-', 'g(h)-', 'ph-' and of zero initial, as compared with others such as 'c, k-', 'l-' and 't-'.

5. The non-occurrence of 'ă' and 'â' in open syllables.[19]

6. (i) The relative shortness everywhere of the vowels spelt 'ă' and 'â'; (ii) the relative length of the vowels spelt 'a', 'ơ', 'e' and 'o' in closed syllables in general as against those spelt 'i', 'u', and 'ư'; (iii) the centring diphthongs found in contextual variation with NV **ɛ** and **ɔ** in open syllables, and the closing diphthongs found in free variation with SV **i**, **e**, **u**, **ɤ**, and **o** in open syllables.[20]

7. (i) The absence in NV of diphthongs beginning with a front vowel and moving towards a closer front vowel, and of diphthongs beginning with a back rounded vowel and moving towards a closer back rounded vowel; (ii) the occurrence in both dialects of diphthongs beginning with sounds represented by 'a', 'ă' and 'â' and moving towards both close front and close rounded back vowels; (iii) the patchy distribution of the finals 'ơi', 'ơu', 'ưi', 'ưu', 'ươu', and 'ươi' as compared with those discussed under (ii) above.[21]

8. (i) The distribution of post-alveolar and velar finals in SV and (ii) the central quality of the SV vowels spelt 'i', 'ê' and 'a' before post-alveolar finals.[22]

9. The pronunciation and phonological interpretation in NV of (i) finals ending in '-ch' and '-nh' and (ii) the finals '-ec' and 'eng'.[23]

10. The pronunciation and phonological interpretation in both dialects of (i) the finals 'oc', 'ong', 'ôc' and 'ông', and (ii) of 'oong'.[24]

11. The distribution of vowels after labial semivowels. (See finals cited under Problem 3.)[25]

12. The uneven incidence of final consonants and of diphthongs in syllables containing a labial semivowel. (See finals 62–79, 81–86, 126–127, 142–145.)[26]

13. Certain seeming discrepancies in the association of vowels and final consonants, e.g. (i) the non-occurrence of 'ơng' and 'ơc'; (ii) the rare occurrence of 'ưn' and non-occurrence of 'ưm' and 'ưp'; (iii) the non-occurrence of 'uôp'.[27]

14. Certain seeming discrepancies, other than those already noted under Problems 3 and 13, in the association of initials and finals, e.g. (i) the limitation of initial consonants before **ɯ** in open syllables; (ii) the rare occurrence of **ɣ** before close vowels or diphthongs beginning with a close vowel; (iii) the non-occurrence of 'gi-' in syllables containing the half-close front vowel **e**; (iv) the frequency, as compared with other consonant sounds, with which **k** appears before a following semivowel; (v) the restriction, especially puzzling in the light of (iv) above, of initial consonants occurring before the finals **ɥe**, **ɥiə** and **ɥiu** to **x** only in NV.[28]

15. The tones and their relation to initials and finals.

16. The very free use made of certain sounds, e.g. initial **k** and the vowel **a:**, as contrasted with others. (There are, for example in NV more than three times as many syllables beginning with **k** as there are syllables beginning with **ɣ**, and three-and-a-third times as many syllables containing the vowel **a:** as there are syllables containing the vowel **e**.)

The remainder of this paper will be devoted to an exploratory examination of a number of the above problems in the light of prosodic theory. Space does not permit the investigation here of the last two problems listed. It may be mentioned in passing, however, that a tentative essay, inspired by Haudricourt's historical thesis,[29] at a prosodic statement to handle Problem 15 appeared encouraging enough to warrant more detailed treatment at a later date. Problem 16 suggests that an attempt to re-state the phonetic exponents of the phonological categories posited in the succeeding section in acoustic terms would be rewarding and might prove more satisfactory than the articulation-based phonetic descriptions adopted here.

Exploratory Statement

As the starting point of our exploratory statement let us take Firth's view that the facts of the phonological structure of a language 'are most economically and most completely stated on a polysystemic hypothesis'[30] by means of a 'plurality of systems of interrelated phonematic and prosodic categories'.[31] We shall thus not find it necessary to postulate one all-embracing phonological system for all the forms of the language, regardless of their origin or function, nor shall we feel constrained to identify systems of units appropriate to one place in structure with systems appropriate to another place in structure. The immediate consequence of this standpoint is, as we shall see later, that Problems 1 and 9 cease to exist.

As a second step, it is accepted that each of the utterances of Vietnamese syllables which form the basis of this investigation constitutes 'one complete act' of speech behaviour, 'a configuration of bodily postures and movements not easily dissected'.[32] For the purposes of phonological analysis, the Vietnamese syllable is here regarded as a structure having 'places'[33] for which systems of phonematic units will be stated, and certain properties characteristic of the syllable as a whole for which prosodic systems will be stated.[34] These properties include such syllable-marking features as tone, and initial, final and medial characteristics which may be referred on the phonetic plane to such phenomena as labialization, palatalization and other manifestations of what Firth called the 'broad distinction of front and back resonance'.[35] Prosodic elements are not regarded as being placed, though they may be referred to one or more 'focal points' in the utterance.[36] Structures are of two or three places. All syllables are regarded as having a syllabic nucleus which is associated with the first place in a two-place structure and the second place in a three-place structure. From the phonic data set out on pp. 168–173 features will be selected as characteristic exponents of terms in systems of phonematic units referable to places in structure and of terms in prosodic systems referable to the syllable as a whole.[37] Such exponents may be 'continuous or discontinuous, discrete or cumulative'.[38] In order to avoid possible confusion between the phonetic and phonological levels of analysis, the terms *consonant* and *vowel* will be reserved for the language of phonetic description. In phonological statements reference will be to *nuclear*, *pre-nuclear* and *post-nuclear phonematic units*, symbolized in Greek fount, and to *prosodies*, symbolized by superior Roman or Roman-based letters.[39]

Since in setting up phonological categories the aim will be to demonstrate syllable structure in terms of 'the mutual expectancy of the parts and the whole' rather than as a 'unidirectional sequence of successive linear segments',[40] it should cause neither surprise nor dismay that the accepted language of phonetic description is frequently ill-suited to the description of the phonetic exponents of such categories, and that new categories of phonetic description are called for.[41]

Problem 1. Approached by way of the polysystemic hypothesis adopted here, this problem, which is common to all languages of the Sino-Tibetan linguistic area in which there are syllables with final consonants, is, in fact, not a problem in phonological terms. The consonantal articulations at the beginnings and ends of syllables are handled partly as exponents of terms of phonematic systems set up in the marginal places in structure, and partly as exponents of terms of prosodic systems. Since there is no particular reason why we should expect the same number of terms in each phonematic system any numerical disparity between them need not concern us.[42] Once it is decided to postulate separate systems for each place in structure the problem ceases to exist. It will, moreover, be found that in the marginal phonematic systems proposed in this paper the ratio of terms is 5:3, which is not by any reckoning a disturbing disparity.

Problems 2, 3 and *4.* To handle the problems raised by the nature and distribution of the initial consonants we shall be concerned with prosodic systems of syllable onset and of onset modification, and, in three-place structures, with the pre-nuclear phonematic system. To take the latter first, it is suggested that it should be conceived of not as referable to phonetic categories relating to the place and manner of articulation and the action of the larynx but to broad articulation types only. For the phonematic commutation system in place one of three-place structures five terms are postulated, as shown below:

Terms	*Phonetic Exponents*
δ	Tense phonation involving complete stoppage of the airstream, followed on release by rapid onset of the following vowel without perceptible intervening breathiness or friction.
ψ	Rather lax phonation with open glottis, involving either complete or partial obstruction of the air-

Terms	*Phonetic Exponents*
	stream followed by slow release, with breathy or fricative onset to the following vowel.
μ	Voiced nasal articulation, i.e. with soft palate lowered and vocal cords brought together to allow continuous escape of voiced air through the nose.
σ	Fricative articulation with marked hissing or buzzing effect. As contrasted with ψ, breath may be either voiced or unvoiced, and there is never complete obstruction of the airstream.
ρ	Voiced oral continuant articulation, with or without perceptible friction.

Associated with the phonematic system in place one are certain syllabic features proper to syllable onset which are stated as a prosodic system of four terms, *dark*, *clear*, *neutral*, and *mixed*, as follows:

Terms		*Phonetic Exponents*
Dark	(w)	Labial or back articulation.
Clear	(y)	Dental, or alveolar apical articulation, produced with the blade of the tongue flat, or dorsal articulation with the front part of the tongue raised towards the hard palate.
Neutral	(ə)	Absence of labiality and of dental or palatal articulation. Typical neutral articulations are (a) either with the tongue tip lowered and the back of the tongue raised towards, or to touch, the soft palate, or (b) with more retracted apical contact than for clear syllables and slightly grooved dorsum.[43]
Mixed (Clear and Dark)	(yw)	Absence of labiality, or dental or palatal articulation, and of the tip-down articulation described for neutral syllables at (a) above. A typical mixed articulation is slightly retroflex, with the tongue tip in contact with or in close proximity to the post-alveolar region.

The initial consonants of Tables A and B on pp. 168–173 may now be interpreted as the cumulative phonetic exponents of pre-nuclear phonematic units and syllable onset prosodies, as follows:[44]

TABLE C

Syllable-onset Prosodies		*Phonematic Units*				
		δ	ψ	μ	σ	ρ
Dark	(w)	**ɓ**	SV.**ph** NV.**f**	**m**	SV **j** < 'gi' NV **z** < 'gi'	**ɣ**
Clear	(y)	**t**	**th**	**ɲ**	SV **s(j)** NV **s** < 'x'	SV **j** < 'd' NV **z** < 'd'
Neutral	(ə)	**k**	**x**	**ŋ**	**h**	**l**
Mixed	(yw)	**ɗ**	SV **tɹ** NV **ch** 'tr'	**n**	SV **ʃ** NV **s** < 's'	SV **ɹ** NV **z** + 'r'

It is here assumed that, providing there are sufficiently cogent linguistic reasons for postulating different elements of phonological structure in a given case, the phonetic exponents of such elements may sometimes converge in what is, from the point of view of general phonetic description, an identical complex of phonetic features. Thus, working from the table above, it may be said that there is convergence of the cumulative phonetic exponents of NV $^{w}\sigma$, $^{y}\rho$ and $^{yw}\rho$; of NV $^{y}\sigma$ and $^{yw}\sigma$; and of SV $^{w}\sigma$ and $^{y}\rho$. The justification for the phonological distinction between SV $^{w}\sigma$ and $^{y}\rho$ lies in the difference observed in the adagio pronunciation of SV 'gi-' and 'd-',[45] and in their occurrence before **w**.[46] Similar considerations, which will be noted in later sections of the text, support the distinction between the NV elements cited.

While there appears to be no serious theoretical objection to the concept of the convergence of the phonetic exponents of phonological categories, the converse hypothesis, i.e. that there may be divergence of the phonetic exponents of the same phonological elements, is only acceptable if the conditions determining such divergence can be stated. It has sometimes been necessary in working through the present material to choose between phonological solutions entailing some convergence or divergence of phonetic exponents. Except in cases where the conditions for divergence were readily discernible, or where strict avoidance of divergence would lead to the postulation of convergence on a very widespread scale, preference has always been given to a solution entailing the statement of some convergence of phonetic exponents.

To return to the problems under consideration, it will be seen from the display of cumulative exponents in Table C on p. 179 that Problem 2 is now resolved to the extent that the system proposed does not require that there should be pairs of voiced and voiceless unaspirated plosives, nor that the phonological relations that obtain between **t** sounds and **d** sounds in other language systems should obtain here.[47] ʸʷδ is related to ʸδ through its clear prosodic component and to ʷδ through its dark prosodic component. Carrying this a little further, it may perhaps be suggested that the apical articulation of **ɗ** is a phonetic exponent of the y-element in the yw- prosody, and that the special resonance effect brought about by the simultaneous glottal constriction is an exponent of the w-element. We may thus interpret the glottalization of **ɓ** and **ɗ** as serving both to ensure the tense phonation and rapid onset to the following vowel that are characteristic exponents of δ as a phonematic unit, and to contribute to the dark resonance effect characteristic of w- prosody. Within such a framework, we do not expect to find further glottalized plosives, since there are no further combinations of tense phonation with dark resonance.

If we turn now to examine the phonetic phenomena to which attention is drawn in Problem 3, we discover that in both dialects there are initial consonants which never occur before labial semivowels; initial consonants which do so quite frequently; and initial consonants which do so less frequently, or very rarely.

(i) The initial consonants which never occur before a labial semivowel are:

NV	SV
ɓ, **z** (< 'r' or 'gi'), **m**, **f**, **v**	**ɓ**, **j** (< 'gi', **ɹ**, **f**, **(b)j**

(ii) Those which frequently occur in such a position are in order of frequency of occurrence:

NV	SV
k x h t ŋ s(< 'x') **th l**	**k h x l ŋ t th s(j)**

(iii) Those which occur less frequently or very rarely are:

NV	SV
ɲ, **ch** (< 'ch'), **ɗ**, **ch**(< 'tr'), **s**(< 's')**z**(< 'd'), **n**, **ɣ**	**ɗ**, **j**(< 'd'), **c**, **ɲ**, **ʃ**, **t**, **n**, **m**, **ɣ**

It will be noted from the above that in neither dialect are labial or labio-dental consonants found before **w**, with the exception of **m** in SV. The two instances of labialized **m** recorded for SV occur in the words 'moa' and 'moå', both first person pronominal forms borrowed quite recently, along with 'toa', from the French 'moi' and 'toi'. Our polysystemic working hypothesis allows us to relegate such partially assimilated loans, which might otherwise distort our picture of the phonology of the language, to special secondary phonological systems.[48] These two words being excluded, it is possible to make the generalized phonetic statement that labially articulated initial consonants are never followed by a labial semivowel. If we seek to make phonological sense of this, we see that we are here dealing with syllables whose onset is characterized by dark resonance, or w- prosody, and may assume that what is dark already does not require to be made any darker. We should therefore not expect any further labial component to be added to the initial complex of such syllables.

Before we go on to examine the non-labial consonants which are never found before **w**, it must be pointed out that although in NV no distinction in pronunciation is made between 'ch-' and 'tr-' (both **ch**), between 's' and 'x' (both **s**), or between 'd-', 'r-' and 'gi-' (all **z**, except in adagio literary style, when 'r' may be pronounced **ɹ**), my NV informants nevertheless kept these apart orthographically with fairly rare cases of uncertainty. The difference in the distribution of **s** < 's' and **s** < 'x', and of **z** < 'r' or 'gi' and **z** < 'd', before **w** or **ɥ** seems to justify separating these consonants for the purposes of phonological analysis.[49]

Of the non-labial consonants which do not occur before a labial semivowel, and which may therefore tentatively be expected to include exponents of w- prosody, i.e. NV **z** < 'r' and 'gi', SV **j** < 'gi'', **ɹ**, and **tɹ**, the interpretation of SV **tɹ** and **ɹ** as cumulative exponents of $^{yw}\psi$ and $^{yw}\rho$ respectively presents no difficulty, and it seems not unreasonable, in view of its absence before **w** and the occasional variant pronunciation **ɹ**, to interpret NV **z** < 'r' as $^{yw}\rho$ for the Northern dialect. It remains to consider NV **z**, SV **j** < 'gi'. Despite the convergence of exponents in SV with $^{y}\rho$, there is phonetic support for the alignment of the sound with σ in the strongly fricative pronunciation observed in adagio speech. The association with w- prosody is harder to defend. The non-occurrence of 'gi-' in labialized syllables leads us to expect that it should be possible to abstract from NV **z** and SV **j** phonetic features referable to dark or mixed syllable onset. The pronunciation of these sounds, however, does not accord well with the phonetic exponents stated above for either of these prosodies and no more accommodating re-statement of the exponents has so far suggested itself. The alignment of the sounds with $^{w}\sigma$ in Table C is therefore no more than tentative gap-filling, pending some more plausible hypothesis.

If we postulate that the phonological presence of dark syllable onset precludes the occurrence at the phonetic level of a labial semivowel after the initial consonant, we might expect that the initial consonant of syllables in which there is a labial semivowel will be such as would in other contexts be associated with clear or neutral syllable onset. A comparison of Table C with the consonants listed under (ii) on p. 180 confirms that this is in the main the case. We have, however, to deal with a number of consonants associated with yw- syllable onset prosody which occur, albeit infrequently or rarely, before a labial semivowel. The number of attested examples of **ɗ**, **n**, SV. **ʃ** and **tɹ**, before **w** is such that it cannot be held that the dark component of yw- onset prosody precludes absolutely the addition of a further dark element, as does w- onset prosody itself. We may, however, maintain that it tends to do so, as compared with y- and ə- onset prosodies.

The alignment of **ɣ** with $^{w}\rho$ accords reasonably well both with the pronunciation and distribution but for one puzzling exception, namely, the word 'góa' *widow, widowed.*[50] This word is of fairly common occurrence, not a recent loan, and not one which can be regarded as belonging to a special class of onomatopoeic, ideophonic or exclamatory forms. It cannot, therefore, on the evidence at present available, be handled as belonging to some secondary phonological pattern for which a different statement is required. Apart from this one word, **ɣ** groups with the labial consonants and with 'r' and 'gi-', and appears a likely candidate for what would otherwise remain a gap in Table C.[51]

Missing from Table C are the NV consonants **ch** < 'ch' and **v**, SV **c** and **(b)j**. These are tentatively put forward as front-modified initial complexes comparable in some ways with the labialized initial complexes already discussed, but differing from them in that they are far fewer in number and that there is no restriction as to the vowels they may precede. There are thus modified and unmodified initial complexes, and this presence or absence of initial modification may be taken as a syllable property and stated in terms of two separate prosodic systems of two terms each, with their focal point in the initial complex. The terms of the first of these systems of syllable onset modification are *dark modification*, symbolized by a superior ^{w} after the pre-nuclear phonematic unit, and *absence of dark modification*, left unmarked. The terms of the second system are *clear modification*, symbolized by a superior ^{y} after the pre-nuclear phonematic unit, and *absence of clear modification*, left unmarked. Using the abbreviation Pr for pre-nuclear phonematic unit, we may make the following generalized statements:

Pr^{w}	precludes	Pr^{y}
^{w}Pr	precludes	Pr^{w}
^{yw}Pr	tends to preclude	Pr^{w}

Arguing from the above, we shall assume that ^{y}Pr precludes Pr^{y}, and that ^{yw}Pr tends to preclude Pr^{y}. NV **ch** < 'ch' and **v**, SV **c** and **(b)j** are interpreted as the cumulative phonetic exponents in the two dialects of ^{ə}Pr^{y} and ^{w}Pr^{y} respectively, and the initials **ch** and **c** before a labial semivowel, as in finals A 67, 141, 143 and B 66–67, 74, 141, 143, as those of ^{yw}Pr^{y}.

To the unmodified initial complexes in Table C we may now add, in Table D below, the modified initial complexes interpreted as combinations of clear or dark modification prosodies in association with pre-nuclear phonematic units and syllable onset prosodies:

TABLE D

Syllable onset prosodies	*Syllable onset modification*					
	System 1					*System 2*
	Pr^{w}					Pr^{y}
	δ	ψ	μ	σ	ρ	
w	—	—	—	—	—*	NV **v**, SV **(b)j**
y	**tw**	**thw**	**ɲw**	**sw**	SV **jw** < 'd' NV **zw** < 'd'	—
ə	**kw**	NV **xw** SV **x(w)**	**ŋw**	NV **hw** SV **ʔw**	**lw**	NV **ch** < 'ch' SV **c**
yw	**ɗw**	SV **tɹw** NV **chw** < 'tr'	**nw**	SV **ʃw** NV **sw** < 's'	—	NV **chw** < 'ch' SV **cw**

* With the one exception discussed on p. 182.

The above at once raises a new question. Why are there five values stateable for Pr^{w} and only one for Pr^{y}? A hint of an answer in historical terms, assuming the gradual convergence of the exponents of ^{w}Pr, ^{ə}Pr and ^{yw}Pr in association with clear modification, is perhaps to be seen in the tendency in modern SV for the labial semivowel to be pronounced very lightly and frequently to be dropped altogether so that we must either suppose that the exponents of $^{ə}\psi^{w}$, for example, converge with those of $^{ə}\psi$ or, alternatively, that $^{ə}\psi^{w}$ does not occur. Note also that for $^{ə}\sigma^{w}$ where NV still has **hw**, SV pronounces **ʔw**, which may be regarded as a step towards the more generalized ^{ə}Pr^{w}.

Our discussions in this section so far have dealt almost exclusively with three-place structures, for the first place of which a system of pre-nuclear phonematic units is stateable. Syllables without an initial consonantal articulation, or with a weak initial glottal stop, are regarded as having a two-place structure. Two-place structures have no pre-nuclear phonematic units. A system of nuclear phonematic units is stated for the first place, and a system of post-nuclear phonematic units for the second place. The system of syllable-onset prosodies stateable for such structures is one of three terms only and is co-terminous with the nuclear resonance system.[52] It is for this reason that Vietnamese syllable structure cannot conveniently be stated in terms of a three-place structure only, with zero consonant as the sixth term in the system of pre-nuclear phonematic units, since the relation of such a sixth phonematic unit with the syllable onset prosodies and the nuclear prosodies would be gravely at variance with those of the other five. Anticipating the phonological description of the nucleus for a moment,[53] this may be expressed as follows:

$$^{w}\mathrm{Pr}\ \text{presupposes}\ ^{w}\mathrm{Nu},\ ^{y}\mathrm{Nu}\ \text{or}\ ^{ə}\mathrm{Nu};\ \mathrm{Pr}^{w}\ \text{precludes}\ ^{w}\mathrm{Nu}.$$

Now the possible phonetic exponents that might be stated for ^{w} zero are *either* an initial labial semivowel, *or* an initial back rounded vowel. But if ^{w}zero = w-, it will be found to preclude ^{w}Nu, and if ^{w}zero = an initial back rounded vowel, it will be found to preclude ^{ə}Nu and ^{y}Nu. Either way, the interior syntagmatic relations of syllable structures containing zero in first place would be quite different from those of syllables containing one of the five pre-nuclear units postulated earlier. In short, the structures of such syllables are different. It has been decided to handle the difference in this paper by describing one set of structures as having three places and the other as having two.

Problems 5–11. It is convenient to look at problems involving vocalic and final consonontal elements together, since there is considerable interplay between the two, especially in SV.

We shall propose a nuclear phonematic system of two terms for the second place in three-place structures, and for the first in two-place structures, and a post-nuclear phonematic system of three terms for place three in three-place structures and place two in two-place structures. To handle syllable resonance qualities we shall require to postulate two prosodic systems, one with its focal point in the syllable nucleus and the other with its focal point in the syllable ending. In the phonological notation of post-nuclear phonematic units, letters already used for the pre-nuclear phonematic units will be avoided in order to emphasize the fact that, despite any phonetic similarity we may detect between the consonant sounds at the beginning and at the end of syllables, no special phonological relations obtain between the pre-nuclear and post-nuclear phonematic systems, other than that both are marginal as opposed to nuclear. With the prosodies it is otherwise, since there are in given cases syntagmatic relations to be stated between syllable onset prosodies and onset modification prosodies, between onset modification prosodies and nuclear prosodies, between both syllable onset prosodies and onset modification and syllable terminating prosodies, and between nuclear prosodies and either one or both of the marginal prosodic systems.[54] We shall thus find it convenient to use the same symbols and some of the same labels as were used in the statement of syllable onset prosodies.

The nuclear phonematic system is as follows:

Terms	*Phonetic Exponents*
ι	Relatively close tongue position.
α	Relatively open tongue position.

The post-nuclear phonematic system is as follows:

Terms	*Phonetic Exponents*
τ	Complete closure of both oral and nasal passages, with abrupt cutting off of airstream.
ν	Closure at some point in the mouth with lowered soft palate, allowing the passage of voiced air through the nose.
ζ	Absence of closure in the mouth, allowing passage of voiced air without audible friction.

The two prosodic systems stateable as having their focal point in the syllable nucleus are as follows:

Nuclear Resonance System

Terms		*Phonetic Exponents*
Dark	(w)	Back of tongue raised, lips rounded.
Clear	(y)	Front of tongue raised, lips unrounded.
Neutral	(ə)	Retracted tongue position, i.e. centre or back of tongue raised, lips unrounded.

Nuclear Extension System

Terms	*Phonetic Exponents*
Central extension (a)	*Either* more open tongue position than when extension is absent, with or without centralized vocalic off-glide, *or* prolongation of vowel with or without centralized off-glide.
Absence of central extension (unmarked)	Absence of prolongation of vowel or of centralized off-glide, with or without closer tongue position than when extension is present.

The syllable-terminating prosodic system is as follows:

Terms		*Phonetic Exponents*
Dark	(w)	Bilabial articulation.
Clear	(y)	Lips spread or neutral, with *either* tip or blade of tongue brought into contact with the denti-alveolar region, *or* dorsum raised towards the hard palate or velum.
Neutral	(ə)	Lips spread or neutral with dorsum either raised towards the soft palate or in neutral position, i.e. rather low in the mouth, not raised to any marked degree towards the hard palate.

Table E below lists the phonematic structures for the penultimate and ultimate places in Vietnamese syllables together with the prosodies having their focal point in the syllable nucleus and ending, and a phonetic transcription of the pronunciations with which they are associated in the two dialects. The statement assumes the same phonological structure for both NV and SV, and handles the differences between them as differences of phonetic exponency only.[55] Where convergence of phonetic exponents is postulated, square brackets enclose the second entry in the table of the relevant phonetic sequence. Where divergence is postulated, the second pronunciation shown is enclosed in round brackets. Pure vowels and diphthongs in apparently free variation (as SV **e** and **ei**) or phonetically determined variation (as NV **ɛ** and **ɛə**) are separated by a comma. In the phonological formulae, the symbols for the prosodies of the nuclear resonance system are placed to the left of the nuclear phonematic symbol, symbols for the prosodies of the nuclear extension system to the right of it. The symbols for syllable

TABLE E

	NV	SV		NV	SV		NV	SV
${}^{ə}\iota\zeta^{y}$	i	i, ɪi	${}^{ə}\iota\zeta^{y}$	əi	ɨi	${}^{w}\iota\zeta^{y}$	ui	ui
${}^{ə}\iota\zeta^{ə}$	iə	iə	${}^{ə}\iota\zeta^{ə}$	ɤ	ɤ, ʌɤ	${}^{w}\iota\zeta^{ə}$	uə	uə
${}^{ə}\iota\zeta^{w}$	iu	iu	${}^{ə}\iota\zeta^{w}$	əu	au	${}^{w}\iota\zeta^{w}$	u	u, ʊu
${}^{ə}\iota\tau^{y}$	it	ɨt	${}^{ə}\iota\tau^{y}$	ət, (ɯt)	ɯk	${}^{w}\iota\tau^{y}$	ut	uk
${}^{ə}\iota\tau^{ə}$	ïik̡	ət	${}^{ə}\iota\tau^{ə}$	ək	ʌk	${}^{w}\iota\tau^{ə}$	uk͡p	ok
${}^{ə}\iota\tau^{w}$	ip	ip	${}^{ə}\iota\tau^{w}$	əp	ɯp, (ɤp)	${}^{w}\iota\tau^{w}$	up	up
${}^{ə}\iota\nu^{y}$	in	ɨn	${}^{ə}\iota\nu^{y}$	ən	ɯŋ	${}^{w}\ddot{\iota}\nu^{y}$	un	uŋ
${}^{ə}\iota\nu^{ə}$	ïiŋ̡	ən	${}^{ə}\iota\nu^{ə}$	əŋ, (ɯŋ)	ʌŋ	${}^{w}\iota\nu^{ə}$	uŋ͡m	oŋ
${}^{ə}\iota\nu^{w}$	im	im	${}^{ə}\iota\nu^{w}$	əm	ɯəm, (ɤm)	${}^{w}\iota\nu^{w}$	um	um
${}^{ə}{}_{\iota}{}^{a}\zeta^{y}$	[i]	[i, ɪi]	${}^{ə}{}_{\iota}{}^{a}\zeta^{y}$	ɯəi, (ɤi, ɯi)	ɯi, (ɤi)	${}^{w}{}_{\iota}{}^{a}\zeta^{y}$	uəi	[ui]
${}^{ə}{}_{\iota}{}^{a}\zeta^{ə}$	[iə]	[iə]	${}^{ə}{}_{\iota}{}^{a}\zeta^{ə}$	ɯə	ɯə	${}^{w}{}_{\ddot{\iota}}{}^{a}\zeta^{ə}$	[uə]	[uə]
${}^{ə}{}_{\iota}{}^{a}\zeta^{w}$	iəu	[iu]	${}^{ə}{}_{\iota}{}^{a}\zeta^{w}$	ɯəu, (ɯu)	ɯu	${}^{w}{}_{\iota}{}^{a}\zeta^{w}$	[u]	[u]
${}^{ə}{}_{\iota}{}^{a}{}_{\tau}{}^{y}$	iət	iək	${}^{ə}{}_{\iota}{}^{a}{}_{\tau}{}^{y}$	ɯət, (ɤt)	ɯək	${}^{w}{}_{\iota}{}^{a}{}_{\tau}{}^{y}$	uət	uək
${}^{ə}{}_{\iota}{}^{a}{}_{\tau}{}^{ə}$	iək	[iək]	${}^{ə}{}_{\iota}{}^{a}{}_{\tau}{}^{ə}$	ɯək	[ɯək]	${}^{w}{}_{\iota}{}^{a}{}_{\tau}{}^{ə}$	uək	[uək]
${}^{ə}{}_{\iota}{}^{a}{}_{\tau}{}^{w}$	iəp	[ip]	${}^{ə}{}_{\iota}{}^{a}{}_{\tau}{}^{w}$	ɯəp, (ɤp)	[ɯp, (ɤp)	${}^{w}{}_{\iota}{}^{a}{}_{\tau}{}^{w}$	[up]	[up]
${}^{ə}{}_{\iota}{}^{a}{}_{\nu}{}^{y}$	iən	iəŋ	${}^{ə}{}_{\iota}{}^{a}{}_{\nu}{}^{y}$	ɯən, (ɤn)	ɯəŋ	${}^{w}{}_{\iota}{}^{a}{}_{\nu}{}^{y}$	uən	uəŋ
${}^{ə}{}_{\iota}{}^{a}{}_{\nu}{}^{ə}$	iəŋ	[iəŋ]	${}^{ə}{}_{\iota}{}^{a}{}_{\nu}{}^{ə}$	ɯəŋ	[ɯəŋ]	${}^{w}{}_{\iota}{}^{a}{}_{\nu}{}^{ə}$	uəŋ	[uəŋ]
${}^{ə}{}_{\iota}{}^{a}{}_{\nu}{}^{w}$	iəm	[im]	${}^{ə}{}_{\iota}{}^{a}{}_{\nu}{}^{w}$	ɯəm, (ɤm)	[ɯəm, (ɤm)]	${}^{w}{}_{\iota}{}^{a}{}_{\nu}{}^{w}$	uəm	[um]
${}^{ə}\alpha\zeta^{y}$	e	e, ei	${}^{ə}\alpha\zeta^{y}$	ai	a:i	${}^{w}\alpha\zeta^{y}$	oi	oi
${}^{ə}\alpha\zeta^{ə}$	ɛ, ɛə	ɛ	${}^{ə}\alpha\zeta^{ə}$	a	a	${}^{w}\alpha\zeta^{ə}$	ɔ, ɔə	ɔ
${}^{ə}\alpha\zeta^{w}$	eu	eu	${}^{ə}\alpha\zeta^{w}$	au	a:u	${}^{w}\alpha\zeta^{w}$	o	o, ou
${}^{ə}\alpha\tau^{y}$	et	[ət]	${}^{ə}\alpha\tau^{y}$	at	ak	${}^{w}\alpha\tau^{y}$	ot	[ok]
${}^{ə}\alpha\tau^{ə}$	ëik̡	ɐt	${}^{ə}\alpha\tau^{ə}$	ak	ɤk	${}^{w}\alpha\tau^{ə}$	auk͡p	ɔk
${}^{ə}\alpha\tau^{w}$	ep	ep	${}^{ə}\alpha\tau^{w}$	ap	ap	${}^{w}\alpha\tau^{w}$	op	op
${}^{ə}\alpha\nu^{y}$	en	[ən]	${}^{ə}\alpha\nu^{y}$	an	aŋ	${}^{w}\alpha\nu^{y}$	on	[oŋ]
${}^{ə}\alpha\nu^{ə}$	ëiŋ̡	ɐn	${}^{ə}\alpha\nu^{ə}$	aŋ	ɤŋ	${}^{w}\alpha\nu^{ə}$	əuŋ͡m	ɔŋ
${}^{ə}\alpha\nu^{w}$	em	em	${}^{ə}\alpha\nu^{w}$	am	am	${}^{w}\alpha\nu^{w}$	om	om
${}^{ə}\alpha^{a}\zeta^{y}$	[e]	[e, ei]	${}^{ə}\alpha^{a}\zeta^{y}$	a:i	[a:i]	${}^{w}\alpha^{a}\zeta^{y}$	ɔi	ɔi
${}^{ə}\alpha^{a}\zeta^{ə}$	[ɛ, ɛə]	[ɛ]	${}^{ə}\alpha^{ə}\zeta^{ə}$	a	a	${}^{w}\alpha^{a}\zeta^{ə}$	[ɔ, ɔə]	[ɔ]
${}^{ə}\alpha^{a}\zeta^{w}$	ɛu	ɛu	${}^{ə}\alpha^{a}\zeta^{w}$	a:u	[a:u]	${}^{w}\alpha^{a}\zeta^{w}$	[o]	[o, ou]
${}^{ə}\alpha^{a}{}_{\tau}{}^{y}$	ɛt	ɛək	${}^{ə}\alpha^{a}{}_{\tau}{}^{y}$	a:t	a:k	${}^{w}\alpha^{a}{}_{\tau}{}^{y}$	ɔt	auk͡p
${}^{ə}\alpha^{a}{}_{\tau}{}^{ə}$	ɛ̈ik̡, (ɛk)	[ɛək]	${}^{ə}\alpha^{a}{}_{\tau}{}^{ə}$	a:k	[a:k]	${}^{w}\alpha^{a}{}_{\tau}{}^{ə}$	auk͡p	[auk͡p]
${}^{ə}\alpha^{a}{}_{\tau}{}^{w}$	ɛp	ɛp	${}^{ə}\alpha^{a}{}_{\tau}{}^{w}$	a:p	a:p	${}^{w}\alpha^{a}{}_{\tau}{}^{w}$	ɔp	ɔp
${}^{ə}\alpha^{a}{}_{\nu}{}^{y}$	ɛn	ɛəŋ	${}^{ə}\alpha^{a}{}_{\nu}{}^{y}$	a:n	a:ŋ	${}^{w}\alpha^{a}{}_{\nu}{}^{y}$	ɔn	auŋ͡m, (ɔŋ͡m)
${}^{ə}\alpha^{a}{}_{\nu}{}^{ə}$	ɛ̈iŋ̡, (ɛŋ)	[ɛəŋ]	${}^{ə}\alpha^{a}{}_{\nu}{}^{ə}$	a:ŋ	[a:ŋ]	${}^{w}\alpha^{a}{}_{\nu}{}^{ə}$	auŋ͡m, (ɔŋ)	[auŋ͡m, (ɔm͡ŋ)]
${}^{ə}\alpha^{a}{}_{\nu}{}^{w}$	ɛm	ɛm	${}^{ə}\alpha^{a}{}_{\nu}{}^{w}$	a:m	a:m	${}^{w}\alpha^{a}{}_{\nu}{}^{w}$	ɔm	ɔm

terminating prosodies are placed after the symbol for the post-nuclear phonematic unit.

The above statement goes a long way towards solving Problems 5, 6, and 7. The system proposed does not require that there should be vowels identifiable with 'ă' and 'â' in phonetically open syllables. The only probable 'gaps' that such vowels, if they existed, might conceivably fill are ᵊιζᵊ and ᵊαζᵊ, which are satisfactorily filled already. The variations in vowel length and diphthongization mentioned in Problem 6 no longer appear haphazard. By and large, shortness or length of vowel occurs where one would expect, and the diphthongization of NV **ɛə** and **ɔə** and of SV **ɪi, ei, ou, ʊu** are not only explicable in terms of phonetic exponents but are even predictable. The apparent gaps in the diphthongs referred to in Problem 7 (i) are seen not to be gaps at all in our system. All diphthongs are exponents of Nuζ structures. Where both nuclear and terminating prosody are of the same type, i.e. both dark, both clear, or both neutral, the cumulative exponents of the nuclear prosody and nuclear phonematic unit may extend through to the end of the syllable without perceptible change. This is commonly the case in NV. In SV there is frequently a slight raising of the tongue towards the end of the syllable so that a narrow closing diphthong is heard. Problem 7 (ii) is one no longer in the light of Table E, since the occurrences mentioned are perfectly systematic and in keeping with those dealt with under 7(i). Problem 7(iii) is more difficult, and I here suggest recourse to the concept of divergence. The recorded instances of 'ưu' in NV are few in number (23 out of a theoretical maximum of 144), those of 'ươu' even fewer (8 out of 144), and there is one solitary example of 'ơu' in the word 'nớu' *gum*. If the attested syllables containing these finals are examined as wholes, taking into account the initial consonants and the tone as well as the final, it is found that the only overlapping forms recorded are 'hươu' and 'hưu'. It is suggested that **ɯəu**, **ɯu** and **ɤu** are to be regarded as divergent sets of phonetic exponents of ᵊιᵃζʷ in NV, and that the conditions under which one form or another is to be expected, which are still to be investigated, will probably turn out to be partly phonetic, i.e. linked with the initial consonant or initial modification or with the tone, and partly a matter of primary and secondary patterns, i.e. there may be a difference in behaviour in this respect between indigenous words of the primary pattern[56] and borrowed words of Chinese origin for which a secondary pattern requires to be stated. From a preliminary check with dictionaries it seems probable that 'hưu' and 'nớu' should be assigned to secondary patterns. It is of interest here that there is convergence of 'ươu' and 'ưu' in SV.[57] My SV informant did not know the form 'nớu' although he believed that he might have heard it. Similar arguments to those used above can be brought to support the grouping together of **ɯəi**, **ɤi** and **ɯi** as divergent phonetic exponents of $^{ə}\iota^{a}\zeta^{y}$. It is noteworthy in this case that of the four recorded instances of **ɯi**, one was recorded by my informant as being in free variation with **ɯəi**, and a second as being in free variation with **ɤi**.

Problem 8. (i) Table E enables us to make the generalized statement that where Nu = ι, there is in SV convergence everywhere of NuPo^{w} and Nu^{a}Po^{w}, and, except when Po = ζ, convergence of Nu^{a}Po^{ə} and Nu^{a}Po^{y}. The final retracted apical contact of SV **ɨt, ɨn, ət, ən, ɐt** and **ɐn** arises from the combination of exponents of ^{y}Nu with those of Po^{ə} and Po^{y} when there is no intervening extension prosody.[58] The velar contact of **ɯk, ʌk, ɯŋ, ʌŋ, ak, aŋ, a:k, a:ŋ, uk, ok, ɔk**, etc. arises from the combination of exponents of ^{ə}Nu and ^{w}Nu and of any nucleus with an extension prosody with those of Po^{ə} and Po^{y}. There is in general no convergence in syllables characterized by absence of nuclear extension, i.e. the exponents of ^{ə}Nu Po^{y} and ^{ə}Nu Po^{ə}, and of ^{w}Nu Po^{y} and ^{w}Nu Po^{ə} do not converge, but variation in usage among SV speakers as regards the finals spelt 'ich', 'êch' and 'ach' supports the suggestion made in Table E that there may be convergence of $^{y}\iota\tau^{ə}$ and $^{y}\alpha\tau^{y}$, i.e. the closeness of **ɨ** in **ɨt, ɨn**, as opposed to **ə** is a cumulative exponent of ι as opposed to α and of Po^{y} as opposed to Po^{ə}. Similarly, **ə** is variously an exponent both of α as opposed to ι and of Po^{y} as opposed to Po^{ə} in Po^{y} syllables, and of Po^{ə} as opposed to Po^{y} in $^{y}\iota$ syllables. We may generalize further by saying that in syllables without nuclear extension extra openness of vowel is everywhere an exponent of Po^{ə} as contrasted with Po^{y}, with convergence of $^{y}\iota$Po^{ə} and $^{y}\alpha$Po^{y} and of $^{w}\iota$Po^{ə} and $^{w}\alpha$Po^{y} except where Po = ζ, viz.:

$^{y}\iota\tau^{y}$	$^{y}\iota\nu^{y}$	$^{ə}\iota\tau^{y}$	$^{ə}\iota\nu^{y}$	$^{w}\iota\tau^{y}$	$^{w}\iota\nu^{y}$
ɨt	**ɨn**	**ɯk**	**ɯŋ**	**uk**	**uŋ**
$^{y}\iota\tau^{ə}$	$^{y}\iota\nu^{ə}$	$^{ə}\iota\tau^{ə}$	$^{ə}\iota\nu^{ə}$	$^{w}\iota\tau^{ə}$	$^{w}\iota\nu^{ə}$
ət	**ən**	**ʌk**	**ʌŋ**	**ok**	**oŋ**
$^{y}\alpha\tau^{y}$	$^{y}\alpha\nu^{y}$	$^{ə}\alpha\tau^{y}$	$^{ə}\alpha\nu^{y}$	$^{w}\alpha\tau^{y}$	$^{w}\alpha\nu^{y}$
ət	**ən**	**ak**	**aŋ**	**ok**	**oŋ**
$^{y}\alpha\tau^{ə}$	$^{y}\alpha\nu^{ə}$	$^{ə}\alpha\tau^{ə}$	$^{ə}\alpha\nu^{ə}$	$^{w}\alpha\tau^{ə}$	$^{w}\alpha\nu^{ə}$
ɐt	**ɐn**	**ɤk**	**ɤŋ**	**ɔk**	**ɔŋ**

(ii) The centrality of **ə** and **ɐ** in Po^{ə} structures may be accounted an exponent of Po^{ə}, but the centrality of **ɨ** and **ə** in Po^{y} structures remains puzzling.

Problem 9. NV ïik̜, ëik̜, ɛ̈ik̜, ïiŋ̜, ëiŋ̜, ɛ̈iŋ̜ are interpreted as cumulations of discontinuous exponents of ^{y}Nu Po^{ə} and ^{ə}Nu Po^{ə} structures in the primary phonetic pattern in which the realization of the nuclear and syllable-terminating prosodies extends over the whole of the final complex. Thus, the centralization of the vowel and the final velar articulation are exponents of neutral syllable termination, while the palatal on-glide to the final consonant and the fronted articulation of that consonant are exponents of clear nuclear resonance. The very few words with final **ɛk** and **ɛŋ** are mostly onomatopes or loans or bound forms[59] and are as such regarded as demonstrating a secondary phonological pattern of which, as contrasted with the primary pattern discussed above, the phonetic exponents are discrete.[60]

Problem 10. A similarity of pattern between the finals under consideration here and those discussed under Problem 9 may be discerned. We are dealing with the cumulative exponents in NV of $^{w}\alpha$Po^{ə} and $^{w}\alpha^{a}$Po^{ə}, and in SV of $^{w}\alpha^{a}$ Po^{ə}, in which the unrounded and central quality of the vowel and final velar articulation are exponents of neutral syllable termination and the rounded back on-glide and final labial closure are exponents of dark nuclear resonance. The final 'oong', which is only found in a few words of fairly recent French borrowing,[61] follows a secondary pattern appropriate to unassimilated loans. It is of interest here that SV **ɔŋ** < 'on' is kept distinct in pronunciation from **ɔŋ͡m** < 'oong'.[62]

Problem 11. Since Pr^{w} precludes ^{w}Nu, it presupposes ^{y}Nu or ^{ə}Nu. We shall expect, therefore, to find phonetic sequences of labial semivowel and vowel which can be associated with $^{y}\iota$, $^{y}\alpha$, $^{ə}\iota$, and $^{ə}\alpha$ in Po^{w} structures. This is indeed what we find, syllables with final 'uy', 'uych', etc., being associated with $^{wy}\iota$, 'uya', 'uyên, 'uyêt' finals with $^{wy}\iota^{a}$, 'uê' finals with $^{wy}\alpha$, 'oe' finals with $^{wy}\alpha^{a}$, 'oă' finals with $^{wə}\alpha$, 'oa' finals with $^{wə}\alpha^{a}$, 'uâ' finals with $^{wə}\iota$, and the final 'uơ' with $^{wə}\iota^{a}$. The limitation of initial consonants before the final 'ư' which is referred to in Problem 14 (i) falls into place when we observe that, with the exception of three words in each dialect,[63] no consonants associated with dark syllable onset occur before **ɯ** in open syllables. This suggests the interpretation of **ɯ** in open syllables as a cumulation of the phonetic exponents of $^{wə}\iota\zeta^{ə}$, leaving the problem of the three exceptions in each dialect for further investigation.

Problem 12. Examination of the phonic data shows that syllables containing a labial semivowel are rarely closed by a labial consonant or by a diphthong ending in a rounded vowel. Furthermore, of the recorded instances, many upon closer investigation turn out to be words which might appropriately be excluded from the primary system such as onomatopes, ideophones, recent loans and the like. There remain, however, a number of forms which cannot, on the face of it, be so excluded. We cannot therefore say that in the primary system Pr^{w} precludes Po^{w} absolutely, but only that it tends to do so. It might perhaps be expected to follow from this that Pr^{w} would presuppose $\mathrm{Po}^{ə}$ and Po^{y} without restriction, but the phonic data for NV[64] suggest otherwise. We find that **wa:** and **wa** appear to occur freely before both **-n** and **-ŋ**, **-t** and **-k**, and before **-i**, but that with very few exceptions other than forms which are clearly assignable to a secondary system, or which are bound forms found in compounds only,[65] **ɥə** and **ɥiə** occur only before final **-n**, and **-t** and **-i**, and **wɛ** and **ɥi** only before final **-ŋ** and **-k**. **ɥe** is very rare in any context, but what examples there are in closed syllables occur before **-k** and **ŋ** and are without exception potential secondary structures. In phonological terms, we find a preference in the primary system for ${}^{wy}\iota\mathrm{Po}^{ə}$ as against ${}^{wy}\iota\mathrm{Po}^{y}$, ${}^{wy}\alpha^{a}\mathrm{Po}^{ə}$ as against ${}^{wy}\alpha^{a}\mathrm{Po}^{y}$, ${}^{wy}\iota^{a}\mathrm{Po}^{y}$ as against ${}^{wy}\iota^{a}\mathrm{Po}^{ə}$, and for ${}^{wə}\iota\mathrm{Po}^{y}$ as against ${}^{wə}\iota\mathrm{Po}^{ə}$. There appears to be no preference as between ${}^{wə}\alpha\mathrm{Po}^{y}$ and ${}^{wə}\alpha\mathrm{Po}^{ə}$, or as between ${}^{wə}\alpha^{a}\mathrm{Po}^{y}$ and ${}^{wə}\alpha^{a}\mathrm{Po}^{ə}$. From the above we may conclude that there is a tendency in Pr^{w} syllables for ${}^{y}\mathrm{Nu}$ to preclude Po^{y} and for ${}^{ə}\mathrm{Nu}$ to preclude $\mathrm{Po}^{ə}$, except where ${}^{ə}\mathrm{Nu} = {}^{ə}\alpha$. We may make the further generalization that there is a tendency in the primary system as a whole to avoid Pr^{w} structures having two dark, two clear or two neutral prosodies focused upon the part of the syllable following the initial consonant, i.e. there is a tendency to avoid such structures as Pr^{w} Nu Po^{w}, Pr^{wy} Nu Po^{y} or $\mathrm{Pr}^{wə}$ Nu $\mathrm{Po}^{ə}$. This hypothesis fails, however, to account for the preference for ${}^{wy}\iota^{a}$ Po^{y} (‘-uyêt’, ‘-uyên), as against ${}^{wy}\iota^{a}$ $\mathrm{Po}^{ə}$. If it is extended to apply in some measure to prosodies focused upon the initial consonant itself, it does, however, go some way towards accounting for the phenomena mentioned in Problem 14 (iv), and also, in Problem 14(v), for the velar articulation of the consonant occurring before **ɥe**, **ɥiə** and **ɥiu** but not for the fact that it is a fricative rather than a plosive.

Some of the questions raised under Problems 13 and 14 have already been touched upon in the preceding pages and tentative answers to some of them given. The patchy distribution of closed syllables containing the vowels written ‘ư’ and ‘ơ’ and of the diphthongs and triphthongs written ‘ưi’, ‘ơi’, ‘ưu’, ‘ơu’, ‘ươu’ and ‘ươi’, together with the number of recorded instances of variation between such finals as 'ưn' ~ 'ân', 'ưi' ~ 'ơi', 'ưng' ~ 'âng', 'ưt' ~ 'ât', 'ươi' ~ 'ơi', 'ơn' ~ 'ân', etc., has prompted the suggestion that in Problem 13 (i) and (ii) we are probably concerned with divergence of phonetic exponents of structural elements, arising in part from the intermingling with the primary phonological system of secondary systems which we are at present unable to sift out. No solution to Problem 13 (iii) has so far suggested itself. A solution to Problem 14 (i) has already been put forward, in the course of the discussion of Problem 11. Problem 14 (ii), (iii) (iv) and (v) remain baffling, despite the faint light shed on the latter two in the discussion of Problem 12. Further study jointly with Problems 4 and 16 is required before a solution can be expected.

Summary

The elements of syllable structure here proposed[66] and the syntagmatic relations within the syllable that have a bearing on the problems under review are summarized briefly below. The symbol π is used to designate the prosodic systems, which are identified by number as follows: π_1 = syllable onset; π_2 = onset modification; π_3 = nuclear; π_4 = nuclear extension; π_5 = syllable termination.

Syllable structure = $^{\pi_1}\mathrm{Pr}\ ^{\pi_2\pi_3}\mathrm{Nu}^{\pi_4}\mathrm{Po}^{\pi_5}$ or $^{\pi_2\pi_3}\mathrm{Nu}^{\pi_4}\mathrm{Po}^{\pi_5}$.

Pr = δ, ψ, μ, σ *or* ρ.
Nu = ι or α.
Po = τ, ν or ζ.
π_1 = w, y, ə or yw.
π_2 = π_{2a} or $\pi_{2b}.\pi_{2a}$ = w or non-w; π_{2b} = y or non-y.
π_3 = w, y or ə.
π_4 = a or non-a.
π_5 = w, y or ə.

π_1 = w precludes π_2 = w, and tends to preclude π_5 = w.
π_2 = w precludes π_3 = w, and tends to preclude π_5 = w.
π_1 = yw tends to preclude π_2 = y or w.
π_1 = y precludes π_2 = y, but π_2 = y does not preclude π_3 = y.
When π_2 = w, π_3 = y tends to preclude π_5 = y.
When π_2 = w, π_3 = w tends to preclude π_5 = w.
When π_2 = w, π_3 = ə tends to preclude π_5 = ə, except where Nu = α.

BIBLIOGRAPHY

W. Sidney Allen, 'Some Prosodic Aspects of Retroflexion and Aspiration in Sanskrit', *BSOAS* XIII (1951), pp. 939–946.

Arthur C. Day, 'Final Consonants in Northern Vietnamese', *Transactions of the Historical Research Institute*, 3, Saigon (1962), pp. 3–22.

Murray B. Emeneau, *Studies in Vietnamese (Annamese) Grammar* (University of California Press, Berkeley and Los Angeles, 1951).

John R. Firth, (1) 'The Structure of the Chinese Monosyllable in a Hunanese Dialect (Changsha)', *BSOAS* VIII (1937); repr. in *Papers in Linguistics* (O.U.P., 1957), pp. 76–91.

(2) 'Sounds and Prosodies', *TPS* (1948); repr. in *PIL*, pp. 121–138.

(3) 'Word Palatograms and Articulation', *BSOAS* XII (1948); repr. in *PIL*, pp. 148–155.

(4) Introduction to *Studies in Linguistic Analysis* (Basil Blackwell, Oxford, 1957), pp. v–vii.

(5) 'A Synopsis of Linguistic Theory, 1930–1955', in *Studies in Linguistic Analysis*, pp. 1–32.

Michael A. K. Halliday, 'Phonological (Prosodic) Analysis of the New Chinese Syllable (Modern Pekingese)', Appendix A in *The Language of the Chinese Secret History of the Mongols* (Basil Blackwell, Oxford, 1959), pp. 192–204.

André G. Haudricourt (1) 'Les Voyelles Brèves du Vietnamien', *BSLP* XLVIII (1952), pp. 90–93.

(2) 'De L'Origine des Tons en Vietnamien', *JA* (1954), pp. 69–82.

Eugénie J. A. Henderson, (1) 'The Phonology of Loanwords in Some South-East Asian Languages', *TPS* (1951), pp. 131–158.

(2) 'The Articulation of Vietnamese -nh and -ch', paper presented to the Fifth International Congress of Phonetic Sciences, Munster, August 1964, and to be published in the proceedings.

Nguyễn Đình Hòa, *Quốc-Ngữ* (Saigon 1955), as cited by Day. I have not been able to consult a copy.

Robert B. Jones, Jr. and Huynh Sanh Thong, *Introduction to Spoken Vietnamese* (American Council of Learned Societies, Washington, D.C. 1957).

Lê Văn Lý, *Le Parler Vietnamien* (Huong Anh, Paris, 1948).

Robert H. Robins (1) 'Vowel Nasality in Sundanese. A Phonological and Grammatical Study', in *Studies in Linguistic Analysis*.

(2) 'Aspects of Prosodic Analysis', *Proceedings of the University of Durham Philosophical Society*, I (1957), pp. 1–12.

Norman C. Scott, 'A Phonological Analysis of the Szechuanese Monosyllable', *BSOAS* XVIII (1956), p. 556–560.

Harry L. Shorto, 'Word and Syllable Patterns in Palaung', *BSOAS* XXIII, 3 (1960), pp. 544–557.

Laurence C. Thompson, 'Saigon Phonemics', *Lg*, 35 (1959), pp. 454–476.

Notes

1 Firth (2), p. 123.

2 Cp. Day, pp. 3–4; Thompson, pp. 455, 473–474.

3 Scott, p. 556.

4 See Allen, p. 945.

5 It would clearly be necessary not only to check the syllable count thoroughly with many more speakers of both dialects but to match it against comparable material from the central dialect, and from as many others as possible. In order to disentangle the primary and secondary phonological patterns which are believed to lie behind much of the apparent divergence of phonetic exponents postulated here (see pp. 178, 188), it would be essential to find some means of tracking down all inter-dialectal borrowings and the odd spellings and artificial pronunciations to which they frequently give rise. It would, furthermore, be desirable to make structural comparisons with related languages, such as Mường, in which Chinese cultural influence has probably been less active, and with Chinese itself.

6 As set forth in Robins (2), p. 3.

7 Firth's adaptation of a passage in James B. Conant's *Science and Common Sense*. See Firth (5), p. 1.

8 Since the material was collected some years ago, it is likely that it is by now old-fashioned in some respects, as regards both pronunciation and usage.

9 But see note 28 on page 195.

10 For a more detailed description of the articulation of Vietnamese 'ch' and 'nh', both initial and final, see Henderson (2).

11 Cp. Emeneau, Preface, p. vii.

12 Such Southern 'mis-spellings', for example, when borrowed into the Northern dialect have sometimes led to what may be regarded either as spelling pronunciations in NV or as alien pronunciations borrowed direct from SV. For example, the Southern mis-spelling 'Chệc' for 'Chệt', a slang word meaning 'Chinese', which is quite regularly pronounced with a final **-t** in SV (see p. 189), has given rise in NV to an aberrant pronunciation **̣cek**, alongside the regular **̣cet** < Chệt. (Cp. Lý, p. 66.) In a footnote on p. 6, Day quotes the Saigon edition of Lý, which I have not seen, as citing yet another orthographic variant of the same word, 'Trệc', which appears to add the further complication of a Northern mis-spelling, 'tr' for 'ch' (see p. 167).

13 My Southern informant, with whom I worked after writing Henderson (1), may have contributed towards the clarification of the irregular Northern forms 'kéc' and 'kẻng' (see p. 174 and Henderson (1), p. 151) when he pointed out that his own regular spelling of the SV word corresponding to NV 'kẻng' was 'kẻn', and that he recognized a variant spelling 'két' for 'kéc'. He was also of the opinion that 'xẻng', for which a Chinese origin is suggested in Henderson (1) (p. 151), is Southern in origin.

14 Missing are the figures for the finals 'ua', '-uôc/-uôt' and 'uôn/-uông', and for finals 20–27 inclusive, and final 104, with initials 20–24.

15 Jones and Thong report (p. 64) that the spelling sequence 'ênh' 'does not occur in SV, being replaced by "inh" and pronounced accordingly'. They also imply (p. 68) that the sequence 'âc' does not occur. My informant produced, without prompting, examples of both spellings. As he confessed to considerable uncertainty as to the 'correct' final consonant letter in such cases, however, it is possible that some of his examples appear in the Jones and Thong material spelt with final '-t'.

16 Cp. Emeneau, p. 12: 'Allophones are few, and the chief problem is the relation between initial and final consonants', and pp. 14–15.

17 Cp. Thompson, p. 469; Emeneau, pp. 6–7, 14–15.

18 Cp. Emeneau, pp. 12–13, 21; Lý, p. 104; Thompson, pp. 474–475; Jones and Thong, p. 66.

19 Cp. Emeneau, p. 15; Day, p. 11; Lý, p. 22.

20 My principal NV informant regularly pronounced **ɛə** and **ɔə** in syllables with the huyền, hỏi and ngã tones. For the differences in vowel length and diphthongization see Emeneau, pp. 5–6, 9–10; Thompson, pp. 461–464, 471–472, 475–476; Lý, pp. 39–40; Day, p. 11; Haudricourt (1).

21 Cp. Day, pp. 9–10; Lý, p. 55; Emeneau, pp. 10, 12–13; Jones and Thong, p. 67; Thompson, pp. 467, 473.

22 Cp. Thompson, pp. 462–464, 467–468; Jones and Thong, pp. 67–68; Hòa, as quoted by Day, in Day, fn. to p. 8.

23 Cp. Emeneau, pp. 6–7, 9, 14–16; Day, pp. 6–9; Jones and Thong, pp. 63, 225–226; Haudricourt (1), pp. 91–93; Lý, p. 45.

24 Cp. Emeneau, pp. 6, 8, 10, 13–14; Day, pp. 7–9; Haudricourt (1), pp. 92–93; Thompson, p. 460, 467–468, 473; Jones and Thong, pp. 2–3.

25 Cp. Thompson, p. 466.

26 Cp. Thompson, p. 466; Emeneau, p. 16.

27 Cp. Day, pp. 7–8, fn. 6 on p. 5; Emeneau, pp. 16, 20–21; Jones and Thong, p. 68.

28 Cp. Emeneau, pp. 12–13, 30. Emeneau notes an example of 'gi' before 'ê' in 'giền' **\zen** *amaranth*.

29 Haudricourt (2).

30 Firth (2), p. 121.

31 Firth (2), p. 137.

32 Firth (1), p. 79. The phonetic transcription in Tables A and B represents an attempt, unsatisfactory in some respects, at dissection in general phonetic terms.

33 See Firth (1), p. 80; Robins (1), p. 88. Cp. Halliday's 'points' or 'positions', Halliday, p. 193.

34 Cp. Robins (2), p. 3.

35 Firth (1), p. 80. Cp. also Firth (1), p. 86; Firth (2), pp. 127, 128, 133; Scott, pp. 556–557; Halliday, p. 193.

36 See Allen, p. 943; Robins (1), p. 88.

37 See Firth (4), p. vi.

38 Firth (5), p. 31. Cp. also op. cit., p. 20.

39 By 'Roman-based' is meant 'turned e' the symbol ə.

40 Firth (5), p. 31.

41 Cp. Firth (5), pp. 15, 25, 31.

42 Numerical disparity is, however, of some concern in phonemic analysis, since

phonemicists usually feel required to decide whether, for instance, final [p] is to be regarded as an allophone of the same phoneme as initial [ɓ], or whether final [t] is to be grouped with initial [t], [th] or [ɗ]. See Emeneau, pp. 14–15; Thompson, pp. 458–460, 470.

43 The term 'dorsum' is used here to designate the upper surface of the tongue excluding the tip and blade; 'dorsal' articulations are those in which the articulating organ is the dorsum; 'apical' articulations are those in which the articulating organ is the tip or blade. Cp. Firth (3), p. 154.

44 It must not be assumed that these exponents are necessarily restricted to the initial consonant articulation. They may on occasion extend into the following vowel, and even beyond. For example, in SV 'vịt' [ˌ**bjit̪**] *duck*, both the fully front pronunciation of the vowel as contrasted with the centralized pronunciation in other contexts (see Table B) and the dental articulation of the final consonant, as attested by palatograms, are exponents of y-onset modification prosody. In SV 'tết' [ˈt̪ət̪] *New Year*, palatograms show that both initial and final consonants are dental. The dental articulation of the final consonant must here be accounted an exponent of y-onset prosody, despite the intervening centralized vowel. That it is not an exponent of y post-nuclear resonance prosody is demonstrated by the fact that elsewhere final **-t** is post-alveolar after y resonance vowels.

45 See p. 166.

46 See p. 180.

47 Cp. Lý, pp. 40–41.

48 Cp. Firth (2), p. 136; Henderson (1), esp. pp. 152–153.

49 My colleague P. J. Honey tells me, however, that there is, in his experience, frequently uncertainty among Northern Vietnamese as to the spelling of words with 'x' or 's', 'ch' or 'tr', and 'r', 'gi' or 'd'.

50 Not recorded for the Vinh dialect by Emeneau, who lists **ɣ** among the consonants never found before **w** (p. 12).

51 At first sight initial **w-** might seem an even more likely candidate, but the non-occurrence of this sound before a following back rounded vowel is out of agreement with the relations of the other phonematic units and onset prosodies with nuclear elements. See p. 184. An alternative solution might be the transposition of **ɣ** and SV **ɹ**, NV **z** < 'r', in Table C, since yw- onset prosody does not preclude a following **w** absolutely. See p. 183.

52 See p. 185.

53 See pp. 185–187. In what follows, the abbreviation Pr is sometimes used for 'pre-nuclear phonematic unit', Nu for 'nuclear phonematic unit', and Po for 'post-nuclear phonematic unit'.

54 This is, of course, why they are regarded as prosodies and not as linear elements.

55 The statement offered here is only one of several, all within the same general phonological framework, that have been explored, each having its own merits and demerits. The choice of the one presented here was dictated by considerations that seem closely akin to the principle behind Thompson's procedure for dealing with asymmetry, namely, the assumption of 'the elimination of asymmetrical features from the phonemic inventory and the distributional table whenever possible, and their treatment on the level of phonetic description'. See Thompson, p. 474.

56 Shorto has proposed (fn. 2 on p. 545) in the interests of clarity that the term 'pattern', rather than 'system', should be used 'to denote the total manifold of

structures and systems'. I have tried to follow this useful suggestion as far as possible.

57 If divergence is accepted as a reasonable explanation of the differentiation between **ɯəu** and **ɯu** in NV, it is, strictly speaking, illogical to talk of convergence of these forms in SV. It might be preferable to assume divergence of spelling under the influence, perhaps, of NV.

58 See, however, n. 44 on p. 196.

59 Viz. 'kéc' *parrot* (see n. 13), 'cù léc' *tickle*, 'leng keng' *nois of a bell*, 'kẻng' *smart* (slang, poss. < *Américain*. Day gives the meaning as *to be American*, see Day, p. 18); 'xẻng' *shovel* (see n. 13). 'méc' *to relate*, *gossip*, which is in free variation with the regular form 'mách', is puzzling. Day and Emeneau also cite 'eng éc' to *squeal* (*like a pig*), see Day, p. 18, Emeneau, p. 16. This form occurs in my SV but not my NV material.

60 For this reason these words are much easier than the primary forms to handle in phonemic terms.

61 Viz. 'boong' (< Fr. *pontin*) *bridge* (of a ship); 'loong-toong (< Fr. *planton*) *office-boy*, 'ba-toong' (< Fr. *bâton*) *stick*. Day (p. 7) and Haudricourt (p. 92) cite other similar forms.

62 My limited observation of Huê pointed to a similar distinction in that dialect between **uk** < 'ut' and **uk͡p** < 'uc'.

63 'bứ', 'giư', 'giữ' in NV; 'bư', 'bự', 'giữ' in SV.

64 The SV is less helpful here both because of the complementary distribution of final **-n** and **-ŋ**, and **-t** and **-k**, and because of the less stable occurrence of labialized initials.

65 The frequency with which rare or seemingly irregular sequences of sounds are marked in my material as occurring only in bound forms, and especially in reduplicated constructions, suggests that these may require to be interpreted as belonging to phonological systems other than that stateable for indigenous free forms.

66 The reader is reminded that the consideration of tone and of concomitant phonetic features such as voice quality is excluded from this study.

The Technique of Prosodic Analysis

T. HILL

I. *Introduction*

In the course of my work at Edinburgh, first as a teacher of phonetics and latterly as a dialect geographer, I have frequently been questioned about Prosodic Analysis: by students who wished to apply it in their research, and by colleagues and visiting scholars who, trained in other schools of structural linguistics, had a sympathetic interest in the theory but could not see what applications it might have in their own research. I have come to the view that, by the side of the numerous examples of research, of high scientific quality, published by the group of linguists associated with J. R. Firth, and R. H. Robins's general description of the theory,[1] there is a need for a *pedagogical* introduction, with sufficient 'worked examples', to make it easier for the student not merely to understand work published by others but to set about doing it himself.

The present article, an attempt to meet this need, started with a term's practical course in Prosodic Analysis, given with the help of a Turkish informant[2] to a class of Phonetics Diploma students at Edinburgh in 1956. My ideas were later embodied in papers read to the Joint Staff Linguistics Seminar at Edinburgh and the Phonetics Department Seminar at Leeds, and from these the present article has developed. It will inevitably fall short of its aim—due, not only to limitations in my grasp of the theory, and in my ability to present it in a clear-cut elementary form, but also to the continuing fluid state of the theory itself. The latter has caused me at certain points to step outside my role of simple expositor, and to attempt my own interpretation of some obscure or little-developed aspect of it; this applies particularly to some of the methodological principles I have formulated at various places in the article, and they are to be regarded as pedagogical devices for which no authority is claimed. I am conscious of how little my exposition reflects the great subtlety and complexity with which Prosodic Analysis has been applied by Professor Firth and his colleagues, and that there are numerous linguists better fitted to teach the theory than myself. In my defence I will merely refer to the story of Columbus and the Egg, and express the hope that this article will be of some help in making Prosodic Analysis *unterrichtsreif.*

II. *Terminology and Method*

The terms *structure* and *system* are used in the senses established by J.R.Firth.[3] The structure of an utterance is a hierarchy of *units* (also called *isolates*, where appropriate), of various *ranks* (I have followed M.A.K.Halliday's practice, as exemplified in 'Categories of the Theory of Grammar',[4] and substituted this term for the traditional *level*, which can thus be reserved for the categories lexis, grammar, phonology, etc.). When talking of a portion of an utterance, picked out as a prospective isolate, I have used the non-committal terms *stretch* and *division*; *segment* and *sound* are used in their normal general phonetic sense, to designate those stretches usually regarded as single articulations. For the phonological unit of structure corresponding to the segment, I have used the established term *place.* At the phonetic level, I have made free use of the terms *cluster* and *group* for a succession of segments which is to be treated as occupying one place in the phonology. That part of the phonic substance corresponding to a phonological element I have termed, as is now customary, its *exponent.* Lastly, where *prosody* might have been expected, the more neutral term *feature* is commonly used: partly to avoid prejudging certain points, and partly so as not to be forced by implication into the choice prosody/phonematic unit.

Prosodic Analysis is a system of analysis applicable to stretches of speech, theoretically of any length whatever—the extreme case would be the whole corpus of a person's utterances in his lifetime. In a complete phonological analysis, the *sentence*, carrying as it does important features of intonation, rhythm, etc., is often the best maximum unit of description; and ideally the present article should start from this. However, for simplicity of exposition, and because the most characteristic and controversial aspects of Prosodic Analysis are best seen at lower ranks, the *word* is the largest isolate discussed. In many languages, an isolate so labelled is the largest to have articulatory 'shape' (in the sense used in section VI below); correlating of course with its great importance in grammatical analysis, as argued by R.H.Robins in 'In Defence of WP'.[5] In most languages, an informant can produce a one-word utterance; when sentence prosodies, etc., have been abstracted, what remains is a convenient unit for analysis. I should add to this two observations. First, many languages, e.g. English, Turkish, German (but not e.g. Nyanja, Arabic) have numerous 'compound words'; though grammatically and lexically, and in certain phonological aspects (especially stress patterns), these may be regarded as single words, the main body of articulatory description will apply to each element in the compound, taken separately. Thus a statement about 'C_1 (i.e. the initial consonant) of a word' must often be understood to mean 'C_1 of a simple word, or of some component part of a compound word'. Secondly, where it is more convenient the units *stem*, *prefix*, and the like are introduced; I have not attempted to justify this in the individual cases.

III. *Some General Characteristics of the Phonic Substance*

If we consider a body of words in any language, we can expect to observe most, indeed often all, of the following phenomena:

1. In pronouncing the word, the speech organs pass through a sequence of distinct articulatory positions; but
2. Some features of the word may continue throughout, or almost so—e.g. voice in English *breadwinner*, lip-rounding in *soup-spoon.*
3. There is a general similarity in all the words of a language, probably best defined in negatives: thus English words have stress at differing points, no implosive consonants, no initial sequences of two plosives, no stressed final short vowels; but
4. Certain sounds occur only in certain grammatical or lexical categories—thus English initial [ð], found only in a group of (mainly) deictic words, e.g. *this, then*; the sequence [wɑ:], found only in some borrowings, e.g. *peignoir*, *coiffure.*
5. Similar sounds occur at different points in the word—thus initial and final [m], [st], e.g. *mass, Sam, step, pest.* They are of course not necessarily identical—English final [m] is normally longer than initial—but common features can be extracted, as here bilabiality and nasality; but
6. Not all sounds occur in all positions—thus English has no final [h] or [tw]; and not all conceivable clusters of (actually occurring) sounds are found—English has [p] and [tw], but no [pw].
7. The alternation of certain articulatory features is correlated with lexical alternance—e.g. *pat*, *bat*, *spat*, *pit*, *pad, pant*; but

8. The same alternances do not necessarily occur in varying contexts in the word—thus English distinguishes *chin* and *shin*, but not [frɛntʃ] and [frɛnʃ], *French*.

If a phonological analysis is dominated by the odd-numbered considerations, it will be a strict phonemic one (and will incidentally form the basis for a practical orthography). If, however, at least as much weight is given to the even-numbered items, the analysis will be of a prosodic type. The rational and appropriate character of such an approach can be demonstrated by the preliminary analysis of some 'languagettes'.[6]

IV. *Reasons for Dividing the Phonic Substance*

Let us postulate a series of languagettes a–d, each having only the words given.

(a) A language with only three possible words, [ɑ], [ŋ], [ɑ̃]. The distinction between these three could obviously be defined in a unidimensional system of three alternants, viz. 'oral', 'nasal', 'nasalized-oral'.

(b^1) A language consisting of [l̡i], [la], [łu]. This also would be covered by a system of three alternants, 'front-spread', 'open', and 'back-rounded'. The observation that each begins with a lateral articulation, though phonetically interesting, would be of no more phonological import than is the fall in amplitude at the end.

(b^2) If the items in (b^1) were instead [li], [la], [lu], ([l] represents [lᵊ] without lip rounding), a phonological definition of these three would be identical with that in (b^1)—the phonetic datum that front-spread and back-rounded articulation respectively set in some time after the initial lateral element would of course be noted, but play no part in the definition.

(c^1) In the case of a larger repertoire [li], [la], [lu], [si], [sa], [su], [gi], [ga], [gu], the most economical definition of the system would take account of independent variation in the initial and the final elements of the words, so that a two-dimensional matrix would be set up. Thus the concepts *structure* and *system* would make their first appearance; the words would have in common a structure of two places, each place having a system of three terms. To look at this from another aspect, segmentation, as a phonological procedure, also appears for the first time—note that it was not necessary in languagettes b^1 or b^2.

(c^2) If the words in (c^1) had been the following—[l̡i], [la], [łu], [ʃi],

[sa], [ʂu], [ɟi], [ga], [ɢu], this, as in (b^2), need not involve any variation in the phonological definitions, but only in the phonetic description. Each word has an initial segment, identified as lateral, apical fricative, or tectal stop (i.e., a stop articulated with some part of the tongue behind the blade); and a following vocoid segment, front close, central open, or back close rounded. These categories are sufficient to identify any of the nine words. At the level of *phonetic* description, it will of course be noted that, in contrast to (c^1), the articulatory postures attributed to the vocoids are present also in the initial elements.

These hypothetical cases suggest two principles, applicable in the analysis of real languages:

1. If a phonetic feature is observed to extend over a more or less large stretch of an utterance, the most immediate and straightforward treatment is to ascribe it phonologically to the whole stretch. This is of course the accepted treatment for e.g. intonation in English, and in principle it may be applied to any kind of feature whatsoever.
2. The procedure of segmentation is dictated by the exigencies of the phonological structure; it does not necessarily agree with the observable succession of phonetic events.

V. *Prosodies of the Word and Syllable*

The principles just given can conveniently be illustrated by an inspection of some Turkish material.[7] As Prosodic Analysis proceeds in the manner indicated, by establishing the features that distinguish utterances, an ideal procedure would be to set up a complete inventory of possible Turkish utterances, then order them in various ways so as to reveal the diverse points of contrast between them. This is clearly impossible: but inventories of limited length can be set up of potentially commensurate units—e.g. words (of all kinds), disyllabic or monosyllabic words only, morphemes, syllables, etc., and by way of defining the differences between them an approach can be made to the phonological structure.

Let us assume that, having made an inventory of native Turkish monosyllabic words, we have extracted the following set of representative items for comparison:

kil, kel, kıl, kal, kül, göl, kul, kol (clay, scurfy, hair, discourse, ashes, lake, servant, arm: in a moderately broad transcription [cil̥], [cɛl̥], [qɯɫ], [qɑɫ], [cyl̥], [ɟœl̥], [quɫ], [qoɫ]).

We note that three parameters are sufficient to specify any one of them *vis-à-vis* the others, thus:

(i) Front vs. back: *kil, kel, kül, göl—kıl, kal, kul, kol.* (It is to be noted that frontness and backness are features of the whole word: the consonants are [c-l̥] in the first four examples, [q-ɫ] in the rest.)

(ii) Rounded vs. unrounded: *kül, göl, kul, kol—kil, kel, kıl, kal.* (Here again, the lip-rounding is present throughout the word.)

(iii) Close vs. (relatively) open vowel: *kil, kıl, kül, kul—kel, kal, göl, kol.*

A complete inventory will also include some words which do *not* fit into these categories, e.g. *kâr*, [cɑr] (profit), which has front articulation of its initial consonant. These will be ignored for the moment.

The next step is to examine a number of disyllables. They fall into two categories, with (in the informant studied) different overall phonetic characteristics, thus:

(i) In the *synharmonic* group the vowel of the first syllable would fall more or less on the periphery of the Cardinal Vowel diagram, but that of the second was perceptibly centralized;[8] words of this group were front or back throughout.

(ii) In the *asynharmonic* group both vowels were peripheral, and *differed* in respect of the front/back contrast. Word pairs to illustrate this are:

Synharmonic	*Asynharmonic*	
[biˈzɩm],	[haˈzin]	bizim (our), hazin (sad);
[mɛçˈtɛ̈p],	[haˈlɛp]	mektep (school), Halep (Aleppo);
[ɛvlɛ̈ˈrɩ],	[ascɛˈri]	evleri (his houses), askerî (military);
[ɟyˈnɛ̈ʃ],	[qɑrˈdɛʃ]	güneş (sun), kardeş (brother).

The synharmonic group comprises mainly the native Turkish lexicon, and the other mainly borrowings from Arabic, Persian and European languages. *Kâr*, quoted above, is to be added to the second group. At present, only the native words of the first group will be discussed.

If now some native Turkish polysyllabic words are contrasted, it will be found that *phonetically* these features occupy different stretches of the word. Numbering them as before, we find:

(i) *göstermelisiniz* (you must show)—*konuşmalısınız* (you must speak): frontness and backness respectively run right through these words (we may note that a corresponding difference in quality can be detected, not only in *k*, *g* and *l*, but also e.g. in *s*, *ş* and *z*).

(ii) Open vs. close vowel must be ascribed to each syllable separately —the evidence for this being essentially negative, i.e. the absence of more comprehensive patterns.

(iii) *koymuştu* (he put)—*kalmıştı* (he stayed): in the first of these examples, rounding runs throughout the word; it is entirely absent from the second. Its extension in the word is, however, limited, in a way that can be illustrated by the two possible plural formations corresponding to the examples:

koymuştular—kalmıştılar; *koymuşlardı—kalmışlardı*. That is, where lip-rounding is present it embraces the first syllable and all successive *close-vowel* syllables, but it is bounded (exclusively) by an open-vowel syllable and is absent from all following syllables.[9]

We now have, phonetically, three features extending over different stretches of the word, viz.:

(i) Front vs. back: over the whole word.
(ii) Close vs. open: over the central portion of each syllable.
(iii) Rounding: over the earlier portion (possibly the whole) of the word.

Features of this kind, extending over more than one segment, are termed *prosodies*. If now they are classified according to their role in the phonology, this list must be modified thus:

(i) Front vs. back: feature of the word.
(ii) Close vs. open: feature of the syllable.
(iii) Rounding: feature of the word.

Thus we may enunciate another principle:

3. Phonetically, a feature may be observed to occupy a certain stretch of the utterance; phonologically, its ascription to a certain subdivision of the utterance is determined by the pattern of alternances, and may not necessarily correspond to the former.

A feature may therefore be ascribed to a stretch of the utterance greater than that over which it manifests itself, as Turkish lip-rounding; of corresponding extension, as Turkish front articulation; or smaller, as nasalization of vowels in Castilian, which is ascribed to the presence of an adjacent nasal consonant. In the latter type of case, the term *focus* has been used to refer to a segment to which a prosody is ascribed.[10]

We may further notice the interesting case in which the two stretches are of corresponding length, but do not coincide in location (phonetically in the utterance, and phonologically in the word structure, respectively): a striking example is nominal tone in Kikuyu.[11] Any Kikuyu noun manifests a more or less great variety of tone patterns,[12] correlated to the type of word preceding it. Thus, when *nothing* precedes it, the noun *mondo*[13] (man) has two low-tone syllables. Three other nouns—*ndigiri* (donkey), *mocinga* (gun), *mokandá* (rope) have tone patterns as indicated (in the system used here and elsewhere in this article for Bantu tone, low syllables are unmarked, high syllables have an acute accent, and rising syllables a haček respectively; thus a, á, ǎ). If we now construct three phrases, in which *mondo* is prefixed by the syllable *wa* (meaning 'of') and by the other three nouns in turn (the phrases then meaning 'the man's donkey/gun/rope'), the following tone patterns occur:

ndigiri wa-móndo
mocinga wá-móndo
mokandá wá-móndo

It can be shown, for these and other phrases (a full demonstration will not be attempted), that *wa* is always associated with high tone on the following syllable—which in other contexts might be low, as noted for utterance-initial *mondo* above. Further, *ndigiri* is associated with low tone in the next-following syllable, and the other two nouns with high. This is accounted for if the three phrases are regarded phonologically as:

/ndigiri wá-mondo/
/mocingá wá-mondo/
/mokándá wá-mondo/

and if it is stated that the exponent of phonological tone on a given syllable is high tone on the *following* syllable. The correctness of this view is shown by its ability to predict various (though not necessarily all) other patterns, such as that of an utterance consisting of /né/ ('it is . . .') and a noun:

Thus *né-ndigiri* is the exponent of /né-ndigiri/
né-mócingǎ /né-mocingá/
né-mókandá /né-mokándá/

The final rise in *né-mocingǎ* is logically enough seen to be due to the 'doubling-up' of phonological low-high on a single phrase-final syllable; whereas in *né-mókandá*, with phonological final high-high, the exponent is a high level tone.

4. A further principle suggested by the case of Turkish is: Some phonological statements will refer to a necessary choice between two or more features; others, to the presence or absence of a feature.

Thus on the one hand there is nothing about the incidence of frontness and backness in the native Turkish word that would lead us to treat either one as the marked member of an opposition. The case of roundedness, however, is different: we can state a rule for its occurrence in the word, but there is no complementary rule, of the same order of simplicity, for the occurrence of spreadness. We can indeed say 'spreadness occurs throughout spread words, and in all syllables after the first non-initial open-vowel syllable of a rounded word'—but this is a mere prolix derivative of the rule for roundedness. To illustrate the point further, we may take verbal tone in Nyanja.[14] In Nyanja words (with certain exceptions that can be ignored here) each syllable has a high or low tone: there are virtually no restrictions of sequence, except that final low-high does not occur; where the phonology would require it, the exponential tones are high-high. If we first consider such examples as *mbálé* (kinsman), *mbale* (plate), *cisanu* (five), *cisánú* (extreme cold), *ine* (I), *íyé* (he), our natural inclination will be to treat high/low as a pair of equipollent alternant features. However, each Nyanja verb tense has a characteristic tone pattern. If we examine its operation with verb stems containing varying numbers of syllables, we shall see that the tense tone pattern is a set of high tones: so many syllables must have them, the rest are unmarked, therefore low. Examples are:

	'eat'	'return'	'talk'	'believe'
'he eats, etc.'	*ádya*	*ábwera*	*álankhula*	*ákhulupirira*

	'eat'	'return'	'talk'	'believe'
'he just eats, etc.'	*ángódyá*[15]	*ángobwéra*	*ángolánkhula*	*ángokhúlupirira*
'he must eat, etc.'	*azídyá*	*azíbwérá*	*azílankhúlá*	*azíkhulupirírá*

As will be seen, the 'present' tense has high tone on the personal prefix *a-*; the 'just' tense, on the personal prefix and the stem initial; and the 'must' tense, on the tense prefix *-zi-* and the stem final.

VI. *Criteria for Division of the Phonic Substance*

In the foregoing, we have already had numerous examples of statements about subdivisions of the word—chiefly about the syllable. It is now necessary to examine the purpose and method of making such divisions. A stretch of speech, isolated for the purposes of investigating its composition, may be regarded in two ways: as being a sequence of two or more sub-units of the same category, or as having a shape with (to use a spatial metaphor) a front, a middle and a back, incommensurable with each other because they are distinct parts of the whole. The idea of *sequence* corresponds to the way one would refer to a number of cars passing successively along a road; *shape* to the composition of a train—it is not *untrue* to say 'the engine passes you before the guard's van does', but it is more meaningful to say 'the train is pulled by an engine and has a guard's van at the back'. Cars passing a point are in principle all alike, having no *predictable* individuality; a locomotive is by definition different in form and function from a carriage, and one aspect of its function is its position in front. To take the metaphor a little further, statements of the kind envisaged are more informative in the case of trains, which have shape: 'this vehicle is the tender' tells us more about it than 'this vehicle is the second car to pass the checkpoint'.[16]

To revert to language: to attribute shape to an isolate is more informative than to say it is a sequence of similar items (*similar* in the sense that each item-place is potentially occupied by the same set of alternants). This suggests the principle:

5. Where possible, an isolate is rather to be analysed as a shape, with unlike parts, than as a sequence of similar sub-units.

The criterion of choice between these alternatives must therefore be considered. It is the degree of, in Firth's term, 'mutual expectancy'. Sequence is suggested by combinatory freedom of the sub-units, shape by limited combinatory possibilities (i.e. a high degree of mutual expectancy).[17] It is probably generally true that freedom decreases with the size of the isolates: thus in English the phonetic character of the initial words of an utterance is as good as unlimited (within the range of possible English words, of course); the two very different articulatory complexes [jɔ:] and [wɒtʃ] occur reversed in the two utterances '*Watch your step*' and '*Your watch is slow*', and a description of one of these sentences would necessarily indicate not merely which words were in it, but in what order they occurred. Thus, in respect of its component sounds a sentence is to be regarded as a sequence (whereas of course for intonation it is often a shape). On the other hand, the constituents of the initial consonant cluster of a word are severely limited in their mutual relations. If we know that such a cluster contains [l], [p] and [s], we know the order *must* be third—second—first, as in *splash*; English has no utterance initials of the form *[psl], *[slp], etc., nor can [p] be preceded by any other articulation but [s]. This is more appropriately regarded as a shape: [p] plus laterality plus alveolar friction, would be a minimal and sufficient characterization. And here the concept of sequence is redundant. We can hardly deny that the tongue is grooved for the [s] at a point of time before it is humped for the [l]—but this need not be stated.

The syllable is usually the isolate in which shape is most clearly dominant. In all languages, the articulations occurring in its nucleus are all (or almost all) distinct from those possible in its margins, being typically vocoids and contoids respectively. If a language has only 'open' syllables, as e.g. Nyanja, the mere mention of two such articulatory features suffices to characterize one of them: a CV structure consisting of [a] plus [t] is necessarily [ta], not *[at], and to specify sequence would be redundant. In a language, such as English, in which syllables have initial and final margins, there are sufficiently great distinctions in the possibilities at these points for them to be regarded as distinguished by shape: the initial margin includes [tw], [spr], etc., the final [lt], [st], [ŋk], etc. It is therefore not surprising that in Prosodic Analysis the greater part of the articulatory features are attributed to the syllable, or if not, then to subdivisions defined by their structural role in its shape.

The syllable and its subdivisions are thus appropriate isolates for illustrating several problems of analysis which may of course occur at all ranks, viz.:

(i) the degrees of subdivision to which the utterance in a given case is to be subjected: this occasionally involves—
(ia), establishing the bounds of the isolate;
(ii) the degree and nature of correspondence between an isolate and the phonic substance, and treatment of junction phenomena occurring between two successive isolates.

VII. *Isolates within the Syllable*

The syllables of English, as of many other languages, may have consonant articulations at both initial and final margins, as in *stop*, *hint*, *pride*—a structure that may be symbolized as C_1VC_2. In deciding whether they should be further divided, and at what points, the mutual expectancy of items at C_1 with those at V, and of items at V with those at C_2, should be investigated. On examining combinations, in RP, of the five short vowels, [ι], [ε], [a], [ɒ], [ʌ] (excluding the comparatively rare vowel [ɷ], which has a very special distribution) with possible simple and complex C_1 articulations, to determine how many conceivable combinations actually occurred in monosyllables, it was found that of 255 possible combinations only 15, i.e. 6%, were not attested.[18] Thus [pι], [prι], [plι], [pε], [prε], etc., etc., occur, in e.g. *pit*, *prince*, *plinth*, *peck*, *press*, but *[skrε] and *[zʌ] do not. A similar test of VC_2 combinations, however, showed that of 225 possibles 73 were missing, i.e. 32%: positive examples are [εlk], [aŋk], as in *elk*, *bank*, negative are *[ɒlk], *[εŋk]. A full inventory, including long vowels and diphthongs, would increase this disproportion—as a number of C_2's are preceded only by short vowels, e.g. [mp], [ŋk], [nθ], [lf]. Mutual expectancy being thus lower between C_1 and V, the primary division of the syllable would be into initial (C_1) and final (VC_2). This applies to English dialects in general, and is the reason why for instance the Phonological Questionnaire of the Linguistic Survey of Scotland (dealing essentially with monosyllabic words) is arranged so as to produce a table of finals, initials being treated as indifferent. In fact the combinations of V and C_2 in an English (or Scots) final are not *usually* so limited as to preclude a further reduction to a sequence of two elements; but in particular cases a feature may be noted that can only be properly attributed to the final as a whole.

The following is a table of monosyllables in the dialect of Gourdon (Kincardineshire), grouped according to the nature of C_2, and including in each group one specimen of each distinct close or mid vowel recorded in that context (but excluding e.g. the open vowel of [mɑn] *man*, and the central vowel of [bɜt] *bit*). The transcribed finals are ordered in two columns, according to whether the transition from V to C_2 involves a very dark C_2 with a more or less prominent shwa glide, or not. It illustrates the great variation possible in (a) the number of V alternants occurring before different C_2's, and (b) the pattern of incidence of the dark articulatory element.

	No shwa	*Shwa*		*No shwa*	*Shwa*
head	[i·d]		*sieve*		[iəv]
trade / *bred*	[e·d]		*leave*		[eəv]
rod	[ɔ·d]		*drove*		[oəv]
road		[oəd]	*move*		[ɷəv]
loud	[u·d]		*stone*		[iən̵]
beef		[iəf]	*pain*		[eən̵]
leaf		[eəf]	*ten*		[ɛən̵]
loaf		[ɔəf]	*John*	[ɔ·n]	
roof	[ɷ·f]		*drone*	[o·n]	
heel		[iəɫ]	*moon*		[ɷən̵]
bail		[eəɫ]	*down*		[uən̵]
Nell		[ɛəɫ]	*freeze*		[iəz]
hole		[oəɫ]	*blaze*	[eːz]	
fool		[ɷəɫ]	*nose*		[oəz]
towel		[uəɫ]	*use* (vb.)		[ɷəz]
			booze		[uəz]

It will be seen that (within the limits of the finals given) (a) some C_2's are never accompanied by shwa, but (b) some C_2's always are; (c) shwa does not seem to be mandatory with any of the vowels given—though there are vowels that *never* have it, e.g. [ɑ] of *man*. There is therefore a case for ascribing shwa to the whole final, as 'dark quality' or the like.

Similar considerations apply to the question whether to subdivide C and V; the issue is usually clearer, as combinatory limitations are more severe. We have already observed the restricted possibilities implied by English [spl-]. If we now place this in an inventory of C_1 items, the latter will be seen to include the following paradigm:

p pr pl b br bl sp spr spl . . .

If they are arranged multidimensionally, this can first be done on the basis of what articulation follows the plosion: thus

lateral	*post-alveolar friction*	*nil*
pl	pr	p
bl	br	b
spl	spr	sp

The other dimension includes three categories—are these to be further sub-grouped? There seems no basis for doing so. They are distinguished multilaterally one from another, thus:

p – fortis (possibly aspirated), voiceless,
b – lenis, partly voiced,
sp – lenis, voiceless, with initial alveolar friction.

Thus, any 'bilabial plosive' C_1 can be exhaustively characterized by specifying, in some such terms as the following:

(i) fortis/voiced/pre-fricative ('sigmatized'?)
(ii) plain/lateralized/rhotacized,

and there is no reason to divide it further.

The general principle applied here might be stated as follows:

6. If there is doubt whether a given point in the utterance should be treated as the boundary of two successive isolates, a positive indication is low mutual expectancy between the sections of the utterance preceding and following it.

It may here be observed that in the foregoing we have been dealing, not with features such as Turkish lip-rounding, which even in pre-Firthian terms might well be termed a prosody by reason of its extension, but with articulatory segments, single or in small groups—distinguished in most work of the Prosodic school by the term *phonematic units*. Thus W.S. Allen, in 'Retroflexion in Sanskrit'[19] defines Prosodic Analysis as 'characterized by the distinction of prosodic and phonematic systems'. But this definition was intended expressly to point the contrast with phonemic analysis, and it may be that we should not regard the dichotomy as fundamental. If the various ranks, from sentence down to place, form one hierarchy, then it might seem more reasonable to speak of frontness and rounding (as in Turkish) as features of the word, plosion and velarity (as in a segment transcribed [k]) as features of the place, and so on.

VIII. *Delimitation of the Isolate*

In the foregoing cases, it has been assumed that for one reason or another the syllables can be not only identified, but also delimited—that is, that it is always clear to which of two syllables a given segment belongs. There are certainly languages of which this is true. It can be shown that all Nyanja syllables are open, thus: in Nyanja, no word ends in a consonant articulation; and all the types of consonant articulation, however complex, that occur between two vowels may also occur initially in the word. Thus, the word *sompha* (imperative of 'to adze out') is seen to be divided *so-mpha*, in that (i) no word occurs with the ending **som*; (ii) its constituent syllables appear transposed in [mphaso] *mphatso* (gift). The point of syllable division will always be placed between a vowel and the first following consonantal articulation.

Again, in Chinese the syllable is of course institutionalized as a lexical and grammatical unit; this would not of itself determine its phonological status, but in fact this is marked almost as clearly as it is in Nyanja. Firth and Rogers, in 'The Structure of the Chinese Monosyllable in a Hunanese Dialect',[20] divide the syllable into initial and final. Whereas, a large variety of consonantal articulations, simple and complex, can be initials, e.g. [p], [ph], [ɟj], [ʂ], [dz], [cw]—finals consist only of vowels (including diphthongs), nasalized vowels, and vowel plus [n]. Thus, in most consonants or consonant groups occurring in the utterance, the syllable division is obvious.

English, of course, is similar to some extent. If we argue from what occurs as C_1 and C_2 of monosyllables, to consonant groups occurring in longer words, the syllabic boundary is sometimes clearly indicated. Thus (choosing words where morphological makeup gives as little help as possible) in *algum*, *chipmunk*, *calumny* (syllables 2 and 3), the only divisions yielding possible C_2 and C_1 are *l-g*, *p-m*, *m-n*. Apart from these cases, we are left with a large body of words like *mascot*, *champerty*, where the consonant groups alone are no guide. Can a rule of syllabification be set up to cover all such cases? It may be significant that possible combinations of V and C_2 in polysyllables resemble those for monosyllables: thus [bɷl] and [-einʤ] occur in both—*bullet*, *bull*, *range*, *danger*—and *[bʌl], *[-aɩnʤ] in neither; further thus divided, *lacquer* gives a first syllable [lak] corresponding to *lack*; whereas a monosyllabic word *[la] is not possible.

But after this criterion had been used, a good number of words would remain to which it did not apply, e.g. *paper*, *holy*, *ballad*—[peɩ] and [hoɷ] can be monosyllabic words, and syllables with final [al] are rare. It seems reasonable to expect that in English and many other languages a great number of words will remain in which no reason can be stated (other than analogy with unambiguous cases) for any particular syllable division.[21] These may be cases where a description in terms of nucleus and onset/interlude/coda (in Hockett's terminology)[22] would be just as adequate for ordering the facts, and avoid the introduction of a speculative element. We may note, for example, that although in 'Vowel Nasality in Sundanese'[23] R.H. Robins uses the term *syllable* and sets out CVC structures for the category, his tabulation of C places with or without *n* prosody does not depend on this division for its validity.

Delimitation of the subdivisions of the syllable is not usually in doubt—being closely correlated to *certain* of the boundaries of the articulatory segments—but the case of the sequence 'consonant plus [j] plus [uː]' in English may be taken to illustrate one such problem. It occurs in e.g. *new*, *feud*, *huge*, and is also considered to be present in words such as *tune*, *dew*, where the articulation actually occurring is commonly an affricate. Now it is noteworthy that these consonant groups occur only before [uː] (or [ɷ], in polysyllables such as *educate*). If the [j] is treated as part of C_1, we therefore have a set of 'iotated' C, alternants with very idiosyncratic combinatory behaviour; it is clearly more reasonable to set up [juː] as a member of the V system, so that e.g. *feud* will be analysed as /f-juː-d/.

IX. *Correspondence between the Isolate and the Phonic Substance*

In order to assert that a portion of the phonic substance is the exponent of a certain phonological feature, we are not restricted to a close correspondence of articulatory categories as set up in the two systems of description (phonetic and phonological). An exponent-isolate correspondence may be asserted because the phonological patterning demands it. Nyanja plosives comprise minimally a closure (which may be voiceless, voiced, or voiceless aspirated) plus or minus various modifications, one of which may be termed w-modification. Thus, side by side with the syllables [ta], [da] there are [twa, dwa]; [tha] is to be linked with [tʍa] which will therefore be treated as /thwa/. A similar series occurs for velars, [kʍa] being analysed as /khwa/. In the case of the bilabial series, there is no *[pwa], etc., by the side of [pa], [ba], [pha]. There are, however, three consonant complexes [pʁa], [bʁa], [pχa]. These are clearly to be treated as the w-modified bilabials, on the ground that: the general symmetry of the system so far (which extends to other features not listed, viz. y-modification and nasalization) provides 'boxes' for them, and there are no more appropriate candidates; uvular modification is unknown elsewhere in the sound system; and there is a minimal similarity of articulation—back stricture—in both cases. The general principle governing this might be stated as follows:

7. When a matrix has been set up for a system of phonological alternances, the location of individual items within it is determined not only by their exponential (phonetic) characteristics, but also by the distribution of occupied and vacant points of intersection in the matrix.

This particular example is commonplace, and nothing has been said about it that would not be acceptable in any structural scheme of phonology. However, because Prosodic Analysis is concerned with the C and V places, or whole syllables, it admits great flexibility in the degrees of extension involved in a phonetic-phonological match. In the lower-class English of central Scotland, for instance, the same system of nasalized plosives occurs as in RP: /mp/, /nt/, etc., and [ŋk] as in *bank* fits into this scheme as /ŋk/.[24] [ŋg], however, does not occur, and words such as singer, longer, finger have [ŋ] alone, thus [sε̈ŋɩr], [ɫɔŋɩr], [fε̈ŋɩr]. This [ŋ] may be regarded as the exponent of /ng/, on criteria like those just stated for Nyanja, viz.: there is a 'box' for /ng/; *[ŋg] does not occur; and [ŋ] having velarity and nasality, is a strong candidate. Thus a single articulatory segment is taken to be the exponent of a complex phonological unit, whose fellows in the system all have complex exponents—[nd], [ŋk], etc.

It must be made clear that we are not asserting that [ŋ] 'is really' [ŋg]—that in some sense a plosion is present though unarticulated; nor indeed even that Nyanja [tʍ] is [thw]. To represent [ŋ] by /ng/ is to indicate symbolically a number of facts about it that can be deduced from the nature of the phonological matrix, and the place of /ng/ in it. These facts are, for instance, that [ŋ] never occurs as C_1 (because nasalization of plosives is only a C_2 feature), whereas [n] and [m] *can* be C_1 (if /n/ and /m/ are to be regarded as having the normal distribution for nasals, [ŋ] does not belong with them); that *[ŋg] does not occur (because the /ng/ place in the matrix is pre-empted by [ŋ]). Similarly, when in 'Prosodies in Siamese'[25] E. J. A. Henderson regards [r] in C_1 position as /Ør/ i.e. rhotacized zero (her own symbol for zero is actually ζ), the intention is to suggest that the correlation of /Ør/ to /Ø/ (i.e. initial vowel) is comparable to that of /pr/ to /p/, etc.

A more complex illustration of this principle is to be seen in a part of the Nyanja class prefix system. As a preliminary, it must be noted that the phonetic data of Nyanja do not include syllables consisting of consonant + [w] + [o] or [u]; that is to say, we find e.g. [ko], but not *[kwo]. From the various series of class prefixes that Nyanja possesses, we will select (i) the characteristic prefix of the individual noun, marking the noun class it belongs to and the agreements it governs; (ii) a prefix found with certain types of noun qualifier classified on their total behaviour as *verbs*, e.g. *chale lo-yera* (a white blanket; *-yera* = white, cf. *li-yera* = it is white, *li-yenda* = it goes); (iii) a prefix linking a pair of nouns, as in *chale la-mfumu* (the chief's blanket: *mfumu* = chief). They will be tabulated in the forms occurring in five noun classes, termed in pedagogical grammars the LI, ZI, KA, MU, and KU classes. Nouns exemplifying these classes are: *lipenga* (trumpet), *zirombo* (weeds), *kanthu* (affair), *ku-Zomba* (at Zomba), *mu-nyumba* (in the house: the last two classes give adverbial function to nouns).

	(i)	(ii)	(iii)
LI	[li]	[loː]	[la]
ZI	[zi]	[zoː]	[za]
KA	[ka]	[koː]	[ka]
MU	[mu]	[moː]	[mwa]
KU	[ku]	[koː]	[kwa]

The prefixes in column (iii) (and those of other classes, not shown here) can be summarised by the formula Ca, C being the characteristic consonant of the class prefix, and a the vowel [a]. Column (ii) can similarly be summarised as Coː, but will only correspond in all respects with (iii) if in the respective classes Coː is interpreted as /loː/, /zoː/, /koː/, /mwoː/, /kwoː/. Correspondingly, the last two items in column (i) will be interpreted as /mwu/, /kwu/.

Just as with C and V alternants, so also with syllables the exponent-isolate correspondence is described in accordance with the structural patterns as a whole. In Skye Gaelic, the words *dearg*, *gorm* [ˈd̥ʒɛrɛ˞g̊, ˈg̊ɔrɔ˞m] (red, green) are fully specified by the phonological transcriptions /djɛrg/, /gɔrm/, representing CVC structures in which certain consonant groups at C_2 are realised with an intervening vowel sound (its quality depending on that of V). Thus phonologically (as in Gaelic metrics) they are to be regarded as monosyllables.[26] Perhaps we should reckon not only with a possible difference between the phonetic and the phonological, but with two (or more) distinct types of phonological division. The words quoted would no doubt be regarded as disyllabic in a study of sentence rhythm, and this may be an indication that we need a syntagmatic syllable (in a series including such terms as utterance, breath-group, foot), and a lexical syllable (a subdivision of the word, or morpheme, or other lexical unit selected)—or indeed a syntagmatic and a lexical phonology, a particular utterance being regarded as the resultant of both together.

Lastly, there are often certain phonetic features of an utterance whose occurrence is to be ascribed, not to any one of the isolates into which it has been divided, but to the presence of two abutting isolates. The phonological elements, of which these features are the exponents, are termed Prosodies of Junction.

In many cases, the number of segments observable at the point of junction corresponds to the number of phonological units ascribed to the two isolates—only the precise exponential character needs to be specified. Thus, the well-known case of RP [ˈhɔːʃːuː] (horse-shoe), with long [ʃː] corresponding directly to the sequence of /s/ and /ʃ/. Cases occur, however, in which a segment of the utterance is itself to be taken as an 'interface phenomenon'. Thus, in the case of English speakers who say [sɔː] or [sɔə] for *saw*, *soar*, and [sɔːrɪŋ] for *sawing*, *soaring*, the [r] will be regarded as a *junction prosody* of the syllables (and therefore as having nothing in common phonologically with the [r] of *rose*).

The contrary case also occurs, in which one articulatory segment represents the junction of two separate phonological items; as where, in Dutch, [ən ˈdoːˈseːp] is the pronunciation of *een doos seep* (a box of soap), the exponent of two like C's in junction being a single articulatory segment. In the dialect of Hyde, Cheshire (where, on grounds not discussed here, [ˀ] is usually to be regarded as an exponent of /t/), in the utterance [ðɩ ˈwɛnˀ ˈfoˀboː maˀtʃ] *They went to the football match*, the first glottal stop is at once the exponent of /t/ the final plosive of /wɛnt/, of /t/ a weak form of /to/ *to*, and of /t/ a weak form of /ðə/ *the*: cf. the sentences [ðr ˈguːɪnˀ ˈfoˀboː maˀtʃ] *They're going to the football match*, and [ðɪn ˈsiːnˀ ˈfoˀboː maˀtʃ] *They've seen the football match*, with only two and one instances of /t/ respectively: it being a rule of junction that any number of successive instances of /t/ have as their joint exponent [ˀ].

When fitting a prosody of junction into a phonological description, two aspects must be considered:

a. Specification of the phonological units abutting at the point of junction, and of the exponent(s): thus in the example *horseshoe*, /s/ + /ʃ/ is expounded as [ʃː].
b. Specification of the syntagmatic structures to which the prosody applies. It may of course not be restricted in this way: thus the English prosody just mentioned can occur in *it was she that did it*, *get this shifted*, etc., etc. In many cases, however, a prosody is restricted to lower-rank grammatical units, e.g. phrases, or simply to particular sub-classes of these. A feature of Scottish Gaelic was noted above (*dearg*, *gorm*), whereby certain C_2 groups have an exponent with a medial vocalic element. Thus, in Skye Gaelic the sequence /n/ /v/ is realised with an intervening vowel in the simple word, e.g. *meanbh* [ˈmɛnɛˑv] 'fine', and in groups consisting of noun preceded by noun or adjective, e.g. *sean-bhean* [ˈʃɛnɛˈvɛn] 'old wife', but not in a group where the adjective follows the noun—e.g. *bean bheag* [ˈb̥ɛn ˈveg̊] 'little woman' (*bean* = wife, woman)—or in other syntagmatic units. A similar restriction applies to liaison in the French nominal group.

X. *Polysystemicity*

It follows, from the attitude to systemic description developed hitherto, that the set of alternances at any specially defined point in the structure is sui generis, and need not correspond in formation to the set at another point. These various sets of alternances are regarded as separate systems, which together make up the phonology of the language. No attempt is made to reduce them to a single all-embracing scheme, and a description of this type is *polysystemic*. Thus, for instance, the same sound, at two distinct places in the word structure, may be taken as the exponent of two different phonological elements, if the matrices into which it fits are different. So in the Nyanja noun or verb stem, the initial syllable alternances include:

[ci][27]		[kwi]
[ce]		[kwe]
[ca]	[ka]	[kwa]
[co]	[ko]	
[cu]	[ku]	

Examples of stems: *cindu* (roof), *cale* (blanket), *coka* (come out), *kasu* (hoe), *kula* (grow), *kwinyata* (shrivel), *kwata* (marry).

This makes it possible for C_1 of stems to be interpreted thus: [ci], [ce] as /ki/, /ke/, and [ca], [co], [cu] as /kya/ etc.—/ky/ being the y-modified counterpart of /kw/. A balanced paradigm results, with complementary blanks.

	/ki/	/kwi/
	/ke/	/kwe/
/kya/	/ka/	/kwa/
/kyo/	/ko/	
/kyu/	/ku/	

In the prefix, on the other hand, where forms such as [ci], [ca], [coː] occur, the same reasoning as was applied to [moː] and [koː] above suggests a slightly different interpretation: thus, arranged as before, we have:

Class	(i)	(ii)	*Phonological interpretation of* C_1
KA	ka	koː	k
KU	kwa	koː	kw
CI	ca	coː	ky

and just as [ku] was treated as /kwu/, [ci] as in *cirombo* (weed: plural *zirombo*) is here taken to be the exponent of /kyi/.

At points of the stem other than C_1, yet other interpretations of the same alveolo-palatal articulations arise: the examples will also illustrate the principle of polysystemicity as applied to different grammatical categories. Thus, for the final stem syllable of nouns the relevant part of the paradigm runs [ci] [ce] [ka] [ko] [ku], e.g. *nthoci* (banana), *mkaka* (milk), *nkhuku* (chicken). In verbs, on the other hand, only the final syllables [ke] [ka] occur (plus a disyllabic element [kei])—these alternances form part of the tense system, thus *wacoka* (he has come out); *acoke* (let him come out); *asacokei* (he must not come out). In each case, therefore, all the syllables can be accounted for in terms of a single series /k/ plus vowel: together with statements about its diverse, grammatically determined exponents.

Similar correlations of grammatical category and phonological structure might be made in respect of some features of English. It has been noted earlier that, in Scottish speech, [ŋ] can be interpreted as /ng/. In RP, both [ŋ] and [ŋg] occur, so that on the face of it this interpretation is barred. But a rule may be set up as follows:

[ŋg] appears internally (sc. in isolates not subdivided for lexical or grammatical analysis), and [ŋ] as word final: [fɩŋgə] *finger*, [sɩŋ] *sing*, [lɒŋ] *long*; in the junction of an adjectival stem and suffix the exponent is [ŋg]; in the junction of a verbal stem and suffix, it is [ŋ]: thus, [lɒŋgə], [lɒŋɩŋ], [sɩŋə]—*longer*, *longing*, *singer*.

Similarly, the presence of both [θ] and [ð] in English word initial can be related to the categories lexical and grammatical word: [ðʌs], [ðoʊ], [ðeɩ] (*thus*, *though*, *they*), as against [θʌm], [θɔːt], [θɩn], (*thumb*, *thought*, *thin*).

In both of these cases, it will be seen that a single phonological alternant /ng/, or respectively, /þ/ (to improvise a symbol), can be linked with a pair of different exponents, if grammatical information is given. The contrary case—two units having in certain circumstances an identical exponent—appears for instance in K. H. Albrow's analysis of the Russian verb,[28] where [tʃ] is variously treated as the exponent of /k/ and of /t/ in different conjugation types, on the grounds of such different paradigms as [kontʃu, kontʃiʃ] (*I*, *you finish*) and [l̥itʃu, l̥it̥iʃ] (*I*, *you fly*).

If the lexicon of a language comprises words from two or more different origins, it may be that in this case also two different phonological analyses will be appropriate. The case of Turkish has already been mentioned; we may also discuss that of German. German has on the one hand a native lexicon, comprising words which may be analysed into

(i) *strong* syllables, identified by having peripheral vowels—e.g. the syllables of *Vormundschaft* (trusteeship), *ausführlich* (exhaustive);

(ii) *weak* syllables, with a central vowel (exponent sometimes zero) or syllabic consonant—e.g. the first, third and fourth syllables of *verzehrende* (consuming), *besonderen* (particular).

A simple word contains one or more strong syllables, and is stressed on the first or second of these, the choice being largely predictable from its grammatical structure: thus, symbolizing strong and weak syllables with S and W respectively, *Abschluss* (ŚS: conclusion), *unerträglich* (ŚWSW: intolerable), *Missetäter* (ŚWSW: evildoer), *missbrauchen* (SŚW: ill-use).

There is on the other hand a large number of learned borrowings, in which almost always every syllable is strong (except for inflexional suffixes), and stress (frequently final) is a lexical feature of the word: thus *Prämaturi'tät*, *Mezza'nin*, *Re'seda* (mignonette), *'Rektor*, *Salon* ([sa'lɔ̃ː] or [za'lɔ̃ː]), *Teint* ([tɛ̃ː], complexion), *Billet* [bɪ'ʎɛt].

The two groups are not identical in the inventory or distribution of their sounds: native words have [pf], e.g. *Pfeife* (pipe), [kn] e.g. *Knüttel* (cudgel), non-initial [ç] only, as in *reich* (rich); learned words have [sk], e.g. *Skandal*, [ʒ], e.g. *Genie* (genius), initial [ç], e.g. *China*. There is therefore reason to discuss the two categories separately (perhaps with a third division for distinctively modern Romance borrowings, in view of the presence of nasal vowels, [ʎ], etc.).

XI. *Phonology in relation to Grammar and Lexis*

In the above examples of polysystemic analysis, it has apparently been assumed that it is right and proper for phonology to conform to grammatical and lexical description. We may note in support of this view that often, unless the data were restricted in this way, phonological patterns would not emerge. When discussing English C_2 groups of nasal and plosive the statement was made, as a necessary step in the interpretation of [ŋ], that these are always homorganic. In fact English monosyllables occur in which this is not so, e.g. *dreamt*, *hanged*. However, all such cases are paradigmatically connected with words lacking this final plosive—thus *dream*, *hang*—and so may be taken as having a structure CVCC, and therefore incommensurable with *hint*, etc. In this respect English may be contrasted with Classical Arabic, which beside *bint-* (daughter) includes such stems as *ḥamd-* (praise), in which the final consonants are not homorganic; further, these stems are paradigmatically connected with others in which the two consonants are separated by a vowel, thus *banât-* (daughters), *ḥamada* (he praised). In contrast with English *hint* (CVC), Arabic *bint-* would therefore be best analysed as CVCC.

But, as J.R.Firth says,[29] 'grammatical classification limits and groups the data *in parallel* with phonological analysis' (our italics).

The two are in principle separate, and grammar is only to be invoked where there is phonological reason to; sometimes indeed the two are best put in definite opposition. On the one hand, the division of English disyllables into CVC–(C)V . . ., as suggested above for *bullet*, *danger*, *lacquer*, corresponds frequently to derivational paradigms—thus *hand/handy*, *range/ranger*, etc., and we have already seen similar considerations applied to words such as *dreamt* above. On the other hand, whereas the Turkish word *köpeği* (his dog) divides morphologically into *köpeğ-* (dog) and a possessive suffix, N. Waterson, however, in her phonological analysis,[30] syllabifies it as *kö-pe-ği*, next deducing a rule of syllabification to account for the different treatment of stem-final /g/ in *köpeği* and *köpekte* (at the dog).

The actual existence of distinct phonological patterns thus appears to be the only *theoretical* justification for describing separately the phonology of a grammatical category in a language. If we analyse the phonology of the Nyanja noun, it should not merely be because the noun is a distinct grammatical category, but because there is in some measure a phonological word-class that corresponds to the noun (there may of course be other, practical reasons for thus restricting the field, but they must not be thought to have a basis in theory).

Where the lexicon falls into phonological sub-groups, it is important to note that the origin of a word does not in itself determine which one it is to be allotted to. Thus *kardeş* (brother) is an original Turkish word—but its anomalous phonetic form puts it into the asynharmonic group; contrariwise *tamam* (complete), of Arabic origin, conforms to the synharmonic class. In analysing English, modern French and classical borrowings might form a distinct category; but Old Norse and Old French borrowings share a common phonetic makeup with the native Old English stock, and would not be distinguished from it. Examples: words treated as 'learned' or 'foreign'—*conceptual*, *sclerosis* (classical), *peignoir*, *ensemble* (modern French); words treated as 'native'—*week* (O.E.), *weak* (O.N.), *beak* (O.Fr.), *holly* (O.E.), *folly* (O.Fr.).

It may happen that, by the criteria of polysystemic analysis, an item forms a distinct class of one member, or just two or three. For instance, whereas in some areas of Scotland the vowels descended from Older Scots ŏ and ǭ are kept distinct, thus *cot* [kɔt], *coat* [kot], in Shetland they have fallen together as [kɔt]. Most Shetland speakers have, however, a word [boət] *boat* (this being a relatively recent English borrowing). Should one therefore say that Shetland too has two midback vowel alternants? Probably not—it is better isolated, as one of what R.B.Lees (in conversation) aptly called 'the queer words'. Again, internally in the Nyanja stem the syllables [ci] and [ce] do not occur, the alternances being [ki], etc., as in verb finals—thus *fikira* (reach), *cokera* (come from)—except for the two stems *pacika* (hang) and *socera* (lose one's way). The phonological structure of Nyanja is most clearly described if these are isolated in a two-item class.[31]

The approach to polysystemic analysis might therefore be formulated as follows:

8. Distinct phonological systems may be set up for any subdivision of the word, or any set of words (of any size from one upwards), if by this means the phonological form of the language is more clearly revealed than in an all-inclusive description.
9. Such phonological sets of words can often be attributed to a grammatical or lexical category, and a description of them may be regarded as the phonology of that category; but it is only in cases of this kind that grammar and lexis should be regarded as relevant to phonology.

XII. *Conclusion*

Because of the circumstances in which it developed, Prosodic Analysis has often been expounded not so much as a complete theory in its own right, but as a reaction to, and corrective of, the Phonemic approach. I have striven to avoid this, and to present it simply as a way—possibly the most reasonable way—of making phonological analyses. At this point, however, I should like to make some brief remarks on its relation to certain other theories of phonology. The view, not infrequently heard, that 'some languages are more satisfactorily described by the one than the other' (scil. phonemic and prosodic techniques),[32] appears to misstate the position. It is true that in analysing some languages a relatively high proportion of phonological features will be ascribed to the 'place', and such an analysis will have considerable resemblance to a phonemicization. It will not, however, have been drawn up in accordance with the strict and detailed protocol of any school of phonemics, and this similarity will be fortuitous and superficial.

The relation to Transformational phonology, as exemplified in R.B.Lees, *The Phonology of Modern Standard Turkish*,[33] is more interesting. Prosodic Analysis made its effective debut with J.R.Firth's

'Sounds and Prosodies'[34] in 1948—effective, in the sense that from this point on there has been a continuous flow of published work from linguists practising it—though what is distinctive about the theory is already visible in his 'The Technique of Semantics'[35] (1935). It will no doubt have struck the reader that, in those numerous and fundamental respects in which Transformational phonology has broken away from Phonemics, it is recapitulating, a decade or more later, the development of Firth's theory. Polysystemicity is an essential element in it, as is the flexible approach to the relation of exponent and phonological item. It is still (like Firth in 1935) attached to the articulatory segment as basic unit—but this is bound to change. It seems indeed especially unfortunate that a theory operating with the data of acoustic phonetics, in which the parameter rather than the segment is the natural basic isolate, should not have followed out the implications of this for analysis.

The essential difference between the two theories is probably the concept of a sequence of operations, found in Transformation phonology. Thus, before Lees can attach the possessive suffix /sín/ (the /s/ is postulated because of such forms as *para-sı* (his money)—the /n/ can be ignored here) to a word such as *köpek*, he must get rid of /s/ (rule 10, p. 28). The suffix, in the form /ín/, can now be added to /köpEğ/, and give köpeí by rule 50 (p. 56): Vg (+)V → V (+)V. If rule 10 were not applied first, /köpEğ/ plus /sín/ would give *köpeksí. With Waterson, the possessive suffix has 'S prosody', of which (p. 584) 'with base final C there is no exponent'. The exponent of the suffix being therefore i after k^h (= Lees's /ğ/), the statement is applicable (p. 583, footnote 1) that the exponent of k^h has 'voice and absence of plosion in syllable initial'. It may well be argued that sequence is concealed in Waterson's characterization of S prosody, and contrariwise that Lees's sequence is an idiosyncratic way of setting out a structure. In any case, the parallelism between the separate assertions is obvious, and the two theories deserve close comparative study.

XIII. *Reading*

For a general exposition of Prosodic Analysis, the student should read R.H.Robins 'Aspects of Prosodic Analysis' (which contains a select bibliography); the article by J.Lyons mentioned earlier is also a very clear elementary statement. When he comes to read works of research on particular languages, the student would do well to begin with two articles by N.C.Scott, 'The Monosyllable in Szechuanese'[36] and 'A Phonological Analysis of the Szechuanese Monosyllable';[37] studied in the order as published, they give two successive stages in the analysis of the same corpus, and so form a graded introduction to the practice of Prosodic Analysis.

Notes

1 R.H.Robins, 'Aspects of Prosodic Analysis', *Proceedings of the University of Durham Philosophical Society* I, Series B (Arts) 1 (1957).

2 Miss Emel Doğramacı, of Ankara, a post-graduate student in English Literature; the Turkish pronunciation represented in my examples (other than those quoted from other writers) is hers.

3 As defined e.g. in 'A Synopsis of Linguistic Theory, 1930–1955', in *Studies in Linguistic Analysis* (Special Vol. of the Philological Society, Oxford, 1957), pp. 1–32, on p. 30, point 5; 'Structure consists of elements in interior syntagmatic relation... Systems of commutable terms or units are set up to state the paradigmatic values of the elements.'

4 M.A.K.Halliday, 'Categories of the Theory of Grammar', *Word* 17.3 (1961), pp. 241–292; ref. p. 248.

5 R.H.Robins, 'In Defence of WP', *TPS* 1959, pp. 116–144.

6 This device, and its name, are borrowed from K.L.Pike, *Language*, Pt. I, Glendale/Cal., 1954, para. 7.741.

7 One should perhaps apologise for yet again using Turkish as a demonstration device. Apart from the full-scale investigations of Waterson and Lees (discussed below), with which the present article does not presume to compete, Turkish material was also used recently by J. Lyons in 'Phonemic and Non-Phonemic Phonology', *IJAL* 28.2 (1962), pp. 127–133; ref. pp. 129–131. But what other language *is* so useful and accessible for this particular purpose?

8 I do not know how general this phenomenon may be—it is not mentioned by writers on Turkish I have consulted. If, however, it *is* at all widespread, it may explain the impression some scholars have received that the Turkish word has initial stress: see the useful summary of theories on pp. 71–75 of R.B.Lees, *The Phonology of Modern Standard Turkish*, Indiana University Publications, Uralic and Altaic Series 6 (1961).

9 These statements are not quite universally true, and in a full description would have to be supplemented—as in particular for such words as *çavuş* (sergeant), where 'labiality' associated with the *v* extends over the whole of the second syllable.

10 E.g. in W.S.Allen, 'Some Prosodic Aspects of Retroflexion and Aspiration in Sanskrit', *BSOAS* 13 (1949–51), pp. 939–946; ref. p. 943.

11 I owe this basic principle of the Kikuyu tonal system to Professor M.Guthrie, of the School of Oriental and African Studies, London, who discussed it in one of his Bantu linguistics lectures during 1946–8.

12 Three levels of analysis are implicit in the use of this term here: (i) the actual pitch pattern of the utterance, a phonetic datum; (ii) the formalization of this (sentence intonation having been abstracted), in terms of a high/low alternance (plus an occasional rising tone) on each syllable—this, already the product of a

process of phonological abstraction, is here treated for convenience as if it were the phonetic data, and is the tone pattern marked in the italicized phrases; (iii) phonological tone as ultimately analysed, retracted by one syllable from that in (ii), is that written in the phrases enclosed in obliques.

[13] My examples are derived from L.E. Armstrong, *The Phonetic and Tonal Structure of Kikuyu* (London, 1940). Of the examples given, *mocinga wá-móndo*, *né-ndígiri*, and *né-mókandá* appear there (pp. 189, 183 and 223 resp.). The others are generated by the tonal rules given by Armstrong, and authority for them can be derived from such phrases as *orito wa-móhendɔ* and *ihetiá reá-wáŋɔmbɛ* (p. 189), and *né-mórodĭ* (p. 210); *orito, morodi* and *ihetia* belong to the same tonal classes as *ndigiri, mocinga* and *mokanda* resp. My spelling corresponds in general to that suggested by Armstrong in the Appendix, except that long vowels, being irrelevant to the tone pattern, are not marked; and hyphens have been introduced to suggest the word division customary in present-day Bantu scholarship.

[14] The Nyanja examples and analysis are all from the writer's unpublished London M.A. thesis 'The Phonetics of a Nyanja Speaker', 1948 (University of London Library); the dialect represented is Mang'anja as spoken by Mr. B. E. Malekebu, of Zomba, Malawi.

[15] The tones marked on this word, at a higher level of phonological abstraction /ángodyá/, are to be referred to the point already noted that Nyanja has exponential high-high in word-final position, where the phonology would indicate low-high.

[16] Thus J.R. Firth, in 'A Synopsis of Linguistic Theory', p. 5, says: 'In these structures, one recognizes the place and order of the categories. This, however, is very different from the successivity of bits and pieces in a unidirectional time sequence.'

[17] This formulation, using the concept 'combination' in respect of stretches of a speech which we may not in fact be going to segment, may appear to be a gratuitous concession to segmental phonology. This is not of course intended. The term happens to be the clearest available, and should be thought of rather as referring to possible successions of sounds in the phonic substance.

[18] These figures have no absolute validity, as their precision is limited e.g. by a large number of *ad hoc* decisions on what is an acceptable English word (proper names? slang? etc.): but they are accurate enough to support the point made.

[19] W.S. Allen, art. cit., p. 556, footnote 4.

[20] J.R. Firth and B.B. Rogers, 'The Structure of the Chinese Monosyllable in a Hunanese Dialect', *Papers in Linguistics 1934–1951* (London, 1957), pp. 76–91.

[21] It may of course prove that an investigation of the utterance from a *phonetic* point of view—based e.g. on the physiological theory of R.H. Stetson, *Motor Phonetics*, Amsterdam, 1951—will make it possible to mark syllable boundaries. How far such phonetic syllables would be relevant to the phonological syllable under discussion is a matter that would then have to be weighed carefully—it is by no means a foregone conclusion that they would; but they would probably be highly relevant to the concept of a syntagmatic syllable (cf. p. 216, supra).

[22] C.F. Hockett, *A Manual of Phonology*, *IJAL* xxi (1955), p. 52.

[23] R.H. Robins, 'Vowel Nasality in Sundanese', *Studies in Linguistic Analysis* (Oxford, 1957), pp. 87–103.

[24] The term 'nasalized plosive' is intended to imply that only one nasal articulation occurs with a given plosive, and is homorganic with it. The phonological

transcriptions /mp/, /nt/, etc., therefore contain some redundancy; more strictly accurate would be some such device as /˜p/, etc.

25 In *Asia Major* (new series), 1 (1949), pp. 189–215.

26 It is interesting to note that F.R.Palmer, in 'Openness in Tigre', *BSOAS* xviii (1956), pp. 561–577, has analysed the Tigre word as having as many syllables as it has consonants—thus having a structure in which each C unit is a single segment, and some of the V's have zero exponent (partly predictable from rules of word structure).

27 Orthographic *c*, *ch*, *j* represent alveolo-palatal affricates.

28 K.H.Albrow, 'The Phonology of the Personal Forms of the Verb in Russian', *Arch L* 14.2 (1962), pp. 146–156.

29 J.R.Firth, 'A Synopsis of Linguistic Theory', p. 23.

30 N.Waterson, 'Some Aspects of the Phonology of the Nominal Form of the Turkish Word', *BSOAS* xviii (1956), pp. 578–591; ref. p. 583, footnote 1.

31 D.C.Scott, *A Cyclopaedic Dictionary of the Mang'anja Language* (Edinburgh, 1892), gives under both of these words alternatives with *k* instead of *c*; they were not, however, elicited from the informant studied.

32 The quotation is from J. Lyons, art. cit., p. 132 (in the context of the discussion to which this article was contributed, it may have been intended merely as the courteous recognition of an opposing point of view).

33 Full reference in footnote 8, p. 9.

34 Chap. 9, *Publications in Linguistics*, pp. 121–138.

35 Chap. 3, *Publications in Linguistics*, pp. 7–33.

36 *BSOAS* xii.1 (1947), pp. 197–213.

37 *BSOAS* xviii (1956), pp. 556–560.

Some Features of Khmer Versification

JUDITH JACOB

Two transcriptions are used below. The one in heavy type, representing the spelling of Khmer words, is based on the transcription usually used for Sanskrit with four main differences:

1. that the inherent vowel is represented by **ɔ̄** when there is no short mark over the final consonant and by **ɔ** when there is a short mark over the final consonant, while the vowel written អា (Sanskrit ā) is represented by **ā** when there is no short mark over the final consonant and by **a** when there is a short mark over the final consonant.

2. that the following vowel-signs are used to represent the symbols added by the Khmers: **ɯ**(អឹ), **uə**(អួ), **ɤ**, (អើ), **ɯə**(អឿ), **iə**(អៀ), **ɛ**(អែ).

3. that although no virama is normally used to mark final consonants in the modern Khmer orthography the final consonants of words are transcribed without the following symbol **ɔ̄** (which would represent the implied inherent vowel).

4. that where a character has the virama, e.g. ភូមិ៍, brackets enclose the corresponding letter in the transcription: **bhūm(i)**.

The transcription in italics is that used by E. J. A. Henderson[1] to represent the modern pronunciation.

The metres which have been used in Khmer poetry have been described elsewhere.[2] The purpose of this article is to discuss in further detail two of the basic features of Khmer versification, the rhymes and the syllables. A description of the recitation of five of the metres, as taught in Cambodia now, is appended.

The rhymes used by Khmer poets are based on both the vowel and final of the metric syllables involved. Nevertheless they do not always seem satisfactory. The 'imperfect' rhymes may be described as follows:

1. those which are orthographically appropriate but which are discrepant in the modern pronunciation. These may indicate that a change in pronunciation has taken place since they were first used.

2. those of which the vowels or finals are orthographically different but are pronounced alike in the modern language. Some rhymes of this category have been noted only in the poetry of the nineteenth century onwards and may therefore reflect modern developments of pronunciation, e.g. **ɛs** with **eḥ**, both now realized as *eh*.

3. those of which the vowels are equivalents neither in the orthography nor in the modern pronunciation. Many of these date back to what is assumed to be the earliest extant poetry and will be discussed in detail in the following pages.

It is the tradition of Khmer poetry that the vowels of one register[3] may rhyme with the corresponding vowels of the same length on the other register. Thus **kɔ̄ṅ**, *kɔːŋ* is as good a rhyme for **bɔ̄ṅ**, *pɔ̀ːŋ*, as is **lɔ̄ṅ**, *lɔ̀ːŋ*, and **gap**, *kɔ̀əp*, rhymes with **kap**, *kap*, just as well as with **rap**, *rɔ̀əp*. Rhymes occur, therefore, in these cases, between vowels which are written with the same symbol. It is possible that at the time when these spelling conventions were established, the corresponding vowels on the two registers were similarly articulated.[4] It seems reasonable to suppose that it was at this same stage in the development of the vowel-system that poetic conventions were being established and perhaps some of the extant Khmer poetry being composed. Thus **ḷāy** and **rāy** (modern pronunciation *laːy* and *rìːəy*), which rhyme together in the 'Chbap Kram', were possibly as perfect rhymes for each other, as far as articulation is concerned, at the time when the poem was composed as the spelling would still indicate them to be. However this may be, and it must of course be largely a matter of conjecture, Khmer rhymes have always been made between corresponding vowels on the two registers as well as between 'identical' vowels. Rhymes across register continue to be tolerated in modern poetry. I know of only one long poem, 'Teav Ek', in which they do not occur at all. Cross-register rhymes are the only examples noted of the first type of 'imperfect' rhymes mentioned above, those which the orthography supports but which modern pronunciation denies.

The second and third types of 'imperfect' rhymes will be dealt with together. Here we are first concerned with rhyming vowels of the same length but orthographically different; some are pronounced alike today while others are not. All common cases of this type of rhyme are mentioned below:

1. Short inherent vowel of either register rhymes with
   (a) **u**. Has been noted before final *k, ŋ, t, n, p, m, r, l, s, h.* e.g. **yəl**, *yẁəl* with **səmpur**, *sɔmbol.* Before final *p* and *m* only, and on the second register, the symbols are pronounced alike today, i.e. both symbols are realized as *ù.*
   (b) **a**. Has been noted before *k, t, p, m, l, s, h,* e.g. **khəp**, *khɔp* with **slap**, *slap.* These symbols are never pronounced alike in modern Khmer.
   (c) **o**. Only before final spirant, e.g. **bəs**, *pẁəs* with **smoh**, *smɔh.* These symbols are always pronounced alike in the modern language, when on the same register.

2. **a** rhymes with
   (a) **ɯ**. Has been noted before the palatals, *c, ɲ, y,* and dentals, *t, n,* e.g. **cañ**, *caɲ* with **mɯñ**, *mùɲ.* These symbols are never pronounced alike in modern Khmer.
   (b) **e** before palatals, e.g. **cañ**, *caɲ* with **ceñ**, *ceɲ.* Before a final palatal plosive the vowels are pronounced alike today, both symbols being realized as *a* (*ɛ̀əc-ɔ̀əc* do not occur).

3. As might be expected because of 2, **ɯ** rhymes with **e** before palatals, e.g. **mɯñ**, *mùɲ* with **ceñ**, *ceɲ.* This coincides with modern pronunciation in which *ɤɲ* and *eɲ*, *ùɲ* and *èɲ* are indistinguishable. The vowels have been transcribed differently in order to maintain the link between spelling and pronunciation.

ɯ, **ɯ̄** and **i**, **ī** occasionally rhyme with **e**, e.g. **cer**, *ce*: with **prambir**, *prampùl.* Although these vowels are of different lengths it is convenient to mention them here.

4. **ī** rhymes with **ay**, e.g. **tay**, *day* with **stī**, *sdɤy.* These symbols are never pronounced alike in modern Khmer.

5. **ɛ**, written with a first register-initial, rhymes with **e**:
   (a) before final **h** and in words of Sanskrit and Pali origin, e.g. **prəhɛs**, *prəhes* with **veh**, *vèh*; **tɛt**, *daet* with **hetu**, *haet.* The modern language supports these pronunciations.
   (b) in native Khmer words before final *k, ɲ, t, n, l* and in open syllables, e.g. **ɛṅ**, *aeŋ* with **leṅ**, *lè:ŋ.* These symbols are never pronounced alike in modern Khmer.

6. **o** rhymes with:

   (a) **u** before *h*, e.g. **soḥ**, *sɔh* with **kuḥ**, *koh*. Modern pronunciation does not support this rhyme. (The word **noḥ**, *nùh*, 'that', is a modern exception as the vowel, **o**, is there pronounced as if it were **u**.)

   (b) the long inherent vowel of either register before *k*, *ŋ*, e.g. **rɔ̄k**, *rɔ̀:k* with **pok**, *baok*. These symbols do not give a rhyme in the modern pronunciation.

It may be that at some time in the past each of the sets of vowels listed above did actually rhyme and that the convention of using the rhymes lingered on after the pronunciation changed (as we have guessed to be the case with rhymes across register). Certainly these rhymes between vowels written with different symbols are still used today, when many of them are not perfect rhymes.

An examination of the poetry of different periods has shown that there has apparently been a fashion in the use of certain of such rhymes. Thus the rhyme, **ī** with **ay**, which does not occur in what are generally taken to be the oldest poems, is used in the poems attributed to the time of King Sri Dhammaraja (reigned intermittently, 1702–1747). The rhyme is not steadily used from then onwards, however. In the poems of King Ang Duong and his contemporaries it rarely occurs. Whether this was mere fashion or a question of dialect cannot perhaps now be known. Again, the rhymes, **ɯ** with **a** and short inherent vowel with **a** were used by King Sri Dhammaraja and the poets of the next generation and by King Ang Duong but not very much by the poets of the late nineteenth and early twentieth centuries; the former seems to be obsolete while the latter is now used again.

The rhyme between **o** and **u** before *h* seems on the other hand to reflect a genuine development. It does not occur in what are taken to be the oldest group of poems; in the next group it occurs only with the word, **noḥ**; finally all the syllables ending with **oḥ** rhyme with **uḥ**.

With reference to 6(b) above, there is evidence from the inscriptions that modern long inherent vowel and *ao/ò*: in many words derive from a vowel written **o**. Thus **mɔ̄k**, *mɔ̀:k*, **rɔ̄k**, *rɔ̀:k* were written **mok, rok** from the seventh century until the early eighteenth. They were probably therefore at some time pronounced the same, with regard to the vowel as other words then and still written with **o**, and now pronounced with *ao/ò*:. This may account for the rhyme.

So far, in discussing the 'imperfect' rhymes which are orthographically discrepant, we have been concerned with vowels which are written with different symbols but are of the same length. Two more rhymes must now be added to the 'imperfect' rhymes of the third type, those, that is, which are different both orthographically and in the modern pronunciation. The two additions are short and long vowels rhyming together. Thus the short inherent vowel rhymes with the long inherent vowel and **a** rhymes with **ā**. This feature persists throughout Khmer poetry. It is possible that the length opposition in the inherent vowel and in **a** in native Khmer words was a comparatively recent development. The short mark, which allows the short and long inherent vowel and **a/ā** to be distinguished in writing, was an eighteenth-century invention. Occasionally **ū** and **u** rhyme together.

It seems then that some of the large variety of 'imperfect' rhymes may have been perfect as regards articulation when they were first used. Once a rhyme was established it set a precedent for later poets; thus any of the above-mentioned rhymes may be used by a modern poet. Nevertheless, it appears that a wide choice of rhyming vowels was required by the poet if he was to fulfil the demands of the metres; for, quite apart from all the rhymes mentioned above, there are occasional instances of completely different vowels being rhymed together (**uə** with **o** and **ɤ** with **ɯ** for example), and of final **k** being unpronounced as in the colloquial language in words such as *mɔ̀:k*, *rɔ̀:k* so as to rhyme with an open *ɔ̀*:. It might be suggested on the other hand that a near-rhyme appeals to the Cambodian aesthetic sense.

The final consonants which give 'imperfect' rhymes are few; all are orthographically different, as follows:

Final **r** with open syllable	Since final **r** is no longer pronounced the modern language supports this rhyme.
Final **s** and **ḥ**	In colloquial speech both are usually realized as aspirates. In reading style they are distinguished.
Final **r** and **l**	Not now pronounced alike.
Final **ūv** with **ū**	Not now pronounced alike.

It has been suggested already that certain rhyming features may be related to a particular period of poetry. It is in connection with the finals that this becomes especially clear. How far is it possible then to date a poem by the evidence of the rhymes? Working from the evidence available to me, I came to the conclusion that, while no one feature or set of features is by itself sufficient to establish with certainty the date of a poem, it may give some indication as to its age. The features enumerated below are thus indicative of age. They are given in order of value.

1. Final **r** and **l** rhyming together. A single example of this in a poem is no proof of its age, since modern poets still use the rhyme occasionally. Frequent use of the rhyme, however, may be taken as a reliable indication that it belongs to the oldest group of poetry.

2. Lack of rhyming between **s** and **ḥ** finals. A negative feature which can prove nothing by itself but which, if it is consistent throughout a long poem, may corroborate other evidence.

3. Lack of rhyming between **ī** and **ay**; between the short inherent vowel and **a**; between **ɯ** and **a**; between **o** and **u**; between the short inherent vowel and **u** before **s**. Again, a negative argument which must be treated with circumspection.

The oldest extant dated poem known to me, written on the inscription No. 40(C), dated 1633 çaka (1701 A.D.) and published in *Ganthamala*, Vol. VIII, *Inscriptions modernes d'Angkor*, shows the above characteristics. The following poems have exactly the same features:—'Chbap Ker Kal', 'Chbap Peak Chas', 'Preah Loeng Mèas', 'Chbap Kram'.[5] Three of them may perhaps for this reason be regarded as being at least as old as, if not older than, the inscription.

The poems of King Sri Dhammaraja are not very much later in date than the inscription, but it would seem that a new set of rhymes were used by him and later poets. Perhaps in the inscription of 1701 an older set of conventions is followed. The following characteristics are noted in the poetry of his poetic successors:

1. **r** and **l** finals are still a common feature but
2. **s** and **ḥ** finals rhyme together.
3. **ɯ** and **a**; short inherent vowel and **a**; **ī** and **ay** rhyme together.

A large group of poems seems to fit into the eighteenth century, having the above characteristics. They are: 'Lboek Nokor Veat', 'Ruong Mea Yoeng', 'Chbap Tunmean Khluon', 'Ream Ker', 'Sisau', 'Chbap Pros', 'Chbap Vithur Bandoet', 'Kbuon Chumreah Utpatavah', 'Chbap Srei' by Moen, 'Chbap Trei Net'.

In the poems by King Ang Duong and other royal persons coming after him in the nineteenth century, final **r** and **l** are no longer rhymed together.[6] As has been mentioned, rhyming between **ī** and **ay** temporarily dropped out during the reign of King Ang Duong but came in again immediately afterwards. The other rhymes used by King Sri Dhammaraja were still used.

The writer's interest in the metric syllable sprang from the desire to answer two questions: (1) How should the syllable, as counted in verse, be defined? (2) Have the Khmer poets kept strictly to the number of syllables required by the metres?

The reader of Khmer poetry who counts all the syllables implied by the orthography is forced to the conclusion that much of it was composed with great freedom, since, while a small number of verses has by this reckoning too few syllables, a very large number has too many. When one hears poetry recited, however, two things become clear. First, no difficulty is encountered in fitting orthographically irregular verses into the rhythm of the required tune. Roeské says,[7] 'Dans la récitation, on abrège le mot s'il y a une syllabe de trop ou on le prolonge s'il y a une syllabe de moins'. Second, when the metric syllable, that is, that part of the verse which is recited on a specific note or series of notes in the tune, is the realization of several orthographic syllables, the structure of the latter is limited to certain types of syllable. After a detailed examination of recitations and of the scansion of Khmer poetry, it was found that, in most but not quite all the poetry which was handled, the following remarks apply. The words which have more written syllables than are required by the metre are almost all of one type; they are words of Sanskrit or Pali origin in which one or more inherent vowels or short vowels occur. When the metre so requires, a syllable with an inherent vowel or short vowel is given a rapid pronunciation, comparable with the colloquial realization of such words,[8] and is thus recited either, together with a long syllable of the word, during the time allotted to one metric syllable or, together with another short syllable, as one metric syllable. Thus **mahā** may be recited either as two metric syllables, *ˈmɔ̀:ˈha:* or as one, *məˈha:*. **bhariyā** may be recited as three metric syllables, *ˈphɛ̀əˈrìˈyì:ə*,[9] or as two, *ˈphɛ̀əˀrìˈyì:ə*. Occasionally a trisyllable of Indian origin needs to be recited as one metric syllable only. Thus, in the following verse from a poem by King Ang Duong in the metre with nine syllables in each verse,[10]

dhvɤ mtec ge luəc pān prān thlay varamɯt
thvɤ̀: məde:c kè: luəc ba:n pra:n thlay vèərəˈmɯ̀t[11]

varamɯt has to be one metric syllable. It would have been possible to reduce **mtec** to one metric syllable, *mdec*, instead of two, *məde:c*,[12] so that **varamɯt** might function as two metric syllables, were it not that the rhythm of the rhyming groups of syllables requires **pān**, rhyming with **prān**, to be the last of a group of three metric syllables.

On the whole it is more usual for a polysyllable to need the colloquial realization in recitation than for it to be required in its full length. No objection seems to be felt to the use of different pronunciations of the same word in verses which occur near together. Thus, in the poem, 'Lboek Nokor Veat', the following verses occur in successive stanzas:

stec prɤ visnukəmm	*sdac praə vìsnùkam*
brəḥ visnukəmm	*prὲəh vìsnùkam*

The metre, *Bat Kakagati*, requires four syllables in each verse. Thus **visnukəmm** has to be pronounced as one metric syllable in the first verse and as three in the second.

Apart from this type of Indian borrowing, then, the syllables implied by the Khmer orthography have in most Khmer poetry the value of metric syllables, with the occasional exceptions now to be discussed. It is normal for two types of word which have hardly more than monosyllabic value in speech to be recited as two metric syllables. Thus **rɔ̄lət, pənlae** (in rapid colloquial speech, *əlẁət*, *pəlae*) are not, even in formal speech or reading style, pronounced with equal stress on the two 'syllables'. *rəˈlẁət*, *bənˈlae* would perhaps be the transcription best representing the pronunciation of the two words in prose reading. In the recitation of poetry, however, the first 'syllable' of such words may have equal stress with the second (*ˈrɔ̀:ˈlẁət*, *ˈbənˈlae*) or may even have a stronger beat in the rhythm of the tune.[13]. Moreover, such pieces may occur as the last syllable in the verse and may bear the rhyme. The following verses from the poem, 'Kakei', by King Ang Duong, contain three instances in succession, all rhyming together:

prɛ prān prɔ̄p prɔ̄-	*prae pra:n prɔ:p prɔ:-*[14]
lom luəṅ kākī	*laom luəŋ ka:kɤy*
metrī trek trɔ̄-	*mè:trɤy tre:k trɔ:-*
kɔ̄ṅ kɔ̄bī pɔ̄-	*kɔ:ŋ kɔ:bɤy bɔ:-*
pos pān thɤp thay	*baos ba:n thaəp thay*

It is only a rare occurrence for these types of word to have their colloquial pronunciation. No example has been noted in the 'Chbap'.[15]

The poem, 'Kakei', provides a few instances, such as in the first verse of the following stanza, written in the metre, Bat Pol:

khəm ət sɔ̄ṅkət nūv kɔ̄ṃhuṅ	*khɔm ɔt sɔŋkɔt nùv kɔmhɤŋ*
kɔ̄ṃsānt tel khuṅ	*kɔmsa:n dael khɤŋ*
kɔ̄ṃtuṅ kɔ̄ṃtau dɔ̄yā	*kɔmdɤŋ kɔmdau tὲəyì:ə*

in which either **sɔ̄ṅkət** or **kɔ̄ṃhuṅ** must count as one syllable. Since the rhyme between the second and fourth metric syllables here requires **sɔ̄ṅkət** to be given disyllable value, **kɔ̄ṃhuṅ** is the word to be uttered in the colloquial style.

The instances of verses with too few syllables are rather rare. Where such poetic licence is taken, the last syllable of the verse, or of the rhythmical section of the verse, is prolonged in recitation in place of the missing syllable.

It seems then that provided that one accepts as normal the frequent abbreviation of suitable syllables in Indian borrowings and the occasional abbreviation of native Khmer words, as demonstrated above, one can state that the written syllable is the metric syllable and that the Khmer poets have kept quite closely to the number of syllables required by the metres.

It was mentioned that the above statements did not apply to all Khmer poetry. So far as the writer knows the only outstanding exception is one long poem, the 'Ream Ker'.[16] This poem does seem in any case to be in a class apart, even from a purely technical point of view; for, while other poetry is recited in schools, homes and on the radio without any accompanying music, the 'Ream Ker' is normally recited with accompanying music and dancing. It does not fit into the category of song, however, since the metres used are those of poetry, not those of song.[17] Certainly it differs from the poems discussed above in the frequency of the need to abbreviate Khmer words and in the greater frequency of the occurrence of verses with too few syllables.

Modern recitations have been used above as the basis of statements which concern poetry composed over two hundred years ago. This seems defensible for two reasons. First, the style of recitation is itself based on tradition and may well be as old as the poetry. Second, the scansion of all the poetry examined can be carried out satisfactorily on this basis.

The recitation of Khmer poetry resembles singing or intoning rather than speaking. Each metre, as taught in modern Cambodia, has its own tune and rhythm. Two Cambodians reciting the same stanza or one person reciting two stanzas may give different versions[18] but the same outline of tune and rhythm will be audible in both cases.

A striking feature of the recitation of Khmer poetry is the humming sound which may occur, it has been found, after the utterance of metric syllables of which the final consonant is either (1) a nasal or (2) a plosive or (3) *h* or *s*. According to whether the final consonant is 1, 2 or 3, the person reciting uses (1) the nasal, (2) the nasal homorganic with the plosive or (3) a velar nasal, to hum on the appropriate note or notes. This humming sound will be referred to as the recitative nasal.

The duration of the utterance of the metric syllable and the recitative nasal which follows it must of course be adapted to the requirements of the tune and rhythm. Thus the utterance of the metric syllable may have to be more rapid than it otherwise would be in order to leave time for the nasal. Syllables which must be uttered on one short note (represented below by semiquavers) are not often followed by the recitative nasal. Syllables which must be uttered on one longer note are usually followed by the nasal if their final consonants are suitable. Syllables which must be spread over two or more notes and whose final consonants permit it are almost always followed by the nasal;[19] and in these cases the latter usually begins with the second note of a descending sequence and the third or last note of an ascending sequence. (Compare *nìh*(*ŋ*) and *rɔ̀:kŋ* in tune 2.) Where a metric syllable which must be recited on one long note is followed by the recitative nasal, the nasal is syllabic. Thus the one long note which is the allotted tune for that syllable is heard as two notes (see *kùt*(*n*) p. 237, tune 1). When, however, a recitative nasal is used, contrary to normal custom, after a syllable which has only a short note (see *tùk*(*ŋ*), p. 238, tune 5), the nasal is not syllabic. The recitative nasal following *h* or *s* is rarely syllabic if the metric syllable is recited on one note only. The taste of the person reciting may vary a little with regard to the recitative nasal; one person may use it in reciting a given metric syllable of a given poem, while another may choose not to do so, especially if a succession of suitable syllables has just occurred.

I recorded in Cambodia the recitation of extracts of five poems of different metres by Miss Nophikoun, a teacher at the Malika School, Phnom Penh. Dr. A. A. Bake, Reader in Sanskrit in the University of London, gave considerable time and thought to the preparation of a musical notation from my recordings, for which I am very grateful indeed. One stanza of each poem is given below. The musical notation and the representation of the recitative nasal are as in the recording of that stanza. Dr. Bake also most kindly wrote some remarks on the musical aspect of the recitations, which are given on pp. 238–240.[20]

1. Bat Kakagati. The stanza is from the poem, 'Chbap Kram'.
Syllable-scheme: 4: 4: 4: 4: 4: 4: 4.

2. Bat Brahmagita. The stanza is from the poem, 'Tumnuonh Trei'.
Syllable-scheme: 5: 6: 5: 6.

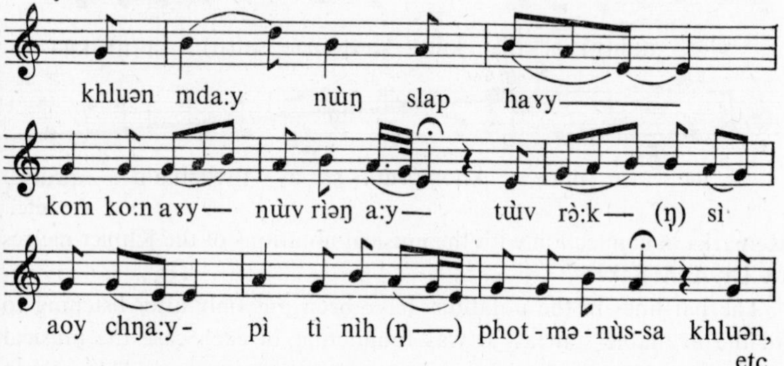

3. Bat Pumnol. The stanza is from the poem, 'Ruong Mea Yoeng'.
Syllable-scheme: 6: 4: 6.

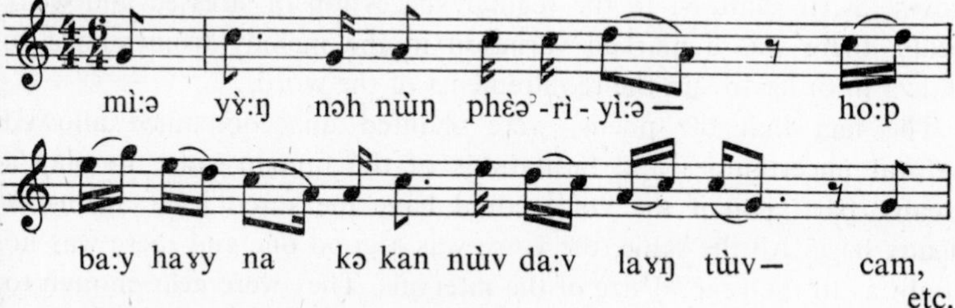

4. Bat Bantol Kak. The stanza is from the poem, 'Ruong Sophea Tunsay'.

Syllable-scheme: 4: 6: 4: 6.

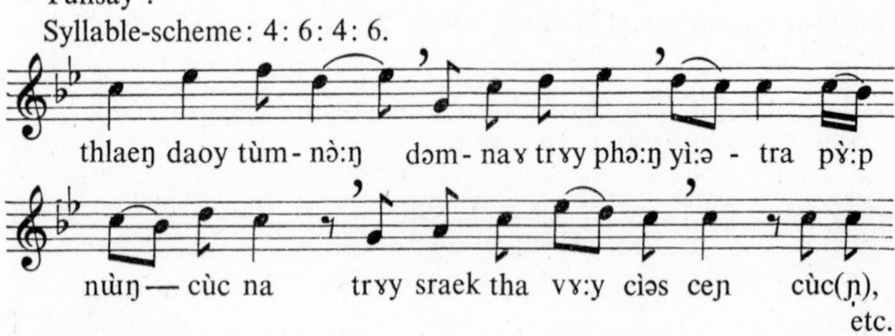

5. Bat Peak Prampoel. The stanza is from the poem, 'Peak Preng Pradau'.

Syllable-scheme: 7: 7: 7: 7.

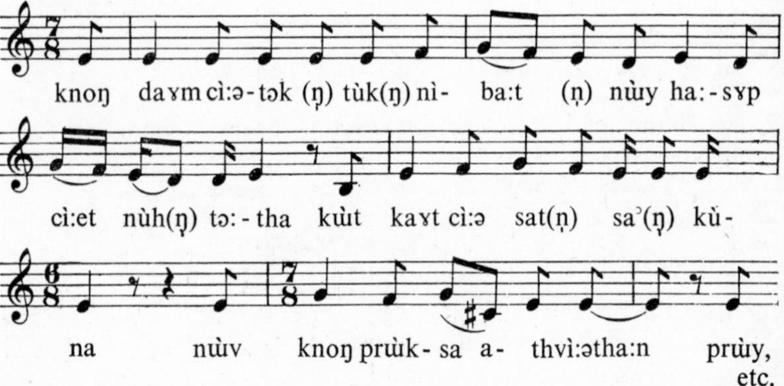

Remarks in connection with the musical notations of the Khmer metres by Dr. A. A. Bake:

The bar-lines in the notations have been put only after listening to all the available stanzas. It was found that in each case the musical time-scheme hardly varied at all from beginning to end. The melody given, however, is only that which fitted the particular stanza noted down, as, in contrast to the regular succession of stressed and weak beats, there was a marked variation in the melody from stanza to stanza in order to suit the requirements of the words.

The fact that the poems were chanted unaccompanied allowed natural uncertainties and hesitations of the human voice to play a greater part than if the voice could have measured itself against a steady base. All the same, the voice was a good one and there was no doubt as to the general size of the intervals. They were near enough to our scale to be represented in ordinary staff notation. The difficulty lay in the nasal syllables on definite notes which were hard to fit into the time-schemes, since they were definitely not grace-notes but, on the other hand, did not seem to have a time-value that could be easily expressed in notation.

The melodies showed a strong tendency to use a scale with one or two degrees missing. As the full octave did not occur, it was impossible to say what the whole octave scale would have been, but the character seemed to be predominantly pentatonic.

As far as the pattern of musical time is concerned, it seems that in the chanting of Cambodian poetry there are two conflicting tendencies —the same as are found in India. On the one hand there is the prosodical scheme where the quantity of each individual syllable in the lines of poetry determines the metrical shape of the melody. A very clear instance of this tendency is No. 4, where the prosodical scheme with two very characteristic successions of short notes is the determining factor. It would be very difficult to fit a regular time-scheme with bar-lines into this pattern. The stanza has a very strong caesura before the fourth quarter, which gives the last line the appearance of an afterthought or a coda with a marked metrical pattern, beginning with a succession of six short notes. This afterthought, however, does not necessarily coincide (any more?) with the sense of the words.

But for the fact that slight changes in longs and shorts occur from stanza to stanza (and that a pause is sometimes filled up with part of a syllable), one might approximate this pattern to that of the classical Indian metres of the śârdûlavikrîdita-type. Perhaps it is even closer to the later Buddhist Sanskrit metres. The general appearance of the underlying metrical scheme of the melody is:

—/—⏑—⏑ ⏑⏑⏑—⏑⏑ —⏑—⏑—[⏑̱]/ ⏑⏑⏑⏑⏑⏑—⏑//

In strong contrast to this purely prosodical melody-pattern stands the purely musical time-pattern, as e.g. in No. 1, a stanza of seven times four syllables, in which, however, the four metrical syllables do not correspond to a musical time of 4/4, but are forced into a pattern of unmistakable bars of three beats. Each stanza of seven quite rigid bars is then divided up into a group of three and two groups of two bars. The closing two-bar phrase is a near parallel to the two opening bars.

The other examples lie midway between these two extremes. The original prosodical scheme is still discernible, but the musical time with its stressed beats has exercised a marked influence on it. The number of syllables in the stanza of the verse does not determine the total number of beats in the groups of bars, nor does the original succession of longs and shorts determine the rhythmic character of the melody from bar to bar.

The scheme 5.6.5.6 (No. 2) is broken up into two distinct phrases with a marked pause between them. Both consequently should have eleven beats. In point of fact, however, the musical time starts on an off-beat and the remaining ten syllables of the semi-stanza are brought into the musical pattern of 6/8, 5/8, 6/8, 5/8, plus a rest. Then the same pattern is repeated to the words of the next two lines, with a rest before the off-beat of the next stanza.

A kindred procedure is followed with the metrical scheme 6.4.6 (No. 3) which is compressed into a pattern of ten beats. This again starts with an off-beat. The counting begins with the stressed second syllable of each stanza. There is a marked rest after the fourth beat, but the beats continue uninterruptedly with a bar of six beats which completes the 10/4 musical scheme.

The same general principle of having a musical line reminiscent of but not identical with the prosodical pattern seems to have been at work in the last of the five examples where, in the metrical scheme of four times seven syllables, the 'seven' appears in the number of beats in each of the six 'bars' of the melody of each stanza.

The recording of the chanting of this particular metre was somewhat faulty and consequently it was more difficult to arrive at a clear picture of what was happening. The notation therefore is definitely a tentative effort.

Notes

1 E. J. A. Henderson, 'The Main Features of Cambodian Pronunciation', *BSOAS* xiv (1952), pp. 149–173.

2 M. Roeské, 'Métrique Khmère. Bat et Kalabat.' *Anthropos* viii (1913), pp. 673–687, pp. 1028–1043. It may perhaps be noted here that modern Khmer poets occasionally use metres which, though not actually described by Roeské, have the same verse- and rhyme-pattern as some of the metres with which he dealt. Thus stanzas consist of 4 verses, each having either 10, 11, 12 or 14 syllables with rhyme-schemes as follows:

1st Stanza	2nd Stanza
________ a	________ d
___ a ___ b	___ d ___ c
________ b	________ c
___ b ___ c	___ c ___ e

The exact position of the internal rhyme varies, cf. the metres with 6, 7, 8 and 9 syllables described on pp. 676–679 of op. cit.

[3] For the use of this term see E.J.A. Henderson, op. cit.

[4] Whether a register-distinction was then in operation is not, I think, known. It must surely be assumed to be possible that the surd and sonant initials once implied voice-opposition and not a register-distinction.

[5] The 'Chbap Kram' is the work of Preah Sugandha who lived during the reign of Sri Dhammaraja; it may therefore be at least slightly later than the poem on the inscription.

[6] One or two occurrences in the poetry of Nong, who wrote during King Ang Duong's reign, are the only exceptions noted.

[7] Roeské, op. cit., p. 673.

[8] The written inherent vowel is realized as *ə* instead of *ɛ̀ə* or *ɔ̀*:, no glottal stop closes the syllable and stress is absent.

[9] As shown on p. 237 in verse 1 of example of Bat Pumnol.

[10] Published in *Kambujasuriya* (1939), No. 5, p. 106.

[11] *vɛ̀ərə'mùt* instead of *'vɛ̀əˀ'rɛ̀ə'mùt*.

[12] See below re abbreviated Khmer words.

[13] See *dɔmnaə* in the stanza from the poem, 'Ruong Sophea Tunsay', p. 238; cf. also the treatment of syllables in Khmer songs.

[14] Here, in the words, **prɔ̄lom** and **trɔ̄kɔ̄ñ**, and on p. 237 in the word, **prɔ̄kham**, the first vowel is transcribed *ɔ*:, not *ə* in order to represent as closely as possible the pronunciation of the words in these contexts of recitation.

[15] It is not surprising that in these poems, written for the moral training of the young, the orthography should be respected.

[16] Khmer version of the Ramayana.

[17] See Roeské, op. cit., pp. 1028–1043, for a description of the construction of Khmer songs.

[18] Compare the variant versions of the same air played on the Cambodian xylophone, by which in fact the musician shows his skill.

[19] This, taken in conjunction with what Dr. Bake writes on p. 239 with regard to the quantitative nature of the prosodical schemes of the metres, would suggest that in Khmer poetry the recitative nasal may have been introduced to create the required long syllables.

[20] It will be observed that no time signature is given in the musical notation for meters 2 and 4. The reason for this is explained in Dr. Bake's notes.

Henry Sweet's Paths Toward Phonemics

ROMAN JAKOBSON

I'll take it down first
in Bell's Visible Speech;
then in Broad Romic . . ..
Bernard Shaw, *Pygmalion*

'The freshness and originality of his mind . . . ever open to new ideas, and fresh points of view . . . the saving virtues of imagination and humour . . . truthfulness, simplicity, and courage';[1] 'unhesitating candour . . . natural simple candour . . . unflinching candour'.[2] While reading these and many similar testimonials in the various memoirs on Henry Sweet, I unwittingly fused these appraisals with the powerful impression I retained from the first, circumstantial conversation with J. R. Firth in a New York tavern toward the end of the 1940s and our last heart-to-heart talk of June 1960 in his enchanting Lindfield home.

When recollecting Firth's pointed views and remarks, when re-reading Sweet's books and papers or when listening to the intent discussions among young English linguists, I once more experience the same salient feature which strikes a foreign observer in English poetry and philosophy from the Middle Ages till our own time. What fascinates me in all these domains and likewise in the centuries of English painting, which so often has been unjustly underrated, is the singular gift of the prominent thinkers and artists: their unusual courage to see the world with their own eyes irrespective of the environmental usage, habit and predilection.

The years when the novelty of Sweet's approach to language and its sound pattern found a particularly clear and explicit formulation were 1876–7. In 1876 he wrote the first version of his treatise on the 'Practical Study of Language' and published an elaborate attempt 'to upset some of the conventional dogmas of philology, logic, and grammar'.[3] In the following year he printed a revised edition of the same study[4] and, probably spurred on by two successive academic defeats, first at

London University College, then in Oxford, and at the same time inspired by his Chairmanship in the Philological Society, Sweet brought out his *Handbook of Phonetics*, prefaced in *Christiania, Aug*. 27, 1877,[5] and outlined a wide research program in his Presidential Address delivered at the anniversary meeting of the Philological Society 18 May 1877.[6]

Sweet's linguistic doctrine proceeds from the thesis that 'language is essentially based on the dualism of form and meaning'. Hence all attempts to disregard this dualism and 'to reduce language to strict logical or psychological categories, by ignoring its formal side, have failed ignominiously. The form of language is its *sounds*. The science which teaches us to observe, analyse, and describe the sounds of language is phonology'.[7] Sweet constantly insisted on the importance of phonology as the indispensable foundation of all linguistic study 'whether that study is purely theoretical, or practical as well'. He was prone to believe that this is now generally recognized, 'except in hopelessly obscurantist circles'.[8]

The same indispensable dualism of form and meaning compelled Sweet to ascertain that the sound shape of language cannot be exhaustively investigated without a constant reference to meaning. Not only in the seventies but in the whole nineteenth century one could hardly find another study of speech sounds which would put forward and utilize the notion of 'significant sound-distinctions' with such a zeal and tenacity, as it is done in Sweet's *Handbook* of 1877. He consistently separates those definite distinctions of sound 'which *may* correspond to differences of meaning' from all other 'differences which are not significant and cannot alter the meaning'.[9]

It is true that this classification of sound-distinctions is confined to those portions of the book which deal with graphic representations of sounds, namely the last Part, entitled 'Sound-Notation', and the Appendix with an Exposition of the Principles of Spelling Reform. It is also true that the system of sound-notation, which under the label *Broad Romic* was introduced by Sweet in order to 'indicate only those broader distinctions of sound which actually correspond to distinctions of meaning in language', was expressively designated by its inventor 'for practical purposes' in opposition 'to the scientific Narrow Romic'. The latter, like Bell's *Visible Speech*, was constructed 'for an accurate analysis of sounds generally' and was 'too minute for many practical purposes'.[10] The idea of a double notation goes back to A. J. Ellis' gradual efforts to complement the explicit system by a more practical one, where 'many of the delicate distinctions which are necessary in a complete phonetical alphabet are neglected' (1848). The last improvement of Ellis' notational experiments was his 'veri eezi' *Glossic* of 1871, coupled with the *Universal Glossic* which aimed 'at giving simbelz faur dhi moast mine·ut foanet·ik anal·isis yet achee·vd'.[11]

Besides the *Broad Romic*, another application of simplified sound notation was Sweet's project of reformed English spelling. He was, like Ellis, a staunch supporter of the reform and vehemently discussed its basic principles. In Sweet's opinion, 'the prejudices, especially of our upper class, are too strong to be overcome by reason', but 'in the end truth and reason will triumph over those arch-enemies of progress', and 'the longer reform is delayed, the more sweeping it will be when it comes'.[12]

Thus the signification of speech sounds was approached by Sweet only within the framework of applied linguistics and merely in connection with graphic questions—the 'practical' variant of sound-notation and the spelling reform. In the *Handbook* these questions are systematically treated with regard to the functions performed by the speech sounds in language, whereas the chapters devoted to sounds and their combinations take no heed of those functions.

Such an inconsistency can be partly explained by the disregard of these questions in the influential contemporaneous writings of German phoneticians. 'The fact that the majority of those who have worked at phonetics in Germany have been physiologists and physicists rather than practical linguists' accounts in Sweet's view for certain defects of the German school.[13] Obviously no attention was paid to the linguistic functions of the sounds by these physiologists and physicists, but also in the authoritarian linguistic trend of that time, in the school of the *Junggrammatiker*, the strictly genetic approach suppressed any functional problem.

Despite that critical attitude to 'the tendencies of German study' which unites Henry Sweet with William Dwight Whitney and Ferdinand de Saussure, and despite his consistently antiauthoritarian, rebellious spirit, neither Sweet nor any other linguist of the Victorian era was able to advance a frontal attack against the narrowly causal, genetic bias of his epoch, and the forerunners' valor and greatness was in bold sallies and flanking movements. Applied linguistics, or in Sweet's terms, 'the practical study of language', was that flank, where he succeeded in raising new problems and in trying new methods.

Although it is the *Narrow Romic* that has been declared 'scientific' by Sweet, he sees that the *Broad Romic* is necessary for what we would call today general phonemics, namely for treating the relations of sounds without going into those 'minute details' on which differences of meaning cannot depend. The *Broad Romic* is further necessary for the 'treating of a single language' and for writing passages of any length in this language.[14] But although the question of relation between sound and meaning is discussed only in connection with notation, we are reminded by the author that 'the notation of sounds is scarcely less important than their analysis: without a clear and consistent system of notation it is impossible to discuss phonetic questions intelligibly or to describe the phonetic structure of a language'.[15] In other words, the phonemic analysis and 'broad' notation imply each other.

J.R. Firth was right when stating that 'the phoneme idea' is implicit in Sweet's *Broad Romic*,[16] yet we could add that the theoretical foundations of phonemics are implicit in Sweet's exposition of the principles which underlie both the *Broad Romic* and the representation of speech sounds in a rational spelling.

It was clear to the author that the reason for the disregard of 'minuter shades', or 'delicate distinctions' does not lie in their smallness but uniquely in their incapacity of changing the meaning. 'Thus the first elements of the diphthongs in "by" and "out" vary considerably: some people sound them broad as in "father", some flat as in "man", with various intermediate sounds. And yet the meaning of the words remains unchanged. The distinction between the vowels of "men" and "man", on the other hand, though really slighter than that of the different pronunciations of "by" and "out", is a distinctive one.'[17]

As a rule, Sweet abstained, according to his own acknowledgment, from 'attempting to settle questions of priority of discovery'.[18] Two world linguists, Henry Sweet and Jan Baudouin de Courtenay, both born in 1845, simultaneously and independently of each other coped with the same problems. In 1877, at the same time as Sweet's *Handbook*, there appeared in the *Bulletin* (*Izvestija*) *of Kazan University* the 'Reports on Baudouin de Courtenay's Studies in Linguistics during 1872 and 1873' with a brief plan of inquiry into 'the mechanism of speech sounds, their correspondencies and their dynamic relationship, based on connections between sound and meaning'. Two 'Detailed Programs of Baudouin de Courtenay's Lectures' of 1877 and 1878 were printed in the *Bulletins* of the same university in 1878 and 1881. They contain a more detailed outline of phonetic studies, expressively divided into two parts—one dealing with the physiological and physical aspect of speech sounds, and the other, 'phonetics in the true sense of the word', treating 'sounds in connection with word meaning'. Whereas Sweet confined his phonemic research to the level of applied linguistics, Baudouin de Courtenay assigned to this reasearch an important place in linguistic theory. He superposed this 'morphologico-etymological part of the science of speech sounds' as a thoroughly linguistic discipline upon the auxiliary description of articulations and their acoustic effects. On the other hand, it was Sweet who opened new vista in his definition and classification of sound distinctions. His rigorous delimitation of both notations—broad and narrow—was a gratifying way toward an empiric implementation of Baudouin's theoretical bipartition of phonetics.[19]

'It would be curious to know what the old school of German philologists think of Winteler's work on the phonology and grammar of one of the dialects of Switzerland', said Sweet in his Presidential Address of 1877.[20] The same work appears among the reference books in Baudouin de Courtenay's Program cited above. Jost Winteler, born in 1846, was the third great precursor of modern phonemics among the linguists of Sweet's and Baudouin's generation and his epoch-making monograph[21] most probably influenced Sweet's use of minimal pairs for commutations tests (e.g. *men-man* or French *pécher-pêcher*) as well as his consistent discrimination between 'distinctive differences' and mere 'variations'. The concept of invariance underlies both Sweet's and Baudouin's phonological studies of the seventies, while the invariants remain nameless in these writings. The term *phonème*, proposed in 1873 by A. Dufriche-Desgenettes simply to translate into French the German *Sprachlaut*,[22] was accepted and popularized by the Romance philologist L. Havet.[23] In his work the young F. de Saussure, striving for a reconstruction of the Indo-European sound pattern, took over this label and used it to designate any element of this pattern which, whatever its articulation may be, proves to be '*distinct de tous autres phonèmes*'.[24] Mikołaj Kruszewski, the closest student and collaborator of Baudouin de Courtenay and one of the keenest spirits in linguistic science of the last century, caught up Saussure's term, proposed to apply it to the various aspects of phonological invariance[25] and jointly with his teacher opened the way to the modern development of this name and concept.

Sweet did not search after names for the invariants in question but only for 'general symbols' to specify these invariants in notation and spelling. 'Thus, the innumerable varieties of diphthongs possible can all be classed under a few general categories . . . and if we simply provide unambiguous signs for these general categories, we can ignore the endless shades of difference within them, because these differences do not alter the meaning or application of the words in which they occur.'[26] He uses two general symbols (ai, au) 'for a variety of diphthongs, all of which may be classed under one of two distinct types, both beginning with back or mixed non-rounded vowels [this 'or' is a deviation from the purely functional approach underlying the Broad Romic] and ending with approximations to (i) and (u) respectively'.[27]

Sweet sought specifying terms not for units but for their relations. His whole definitely relational conception of phonological invariance is based on the notion of 'significant distinctions', opposed to 'not significant', 'superfluous', or as we would say now, redundant differences. What matters on this level is not the sound but its distinctive properties. 'Hence we have to distinguish not so much between *sounds* as between *groups of sounds.*' As an example of the 'important distinctions of these groups' Sweet quotes that of 'close' and 'open'.[28] A further radical and valuable contribution to the sifting of 'superfluous sound-distinctions' is Sweet's 'general rule that only those distinctions of sounds require to be symbolized in any one language which are *independently significant*'. Thus, in English, it would be superfluous to indicate the distinction of narrow and wide since 'the quantity would always imply the distinctions of narrow and wide'. Of 'two criteria of significance' only one proves to be relevant.[29]

Sweet is fully aware that 'if we confine our attention to definite distinctions . . . which may correspond to differences of meaning, we find that each language utilizes only a few of these distinctions'.[30] But in addition to such intralingual restrictions in the inventory of 'independently significant distinctions' there are universal restrictions. If two vowels, even 'formed in a totally different way', 'are never employed together in the same language to distinguish the meanings of words, . . . they may be considered as variations of the same vowel'.[31] Thus, the extraction of invariants from intralingual variations is quite logically complemented by a daring and novel search for interlingual, universal variations and for corresponding invariants. Of course, this kind of consideration is claimed by the author to serve merely 'practical purposes', but at present it is clear that under the narrowly genetic and causational orientation of that age only an emphasis on 'ordinary practical purposes' gave a chance to the linguist to tackle the purposiveness of language and opened up to him some insight into its means-ends model.

Both for Baudouin de Courtenay and for Sweet it was self-evident that differences of word meaning could not depend on the stress automatically tied to the first or some other syllable of the word. Hence, according to Sweet's 'common-sense principle', 'if a language always has the stress on the first syllable, the stress does not require to be marked at all'. But this principle is applied by Sweet not only to the cases of probability one but also, and this is a pertinent innovation, to the specimens of a probability less than one: 'If the majority of words have the stress on the first syllable, then it is necessary to mark it only when it falls on some other syllable.' For example, in English, 'it need not be marked in *foutograf* (photograph)'.[32]

Binary oppositions requiring a symbol only for the mark but not for its absence were clearly viewed by Sweet: Since in Greek 'there are only two breathings, . . . the absence of the rough breathing is enough to show that the other one is meant'.[33] The same rule is applied to the pair of Swedish word-tones where the simple tone 'is practically merely the negation of the compound tone, and may therefore be either a rise or fall according to the context'.[34]

The 'less accurate' Broad Romic was conceived by its author 'as a kind of algebraic notation'[35] and thus was seen to be an advanced and generalized scientific operation. A similar tendency toward an algebraization of linguistics was professed by Baudouin de Courtenay and F. de Saussure.[36]

Sweet's phonetics and especially its avowedly practical sections have played an outstanding international role. Since the late eighties Paul Passy's campaign for a reform of French orthography and his leading activities in the International Phonetic Association, especially his continuous struggle for the 'golden rule' of broad notation affirm and develop Sweet's principles. At the beginning of our century closer links were established between Baudouin's school and Sweet's followers in the Phonetic Association, especially between Lev Ščerba and Passy, and the former's theoretic and descriptive studies, a transitional stage from Baudouin's doctrine to modern phonemics, were inspired by Sweet's and Passy's elicitation of significant distinctions. From 1900 there arose an abundant linguistic correspondence between Sweet and Baudouin de Courtenay partly due to the latter's concern with the relation between language and writing. If these letters still exist, they should be published, and in general one can only emphatically repeat the concluding words of A. Brandl's obituary notice on Sweet: 'Möge sein Nachlass treue Herausgeber finden!'[37]

When in 1943 L. Bloomfield was asked what were the works that gave an impulse to the phonemic part of his manual,[38] he referred to Sapir and Trubetzkoy, but first and foremost to Sweet's note on 'Significant Sound-distinctions',[39] from which, as the author of *Language* confessed, actually arose his term and idea of 'distinctive features'.

Another trait closely linked with Sweet's functional attitude toward speech sounds and likewise connecting the 'science man' of the 1870s with modern research, is his predilection for descriptive linguistics. It is characteristic that even in the preface to his *History of English Sounds from the Earliest Period*, the author blamed the 'one-sidedly historical spirit' of the German philological tradition[40] or, as he said in 1874, the 'mainly historical and antiquarian' tendencies of German study.[41]

In his famous Presidential Address of 1877 Sweet condemned the exclusively genealogical orientation of comparative philology which values 'the forms of later languages solely according to the amount of light they throw on older forms'.[42] Both in his address, and in a later study devoted to Linguistic Affinity,[43] Sweet displayed a new set of comparative problems. On the one hand, 'divergence between cognate languages ... raises the question, how far does the possibility of change of structure extend?'[44] On the other hand, 'nothing can be more important than the comparison of the "parallel developments" in such distinct languages as the Romance and the Neo-Sanskrit, English and Persian, etc.'.[45] The diffusion of linguistic phenomena asks for a systematic study, since the possibilities of mixture proved to be 'greater than was suspected by the founders of comparative philology'. 'There is no necessary limit to mixture of vocabulary. ... The possibility of syntactic influence is clearly proved' and 'there is clear evidence that different languages may influence one another morphologically'.[46]

Again it was Sweet who had broached an unwonted problem which became a crucial topic in present-day linguistics: 'In the first place, there can be no doubt that contiguous languages often show striking phonetic resemblances even when they are not cognate or only remotely so.' This statement is supported by references to 'marked phonetic peculiarities' spread out 'without regard to linguistic relationship' in the Caucasus, in Eastern Asia or in Southern Africa.[47]

Beside similarities due to kinship or contiguity of languages Sweet observed genetically independent 'agreements in general structure' and for instance proposed a comparison of some features of Modern English 'to those of Chinese, the Turanian, and even of some savage languages'. From such a typological comparison independent of genetic relations, Sweet infers 'the all-important principle that every language and every period of a language has an individuality of its own, which must be respected'.[48] The corollary of this principle is 'the recognition of a science of *living*, as opposed to dead, or antiquarian philology'. This general conclusion of Sweet, exactly like his *Broad Romic*, is tied for him with the practical study of language; he lucidly foresees, however, that this science 'is the indispensable foundation' of the various linguistic branches, and even 'of historical and comparative philology'.[49]

On the practical level Sweet displays a consistently functional approach, and discussing 'the delicate distinctions of the English verb' he asks ironically: 'What can historical philology contribute to the analysis of *will love*, *shall love*, *is loving*, etc.?' The 'injurious' misuse of the historical viewpoint is drastically attacked by Sweet and appears to him 'as reasonable as it would be to insist on every one having Macaulay's *History of England* permanently chained round his neck, because history is an improving study'.[50] Meanwhile Sweet's view of synchrony is far from deadly statics, and 'changes in progress' are discussed by him with a gripping ingenuity.[51]

There appears one more concept, conjugate with the functional method of approach and quite alien to the predominant linguistic doctrine of the late nineteenth century. This was the idea of totality, emphasized by Sweet against the disintegrating spirit of the current dogma: 'I, for one, am strongly of the opinion that our present exaggeratedly analytical methods . . . are a failure compared with the synthetic methods of the Middle Ages, by which sentences were grasped as wholes', whereas at present they are 'put together like pieces of mosaic work'. The critic concludes that 'any real reform will involve, partially at least, a return to these older methods'.[52] It is remarkable that similarly to Sweet, his older American contemporary Charles Sanders Peirce also, while anticipating the build-up of a semiotic science in the future, deplored and assailed its present status and invoked the Schoolmen's superior legacy.

Neither of these two giants received a chair from his alma mater or from any other university. After a long 'series of academic disappointments and rebuffs' and '1901—the year of the most incredible of all his academic defeats, . . . Oxford's failure to offer to Sweet what was then the sole professorship of comparative philology' in England,[53] he vainly tried to persuade the Vice-Chancellor of Oxford University that beside the Chair of Comparative Philology, 'there ought to be another Professorship of the Science of Language (philosophical grammar, etc.)'.[54] In H. C. Wyld's opinion, 'no man surely was ever more sensitive, and more easily wounded by maliciousness, callousness, and brutality, even when these were veiled by a soft voice and sleek manners'.[55]

In an earlier note, commenting on Sweet's failure of 1901, Wyld reports that in a company of prominent German *Junggrammatiker* the only explanation considered satisfactory for the shocking and unbelievable fact that Sweet never became professor was the whimsical surmise 'that *Sweet* stood for *Süss*, which was clearly a Jewish name, and that Israelites were not much more popular in England than in Germany'.[56]

As I wrote in my afore-cited paper about Baudouin de Courtenay and his school, 'the proverb says that it is wrong to discover America too late, after Columbus, but also a too early discovery may be detrimental'. The great precursors of the modern science of language—John Hughling Jackson (1835–1911), Charles Sanders Peirce (1839–1914), Henry Sweet (1845–1912), Jan Baudouin de Courtenay (1845–1929), Jost Winteler (1846–1929), Mikołaj Kruszewski (1851–1887), and Ferdinand de Saussure (1857–1913)—each of them in his own way bears a stamp of tragedy on his whole life.

In the final Annual Address of the President, delivered by Henry Sweet at the Anniversary Meeting of the Philological Society, 7 May 1878, under the eloquent heading 'The Future of English Philology' it was stated:

> There is one form of charlatanry to which I will call your attention, and which is specially insidious and dangerous, veiling itself under the disguise of conscientiousness and accuracy. It may be termed the *mechanical* view of language, and is based on the assumption that language . . . is not governed by general laws, but consists merely of a mass of disconnected details.[57]

The scholar who dared to look far ahead and to defy the creed of his time was proscribed to become *le savant maudit*.

Notes

[1] Henry Cecil Wyld, 'Henry Sweet', *Archiv für das Studium der neueren Sprachen und Literaturen*, N.S. xxx (1913), pp. 1–8.

[2] C.L. Wrenn, 'Henry Sweet', *Transactions of the Philological Society* 1946, pp. 177–201.

[3] Henry Sweet, 'Words, Logic, and Grammar', *Transactions of the Philological Society* 1875–6, pp. 470–503. Reprinted in: Henry Sweet, *Collected Papers*, arranged by H.C. Wyld (Oxford, 1913), pp. 1–33.

[4] Henry Sweet, 'Language and Thought', *Journal of the Anthropological Institute* (May, 1877).

[5] Henry Sweet, *A Handbook of Phonetics* (Oxford, 1877).

[6] Henry Sweet, 'Presidential Address on English Philology and Phonology', *Transactions of the Philological Society* 1877–9, pp. 1–16. Reprinted in: *Collected Papers*, pp. 80–94.

[7] *Collected Papers*, p. 85.

[8] *A Handbook*, p. v; *A New English Grammar Logical and Historical* (Oxford, 1892), p. xii.

[9] *A Handbook*, see especially pp. 103 f., 182 f.

[10] Ibid., pp. 103, 105.

[11] Alexander John Ellis, *The Ethnical Alphabet, or Alphabet of Nations* (London, 1848), p. 1; idem., *On Early English Pronunciation* III (London, 1871): 'Glossic', pp. xiii–xx; see p. xiii f. In 1878 Sweet himself acknowledged and determined his indebtedness to 'the pioneer of scientific phonetics in England': 'I thus formed the two systems, *Broad* and *Narrow Romic*, mainly on the basis of Mr. Ellis' *Paleotype*, from which the latter differs mainly in the values assigned to the letters. To the relation between my two systems corresponds that between Mr. Ellis' *Glossic* and *Universal Glossic*, which are, however, based not on the Roman values of the letters, as in the case with Paleotype, but on an attempt to retain their present English value' (*Collected Papers*, p. 117 f.). Both *Glossic* and *Broad Romic* carry out a 'rougher phonetic notation and for purely practical purposes' (ibid., p. 120).

[12] *Collected Papers*, p. 88; cf. *A Handbook*, p. 169 ff.

[13] *A Handbook*, p. vi f.

[14] *A Handbook*, p. 103; cf. *The Practical Study of Languages* (New York, 1900), p. 25.

[15] *A Handbook*, p. 100.

[16] J.R. Firth, 'The word "phoneme"', *Le Maître Phonétique*, Third Series, XII (April, 1934), pp. 44–46.

[17] *A Handbook*, p. 182.

[18] For more detailed data on 'the Kazan School of Polish Linguistics and Its Place in the World development of Phonology' see my paper in the *Bulletin de la Société Polonaise de Linguistique* xix (1960), pp. 3–34.

[19] *A Handbook*, p. 105. Baudouin hinted for the first time at the need of discrimination between two ways of transcription only in 1881, when his selected lectures on Slavic comparative grammar appeared in the review *Russkij Filologičeskij Vestnik*.

[20] *Collected Papers*, p. 87.

[21] Jost Winteler, *Die Kerenzer Mundart des Kantons Glarus in ihren Grundzügen dargelegt* (Leipzig, 1876).

[22] See *Revue Critique* I (1873), p. 368.

[23] Cf. L. Havet, 'OI et UI en français', *Romanie* (1874), p. 321.

[24] Ferdinand de Saussure, *Mémoire sur le système primitif des voyelles dans les langues indo-européennes* (Leipzig, 1878–9), p. 121.

[25] Mikołaj Kruszewski, Über die Lautabwechslung (Kazan, 1881), p. 14. Cf. my above-named article, pp. 11 ff.

[26] *A Handbook*, p. 103.

[27] *The Practical Study*, pp. 18 f.

[28] *A Handbook*, p. 183.

[29] Ibid., p. 104

[30] Ibid., pp. 103, 182.

[31] Ibid., p. 183.

[32] *A Handbook*, p. 190; *The Practical Study*, p. 19. Cf. the question of absolute and relative predictability discussed by A. A. Zaliznjak in *Simpozium po strukturnomu izučeniju znakovyx sistem* (Moscow, 1962), p. 55.

[33] *The Practical Study*, p. 19.

[34] *A Handbook*, p. 155.

[35] *A History of English Sounds from the Earliest Period* (Oxford, 1888), p. x.

[36] Structure of Language and its Mathematical Aspects. *Proceedings of Symposia in Applied Mathematics* XII (American Mathematical Society, 1961), p. v f.

[37] *Archiv für das Studium der neueren Sprachen und Literaturen*, N.S. XXX (1913), p. 11.

[38] Leonard Bloomfield, *Language* (New York, 1933), Ch. V–VIII.

[39] *The Practical Study*, p. 18 f.

[40] *A History*, p. xi.

[41] Henry Sweet, 'Report on Germanic and Scandinavian', *Transactions of the Philological Society* 1873–4, pp. 439–446. Reprinted in *Collected Papers*, pp. 73–79. See p. 75.

[42] *Collected Papers*, p. 92.

[43] Henry Sweet, 'Linguistic Affinity', *Otia Merseiana* ii (1900–1), pp. 113–126. Reprinted in *Collected Papers*, pp. 56–71.

[44] *Collected Papers*, p. 63.

[45] Ibid., p. 92.

[46] Ibid., p. 60 f.

[47] Ibid., p. 61 f.

[48] Ibid., pp. 62, 92.

[49] Henry Sweet, 'The Practical Study of Language', *Transactions of the Philological Society* 1882–4, pp. 577–599. Reprinted in *Selected Papers*, pp. 34–55. See p. 49 f.; cf. p. 91.

[50] Ibid., pp. 34, 36; *A Handbook*, p. 201.

[51] *A Handbook*, p. 195 f.

[52] *Selected Papers*, p. 34.

[53] C. L. Wrenn, op. cit., pp. 182, 193, 195.

[54] J. R. Firth, 'The English School of Phonetics', *Transactions of the Philological Society* 1946, pp. 92–132. See p. 131.

[55] H. C. Wyld, op. cit., p. 8.

[56] H. C. Wyld, 'Henry Sweet', *The Modern Language Quarterly* iv (1901), pp. 73–79.

[57] Henry Sweet, 'English and Germanic Philology', *Transactions of the Philological Society* 1877–9, pp. 373–419. Reprinted in *Collected Papers*, pp. 95–140.

Indian English: A Study in Contextualization[1]

BRAJ B. KACHRU

INTRODUCTION

This paper is primarily an investigation in sociolinguistics, restricted to one aspect of the language contact situation in India. It is a study of a *variety*[2] of the English language used as a foreign language (L^2)[3] by English-knowing bilinguals in an Indian cultural and linguistic setting. In order to examine the effects of such a cross-cultural situation on the language features of an L^2 we have included two types of statements: (i) formal, and (ii) contextual.[4] A statement about (ii) may be possible if certain categories are adopted for the contextualization of a text. The contextual categories may form part of the general linguistic theory at the (inter-)level of context. The necessity to include context as a relevant (inter-)level of description motivated the second aspect of this paper, which is a programmatic study towards the setting up of a construct for contextualization.

This paper, then, includes both theoretical preliminaries and descriptive statements. There is no attempt to present a theory of context, although we hope that the categories suggested here may contribute towards such a theory. The categories have been set within the framework of linguistic science, the aim being to 'make statements of meaning so that we see how we *use* language to *live*'[5] (our italics). This approach has contributed towards bringing out the *Indianness* of the Indian idiom of English as opposed to the *Englishness* of British English and the *Americanness* of American English.

The illustrative material (cf. Appendix) has been abstracted from the English texts written by Indians (henceforth termed Indian English).[6] The term Indian English (abb. IE) is used here as a cover-term for that variety of the English language which is used by 'educated' Indians. In terms of their proficiency in English, care has been taken to include only the users of the *standard* form of IE. A standard user of IE is one who ranks somewhere between the *central* and *ambilingual* points on the *cline of bilingualism.*[7] The form of English used by educated Indians could perhaps be called, alternatively, 'standard Indian English'. By the term IE we do not, however, imply a status equal to those varieties of English which are used as *primary* or *first* languages.

English in an Indian Setting

Perhaps it should be mentioned here that in India the English language functions in the following sociolinguistic setting: (i) it is a foreign language used under the influence of a number of substrata, (ii) it is used in cross-cultural (and cross-religious) contexts, as well as for describing both these and native contexts; (iii) it is used in IE writings (i.e. fiction, newspapers, etc.).

The above (i–iii) assign specific roles to IE which, on the whole, are different from the ones assigned to English where it is used as the first language. It may then be said that Indians are bilinguals in the sense that they are using English as a *complementary language* in typically Indian contexts.

In the use of the written medium of IE a distinction is possible along the lines of writer/reader relationship. An Indian bilingual's use of English may be conditioned by the reading public of his work. This is clear in the creative work of IE writers, especially of the novelists and short story writers. Thus, on the *writer/reader* relationship we have two forms of IE: one which is written in India, the reading public of which is exclusively Indian, and another which is written either in India or outside India, for Indians or non-Indians. (The second form of IE may be written with a view to a reading public having English as L^1. This distinction is significant in the sense that these two forms vary in their degree of 'Indianness' and in their use of 'Indianisms'.[8])

I. TRANSFER AND CONTEXT

1. *Process of Transference in an Indian Language Contact Situation*

1.1. In linguistic terms a study of a language contact situation involves a study of transfer (or transference) at different levels. In such a situation there are at least two languages (L^1 and L^2) and, in certain cases, two cultures (C^1 and C^2) involved.[9]

1.2. In IE the process of transference may result in the following: (i) items of L^1 may be transferred to L^2 to form hybridized formations; (ii) formal exponents of the contextual units (see below 3.2) may be transferred to L^2 (in this case British English) at different ranks (cf.

fn. 4); (iii) extensive use may be made of the *open set* items of different L^1's to contextualize the text in Indian situations, which are part of C^2 for an English L^1 speaker (see 7.0 to 9.6); (iv) items of L^2 may be collocated[10] in 'un-English' collocations (cf. 6.0).

1.3. This process (cf. 1.2) involves transfer of two types: transfer of linguistic items from L^1's; and transfer of certain non-linguistic features, i.e. the *non-belonging elements*[11] of the C^2.

1.4. The above (i–iv) may be better explained if we take into consideration the 'meaning'[12] of an utterance and its *use* in actual Indian contexts, in addition to the formal features of IE. In order to show the effects of the Indian setting of IE we shall treat one variety of English, which is spoken as the *first* language, as the norm for marking the deviations in the variety used as an L^2. There are, we think, strong reasons for treating British English as the norm for IE. A distinction may also be made between a 'mistake' and a deviation.[13]

1.5. The types of transfer discussed in 1.2 may be termed: A. Transfer of context; B. Transfer of formal items; C. Transfer of form/context components.

A. *Transfer of Context*

This refers to the transfer of 'elements' of certain contexts from C^1 and L^1 to L^2. A further distinction may be made in terms of the culture of the participants. If the participants are speakers of (say) Hindi and Marathi, or Tamil and Telugu, or French and English, there may be transfer at the formal levels only, without necessarily any transfer at the contextual level. If the participants, however, belong to different cultural and language backgrounds (e.g. Hindi-English, Tamil-English, French-Russian), this may involve the transfer of certain contextual units (see below 3.2) which may be non-belonging elements of the culture of L^2, such as the caste system of India, social and religious taboos, notions of superiority and inferiority, and the like.

In terms of the *performer/addressee* relation, in the case of IE the process may be explained as follows:

Medium	Performer	Addressee	Situation of Transfer
Written and/or spoken	Indian	Indian and/or non-Indian	C^1 and L^1 items transferred to L^2.

B. *Transfer of Formal Items*

This may be of two types:

(a) Formal items from different ranks may be transferred from L^1 to L^2, e.g. sentences, clauses, phrases, fixed collocations, compounds: *salt-giver* (*Kanth*, 32), *spoiler of my salt*, (*Un*), *sister-sleeper* (*V of G*, 130), *bow my forehead* (*Un*), *turmeric-ceremony* (*MM*, 70).

(b) L^1 meanings may be transferred to L^2 items. For instance, the term *brother-in-law* has one restricted meaning in British English as a kinship term; in IE it has acquired three distinct meanings (cf. 7.6) as a term of (a) abuse, (b) affection or intimacy, and (c) kinship. The terms *sister* and *mother* have extended collocations as terms of regard and respect used without relationship, e.g. 'Now you know what your duties are, and how to do them, sister, you will receive our instructions.' (*WM*, 93.) In the use of the items *flower-bed*, *government*, etc. there is a change of register in IE with the result that a native speaker of English will not understand these items without understanding the defining-context. Examples are:

> 'On this, her *flower-bed*, her seven children were born.' (*MM*, 109.)
> '*Government*, she knows nothing about drinks. She is hardly sixteen and completely innocent.' (*TP*, 40.)

The item *government* is used here as a mode of address for a person who represents the State, and hence authority. Contextually and collocationally the items *brother-in-law*, *sister*, *mother*, *flower-bed*, and *government* each belong to one or more lexical sets in IE.

C. *Transfer of Form/Context Components*

Socially determined speech-functions (see 6.4, 7.0) such as *modes of address/reference*, *greetings*, *blessings/prayers*, *abuses/curses*, are related to the C^1 in the Indian context of culture. In Indian languages there are fixed formal exponents for these contexts, and these may be transferred to L^2 for those contextual units which are absent in the culture of L^2. This might involve transfer at two levels, both formal and contextual, since it is transfer of a contextual unit with the formal exponents which function in such a unit. Formally this may result in collocational deviation.

2. *Contextualization of a Text*

2.1. We should, however, hasten to say that a linguistic statement which takes into consideration the contextual units (see below 3.2) of a language cannot be as definitive as a formal statement, since this aspect of linguistic science has as yet no rigorous methodology. It has, however, been realized for some time now that for a complete linguistic description the (inter-)level of context (in traditional terminology 'semantics') can be of crucial importance, and certain theories have been suggested.[14]

2.2. A description which incorporates the (inter-)level of context as a relevant level for a formal statement has to ask certain basic questions, for instance: Is it possible to establish contextual categories on, more or less, the same basis on which the categories at the grammatical level are set up? Is there a methodology which could be used to relate the formal features of a text with the (inter-)level of context? This then involves both theoretical and procedural problems.

2.3. We have drawn on the theoretical work of the late J.R.Firth for an examination of the above relationship. A tentative classification for contextualization is found in his work,[15] and in the work of others[16] who further developed or discussed his concept. In his approach[17] Firth does not accept the dichotomy of *form* and *meaning* and he rejects the suggestion of the hierarchical direction among the linguistic levels; instead he adopts a 'hierarchy of techniques'.[18] In Firth's view, then, the end product of linguistic analysis should be to relate the text to the *context of situation*, as language is 'not merely a process parallel with culture', but 'an integral part of it'.[19]

3. *Categories for Contextualization*

3.1. A contextual statement may be made about a large text, in a general sense, in terms of the context of culture, or about delimited parts of a text. A restricted statement which marks a 'piece' of language for a specific operation is the first step towards establishing what we are here calling, for lack of a better term, a *contextual unit*.[20] This, however, is not of the same nature as the categories at the formal levels.

3.2. A contextual unit is set up in an attempt to demarcate the textually relevant features of a 'situation' in terms of the *contextual parameters*.[21] It may be viewed as an abstraction on two axes: the syntagmatic and the paradigmatic. Syntagmatically we think of a contextual unit as having clear endpoints in the time dimension; paradigmatically, it is a bundle of features comprising one or more contextual parameters.

3.3. The contextual parameters are definable, both formally and contextually, as variables which determine the effective operation of a text in a contextual unit. The value of each parameter is seen in terms of the change it entails in a language-text in a particular contextual unit. If the formal markers associated with a text are altered it should entail the change of the parameters too (barring those situations where the same parameter may operate in two or more contextual units). 'The *placing* of a *text* as a constituent in a context of situation contributes to the statement of meaning since situations are set up to recognize *use*.'[22]

3.4. For contextual meaning, then, the relevant features of a text may be determined by two methods: *contextual substitution* and *textual substitution.* In *contextual substitution* we ask whether, for example, sex or the social status of a speaker is a relevant feature. Does the introduction of a participant of different sex, or a person from a higher or lower social status, entail a textual change? In *textual substitution* we ask: if another text is substituted, does that lead to contextual change?

3.5. A delimited text may be said to be the exponent of a contextual unit on the basis of those formal features which mark it off from other delimited texts, and which make it 'effective' in a particular context.

3.6. We may regard a contextual unit as a *frame* (in some ways analogous to a 'substitution frame')[23] and the parameters as the *distinctive* markers of the frame which determine the formal exponents for it. A sentence may be treated as the highest unit for contextualization and as a component of a restricted language (cf. 4.2); this, however, does not mean that the units of lower rank cannot be contextualized (e.g. markers of *sex*, *age*, *caste*, etc.). There are cases when pronouns, modes of reference/address, etc., may be language correlates of certain parameters, e.g. *government* (*TP*, 40), *mother of Onu* (*SMH*, 111), *twice-born* (*Un*, 14). A formal item may be correlated with one parameter and contextual unit in one culture, but in another culture that particular unit may be absent; for instance, *I bow my forehead* (*C*, 14) will have no specific contextual unit in British culture, but in Indian culture it is a distinctive item operating in the contextual unit of *greetings*.

3.7. We have set the following parameters for this restricted study of IE, and these can be correlated with the formal exponents from the text. In fact, it is the text which is used as the basis for finding the parameters. This then gives us a frame for placing certain items in the context of culture. We have used Ellis' concept of 'wider situation' and 'immediate situation'.[24]

A. General Cultural Factors ('wider situation'):

1. Social status of the individual in the group. This has two dimensions:
   (a) Position in the hierarchy of caste.
   (b) Political status and economic position.
2. Religion. In the Indian setting it is important to know whether a participant is a Hindu, Muslim, etc. (cf. 9.3).
3. Speaker/addressee relationship: *wife/husband*, *children/parents*, *teacher/pupil*. For instance, in conservative circles in India a wife is not addressed by name but in a very indirect way as *mother of* . . . (*mother of Onu, SMH*, 111). The same is true when an orthodox wife refers to her husband. Instead of using his name she might only use a pronoun *he* or an honorific pronoun.

B. Individual or Personal Factors ('immediate situation'):

1. Sex of the participants.
2. Age of the participants.
3. Educational background of the participants—whether or not a person has received a formal education or a university education.
4. Characteristics which localize persons.
   (a) Linguistic: Accent and other language traits.
   (b) Non-linguistic: Food habits, dress, etc.

Linguistic characteristics may link up with religion. There are religious dialects (e.g. Hindu Kashmiri, Muslim Kashmiri) as well as social dialects (e. g. Brahmin Tamil, non-Brahmin Tamil). Certain language features may thus correlate with more than one parameter.

4. *Context Versus Sub-languages*

4.1. Contextually delimited language types may be termed *restricted languages*,[25] *registers*[26] and *speech-functions*. A statement about these is better considered as a statement of the *operation* of a language in specific contexts involving, at least, two participants (*performer/addressee*). The grouping is based on (a) the language features which mark one text from the other class of texts, and (b) the function of the text in specific contextual units. This grouping may give us sub-languages recognized in terms of vocation, participants or attitudes: e.g. languages of (a) *administration*, *newspapers*, etc., (b) *wife/husband*, *parents/children, buyer/seller,* (c) *abuses/curses, flattery/persuasion,* etc., (d), *phatic communion,* (e) *radar, railways,* etc., (f) *Hindu rituals/Muslim rituals,* etc.

4.2. A *restricted language,* then, is a delimited 'sub-language' which is 'functionally' and formally distinct from other sub-languages. It cuts across idiolects and regional varieties and may be used for specific functions by all the speakers/writers of a tongue.[27] For instance, in IE the restricted language of *administration* and *law* is pan-Indian in the sense that all the speakers/writers of different regional varieties of IE, with different IE backgrounds, use it in this context. It is distinct from an idiolect or 'style' (cf. 4.5) in the sense that it does not necessarily show the individuality or idiosyncrasies of persons, and it does not mark just one person from another.

4.3. A *register,* in our sense, is a further step in delicacy in terms of sub-grouping. For instance, in the restricted language of newspapers one would expect that *editorials, legal reporting, women's pages,* etc., may be further subgrouped on formal grounds.[28]

4.4. We may find that we need another term to explain certain special types of registers. While demarcating the restricted language of social roles, at first, we may include the following in it: *greetings, modes of reference/address, abuses/curses, flattery/persuasion.* Soon it will be evident that there are enough formal and contextual reasons for grouping such socially determined speech-events separately. We shall use the term *speech-function* for such items. By speech-functions we mean those items (i) which reveal the personal attitude of a speaker/writer in a particular culture (e.g. *abuses/curses*); (ii) which convey social attitudes in favour of or against a person or persons (e.g. *greetings, modes of address/reference*); (iii) which are repetitive and socially determined; and (iv) which mark a person as 'inside' or 'outside' the culture of a speech-fellowship or a speech-community.

4.5. We may now ask: In the restricted language of newspapers, to take one example, shall we consider *editorials, legal reporting,* etc., in *The Times* and the *Guardian,* and in the *News of the World* and the *Daily Express* as the same registers? In such cases perhaps it would be useful if we accept a 'style scale' on which we mark different registers according to different styles. We may then have one register in *different* styles; for instance, following Joos,[29] we may have *intimate, casual, consultative, formal, frozen* styles for one register operating in a specific contextual unit. The difference in the above newspapers would then be a difference in style if two papers are reporting the same event but using different types of languages. Two texts may belong to the same contextual units and be distinguished only in style.

4.6. In selecting a register for a particular contextual unit a person makes a *register choice* out of his total *register range*.[30] A register range is the repertory of registers at the command of a person at a given time. This distinction is useful in a language contact situation, since a wrong choice of a register may lead to *register confusion*. By register confusion we mean the use of a register which does not belong to a particular contextual unit. There are many Indian formations which stand out as deviations because the items do not normally function in the register concerned when used by a native speaker of English.

4.7. The other manifestation of this 'confusion' is at the lexical level: it may be explained as the use of a lexical item in a restricted or extended sense by an L^2 user of a language. (For example, the Indian use of lexical items like *thrice*, *nice*, *purchase*, *shift*, *bawl*, etc.)

II. LEXICO-GRAMMATICAL TRANSFER

5. *Types of Transfer*

5.1. In IE the lexico-grammatical transfer may be of the following types:

A. **Lexical transfer** (or borrowing): This is what is usually termed lexical borrowing. It may be explained as the use of L^1 lexical items in L^2, not necessarily involving any formal change. This includes Indian loan words in IE.

B. **Translation**: Translation is establishing equivalent, or partially equivalent, formal items at any rank in L^2 for the formal items of L^1. For instance, in IE in translating the following items an attempt has been made to establish equivalent items in L^2: *dvij* 'twice-born' (*Un*, 14); *namak-harām* 'spoiler of my salt' (*Un*); *ishwar-prem* 'god-love' (*Un*, 205).

C. **Shift**: *Shift* (or adaptation) is distinguished from translation in the sense that in a shift there is no attempt to establish formal equivalence. The 'new' formation may be an adaptation of an L^2 item or may provide the source for an elaborate adaptation. The motivation in this case is that the contextual unit in the L^2 demands a formal item and a bilingual uses an L^1 item as the source for it. For example, *may the vessel of your life never float on the sea of existence* (*C*); the source item for this shift is *terā beṛā gark ho*. It may sometimes involve the shift of fixed collocations (idioms) of L^1, e.g. *a dog is a lion in his own street* (*ABW*, 71), *a crow tried to strut like a peacock* (*BH*, 224), *speak to the sky* (*P of D*, 107).

D. **Calques**: Calques are those items which have L^2 phonology and grammar, but involve transfer of the contextual meaning from the C^1, in addition to the transfer of the collocation from L^1, e.g. *flower-bed* (*MM*). In other words, a calque may be defined as rank-bound translation which may be parallel in terms of the units of L^1 and L^2, but may also be item-bound. That is, an attempt may be made to find equivalence in the open-set items which operate in the structures concerned. Sometimes, this may result in *register confusion* or formal (collocational) deviation from the norm. For instance, *flower-bed* (*MM*) is rank-bound in the sense that the L^1 and L^2 items belong to the same unit ('word', compound), but, in addition to this, it has another characteristic: it is item-bound, too. That means that the writer, B. Bhattacharya, has translated the lexical items *Phūl* (flower) and *shɔjjā* (bed) and has used *flower-bed* in the same contextual unit in which *phūl-shɔjjā* operates in Bengali culture. This results in contextual ambiguity in English, since the item *flower-bed* is restricted to the register of gardening in English. This difficulty of *register confusion* could be resolved by translating it as *nuptial-bed*, which would be rank-bound translation but not item-bound; hence there would be no contextual difficulty.

5.2. Lexical borrowing in IE has been discussed by Yule and Burnell, and Rao.[31] We shall now discuss the process of translation with special reference to the language contact situation in IE. It should be made clear here that translation in a language contact situation is different from contextual translation from a source language to a target language.[32]

5.3. In a language contact situation translation may be of the following two major types (further delicate analysis, however, is possible in terms of the structures involved).

A. **Rank-bound**: In rank-bound translation a writer translates formal items of L^1 at the 'same' rank into L^2. (That is if we presuppose that the number of units in the two languages is the same.)

In the following examples in IE the unit 'word' (compound) in L^1 has been translated at the 'same' rank into L^2: *rathyātra* 'car-festival' (*OR*, 15.7.59); *gopūjā* 'cow-worship' (*V* of *A*, 122); *grih-devatā* 'family-protector'; *ishwar-prem* 'god-love' (*Un*, 205); *kaṭiḍorā* 'waist-thread'

(*He Who*, 190); the unit 'group' (class 'nominal') has been transferred as follows: *ghoṛārḍim* 'horse's egg'; *motiyāṃdā bādshāh* 'king of pearls' (*TP*, 90).

A few examples are given below from the formal items of higher ranks from speech-functions and phatic communion:

(i) *May the fire of your ovens consume you* (*C*), (*bhaṭṭhī mẽ jā*);
(ii) *Where does your wealth reside*? (*TP*), (*āpkā daulat khānā kahā̃ hai*?);
(iii) *What honourable noun does your honour bear?* (*TP*), (*āpkā shubh nām kyā hai*?);
(iv) *Beat me on my head till I go bald* (*C*), (*kūṛ kūṛ ke mainū̃ ganjā-karde*).

These are the examples of what may be termed 'ornamental style'. The sources again are the L[1] items. The above (ii) and (iii) respectively mean: 'Where do you live?' and 'What is your name?'

B. **Rank-changed**:[33] In rank-changed translation the items of L[1] are translated at different ranks into L[2]. This may be transfer at a higher rank or a lower rank. The following items of the word rank have been transferred into L[2] at the rank of group ('nominal'): *bhaiyā-dūj* 'brother-anointing ceremony' (*He Who*, 160); *yajñopavīt* 'nine-stranded thread' (*He Who*, 45); *shuddhi* 'cleansing-bath'; *godhūli* 'cow-dust hour'; *munḍan saṃskār* 'hair-cutting ceremony' (*Kanth*, 56); *bad-baxt* 'you of evil star' (*Un*).

There are other items which do not involve a rank change. In such items words of L[1] are transferred as compound words: e.g. *pattal* 'dining-leaf' (*WM*, 84); *tilak* 'forehead-marking' (*Mr S*, 206); *janeo* 'holy-thread'; *coṭī* 'tuft-knot' (*C*, 180); *dvij* 'twice-born' (*Un*, 14).

6. *Indian English Collocations*

6.1. Further, the process of Indianization of the English language has formally resulted in Indian collocations, which are sometimes termed (in a derogatory sense) 'Indianisms' (cf. fn. 8). These include those compounds and collocations which may have one or more of the following characteristics:

(i) they deviate grammatically from British English compounding; (ii) they are 'loan shifts'[34] from Indian languages; (iii) they are collocationally Indian; and (iv) they have contextual units assigned in Indian culture which are absent in British culture.[35]

6.2. By Indian collocations we mean those formations which are contextually Indian, and/or which are collocationally uncommon in British English. In both these cases there is deviation from the norm. In the first case it is contextually determined deviation, and in the second, it is formal deviation in terms of the sets which operate in the structure of a collocation.

We may then say that collocationally IE deviations have the following possibilities:

Item	Collocation of items	Contextualization of Items	Deviation
(i) Usual	Usual	Unusual	Contextual
(ii) Usual	Unusual	Unusual	Formal/Contextual
(iii) At least one unusual	Unusual	Unusual	Formal/Contextual

In (i) we consider forms like *flower-bed* (*MM*, 105), which have normal collocation of two items, and are accepted by a native speaker as 'usual', but whose contextual meaning is entirely different from what a native speaker of English would understand. The meaning of such formations is intelligible only when they are related to appropriate contextual units in Indian culture.

In (ii) a collocation is formally 'unusual' in the sense that the items used in IE to form such a collocation do not collocate in British English. It may be contextually deviant in the sense that in British culture it would not function in the same contextual unit which is assigned to it in India; or in certain cases, there may be no contextual unit at all for such collocations in British culture. For example: *sister-sleeper* (*V of G*, 130); *separate-eating* (*Kanth*, 51); *dining-leaf* (*WM*, 84); etc.

The collocations like *sister-sleeper* are not deviant in terms of the structures, but only in terms of the class assignment of the items. The construction N + V is very productive in English compounding (e.g. *fan dancer*, *baby sitter*, etc.) and structurally, it falls under this class,[36] but the item *sleeper* in IE sense is un-English and (in this sense) cannot occur alone in British English or IE. On the other hand, *rape-sister* (*BH*, 46), which has V + N construction, is no longer productive in

English although we have examples like *cutthroat*, *cutwater*, *do-nothing*, *spoilsport*.[37]

In (iii) an 'unusual' item is collocated with an item which is normal in that context; for instance, *mango-breast* (*TP*, 15). In this item the deviation is in the sense that *mango* does not collocate with *breast* in British English. Perhaps the reason is that contextually *mango* as a fruit is exotic in Britain. Hence the 'secondary' meaning of this lexical item is absent in British English.

6.3. In addition to the collocational differences there is another formal difference which has resulted in many 'Indianisms'. In IE there is a very productive device by which a syntactic unit of a higher rank is 'reduced' so as to create a compound word. In other words, at places where a native speaker of English tends to use a group or a clause an IE user might choose a unit of word rank. Thus many nominal formations with qualifiers are reduced to endocentric nominal compounds. Another point here is that many forms which are register-restricted[38] in British English may be used in IE without such restrictions.

6.4. In the 'reduction' of the item the order of the components is changed, e.g.: *an address of welcome* ~ *welcome address* (*IE*, 14. 8. 59); *a bunch of keys* ~ *key-bunch* (*AD*, 178); *a box of matches* ~ *matchbox*;[39] *lady from the mission* ~ *mission-lady*; *strength of class* ~ *roll-strength*; *the basis of caste* ~ *caste-basis* (*H*, 25.11.63).

It is difficult to be dogmatic about the cases of 'reduction' as some of the following formations might not be regarded as 'reduction' by British English speakers, e.g. *caste-proud* (*He Who*, 17). This might be regarded simply as collocationally and contextually IE, though formally equivalent to such an item as *house-proud*.

6.5. The contextually deviant formations are those formations which function in IE contextual units, and would perhaps be unintelligible to a native speaker of English only because he is not acquainted with Indian contexts of culture. A parallel to this linguistic situation is found in America and Australia, where the English-speaking settlers had to coin a large number of words to name the local contextual items, which resulted in such forms as: *friar-bird*, *frogs-mouth*, *ground-lark*, *thousand jacket*, etc.[40] In India the situation is, however, different. It is not a group of new settlers using their L^1 in a new country, but an L^2 being used by the natives in their own contexts. The early English travellers to India borrowed a number of Indian words and hybrid forms into English for such contexts. But on the whole the IE formations (hybrid or non-hybrid) were coined by the Indians themselves. A few examples of such formations are:

alms-bowl (*He Who*, 44), *alms-taker* (*Mr S*, 154), *bangled-widow* (*Kanth*, 233), *bath-fire* (*Kanth*, 45), *bath-milk* (*He Who*, 130), *betel-bag* (*Kanth*, 31), *betel-case* (*V of G*, 20), *car-festival*[41] (*ORI* 5.7.59), *dung-cake* (*N in S*, 47), *leaf-bag* (*C*, 149), *sacred-ash*[42] (*FE*, 52), *sacred-tuft* (*1000 Nights*, 142), *upper-cloth* (*AD*, 223).

6.6. We have not considered here those hybridized (or mixed) formations which comprise elements from English and an Indian language. There is a large number of such formations which warrant a detailed separate treatment. These include two types of items:

(i) **Open set**: e.g. *lathi-charge* (*HS*, 15.6.59), *bidi-smoking* (*S and R*, 198), *City-Kotwali* (*HIS*, 261), *Congress-Pandal* (*Un*, 212), *Police-Jamadar* (*Kanth*, 29), *rail-gadi* (*BH*, 75), etc.

(ii) **Closed system**: e.g. *cooliedom* (*C*, 44), *goondaism* (*H*, 2.3.64), *piceworth* (*SMH*, 161), *policewala* (*SMH*, 61), *Sadhuhood* (*Un*, 59), *Upanishadic* (*S and R*, 25), etc.

The 'mixed' forms may be classified on the basis of their function in a context or on the basis of their form. In a formal classification the categories of lexis may be adopted to classify such items.

III. INDIAN ENGLISH IN INDIAN CONTEXTUAL UNITS

7. *Indian English and Restricted Languages*

The other interesting aspect of the English language in India is its *use* by Indians in typically non-British contextual units of Indian culture. This use has evolved an Indian 'idiom' of English different from British English; and, what is more important, this 'idiom' is now used even outside India to refer to such Indian contexts. In this section we shall describe briefly the language features of three restricted languages of IE which are used in the Indian socio-cultural context: i.e. speech-functions (7.0); the Indian caste system (8.0); and social roles (9.0). The description that follows is neither exhaustive nor fully illustrated; it does, however, suggest further research possibilities in this area.

7.1. *Speech-functions*. In (4.4) we have suggested that the term speech-function[43] may be restricted to special language types with particular characteristics. An IE text may provide us one or more of the following types of contextual data about which linguistic statements can be made:

(i) text of attitudes, e.g. *modes of address/reference, blessings, flattery*, etc.
(ii) text of status and social position: *superiority/inferiority, caste system*, etc.
(iii) text of social roles, *rituals, ceremonies*, etc.
(iv) text of individual habits (which are not socially determined).

7.2. In describing speech-functions we have first to 're-create' the non-linguistic environment; this should provide us with the 'situational data' from which the relevant definable contextual features for a speech-function may be abstracted. The 'situational data' may be defined as the context of culture in which a speech-function operates. In the following we have described three speech-functions (i.e. *abuses/curses, greetings* and *modes of address/reference*) to illustrate this point.

7.3. The following variables have been used for abuses/curses: (1) the geographical location; (2) the L^1 of the writer; (3) the speaker/addressee relation; (4) distinctive points about the participants, i.e. age, status (economic and social), position in the caste hierarchy, sex; (5) religion.

By geographical location we mean localization of a text in terms of the north of India or the south of India. This is the first broad division. The second step would be to localize the text more specifically, say in terms of the Punjab, Uttar Pradesh, Bihar, Bengal. This is important on formal grounds, as it will be found that the item *eater of your masters* (*C*, 18) is common in the Punjab only. Again, the abuses *eater of your masters* and *would that you had died in my womb* (*He Who*, 195) can be further identified. In the first, the position and the status of the participants are involved (i.e. *master/servant* relation). The text also shows that it is a feminine abuse. The second abuse involves the relationship of *mother/child.* Another example, *keep to the side of the road, you low caste vermin* (*Un*, 39), involves two persons, an upper caste Hindu and a low caste Hindu. It is not difficult to guess the geographical location of the text. *You circumcised son of a pig* (*DD*, 202) may result in Hindu-Muslim discord in India if it is used by a non-Muslim to a Muslim. *May thy womb be dead* (*He Who*, 212), is obviously limited to women addressees.

7.4. A further sub-grouping is possible on the basis of some formal (lexical) exponents. We have divided the *abuses/curses* under the following heads:

(a) From masters to servants:

you eater of your masters (*C*, 18); *you spoiler of my salt* (*Un*); *you of the evil star* (*C*, 16); *son of a concubine* (*Kanth*); *you donkey's husband* (*Kanth*).

(b) From parents to children:

you have eaten my life (*C*); *would that you had died in my womb* (*He Who*, 159); *why did I rear a serpent with the milk of my breast* (*He Who*, 159); *oh . . . you dead one* (*C*, 24); *when you are married I shall drink a seer of frothing warm milk, you widow* (*S and R*).

(c) Addressed to women only:

may thy womb be dead (*He Who*, 212); *eater of my child* (*He Who*, 212); *ari . . . you prostitute* (*Un*); *oh you prostitute of a wind* (*Kanth*, 170); *go and lie with a licking male dog* (*C of B*).

(d) Used by men to men:

the incestuous sister-sleeper (*V of C*, 13); *you lover of your mother* (*C*, 119); *that penis of a pig who sleeps with his mother, pimps for his sister and daughter* (*TP*, 144).

(e) Mostly used by women:

may the vessel of your life never float in the sea of existence (*C*, 20); *may you never rest in peace neither you nor your antecedents* (*C*, 78); *may the fire of your ovens consume you* (*C*, 78); *you cock-eyed son of a bow-legged scorpion* (*Un*, 38).

(f) Used between members of different religious groups:

you circumcised son of a pig (*DD*, 202); *a lecherous cow-eater* (*C*, 226).

(g) Addressed to one's own self:

I am a leper if there is a lie in anything I say (*AD*, 54); *may my limbs be paralysed and my tongue dumb and my progeny forever destroyed* (*Kanth*).

(h) Showing repentance, friendship, intimacy or affection:

father of fathers, I could kill that man (*Un*); *brother-in-law, you are lucky* (*Un*); *give, obey, brother-in-law, give us some of sweets* (*Un*).

(i) Used for threat and challenge:

that incestuous lover of your sister (*TP*, 25); *what seducer of his mother can throw bangles at me* (*TP*, 72); *if I don't spit at his bottom* (*TP*, 186); *if I do not spit in Mali's mouth my name is not Juggat Singh* (*TP*, 187); *a crocodile in loin cloth* (*He Who*, 217).

(j) Showing jealousy (man/woman relationship):

call yourself a priest with so filthy a heart? The sacred thread is blackened by the sweat of your pores (*He Who*, 93–94).

(k) Of neutral type (as to participants):

this heartless blackguard (*AD*, 50); *filthy brute* (*AD*); *heartless devil* (*AD*, 50); *dung-eating curs* (*Kanth*, 220); *you son of my woman* (*Kanth*, 129).

7.5. For contextualizing greetings in IE we need roughly the same parameters which we need for abuses/curses. The speaker/addressee relationship is more revealing here since it helps us to classify greetings according to a person's religion, his caste, and his position in the caste hierarchy and social status.

We have grouped greetings under the following heads:

(a) Greetings addressed to elders and upper-class:

bow my forehead (*C*, 14); *I bow at his feet, I lick the dust of road on which he passes* (*SMH*, 70); *fall at your feet* (*C*, 14); *touch your feet* (*Un*).

(b) Greetings addressed to persons of equal status but elders:

jay-deva (*C*, 126); *long live the gods* (*C*, 14).

(c) Greetings addressed to superiors (officer/subordinate relationship):

salam Huzoor (*TP*); *well, inspector sahib, how are things?; God is merciful, we only pray for your kindness* (*TP*, 19).

(d) Greetings used by prostitutes and sycophants:

welcome, my eyes have gone blind looking at the way along which you were to grace my house (*C*, 202); *you have blessed my hovel with the good dust of your feet* (*SMH*, 55).

Further points to note about the greetings are:

(a) In different social relations, e.g. *master/servant*, *age/youth*, a greeting does not evoke the same echo response in India as in English society, e.g. *good morning—good morning*. In Indian society the response may be as follows:

'Salam, Havaldarji.'
'Come, ohe, Bakhia, how are you?' (*Un*).

(b) The verbal exponents have other non-verbal cues which help us to assign a text to a contextual unit. For greetings used in *master/servant* relations the non-verbal cues may be *joining hands, dusting his feet*, etc.; but in the greetings addressed to people who are of equal status but elders, the *folding hands* are the exponents of the same social position although the participant who is greeted is senior in age.

(c) The markers of caste, religion, occupation, etc. indicate further context restrictions:

'*Ram, Ram, Panditji.*'
'*I touch your feet Panditji.*'

(d) Greetings may precede or follow markers denoting caste, profession, religion, sex or the kinship of the participants. These may further be followed by honorific suffixes (e.g., *ji*) as in Table I.

TABLE I

SHOWING MARKERS WITH GREETINGS[44]

Caste	Profession	Religion	Kinship (cf. 7.7)
pandit	*babu*	*khwaja*	*brother-in-law*
thakur	*havaldar*	*sardar*	*mother*
			sister
			grandmother
jamadar	*inspector*		*father*

7.6. The *modes of address* and *modes of reference* are essentially determined by the systems of L^1 and the social pattern in which that system functions. A term restricted to the kinship system of a language may be used with extended meaning in another culture and transferred to an L^2. The extended use of the term in L^2 may cause contextual ambiguity.

The following items have been used in non-English contexts in IE.

1. Superiority/inferiority:

(a) *Cherisher of the poor*:	'Cherisher of the poor, what does your honour fancy?' (*TP*, 37)
(b) *King of pearls*:	'King of pearls, you can say what you like but this time I am innocent.' (*TP*)
(c) *Government*:[45]	'Government, she knows nothing about drink. She is hardly sixteen and completely innocent.' (*TP*, 40)
(d) *Huzoor*:	'Would huzoor like to sleep on the verandah?' (*TP*, 99)
(e) *Ma-bap*:	'The government are just and bounteous, they are your ma-bap (mother-father).' (*SMH*, 48)
(f) *Friend of the poor*:	'Take care of yourself, friend of the poor.' (*S of J*, 228)

2. Professional:[46]

(a) *Inspector sahib*:	'Come along, inspector sahib,' said Hukum Chand. (*TP*, 128)
(b) *Deputy sahib*:	'The deputy sahib has already sent orders to all police stations to keep a lookout for Jugga.' (*TP*, 55)
(c) *Policewala*:	'Policewala, badman, wildman, burn-face man.' (*SMH*, 61)

3. Caste/religion:

(a) *Pandit*:	'Hey, Pandit, can't you remain at peace with yourself for a moment?' (*FE*, 185)

4. Kinship:

The IE kinship system has been discussed elsewhere (cf. below 7.7). The following examples, however, show that items operating in British English kinship terms may be used with an extended meaning in IE; for instance, *mother* as a term of respect, *sister* of regard, and *father-in-law* in the sense of abuse. *Bhai* (brother) is used for any male of equal age, *father* for all elder persons, and an uncle may be referred to as *father*:

(a) *Mother*: 'Mother, a betel-leaf for you,' she hailed. (*SMH*) (Shopkeeper addressing a customer.)

(b) *Father*: 'Father,' said the old man as he held out his card ... (*SMH*, 165) (Addressing a social worker.)

(c) *Sister*: The coolie said: 'Are you travelling alone, sister?'
'No, I am with my master, brother.' (*V of G*, 19)

(d) *Mother of my daughter*: 'Oh, I say, the mother of my daughter,' said the burra Babu, in the archaic conversation of Indian family life. (*C*, 29)
(In certain circles this is the normal mode of address or reference.)

The third person pronoun *he* may be used referring to one's husband. In orthodox circles it is not modest for a lady to refer to her husband by name; in such cases the pronoun *he* is used, e.g. 'He, now in jail-house would not have eaten.' (*SMH*, 90)[47]

5. Flattery/affection:

(a) *Jewel of jewels*: 'You will hear the jewel of jewels screaming.' (*SMH*, 1)

(b) *Mother of ...* 'Why do you stick your eyes to my kitchenpot, mother of Onu ...' (*SMH*, 111)
(In certain situations a woman may be referred to (or addressed) as mother of ... (name of her child).)

(c) *Brother-in-law*:
(a) 'Brother-in-law, you are lucky.' (*Un*)
(b) 'Give, obey, brother-in-law, give us some of the sweets,' said Chota. (*Un*)

6. Neutral (as to participants):

(a) *Babu-sahib*:[48]	'Where does your wealth reside, Babu sahib?' (*TP*, 53)
(b) *Bhai*:	'No, Bhai, no. If I knew, why would I not tell you?' (*TP*, 99)
(c) *Master*:[49]	(a) 'Yes, master, I do pay.' (*FE*, 4) (b) 'Do not take my boat, master, you have taken all. Spare this one, master.' (*SMH*, 48)
(d) *Dada*: (M)	'Dada, I am dead serious.' (*SMH*, 3)
(e) *Didi*: (F)	'Speak didi,' he moaned. (*SMH*, 130)
(f) *Sab*:[50]	The proprietor, a genial Bombay man, was a friend of his and cried: 'Ishwarsab, the results were announced today.' (*AD*, 85)

7.7. In the speech-functions in IE the effect of culture on the use of kinship terms is contextually significant, and, as mentioned earlier, may differ from the use of kinship terms in British English. In British English the lexical set of kinship terms may comprise, among other items, the following items: *brother*, *brother-in-law*, *cousin*, *father*, *mother*, etc. In IE these terms need different formal and contextual statements since (i) the members of one British English set operate in three sets in IE; (ii) the members of a set, in IE, have been increased; (iii) the meaning of the items has been extended. The extension of items of one British English lexical set to more than one lexical set in IE means that items like *brother*, *sister*, *mother*, *brother-in-law*, may operate in any of the following sets: (i) modes of address/reference; (ii) terms of endearment; (iii) terms of regard and respect as well as in the usual British English sense as (iv) terms of kinship.

In British English the item *cousin* has no marker of sex; in IE, however, *cousin* may be followed by a sex marker, i.e. *cousin-sister* (*RH*, 29), *cousin-brother* (*F of F*, 131).

8. *Indian Caste in Indian English*

8.1. References to the Indian caste system in English (not only in IE) show how the items of a foreign language may be used to describe an entirely alien contextual unit. The contextual unit of caste in the typical Indian sense is absent in British culture, and any reference to it may mean either a lexical borrowing from Indian languages or an extension of the collocability of the lexical items of British English. It may also entail a rank-bound (cf. 5.3(a)) or rank-changed (cf. 5.3(b)) transference from Indian languages.

In IE fiction or newspapers (especially legal and administrative reporting) we observe that over the years a restricted language of the caste system has evolved. This would be a topic for an independent study: here we have only touched upon a few features of this restricted language.

8.2. In English the item *caste* or the *caste system* is used in any of the following senses:[51]

(i) for reference to the hereditary classes of the Hindu society (i.e. *Brahmin, Kshatriya, Vaisha, Sudra*);
(ii) for reference to social grouping, in any culture, on the analogy of the Indian caste system;
(iii) for reference to the sub-castes in any of the four castes in (i).

In IE the item *caste*, when treated as a node of a collocation, collocates with the following items:

Items following 'caste':

-basis (*H*, 25. 11. 63); *-brotherhood* (*BH*, 125); *-dinner* (*Kanth*, 89); *-distinction* (*Un*, 210); *-domination* (*L*, 19.3.61); *-elders* (*He Who*, 17); *-feast*, *-feeling* (*Un*, 193); *-following* (*L*, 19.3.61); *-less* (*Un*, 143); *-mark* (*RH*, 204); *-proud* (*He Who*, 171); *-sanctity* (*He Who*, 155); *-well* (*Un*, 33); *-union* (*MM*, 190); *-vermin* (*Un*, 68); *-waif* (*He Who*, 203).

Items preceding 'caste':

high- (*He Who*, 94); *inter-* (*MM*, 190); *low-* (*MM*, 163); *lowest-* (*Un*, 35); *out-* (*Un*, 39); *professional-* (*MM*, 142); *sub-* (*AD*, 10); *upper-* (*Un*).

In *modes of address/reference* in the caste system the following items are used:

(a) for upper caste: *high-born*; *high-caste* (*He Who*, 94); *twice-born* (*Un*, 14);[52] *uppercaste* (*Un*, 33).
(b) for lower caste: *caste-less* (*Un*, 229); *lowcaste* (*Un*, 67); *lower-caste* (*C of B*, 9); *untouchable* (*Un*, 177).

In the social roles also items of different ranks in IE are used for the two main castes, the upper caste and the lower caste. For example, there is an *ordered series of words* restricted to the upper caste in which the item *Brahmin* precedes:

Brahminhood (*S and R*, 20); *-corner* (*Kanth*, 106); *-guru* (*S and R*, 223); *-house* (*S and R*, 28); *-priest* (*RH*, 106); *-land* (*S and R*, 285); *-quarter* (*Kanth*, 132); *-restaurant* (*SIF*, 161); *-role* (*He Who*, 109); *-street* (*Kanth*, 21); *-section* (*S and R*, 50).

Then we have another series in which the item *Brahmin* follows another item, e.g. *sacred brahmin* (*S and R*, 11). In the context of the upper caste a large number of items are assigned *restricted* semantic areas: e.g. *forehead-marking* (*Mr S*, 206); *nine-stranded thread* (*He Who*, 45); *red-paste trident* (*He Who*, 98).

The following sets are used for the lower caste:

(a) *chamar woman* (*He Who*, 107), *-people* (*He Who*, 107);
(b) *paria children* (*Kanth*, 225), *-girl* (*Kanth*, 219), *-kids* (*Kanth*, 219), *-looking* (*Kanth*, 242), *-mixer* (*Kanth*, 63), *-polluter* (*Kanth*, 127), *-quarter* (*Kanth*, 19), *-street* (*Kanth*, 219), *-woman* (*Kanth*, 219);
(c) *sudra corner* (*Kanth*, 118), *-lines* (*Kanth*, 242), *-street* (*Kanth*, 31), *-woman* (*Kanth*, 24), *-quarter* (*Kanth*, 25).

8.3. In some formations one component may be the item *caste* which may help in contextualizing a text and assigning it to the proper contextual unit. The difficulty arises when L^2 items like *defile, pollute, touch*, etc., are used contextually and collocationally in an un-English sense. The following three 'sets' will make this clearer:

1. **Defile**: *touched me and defiled me*; *the defiled one*; *defiled by contact*; *defiled my house*; *defiled my religion*; *...feet become defiled*; *defiling distance.*
2. **Touch**: *the touched man*; *touch-purify*; *fear of touch*; *untouchable*; *touched the dust of his feet*; *touched me and defiled me*; *touched each other while dining*; *touched our low-caste feet.*
3. **Pollute**: *polluting myself*; *polluting kitchen*; *fear of pollution*; *pollution of progeny*; *our community polluted*; *pollute the food*; *polluting distance.*

These items could perhaps be termed *context-specific items*' (cf. 9.7) since their meaning is essentially determined by the contextual unit in which they operate. Once the contextual unit is changed they become unintelligible to a native user of English.

8.4. As a preliminary study in quantitative method for classification of deviations in a variety of a language we took one text (*Untouchable*, a novel by M. R. Anand, London, 1935) of an IE writer. A selected number of items (*caste*, *defile*, *high*, *highest*, *low*, *lowest*, *out*, *pollute*, *touch*, *upper*) were abstracted and the following study made:

(i) the total range of collocations (cf. Table II);
(ii) the frequency of 'usual' and 'unusual' lexical environments of these items.

TABLE II

SHOWING DEGREES OF 'INDIANNESS' OR 'CASTENESS' OF CERTAIN ITEMS IN INDIAN ENGLISH

Item	Total Frequency	Usual collocations (i.e. as in British English)	Unusual collocations (i.e. special Indian English collocations)
		Frequency	Frequency
Caste	99	—	99
Defile	20	—	20
High	9	2	7
Highest	2	1	1
Low	12	5	7
Lowest	3	2	1
Out	42	18	24
Pollute	35	—	35
Touch	84	15	69
Upper	2	1	1

9. *Indian English in Indian Social Roles*

9.1. In treating social roles separately in this section we are not creating a dichotomy between (i) restricted languages, (ii) speech-functions, and (iii) the language of social roles. These may cut across each other, and this distinction is made for classificatory convenience. There is, however, some difference between the speech-functions and the language of social roles in general: social roles do not necessarily include the socially determined repetitive events; and social roles are not limited in the same sense as the speech-functions are.

9.2. The division of social roles into contextual units is very arbitrary. In order to find language correlates in language contact situations we may define social roles as those demarcated 'areas' of activity which are brought under the focus of attention of the linguist, and for which he finds formal exponents in the text under description.

9.3. The following are some of the social roles in which IE is used in India: (a) religion, (b) ceremonies and rituals, (c) dress and ornaments, (d) food and food habits, (e) marriage, (f) politics.

We shall consider here only a few collocations which show the religious attitude of the two major Indian communities, Hindus and Muslims. As the item *caste* has become the node of all the caste collocations in IE, in the same way the item *communal*[53] is used in Hindu-Muslim relations. It may be used with the suffixes *-ism* (*BJ*, 7.6.59) and *-ist* (*1000 Nights*, 140). The range of collocability of *communal* is entirely different in IE from what it is in British English (in *OED* and other dictionaries of English one Indianized meaning of *communal* is usually given). The following formations with *communal* as node have been abstracted from different *ordered series of words* (which in this case are also lexical sets) of IE.

Communal attitude (*L*, 9.4.51); *-bodies* (*IN*, 8.7.61); *-coloring* (*IN*, 7.2.64); *-consideration* (*IN*, 7.2.64); *-disturbance* (*L*, 26.3.61); *-distinctions* (*1000 Nights*, 141); *-parties* (*L*, 26.3.61); *-passion* (*L*, 26.3.61); *-press* (*L*, 26.3.61); *-riots* (*V of G*, 84); *-trend* (*HS*, 1.7.61); *-unity* (*IN*, 8.7.61). (Also *communally named* (*L*, 9.4.61); *inter-communal* (*IN*, 8.7.61); *communal leader*.)

Reference to any clash between the religious communities, especially the Hindus and Muslims, is made by the item *communal riots* (*V of G*, 84) or *riots* (*1000 Nights*, 121). In IE, the item *riot* has more or less a restricted meaning referring to the disturbances of a 'communal nature'.

This difference may come up not only in the register of politics, but also in other social roles like eating and marriage, and in speech-functions, such as abuses/curses (cf. 7.4(f)), modes of reference/address, and greetings (cf. 7.5). In the relationship of two religious groups in eating we have forms like *inter-dine*, *separate-eating* (*Kanth*, 51), *cow-eater* (*V of G*, 124), *cow beef eater* (*F of F*, 157), *cow-worship*, *forbidden meat* (*MM*, 31), and in social relations *inter-marriage* (*MM*, 11). (*Inter-marriage* is also used for marriages between two castes, but is less frequent for what are called international marriages—those between an Indian and a foreigner.)

9.4. The ceremonies may be of two types, (i) individual and (ii) social.

(i) Individual: *hair-cutting ceremony* (*Kanth*, 56); *rice-eating ceremony* (*Kanth*, 171); *turmeric-ceremony* (*MM*, 70); *naming ceremony* (*SMH*).

(ii) Social: *aroti-time* (*He Who*, 207); *bath-milk* (*He Who*, 130); *car-festival* (*OR*, 15.7.59); *shagan-ceremony* (*BH*, 124); *brother-anointing ceremony* (*He Who*, 160); *rain-bringing ritual* (*F of F*, 88); *vinayaka-festival* (*ET*, 21).

95.5. In the restricted language of politics in IE the problem is not of 'redefining' the items: what interests us here is that some lexical items and formations have acquired specific meanings. In a Gandhian context the following lexical items are used: *ahimsa, satyagraha, khadi* or *khaddar*. These items have now been borrowed in British English, too, and are listed in the *OED*. These three give us the following lexical sets, which, incidentally, are also ordered series of words.

Ahimsa camp, -leader, -soldier (*WM*, 78); *-sweeper* (*Un*, 218). *Ashram disciple* (*MM*, 82), *-camp* (*WM*, 82); *khadi board* (*SL*, 8.6.59), *-clad* (*SL*, 6.6.59), *-competition* (*WM*, 97), *-coat* (*Kanth*, 148), *-cloth* (*Kanth*, 109), *-shop* (*Kanth*, 135); *Khaddar clad* (*1000 Nights*, 14), *-jibba* (*WM*, 44), *-sari* (*WM*, 48); *Swadeshi movement, -cloth* (*Un*, 208); *Satyagraha movement*[54] (*SMH*, 73); *Satyagraha campaign* (*BJ*, 7.6.59).

9.6. The following formations are used in connection with (i) village parties or village politics, (ii) trade unions and (iii) other societies:

Congress-panchayat committee (*Kanth*, 119); *Dehati Janata Party* (*SL*, 15.6.59); *Grain Gola Committee* (*OR*, 15.7.59); *Gram Sahayak Refresher Course* (*Hit*, 28.12.59); *Kisan Candidate* (*V of G*, 13).

9.7. In describing social roles in IE it will be useful if we treat certain items as *context-specific items* (cf. 8.3). A contextual item, in our sense, would be a formal item of any rank (up to a sentence) the meaning of which is entirely dependent on the Indian context. We have taken a few excerpts to illustrate this point.

(a) 'She pulled a dining-leaf out of the bundle in the kitchen rack, spread it on the floor . . .' (*WM*, 84).

(b) '... called for coffee ... brought in brass tumblers ... poured it back and forth ... forth and back in the perpetual concertina motion.' (*DD*)

The above (a) is contextually parallel to what in the English society would be *she took a plate and laid it on the table*. In this case, then, there is unintelligibility for an L[1] speaker of English because the items and the collocations that fill the structure are not usual, and because this contextual unit is absent in British English. The unintelligibility at the cultural level may leave the following 'meanings' uncomprehended:

(i) that the person is from the south of India (because the *dining-leaves* are not, normally, used in the north of India);
(ii) that it is a middle-class orthodox Hindu speaking about a conventional household.

10. *Conclusion*

In the preceding sections we have attempted to illustrate briefly how the Indian socio-cultural and linguistic setting has affected features of the English language in India. It has been argued that a statement which includes context as a congruent level for such a language contact situation is not only more powerful, but it also helps in the classification of those formations which some scholars, in India and elsewhere, have termed *Indianisms*. Indianisms have been considered 'sub-standard' because such items are not used in British English, and hence should not form part of 'standard English'.

In a comparative description of the variety of a language, what is important is that in addition to the comparison of the structures and systems, at one or more levels, the contextual units in which the varieties function should also be considered as crucial for a complete description. A comparison involving the contextual units of a variety may be explained as a study of the effects of the context of culture (both 'wider situation' and 'immediate situation') on a variety of a language.

We have considered some selected and restricted formal and/or contextual aspects of IE to illustrate how IE has acquired an Indian characteristic which manifests itself at other than the phonetic or the phonological levels. In the spoken medium IE has by now established itself into an Indian variety of English (which, however, varies significantly on the cline of bilingualism). At the other levels too the Indian contextual units, in which the English language has been increasingly used even after 1947, have influenced the formal features of IE. IE has ramifications in Indian culture (which includes languages) and is used in India towards maintaining appropriate Indian patterns of life, culture and education. This, in short, we might call the *Indianness* of Indian English, in the same way as we speak of the *Englishness* of British English.[55]

Notes

[1] The idea of this study, in the present form, originally came from the late Professor J.R.Firth. I am indebted to him for the encouraging interest he took in my work (a part of which is presented here) in spite of his indifferent health, during 1958–60, first at Edinburgh and later at his home at Haywards Heath (Sussex). My thanks are due to M.A.K.Halliday for his stimulating guidance and detailed comments, to J.C.Catford, Miss Yamuna Keskar and R.Narasimhan for reading an earlier draft of this work and for their criticisms. Many ideas of Halliday have been incorporated here without any special mention; this does not, however, mean that Halliday would necessarily agree with all my interpretations and views as set forth in this paper.

[2] By varieties of a language we mean two or more forms of a language as 'developed' in different contextual settings. A good example is the English language in America, Australia, Canada, etc. The varieties of English used as foreign or second languages (L^2's) would include English in India, parts of Africa, Malaya, etc. Another example is Hindi, as developed in the South of India, especially Hyderabad, and other such non-Hindi speaking regions of India. See J.Gumperz and A.Ferguson, 'Linguistic Diversity in South Asia', *IJAL* supplement 26.3 (1960); also J.C. Catford, *Applied Linguistics in the Teaching of English as a Secondary Language* (mimeographed).

[3] The terms L^1 and L^2 have been suggested by J.C.Catford as abbreviations for a primary language and a secondary language: see his 'The Teaching of English as a Foreign Language' in *Studies in Communication* 3 (London, 1959). It should, however, be made clear here that the relative status of a bi- or multi-lingual person's language is difficult to establish. For most multi-linguals, one language is clearly dominant, in the sense that it is used with greater facility, most of the time, in the widest range of situations. The dominant language is the primary language (L^1)—other languages are secondary languages (L^2's). For some Indians, perhaps, English has equal status with an Indian language. Even so, there are important spheres of language use—notably in the private and emotional life of such persons—where an Indian language is L^1. For most, English is clearly L^2. In any case English functions as L^2, and can for the purpose of this study generally be regarded as such.

In the Indian context we find the distinction between *first language*, *second language*, and *foreign language* useful. A *first language* may be defined as the mother tongue, or broadly, the regional language. A *second language* is a language which belongs to India both culturally and linguistically: for instance Tamil or Kannada in Uttar Pradesh, or Hindi in Andhra Pradesh or Tamilnad. A *foreign language* is any language which is not used as the *first language* in any part of India.

[4] The terms *context*, *level(s)*, *inter-level*, *rank* and other technical terms (excluding

exponent and *exponence*) have been, generally, used in the sense in which these are used by M.A.K.Halliday in his 'Categories of the Theory of Grammar', *Word* 17.3 (1961) (hereafter, *Categories*). See also ibid., pp. 244–245, for the use of the terms *formal meaning* and *contextual meaning*.

[5] See J.R.Firth, 'A Synopsis of Linguistic Theory', in *Studies in Linguistic Analysis* (Blackwell, Oxford, 1957), p. 23 (hereafter, *Synopsis*).

[6] The term Indo-Anglican (or Anglian) writing has been used by some scholars. (See K.R.S.Iyengar, *The Indian Contribution to English*, Bombay, 1945.) We prefer the term Indian English writing, as it makes clear that L^1 speakers of Indian languages are using IE as an L^2, and, more important, the English language is operating in Indian contexts which are 'un-English'. In our use there is no value judgment attached to the term as there is in the use of Whitworth (see G.C.Whitworth, *Indian English*, Lahore, 1932).

[7] The 'cline' of bilingualism may be defined as an arbitrary scale on which the competence and proficiency in L^2 may be 'measured'. The three crucial points on the 'cline' are: (i) the *zero* point; (ii) the *central* point; and (iii) the *ambilingual* point. The zero point is significant in the sense that a speaker of an L^2 who ranks *above* this point may be considered a bilingual. The criterion for ranking a person as a bilingual is that a native speaker of a language accepts the medium (written or spoken) he uses as 'intelligible' at all the formal levels. That a person is intelligible does not imply that he has a 'native-like control' over a language: it simply means that a person is able to use an L^2 for what we term 'effective' social control in all social roles. It certainly does not mean that he is *ambilingual*. The *zero* point is not necessarily the end point of the axis at the bottom. A person may have some *competence* in a language, but still he may rank at some point *below* the zero point. When certain speakers and writers of IE are considered to use *Baboo English*, or *Butler English*, we are, in a way, making a statement about the 'proficiency' of the users, which in the case of *Baboo English* or *Butler English* is not only insufficient, but also produces very amusing results. The term 'cline' has been borrowed from Halliday, *Categories*, pp. 248–249.

[8] *Indianisms*, as used traditionally, include those expressions which are rejected by some scholars as 'sub-standard' though these are widely used by educated Indians. The examples given are: *pin-drop silence*; *B. A. Pass*; *England-returned*; *Himalayan-blunder*; *nation-building*; *change of heart*; *dumb millions*; *to marry with*; *to make friendship with*, etc. (cf. R.C.Goffin, *Some Notes on Indian English*, S.P.E. Tract No. XLI, p. 31; and S.Mathai, 'The Position of English in India', in *British and American English Since 1900* (London, 1951), p. 99). Note that in their use 'Indianisms' include not only formally deviant items, but contextually deviant items too.

[9] C^1 is used here as an abbreviation for the native culture of an L^1 speaker, and C^2 for the culture of the native speaker of an L^2. These are used as parallel terms with L^1 and L^2 at the contextual level.

[10] Firth suggested 'collocation' as a technical term in *Modes of Meaning* (1951), and discussed it further in the *Synopsis*, pp. 11–13. Also see T.F.Mitchell, 'Syntagmatic Relations in Linguistic Analysis', *TPS* 1958, p. 108; Halliday, *Categories*, p. 276; B.B.Kachru, 'An Analysis of Some Features of Indian English: A Study in Linguistic Method', Ph.D. Thesis, Edinburgh University, 1961, pp. 57–81.

[11] U.Weinreich, *Languages in Contact* (New York, 1953). 'The non-belonging

elements can be separated as "borrowed" or *transferred*. This is one manifestation of linguistic analysis', p. 7. In this study, 'transfer' includes non-linguistic features too, for instance transfer of the contextual units which are foreign to the culture of the native speaker of an L^2 (in the Indian situation these would be British speakers of English).

[12] Used as a technical term. See Firth, 'Technique of Semantics', in *Papers in Linguistics*, 1934–51, p. 54 (hereafter *Papers*).

[13] A 'mistake' is any 'deviation' which is rejected by a native speaker of a language as out of the linguistic 'code' of that particular language and which may not be justified on formal or contextual grounds. A 'deviation' may involve differences from the norm, but may be necessary in the cultural context in which a language functions.

[14] Of special interest is 'The Structure of a Semantic Theory', by J.J.Katz and J.A.Fodor, *Language* 39.2 (1963), which presents a semantic theory of language on the basis of Chomsky's linguistic theory. Also see the review of the above by R.M.W. Dixon under the title, 'A Trend in Semantics', *Linguistics* 1 (1963).

[15] See *Speech* (London, 1930), pp. 38–45; *The Tongues of Men* (London, 1937); pp. 126–130; the following papers in *Papers*: 'The Technique of Semantics', 'Modes of Meaning'; 'General Linguistics and Descriptive Grammar'; *Synopsis*, pp. 7–11; 'Ethnographic Analysis and Language', in *Man and Culture* (London, 1957), pp. 83–118. Also see G.L.Bursill-Hall, 'Levels analysis: J.R.Firth's Theories of Linguistic Analysis', *JCLA/RACL* 6.2–3 (1961).

[16] e.g. T.F.Mitchell, 'The Language of Buying and Selling in Cyrenaica: A Situational Statement', *Hesperis* 1957, pp. 31–71; M.A.K.Halliday, 'The Language of the Chinese "Secret History of the Mongols"', Philological Society Publication No. 17 (Oxford, 1959), section on 'Contextualization'; B.B.Kachru, op. cit. (n. 10); J.Ellis, 'On Contextual Meaning' (in the present volume).

[17] See Firth, *Synopsis*, p. 2, 'In the most general term the approach may be described as monistic.'

[18] See 'Personality and Language in Society', in *Papers*, p. 44.

[19] Firth, 'Linguistics and the Functional Point of View', *English Studies* 16 (1934).

[20] A contextual 'unit', however, is not of the same nature as a 'unit' at the formal levels. Earlier the term 'sector' was suggested for it; cf. Kachru, op. cit., p. 89.

[21] The use of this term in this context was suggested to me by Firth, in 1960, after he visited the PAT (speech synthesizer) laboratory in the Phonetics Department of the University of Edinburgh.

[22] See *Synopsis*, p. 11 (Firth's italics).

[23] The concept of 'substitution frame' has been used by D.Metzger and G.E. Williams in their ethnolinguistic work. See 'A Formal Ethnographic Analysis of Tenejapa Ladino Weddings', *American Anthropologist* 65.5 (1963). Also see Madeleine Mathiot, 'A Procedure for Investigating Language and Culture Relations' (mimeographed). She suggests the term 'behavioral unit'.

[24] J.Ellis, op. cit. (n. 16).

[25] Firth used this term for those sub-languages which are 'restricted by scientific method conforming to functions of language in life'; see his 'The Treatment of Language in General Linguistics', *The Medical Press*, August 19, 1959, p. 146.

[26] See T.B.W.Reid, 'Linguistics, Structuralism and Philology', *ArchL.* 8 (1958), pp. 28–37.

[27] See T. Hill, 'Institutional Linguistics', *Orbis* 7.2 (1958). 'The word *tongue* will be used as a neutral term for any of the entities commonly styled dialect, language . . .' (p. 442).

[28] The following studies submitted for the Diploma in Applied Linguistics, Edinburgh University, have shown interesting register differences: R. P. Aronson, 'A Comparative Analysis of English Verb Usage in the Restricted Languages of Fiction and the Natural and Social Sciences as Represented by Three Contemporary Written English Texts', 1959; M. M. Claxton, 'A Study of Nominal Groups', 1960; P. J. Seccombe, 'Styles of English Encountered Within the Register of Obstetrics and Gynecology Related to the Linguistic Problems of the Overseas Post-graduate Students', 1961.

[29] M. Joos, 'The Isolation of Styles', in the *Report of the Tenth Annual Round Table Meeting of Linguistics and Language Studies*, 1960. See also J. C. Catford, *Applied Linguistics in the Teaching of English as a Secondary Language*. (See *n. 2*.)

[30] J. Ellis, op. cit.

[31] N. Yule and A. C. Burnell, *Hobson-Jobson* (London, 1903). Also G. S. Rao, *Indian Words in English* (London, 1954).

[32] The categories of a general theory of translation may, however, be applied to the process of translation in a bilingual situation.

[33] Note that the use of rank-changed is not the same as Halliday's *rankshift*; see *Categories*, p. 251.

[34] This term is used here both for compounds and collocations.

[35] (iii) and (iv) are not mutually exclusive. What is contextually 'un-English' is often 'collocationally un-English'.

[36] R. B. Lees has described such cases in his *The Grammar of English Nominalisations* (*IJAL* supplement, 26.3 (1960)). '. . . in a great many cases it will be possible to construct on the basis of the given transformations an indefinitely large number of compounds which do not occur in any corpus of English not because they are excluded by the grammatical rules of English, but rather because of various conventions of usage and of historical vicissitudes', p. 121.

[37] Ibid., pp. 148–152.

[38] A register-restricted form is one which is accepted in a specialized register, but would not be accepted in common speech or writing; for example, *dying declaration* may be used in a legal document but not in non-legal registers.

[39] In British English *match-box* is used for a box without matches. In IE it is substituted for what in British English would be *a box of matches*.

[40] See E. E. Morris, *Austral English* (London, 1898), p. 160. Also H. L. Mencken, *The American Language* (New York, 1945).

[41] The reference is to annual *ratha-yatra* of Lord Juggernatha, a deity in Puri, Orissa. The image of deity is carried in a procession on an enormous car adorned with paintings.

[42] This item is a member of an ordered series of words which also form a lexical set. The other members are: *sacred lamp*; *sacred thread*; *sacred paste*; *sacred tuft*; *sacred fan*.

[43] Firth has used this term in his work, but there is no suggestion about the specific use and its distinction from 'restricted language'.

[44] The categories in the Table are not mutually exclusive; for instance *Pandit* is an exponent of both religion and caste.

45 Used here for a person representing official authority, i.e. one who is a symbol of the government. This is a transfer of Hindustani *sarkar*.

46 Sometimes peddlers may be addressed by naming the goods they are selling; for instance *tooth-powder* in 'Hey, tooth-powder, come here, give me a packet'. (*FE*, 80).

47 Other example: 'He (you wouldn't speak your groom's name even in your heart, you said he)', (*SMH*, 76).

48 Spelled as *babu* or *baboo*. A term of respect used frequently in the north of India. In the south of India it is used for *sir, your honour*. In many parts of India it is used as a mode of address for a native clerk. Cf. Yule and Burnell, op. cit., p. 44.

49 May be used as a mode of reference by orthodox women for their husbands.

50 In colloquial language *sab* is used as the weak form of *sahib*. It is equivalent to *master* and may be used without religious or status restrictions when one wants to show respect. Originally it was used for Europeans in India.

51 Cf. A.C.Basham, *The Wonder That Was India* (London), pp. 137–187.

52 This is a loan-shift from Sanskrit *dvija*. The three castes, Brahmin, Kshatriya, Vaisha, are 'twice-born' in the sense that they have their natural birth and then, at their initiation, are invested with the sacred thread which implies acceptance in the caste; hence, re-birth. See ibid., p. 138.

53 In *O.E.D.* and other standard dictionaries of English the extended Indian meaning is normally found.

54 *Satyagraha* is usually translated into English as 'non-co-operation'. This is not the 'correct translation'; *satya* is 'truth' and *āgraha* 'demand'.

55 The crucial questions such as how much 'deviation' from the norm is 'allowable' in an L^2 variety at the different formal levels, and the necessity (and problems) of standardization of a variety, have not been discussed here. These, of course, are directly linked with the interpretation and classification of a 'deviation' or a 'mistake' in a L^2 variety (cf. n. 13).

APPENDIX

List of the Indian English sources used in this study. The abbreviated forms used in the text are given in brackets. The place of publication is London unless otherwise indicated.

Abbas, K. A., *One Thousand Nights on a Bed of Stone*, Bombay (*1000 Nights*); Anand, M. R., *Untouchable*, 1935 (*Un*); *Coolie*, 1936 (*C*); *The Big Heart*, 1947 (*BH*); *Seven Summers*, 1951 (*SS*); *Across the Black Waters*, Bombay, 1955 (*ABW*); *Power of Darkness*, Bombay, 1958 (*P of D*); Bhattacharya, B., *So Many Hungers*, 1959 (*SMH*); *Music for Mohini*, 1959 (*MM*); *He Who Rides a Tiger*, 1960 (*He Who*); Ghosh, S. N., *The Flame of the Forest*, 1955 (*F of F*); Markhandaya, K., *Some Inner Fury*, 1955 (*SIF*); Narayan, R. K., *The Bachelor of Arts*, 1931 (*BA*); *Mr Sampath*, 1952 (*Mr S*); *The Financial Expert*, 1952 (*FE*); *Waiting for the Mahatma*, 1955 (*WM*); Rajan, B., *The Dark Dancer*, 1958 (*DD*); Rao, Raja, *Kanthpura*, 1938 (*Kanth*); *The Cow and the Barricade and Other Stories*, 1947 (*C and B*); *Serpent and the Rope*, 1960 (*S and R*); Singh, K., *Train To Pakistan*, 1956 (*TP*).

Newspapers: *Bharat Jyoti*, (*BJ*), Bombay; *Hindu* (Weekly Review), (*H*), Madras; *The Hindustan Standard*, (*HS*) Calcutta; *Hitwada*, (*Hit.*), Nagpur; *Indian News*, (*IN*); *Link*, (*L*), New Delhi; *The Mail*, (*M*), Madras; *The National Herald*, (*NH*), Lucknow; *The Search Light*, (*SL*), Patna; *The Tribune*, (*T*), Ambala; *Vakil*, (*V*), Srinagar.

Firth's Theory of "Meaning"

JOHN LYONS

It has been said that: 'The two developments in linguistics that will always be associated with Firth's name are his theory of context of situation or, more generally, the contextual theory of meaning, and prosodic analysis in phonology.'[1] 'Prosodic analysis' has been exemplified by Firth and his followers in the phonological description of a number of different languages. For that reason it is quite widely known; and many linguists would agree that it provides a more satisfactory approach to the description of the phonological structure of certain languages than 'orthodox' phonemic theory.[2] The 'contextual theory of meaning', on the other hand, has not been exemplified by any considerable body of practical analysis and, outside the somewhat restricted circle of Firth's declared adherents, seems to have been dismissed out of hand as involving an idiosyncratic, unmotivated or even mischievous reinterpretation of the term 'meaning'. It is time that we had a critical examination of the theory, the more so as there are signs of a renewed interest among linguists in the rehabilitation of semantics as an integral part of their science. Firth himself frequently claimed to have established, and to have maintained in all his work, the proper linguistic approach to the treatment of 'meaning';[3] and this claim has been reiterated by his followers.[4] It is the purpose of the present article to examine Firth's theory of 'meaning' and to see whether it has anything of value to contribute to contemporary linguistics. I will suggest that, although the notion of 'context', in particular the notion of 'context of situation', is essential to a materially adequate theory of semantics, it cannot be made to bear all the weight that Firth placed upon it. Further, I will maintain that Firth either failed to see or rejected without mentioning, and for reasons which it is difficult to discern, certain distinctions which must be drawn before the theory of semantics can make any claims to precision and empirical adequacy.

The first point which must be made is that in discussing Firth's theory of 'meaning' one is concerned with an all-embracing theory of language structure, and not merely with semantics as this term is customarily understood. According to Firth, the most important fact about language is its social function: 'normal linguistic behavior as a whole is meaningful effort, directed towards the maintenance of appropriate patterns of life'.[5] Every utterance occurs in a culturally determined 'context of situation'; and the 'meaning' of the utterance is the totality of all the features in it that can be identified as contributing to the maintenance of the 'patterns of life' in the society in which the speaker lives and to the assertion of the speaker's social role and personality within the society. These features are not of course 'given' in the data, but must be 'abstracted' from it by a careful study of the contrasts that hold between utterances in the same or different contexts of situation. In accounting for the total 'meaning' of utterances, the linguist makes abstractions from the data at different, hierarchically-ordered, 'levels of analysis'—phonetic and phonological; grammatical, lexical and semantic—and describes the 'meaning' of units of each level in terms of their 'function' as elements in the structure of units of the level above. The structures of the higher-level units are the contexts in which the lower-level units 'function' and 'have meaning'. 'Meaning . . . is to be regarded as a complex of contextual relations, and phonetics, grammar, lexicography, and semantics each handles its own components of the complex in its appropriate context.'[6] Thus all branches of linguistics necessarily deal with 'meaning'. And Firth can make such statements as the following, which are apt to puzzle, if not scandalize, any reader who fails to take the point of the definition of 'meaning' as 'a complex of contextual relations': 'Phonology states the phonematic and prosodic processes within the word and sentence, regarding them as a mode of meaning. The phonetician links all this with the processes and features of utterance. Such processes are characteristic of persons, of social groups, even of nations. Moreover the general feature of voice quality is part of the phonetic mode of meaning of an English boy, a Frenchman, or a lady from New York. Surely it is part of the meaning of an American to sound like one.'[7] At first sight, assertions of this kind might seem to depend upon a perverse and wilful extension of the term 'meaning'. However, in the light of the outline of Firth's theory of 'meaning' given above, we can see that his use of the term in the passage quoted and in similar passages is consistent with his general view of the analysis of 'meaning' as 'a serial contextualization of our facts, context within context, each one being a function, an organ of the bigger context and all contexts finding a place in what may be called the context of culture'.[8] Whether Firth always uses the term 'meaning' in a way that is consistent with this conception, it would be difficult to say. A more interesting question is the degree to which the term 'meaning', in the general sense in which Firth uses it and which is exemplified in the quotations, is compatible with its more common use in the other theories of semantics and in everyday discourse. Before we turn to this question, however, we must develop a little further the implications of the 'the contextual theory of meaning'.

When we look in Firth's writings for clarification of the key terms 'function' and 'context' we cannot but be struck by the extreme vagueness with which they are introduced and employed. In his earliest paper on the subject he says: 'I propose to split up meaning or function into a series of component functions. Each function will be defined as the use of some language form in relation to some context.'[9] In one of his latest articles he talks of 'the application of the word "meaning" to the function of an element with reference to the specific system of which it is a "term", "unit" or "member" in a given language'.[10] When he attempts to describe the way in which the linguist might go about 'splitting up meaning into its component functions' he has recourse to analogy: 'Having made the first abstraction by suitably isolating a piece of "text" or part of the social process of speaking for a listener or of writing for a reader, the suggested procedure for dealing with meaning is its dispersion into modes, rather like the dispersion of light of mixed wave-lengths into a spectrum.'[11] The analogy is not very helpful. In order to see what is meant by 'splitting up meaning into its component functions' we have to examine the instances of the several 'modes of meaning' given by Firth.[12] I do not propose to carry out a detailed examination of Firth's examples here. This would take up too much space. I will merely say that an examination of his examples suggests that 'meaning', or 'function in context', is to be interpreted as acceptability or appropriateness in that context: an utterance or part of an utterance is 'meaningful' if, and only if, it can be used appropriately in some actual context. The task of the linguist describing a particular language is to distinguish the different component levels of acceptability—phonetic, phonological, grammatical, lexical and semantic—and to show that for an utterance to be fully 'meaningful' it must be acceptable at all levels. If we take 'meaning' in this sense, keeping in mind Firth's strong emphasis on the social aspect of linguistic behaviour, we can give a consistent interpretation to most of his theoretical statements and to his examples. We may now go on to enquire whether his notion of 'meaning' will enable us to deal satisfactorily with the properties and functions of language which are customarily held to fall within the scope of semantics.

The first generally-accepted semantic notion which may be mentioned in connection with Firth's theory of 'meaning' is the notion of 'significance'. We must of course start with some intuitive idea of what is meant by this term. Let us assume that the grammatical analysis of a particular language has been carried out to whatever degree of refinement is considered desirable. Let us assume further that a large set of sentences has been constructed in accordance with the rules of the grammar, taking account of the relations of 'collocation' holding between particular lexical items only in so far as these can be interpreted as relations of syntactic 'colligation' holding between distributional classes. All these sentences are by definition grammatically well formed. Some of them will be significant, or 'meaningful', in the sense that they will be understood and given a consistent interpretation by native speakers of the language concerned; others will be nonsensical, or 'meaningless', in the sense that they will not be understood at all by native speakers or, if understood, not interpreted consistently. There are obvious difficulties here. However, we need not assume that there is always a clear distinction between sentences that are both grammatical and significant, on the one hand, and those that are grammatically well formed, but nonsensical, on the other. It suffices that the distinction can be made satisfactorily in a fair number of cases.[13] Some linguists, it is true, would reject entirely the distinction of grammaticality and significance.[14] But this is surely a minority view. And, as we shall see, it is not Firth's view; so we may neglect it here.

If we now look in Firth's theory of 'meaning' for an explication of the intuitive notion of 'significance', it is not difficult to see that for him this is acceptability at the highest level of analysis; acceptability in a context of situation. It is because he cannot envisage such sentences as Jespersen's 'A dancing woman charms' or Sapir's 'The farmer kills the duckling' ever being employed in some actual context of use that he describes them as 'nonsense'.[15] They do not have the 'implication of utterance'; they cannot 'be referred to typical participants in some generalized context of situation'.[16] We may think that Firth is wrong in either, or both, of these particular instances. But his principle is clear. Sentences may be perfectly well formed from a grammatical point of view—to put it in his own terms, they may have 'meaning . . . at the grammatical level of understanding'—and yet, if they do not have the 'implication of utterance', from the semantic point of view they will be 'just nonsense'.[17]

Now this view has much to commend it. It is certainly more attractive than theories of semantics which define 'significance' in terms of the 'designation' of 'states of affairs', or of the 'expression of propositions' —theories which Firth aptly characterized as 'dualist'.[18] However, it is clear that Firth's view of significance depends very heavily, as he himself recognized, upon the ability of linguists to identify and describe the contexts of situation in which utterances function and have 'semantic meaning'. Firth assumes that this is in fact possible; and he gives some indication of the different ways in which contexts of situation might be classified.[19]

It is easy enough to criticize Firth's notion of 'situation' as vague and ill defined. At the same time it seems clear that there *are* very many different and identifiable 'situations' in which we engage as participants in our various social roles; and that what we say is often to a considerable extent determined by situational factors. The language we use at home is different, and describably different, from the language we use at work; different again from the language we use in church, or on the playing field or golf course, when talking to women or children or to the other men, to our social superiors or inferiors; and so on. It is, I think, undeniable that the notion of 'situation', however difficult it might be to formalize or even to discuss satisfactorily in general terms, is essential to any comprehensive theory of linguistic behaviour. Firth must be given credit for his recognition of this fact and for his insistence that situational correlations are to be taken into account as an integral part of the description of language (and at all levels of analysis) and not treated as a secondary 'paralinguistic' phenomenon. We are no doubt a long way from being able to account systematically for contexts of situation. But the analysis of situation is a programme that should be pushed forward by linguists. Until this has been done we are perhaps in no position to judge the complete adequacy of the explication of significance in terms of situational correlations. It may be suspected even now, however, that the notion of 'significance' is too complex to be handled solely in this way; that a good deal of significance cannot be accounted for satisfactorily except in terms of the semantic compatibility of the constituent elements of utterances. This is, of course, the way in which significance has always been handled by traditional grammarians and logicians. Although Firth was undoubtedly right to criticize logicians for their tendency 'to think of words and propositions as having "meaning" somehow in themselves, apart from participants in context of situation', he went too far in suggesting, as he certainly seems to suggest, that all utterances can profitably 'be referred to typical participants in some generalized context of situation'.[20] If the notion of 'situation' is extended to the point to which Firth appears at times to wish to extend it,[21] it is in danger of losing its usefulness altogether. However, let us turn now from the notion of 'significance' to that of 'reference'.

The term 'reference' has been employed by semanticists in many different senses. Here I am using it in the sense in which it is used, and has been formalized, by a number of modern logicians.[22] Reference (or denotation, or extension—the three terms are used equivalently) is the relation that holds between expressions of a language and observable entities (objects or properties of objects) outside the language. The reference of the word *cow*, for example, is the class of all animals to which this word is applied by speakers of English. In traditional 'conceptual' semantics this relationship is taken into account only indirectly. Words are said to 'denote', or 'signify', not material objects or classes of objects, but the intermediate 'concepts' in the minds of the speakers and hearers which subsume these objects or their properties. Moreover, after setting up universal 'concepts' to account for the relationship which undoubtedly exists for all natural languages between some items of their vocabularies and entities in the 'outside world', traditional semanticists then go on to postulate such 'concepts' for all vocabulary items, thus arriving at the dualistic 'mentalism' against which empirically-minded philosophers and linguists alike have inveighed so much recently. What is wrong with traditional 'conceptual' semantics is not the dualist principle itself, but its extension beyond the limits within which it is empirically applicable, and of course the unnecessary postulation of intermediate concepts.[23] No theory of semantics would be complete unless it made provision for handling reference, where reference does in fact hold. This point need not be argued, since it is generally accepted by semanticists. Restriction of the notion of reference to observable entities (describable, if necessary, in a neutral metalanguage) removes any reservations one might have about its incorporation in an empirical theory of semantics. I would submit that Firth's 'monistic' theory of 'meaning' leaves no room for the relation of reference and therefore cannot be considered to be a complete theory of semantics.[24]

Many modern logicians and philosophers of language distinguish sharply between reference and what they call meaning. This distinction involves a deliberate restriction of the scope of the term 'meaning'. The theory of reference, as I have said, treats of the relation that holds between expressions of a language and observable 'things' or 'properties' to which these expressions refer or which they denote. The theory of meaning deals with such notions as synonymy and analytic implication.[25] It accounts for implications such as the following: if x is a *bachelor*, then x is *not married*; if x is the *husband* of y, then y is the *wife* of x; if x is *higher* than y, then y is *lower* than x; if x is *scarlet*, then x is *red*; if x is *red*, then x is not *blue*, *green*, *white*, etc. In other words, it accounts for a set of meaning-relations of various logical types (including antonymy, inversion, inclusion, incompatibility, synonymy, etc.) holding within sets of vocabulary items. Such relations are generally treated by semanticists in terms of a prior notion of 'meaning' independently defined. I have suggested elsewhere that the meaning of an item ('meaning' being used here in the restricted and technical sense in which it is distinguished from 'reference') should be regarded as a function of the several meaning-relations into which it enters as a term; that two lexical items are synonymous, antonymous, incompatible, etc., not because they have, severally and independently, such-and-such a meaning, but because their synonymy, antonymy or incompatibility is part of their meaning; in other words, that the notion of 'meaning' should be regarded as logically secondary to the notion of 'meaning-relations' and that the different meaning-relations in terms of which the vocabulary is structured can be described as holding (under implication, assertion and denial) within transformationally related sentence-frames.[26] Whether or not this treatment of the question is accepted, it is evident that any theory of semantics must take account of such meaning-relations as I have mentioned. However, there would seem to be no more room in Firth's theory of 'meaning' for these meaning-relations, than there is for the notion of 'reference'. Since reference and meaning (in the sense in which these two terms are being employed here) together cover the greater part of what is ordinarily understood by 'meaning', when one asks, for instance, 'What is the meaning of the word x?', it is clear that Firth cannot reasonably claim to have provided us with a comprehensive theory of semantics.

In saying that Firth pays no attention to the meaning-relations which support analytic implications holding between different sentences of a language, I have not failed to notice two passages in which he does in fact make reference to such relations.[27] In the first of these (in his discussion of Swinburne's poetic diction) he talks of 'the association of synonyms, contraries and complementary couples in one collocation', of 'associated words', of 'instances of reversed and crossed antitheses', and of 'polarities'. In the second (in his commentary on the Report of the Commission set up by the International Council for Philosophy and Humanistic Studies) he refers to the establishment of 'ordered series of words' and asserts: 'Ordered series of words (o.s.w.) include, for example, paradigms, formal scatter, so called synonyms and antonyms, lexical groups by association, words grouped by common application in certain recurrent contexts of situation, and groups of phonaesthetic association'. Nowhere does he give any indication of the principles whereby 'synonyms, antonyms, contraries and complementary couples' or 'lexical groups by association' are to be established within the terms of his general theory. And yet it is precisely such lexical sets which a theory of meaning should enable us to establish.

The first of the two passages which I have just quoted comes from the article in which Firth introduces 'collocation' as a technical term. Although he devotes considerable space to a discussion of this concept and constantly refers to the 'collocational level' as intermediate between the grammatical and the situational, he never makes clear how the notion of collocation fits into his general theory. His assertion that 'one of the meanings of *night* is its collocability with *dark* and of *dark*, of course, collocation with *night*', would seem to bring 'the statement of meaning by collocation' in line with the distributional theory of meaning advocated by Harris and Hoenigswald.[28] And the distributional theory of meaning is very quickly disposed of on at least three counts: firstly, it does not satisfy the conditions of material adequacy governing the use of the term 'meaning'; secondly, it appears to involve the identification of language and text (or of 'langue' and 'parole'); and, finally, even if it were true that similarity and difference of distribution could be correlated with similarity and difference of meaning, there are many other more important meaning relations (some of which I have mentioned above) which must be accounted for in a theory of meaning, and these relations cannot be derived by purely distributional, or collocational, criteria unweighted by concentration upon certain 'diagnostic' frames in which occur various 'logical constants' such as negative, adversative, conditional and causal particles.[29]

In saying that the collocations of a word are not part of its meaning (in any generally accepted sense of the term 'meaning'), I am not of course denying the obvious fact that the meaning of a word can often be conveyed to someone who already has a partial knowledge of the language by listing a well-chosen set of collocations in which the word in question is used. We do come to learn the meaning of many words by virtue of hearing them, or seeing them, in various verbal contexts. But our ability to infer their meaning from the contexts in which they are employed, verbal or situational, depends upon our intelligence or 'sentiment linguistique', upon our knowledge of the meaning of other words in these contexts and upon our realization of the paradigmatic oppositions and equivalences that hold between the word in question and other words which might have occurred, but did not in fact occur, at the same point in the text.[30]

It will be clear to the reader that this criticism of the definition of the 'meaning' of a word, or of part of the meaning of a word, in terms of its collocations has been based upon a more usual interpretation of the term 'meaning' than that given to it in Firth's general theory of language-structure. Let us now consider briefly the question of 'collocation' from the point of view of Firth's own interpretation of the term 'meaning'; that is to say, from the point of view of acceptability. I have already said that Firth splits up the 'spectrum' of total acceptability into its component 'modes'—phonetic, phonological, grammatical, lexical and semantic. (The term 'semantic', it will be recalled, is restricted to the contextualization of the utterance in 'situation'; the later term 'collocational' is presumably to be equated with the earlier term 'lexical'.) Now Firth does not in fact have very much to say, in the article in which he introduces and exemplifies the notion of 'the statement of meaning by collocation', about the question of determining what collocations are synchronically acceptable or unacceptable. His analysis of Swinburne's poetic diction and of certain letters of the eighteenth and early nineteenth century is directed primarily towards the establishment of two points: first, that the frequency of particular collocations is an identifiable feature of the style of a particular author; and, second, that certain collocations remain current over long periods of time, whereas others do not. Both these points are interesting and should be taken into account, and indeed often have been, in comparative stylistics and in diachronic linguistics. However, they are clearly not relevant in the synchronic analysis of a language. It is true, as Firth suggests, that at some place in the synchronic description of a language mention should be made of phrases which occur with very high frequency. At the same time, it must be remembered that many such phrases are, synchronically speaking, no longer to be considered as collocations of units at all, but as simple grammatical units; as 'idioms' or 'primes'.[31] Though they were presumably formed at one time in accordance with the regularities holding for the 'état de langue' of that time, they have now become what Saussure called 'locutions toutes faites, auxquelles l'usage interdit de rien changer, même si l'on peut y distinguer, à la réflexion, des parties significatives';[32] and are to be listed as such in the lexicon. Somewhat different from 'les locutions toutes faites', and well worthy of study by the semanticist—as Porzig pointed out many years ago[33]—are collocations of pairs of particular items between which there holds a strong relation of unilateral, or bilateral, syntagmatic presupposition, which is distinct from, and in the case of unilateral presupposition frequently at variance with, syntactic dependency. Instances of this are the presuppositions that hold between *bark* and *dog*, between *rancid* and *butter*, *addled* and *egg*, and so on. Syntagmatic presuppositions of this kind, which Porzig called 'wesenhafte Bedeutungsbeziehungen', seem to be a characteristic feature of all languages; and they are, as is well recognized, the source of a good deal of metaphor and other stylistic effects. There is, in short, good reason to promote the study of collocations in both the synchronic and the diachronic analysis of language. It is doubtful, however, whether the right method of doing this is to set up a 'collocational level' as such. There are many different factors which determine the acceptability or unacceptability of particular collocations: logical consistency, material motivation, social convention, and so on.[34] And there are in any case many different points of view from which collocations may be studied other than from the point of view of their acceptability or unacceptability. Rather than set up one structural level to handle the co-occurrence of particular lexical items, presumably on a statistical basis, it would seem preferable to distinguish these several factors and these various points of view, and to investigate them separately.

Before we go on to enquire what is *the meaning* of a particular element in a given context, we must be satisfied that it does in fact *have meaning*. That this is not always realized is probably due to the traditional 'dualist' theory of language-structure, which maintains that the linguistic 'sign' is a complex of 'form' and 'meaning' and that every 'form' necessarily has associated with it some definite 'meaning' in all contexts in which it occurs. However, an alternative view of meaningfulness has been proposed in recent years. According to this view, which is based on the principle that 'meaning implies choice', an element has meaning (is meaningful) in a given context only if it has been selected from a set of elements any one of which might have occurred in that context.[35] In other words, any element whose occurrence is not wholly determined by the context in which it occurs has meaning in that context. Conversely, if the occurrence of an element is determined by its context, the element in question has no meaning in that context. Moreover, the greater the contextual determination, the less meaning the element has. To make the point in the now familiar terms of information-theory: the amount of 'information' carried by a given element in a given context is inversely proportional to its probability of occurrence in that context.[36] There are, of course, immense, and perhaps insuperable, practical difficulties in the application of the principle to the precise calculation of the relative amounts of 'information' carried by each element in an utterance. We do not generally know what are the actual selection-units that have been incorporated in particular utterances and we cannot take account of all the relevant situational features affecting the probabilities of occurrence.[37] However, the practical (and perhaps theoretical) impossibility of summing over the transitional probabilities of occurrence at each level of analysis, and so quantifying precisely the amount of information carried by every element in an utterance, should not prevent us from accepting the principle that the meaningfulness of an element is a function of its probability of occurrence in particular contexts. We can satisfactorily apply the principle in the limiting case in which the occurrence of an element is totally determined by its context: saying, for example, that the grammatical 'formative' *to* has no meaning in utterances such as *I want to go home*, but is an automatic consequence of the selection of the verb *want*, which requires this particular form of complementation.[38] And we can often say, without, however, being able to give a quantitative formulation to our statement, that a given element has more meaning than some other element would have had in the same context because its probability of occurrence is lower. The principle is well recognized in stylistics.

Now, Halliday has asserted that Firth's 'formal meaning [as distinct from contextual meaning[39]] is the "information" of information-theory'.[40] As evidence for this statement he quotes Firth: '"linguistic forms" are considered to have "meanings" at the grammatical and lexical levels, such "meanings" being determined by the interrelationships of the forms in the grammatical systems set up for the language. A nominative in a four-case system would in this sense necessarily have a different "meaning" from a nominative in a two-case or fourteen-case system, for example.'[41] There is, however, a vital difference between the 'information' of information-theory and 'formal meaning', as the quotation from Firth makes clear. In information-theory the amount of 'information' carried by an element is not a function of the *number* of elements in the system of which it is a member, but of their *relative probabilities of occurrence*. It follows that the nominative in a four-case system might very well carry the same amount of 'information' as the nominative in a two-case, or even fourteen-case, system. 'Formal meaning' and 'information' can be equated only on the assumption of equiprobability.

There is a further difference between Firth's 'formal meaning' and the 'information' of information-theory. Some of the examples used by Firth suggest that he does not distinguish in respect of 'formal meaning' between the oppositions that hold between elements occurring in the same context and the oppositions (if indeed we call them 'oppositions') which hold between elements which cannot, or do not usually, occur in the same context: between paradigmatic and syntagmatic relations. He talks, for instance, of the 'meaning' of the category 'noun' in a system of three word-classes, 'noun', 'verb' and 'particle'.[42] And in the operational establishment of the 'formal meaning' of a lexical item, he does not appear to distinguish between contextualization in what he calls 'formal scatter' and contextualization in 'verbal context'.[43] This is surely an abuse of the notion of 'context'. However that may be, it is clear that Firth's 'formal meaning' is *not* to be identified with the notion of 'information', or meaningfulness. To the present writer at least the interpretation of 'meaningfulness' according to the principles of information-theory seems immensely more profitable for linguistic analysis.

The term 'meaning' is employed in so many different senses in everyday usage that it would be impossible, even if desirable, to embrace them all in one consistent definition. In the course of this paper, I have distinguished the four notions of 'meaning', 'reference', 'significance', and 'meaningfulness', all of which are confused in the everyday use of the word 'meaning' and all of which (doubtless with other notions) must be taken into account in a complete theory of semantics. I have attempted to show that Firth, despite his own assertions and those of his followers, does not provide us with a complete theory of semantics, but rather with a theory of linguistic structure in which the term 'meaning' is given several different and peculiar interpretations; that the only true semantic notion that Firth's theory can make any claims to have captured, and that only partially, is the notion of 'significance'; and that the use of the term 'meaning' in some of the senses in which it is employed by Firth cannot but lead to confusion with more-established uses, and should be abandoned. At the same time I have sought to do justice to what is of value in Firth's theory of language-structure: his insistence upon the multiplicity of social situations in which language functions and the degree to which what we say at any time is determined by the situation we are in and the particular social role we are playing at the time; and his refusal to describe languages as monolithic, unified systems, writing off as paralinguistic and outside the range of linguistic description everything that distinguishes particular 'styles' and 'registers'.

Notes

1 R.H.Robins, 'John Rupert Firth' (obituary article), *Lg* xxxvii (1961), p. 194.

2 Cf. J.R.Firth, 'Sounds and prosodies', *Transactions of the Philological Society* 1948, pp. 127–152; for discussion and bibliographies, R.H.Robins, 'Aspects of prosodic analysis', *Proceedings of the Durham University Philosophical Society* I, Series B (arts) (1957), pp. 1–12; 'General linguistics in Great Britain 1930–1960', in *Trends in Modern Linguistics* (ed. Christine Mohrmann *et al.*, Utrecht and Antwerp, 1963); J.Lyons, 'Phonemic and non-phonemic phonology', *IJAL* xxviii (1962), pp. 127–133.

3 *Papers in Linguistics 1934–1951* (London, 1956), pp. 225 ff. This volume contains most of Firth's important theoretical articles: 'The technique of semantics' (*TPS* 1935); 'The semantics of linguistic science' (*Lingua* i (1948)); 'Personality and language in society' (*Sociological Review* XLII (1950)); 'Modes of meaning' (*Essays and Studies*, The English Association, London, 1951). Two later articles of importance are: 'A synopsis of linguistic theory', *Studies in Linguistic Analysis* (Special Volume of the Philological Society, Blackwell, Oxford, 1957), pp. 1–32; 'Ethnographic analysis and language', *Man and Culture: An Evaluation of the Work of Bronislaw Malinowski* (ed. Raymond Firth, London, 1957), pp. 93–118. Page references to articles other than to the last two mentioned here will be to their reprints in *Papers in Linguistics*, abbreviated hereafter as *Papers*.

4 See, for example, R.H.Robins, 'A problem in the statement of meanings', *Lingua* iii (1952), pp. 121–137; M.A.K.Halliday, 'Categories of the theory of grammar', *Word* xvii (1961), pp. 241–292, esp. pp. 244–245; 'Linguistique générale et linguistique appliquée à l'enseignement des langues', *Études de Linguistique Appliquée* (Publications du Centre de Linguistique Appliquée, Faculté des Lettres, Univ. de Besançon), i (Didier, Paris, 1962), pp. 5–48, esp. pp. 42 ff.; W.Haas, 'The identification of linguistic units', *TPS* 1954, pp. 54–84, esp. pp. 79 ff.; R.M.W. Dixon, *Linguistic Science and Logic* (Janua Linguarum. Series minor. No. 27, The Hague, 1963), esp. pp. 35 ff.

[5] *Papers*, 225.

[6] *Papers*, 19. (Note that in his earlier work Firth did not distinguish as clearly between phonetics and phonology as he did later.)

[7] *Papers*, 191–192; also 225–226.

[8] *Papers*, 32.

[9] *Papers*, 19.

[10] *Papers*, 227.

[11] *Papers*, 192; also 183.

[12] As I have said, there is very little in the way of practical description carried out by Firth's followers to which we can refer for guidance in the interpretation of 'function' at the higher levels of analysis. T.F. Mitchell, 'The language of buying and selling in Cyrenaica: A situational statement', *Hespéris* xliv (1957), pp. 31–71, is a brilliant exception. This article does indeed demonstrate the value of the notion of 'contextualization' of utterances in recurrent and identifiable situations, each culturally determined. It does not, however, lead us to expect (and perhaps does not intend to suggest) that the notion of 'context of situation' can be extended to the point that Firth's theory demands. In 'General linguistics in Great Britain 1930–1960' (p. 35, n. 16), Robins cites, as 'examples of the application of Firth's context of situation analysis to semantic statements', in addition to Mitchell's article, his own 'A problem in the statement of meanings'; W.S. Allen, 'Structure and system in Abaza', *TPS* 1956, pp. 164–169; M.A.K. Halliday, *The Language of the Chinese 'Secret History of the Mongols'* (Publications of the Philological Society, 17, Blackwell, Oxford, 1959), chapter 3. However, these examples are of extremely limited scope; and Halliday's use of the term 'context of situation' seems to be quite different from Firth's.

[13] N. Chomsky, *Syntactic Structures* (Janua Linguarum. Series Minor. No. 4, The Hague, 1956), p. 14.

[14] See R. Jakobson, 'Boas' view of grammatical meaning', *AmA* lxi (1959), pp. 139–145. For a particularly good discussion of this question, see H. Putnam, 'Some issues in the theory of grammar', *Proceedings of Symposia in Applied Mathematics* XII (American Mathematical Society, Providence, Rhode Island, 1961), pp. 25–42, esp. pp. 30 ff.

[15] *Papers*, 24.

[16] *Papers*, 226.

[17] *Papers*, 24.

[18] *Papers*, 217, 227.

[19] *Papers*, 29–31.

[20] *Papers*, 226.

[21] Despite his reference to 'the interrelations of the terms of the actual *observable* context itself' (my italics), *Papers*, 19.

[22] See Y. Bar-Hillel, 'Logical syntax and semantics', *Lg* xxx (1955), pp. 230–237; N. Chomsky, 'Logical syntax and semantics: Their linguistic relevance', *Lg* xxxi (1955), pp. 36–45. Further references are given in these two articles.

[23] In saying that it is unnecessary to postulate 'concepts', I am of course speaking as a linguist, and not as a psychologist or philosopher. The linguist can describe a language satisfactorily without invoking 'concepts' in the 'minds' of the speakers.

[24] No one would wish to suggest, I assume, that the proposed situational category of 'the relevant objects' should be interpreted referentially (*Papers*, 182). I find

nothing in Firth's own writings to support this interpretation; and it would be a most unsatisfactory way of dealing with reference.

[25] The necessity of distinguishing between reference and meaning is usually said to depend upon the fact that two expressions with the same referent need not be synonymous. A more important reason, in my view, is that the analytic implications holding between the expressions of a language which have referents do not differ in kind from the analytic implications holding between expressions without referents.

[26] See J. Lyons, *Structural Semantics: An Analysis of Part of the Vocabulary of Plato* (Publications of the Philological Society, 20, Blackwell, Oxford, 1964), chapter 4.

[27] *Papers*, 197–199; 228.

[28] *Papers*, 196. Cf. Z. S. Harris, *Methods in Structural Linguistics* (Chicago, 1951), *passim*; and H. M. Hoenigswald, *Language Change and Linguistic Reconstruction* (Chicago, 1960), pp. 16 ff.

[29] See my *Structural Semantics*, chapters 1 and 2, and my review of Hoenigswald, *Language Change*, in *BSOAS* xxiii (1961), pp. 621–622. See also F. W. Householder's review in *IJAL* xxviii (1962), pp. 69–79, with comments by Hoenigswald.

[30] To identify the meaning of a word with the set of its collocations, its distribution, is rather like identifying the meaning of a word with that to which it refers. Wittgenstein has observed that the meaning of a word can frequently be given by pointing to something which it denotes (that is, by 'ostensive definition'), but that the success of the demonstration depends upon the intelligence of the enquirer and his ability to see what the demonstrator is getting at. Cf. L. Wittgenstein, *Philosophical Investigations*. Translated by G. E. M. Anscombe (Blackwell, Oxford, 1953), pp. 3 ff., pp. 13 ff.

[31] See C. F. Hockett, *A Course in Modern Linguistics* (New York, 1958), pp. 171–173; and F. W. Householder, 'On linguistic primes', *Word* xv (1959), pp. 231–239.

[32] F. de Saussure, *Cours de linguistique générale* (5th ed., Paris, 1955), p. 172.

[33] W. Porzig, 'Wesenhafte Bedeutungsbeziehungen', *Beiträge zur Gesch. d. deutschen Sprache* lviii (1934), pp. 70–97. Cf. Porzig, *Das Wunder der Sprache* (Berne, 1950), pp. 68 ff.

[34] Cf. C. E. Bazell, *Linguistic Form* (Istanbul, 1953), p. 83.

[35] See Bazell, *Linguistic Form*, p. 81; and P. Ziff, *Semantic Analysis* (Ithaca, 1960), p. 42.

[36] For an informal and accessible account of the principles of information-theory, see C. Cherry, *On Human Communication* (New York, 1957), pp. 40 ff.

[37] See *Psycholinguistics: A Survey of Theory and Research Problems*. Indiana Univ. Publications in Anthropology and Linguistics (Bloomington, Indiana, 1954), pp. 50 ff., pp. 93 ff.

[38] See Ziff, *Semantic Analysis*, p. 81; and Lyons, *Structural Semantics*, 23–28.

[39] The distinction between 'formal' and 'contextual' meaning does not appear to be made in quite these terms in Firth, but it seems to be implied in several places.

[40] 'Categories of the theory of grammar', 246–247. See also Dixon, *Linguistic Science and Logic*, pp. 35 ff.

[41] *Papers*, 227.

[42] *Papers*, 22.

[43] *Papers*, 25 ff., 36 ff., 228.

Predictive Statements

ANGUS McINTOSH

I

I propose in this paper to discuss some of the problems of choice with which a speaker or writer of English is confronted when he wishes to make a statement which is predictive in implication. By 'predictive' I do not necessarily mean something which is without a well-founded basis in reason or in observation; I merely wish to separate statements which simply convey judgments or assessments about what is going to happen from others which carry other implications as well, e.g. those which we might describe as 'decision' or 'promise'. I do not intend here to deal with predictive statements which 'carry' an assessment of the *probability* of something happening:[1] in other words I shall be dealing with statements of the type 'It is going to rain' or 'He is about to fall' rather than those of the type 'It may rain' or 'He might fall'.

In a study of this kind I see no reason to be apologetic about taking context of situation into account. For it is on the basis of the scrutiny of instances of statements in relation to contexts that I am able to consider the nature of the problems of choice with which I am concerned. Within the confines of what is actually spoken or written, I have found it necessary to consider the influence of elements in the co-text[2] (i.e. in the textual environment of the constructions under actual scrutiny), for some of these override an interpretation which would have been made had they *not* been present.

As to the formal status of the constructions with which I deal, I have confined myself to statements in which the prediction may be said to be effected *grammatically*, excluding on this ground such things as 'I prophesy rain' or 'I predict a very difficult time for him shortly'. In fact it emerges that there is a good case for maintaining that all or almost all the constructions which I have found it necessary to consider on this basis involve the use of verbal groups. It is true that not everyone would agree about the definition of 'verbal group'. But my primarily contextual approach has associated a number of rather distinct grammatical patterns and I have been surprised to find that all these are such as would by some scholars now be associated on purely formal grounds within the general category of 'verbal group'.

II

The making of purely predictive statements seems to be somewhat complicated, in everyday circumstances,[3] by the fact that most of the available constructions have some other, often more primary, function which makes them unambiguously usable for prediction in certain cases only. There appears to be no tense, in the ordinary sense of that word, which is reserved for 'pure' prediction.

We may say that there are two main tense-types which can be used for this purpose. But with both of them restrictions are imposed by the fact that certain of their exponents may carry some other (and, in this case, unwanted) implication. The two types are:

1. *be going to* + inf. (and *be going to be* + *-ing*[4]). A frequent implication of this is that of 'action already arranged or decided upon'; so it is not automatically available for pure prediction except where there can be no question of the action having already been arranged, etc., or at least where it would not be assumed that it had. We may therefore say, for the purpose we are considering: 'it is going to rain', 'the baby's going to cry', 'she's going to be sick'. But we may not say, with the same purely predictive intent, 'my daughter's going to sing for you' or 'I'm going to give him a piece of my mind'. The particular infinitive which happens to be involved is therefore critical. There are of course marginal cases which, according to the context (and sometimes co-text), may have either meaning. E.g. 'I'm going to cry': 1. (I feel it in my bones) 2. (I have decided to burst into tears to win his sympathy).
2. *will* + inf. (and *will be* + *-ing*).[5] With the tense—*will* + inf.—there are two implications which may be said to get in the way of pure prediction, viz. 'determination now' and 'agreement'. With *will be* + *-ing* there is a different non-predictive ingredient much closer in implication to tense-type 1. above. E.g. 'I'll be leaving tomorrow night' (it has all been fixed up). The use of both *will* + inf. and *will be* + *-ing* for purely prescriptive purposes is therefore restricted.

It is naturally the case that the infinitives ineligible for purely predictive use in each of these two tense-types largely coincide. For most verbs which can carry the implication of arrangement or decision can also involve that of determination or agreement. So it is not normally possible, with simple predictive intent, to say either:

I'm going to leave tomorrow night

or: I'll leave tomorrow night.

It is possible, on the other hand, to say both:

I'm going to collapse before long

and: I'll collapse before long

because *collapse* is not one of the verbs ineligible for this kind of purpose.

A full analysis of this problem would have to take account of differences between first, second and third person. In general (when such verbs are used) statements involving the second or third person (and especially the latter) can more readily be predictive than those involving the first. E.g.

You'll/he'll leave her within a year
He'll come to see me soon

as against:

I'll leave her within a year
I'll go to see him soon

which would often imply some kind of agreement, undertaking or threat.[6] Furthermore (again where such verbs are used) W-constructions can more readily be purely predictive in implication than G-constructions.[7] In

You're/He's going to leave her within a year

and especially with the third person, there is a probability of an implication of something having already been decided on, either by the speaker or the subject or someone else.

What we have so far discussed raises two questions. First, given that the last two examples are both predictive statements, are the two constructions which they exemplify in free variation, or have they (whether slightly or greatly, whether rarely or generally) different meanings? Secondly, are there other constructions available for prediction in cases where those we have discussed seem to fail us?

We may consider the first question. The two constructions are not in free variation, though in many instances (like those cited) it may make little difference which we choose. English, in predictive statements, seems to make allowance for distinguishing between two attitudes towards the event as looked at from each of two different points of view:

1. Whether the event predicted is thought of as being contingent upon or associated with some other event or not. This event may or may not be explicitly alluded to. This distinction may be labelled *contingent/absolute* and abbreviated as C/A.
2. Whether the event predicted is more closely or less closely associated with the present, in rather the same sense as we can say that the perfect is more closely, the preterite less closely associated with the present.[8] This distinction may be labelled present-orientation/future-orientation and abbreviated as P/F. Furthermore, and in some measure irrespective of anything we might describe adequately as 'present-orientation', P is also likely to be favoured over F when the event in question is imminent.[9] For convenience, however, we shall use the label P for both 'present-orientation' and 'imminent' and F for 'future-orientation'.

Other things being equal, the C/A distinction seems to have as its exponents the *will/be going to* tense-types. Without presenting any qualifications to this for the moment, we may say that statements using the G-construction carry no reservations arising out of contingent circumstances:

He's going to cry.

Here the possibility that he may not cry after all is not (or need not be) envisaged at all; this kind of statement can be followed normally and naturally by 'and when he does . . .', less normally and naturally by 'and if he does . . .'. It is true that this A-implication may be overridden by such additions as 'if you don't give him the sweet' but there are many statements in which this kind of addition would come more naturally (as a reinforcement) after a W-construction than (as an overriding element) after a G-construction. Where this is *not* the case, and G is in fact used, it is usually because the need to stress P as against F is very strong.[10]

Statements containing W (if once more we may present an unqualified account first) more often either cite or imply reservations arising out of contingent circumstances:

He'll cry.

This *can* be followed normally and naturally by 'and if he does . . .'. It can also be the answer to 'What'll he do if I drop him?' In general, the fact that he may not cry after all is clearly envisaged, though the circumstances or countermeasures which may prevent it need not necessarily be expressed.

So far we have a basic system in which W is the exponent of C and G of A. But there is a complication when we turn to the question of how a distinction between P and F is made. For it would seem that this distinction has *also* to be carried by the exponents G and W. When the predicted event is presented with present-orientation or with an implication of immediacy, then G is used; when it is presented as future, then W is used. The contrast may be illustrated by examples:[11]

P	F
You're going to beat him easily[12] (suggestion that the match has started: you've won the first set 6–1 already).	You'll beat him easily (when the time comes).
He's going to have an awful time when he marries her (even now, the writing is on the wall).	He'll have an awful time when he marries her (though things may look all right at present).
He's going to be a complete crock in six months (look what he's like already).	He'll be a complete crock in six months (he may be all right here, but life in the tropics will finish him).

It should be noted that such distinctions between present- and future-orientation are often of no great importance; there are many situations in which it is a matter of indifference which construction is chosen. But more generally critical is the choice of G-constructions, other things being equal, for the expression of something imminent:

She's going to faint.

We have noted that there are occasions when any one of the distinctions PA, PC, FA, FC may be required and that there is an obvious difficulty here because G has to carry both P and A, W both F and C. What then happens if we wish to 'convey' PC or FA?

If we draw only upon the resources offered by the alternative constructions G and W in these circumstances we are forced to sacrifice either the opposition P/F or A/C in these two situations. In other words PA is readily carried by G:

You are going to beat him easily

and FC is readily carried by W

You'll fall!

But in the other two cases of PC and FA there will normally be a conflict of implications. This can be overridden by things in the co-text:

You're going to fall / if you don't look out PA > PC
You'll fall / that's a certainty[13] FC > FA

Otherwise what happens is that one or other of the oppositions takes primacy.

It would appear that the conveying of the A/C distinction tends to take primacy over the P/F distinction. Hence a statement

You'll fall

is more likely to indicate (P!)C than F(A!).[14] And a statement

That's not going to improve matters

given that it does *not* carry the PA implication that is basically associated with a G-construction, is more likely to indicate (F!)A than P(C!). Examples of the opposite tendency will be considered shortly. In spoken language, as we shall have occasion to note later, ambiguities of the above kind are often resolved by (P)C and F(A) statements having distinctive intonational patterns and so with (F)A and P(C).

The general situation may be made clearer by two diagrams. The first shows what happens when the A/C distinction has primacy, the second when the P/F distinction has.

(i)

		SECONDARY	
		P	F
PRIMARY	C	WILL overruling *GOING TO* C(P!)	WILL
	A	GOING TO AP	GOING TO overruling *WILL* A(F!)

(ii)

		PRIMARY	
		P	F
SECONDARY	C	GOING TO overruling *WILL* P(C!)	WILL CF
	A	GOING TO AP	WILL overruling *GOING TO* F(A!)

We may now consider some examples where overruling occurs:[15]

1. Where A (as against C) is being stressed and G (as against W) is therefore used despite there being no implication of present-orientation:

   You're going to regret this in a year or two

   Here if one used W:

   You'll regret this in a year or two

   it would normally be implied that it was still possible to avoid or make amends for the action, etc., which would lead to regret.

   Or again:

   It's going to rain tomorrow.

   Here if one used W:

   It'll rain tomorrow

   there would normally be at least some implication of an association with something else in the context of situation. In cases like references to the weather, where what is going to happen is beyond our control, the implied association is often with some concomitant action that must be taken to make the best of it. Such a sentence can normally and naturally be followed by, e.g., 'so don't go off without a good raincoat'.
2. Where C (as against A) is being stressed and W (as against G) is therefore used despite any imminence of the action, or present-orientation. This is particularly common in predictive statements which may be classed as warnings or threats with the implication 'unless . . .!' E.g.

   We'll miss the train!

   Here the implication is 'if something isn't done about it'. If one used G:

   We're going to miss the train

   the implication would tend to be (unless this were cancelled by a special intonational pattern)[16] that nothing could now be done about it.

3. Where F (as against P) is being stressed and W (as against G) is therefore used despite the absoluteness of the event:

He'll lose the match against Hoad
It'll get a little warmer in August

There is more than one intonational pattern which can have an A-implication in such cases: when such a distinctive pattern is used sentences may be labelled FA instead of F(A!).

4. Where P (as against F) is being stressed and G (as against W) is therefore used, despite the contingency of the event. This, like 2. above, is particularly associated with warnings or threats:

He's going to fall! (every sign of it
but something *may* still be done).

As has already been suggested under 2 above, the use of a distinctive intonation pattern here will override an A-implication that would otherwise normally be present. When such a pattern is used, both the P and the C implications are formally conveyed in full and the sentence may be labelled not P(C!) but PC.[17]

III

We may now turn to the second question we asked on page 305. Are there other constructions available for predictive statements in cases where those we have discussed seem not to be available for this purpose? We have seen that G- and W-constructions are of least use for pure prediction in those cases where to employ them would (at the very least) be to run a risk of implying such other things as arrangement, decision, determination now, or agreement. This explains why in the last few pages our examples have been confined to verbs where this difficulty does not normally arise. But it is not possible to use all verbs in this way, because of the intrusion of extra implications, e.g.

I am going to see him tomorrow

or: I'll meet you at the club.[18]

How then do we get around this difficulty? First of all we may note that we can often as it were 'rescue' G- and W-constructions for purely predictive purposes by adding something in the co-text. E.g.

I'm going to meet him tomorrow,
I feel it in my bones.

Here we may say that the second clause overrides any suggestion of 'action already arranged or decided upon' such as the first clause would normally have implied by itself. So also with:

I'll see him tomorrow, I'm quite sure.[19]

Those concomitants which override in this way some otherwise different interpretation are numerous, and clearly deserve some investigation; some classification of them is certain to prove indispensable in M.T. procedures where clues are being sought, in a given instance, which would establish which 'use' was in question (i.e. whether purely predictive or otherwise). We must here be content to regard all examples of G-constructions wherein the infinitive can imply 'arrangement, etc.' as not purely predictive in themselves, noting at the same time that they can be made so by appropriate elements in the co-text.[20] And so *mutatis mutandis* with W-constructions.

If we examine the various other 'tense' resources which might seem to offer us what we need for pure prediction it soon becomes clear that there are many cases in which to attempt to use these would commit us to the implication of overtones similar to those we have noted as often characterizing G- and W-constructions. Any alternative constructions that are to be eligible for what we need (at least systematically and generally) must be without this drawback. Or if they are not, we must once again at least be able to override the unwanted implications by adding certain co-textual concomitants or to use some distinctive intonational or stress pattern.

These conditions rule out a number of tenses except in special cases:[21]

1a. The type *to be* + inf. E.g.

They're to fly to London tomorrow.

Here the implication may either be 'arrangement already made' ('It's all laid on') or (rather less commonly) 'requirement' ('somebody, not necessarily the speaker, says they must'); neither of these is normally capable of being cancelled.

1b. The type *to be* + *-ing*. E.g.

He's to be speaking in Edinburgh on Monday evening.

With this tense 'arrangement already made' is the regular implication and this is not easily cancelled.

2a. The type 'present tense'. E.g.

She arrives next Monday.

Here again there is an implication of 'arrangement already made' which cannot readily be cancelled.

2b. The type *be* + *-ing*. E.g.

He is sailing for Bombay shortly.

The remark made about 2a applies here.[22] There are in any case obvious restrictions on 2a and 2b for future use because of their common tendency to refer to present events. The tense resources generally available for purely predictive purposes are therefore surprisingly limited.

In a fairly wide range of situations it is possible to use the type *will* + *have* + ppl.—the tense which normally indicates completion of action before some point of reference in the future.[23] E.g.

I'll have finished it by tonight
They'll have made up their minds before then.

It will be noted that no implication of 'determination now', etc., such as we have associated with W-constructions like

I'll finish it by tonight

attaches to these examples.[24] But this construction is not universally available for purely predictive purposes; a (usually explicit) point of reference in the future is generally required.[25] Consider also:

I'm going to have it finished by tonight.[26]

This normally carries much less possibility of an implication of arrangement or decision than

I'm going to finish it by tonight.[27]

It would appear that the W/G alternatives exemplified by 'I will have finished it by tonight' and 'I'm going to have finished it by tonight' are chosen in more or less the same way as the other W/G-constructions we have considered earlier. Here, as with our original W- and G-constructions, though perhaps less strongly, A/C and P/F considerations are involved.

Since the total number of 'tense' resources available for predictive statements in ordinary circumstances is severely restricted, the superimposition of distinctively predictive intonational and stress patterns on otherwise ambiguous constructions is therefore a comparatively limited matter. We have already noted the association of special intonational patterns with threats and warnings, and there are other circumstances in which a distinctive intonation marks, or helps to mark, a predictive statement. Examples are

He'll starve the poor thing before he's finished.
He'll be getting engaged before long.[28]
He's going to ruin the poor child before long.

And at least in some cases this marking is achieved solely by intonation:

He'll starve the poor thing.

So also perhaps in

He's going to kill the poor thing,

where, however, the same intonation might not cancel the implication 'he has made arrangements to kill the poor thing', and is certainly not a reliable guide in itself.

In any case, this particular pattern does not seem to have a general relevance to our problem. It has its own implication of 'disapprobation' or 'alarm', and though the correlation between this and 'prediction' may be fairly close in certain types of instances, it is probably not usually a conclusive prediction-marker in itself.

In general it would not appear that intonational patterns normally serve by themselves to mark a purely predictive use of 'future-ingredient' tenses, though they may sometimes contribute to that total body of evidence which enables us to identify such a use in a particular instance.

As far as stress features are concerned it is probable that there are few markers of predictive use. There are on the other hand numerous stress features which are sufficient to indicate in many instances that we are dealing with some use of G or W which is *not* purely predictive. E.g.

I wíll see him tomorrow.
She's góing to learn French thoroughly.

IV

We may now consider some constructions of a different kind. Where there is a danger of G or W being misinterpreted as implying arrangement or determination or agreement, or some similar difficulty with other tenses, it is possible to use *be sure/certain to* + inf. or *will be sure/certain to* + inf.[29] E.g. in:

She's going to learn French thoroughly

there is a strong possibility of an interpretation 'she has arranged to ...', and of another 'I am determined that she shall ...'. But the construction can (with certain reservations) be replaced by

She's sure/certain to learn French thoroughly.

Similarly

Don't worry, he'll ask you to marry him,

where there is a danger of an interpretation 'I'll see to that', can (again with certain reservations) be replaced by

Don't worry, he's sure/certain to ask you to marry him.[30]

Though this construction may be regarded as perhaps the most valuable for the making of predictive statements that we have in the language, it cannot always replace other constructions we have discussed without involving a change of meaning; it may be said, however, that in most cases where it can, it would seem to achieve a more purely predictive meaning than the others. In particular, it tends to carry the extra ingredient either of assurance or foreboding:

'She's sure to drive safely (don't worry!)'
'He's sure to catch his death of cold (alas!)'

This makes it ineligible for use for purposes which need to be neutral in this respect. Furthermore it will not serve where there is any implication of the carrying out of such intentions as are characteristic of many kinds of threats or warnings. E.g. it is not usually possible to say

He's sure to fall!

with a C implication such as 'if you don't do something about it' unless it is specifically accompanied by some such qualification. One can, however, say

Careful, there are sure to be snakes in that hollow,

or

It's sure to rain,

where no contingent circumstances of a kind which *control*[31] the event are involved. This seems to be because this construction has an A (rather than C) orientation. Here again, however, a C implication can in some cases be induced by explicit mention of such controlling factors:

It's sure to rain if the wind drops.

The possibility, not only of the above, but also of

I'm sure to get lost if you don't come with me

as against the abnormality of

I'm sure to call the police if you don't leave at once

requires consideration. This has to do partly with a normal association of this construction with events, etc., that are not looked upon as capable of being arranged or decided upon. But this is not everything, for we can say

He's sure to give you an interview.

Here there is a difference between uses with the first, second and third persons: when it is a question of events that can be arranged or decided upon, it is with subjects in the third person that statements can most readily be purely predictive. The reasons for this are fairly clear and need not be gone into here.[32]

In general the facts would suggest that the *sure/certain* construction as well as having an A rather than a C orientation has also an F rather than a P orientation.[33] It therefore normally has the A implications of a G-construction and the F implications of a W-construction. So from these points of view (though at the risk of implications of foreboding or assurance) it is suitable as an alternative to W in such sentences, when they have F(A!) implications, as

He'll lose the match against Hoad

and

It'll get a little warmer in August.

A more clearly 'full' F orientation is supplied, however, by *will be sure/certain to* + inf.:[34]

She'll be sure to have trouble with that leg.

But this *will be* construction with *sure* (as distinct this time from *certain*) does not serve to replace with an unambiguously pure predictive implication such G or W statements as might be interpreted as not purely predictive. Consider the G and W statements:

I'm going to see him tomorrow

and

I'll see him tomorrow.

If we replace these by

I'll be sure to see him tomorrow,

we have not escaped the possibility of other than predictive implications.[35] This construction cannot therefore be regarded as a replacement with the same value for predictive purposes as *be sure/certain to* + inf. No similar objection would seem to apply to *will be certain to*, as in:

I'll be certain to see him tomorrow.[36]

Two tenses which have certain similarities to *be sure/certain to* (notably that of being free of the implications of arrangement or decision which we have so often encountered) are *must* + inf. and *must be* + *-ing*. E.g.

Then they must arrive here about noon on Tuesday.
He must be coming back to Europe sometime about March.

In these constructions there is a strong implication of inference: 'All the evidence suggests that they/he will . . .'.[37] Where something imminent is involved they seem to have an A rather than a C implication; this is more readily cancelled with *must be* + *-ing* than with *must* + inf.

It is possible in certain cases to use *be about to* + inf. for predictive purposes:

She's about to fall.
He's about to enter the auditorium.

This type of construction seems in many instances to carry, like G-constructions, the implication of 'action already arranged'; e.g.

He's about to come and see me.

It should also be noted that this construction too usually has an A rather than a C orientation: this makes it abnormal to say such things as

She's about to fall if you don't look out.[38]

Similar remarks might be made of *be* + *on the point of* + *-ing*.

APPENDIX

Note on a form of 'prediction' not relating to the future

There are cases where a person's knowledge about something going on *at present* may be as deficient as it is about anything in the future. In such cases we may speak about prediction relating to the present, though 'conjecture' might be a better word. The main characteristic of this is that it is a W-construction and it is only at first sight surprising that this normally F-oriented construction should be the one used in this situation. Characteristic examples are:

He'll be earning a lot of money over in the States (no doubt, etc.).
They'll be having a wonderful time in St. Moritz (no doubt, etc.).
It'll be raining in Manchester (no doubt, etc.).

These constructions can be replaced by *be sure/certain to be + -ing*. We should also note the alternative possibility of using *must* + inf. and *must + be + -ing* in similar circumstances.

Notes

1 See, however, note 30.

2 I owe this term to Mr. J. C. Catford.

3 Reference will be made later to situations specifically involving prophecy or prediction, e.g. those associated with weather reports, telling fortunes, etc. Cf. notes 18 and 21.

4 The alternative use of the latter sub-type, and of *will be + -ing* with the intention of laying a different kind of emphasis on the time or the duration of the event in question, must be remembered. But in what follows this is assumed and examples are not given.

5 I avoid here the difficult problem of *shall* and *will*, partly because of the amount of disagreement between different speakers as to the selection of one or the other. It should be noted that many speakers make little use of *shall* except in questions with a first person subject, of the type 'shall I/we get you an extra blanket?'

6 This difference between persons has not been explored in the present study, but cf. p. 315 and note 29.

7 W-constructions are those with *will/shall*, G-constructions those with *going to*.

8 The parallel is not precise, and (for reasons connected with the extra 'ingredients' frequently carried by G) the distinction is vaguer than that between perfect and preterite: the degree of precision of the parallel requires further investigation, logical as well as linguistic. Cf. the treatment in W. E. Bull, 'Time, Tense, and the Verb', *University of California Publications in Linguistics* 19 (1960).

9 In this respect G has on many occasions a function closely similar to that which is regularly performed by *be + about to*, with which I deal later (see p. 316).

10 Note also that the G-construction does not readily admit certain even mild reservations such as 'I expect I'm going to be ill when the cold weather sets in' whereas it is perfectly normal to say 'I expect I'll be ill when the cold weather sets in'. It is possible, on the other hand, to say 'I think I'm going to be sick' or 'I

believe he's going to recover' where the need to convey an implication either of immediacy or of present-orientation is strong.

11 The implications indicated in brackets are not to be taken to be pertinent to all possible interpretations of the examples cited, but only to those interpretations which fit the above preliminary statement.

12 It is to be noted that this and the following P examples can quite naturally be followed by such phrases as 'at this rate' or 'to judge by the way things are going'; this is one index of the intended closeness of tie-up with the present. We may say that 'at this rate', etc., in G-constructions tends to reinforce an implication that is already there. If it occurs in W-constructions it supplies an implication that would not usually be present without it.

13 It may be noted that certain kinds of negation have the same sort of A effect as things like 'that's a certainty'. E.g.

You'll never catch that train A

Contrast:

You won't catch that train
(unless, if . . . not, etc.) C

14 The exclamation marks after letters call attention to an implication contrary to that normally carried by a particular construction.

15 We must again here (cf. note 11) stress the fact that the implications we are taking these examples to carry are not necessarily those they would carry in all contexts.

16 See 4, p. 310. Note that this is the same intonational pattern as is normally associated with

We'll miss the train!

It reinforces the C implication already present in the W-construction here, instead of cancelling an A implication.

17 In connection with situations involving A(F!), C(P!), F(A!) and P(C!) it might be worth while to explore further the possibilities of notations like the following:

He'll win his first set — F(A!) | but he's going to lose the match — A(F!)

He's going to win this first set — PA | but he'll lose the match — F(A!)

The availability in spoken language of an intonational means of supplementing G and W, and therefore clarifying both A/C and P/F distinctions, would suggest something that could be verified: that written language, far more than spoken, must resort to alternative (co-textual) devices wherever it is important to clarify these distinctions. E.g. 'He's going to fall if you don't look out' or 'He'll lose this match as sure as eggs are eggs'.

18 Mention has already been made (note 3) of special 'contexts of prophecy' in which such uses are possible. Cf. also note 21. In such situations, if a W-construction is employed, it is normal to use the strong form of *will*: 'You will meet a tall dark woman.'

[19] These cases may be contrasted with others wherein another kind of addition to the text *reinforces* rather than overrides the other, non-predictive implications in the 'main' statement. E.g.

I'm going to see him tomorrow, it's already been arranged

or: I'll see him tomorrow, I promise you.

[20] The overruling concomitants will of course usually have other functions as well.

[21] The main exception is in prophecy-situations, where (with varying degrees of frequency) all four of the tenses here discussed may be used:

1a. You're to meet a tall dark man.
1b. You're to be getting married shortly.
2a. (rare) Your husband-to-be comes into your life very shortly.
2b. Your period of suffering is coming to an end this summer.

The implication of 'arrangement (etc.)' is so strong in all these tenses that none of them is readily available (outside prophecy-situations) with verbs relating to an event where arrangement, etc., would be out of the question. In this way they differ from G- and W-constructions.

[22] All the above tenses may be regarded as A rather than C, though this can be overridden by elements in the co-text, as with G-constructions.

[23] This tense may also be used for conjectures regarding events terminating in the present. E.g.

He'll have finished his supper by now.

[24] Note, however, that such implications are not removed if we say 'I will have it finished by tonight'. Indeed here a further possible implication ('by somebody else'?) is introduced.

[25] This need not be a 'chronologically' definite point; e.g. *soon*, *before long*, *by the time we arrive*, etc., are adequate.

[26] Again the ambiguity is not resolved by:

I am going to have it finished by tonight.

And, as with the other case, a new and quite different ambiguity (by somebody else ?) may arise in many instances of this pattern, including that cited.

[27] We may note that 'I'm going to finish it by tonight' is rather less likely than 'I'll finish it by tonight' to be taken as a predictive statement, other things being equal. Certain intonational patterns increase the probability of either being intended as predictive, but it is doubtful whether any of these is decisive, i.e. they can probably all, in certain circumstances, be used when the statements are intended non-predictively.

[28] Here we should perhaps notice the somewhat restricted availability of *will be going to* + inf.:

He'll be going to buy a Rolls-Royce next.

This construction tends to have an overtone of disapprobation.

[29] To these we should also add *bound to*, noting, however, that this sometimes has another meaning, especially in association with the first person: 'But I'm bound to go and see Aunt Susan when I'm in London.' Even more severe, for predictive purposes, are the restrictions on *must*; for the role of *must* in conjectural statements relating to the present, see Appendix.

[30] A G or W statement containing 'probably' may similarly be replaced by *be likely to* + inf. or *will be likely to* + inf. E.g.

He's likely to ask you to marry him

instead of

He'll probably ask you to marry him.

The weakest corresponding negative to *be sure/certain to* is *not be* (*is not*) *likely to* or *be unlikely to*.

[31] But cf. p. 309 on 'It'll rain tomorrow'.

[32] Cf. p. 305.

[33] For instance 'He's sure to fall!' does not carry the implication of imminence which we should normally associate with 'He's going to fall!'.

[34] This makes it impossible to say:

I'll be sure to call the police if you don't leave at once.

[35] When not, it appears often to carry the implication of assurance about the carrying out of something. Again implications of foreboding are possible: 'I'll be sure to run into the blighter tomorrow (just my luck!).'

[36] In other words, in my own English at any rate, *be sure* in such a construction can often mean the same as *make sure*, whereas *be certain* cannot pair off in a similar way with *make certain*, which cannot take an infinitive after it.

[37] It is perhaps unnecessary to point out that *must* + inf. is often liable to the alternative implication 'It is necessary that they should . . .' whereas *must be* + *-ing* is less commonly so.

[38] It is odd that in reference to past events this A orientation is not strong. Here it is perhaps more normal to use sentences of the type 'she was about to fall, but someone managed to catch hold of her' than of the type 'she was about to fall, and when she did . . .'. The same is true of 'she was on the point of falling'.

Hypostatization

G. B. MILNER

> La parole et l'écriture sont les instrumens de l'esprit; souvent l'ouvrier guide l'instrument; souvent aussi l'instrument guide l'ouvrier.
> Ch. de Brosses[1]

The term which has been chosen as a title for the present article is one which J.R. Firth was known to use in conversation as well as in his weekly lectures on general linguistics.[2] There was a fairly high degree of expectancy that in any discussion on the general theme of semantics he would set up a number of targets, which he would then proceed to demolish with the concentrated fire of his eloquence. One of those he referred to succinctly as 'the cowness of cow'[3] and the other was hypostatization.

In his lifetime it would have been rash for one of his colleagues to give any but a guarded and qualified rendering of the linguistic views subsumed under those two (and a number of other) headings. The certainty that the rendering would be disowned was the only certainty one could hope for. Those who knew him will agree, however, that to say this is not to disparage, but only to remind oneself that he was at his best in the atmosphere of the lecture room and of the senior common room. Given a small but appreciative audience, he would arrive, apparently without effort, at new and stimulating ways of looking at language. More often than not, however, he was inclined to leave the actual investigations and the publication of the results to others. Because of his predilection and natural gift for oral controversy, his theoretical position was seldom entirely static, and once stated, his views might soon be replaced by others which gave him greater satisfaction, because of a change in preoccupation or in weight of emphasis. It would therefore be imprudent to claim that the problem presently to be set out does justice to the concept of hypostatization in J.R. Firth's system of linguistic theories. It is legitimate, however, to claim that the two are germane as it is proper to acknowledge that this view of the problem owes a great deal to my association with him, first as a postgraduate student and later as a colleague.

In the literature of travel and exploration in Asia, Africa and in the New World, a certain linguistic device has a very long history. I am referring to the use of a term taken from a vernacular in a passage of prose in order to describe an object, concept or person for which there is no ready equivalent in the cultures of Western Europe. In the ethnographical literature concerned with the peoples of the South Pacific, it has a long tradition which goes back to Alvaro de Mendaña's accounts of his discovery of the Solomon Islands in 1568.[4] Thus in the first narrative, addressed to the Lord President of the Kingdoms of Peru, there is a description of the arrival of the ships in the island of Ysabel. On Saturday 7 February 1568, the coast is sighted for the first time, and many small canoes come out to meet the ships. The 'Indians' make 'signs of peace', saying many times '*tabriqui*, *tabriqui*'. Mendaña thinks that the natives must be asking for the captain and tells some soldiers standing near by to point to himself if the word should be repeated. He then throws a red cap overboard which is picked up and given to 'a chief who was in a canoe' and who puts it on his head, and the rest return to beg for more. 'Upon this, other canoes came out with other *tabriquis*'.[5] Thus, within a very short time after his arrival in the Solomon Islands, Mendaña has isolated a vernacular word (or words), he has equated it (or them) with 'chief' and, since he is writing in Spanish he gives *tabriqui* a plural morph where he feels it to be necessary (*tabriquis*).

A little later there occurs an account of an interview between Mendaña and 'Bileban Arra', a chief of Ysabel:[6]

'I told him also that His Majesty' (i.e. the King of Castille) 'had many *tabriquis* for *naclonis*' (*nacloni* has previously been translated by: vassal) 'and I myself was his *nacloni*. Then he gave his allegiance to His Majesty, saying that he and his *naclonis*, and his *paces*, which signifies women, and his *sulis*, which signifies children, wished to be the *naclonis* of His Majesty and to serve him'.

It is of interest to note that although a number of the Melanesian words from Ysabel recorded by Mendaña have been identified as occurring in languages still spoken roughly in the same area,[7] *tabriqui* or *taurique* has not been recognized. A possible interpretation (Polynesian *te ariki*, the chief) is somewhat doubtful since at the present time no Polynesian language is spoken on the island of Ysabel. One possibility which cannot be ruled out, however, is that the word did not connote a chief at all in the language of the area, but that the Solomon Islanders may themselves have assumed that it was the Spanish for a chief. An argument in support of this view is that the individual with whom Mendaña exchanged names and whom he calls variously Bileban-Arra (p. 112), Bileban Arra (p. 130), Bile-Banharra (p. 166) or simply Bile (*passim*) was in all likelihood actually called Bile, *bangara* /baŋara/ being a word for chief commonly found to this day in the Western Solomons.[8]

Exactly two centuries later the same process of linguistic naturalization can be observed in the journal of Joseph Banks (in later life Sir Joseph Banks, President of the Royal Society) who as a young and wealthy patron of the sciences accompanied Cook on his first voyage of Australasian exploration between 1768 and 1771.[9]

The *Endeavour*, which was to take him round the world, anchored in Tahiti on 13 April 1769. With his lively interest in all natural phenomena, Banks at once set out to study fauna and flora, the native polity, and as much as he could of the Tahitian language. By 5 May the following sentence occurs in his journal (p. 89): 'We understood that he was some officer belonging to Dootahah and was called his *Tomite.*'[10] In the entries of 9 and 10 June, Banks notes that he has taken an active part in a mourning ritual and the following words are found in his description of what occurred (pp. 97–98):

> (9 June) 'Yesterday and to-day the *Heiva no Metua*, or Chief mourner, walked.'
>
> (10 June) 'Tubourai was the *Heiva*, the three others and myself were to be *Nineveh*.' . . . 'We, the *Ninevehs*, had orders from the *Heiva* to disperse them;' etc.[11]

It will be noted that less than two months after first landing on Tahitian soil Banks has already naturalized Polynesian words to the extent of giving them a plural in *-s*. The following quotations taken from the general description of Tahiti in the same work (pp. 176–177) illustrate even more clearly the procedure by which some of the very first Polynesian words to be used by an English scholar were given meaning in a passage of English prose:[12]

> 'Their orders are *Earee ra hie*, which answers to king; *earee*, baron: *manahouni*, vassal; and *toutou*, villain.'
>
> '. . . in Otaheite there may be about a hundred such districts, which are by the *earees* parcelled out to the *manahounis*.'
>
> 'Inferior to the *manahounis* are the *toutous*.'[13]

Nearly two hundred more years have passed since Banks's stay in

Tahiti and the process of naturalizing exotic words into English and other modern European languages has such a long history that it is seldom even noticed, let alone called into question. Is there any reason why it should be? Is a word not a widely-accepted unit of grammatical analysis in many different types of linguistic structure? To the linguist and to the layman alike, is a word not, by common consent, an indispensable concept for purposes of lexical nomenclature, a sign fixed by conventional orthography and institutionalized in dictionaries? Therefore, when the meaning of an exotic word is not easily and immediately conveyed into English by means of a single word or short paraphrase (by reason of the unfamiliar, strange or exotic nature of the concept which the word denotes or signifies) is it not, surely, legitimate for an author first to give a paraphrase (or more or less brief explanation of the semantic range covered by that word) and then to use the vernacular term itself (in italic or roman characters) as a kind of shorthand reference to his original paraphrase or explanation?

On the other hand, when an exotic term is removed from its matrix and inserted into a linguistic construct which rests on a totally different set of phonological, grammatical and lexical categories, it is also legitimate to ask what the linguistic and semantic consequences are likely to be, that is to say it is a situation in which it is essential to determine to what extent the meaning of a word is lexical and to what extent contextual.

In his article on 'The Technique of Semantics'[14] J.R. Firth quotes with evident agreement a sentence from Dr. Johnson's dictionary:[15] 'Words change their manners when they change their country',[16] while at the very outset of his article Firth had stated that . . . '(Secondly) the complete meaning of a word is always contextual, and no study of meaning apart from a complete context can be taken seriously'.[17]

Let us examine, then, what consequences can be expected when a word taken from, say, an Oceanic language is introduced by an author into his discussion of social organization, religious belief or whatever his topic may be. Firstly, the native word is lifted out of its phonetic and phonological context, out of its grammatical context, out of its lexical context by a process of linguistic surgery which is often not discussed. The principles of the anatomy upon which the surgery is based are frequently not understood. The word is then inserted or grafted into the texture of a sentence in an Indo-European language. This double process must therefore represent on the one hand a loss and on the other a gain of meaning. The word loses meaning, first, because the sounds of the word cease to have the emotional or associational overtones[18] which they had in their original context. The word loses meaning, secondly, because it is divorced from its morphological and syntactical framework of categories and therefore it loses its derivational flexibility and its potential share in the formation of other words by compounding and other processes. It loses meaning, thirdly, by losing its place in a semantic system which, according to the context, may vary considerably in the rigour with which it is used but the members of which are interdependent. It loses meaning, fourthly, because out of the total field of semantic usage, certain areas are arbitrarily chosen to the exclusion of others. For instance in a work of anthropology, history or geography the word is likely to be used in a technical or, at least, specialized as opposed to an everyday context.

Similarly, in its language of adoption, the word acquires new meaning by reason of the phonetic context in which it is placed, the grammatical uses to which it is put, the definitions or explanations given by the writer who happens to be its original foster-father: all these factors must inevitably lead to a slow and imperceptible but continuous process of semantic change and growth. It need not, of course, affect the understanding of the author who first introduces an exotic word and who may have a very extensive knowledge of the language from which he has borrowed it. Yet it cannot help but influence his readers or listeners who do not share his knowledge either of the language or of the culture concerned, and whose understanding of the word must usually depend solely on its appearance in a foreign linguistic matrix. In effect this process often leads to the coining, let us say, of a new English word, the meaning of which is determined, not only by the total history and present development of the English language, but also by the use which its first sponsors make of it when they first present it for linguistic naturalization. This can be illustrated from two of the Samoan words used by Margaret Mead in her books entitled *Coming of Age in Samoa*[19] and *Social Organization in Manua.*[20] The first of those words, *fono*, occurs in the following four grammatical, semantic and typographical contexts on p. 10 of the latter work:

(i) The 'Great Fono' (formal gathering)
(ii) any fono
(iii) this Great Fono
(iv) smaller fonos

Already the Samoan word *fono*, written not in italics but in roman, with or without a capital letter, with or without quotation marks, has been naturalized into English to the extent of having a plural in -s. Certain consequences must now follow. The word will be aligned with a series of English nouns that have a voiced as opposed to a voiceless spirant as exponent of a plural morpheme e.g. /foutou/—/foutouz/; /roubou/—/roubouz/. Or perhaps the first vowel of the Samoan word will be 'assimilated' differently and the pronunciation will be /fɔnou/—/fɔnouz/ on the model of /mɔtou/—/mɔtouz/. The original word, as it happens, does have a plural, though it goes without saying that it is formed quite differently, but it also has a verbal as well as a nominal range of extensions. Indeed, semantically, *fono* has a much wider range than that of 'formal gathering'. As the remainder of its semantic field could conceivably be irrelevant to the purpose of the author, this reduction might be thought not to be of great consequence. Yet we must not expect more than a very limited degree of communication. Unless we know the Samoan language, *fono* will mean to us what the author has chosen to tell us and, having acquired an additional item in our English vocabulary, we may be expected to use it more flexibly, or less flexibly, than the author has done. For he (or she) is likely to have keyed the word to a particular context of situation which happens to be relevant to his purpose. Ordinary readers, however, not being familiar (as she is) with the Samoan language and culture will almost inevitably go beyond, or fall short of, the limited semantic area circumscribed by the author.

In *Coming of Age in Samoa*, Margaret Mead refers to *moetotolo* (p. 76), a type of endemic nocturnal activity, in the following terms: 'The curious form of surreptitious rape, called *moetotolo*, sleep crawling, resorted to by youths who find favour in no maiden's eyes.' The social significance of this phenomenon is then discussed and a few pages later the word already seems to be well on its way to earning a right of entry in *Webster's International Dictionary* (pp. 79–80):

(i) The *moetotolo*
(ii) Catching a *moetotolo* is counted great sport
(iii) The *moetotolo* problem
(iv) (As) some of the boys (who) were notorious *moetotolos*, etc.

It is necessary to ask what has been gained by the introduction of this word, other than a certain amount of local colour and perhaps a blank, and therefore convenient, linguistic label. Otherwise it is difficult to see what is achieved by a phrase like 'notorious *moetotolos*' that is not also achieved by 'notorious sleep crawlers'. Moreover one wonders whether this process does not owe the wide favour it enjoys to a misconception about the semantic range of a word once it has been taken out of its vernacular context. What is called in question here is the semi-explicit belief that *for the reader or listener* the very use of an exotic word in English, quite apart from what is said about it and from the grammatical and lexical uses to which it is put, must *ipso facto* carry with it the same semantic range that it carries *for the writer or speaker who is familiar with the language and culture of origin.* This distinction is of some importance, for it is not the understanding of a writer or speaker using a word from first-hand knowledge which is impugned. He often has a more than adequate command of the language from which he has taken a certain term. As a rule, however, his readers or listeners do not share his knowledge of the language and culture concerned and therefore their understanding is wholly dependent on its appearance in a foreign matrix.

It would of course be quite unfair to suggest that all authors who write about exotic cultures suffer from the same misconception. In fact many of them when they have occasion to use vernacular terms are most careful to define their context, to make a rigorous use of italics, parentheses, quotation marks and other devices serving to indicate that they are having recourse to two separate linguistic media and not to one. Or they will state that a certain exotic word is presented as a kind of technical term in limited use, and is therefore not to be confused with its currency in the language of origin.[21] The history of the term *mana* is a good example of the great confusion which is to be expected when that distinction is not made.

The earliest occurrence of *mana* in English recorded by the *Oxford English Dictionary* is in a book published in 1855.[22] One of the first scholars principally responsible for the wide adoption of this word outside the context of Melanesian and Polynesian ethnography was Dr. R. H. Codrington, an Oxford scholar who was at that time a member of the staff of the Melanesian Mission on Norfolk Island. One of Codrington's duties was to reduce the then almost unknown languages of the Solomon Islands and of the New Hebrides to writing with the help of native informants, with the object of providing simple religious literature in the language of each area. Perhaps as a result of the experience of translating, or helping to translate, the Lord's Prayer into many different tongues,[23] as well as of ensuring that as far as possible no undesirable semantic overtones adhered to the word chosen to render the Christian concept of 'power', Codrington seems to have reached the conclusion that a certain complex of beliefs, which in many languages of the area were implicit in the widespread term *mana*, figured prominently in the religious systems of eastern Melanesia. In 1877 he is on record as having been in correspondence with Max Müller, who was then preparing to give the Hibbert Lectures for 1878.[24] For Max Müller, who reproduces the relevant part of a letter from Codrington verbatim,[25] *mana* is defined as 'a Melanesian name for the infinite'. In Codrington's principal work of ethnography[26] *mana* is discussed in considerable detail, the word (written in italics) occurring frequently in the English text[27] and already in so flexible a manner that it indicates familiarity with the languages from which the author has taken the word. Thus according to him one can 'have *mana*' (p. 56), '*mana* gets a man on' (p. 103), 'an object is said to be *mana*'.[28] *Mana* may or may not be preceded by an English definite article (p. 120), an indefinite article (p. 119), a possessive (p. 120) and it can also be an adjective (p. 201).

From then onwards the process of hypostatization gathers momentum. *Mana* is no longer associated only with the ethnography of the South Pacific but acquires currency in the terminology used by students of primitive religion and even by philosophers. From English, *mana* also passes into other European languages. It becomes masculine in French: *le mana*, and neuter in German: *das Mana*. The following is a quotation from Wundt:

> 'Hält man sich an die Beschreibung dieses Autors, so geht aber aus ihr durchaus nicht hervor, dass das Mana eine einzige übersinnliche Macht sei, wie es von Müller gedeutet wird.'[29]

In this work *das Mana* can enter into the formation of a compound, as in: *die Mana-Theorie*, but apparently does not occur as an adjective or as a verb. In French, however, Hubert et Mauss have no such restriction. In their *Esquisse d'une Théorie Générale de la Magie*[30] one finds for instance the following: *un acte mana* (attributive adjective), *il est mana* (predicative adjective), *du mana* (partitive), *individu à mana*. As a noun, *mana* also has a plural: *les divers manas, les manas génériques* (pp. 108–111).[31] Similarly in Italian, Bruno speaks of *il mana* (masculine substantive) and of *potenzialità mana* (adjective).[32] Indeed the further *mana* is removed from its vernacular context the greater the confusion and the sharper the controversy.[33]

By contrast, in the language of the New Zealand Maori from which the word was originally borrowed into English, *mana* is used in contexts that may appear strange to those who are only acquainted with it in the literature of anthropology and philosophy. Thus in a New Zealand white paper of 1945[34] published in both English and Maori, the word *mana* or its derivatives are used in the latter in translation, for instance, of the following English words and phrases:

authority:	'by the authority of the same'
control:	'control of the Tribal Executive'
force:	'the Act shall come into force'
power:	'such powers as may be delegated to them by the Committee'
pride:	'pride of race' (i.e. self-respect)

In a modern translation of the *Merchant of Venice* into Maori[35] the word *mana* also occurs a number of times, notably four times in Portia's speech on the quality of mercy.[36]

In an important article[37] Professor Raymond Firth has made a complete reappraisal of the meaning of *mana*. Commenting on a statement by Hubert et Mauss that 'l'idée de mana se compose d'une série d'idées instables qui se confondent les unes dans les autres' he makes the apposite comment that 'the confusion and instability... seems to be the result of the anthropologists' analysis rather than a property of the native idea'.[38]

Using a strictly pragmatic and empirical approach, and confining his analysis to the use of a term in a particular culture (with which he had become personally acquainted in the course of a prolonged period of field-work) Raymond Firth found that far from being an intractable riddle (as it had become after sixty years of uncontrolled usage by scholars in several European languages) the meaning of *mana*, in a given language and in a given universe of discourse, could be stated relatively simply. Some of the most important conclusions he reached are relevant to the problem under discussion:

Firstly, attempts to arrive at the meaning of a vernacular term by elaborating and extrapolating dictionary definitions (while engaging in armchair discussion) are likely to end in absurdity and failure (pp. 483–484, esp. footnote 1 on p. 484). Secondly, to assume that merely because a vernacular term like *mana* is widespread in a linguistic area, there is necessarily a generalized concept which subsumes a host of individual aspects or facets of a 'transcendental' meaning, is to be the victim of an illusion.[39] Thirdly, the degree of abstraction which has, in the course of time, been applied to a term such as *mana* by students of primitive religion and philosophy, has turned it into a technical term. In this process much has incidentally been learnt about primitive religion, but the word has become estranged from its original usage in communities where such a degree of intellectual analysis is quite unknown (pp. 487–488). Fourthly, much of this process of abstraction has taken place in an unrealistic manner inasmuch as in the past, meaning had been discussed without direct reference to linguistic context and situation. Fifthly, Raymond Firth has come to the conclusion that this lack of linguistic perspective can only be overcome by supplying a body of empirical material, from one particular area, illustrated by reference to actual situations, by statements of informants, supported if necessary by the text of their utterances (pp. 488–489).

He shows that it is virtually impossible to give the meaning of *mana* in the language of Tikopia except by giving examples of the use of this term in contrast to that of other terms such as *mara*, *manu*, etc., which function in the same universe of discourse, and by showing how each could occur in particular contexts of situation (pp. 489–497). Some of the particularly relevant utterances are translated in the body of the article and the Tikopian originals are given in an appendix (pp. 509–510).

Sixthly, the assumption that a fundamental concept necessarily underlies each and every occurrence of a particular term in a certain language (let alone in a group of languages) is gratuitous and must be guarded against. As Raymond Firth states: 'All my inquiries for the *Ding an Sich* came to nothing' (p. 497) and 'The interpretation in terms of such abstraction can only be the work of the anthropologist. The Tikopia is content with concrete description of the results of activity and does not pursue the intellectual problem as to the nature of that activity' (p. 498).

It is not the purpose of the present article to suggest that the use of exotic words as such is to be condemned. It cannot be doubted that if they were entirely abandoned in the social sciences, especially perhaps in anthropology and history, the substitution of English words (for instance) would be fraught with great difficulty. Different workers in the same field might not only disagree as to the most suitable term to be used in translation, but also have to overcome the difficulty of 'closing the gap' between the general acceptation of an English word and the particular, perhaps novel, shade of meaning they might desire to attach to it. The use of vernacular terms therefore provides a convenient method of checking one field-worker's findings with another's, especially if they use different European languages. The present writer's plea, however, is that if the dangers of hypostatization are to be avoided, a much more rigorous, and as it were, controlled use be made of vernacular terms in Western languages. When a writer takes them out of their original context, it is desirable that he should decide whether their importance does not warrant the decision to naturalize them into English for instance. If there is nothing in the total resources of the English language that quite meets his need, it seems perfectly legitimate for him to take an exotic word and anglicize it. He can then declare it to be an English noun or verb, or adjective, or all three, and he can then decide under what other parts of speech the word ought to be considered. It will then have full linguistic citizenship, it will decline, conjugate, have comparative and superlative forms, etc. It can then be printed in roman and used without any restrictions other than those originally imposed upon it by its sponsor.

Alternatively, if the importance of a word and corresponding concept or concepts is not such as to warrant its introduction into English, that word can be quoted in brackets, perhaps also in italics, either in the body of the text or in footnotes, as a method of building a bridge between the language of information and the language of description. It might even be possible to effect a compromise by using a system of code letters or names (linked possibly to a key in an appendix). This would obviate both the need to anglicize exotic words and the danger of confusing their technical and non-technical uses.

It would seem appropriate to conclude an article on a particular aspect of hypostatization, as it began, with a quotation from the same work by de Brosses:[40] 'Toute expression figurée dont on se sert dans le discours . . . est sans danger tant qu'on la prend comme on la doit prendre, c'est-à-dire comme une comparaison; sans s'écarter de son origine, ni du simple but qu'on avoit en l'employant. Mais on ne s'en tient pas toujours là. On perd le fil de l'application, quand l'expression a pris force par l'usage habituel, quand elle frappe des auditeurs ignorans ou enthousiastes. Les opinions des hommes font un étrange chemin, dès que les abstractions, les métaphores, les métonymies et autres figures sont regardées comme existences réelles, sont employées comme principes et deviennent la base du raisonnement.'

Notes

1 *Traité de la formation méchanique des langues*, 1765, I, 22.

2 I wish to acknowledge my debt to Professor Raymond Firth, who saw the

original draft of this article and at whose suggestion certain corrections and additions have been made.

[3] The expression 'cowness of cow' implied a rejection of the view that a word has a central 'core' of meaning which makes it possible to refer every recurrence of a word like 'cow', for instance, to a four-legged, herbivorous animal. The existence of this nuclear semantic content was an illusion. If one attempted to arrive at a definition of the 'cow-constituting' qualities or 'cowness' of a cow, he would say, one would be driven to define the 'cowness of the cowness of cow', with absurd or trivial consequences.

[4] *The Discovery of the Solomon Islands by Alvaro de Mendaña in 1568*, edited by Lord Amherst of Hackney and Basil Thomson (Hakluyt Society, 2nd series, vol. I, London, 1901).

[5] op. cit., 107–108.

[6] ibid., 130.

[7] Cf. op. cit., lxxix–lxxxv.

[8] Cf. J.H.L. Waterhouse, *A Roviana and English Dictionary* (Sydney, 1949), *bagara-na*, a chief.

[9] *Journal of the Right Hon. Sir Joseph Banks*, edited by Sir Joseph D. Hooker (London, 1896).

[10] In the modern spelling of Tahitian: *tamaiti*, 'child' or 'son'.

[11] The two dictionaries of Tahitian which I have been able to consult are those of J. Davies (*A Tahitian and English Dictionary*, Tahiti, 1851) and E. and I.D. Andrews (*A Comparative Dictionary of the Tahitian Language*, Chicago Academy of Sciences, 1944). Davies gives the following information: *heiva*, a dance, an assembly for dancing; *no*, of, belonging to; *metua*, parent. *Heiva no metua* would therefore be a dance (?) for the parent; *neneva*, a fool or foolishness; giddiness. Andrews gives in addition, for *heiva*, performance of drama.

[12] In fairness to Sir Joseph Banks it should be noted that these words occur in the entries of a private journal kept during a period when a host of totally new and unfamiliar experiences were crowding into his mind.

[13] Davies gives *arii* (*ari'i* in Andrews) as 'head or principal chief, king' and *rai* (not found in Andrews) as 'highest chief, or king'. The other two words do not appear in Davies but Andrews gives the following: *manahune*: plebeian, low, humble; dwarfs or inland people, possibly the indigenous inhabitants of the islands; *tutu*: slave, mean, base, bow-born (*sic*), servant.

[14] *TPS* 1935, pp. 36–72.

[15] Samuel Johnson, *A Dictionary of the English Language*, 2 vols. (London, 1755), p. 3 of the preface. The full passage reads as follows: 'The words which are represented as thus related by descent or cognation, do not always agree in sense; for it is incident to words, as to their authours, to degenerate from their ancestors, and to change their manners when they change their country.'

[16] *TPS* 1935, p. 42.

[17] ibid., p. 37.

[18] J.R. Firth was puzzled by the fact that *drape*, a loan-word from French, had become assimilated to the same phonaesthetic series as words like *drip*, *drop*, *droop*.

[19] Reprinted as a Pelican Book, London, 1954.

[20] Bernice P. Bishop Museum Bulletin no. 76 (Honolulu, 1930).

[21] This particular point has not infrequently been made in the case of taboo as opposed to Polynesian *tapu*; s. for instance A. R. Radcliffe-Brown, 'Taboo' (Frazer Lecture 1939), reprinted in *Structure and Function in Primitive Society* (London, 1952), pp. 133–152, esp. p. 134.

[22] R. Taylor, *Te ika a Maui, or New Zealand and its inhabitants* (London, 1855), p. 279. 'The natives . . . feel . . . that with the land, their *mana*, or power, has gone likewise;' (Supplement, Oxford, 1933).

[23] In a pamphlet published by the Melanesian Mission in 1945 and entitled 'The Lord's Prayer in Thirty-Three Languages, as used in the Diocese of Melanesia', the word *mana* or a possible cognate occurs in fifteen out of the thirty-three versions.

[24] F. Max Müller, *Lectures on the Origin and Growth of Religion* (Hibbert Lectures 1878, London, 1880).

[25] 'There is a belief in a force altogether distinct from physical power, which acts in all kinds of ways for good and evil, and which it is of the greatest advantage to possess or control. This is Mana' (p. 53). This quotation from Codrington is made to support the following assertion (on the same page): 'How the idea of the infinite, of the unseen, or as we call it afterwards, the Divine, may exist among the lowest tribes in a vague and hazy form we may see, for instance, in the *Mana* of the Melanesians'.

[26] R. H. Codrington, *The Melanesians* (Oxford, 1891).

[27] See especially pp. 51–58, 111–134, 191, 194–206 *et passim.*

[28] This is taken from a footnote on p. 119, the relevant part of which reads as follows: 'The word *mana* is both a noun substantive and a verb. . . . An object in which *mana* resides, and a spirit which naturally has *mana*, is said to be *mana*, with the use of the verb; a man has *mana*, but cannot properly be said to be *mana*.' It seems likely that here Codrington was referring to the uses of the term *mana* in the framework of Melanesian grammar, a subject on which he spoke as an expert. Whether he regarded those statements as applying in equal measure to *mana* as a loan-word in English, is not clear.

[29] Wilhelm Wundt, *Völkerpsychologie, vi, Mythus und Religion* (part 3, p. 36).

[30] H. Hubert and Marcel Mauss, *ASoc* vii (1902–3), pp. 108–116.

[31] 'le mana n'est pas simplement une force, un être, c'est encore une action, une qualité et un état. En d'autres termes le mot est à la fois un substantif, un adjectif, un verbe' (p. 108).

[32] Allessandro Bruno, 'Sui fenomeni magico-religiosi della communità primitive', *Rivista italiana di Sociologia*, Twelfth Year, vol. iv–v, pp. 568–576. The same author also speaks of *la nozione di mana* (p. 572) and of *la nozione del mana* (p. 576).

[33] De Brosses in his *Traité de la formation méchanique des langues* had already recognized the hidden pitfalls of the uncontrolled adaptation of exotic words: '(Mais) ceux qui voyent quelque objet nouveau, et l'entendent nommer en la langue du pays où ils se trouvent, ont plutôt fait de répéter le mot que de l'expliquer par une traduction; et il passe ainsi dans l'usage, sans que la plupart des gens sçachent ce qu'il veut dire. Les sçavans ont beaucoup contribué à cet abus, par les noms qu'ils ont les premiers imposés à grand nombre de choses nouvelles dont ils avaient à parler' (ii, pp. 66–67). Dr. Johnson was much more outspoken in the preface to his Dictionary: 'The words which our authors have introduced by their knowledge of foreign languages, or ignorance of their own, by vanity or wantonness, by compliance with fashion, or lust of innovation, I have registered as they occurred,

though commonly only to censure them, and warn others against the folly of naturalising useless foreigners to the injury of the natives' (p. 4).

[34] Act 9 George VI, Maori Social and Economic Advancement Act, 1945 (9 Hori VI, Te Ture Toko i te Ora me te Pai mo te Iwi Maori).

[35] *Te Tangata whai-rawa o Weniti* (Merchant of Venice) by William Shakespeare, translated into Maori by Pei Te Hurinui (Palmerston-North, 1946), Act iv, scene 1, p. 59.

[36] (i) *Ko nga mana nunui, tino pai ratou ina mau ki te aroha* ('Tis mightiest in the mightiest: it becomes, etc.).

(ii) *Ko tona tokotoko he tohu no tona mana tangata* (His sceptre shows the force of temporal power).

(iii) *Engari, ko te aroha keitua noatu i tenei mana kingi* (But mercy is above this sceptred sway).

(iv) *Noreira, nga mana o te ao, e rite atu ai ki to te Atua* (And earthly power doth then show likest God's).

[37] Raymond Firth, 'The Analysis of *Mana*: An empirical approach', *JPS* 49 (1940), pp. 483–510.

[38] op. cit., fn. 3, pp. 484–485.

[39] 'Attempts at recovery of the "original notion" from which others have been derived rests implicitly upon a projection of a sequence in the mind of the analyst into the phenomena analyzed' (p. 485, fn. 4).

[40] op. cit., i, p. 289.

Some English Phrasal Types[1]

T. F. MITCHELL

There seem to be three interconnected aspects of meaning particularly relevant to descriptive linguistic analysis: these are meaning as observable, more or less shared usage, meaning as contrastive distributional relationships of various kinds, and meaning as the process by which the analyst selects data for comparison from an infinite range of possibilities. Selection and observation, mostly self-observation, involve not only the perceptual training of the linguist but also the exercise on his part of imaginative insight in seeking and evaluating contrastive relations between linguistic elements; the schemes by which he subsequently displays the formal differentiation of meaningful units and classes of units are truly part of him and in this sense the commonly held view of meaning on the one hand dissociated from form on the other is wholly inappropriate to *descriptive* linguistics, whatever its relevance may be to other branches of the general subject. The descriptive linguist does not have to account a priori for the selection of relational contrasts to which he draws attention nor is he obliged to state his reasons for the choice of this term or that from his stock of general experience to designate units and classes of units established in the analysis. This choice will doubtless relate to notions and extra-linguistic experience of many kinds but the terms, though answering a real mnemonic need, are not the object of the description but rather a posteriori headings for the sets of comparisons appearing under them. In the situation most favourable to descriptive linguistics, namely that in which the linguist describes his own language and the description is evaluated by other native users of that language, the reader is asked to make a series of value-judgments on the relevance to his own experience of the intra-lingual relational contrasts set out in the analysis, and it would be unreasonable to expect anything like complete agreement in all cases. Some may say 'But there is more to meaning than this. If, for example, any number of men are asked to draw a tree, they will all produce something recognizably similar, with trunk, and leaves, and branches.' No doubt this is so, as it is true also that language is used for the multifarious purposes of personal and social activity, but such considerations are of no direct concern to the descriptive linguist. To take a simple example, if he is concerned to define in descriptive terms, let us say the form *tree*, then he is interested in its total collocability, including its occurrence in *trunk* —, *leaves* —, *branches* —, etc. He selects inter alia

the *trunk* of a $\left\{\begin{array}{l}\textit{tree}\\ \textit{elephant}\end{array}\right.$ the *leaves* of *a* $\left\{\begin{array}{l}\textit{tree}\\ \textit{book}\end{array}\right.$

the *branches* of a $\left\{\begin{array}{l}\textit{tree}\\ \textit{family}\end{array}\right.$

and is thus ultimately able to display unique distribution in collocation for the form.[2] He can then if he likes sum it up with a picture, but he is not as a consequence obliged to believe in the relevance of images or universals to the analysis of meaning in descriptive linguistic terms. The picture of a tree would be on a par with a 'definition' of the form *tree* in arboricultural terms or, say, with the use of such a term as 'noun of personal reference' to designate a formally established nominal sub-class, or again with the more prolix reference to the active participle of certain forms of colloquial Arabic as 'relating to a past act creating a state which has remained unbroken up to the present', which is in effect no more than an extended mnemonic heading for the contrastive linguistic behaviour of participle and tense forms which is subsequently described. It need hardly be said that memorizing or summarizing devices of this kind are not to be confused with the descriptive statement of meaning in terms of contrastive distribution.

Generality in analysis has many dimensions; it relates either to the amount of material or number of items covered by a given generalization, or to the number of restricted or sub-languages so covered, or to the number of speakers who recognize the distinction/s, or to the frequency of occurrence or association of elements. It is, moreover, of the nature of a continuous scale, which has no fixed terminals such as are suggested by the traditional division of grammar and dictionary. The desirability of generalizing linguistic distinctions within permissible limits should not conceal the fact that a generalization is based on a given set of particularities, and although some measure of 'editing' is unavoidable, indeed even desirable to the extent that it eliminates or reduces reference to non-linguistic cues to meaning, it is none the less important both to guard against gross over-generalization, and to recognize that our grammatical descriptions are for the most part 'blunt' and divisions within the dictionary often made on the basis of criteria which remain unstated. Not only is a generalization made in relation to a given selection of data but one is constantly redividing the corpus of material and selection is rarely the same for both colligational (general) and collocational (particular) statement. The association of *dog* with *bark* in *the dog's barking* is just as regular as that of the singular noun *dog* with the singular verb *is*; *dog* does not as a rule occur with *neigh* or *whinny*[3] any more than it does with *are* but this statement relies for its truth on comparisons made within different sets of data. In turn, *the dog's barking* differs from *the dog's down the road* in that the closeness of the link between *dog* and *bark* is not matched by that between *dog* and *down the road*; degrees of solidarity between linguistic elements are infinitely varied and that between *dog* and *bark* is such that *dog bark* may reasonably be regarded as a single linguistic unit or collocation, itself in part definable by the linguistic company it habitually keeps. Within the restricted range of data to which it relates, the collocation often cuts across colligational boundaries established elsewhere: *smell* and *sweet*, for example, belong to the same collocational unit in *it smells sweet* and *sweet-smelling*; again, although the occurrence of passive marks with intransitive verbs is limited to colligational association of the class with prepositional phrases (cf. *to stroll in the garden* : *a garden* (*made*) *to be strolled in*[4]), nevertheless collocations, as *gentle stroll* and not **rapid stroll*, are not limited to that colligation; in the same way, a unit *heavy* ~ *damage* (~ = 'transposable with') is a collocation whose grammatical distribution includes *heavy damage* (adjective + noun), *to damage heavily* (verb + adverb), *heavily damaged* (adverb + passive participle). That the collocation, as *heavy* ~ *damage*, is not to be confused with mere exemplification of a colligation, as adjective ~ noun, is perhaps more clearly demonstrated by the comparable collocation *heavy* ~ *drink* in the colligational scatter *to drink heavily* (verb + adverb), *heavy drinker* (adjective + agentive noun), *heavy drinking* (adjective + verbal noun), from which it will be seen that **heavy drink* and **heavily drunk* are excluded in the way that **heavy damager* and **heavy damaging* do not appear in the (*heavy* ~ *damage*) set of relata. The naming of relationships at whatever level is inherently difficult; at the collocational level, units are not so much of words as nameablep rimarily by means of words but this should not, of course, lead to the conclusion that the linguistic value of, say, *heavy* ~ *drink* derives from a mixture of distilled conceptual essences or of otherwise defined stimuli labelled *heavy* and *drink*.

Characteristic, too, of what Firth called a 'monistic' approach to linguistic description is the view of phonology, grammar and lexicon in one important sense as mutually extending areas of definition of linguistic units and classes of units. The field of intonation, still awaiting thorough cultivation, provides some apt illustrations. Our usual, somewhat arbitrary procedure is to arrive at a set of distributable units of intonation by comparing some utterances which differ meaningfully in terms of pitch feature and then to apply this framework of distinctions passim and more especially in vacuo, that is with intonation dissociated from other formal features of texts. Space does not permit detailed exposition and the following remarks are limited to the topic of tonicity or placement of the nuclear tone. In the matter of compounds, for example, consider the difference between what have been called *foretones* and *hindtones* in comparable contextual occurrence of the following pairs, representative of generalizable relations: *a tóy factory* (*sc.* where toys are made) and *a toy fáctory* (*sc.* which is a toy), *a shóoting stick* and *a shooting stár*, *líght-coloured* and *light-fíngered*, *níce-looking* (a person who looks nice may, of course, be rather ugly) and *nice-lóoking*, *fíghting-mad* (*sc.* mad about fighting) and *fighting-mád* (*sc.* uncontrollably angry), *a Gérman scholar* and *a German schólar*, *a Chrístmas carol* and *A Christmas Cárol* (*sc.* by Charles Dickens),[5] *trée-lined* and *British-máde*, *a lét-down* and *a lie-dówn*, *a dréssing-gown* and *a dressing-dówn*, *a tálking-to* and *a set-tó*. Such distinctions should, of course, be seen within total schemes of differential relationship but the conclusiveness of further typological differentiation such as that between, say, on the one hand, *a wine-glass*, *a glass of wine*, and, on the other, *a stone wall*, should not be allowed to obscure the fact that *a wíne-glass* and *a stone wáll* are also typologically distinguished in the matter of nuclear placement. Such placement is important in other multi-word complexes, in many so-called idioms, for example; it is for instance relevant to the identity of the idiom *to take someone down a peg*, that, although the nucleus may be associated with components other than *down*, it may not be associated with *a peg*; the idiom thus contrasts with, say, *take her down the páth* and, if the example be admitted, with *take her down a pég* (*sc.* to the bottom of the garden, to help her hang out the dress she has just washed).[6] Again, the type of adjectival association exemplified by *dear little* (*house*), *pretty little* (*cottage*), *nice old* (*man*), the slangy *dirty great* (*boots*), etc. is also characterized by the facts of nuclear incidence; that the 'ictus' does not typically fall on *little* in *a dear little house*, for example, but may be associated with either *dear* or *house* is certainly relevant to the unitary nature of *dear little* and perhaps also to the view propounded below in accordance with which *a dear little house* is regarded as compounded of *dear little* and *a little house*. Nuclear placement in 'multi-compounds' also offers interesting possibilities for research: there are, for instance, those cases exhibiting difference of tonicity between compound and including compound, e.g. *the Nórth Country* and *a North Cóuntryman,*[7] *égg marketing* and *The Egg Márketing Board, Hígh Street* and *High Street, Sévenoaks,* and those wherein tonicity varies within certain limits, as *The Railway (´)Season (´)Ticket Inst(´)alment Company Limited,*[8] and again those which in comparable contexts exhibit comparative tonic 'stability' as *flówer-pot* and *flówer-pot stand* or *bílliard balls; ivory bílliard balls;* (*ivory*) *bílliard ball supply; The Ivory (´)Billiard Ball Suppl(´)y Company Limited.* It seems likely that difference of these and other kinds is attributable in considerable measure to the constituency of the multi-compounded structure and that this constituency may be determined by techniques available to us. It is likewise certain that placement must be related to contextual categories in the way, for example, that *The Egg Márketing Board* is broadly relatable to a context of 'first mention' and *The Egg Marketing Bóard* and *The Égg Marketing Board* are associated with contexts of 'further mention' (cf., for example, *If you want to market eggs, you should get in touch with The Egg Marketing Bóard*). The following final illustration is intended to show how tonicity may sometimes work in the manner of word-order. If, given a spoken sentence like *I saw Joan*, the adverbial element *only* is interpolated pre-verbally, then the incidence of the nucleus marks the phrasal association of *only* either with the verb or with the object; cf., for example,

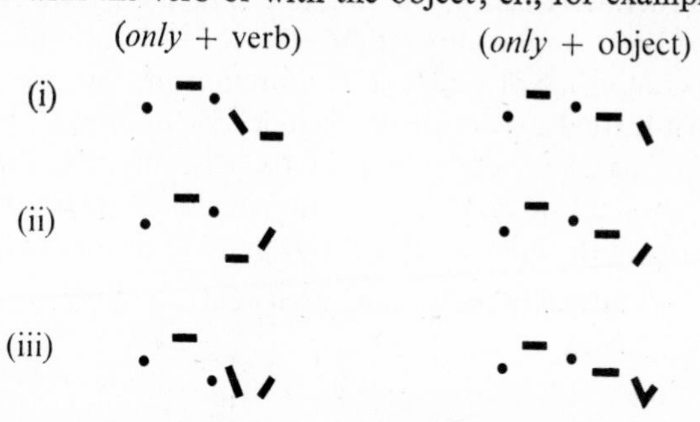

Other patterns, e.g. [pattern], may be ambiguous and analysis in

such cases would depend on the extended context or on the development of more refined analytical frameworks than those at present available.[9] But the fact of some apparent 'untidiness' cannot be allowed to prevent generalization as far as it will go, and there is no doubt that, for example in the case of the falling nucleus and with *only* in pre-verbal position, the association of the nucleus with *Joan* results in a sentence which is no more ambiguous than *I saw only Joan*, with a difference of word-order.[10] Clearly, intonation is only considered apart from the rest of the formal complex at the cost of impoverishing the analysis.[11] Phonological criteria, then, are no less relevant to the analysis of meaning in descriptive terms than those of a grammatical kind, and, although the examples given in the rest of this paper are primarily grammatical, no priority is envisaged as between the different orders.

The process of analysis appears to involve the comparison of texts which are in some way similar (even apparently ambiguous) and the contrastive relationships into which they enter; contrast may be made not only between the relata of a given set or sets of related texts but also between sets. Within an overall framework of acceptability and unacceptability, textual comparison is often made in terms of what may be metaphorically called 'operations'. One such 'operational' type is *substitution.* To take Lees' example of ambiguity—*it's too hot to eat*,[12] substitution in turn of, say, *touch*, *play football*, and *raise its head* for *eat* may be used to demonstrate the existence of overlapping series with *eat* a member of more than one such series. Substitutions may be multiple, involving a number of textual elements simultaneously, as between, say, *to have philosophical inclinations* and *to be philosophically inclined.* Texts between which the relation of substitution obtains contain the same number of structural places or 'slots' in the same sequential order. *Expansion*, subdivisible into pre-, intra-, and post-textual expansion and combinations thereof,[13] is another common type of 'operation'. Not only the substitution of, say, *the dog* for *it* but also post-textual expansion to include, for example, *today* would reveal further parallel overlapping in the case of *it* in the previous example. The establishment of some adverbial sub-classes provides an apt illustration of the manner in which expansion may be employed, cf.

suddenly	(they)	*suddenly*	(went)	*suddenly*
back				*back*
		rarely		*rarely*
		just		
				singly

The reverse process of *contraction* (omissibility) appears to involve the same comparisons and need not, therefore, be typologically distinguished. Unexpanded and expanded texts are nevertheless considered to be related mutually and it will sometimes be convenient to employ terminology of contraction. Texts standing to each other in a relation of expansion or contraction do not contain the same number of structural places. A third major 'operation' is that of *transposition*. Transposed elements may belong to the same or similar structural places as in, say, *he does usually* and *usually he does*, *he likes his hard boiled eggs* and *he likes his eggs hard boiled* or *he likes his eggs boiled hard*, or elsewhere to different places as in, for example, *a born German scholar* and *a German-born scholar*, *the red Spanish soil* and *Spanish red wine* (where *red wine* is a unitary element). Comparison is often, of course, made in terms of combined operations; a combination of expansion and transposition, for example, may be separately termed *transformation* and *to paint the door red* and *a red-painted door* or the earlier *a wine-glass* and *a glass of wine* considered as transformationally related. *Transformation* in this sense does not, of course, conform to transatlantic usage. Once again, a transformational relationship may be regarded as mutual between transforms and not as unidirectional.

The use of the above-mentioned operational types inter alia is generally well illustrated in the field of English comparison. Comparative and superlative structures are here disregarded and attention concentrated rather on similative constructions characterized by an element *as-as-* and by the presence of an adjectival form in inter-*as* position.[14] There are three main types of relationship between the inter-*as* adjective and post-*as* elements. For the most part all three types occur either predicatively following such verbs as *be*, *become*, *look*, *feel*, *seem* or as post-nominal qualifying phrases, e.g. *a yellow as bright as Van Gogh's brightest sunflower*.

The three types are:

	Inter-*as* adjective	Post-*as* element
(1)	Restricted membership of class	Inclusive of all adjectivals

e.g. *as good as new*, *as good as done*. *as good as* is a separable adverbial element, cf. the substitutions *virtually new*, *almost done* and the transform *it's not new but as good as*.

(2)	Unrestricted	Unrestricted nouns, pronouns, adverbs, verbal phrases

e.g. *as good as Tom, as good as him* (or *he is*), *as good as ever* (*it was*), *as good as you'll find.* Criteria of differentiation are many;[15] they include, for example, associability with numeratives, cf. *half/twice as good as Tom*, expansions of the kinds illustrated by *neither as good nor as bad as he suggests, as good a man as you'll find anywhere, it's as up-to-date an introduction to atomic physics as anyone could ask for*, substitutability with other types of comparison, e.g. *as good as/better than Tom*, a range of intonational possibilities characteristic of the class, and so on.

(3) Restricted — Restricted nouns

Restriction is in terms of fixed accompaniment between inter- and post-*as* elements.

e.g. *as good as gold.* The class in general does not share the associability sketched under (2), nor, for example, does it permit the negative expansion[16] or the interrogative transformation; omissibility of the first *as* is also noteworthy. The class, though restricted, is very productive, cf. *as deaf as a post*, *as pleased as Punch*, *as mad as a hatter*, etc., etc.

It would be plausible to regard, for example, *-deaf-a post* as a discontinuous adjectival element belonging to a class of such elements regularly associated with a discontinuous affix (*as*)-*as*-. Collocational 'refinement' is often necessary before analysis on an extended scale can be completed; *a miss*, for example, is *as good as a mile* and cannot, like the baby, be *as good as gold*; again, materials may be *as dry as tinder* but people and their writings *as dry as dust*. Examples of the class aptly illustrate differences of restricted language, as, for example, between idiolects, between British and American usage, between dialect and standard (*as daft as a handcart* and *as red as rats* belong to the Devonian speech of the Torbay area and presumably *as yellow as a guinea* belongs only to the educated standard), between humoristic (*as red as Russians*), advertising (*as soft as a caress/whisper*), and literary (*as tall as a spire*) language, etc. A sub-class of (3), notionally superlative, contains certain fixed verbal phrases and/or the repetition of the adjectival element, cf. *as nice as can be, as mean as they come, as brazen as you like, as pretty as pretty* (*can be*). A further sub-class of expletives also properly belongs here, cf. *as hot as hell, as hot as blazes*. Alliterative reduplication, as in the case of *as good as gold, as dead as a* *doornail*, etc., is not infrequent throughout the class but is by no means a sine qua non among its characteristic features.

The phrasal type just considered also provides examples of an interesting transformational difference between the form of adjectival elements in pre- and post-nominal position in the adjective-noun phrase. *as white as snow* and *snow-white* are mutually exclusive in terms of post- and pre-nominal occurrence respectively in, say, (*he had*) *hair as white as snow* and (*he had*) *snow-white hair*.[17] This type of behaviour is paralleled widely elsewhere in the language; with *as-as-* of *as white as snow/snow-white* compare the similar presence and absence of *the-of-* in, say, *the felling of trees/tree-felling* or *the colour of straw/straw-coloured*, and of *-of the-* in, say, *the handle of the door/the door-handle*. Transformation of the kind illustrated is highly relevant to compounding in English and also noteworthy is the typical 'singularity' or, better perhaps, 'neutrality' of pre-final components of compounds, cf. *tree-* (not **trees-*) in *tree-felling* above. Thus, plural and genitival *-s* is noticeably absent from, say, *a billiard table* (cf. *a game of billiards*), *Parent-Teacher*(*s*) *Association* (cf. (*our*) *parents' teachers*), *Five Oak Green* (village name), *eagle-eyed* (not **eagle's-eyed*), *indoor cultivation* (cf. *cultivation indoors*), and so on. Idiolectal and dialectal differences are fairly common; the publican, for example, will almost always talk of *a dart match*, to which the speakers of 'standard' among his patrons are likely to refer as *a darts match* (possibly by hypercorrection). Adverbial -(*al*)*ly* is likewise omissible or absent from, say, *its characteristic*(*ally*) *sweet smell*, *sweet-smelling*, *the immediate past president*, *new-laid eggs*, etc.,[18] and a parallel is possibly to be seen in the exclusion of adverbial *very*, *extremely*, etc., from association with adjectival compounds of the type *fighting-mad*, *piping-hot*, *streaming-wet*, *icy-cold*,[19] etc. Perhaps the 'mensurative' phrase is the commonest phrasal type exhibiting this feature of 'neutrality', cf. *a steel pin three inches long* and *a three-inch-long steel pin*, and such other examples as *a 20-cigarette-a-day man*, *a six-man team*, *a four-year honours course*, *a three-stage rocket*, *a five-finger exercise*, *two foot six*, *ten stone twelve*, etc.

The technique of exhibiting difference between prima facie similar texts by showing the correspondences into which they enter with other comparable texts is well illustrated by nominal phrases containing *the-of-*. In the following examples of related transforms, generalized use is made of the symbols / and :. Phrases flanking / are in free variation at least over some range of their occurrence, and those separated by : are in complementary distribution:

the shooting of pigeons/shooting pigeons/pigeon-shooting[20]
the House of Windsor: *Windsor's house*[21]
the love of God: *God's love*[22]
the name of God/God's name
the colour of straw: *straw-coloured*[23]
the lid of the teapot/the teapot lid
the rim of the glass: *the glass rim*[24]
the fifth of August/August the fifth

Other cases, for example *the bottom of the garden*, *the kind of girl*,[25] *the size (of) hat*,[26] *The son of a gun!*, etc., exhibit more complex patterns of transformation but might equally be demonstrated to differ among themselves in the manner of their relatability to comparable texts. The same principle may also be applied in establishing typological difference between compound nouns in the adjective-noun phrase; cf., say,

a nice coffee-smell/a nice smell of coffee
a fine rose-show: *a fine show of roses*
a red wine-glass: *a glass of red wine*
a heavy lorry driver: *to drive heavy lorries*

To take another example, and to turn henceforth exclusively to consideration of adjectival compounds and sequences, *hot buttered toast*, *hot-headed Irishmen*, and *hard-boiled eggs* might perhaps be regarded as grammatically homologous (adjective + participial or adjectival *-ed* form + noun), yet the phrases contrast strongly in grammatical value, as the following selection of relations shows:

to butter toast	**to head Irishmen*	*to boil eggs*
toast buttered hot	**Irishmen headed hot*	*eggs boiled hard*
*(*I like*) *toast hot buttered*	(*I find*) *Irishmen hot-headed*	(*I like*) *eggs hard-boiled*
hot butter	*hot-head/s*	**hard boil/s*
the toast is hot and buttered	**the Irishmen are hot and headed*	**the eggs are hard and boiled*
hot toast	*hot Irishmen*	*hard eggs* (?*)
buttered toast	**headed Irishmen*	*boiled eggs*

hot buttered toast exemplifies a common pattern containing two 'separable' adjectives and is classifiable, at least as far as separability is concerned, with e.g. *cold frosty weather* and *a fine sunny day*. The adjectival sequence *hot buttered* has, of course, a different junctural potential from the necessary close juncture of both corresponding sequences in *hot-headed* (*Irishmen*) and *hard-boiled* (*eggs*). *hot-headed Irishmen*, like *long-haired intellectuals*, *white-walled cottages*, *oval-shaped faces*, etc., etc., belongs to a very productive class of which some further details are given subsequently. Broadly classifiable with *hard-boiled eggs*, at least in the writer's usage, are, for example, *fresh-cooked vegetables*, *fresh-picked strawberries*, *fresh-cut sandwiches*, *new-mown hay*, *close-cropped hair*, *soft-boiled eggs*.[27] In the absence of subtler analysis leading to classificatory refinement, there seems nothing for it but to rely on analogy in the cases of, say, *new-fangled ideas*, *clean-cut features*, etc., for these phrases do not fit at all into the framework of differentiation set out above. The intricacy of the ramifications of differential relationship has, of course, to be recognized and patterns of selected relationship are rarely matched point for point in any two cases. Nevertheless, on the basis of such 'scatters' as those displayed above, sound value-judgments, quasi-statistically based, may be made as to the classifiability of textual elements.

A compound type sharing the adjectival and participial forms of the first and second components of *hard-boiled* (*eggs*) is that which relates to places, and especially countries, of origin, e.g. *French-made*, *British-born*. Junctural differences play their part in establishing the unity of such compounds; cf., for example, the potential distribution in time of *German* and *armed* in *the German armed forces* and *the German-armed Italian forces*. Comparison in these cases is to be made, not with corresponding adverbial forms (the absence of adverbial cognates is characteristic of adjectives of origin) but rather with postposed periphrases as in *Made in France*. *French-made* and *Made in France* are not, of course, equivalents but may reasonably be compared. As we have already in some measure seen, comparison is validly made on a broad front between a monomorphemic form which is preposed (attributive) in relation to a given element and a postposed prepositional or similarly periphrastic 'qualifier'. Transformational relationship of this kind provides a more powerful criterion for the recognition of compounds than, say, uninterruptability or mobility in the sentence. For reasons of space, detailed comparison may not be made here between pre- and postposing, but cf., for example, *hand-picked* and *picked by hand*, *tree-lined* and *lined with trees*, etc. Relevant contrasts would include *a tree-lined avenue* (**a lined with trees avenue*) and *an avenue lined with trees* (**an avenue tree-lined*), and it would also be necessary to notice that if the nominal element (*tree* in the example) were itself complex, then postposing would be the rule, cf. (*an avenue*) *lined with acacia trees* (**an acacia tree-lined avenue*).

One type of adjectival compound is marked by a suffix *-ed* and in colloquial English appears primarily to relate to bodily parts and personal characteristics. The suffix belongs to a system of affixes, in some cases discontinuous, which are associated with adjectival compounds. The affixes are:

- *-ed*
-en -ed
-y -ed
-y/-ish -

More particularly in the written language, the suffix *-ed* occurs with otherwise monomorphemic forms, cf. *a kilted man*, *uniformed guards*, and the co-ordinate *booted and spurred*; it is especially frequent, however, in both spoken and written English, as the final element of such adjectival compounds as *bone-headed*, *fair-haired*, *good-hearted*, etc. The second component of these compounds rarely has independent or quotable status in the language. In contrast with the case of most compounds, the first component may be inflected, notably with the comparative and superlative marks *-er* and *-est*, and, again in contrast with other types, the total compound may be associated with foregoing adverbial forms as *very*, *rather*, *extremely*. The unity of some examples of the type seems to be quantitatively marked in the speech of some, the writer's included, wherein a disyllabic pronunciation of the second component of *long-legged* [**ˈlegid**] corresponds to monosyllabic [**legd**] in *longer-legged*.

Participial *-ed* and *-en* are excluded from association with the first component of the foregoing compounds; we do not find, say, **damaged-fronted* or **crushed-legged*, and similarly we tend to talk of *a man with a broken arm* and not of **a broken-armed man*. The exclusion of participial *-en* from, e.g., **broken-armed* may be seen partly in relation to the common affixal pattern *-en -ed* which is applicable to adjectival compounds of the type under consideration, cf. *flaxen-haired*, *waxen-faced*, *shaven-headed*, *leaden-footed*, *ashen-faced*.[28] This type again appears to belong mainly to the written language.

A further affixal pattern *-y -ed*, as in *glassy-eyed*, *bleary-eyed*, *steely-*

eyed, mealy-mouthed, woolly-minded, spindly-legged, sandy-haired, also seems to relate principally to bodily parts.[29] The affixes *-en* and *-y* both apparently concern what is traditionally termed 'metaphor', and the impossibility of the earlier example **broken-armed* may be contrasted with the metaphorical *broken-hearted.* The affix is more often than not associated with a class of 'material' nouns (cf. *steely, glassy, silky, silken, ashen,* etc.) and resultant adjectival forms tend to occur attributively (cf. *a steely look, a glassy stare*) rather than predicatively (**it/he is steely/glassy*). Predicative use tends to be 'non-metaphorical' (cf. *it's snowy,* sc. *it looks as if it's going to snow*). The distinction is perhaps especially clear in the compound adjectival forms under discussion; contrast, for example, (*a*) *glass-fronted* (*bookcase*) and (*a*) *glass eye* with *glassy-eyed* (not **glass-eyed*). Meaningful in the same terms is the contrast between *woolly-minded* and *wool-minded,* between which difference of nuclear placement may be one further distinguishing feature.[30]

An infix *-y,* often freely variant with *-ish,* is characteristic of colour compounds like *greeny grey/greenish grey,*[31] *reddy brown/reddish brown.* This is perhaps the most important class of adjectival compounds in which an infix occurs in the absence of any other affix.[32] A class of forms including *pale, dark, light, deep* behaves like, let us say, *red* in the compound *red brown,* cf. *pale pink,* and is similarly associable with the infix *-ish,* cf. *pale-ish pink wallpaper,* with which *pale, pinkish wallpaper* contrasts in many respects, including those of juncture and tone. Complete analysis should envisage refinement in a number of directions: for example, the *pale*-class does not accompany all colour adjectives—*pale green, pale blue,* etc., occur but not **pale red, *pale brown,* etc.; again, certain compounds are transposable, cf. *greeny grey* and *grey(e)y green,* others are not, cf. *reddish brown* but not **brownish red.* It would be necessary, too, to consider the distribution of forms among different restricted languages; in the language of women's fashions, for example, many colour compounds, e.g. *brutal red,* come and go almost overnight, while the catalogues of rose-growers likewise contain a number of characteristic compound forms.

Reference to transposition (word-order) in most textbooks of linguistics has often been restricted to pointing out such differences as that between *Tom hit Bill* and *Bill hit Tom,* differences, that is, which are more or less trivial from an intralingual descriptive standpoint. Transposition is of considerable relevance to the analysis of the adjective-noun phrase in English.[33] Variation in the categorial order, i.e.

noun-adjective contrasting with adjective-noun, is of some significance; the order noun-adjective is characteristic of headings, styles of designation, captions, catalogue language in general[34] and in particular with reference to agricultural and horticultural types, cf. *William the Bold* (book-title; notice the inclusion of the definite article and contrast *the bold William*), *Charles the Bald, George the First, August the Fifth, Catamarans Past and Present* (title of article), *Light Sussex cockerels, February-hatched* (caption), (*a*) *Laxton Superb*, (*a*) *Rhode Island Red*, etc. The order adjective-noun, however, is undeniably more frequent and it is with examples of this order that the remainder of the paper is concerned, and especially with the frequent case of two adjectival forms preceding the noun.

To take first the examples *a German-born scholar, a born German scholar, pure English vowels* and *English pure vowels. German-born* and *pure English* are recognizable as compound adjectival forms on the basis of such criteria as the close juncture marking their association, the inadmissibility of expansion to include preceding adverbial forms *very, extremely*, etc., similar inadmissibility of the marks of comparison (*-er, -est, more, less*, etc.), uninterruptability (cf. *a German-born French scholar*), parallelism with numerous other such compounds (e.g. *German-made*: *Made in Germany*), predicative occurrence in the same form (cf. *he's German-born but British-naturalized, his French vowels are pure English*). A number of these criteria also justify the view of *German scholar* (in *a born German scholar*) and *pure vowels* as fused, and other criteria are available in support: cf., for example, the parallelism between *a German scholar*: *a scholar of German, car sales*: *the sale of cars, a French teacher*: *a teacher of French*, etc., and, in the case of *pure vowels*, the lack of a predicative transform—*his vowels are pure* is not a comparable text; the junctural (including qualitative) difference is also noteworthy between *pure vowels* in *English pure vowels* and in *he has such pure vowels* (naïve comment on speaker's clarity of diction). A particularly powerful criterion is sequential order, as will be seen from the subsequent treatment of this topic below. The four examples thus illustrate four different types of constituency as follows:

Adjective	Noun
German-born	*scholar*
born	*German scholar*
pure English	*vowels*
English	*pure vowels*

Within the framework of the same phrasal type, there is a 'meliorative-pejorative' class in which the two adjectival forms display a special kind of compounded association. Examples are *a dear old lady, a sweet little baby, a pretty little house, a fine big boy, a nice young man, a nasty old man, a silly old fool, a dirty little blighter*, etc.[35] Contrast the close juncture of all these cases with the open juncture of, say, *fine + black + hair* (cf. *a fine₌big₌boy*)[36] and, again, compare the incidence of the nuclear tone in, say, *a pretty little house* (nucleus rarely associated with *little*) with that in the case of adverbial *pretty* in the orthographically similar form. The limited membership of the adjectival classes concerned is also relevant to the view that a compound relationship exists between them, and this view is further supported by the 'removal' of the second adjective from immediate juxtaposition with the noun in, say, *a pretty little Georgian house*. Other criteria include the inadmissibility of comparative and superlative marks for the final adjectival form of the group, cf. *a sweeter* (*more charming*) *old* (not **older*) *lady I've never met*, although this may also be seen as a reason for regarding *old* and *lady* as specially linked, so that *a dear old lady* may be regarded as compounded from *dear old* and *an old lady*. Although the collocability of a unitary *old lady* is not the sum of the collocability of *old* and of *lady*, there is nevertheless significant collocational overlapping which might be represented so:

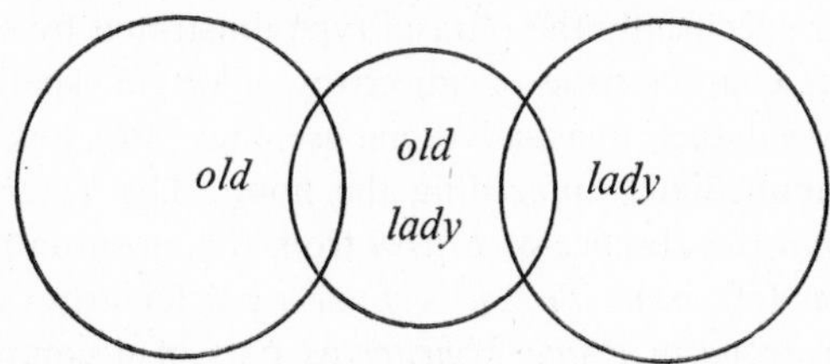

Cf., say, *Mrs. X is a dear old lady—she must be 80 if she's a day but . . .*, wherein *Mrs.*, *lady*, and *she* are collocationally bound in the same way as *old* and *80 if-a day*. The uninterpolability before the second adjectival form of such adverbs as *very, extremely*, etc., is relevant to the identity of the phrasal type of *dear old* in the same way as the exclusion of comparative and superlative marks; contrast, for example, *it's a very pretty* (**very*) *little house* with, say, *he's got a very ugly, very bad-tempered face*. Most such adjectival sequences do not occur predicatively, even with a co-ordinator (*and, but, or*, etc.); there is no **it's*

pretty and little or **it's little and pretty* corresponding to *a pretty little house*, although *he's nice + and young* (afterthought) may perhaps be taken to relate to *a nice young man*[37] and *he's old + and nasty* (with difference of order) to *a nasty old man.*

We have seen that *little* in *a pretty little Georgian house* is separable from *house*, yet it must nevertheless always stand in closer proximity to the noun than the preceding adjective *pretty*; cf., too, *a tall young man, a promising young man* (not **a young tall man, *a young promising man*). This fact of irreversibility distinguishes the 'meliorative-pejorative' phrasal class from that which includes, say, *prime British beef, a hot African sun*, etc.; *a hot African sun* contrasts with (journalese) *an African-hot sun*, where *African-hot* belongs in part to the earlier type of *German-born.* We have seen that the *African-hot* type is generally relatable to corresponding periphrases (cf. *as hot as* (*anywhere*) *in Africa*) and is 'adverbial' in the sense that it may not be immediately preceded by adverbial forms. This kind of adverbial behaviour, common with adjectives of origin like *African*, is also observable in, say, *piping-hot, hellish-hot, icy-cold, ice-cold, pure English*, etc., [38] and it is partly in this light that the irreversibility of *a cold frosty morning, a fine sunny day, a full yearly statement*, etc., should be seen. These last examples are, however, more surely classified with, say, *a long jagged scar*, as illustrating a strongly marked tendency to place shorter (usually monosyllabic) forms first in adjectival sequences.

To consider specifically the phrasal type illustrated by *a hot African sun*, it appears characteristic of adjectives of origin (spatial and temporal) that, save in their quasi-adverbial use, they must generally occupy the position immediately preceding the noun. The generality of this rule is such that the absence of *British* from this position in *the British Prime Minister* (cf. *prime British beef*) is a particularly cogent reason for regarding *Prime* in *Prime Minister* as part of a compound form; supporting criteria would include a possible pronunciation **[prai ˈministə]**. Similarly, *an old Roman coin* is classifiable sequentially with *a hot African sun* and contrasts with the type of *a dear old lady.*

A class of colour adjectives is also recognizable, like adjectives of origin, on transpositional grounds. The contrast has already been shown—at least by implication—between the type of (*a*) *jet-black* (*cat*), involving an adjective and a noun and transformational relationship with the type of (*a cat*) *as black as jet*, and the adjectival sequential type of (*a*) *pretty little* (*hat*); both types, and especially the latter, are in turn to be contrasted with the sequence of adjectival forms in, say, (*a*) *little black* (*hat*), *coarse brown sacking, heavy red curtains*, in which colour adjectives occupy the position of closer proximity to the noun. Colour adjectives 'give way', however, to adjectives of origin, cf. *the green English countryside*. Both non-colour and colour adjectives may, of course, be compounded with the noun, so that such examples as *Spanish red wine* (cf. *the red Spanish soil*) and *black beady eyes* (cf. *long black hair*) are only prima facie irregular. Consideration of such complexes as *silk scarf, stone wall, glass beads*, etc., leads to further refinement in the statement of the facts of sequence. The complex is usually regarded as an adjective-noun sequence incorporating a special class of forms (*silk, stone, glass*, etc.) relating to materials. As a rule this view relies principally on the patterns of stress (rhythm) and tone with which such complexes are associated and is probably defensible, although the material class does not behave wholly in the manner of other adjectives. 'Material' forms may be compound, as, say, *solid mahogany* in *a solid mahogany table*[39] or *blue glass* in *pretty little blue glass beads*, for which a threefold constituency of *pretty little, blue glass* and *beads* is suggested both by the rhythmic pattern typically associated with the whole and by the transform *pretty little beads of blue glass*. In the matter of proximity to the noun, material forms take precedence over all others, cf. *a large black Indian silk scarf*.

In contrast with the above examples of sequential determination, *an ugly bad-tempered face* and *a long cold winter* illustrate the case of freely transposable adjectival forms. Transposable sequences are often associated with co-ordinators, cf. *a dry but cold summer*, and are, of course, distinguished, not least in the matter of juncture, from such compound forms as *hot=and=cold* (*water*).

Within the limits of the short adjective-noun phrase containing two adjectival forms, the following principal types have therefore been distinguished:

(1) sequences comprising two major constituents, one of which is compound, as

1	2
(*a*) *German-born*	*scholar*
(*a*) *born*	*German scholar*
pure English	*vowels*
English	*pure vowels*

(2) sequences comprising three constituents, in which

(a) the adjectival forms are not transposable, as

1	2	3
(*a*) *dear*	*old*	*lady*
(*an*) *old*	*Roman*	*coin*
(*a*) *little*	*black*	*hat*
green	*English*	*fields*
(*an*) *Indian*	*silk*	*scarf*
(*a*) *long*	*jagged*	*scar*

Notes (i) Transposition, where feasible, of forms at 2(a) tends to result in sequences as at (1); cf. *a hot African sun* (like *an old Roman coin*) and *an African-hot sun* (journalese).

(ii) Compound elements may, of course, occupy either first or second adjectival place at 2(a), cf. *a black and gold lacquer box, a Chinese blue and white porcelain jar.*

(b) the adjectival forms are freely transposable, as

1	2	3
(*an*) *ugly*	*bad-tempered*	*face*

The fact of relationship between class of pre-nominal element and sequential order is abundantly illustrated by the antique dealers' advertisements in the 'glossy' magazines, which are a mine of adjective-noun phrases, generally of greater length than those that have been considered. In the following examples selected at random from *Country Life* compounded elements are indicated either by an orthographic hyphen or by a superscript horizontal brace, but for reasons of space no attempt is made to justify the view of such elements as compounds

a Georgian mahogany 'flap top' dumb waiter, an early 19th century mahogany cross-banded breakfast table, a very attractive small Antique Hepplewhite mahogany chest, a fine Antique Sheraton mahogany sofa table, a Hepplewhite mahogany tub-shaped writing chair, an Antique Sheraton mahogany double corner cupboard an unusual Regency rosewood lyre-ended sofa table, a set of 6 attractive Antique Hepplewhite mahogany single chairs, an

Antique Sheraton roll top secretaire and bookcase, a Regency period rosewood writing table, an Antique Georgian mahogany wine cooler, a mid-18th century carved pinewood chimneypiece, a Charles II period oak gate-leg table, a Hepplewhite period mahogany bow front chest of drawers, a late 18th century continental walnut centre table.

The position of pre-nominal forms in relation to the noun appears to be as follows: shape or design (N-1), material (N-2), colour (N-3). A comparatively rare class of origin (*continental*, *French*, etc.) is associated with place N-4. The forms *Sheraton*, *Hepplewhite*, *Chippendale* occur with a preceding *Antique* but do not follow any other term of period reference; *Antique* must be followed by a maker's name or a period term such as *Georgian*, never by elements belonging to classes N-1 to N-4; it seems reasonable, therefore, to consider both *Sheraton*, *Hepplewhite*, *Chippendale*, with or without *Antique* preceding, and *Antique Georgian*, *Georgian*, *early 19th century*, *Regency period*, *Hepplewhite period*, etc., as members of one class having reference to period or combined make and period (N-5). An example like *a late 18th century* (N-5) *continental* (N-4) *black* (N-3) *lacquer* (N-2) *bow front* (N-1) *chest* (N) is the exception rather than the rule, for it is rare to find more than three of the classes exemplified at once and certain of them occur more frequently than others; thus, the class relating to period and/or make is a sine qua non and so for practical purposes is the material class; origin, colour, and shape/design, on the other hand, are, so to say, expendable. There are, moreover, constraints or restrictions of association between members of the different classes, and a complete analysis should also attempt to establish some regularity between the occurrence of preposed forms and postposed periphrases.

The examples, as far as we have briefly considered them, might perhaps occur in written English elsewhere. It is such elements as *fine*, *fine quality*, *attractive*, and even *small* that characterize the advertisement as such and that are therefore separable in the total phrase. The 'advertising' class occupies place N-6 and includes among its membership *rare*, *unique*, *simple*, *fine*, *fine quality*, *attractive*, *unusual*, *superb*, *important*, *interesting*, *very/extremely/exceptionally/particularly fine*, *most pleasing*, *small*, *small and attractive*, *very pretty small*. There remains to be noticed in this very brief account one final class, namely the quantifier (N-7); this class includes *a/an*, *a pair of*, *a set of* (±

numeral), *a collection of*, *one/two of a collection of*. Advertising elements, when associated with composite quantifiers, are either interposed (cf. *an unusual set of*—) or postposed (*a set of unusual*—). In the usage of many dealers the element following the advertising element (usually, therefore, a member of the period/make class) appears with a capital letter (cf. *a small Antique Chippendale mahogany secretaire*), which thus marks the division of the total phrase into two parts, 'eulogistic' on the left of the capital, 'descriptive' on the right.

Notes

1 The present paper is intended primarily to draw attention to what is felt by the author to be the present need for greater explicitness in the definition of linguistic items and their classes; no attempt has been made to write up rules to cover the relationships between the phrases considered.

2 The collocations, say, *trunk-tree*, *leaves-tree*, etc., are themselves different linguistic elements from their component forms, e.g. from *tree*, and are differently collocable from other comparable elements; one *lops* the *branches* of a *tree* but not the *branches* of a *family*, for example, and *leaves fall* from *trees* in a way that *leaves* of *books* do not, and so on. The method of reference is, of course, quasi-metaphorical; in the way that one adds *-s* to *dog* and not to the animal, so *lop* is associated with the complex linguistic form *branch-tree* and with no arboricultural operation.

3 Attention is drawn to the fact that the linguistic form *dog* tends not to occur with the forms *neigh* and *whinny*; that in the real world dogs neither neigh nor whinny is immaterial. One is surely concerned at all times in descriptive linguistic analysis with contrastive distributions, with what is acceptable and what is not, at whatever level one is working. It is not enough to say, for example, that the sentence *There is a bird with 28 wings over there* is grammatically 'well formed'; this is no doubt so, but is it more than to recognize that we are constantly analogizing in our use of language and that the grammatical well-formedness of the example derives in part from its cumulative analogy with, say, *There is a bird with a broken wing over there*, *There is a woman with a broken suitcase over there*, *There is a woman with 28 suitcases over there*? If this is so, it is surely reasonable, while accepting the sentence *There is a bird with 28 wings over there* as grammatically well formed, to reject the lexical form of *a bird with 28 wings*. One cannot help but be puzzled by the refusal of American transformational-generative grammarians to incorporate in their valuable work collocational study of the kind envisaged here; in this connection, see particularly P.H. Matthews, 'Problems of selection in transformational grammar', *Journal of Linguistics* 1.1 (April, 1965), pp. 35–47.

4 Or, of course, ... *to stroll in* or . . . *for strolling in.*

5 This distinction is not maintained by all speakers.

6 The best hope of defining idioms seems to lie in their (comparative) immutability in contrast with non-idiomatic relata; one may, for example, transpose the non-idiom and talk of *the peg I took her down*. Is it, however, the whole of, say, *to get someone into hot water* that is idiomatic or, as seems more plausible, *hot water* alone in the collocation inter alia *to get someone into* ~ *hot water*? Unidiomatic *hot water*, so to speak, is transposable as in *the water's hot* or expandable as in *hot and cold running*

water. Such contrasts are, of course, as necessary to the definition of idioms as to that of any other linguistically meaningful item.

[7] This form, together with *the Nórth Country* (or *the North Cóuntry*), *a North Cóuntrywoman* and *North Cóuntry people*, appears to be unknown to people from the north of England but regularly occurs in the speech of southerners.

[8] A somewhat unexpectedly named company in London's St Martin's Lane.

[9] Categories of voice quality, for example, and agreement on the facts to which they relate, are clearly required even in anticipation of the ability to describe relevant articulatory activity. We should probably, too, recognize differences of voice-register in English—much of the present intonational distinction between *low rise* and *high rise* may perhaps be better regarded as register difference, once the importance of register has been recognized. To quote a few examples: to the man joining you in the lift whom you politely ask which floor he wants prior to pressing the button on his behalf, it would be downright rude to accompany your pressing of the appropriate button with a low rising echo of the number he gives you, cf. *A. Which floor? B. Third, please. A.* (pressing button) *Third?*; similarly, the use of a low rise for the 'tag' component of, say, *Phone me at midnight, will you?* would relate to a threat rather than a request; compare, too, in terms of register the rising tone used in association with a telephone number when (a) answering the phone and announcing your number and (b) calling a number and enquiring whether response is indeed from that number; again, compare the strong implication that the speaker does not wish to bother if he utters the words *or not bother* of, say, *Shall I close the gate or not bother?* on a very low, 'sub-vocal' fall, with the request for instructions associated with the same pattern in a higher register (the degree of pause following *gate* may also be relevant, together with the distribution in time of that which follows).

[10] If *only* is initial in the sentence, then contrast between 'no one else saw her' (falling nucleus on *I*) and 'that's why I mention the subject' (*only I*, and possibly also *saw*, uttered rapidly on a low level monotone) would be relevant to the establishment of a class of sentence-initiating elements (including *well*, *only*, *now*, etc.).

In general, the distribution of utterances and parts of utterances in time is a subject that would repay closer study than has hitherto been devoted to it. For example, the aggressive *Do you mind!* of the teenager derives its identity partly from the slow (even decelerando) tempo with which it is most often associated as well as from intonational contrast with comparable forms of words. The recognition of identity depends, of course, on a complex of criteria—tonal, temporal, grammatical—some of which are likely to be only potential to the entity in the instance. The category of juncture seems to be essentially a matter of protraction versus contraction in time. It is not proposed to enter here into a detailed discussion of juncture: protraction corresponds roughly to open or plus juncture elsewhere (symbol +) and contraction to close juncture (symbolized where appropriate in this paper by the double hyphen). If protraction tended to confer unity to the above protestation, it is contraction that distinguishes, say, *a red=admiral* (butterfly) from *a Red + admiral* (*sc.* a Russian sailor), or *a high=chair* (for the baby) from *a high + chair*, or that characterizes co-ordinates like *a knife=and=fork*. Other features of phonetic form are, of course, frequently relevant, as for example the possibility of a whispered vowel in the penultimate syllable of *I'll be there from ten=to=2* (*sc.* 1.50), which contrasts juncturally with *I'll be there from 10 + to=2* (*sc.* 10 o'clock to 2 o'clock), or, again, the quality of the vowel in the first *-men* syllable in *Frenchmen and women* as opposed to *French men and women*, an orthographic distinction that is by no means always made, or finally, the total form of *old* in *an old* + *Roman* (*coin*), on the one hand, and (*it's only*) *an old=Roman* (*coin*), on the other.

11 All that has been briefly considered in the present paper is the question of tonicity or nuclear placement. Attention might rather have been paid to the variant possibilities of tune or pattern, in order to contrast, say, the typical fall + rise of the comment *I like that* both with use of the falling-rising tune (*sc.* 'I like it but I'm not crazy about it') and with the characteristic fall of the comparable protestation.

12 See R.B. Lees, 'A Multiply Ambiguous Adjectival Construction,' *Lg* 36.2, Pt. 1 (April–June 1960), p. 207.

13 Such threefold distinction is parallel to that of *initial*, *medial* and *final* elsewhere. The terms *initiating* (see n. 10), *mediating* (cf. *he's a sort of—er—what do you call it—you know what I mean—*. . . .) and *terminating* also suggest themselves as terms for the designation of certain classes of elements more or less clearly recognizable in English discourse. Junctural and tonal differences between, say, *it was a good=job=too* (falling nucleus on *too*) (*sc.* serve him right) and *it was a good job* + *too* (falling tone on both *job* and *too*) concerns the behaviour of a class of terminating elements including *too*, *either*, *though*, etc. Other comparable elements, e.g. *you know*, *I think*, etc., are characteristically transposable, cf. (with transposable elements bracketed) (*I think*) *you know* (*I think*) *what I'm talking about* (*I think*), (*you know*) *I think I know what I'm talking about* (*you know*).

14 It would be necessary in a thoroughgoing analysis to distinguish between adjectival and adverbial constructions. Adverbials would be recognizable not only by the shape of the inter-*as* element (cf. *as soon/quickly as possible*, *I'll go as soon as/immediately he arrives*) but also by features of grammatical distribution, e.g. association with verbal elements, cf. *he may sing as well as* (*sc.* in addition to) *dance* (note repetition of non-finite verbal form), *he may sing as well as* (*sc.* as competently as) *he dances*, *he may as well sing as dance*.

15 Some are given in my 'Syntagmatic Relations in Linguistic Analysis', *TPS*, 1958, p. 111.

16 Negation involving the so-called 'operators' in English might be regarded as a matter of substitution rather than expansion, for there are good grounds for recognizing a separate negative conjugation in the language.

17 Analysis is not taken beyond the fact that the type of *as white as snow* is excluded from pre-nominal occurrence. 'Material' nouns and 'sensory' adjectives appear in a very common type of noun-adjective compound, cf. *pearl-grey*, *granite-hard*, *crystal-clear*, *stone-deaf*, etc., but the relationship exhibited by *snow-white* and *as white as snow* is not paralleled in the case of any of these examples. Moreover, of course, not only should notice be taken of difference between such generalizable types of relationship as *snow-white: as white as snow*, *stone-deaf: *as deaf as stone* (cf. *as deaf as a post*), but also of more particular distributional differences, illustrated in the case of, say, *stone* by (*a*) *stone*(*wall*), (*a*) *stony* (*stare*), (*a heart*) *of stone*, etc. In passing, attention is drawn to the difference in respect of tonicity between the compound type of *stone-deaf* above and the type of *work-shy*, *fashion-conscious*, *house-proud*, *boy-mad*, which is in parallel with the participial and predominantly literary type of *storm-swept*, *travel-stained*, *wind-blown*, etc.

18 Differences like that between *du vrai bon café* and *le café est vraiment bon* (cf., too, *du café fin moulu*) suggest the existence of similar features in French.

[19] Not all speakers of British English, it seems, would recognize the form *icy-cold* but it is regularly used by the writer in, say, exclamatory reactions to tactile sensations of cold.

[20] E.g. *the shooting of pigeons/shooting pigeons/pigeon-shooting is encouraged by the Government*. The exclusion of *the-of-* from, e.g., *I went shooting pigeons/pigeon-shooting* no doubt partly justifies the recognition of *the-of-* as a nominalizing device associated with gerundial form, but this is certainly not the whole story.

[21] Like *The House of Windsor* are, for example, *The Wife of Bath, The Book of Esther, the month of May, the character of John* (*sc.* in a play); titles and proper names are regularly involved.

[22] In spite of the presence of the colon in both cases, contrastive relationship in this example is not parallel to that of the preceding pair, between which no distributional similarity obtains. Cf., too, for example, the contrast between *the love of God/loving God* and *The House of Windsor: housing Windsor.*

[23] Mutual exclusion operates as between post- and pre-position in relation to a 'qualified' noun, cf. *he had hair the colour of straw: he had straw-coloured hair*, but compare the fact of free variation in the predicative *his hair was the colour of straw/straw-coloured* (cf. *his hair was as white as snow/snow-white*).

[24] E.g., of or around the table.

[25] As in, say, *she's not the kind of girl to take home.*

[26] An interesting type characterized by the omissibility of *of*, cf. *that's the size* (*of*) *shoe she takes*. 'Defining' nouns, *size, shape, colour, length, width*, etc., are regularly involved, cf. *that's the colour dress I like.*

[27] A class of quasi-adverbial monosyllabic adjectives (*hard, new, fresh*, etc.) exhibit in certain collocations the neutrality of form already noted for the pre-final component of compounds, thus *new-laid* (not **newly laid*) *eggs*, but, with collocational difference, *newly planted* (not **new-planted*) *wallflowers*, or again, *fresh-picked strawberries* but *freshly sown cabbage*. That *new-laid eggs* and *fresh-picked strawberries* are usually associated with eye-catching notices in shops or on country roads is probably not irrelevant. Similar behaviour of members of the class is noticeable in the differently compounded phrases *long drawn out, hard done by, hard put to it to . . .*, etc.

[28] *ashen-fáced* may be compared with the differently constituted *ásh-coloured* (like *stráw-coloured, péar-shaped*, etc.); notice inter alia the difference of tonicity.

[29] *snowy hair* is unlikely to occur save perhaps in literary texts (cf. *snow-white hair*) but *snowy-haired* is an attested example.

[30] It is tempting to see the *-s* of the comparable *woollens-minded* as obviating any possible confusion with the *-en -ed* pattern, but, in the absence of a corresponding singular form, *woollens* is an 'imperfect' plural. This *-s* is often part of a collocational unit, e.g. *heavy damages, the United Nations*, and as such regularly appears in compounds, cf. *United Nations-minded* (contrast *computer-minded*). The seeming adverbial form in, say, *internationally-minded* is also interesting and is possibly to be seen in the light of a complex substitutional relationship as follows: *to have* + (adjectival x + nominal y) corresponding to *to be* + (adverbial x + -ed participial y), e.g. *to have philosophical inclinations* and *to be philosophically inclined, to have a descriptive orientation* and *to be descriptively oriented.*

[31] The co-ordinate *grey and green* belongs to yet another category.

[32] Certain 'expletive' adjectival compounds exhibit similar features, cf. *hellish hot*

(*:as hot as hell*). It may be that *-ing* in the type of *streaming-wet*, *hopping-mad*, *piping-hot*, etc., mentioned elsewhere is likewise to be considered infixal.

33 The scope for research offered by comparable material in languages other than English is also, of course, considerable. To what facts of detailed linguistic organization, for example, do the following cursorily selected examples of the adjective-noun phrase in French relate: *du vrai bon café*, *l'anglais pur comique*, *un vrai connaisseur professionnel*, *le principal producteur mondial* ('the chief world supplier'), *le code mécanographique standard*, *une ligne élégante et moderne*, *une amère et noire décoction*, *des cheveux brun foncé*, *la dose de café moulu nécessaire*, *les possibilités limites des machines*, *des boîtes de fer soigneusement closes*, *des feuilles d'un beau vert brillant* ('beautiful brilliant green leaves'), (*avoir*) *des larmes plein les yeux*, (*un tamis fait d'*) *une très fine et très solide toile métallique de nickel pur*, etc., etc.?

34 Perhaps the classic example is the G1098 equipment scale of the Army Quartermaster.

35 Cf., too, the slangy, semi-expletive *dirty great boots/lie*, etc. *Good old* and *poor old* as in, say, *good old Joe!*, *poor old fellow!* probably also belong here.

36 The degree of juncture between the second adjective and the noun is also, of course, relevant. It is the timing of the whole that matters.

37 Compare from the standpoint of juncture the adverbial *nice=an(d)=* in, say, *he's nice=an(d)=young*, which, in turn, may not be used attributively.

38 These forms are, however, frequently preceded by the adverbial *absolutely* in the writer's speech. See also fn. 32.

39 Notice the close juncture of *solid=mahogany*, *solid=silver*, etc., and contrast, for example, *a solid + sober citizen*.

On Scales of Contrast in Connected English Speech

RANDOLPH QUIRK and DAVID CRYSTAL

If we were to ask a group of native English speakers whether

(*a*) Throw it into the garden

was more like

(*b*) Throw it from the garden

or more like

(*c*) Throw it in the garden

we can assume that more would equate (*a*) and (*c*) than (*a*) and (*b*), and that this would constitute evidence that there was a scale of importance within the differences between 'different' prepositions. Whatever difference there may be between *into* and *in*, we could say, there are environments in which they come together in contrast with *from*, and we might postulate within the 'system' of prepositions such a 'subsystem' as

from :: in(to)
in : into

In an attempt to see whether there was a scale of importance for some of the many possible types of difference manifest in the prosodic features of connected speech, we recorded the utterance:

> A few minutes later, the fellow came; he walked up slowly, and said 'Oh, it wasn't you that I wanted.'

A transcription of this recording, narrow enough to register all the features relevant to the experiment, is given in line II of Table 1. Forty-six native English informants in turn heard the recording twice, first as a whole and then in two parts; they were asked simply to repeat it in the same two parts, the break being at point 5 (Table 1, line I). Their versions were recorded and transcribed in the same type of notation, and these were then scrutinized for the various kinds and

TABLE 1

Showing the distinctions relevant to the experiment and the extent to which the 46 informants observed them

A few minutes later, the fellow came; he walked up slowly and said 'Oh, it wasn't you that I wanted'.

Model	I	1	2	3	4	5	6	7	8	9	10	11	12	13	14	
	II	. • • . ⌣ .			• .	⌢ ♩ .		•	•	∼ . . .	∽	♩ .	• .	⌢ . .	⌣	
	III	/ '		⁄ #	/	:\# .		/	'	∨#	|^	#.		\	⁄ #	
Informants: Tone Unit	IV			*34*		4	n.a.			*41*		*42*		1		n.a.
Tonicity	V	2		*33*	16	*34* (+4S)				*41*		*42*		*40*	*38* (+5S)	
Onset	VI	*46*			*34*		4 (+4S)	*46*			32	*9*	*43*		1 (+5S)	
Nucleus	VII	1\ 1\(+/)		*28* 3∨ 2\	14\ 2∨(+3S\ 1S-)	*32* 2/				*17* 12/ 12\		*10* 29\ 2∨ 1/		*29*(+/) 2^(+/) 9\	(\+)*29* (^+) 2 1/ 6\ (+5S\)	
Stress	VIII		*15*						*5*							
Stress replacing nucleus	IX													3		
Stress plus nucleus	X					1						19		2		
Booster	XI			5(∨ *or* \)		*21*				11				23	1 (\)	
Booster replacing onset	XII				10							33				
Pause	XIII			1			n.a.				3		*26*			
Range	XIV			*15* 17 N/ 1 N\		*28* 4 N\ 2 N/				*29* 2 N∨ 7 N/ 3 N\		*38* 2 N∨ 1 N\ 1 N/		*39* 1 N\	*30* 7 N/ 1 N\	

Notes: The italicised numbers show agreement with features in the model; unitalicised numbers are deviations.
n.a. = 'not applicable', since informants reacted to a recording of the model in two parts bounded at these points.
S = 'subordinate', on which see p. 364 below and note 6.
Range in line **XIV** refers only to a contrast between 'not narrow' and 'narrow' (N); that is, a range equal to or greater than that of the model is here regarded as agreement and distinguished from instances of narrowed range in (non-subordinate) nuclei.

degrees of similarity and dissimilarity to the original version (hereafter referred to as the 'model') in terms of the following key features:[1]

Points 3, 5, 9, 10, 13, 14 as 'nuclei', similarity being noted in terms of occurrence, location, pitch height at beginning of nucleus, pitch range, and direction of pitch movement;

Points 1, 4, 7, 10, 12 as the first points of pitch prominence ('onset') after beginning of utterance and after each nucleus, points 13 and 14 being considered correlative and interdependent, forming a complex without the possibility of an intervening onset;

Points 2, 8 as points of syllabic prominence without a step-up in pitch ('stress');

Points 6, 11 as pauses, similarity noted simply in terms of 'pause' or 'no pause', regardless of precise duration.

For example, the following is a selection of agreements over a stretch of the utterance up to the first nucleus, 'A few minutes later':

1(*a*) 3 out of 46 informants had: onset on *few*; stress on first syllable of *minutes*; rising nucleus (with same range as model) on *later*.
(*b*) 11/46: onset on *few*; rising nucleus (with same range as model) on *later*.
(*c*) 28/46: onset on *few*; rising nucleus on *later*.
(*d*) 33/46: onset on *few*; nucleus on *later*.
(*e*) 34/46: onset on *few*; nucleus within the stretch.

To illustrate the fact that the two conditions remaining in 1(*e*) are not universally liable to equal agreement, we may give the comparable points in the selection for another stretch, admittedly least typical in the amount of disagreement over the placing of the onset, 'and said "Oh"':

2(*d*) 7/46: onset on *oh*, nucleus on *oh*.
(*e*) 42/46: nucleus on *oh*.

Applying such tests of agreement throughout the material, it was found, as we see in Table 1, first that different substantial criteria produced sharply different amounts of agreement, and secondly that the same substantial feature produced differing amounts of agreement at different points in the utterance. These two factors taken together suggested that we were dealing with different systems and not merely expansions of a single system. It was further found that the series (*a*)–(*e*) given for one particular stretch above had regularity and consistence in the correspondence of agreement to substantial features when compared with the series set up for the other stretches. Since, therefore, there was non-randomness in the kind of feature noted and the agreement observed, it is possible to re-state generalized forms of these series, accounting for all the data in the test material, as inverse hierarchies of systems.

The systemic statement which accounts for the highest level of agreement concerns what is common to 1(*e*), 2(*e*) above: the occurrence of an unstipulated nucleus at an unstipulated point within a stretch of speech. That is, the barely delimited 'tone unit'[2] or what Trim has called 'tone cum rhythm group'.[3] There was 84·8 per cent agreement in this respect, though such a level was not evenly spread over all tone units, yielding a point of subsidiary interest to which we shall return.

The next highest level of agreement, 81·6 per cent, was to be found in 'tonicity', the abstraction that relates to the location of the nucleus, without regard to the range or direction of the pitch movement.

The third highest level of agreement, 77·3 per cent, concerned the onset location—the first point of pitch prominence in the tone unit.

When we come to the exponent of nucleus, we find more difficulty in deciding what we should regard as agreement. In terms of a widespread typology that is based on direction of pitch movement alone, we have in the model five types of nucleus: rise (at Point 3), fall (5), fall-rise (9), rise-fall (10), and fall-plus-rise (13, 14). Examined in the light of this typology, the data of the experiment yield 61·6 per cent agreement. This is a sharp drop from the agreement reached in respect of the previous feature considered, and probably most speakers would agree that they are intuitively aware of less randomness in nucleus selection than this figure would imply. Our uneasiness is confirmed when we examine the grossly uneven way in which agreement is registered in the test material by means of this typology. At one extreme, in the tone unit 'the fellow came', we find (with tonicity at *fellow* or *came*) that there is 95 per cent agreement on the nucleus type 'fall'. At the other extreme, in the tone unit 'and said "oh"', we find only 22 per cent agreement on a rise-fall nucleus. But scrutiny of the area of disagreement in the latter case reveals significant regularities. Where the model had a rise-fall on *oh*, 39/46 informants registered a step-up in pitch at this point, and of the 32/46 who did not repeat the rise-fall, no fewer than 29 made a fall nucleus here, 26 of them with a 'high' step-up in pitch (that is, to a point higher than the level of the previous pitch-prominent syllable), followed by a wide-range fall. It would seem, therefore, that an essential feature of a rise-fall is the attainment of a high pitch level (not at all necessarily by means of a pitch glide), and that even conservatively we can equate a high step-up plus wide fall with a rise-fall nucleus. Thus:

model: ôh informants: ôh 10× !òh 26×

If we now bracket !\ with ^ as variant exponents of the 'same' nucleus, we find we have an agreement figure of 74·4 per cent for nucleus types.

Agreement levels of the four types so far noted may now be summarized as follows:

(*a*) Tone Units:

.......#.......#.......#.......#.......# 84·8%

(*b*) Tonicity:

...Ton..(#)...Ton..(#)...Ton..(#)...Ton..(#)...Ton..(#) 81·6%

(*c*) Onset:

./.(Ton..#)./.(Ton..#)./.(Ton..#)./.(Ton..#)./.(Ton..#) 77·3%

(*d*) Exponence of Nucleus:

.(/)Nuc(#).(/)Nuc(#).(/)Nuc(#).(/)Nuc(#).(/)Nuc(#) 74·4%

Since a high starting point plus wide range would seem to be significant features capable of distinguishing between a fall and a rise-fall, it is worth looking at the distribution of range characteristics elsewhere in the material. It is possible that we should associate range with the relatively low agreement found at another nuclear point, the fall-rise in 'he walked up slŏwly'. The fall-rise is repeated here by only 17/46 informants, while 12/46 had a rise and a further 12/46 a fall. But this scatter of results is perhaps not as random as such figures might suggest. Of the 24/46 repeating a nucleus but not a fall-rise, 10 had narrow range and 7 of these had the narrow range with a rise. Although the evidence from this particular experiment is slight, it seems possible that in a given grammatical environment a narrow-range unidirectional nuclear tone—especially a rise—may operate in a system of variants of fall-rise; further investigation may be expected to reveal the terms of such a subsystem and the conditions under which they are selected.[4]

The part played by range is seen less equivocally in the data for the first tone unit in the experimental material, 'a few minutes later'. In the first place, it is to be noted that while the model had a full-range rise on *later*, 12/46 informants did not observe a tone unit at all in this instance. This is perhaps not surprising in view of the relatively low predictability that a front-placed verbless adjunct (as opposed to a finite or non-finite verb adjunct) should constitute a tone unit.[5] More importantly, while 28/46 not merely observed a tone unit but repeated a rise on *later*, 17 of these informants gave the rise a narrow range. In view of what was said in the previous paragraph, it is worth adding that a further three informants gave a fall-rise on *later*. Even if this constitutes little additional evidence on the relation of ˇ and Nˊ, it surely indicates that Nˊ has a place in a subsystem of nuclei, grammatically conditioned: that, in other words, the rise of yes-no questions is characteristically different from the rise of front-placed adjunct exponents.

Range has an evident relevance to the phenomenon of tonal subordination.[6] In the experimental material, subordination chiefly occurred when informants moved a nucleus forward from its place in the model; for example, from *came* to *fellow* in 'the fellow came'. A quarter of those who thus moved the nucleus retained a nuclear tone on *came* but gave it a narrower range than that of the fall on *fellow*. For example:

transcribed as ˋ[ˋ]#

In one case, the exponent of the subordinate nucleus was level,[7] and interestingly enough it was an instance when the superordinate nucleus was itself narrow. Thus we might postulate a parallel series

= ˋ Nˋ systematized as ˋ[ˋ]#

= Nˋ ‾ systematized as Nˋ[ˋ]#

where the final pair of transcriptions has reduced the substantial differences to a single determining distinction. It is clear that we might further generalize to the point of equating these as both

ˋ[ˋ] in contrast with ˋ

or, at a still higher level of abstraction, as both

ˋ in contrast with ˊ, ˊ[ˊ], [ˊ]ˊ, etc.

Finally, a narrowed range seems to be commoner than merely random in the second nucleus of the correlative pair in the sequence

it wasn't yòu that I wánted #

where 7 of the 29 informants who repeated a rise on *wanted* made it narrow.[8] This may indeed suggest an affinity between the sets of 'correlative nuclei' (rise-plus-fall as in 'he walked áll the way hòme', fall-plus-rise as in 'the òld men tríed') and the phenomenon of 'subordination'.

The area of minority disagreements is, in its own way, as informative as that of majority agreements. Thus in the tone unit 'the fellow came', the fall nucleus of the model is repeated by 44/46 informants, while 2 substitute a rise. In the unit 'a few minutes later', 28/46 repeat a rise and three substitute a fall, while a further three substitute a fall-rise. In the unit with correlative nuclei, 'it wasn't you that I wanted', a fall on *you* is repeated 38 times and the only alternative nucleus type that occurs is a rise-fall in two cases, and these—as we have seen—should be treated as variants of a fall. The correlative rise on *wanted* presents a very different picture. While 32 repeat a rise (31 completing the fall-plus-rise correlation), no fewer than 11 informants substitute a fall. These 11 fall into two important groups. The first, numbering five, make the fall subordinate to that on *you*:

. . . yòu that I [wànted] #

The other six make the fall the primary nucleus, usually of the whole original unit ('. . . you that I wànted#'), but in one case with the formation of a new unit ('. . . yòu# that I/wànted#'). In the unit 'he walked up slowly', as we have already noted, the fall-rise is twelve times replaced by a rise and twelve times by a fall. Finally, we have the unit, 'and said "Oh"', in which—again as already noted—the principal disagreement is a majority one: 29/46 informants substitute a fall for the rise-fall; the minority disagreements here are a fall-rise twice and a rise once.

It is clear from the previous paragraph that the polarity is most extreme between fall and rise: the distinction between these two has clearest phonological status, with a contrastiveness most resembling that between, let us say, voiced and voiceless consonants in English phonology or between singular and plural in English grammar. A fall may be replaced by a rise-fall or it may even be ignored occasionally (at any rate in the correlative fall-plus-rise sequences); but it is very unusual to find it replaced by a rise. The other pole, the rise, has slightly less stability, and it can be replaced by a fall fairly readily as the second part of a correlative sequence, though such replacement seems rare elsewhere.[9]

By contrast, the fall-rise admits replacement by both fall and rise quite frequently, and we find it three times replacing a rise, twice replacing even a rise-fall,[10] and being introduced a further twice where there was no nucleus in the model:

the /fĕllow# /càme#

Its phonological status seems to be indicated most by its apparently strong tendency to co-occurrence with 'contingency' or close grammatical relationship with what follows.[11] Contingency is even more obvious, of course, in the correlative nuclei of fall-plus-rise units in contrast (not infrequently neutralized) with fall units.

Further study is required to validate the hypotheses suggested by the present material, but it would seem that systems of nuclei operate in a set of relationships somewhat in the manner postulated for the present limited material in the two-dimensional model represented in Table 2.

TABLE 2

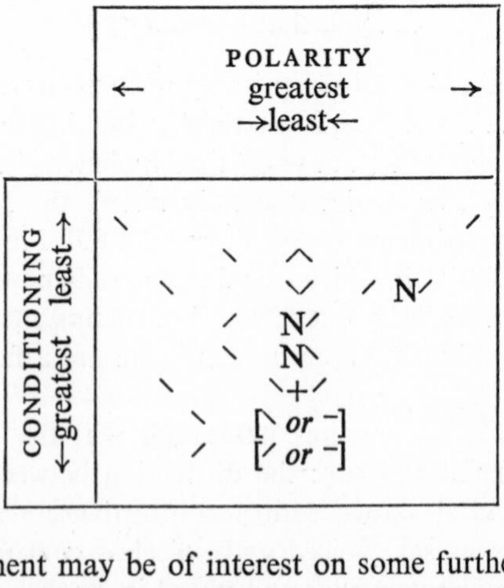

	POLARITY ← greatest → →least←				
CONDITIONING ←greatest least→	ˋ				ˊ
		ˋ	ˆ		
	ˋ		ˇ	ˊ Nˊ	
		ˊ	Nˊ		
		ˋ	Nˋ		
	ˋ		ˋ+ˊ		
		ˋ	[ˋ *or* ¯]		
		ˊ	[ˊ *or* ¯]		

A brief comment may be of interest on some further disagreements relating to tone-unit limits, tonicity, and onset location. Four informants make a new tone unit begin with *came* (Table 1, line IV), thus tonally separating subject and verb, three making the exponent of subject alone ('the fellow') constitute a unit. The rarity of this type of break in clause structure (where the subject is a simple nominal group) is to be contrasted with the situation in which 42 informants follow the model in tonally interrupting the exponent of complement in 'and said . . .' where, however, the complement itself has clause structure in which the tonal interruption is between adjunct and SVC. As to tonicity, it was noted in *Proceedings*, p. 683, that a nucleus fell only rarely on an element preceding the head in group structure. In the present material, it is noteworthy that there are only two disagreements with the model in this respect: the placing of a falling nucleus on the premodifying *few* in the adverbial group 'a few minutes later' (Table 1, line V), and one of these appears less exceptional when it is pointed out that the fall is correlative to a rise on *later* (Table 1, line VII). Disagreements on onsets are in some cases unimportant: thus the relatively low agreement figure at *fellow* is a simple consequence of the relatively low level of agreement on the first tone unit's limits (Table 1, line IV). The shift of onset from *oh* to *said*, however, is very striking. In the model, it happened that the onset fell in four cases on the verb exponent or on the first lexical item in group structure (alternatively, but doubtless trivially, on the second syllable of each tone unit). The one exception was, so to say, 'regularized' by many informants:

and said /oh 9× *but* and /said oh 32×

The experimental material yielded little information on other aspects of agreement and disagreement. The pause at point 11 was repeated 56·6 per cent of cases, the booster[12] at point 5 in 45·6 per cent, and the stresses (prominence without step-up in pitch) at points 2 and 8 in 21·7 per cent. The chief interest that these features presented was their co-occurrence with others. Thus new pauses were introduced in several cases but only at tone unit limits. New boosters were introduced liberally. Apart from those already mentioned which co-occurred with a fall replacing (and thus jointly representing) a rise-fall, forty were introduced before falls and fall-rises and it would seem that : or ! plus ˋ or ˇ can be regarded as variants of ˋ or ˇ respectively with a distinctiveness of an utterly different (and 'lower') order from the distinctiveness of ˋ and ˊ, ˋ and ˇ, ˇ and ˊ, or even ˊ and Nˊ. On stress there is very little to say: in a few cases it was found replacing a nucleus at *you*, and in a few it was itself replaced by a booster at *up*; extra stress (ˈˈ) co-occurred with nuclei on a few occasions: *came* 1×, *you* 2×, *oh* 19×.

To conclude, it is clear that there is high predictability as to what will constitute a tone unit. This will be grammatically determined in two ways—internal structure, and the external relations of this structure. There is a comparably high predictability in tonicity, but this is not directly related to the predictability of tone unit. Tonicity is again grammatically determined primarily, but probably chiefly in respect of the internal grammatical structure of the tone unit. There is rather less predictability over the selection of nucleus type, but it is still high. The selection seems to be determined primarily by the external relations of the tone unit,[13] but certain subsystems seem conversely to be determined primarily by internal relations.

Notes

[1] The recordings of the model and of the informants' versions are filed in the Survey of English Usage and may be heard at University College, London. The technical terms and the type of transcription used in this paper are explained in the paper by Quirk and others, 'Studies in the Correspondence of Prosodic to Grammatical Features in English', *Proceedings of the Ninth International Congress of Linguists* (The Hague, 1964) (hereafter referred to as '*Proceedings*'), pp. 679 ff., and with more detail in Crystal and Quirk, *Systems of Prosodic and Paralinguistic Features in English* (The Hague, 1964).

[2] See *Proceedings*, pp. 680–681. Cf. also M.A.K. Halliday, 'The Tones of English', *ArchL* 15 (1963).

[3] *MPhon* 112, July–Dec. (1959), p. 27.

[4] In one of the unscripted texts in the Survey of English Usage collection (5b.51), for example, we find several examples like the following:

(*a*) the Advisory Council to which you re*ferred* # expressed an opinion #

(*b*) and in*deed* # flies # in the face # of the very considerable body of factual evidence that exists #

(*c*) have any crimes # in *prac*tice # been punishable by judicial beating #

(*d*) in nineteen forty *eight* # judicial beating was abolished #

In each of these, the italicized syllable bears a narrow range rising nucleus (N⁄). The first terminates a postmodified nominal group operating as subject, the other three a preverbal adjunct, that in (*b*) being followed by a similar one uttered by the same speaker a few seconds later, 'in actual fact', with a nucleus ∨ on *fact*. It is probable that if informants were asked to repeat these utterances (*a*)–(*d*), they would frequently replace N⁄ by ∨.

[5] See Table I in *Proceedings*, p. 689.

[6] See further, Crystal and Quirk, *Systems of Prosodic and Paralinguistic Features in English*, pp. 52ff.

[7] But this is not to say that a 'level' nucleus is to be related solely to 'fall' in systemic description. Although our present materials offer much evidence for linking level with fall, an alternative link with rise is also suggested. Levels seem undoubtedly to have a place in a subsystem of rising nuclei, though perhaps rather

in prosodic co-ordination than subordination. To illustrate again from the text referred to in footnote 4:

(*a*) with having their trousers taken dōwn # and their backsides bírched #
(*b*) between eighteen nīnety # and nineteen thirty fòur #
(*c*) it is subject to the final prerōgative # of mērcy # of the Home Sēcretary # who may recommend a reprìeve #

In these instances, the level nuclei seem more readily replaceable by rising nuclei than anything else and might ultimately be best viewed as exponents of narrow terms in a subsystem of rise relatable to a particular rhetorical register of speech.

[8] It is worth mentioning that in the first tone unit one informant gave such a correlative pair on *few* and *later*, making the rise of narrow range. There are several examples of ⸌ + N⸍ in the Survey text 5b.51 from which other supplementary materials have already been quoted. For example:

(*a*) if they dìd these dreadful *N* thíngs # they might . . .
(*b*) the plàin fact of the matter *N* ís # they have not . . .
(*c*) the vast majòrity of *N* múrderers # are . . .

[9] Compare the table given in *Proceedings*, p. 691, which shows that falls are not only twice as common as rises but that they frequently occur in similar environments, presumably indicating an area in which the contrast between fall and rise is neutralized.

[10] Both irregularities, however, occur with informants who seem to be unusual and unreliable in some of their other responses as well, ignoring or replacing the nuclei on *slowly*, *you*, and *wanted*.

[11] Cf. *Proceedings*, pp. 684 f., 690 f.

[12] A booster is a step-up in pitch; see further, *Systems of Prosodic and Paralinguistic Features in English*, p. 46.

[13] This is a matter that is developed further in a forthcoming University of London thesis by David Crystal. Survey of English Usage materials show several kinds of pattern in tone-unit sequences. For example, there is a high expectation that a tone unit with fall-rise nucleus will be followed by one with a high boostered fall nucleus, and that tone units of the latter type are equally expected after sequences of tone units with rising nuclei. Similarly, a rise-fall tone unit is more frequently than random followed by a fall unit, while a rise-plus-fall unit is more frequently than random followed by a fall-plus-rise unit and almost never by a fall-rise unit.

Language-Planning in Seventeenth-Century England; Its Context and Aims

VIVIAN SALMON

One of the most interesting features of the intellectual background of the seventeenth century was an almost obsessive desire for the advancement of human knowledge by the construction of a system of universal symbols which would be comprehensive, unambiguous and entirely free from redundancy. The earliest attempts at such a system, adumbrated in the previous century, were limited to the invention of a set of written symbols which would be interpreted in the reader's own tongue, providing merely a basic vocabulary; models frequently cited included Arabic numerals, hieroglyphics, the Chinese character and signs of the zodiac. Later, there were suggestions for a universal spoken vocabulary based on the 'primitive roots' of Hebrew. During the course of a century the aim of language planners became more sophisticated; they sought a notation which would comprehend the whole of human knowledge, divided into conceptual classes, each symbol unambiguously indicating the properties of the object symbolised, and possessing its own standard pronunciation.[1] A number of efforts between about 1630 and 1660, chiefly in England and France, culminated in the work of John Wilkins, the *Essay Towards a Real Character and a Philosophical Language* (1668), which was published under the aegis of the Royal Society. None of these attempts has ever been reprinted, but of the authors Professor Firth remarked: 'it is a mistake to regard their works merely as interesting linguistic freaks. All subsequent standardization of scientific nomenclature according to a reasoned system is in continuation of the need then felt and expressed.'[2] Wilkins's work is certainly more than a mere curiosity; it is historically significant not only because, as Firth noticed, it influenced modern linguists like Bally, via Roget's *Thesaurus*, but also because it forms a compendium of many of the ideas on language which had been developing since the Renaissance, and which were so closely bound up with contemporary views on literature and philosophy in Western

Europe. But even if we now have nothing more to learn from the *Essay* we can regard it with sympathy and interest as an attempt to solve a problem which is still with us—the international dissemination of scientific knowledge. When experimental science was in its infancy, scientists were faced with the kind of difficulty discussed by a doctor-botanist to whom Wilkins acknowledges a debt in the *Essay*:

> monitum volo lectorem, ne in tanta nominum varietate . . . confundatur . . . Nam interdum unaquæque res multis nominibus à quibusdam designatur . . . Quapropter ego non sine ratione cum Galeno optavi aliquando, res posse tradi sine nominibus, ut sophistis eriperetur decertandi & calumniandi occasio.[3]

and it has usually been assumed that Wilkins, as a devoted Baconian, was setting out to solve the semantic problems posed by his master as his contribution to the scientific research of the early Royal Society.

Within the last decade, however, the scientific purpose of the work of Wilkins and of the other language planners has been seriously questioned. It has been suggested that Wilkins was primarily motivated by a desire to promote religious unity among the reformed Protestant churches of Europe by attempting to remove the verbal ambiguity which he considered to lie at the heart of theological disputes, and that he wrote the *Essay* under the influence of John Amos Comenius, the Moravian religious reformer who published a demand for an international constructed language in the same year as the *Essay*. If we accept this suggestion, the effect will be 'to reduce sharply the amount of credit (or blame) that can be assigned to English authors for opening the field of linguistic reform'.[4] Professor Otto Funke has already made a brief reply to the argument, without convincing the most recent scholar to investigate seventeenth-century universal languages;[5] the evidence will here be examined afresh in the hope of re-establishing the older view of Wilkins as primarily a scientific linguist worthy to be numbered among those many Englishmen who, as Professor Firth believed, made such weighty contributions to the development of linguistic thought from the age of Elizabeth to that of Sir William Jones.

In the earlier part of the seventeenth century the virtual disappearance of Latin as a means of international communication created major difficulties for the growing body of scientists in Europe; almost as adversely affected were the religious reformers in Germany, Poland, Scandinavia, the Low Countries and Britain, who were trying both to heal sectarian disputes and to modernize the mediaeval learning which was still current in many schools and universities. The most influential of these Protestants was Comenius, who spent some time in England in 1641–2 as the guest of Samuel Hartlib, an idealist of German origin who was concerned with almost every scheme for the reform of learning which was mooted in England in the mid-seventeenth century.[6] While he was in London Comenius composed a plea for the foundation of a 'Baconian' college for the advancement of learning, which included an impassioned demand for the creation of a universal language to unite all Christians in the love of God, all cause for religious dispute being removed through the abolition of verbal ambiguity. When Comenius left England in June 1642 the manuscript of this work, the *Via Lucis*, remained here for transcription, and it was not published until 1668;[7] but it has been suggested that it was circulated by Hartlib to his friends, who included some of the language planners, and became their major source of inspiration. The greatest of these linguists, John Wilkins himself, might even have met Comenius and discussed his universal language in 1641–2. In addition, a colleague of Comenius, Cyprian Kinner, is alleged to have suggested to Wilkins indirectly via Hartlib one of the most important features of the *Essay*—the 'technical word' which indicated by its alphabetical components the qualities of the object it symbolized: the suggestion was made in a letter from Kinner to Hartlib of June 1647 which Hartlib may also have passed on to his friends, and in particular William Petty; it involved the symbolization of various categories of reality by individual letters of the alphabet, 'technical' words resulting from a combination of several.[8]

The argument for Comenius's influence on the English language planners may be briefly recapitulated here. Before his visit, English scholars had been interested in the construction of simple universal characters—basic vocabularies of existing languages with conventional symbols; among them were Bacon, William Bedell, Bishop of Kilmore, with his collaborator Johnston and John Wilkins himself (in an early work entitled *Mercury*). After his visit, their interest turned to the construction of new languages based on a scientific classification of reality which would prevent verbal ambiguity; such languages were adumbrated, or actually produced, by a group of Oxford scholars and their associates including William Petty, Seth Ward, George Dalgarno and John Wilkins, all of whom, it is claimed, were motivated by the desire to prevent religious strife which Comenius had put forward in the *Via Lucis* as the prime end of a universal philosophical language.[9] Thus Comenius is seen as a vitally important figure in the development of

English ideas on language; his influence, it is said, changed the whole nature of the quest for a means of international communication from what was little more than a type of shorthand to a sophisticated semantic investigation; and the marks of this influence are threefold; the emphasis on its value for preventing religious disputes, the necessity for the classification of reality, and the desirability of a vocabulary which would show its meaning by its form. So persuasive was his argument, it is claimed, for the religious significance of a constructed language, that no language planner who had been subjected to its 'merciless iteration' in the *Via Lucis* could ever have forgotten the theme.[10]

It is precisely this statement which throws doubt on the argument; certainly no modern reader would dispute the 'merciless iteration' and its likely effect. But the very man who was most closely connected with Comenius in England, and the most enthusiastic supporter of his schemes, seems to have done precisely what seems impossible; with the manuscript of *Via Lucis* in his possession, as it is claimed, and only five years after it was written, Samuel Hartlib encouraged and actually himself published in 1647 a project for a universal character which totally ignored the superior claims of a philosophical language—and sent it to Comenius for his criticism. What is even stranger is Comenius's reply to Hartlib when he received Francis Lodowick's *Common Writing*. 'Conatus Vester', he says, believing that the work is Hartlib's

> de communi omnium gentium et linguarum scriptura bene me oblectavit, tametsi ab illo non tantum sperem, quantum optari video. Millies praestaret habere linguam novam . . . Monuit quidem sapiens ille Mersennus noster . . . dubitare se, an dignum sit, tantos in linguae Latinae culturam impendere labores, cum faciliori opera effingere queamus novam tanto perfectiorem.[11]

In thus declaring that he prefers a new language to a common writing, Comenius cites, not his own views in the *Via Lucis*, but ideas which Comenius had received from Mersenne in a letter of 22 November 1640. The French scholar, friend of Descartes and centre of intellectual life in Paris in the 1630s and 1640s, had been brought into touch with Comenius in 1639 through a common friend, and in this letter Mersenne was giving his opinion on the reformer's new system of teaching Latin in his *Janua Linguarum*, first published in 1631. He also described to Comenius the attempt at producing a universal character, on which his friend Jean Le Maire had been working for some twenty years, and the words he used must have echoed in his correspondent's mind when he too was called upon to pronounce on the merits of a universal character seven years later: 'Quanto enim facilius esset novam linguam condere, quam omnes mortales, si non loquerentur, saltem intelligerent.'[12] And he goes on to recommend to Comenius a work which he had recently written, which described briefly the principles on which a universal language could be based. In commenting on Lodowick's *Common Writing* Comenius chooses, therefore, to refer not to the *Via Lucis*, which contains a passionate plea for a universal language, but to a chance remark of Mersenne's made some seven years previously; yet in the same letter to Hartlib, Comenius does refer to other sections of the *Via Lucis*, in particular to the only chapter (XVIII) which we know for certain that Hartlib possessed, since it was found among his papers. If the remainder of the manuscript was also in his possession at that time, and if it contained the chapter on universal language, then it is incredible that Comenius should make no reference to it whatsoever. We must suppose that the 'merciless iteration' had been forgotten by both author and reader.

This failure to acknowledge the existence of the language chapter in the *Via Lucis*, by both Comenius and Hartlib, suggests the desirability of reopening the enquiry into Wilkins's debt to Comenius, and there are three major lines of investigation open to us. First we may examine the works of the language planners to see to what extent the influence of Comenius is actually acknowledged; even if the *Via Lucis* were not in print, they could still have made some reference to it, as Wilkins did in the *Essay* to the unpublished papers of Holder and Lodowick. Secondly, we may enquire what grounds there are for believing that Hartlib kept the manuscript of the *Via Lucis* and circulated it among his friends, or that Wilkins might have belonged to the Hartlib circle in 1641–2 and have discussed it with Comenius personally. And lastly, we may ask whether the language planners could have obtained the ideas they are said to have derived from Comenius from any other source—either by a logical development of attempts at a universal character in the light of the seventeenth-century intellectual background, or by the special influence of any other scholar not necessarily motivated by religious ideals.

If the language planners were in fact indebted to the *Via Lucis*, there should be references in their work to both Comenius's ideas on universal language and to his views on the solution of religious strife by its means; and it must be remembered that, according to DeMott, it was precisely in order to achieve the goal of religious unity that Comenius advocated a constructed language and thus changed the direction of

English enquiries from characters to languages; so that references to the solution of religious disputes in works on the universal character cannot in any case be regarded as evidence of Comenius's influence. There are indeed a number of references to Comenius in the writings of Ward, Dalgarno, Beck and Edmundson, but they offer less than one might expect. They all relate to Comenius's most famous work, the *Janua Linguarum* (1631), a text-book for Latin-teaching which owed its enormous success to its insistence on the learning of whole sentences rather than paradigms; as Comenius himself said 'it happened that it was accepted with much applause, and unanimously approved by the learned, as the true, and most genuine way of teaching the languages'.[13] Every schoolmaster in England must have known the work, which went into edition after edition. In his defence of learning at Oxford, and in particular, of language-teaching, Seth Ward remarks '*Comenius* I know, and that his way is usefull' (*Vindiciae* 43), Cave Beck refers to the *Janua*, Dalgarno calls his own character a 'Janua' to language-study, and Edmundson comments on the '*great Benefactor to Schoole-Masters*' of whose works he cites both the *Janua* and his *Methodus Novissima* (1648). In only one case is the name of Comenius connected with a universal language, in a printed broadsheet in Sloane 4377. Here Dalgarno lists the men who have desired such an invention, and he cites Bacon, Ward, Petty, Comenius and Lodowick—in that order. The *Via Lucis*, had he known it, should have been given pride of place, containing as it does the most fully formulated discussion of the subject; Dalgarno may have had in mind Comenius's mention of the universal language in the *Methodus Novissima*, where he acknowledges its desirability but thinks it to be impossible of attainment. Edmundson notes that a common language has been much desired, but by 1658 there were at least two English projectors whom he could have had in mind, Lodowick and Ward, the latter being a member of his own university.

The language projectors are strangely silent on their debt to the *Via Lucis*, but they are scarcely less reticent on the value of a universal language for solving religious disputes; only one mentions quite explicitly its help in clearing 'Modern differences in Religion', and this was Wilkins, who as a bishop in the Church of England might be expected to be particularly aware of the problem. It has been suggested that William Petty was also influenced by Comenius when he composed his *Dictionary of Sensible Words* (1685) and his *Explication of 12 Theological Words* (1686), but these are not attempts at a universal language—they are only putting into practice an idea suggested by Bacon, that words should first be defined before arguments are entered into.[14] The *Dictionary* is not specifically religious in tone. About a third of its contents are of theological interest, but the remainder are legal, political (e.g. Whig, Tory, trimmer) and the like. The theological words became of topical significance in the following year with the contentious accession of James II, and Petty manifests here a debt, not to Comenius, but to his great friend and master, Thomas Hobbes, since several of the definitions are inspired by similar ones in *Leviathan*. Petty's closest connection with universal language schemes is his reputed invention of 'technical words' in the late 1640s; but we have no knowledge of his intentions, and his choice of subject, botany, seems to indicate that they were purely scientific. Other scholars with linguistic interests have also been said to show the influence of Comenius in their desire for the settlement of religious disputes by a universal language, but they were working on characters, not on philosophical languages. The earliest of these is William Bedell, Bishop of Kilmore, who set one of his clergy to work on a universal character in the early 1630s; it has been suggested that he did so in order to assist the work for religious unity among Protestants in Europe which was being carried out by Hartlib's friend, John Dury, to whom he gave financial support; but it is interesting to note that Dury's avowed linguistic interests had a rather different end from the solution of disputes. He desired 'A Magicall Language wherby secrets may bee delivered and preserved to such as are made acquaint with it traditionally'.[15] Such an aim seems more in keeping with what we learn of Bedell's work from Hartlib's *Ephemerides*; in the late 1630s he was engaged in 'setting forth Jhones Herbarium Angliae'. Another linguistic projector, Francis Lodowick, is talking about a 'Universall Reall Caracter' when he comments that it will 'assist to the true knowledge of things ... in the diffinition ... whereof there is so much trouble and dispute';[16] when one of Cave Beck's friends, in a dedicatory poem, mentions strife, 'Bout all that should reduce to unitie', it is to Beck's *Universal Character* that he attributes a solution, and Bacon that he names as Beck's inspiration; and Dalgarno, speaking of 'Rhetoricall flourishes of words' which 'doe often obscure best literature', notes 'what strife hath been in the world meerly about words' when recommending the use of his earlier universal character—not his *Ars Signorum*.[17] Since these quotations all refer to attempts at universal characters, they are not admissible as evidence of Comenius's influence on the construction of universal language.

Difficult as it is to see the special influence of Comenius in these references to strife about verbal ambiguities, when they occur in works on both universal character and universal language, it is clear that projectors of both felt a strong distrust of words and were well aware of the arguments to which they might lead. Why this was so we shall discuss later, but we should first see what positive evidence there is of aims and sources in the works of the projectors. Ward, Dalgarno and Wilkins describe in some detail the genesis and aims of their efforts. Ward claims that he was inspired by the new symbolic methods used in mathematical notation, which were 'more comprehensible and mannageable' than the 'verbose' way of earlier mathematicians, to take the same course in other things; 'Symboles might be found for every *thing* and *notion*.' But a universal character demanded too much of the memory, so that he was forced into a classification which would avoid an excessive number of symbols. The purpose of the universal language was to provide 'a speedy way . . . to the attainement of Knowledge . . . by making a shorter, and clearer cutt to the understanding (by the way of signification) then that which is travailed now by words'. 'This designe', he continues, 'if perfected, would be of very great concernement to the advancement of Learning.'[18] Dalgarno is even more explicit about the genesis of his work; he describes how he was meditating on the Hebrew method of indicating whole phrases by a single character, when it occurred to him that it would offer an improved version of shorthand; 'That drove me before I was aware upon a real Character; That again after a little consideration resolved it self into an Effable language.' By this account, the development of his interest would seem to have been accidental; having considered means to a 'Real Character', he then realized that it would be useful '*to remedy the difficulties and absurdities which all languages are clogg'd with ever since the . . . fall; . . . to cure even Philosophy it self of the disease of Sophisms, and Logomachies*'.[19] About the aims of his universal character Dalgarno provides much information. It will serve as a 'Brachygraphy' applicable to all languages which will improve on ordinary shorthand for brevity and for speed, and will moreover be capable of pronunciation by all nations. It will also act as a *Janua* to language study, and, more ambitiously, it will be suitable for 'an emphatick delivery of real Truths, and the grounds and precepts of Arts and Sciences'. Dalgarno lists nineteen characteristics and advantages of his work; not until the sixteenth do we find mention of its usefulness in the propagation of the Gospel, while the eighteenth claims that it will 'unite the Nations . . . by a more familiar and frequent intercourse and commerce'.[20] But it must be noted that all these aims, religious and otherwise, relate to a universal character and not a philosophical language, and cannot therefore be regarded as fulfilling the demands of the *Via Lucis*.

Wilkins, the last of the three language planners to describe his aims in detail, produced two works on universal communication, in the earlier of which, *Mercury*, he discusses merely a simple character based on Hebrew roots; even so, it has been suggested that he borrowed the title from the *Via Lucis*, where Comenius refers to his international language as 'this Mercury, this messenger'. But *Mercury* was published in 1641 and Comenius was writing his manuscript between November 1641 and April 1642; and as Wilkins acknowledges that he writes in continuation of Godwin's work on codes entitled *Nuntius Inanimatus*, his title seems obviously derived from Godwin's.[21] In the *Essay* Wilkins describes the functions of a universal language: to eliminate the necessity for learning many foreign languages, to ease '*mutual* Commerce' among nations, to improve 'Natural knowledge', to propagate true religion, and, as almost the last consideration, to assist '*the clearing of some of our Modern differences in* Religion' by preventing '*impostures and cheats*' from misleading us '*under the disguise of affected insignificant Phrases*'. (f.b.1.) Such a statement is exactly what might be expected from a supporter of the seventeenth-century movement, entirely unconnected with Comenius, for the simplification of prose style, and it is interesting to note that not one of the sources he quotes (including Bacon, Vossius and Hermannus Hugo) is of a religious nature. Wilkins explains how he came to undertake his task. Having discussed the subject generally with Seth Ward, who first gave him a '*distinct apprehension of the proper course to be observed*', he set to work to help Dalgarno—probably when the latter had turned from the construction of a character to the project of a language. No credit whatsoever is given to Comenius, and Wilkins sees his work as having so little connection with religious purposes that he finds it necessary to apologize for its production by a bishop of the Church of England. His excuse for undertaking it is not that it might be useful in the solution of religious disputes, but that it was begun when he was '*in an Academicall station*' and engaged in frequent discussions with his colleague Ward on '*the advancement of several parts of Learning*'. (f.b.2r.)

Thus not one of the language planners acknowledges a debt to

Comenius other than as the author of Latin text-books, and only Wilkins connects a universal philosophical language with the solution of religious disputes, although others, including Dalgarno, Edmundson, and a friend of Cave Beck, refer to disputes of various kinds due to verbal ambiguity and rhetorical obscurity, sometimes in connection with a universal character (as in the case of Beck); that mere awareness of verbal ambiguity is no evidence of a debt to Comenius will be shown later, when the language planners' debt to Bacon is outlined, and another source for Wilkins's ideas will be suggested.

The second problem to be examined involves two enquiries: the role of the original manuscript of the *Via Lucis*, and the possibility that Wilkins, and perhaps Ward, not only knew the manuscript but met Comenius himself during his visit to England. It is known that the manuscript of *Via Lucis* was left in England for transcription (perhaps of a fair copy) when Comenius went abroad in 1642, and it was returned to Hartlib by the copyist in August of that year. In the following September Comenius writes to a friend that he has recently shown someone the *Via Lucis*, so that Hartlib must have sent at least one manuscript on to him from England.[22] But there is no evidence that the whole of the *Via Lucis* remained here to be circulated among Hartlib's friends; the evidence, such as it is, points rather to Hartlib's having copied only the one chapter which was of prime interest to him—the plan for a universal college, which was found among his papers. But even if the whole manuscript remained here, we still do not know for certain that it was identical with the printed version of 1668; it is obvious that Comenius added the lengthy dedication in that year, and it is at least possible that he revised or added to the rest (particularly as the chapter on universal language is almost at the end of the work). It is certainly odd that in all other publications of about the same period Comenius emphasizes the importance of *Latin* as the ideal universal language, and though he considers the possibility of a constructed language in his *Methodus Linguarum Novissima*, he finally dismisses it as impractical. He even departs from the ideal of the abolition of 'rhetorical flourishes' dear to the English language planners, by producing an *Ars Ornatoria* (1664) in which he claims that no one can speak forcefully on any subject unless he can first speak with variety and elegance; and he may also have inspired an attack on Dalgarno's universal language which appears in the preface to an edition of the *Janua* in 1662.

But whether or not this chapter was written in 1641–2, there still remains the problem of whether Wilkins and Ward could have seen the manuscript or met its author. In all the documents which R.F.Young has printed concerning Comenius's visit to England,[23] there is no reference whatsoever to either of them as belonging to Hartlib's circle at the time; Hartlib does not mention them in his *Ephemerides* until eight years later, and we have no evidence at all that he knew them earlier than this. The only facts of which we can take account are that a copy of one chapter of *Via Lucis* was found among Hartlib's papers, and that he was acquainted with Wilkins and Ward by 1650. All else is conjecture.

External evidence hardly justifies the important role which has been assigned to Comenius in the development of language-planning in the seventeenth century, but it may still be asked whether the fundamental change in direction which took place after about 1650 could have come about entirely without the inspiration of the *Via Lucis*, or whether there are other features of seventeenth-century thought which could account for the increased sophistication of the linguists' aims.

It must first be acknowledged that such a development might have come about spontaneously. The oft-cited model for a universal character was Chinese, which had aroused an interest in England in the preceding century which had been reinforced, not only by Bacon in the *Advancement of Learning*, but also by the publication in 1616 of an account of missionary journeys to the East.[24] This work, originally in Latin, was translated into several modern languages and was partially incorporated in *Purchas his Pilgrimage* (1628). But those who took the Chinese character as their model in constructing universal characters soon realized an almost insuperable difficulty—the enormous number of symbols which would need to be memorized for any but the most limited vocabulary. The problem, mentioned by both Bacon and Descartes,[25] was discussed by many of their successors, including Ward and Dalgarno. The solution was obvious. Some sort of classification must be devised which would denote associated objects by like symbols; and it seems that such a step was taken by more than one linguist the progress of whose work we can follow.

Timothy Bright, the earliest known English shorthand writer, first invented a simple mainly phonetic shorthand which was not even as sophisticated as a universal character; but he changed to a system which was a rudimentary universal language in that objects were grouped in classes denoted by a primary symbol, derivatives being shown by points and lines.[26] Johnston's character was also altered during composition and we are told in the *Ephemerides* that the second draft was a great improvement on the first; this may have been a change in the direction of classification. Lodowick certainly changed from a character to advocacy of a language between 1647 and 1652 (although his inspiration may have come from Comenius's suggestion in his letter to Hartlib); and Dalgarno relates how his universal character developed into a philosophical language as a result, it seems, of little more than introspection. At any rate, he writes to Hartlib in a letter preserved among his manuscripts (1659):

> My spare houres I wholly employ in revising and endeavouring a farder perfection of my first thoughts & truly I have found by experience that solitarines does fitt and dispose an Inventors spirit to dive to the bottom of his invention.

He enquires whether Hartlib has any news of Wilkins's effort and remarks:

> if he attempt anie thing on this subject he shal have small credit of it for besides y[t] all he wil doe wil be to discover another mans Labors, . . . he wil doe it w[t] several material defects . . . since the tyme of my retirment I have discovered advantages wh[ch] I perswade my self have not fallen under his Consideration.

Whether spontaneous or not, these developments must have been assisted by several intellectual interests of the seventeenth century to which reference can be made only briefly here, though each merits a full investigation for its contribution to linguistic studies. They include certain treatments of lexis for language-learning, the development of shorthand in England, the interest in codes, ciphers and methods of communication at a distance engendered by the Civil War and the long-lasting fascination, which reached its peak in the seventeenth century, of the methods of organizing knowledge devised by Lullism and the Cabbalah.

First, although Comenius is credited with inspiring the English linguists with the desire to classify reality for the purposes of a philosophical language, English grammarians had long been accustomed to arranging Latin vocabulary in conceptual classes for greater ease of learning. In the *Lingua Linguarum* Henry Edmundson actually suggests that Comenius adopted the custom of '*throwing the words into Philosophicall Heads of Matter*' from our own grammarians Hunter and Stanbridge, and in Hartlib's papers we find this among several similar comments: 'Dieser Doletus ist der erste gewesen, der sein Lexicon secundum titulos rerum præcipuos disponiret, e.g. De re Rustica, re

Militari, re Navali etc. welches gewiess ein gueter Modus ist.' (Sloane 417 f. 127, 1637.) Alsted's great *Encyclopaedia*, very well known in England as Hartlib's papers testify, notes especially; '*Inter omnes Lexicographos illi maximam merentur laudem, qui ordinem verborum conformant ordini rerum, tanquam normæ & mensuræ* . . . non solùm dictionum ipsarum significationes potes comprehendere, sed rerum etiam naturam.'[27] This attempt to range real objects in classes as a practical measure in language-learning was supported by the common contemporary belief in the 'great chain of being' which saw creation as a hierarchy of classes, each linked to the one above and below it.[28] This doctrine, of classical origin, was still held by the young Descartes and formed the theoretical background for much of Comenius's thought on 'words and things', but it was losing its hold in the new scientific age of the mid-seventeenth century and led to the kind of criticism of Comenius which we find in the *Ephemerides*: 'If their bee not a perfect gradation so that but one bee missing all is spoiled' (1639). More to our purpose is a reference to the philologist Henry Jacobs of Merton, friend of a founder-member of the Royal Society and acquaintance of Seth Ward. Jacobs's opinions in the 1630s are reported by the grammarian Thomas Hayne: 'ipse profitetur se methodo sua & hactenus intentata, per certas proprietatum classes subordinatim velle istas disponere, donec in paucissimis desinant Principiis: ut hæc verborum Philosophia exactè imitetur illam rerum.'[29] This was the principle followed by Dalgarno and Wilkins—not only to 'distribute' words into classes, but to see that the 'philosophy' of words answered exactly to that of things.

Closely allied to this idea of semantic classification was the attempt to systematize all human learning and to indicate the various branches by universal symbols. This was particularly the aim of the Cabbalists, as a French contemporary of Wilkins explains:

> Quoy que beaucoup de gens n'ayent pas eu la force de s'imaginer, qu'il y ait quelque ordre vnique pour les Sciences, les Grands-Maistres l'ont tousiours recherché . . . Les Rabbins . . . auoient autrefois leur Caballe . . . dans laquelle on dit que toutes les Sciences estoient contenuës. Ils luy donnoient deux Parties, dont la premiere . . . traittoit des choses . . . la seconde Partie . . . traittoit des Noms . . . cela n'a point esté inuenté pour traitter de toutes les Sciences . . . Cela n'a du rapport qu'à vne seule, qui est d'expliquer toutes les choses . . . selon les accouplemens & les transpositions des Lettres, pour en faire diuerses significations.[30]

The Cabbalah was as familiar in England as in France since most linguistic scholars knew Hebrew, and there are two specially close links with the work of Wilkins; the earlier is to be found in the *Vindiciae Academiarum* of Seth Ward, to whom Wilkins attributed his earliest interest in universal language, and who comments on Cabbalism in these terms:

> The use of Symbols is not confined to the Mathematicks only, but hath been applied to the *nature of things* by ... the Cabalists ... the Combinatorian Jews ... and others, have made Symbols of the Letters of the Alphabet ... Such a Language ... would afford that which the *Cabalists* ... have vainely sought for in the Hebrew (pp. 19, 22).

Another link appears in Hartlib's *Ephemerides* of 1651, where he reports that the 'Club-men' at Oxford (the group including Wilkins which later became the Royal Society) are making summaries of, among others, the works of Kircher—and Athanasius Kircher was a noted linguist and Cabbalist. Cabbalists were interested in literal symbols in the same way as the Lullists, disciples of the fourteenth-century monk Raymond Lully who had invented a simple kind of logical device for analysing knowledge; even Descartes bore it in mind when he conceived his new method of constituting a universal science, and it played no small part in Leibniz's *De Arte Combinatoria.* Ward also comments on '*Lully*, and others [who] have made Symbols of the Letters of the Alphabet, so that א signifies with them *God*' (p. 19). Just as Wilkins used letters of the Roman alphabet to symbolize the various branches of knowledge and objects in the universe, so the Cabbalists and the Lullists used alphabetical symbols. Kircher, for example, used 22 letters of the Hebrew alphabet, each with a precise meaning; aleph = 'doctrina', beth = 'domus', ghimel = 'plenitudo', etc. And he ended his alphabet with the remark 'quo quidem totius tam intelligibilis, quam sensibilis naturæ ordo exhibetur'.[31] Lully himself used an alphabet of nine letters, each symbolizing an area of reality, and each significant in various classes such as 'absoluta' and 'relata' according to the position in which it occurred.

Seth Ward and Dalgarno used purely alphabetical symbols for their attempts at a universal language, but Wilkins also used a notation of lines and points, one object of which was to remove the 'second curse' of the confusion of tongues, as he called it—the difference in alphabets. It looks somewhat like a form of shorthand, and there is no doubt that the intense interest in this subject in early seventeenth-century England was closely bound up with the development of a universal character;

indeed, the association was noticed at the time.[32] One early member of the Royal Society, John Beale, wrote to Hartlib in 1657: 'I verily beleeve, that a progresse in variety of attempts for the advancemt of short-writing will in the end bring foorth an Vniversall Character';[33] and Hartlib noted in 1640 concerning Bright's 'brachygraphy' that Sir William Boswell 'was persuaded this Art might bee notably perfected. For they are rather Reales Cherienses then those other stenographical characters'. Comenius was amazed at the English interest in shorthand when he arrived here in 1641, and wrote home almost at once commenting on it; Mersenne too discussed it in his correspondence (preserved among the Hartlib manuscripts) with Theodore Haak, reputed founder of the Royal Society, in the year when Boswell was commenting on Bright. Mersenne does not altogether approve of 'brachygraphy' because some of the characters take as long to write as the ordinary word; the system on which he is commenting (which Haak had probably sent him) seems to aim at an analogy between word and object. It might be possible, he thinks, to 'baptizer chaque chose d'un caractere bien court . . . mais quand il sera question d'un cheval, d'un lion . . . l'on aura de la peine a trouver des propres Caracteres assez intelligibles'. Undoubtedly the problems of symbolization raised by non-phonetic shorthand must have created much interest in, and discussion of, matters linguistic among seventeenth-century Englishmen, and not only among grammarians. Robert Boyle, for example, was reported by Hartlib in 1650 to be perfecting his shorthand so as to use it for writing up experiments; likewise the essential use of codes and ciphers during the Civil War, when the opponents both spoke English, made men acquainted with other aspects of language, such as the structure of words and frequency of sounds. It is interesting to note that another founder-member of the Royal Society, the mathematician John Wallis, who had advised Dalgarno on his universal language, won a good deal of fame (and opprobrium) for deciphering the documents captured from Charles I after the battle of Naseby; Leibniz tried to discover his method, but without success.[34] Cryptography may seem a far cry from universal language, but it sometimes used symbols for whole concepts in a suggestive way, as is shown by Juan Caramuel's remark: 'In Germaniâ & tempore turbato haec scribimus, & proderit notas . . . quibus, aut similibus, uti solemus.' He then gives three different symbols for *Pedites mittam ad vos, Equites mittam ad vos, Pedites mittite ad me.*[35]

When John Wilkins began work on his *Essay* in the 1650s there was thus available to him, via his colleagues in the Oxford Philosophical Club and elsewhere, a wide body of knowledge which could affect the way he planned his task. There was the organization of vocabulary of the teachers of classics, and the systematization of knowledge of the Lullists and Cabbalists who labelled concepts by letters of the alphabet; and there was also the non-alphabetic symbolization of the shorthand writers and cryptographers. In the final section of this enquiry we shall see to what extent the works of Wilkins and the other linguistic reformers might have developed spontaneously in such an intellectual background, and to what extent they were the fruition of ideas adumbrated by earlier, and better known, philosophers and linguists.

The seventeenth-century quest for a universal language has until recently been ascribed to Bacon's views on semantics and the 'Real Character'. But two objections have now been raised to this attribution. One is that Bacon did not accept the possibility of a constant relationship between word and object necessitated by a universal language, and the other is that he advocated merely a universal character, not the kind of philosophical language which Wilkins actually produced. It must be pointed out, however, that both Bacon and the linguistic reformers distrusted *words* as symbols, and it was an entirely different kind of symbol that they were seeking, which would be inherently associated with its object in a way not possible with normal vocabulary—hence the invention of the 'technical word' or the non-alphabetic symbols of Wilkins. Ward explicitly stated that he was seeking 'a shorter, and clearer cutt to the understanding (by the way of signification) then that which is travailed now by words' (p. 20). It must also be pointed out that, however mistaken they might have been, the English linguists certainly thought that Bacon inspired their undertakings, and one scholar in Hartlib's circle even objected to Comenius for not giving sufficient credit where it was due:

> I dislike this chiefly in Mr. Comenius Worke, that he giveth not therein that honour to my Lord Verulam, which is due to soe worthy a Gentleman and whom Comenius is so much be holding to, because all what good he hath in this his præface, he hath taken out of my Lord Verulams his Works.[36]

The reference is to a general work on education, but is typical of the kind of attitude adopted towards Bacon by scholars of the seventeenth century; linguists cite his name over and over again, among them Wilkins.

Bacon certainly adumbrated a character rather than a language, but he throws out fruitful hints for his successors. He mentions 'a kind of grammar which should diligently inquire, not the analogy of words with one another, but the analogy between words and things, or reason' and calls for a universal grammar, 'the noblest species of grammar as I think', which would 'handle the various properties of *languages* . . . so . . . the several beauties of each may be combined . . . into a most beautiful image and excellent model of speech itself'.[37] In these passages Bacon considers a vocabulary based on analogy between word and thing, as well as a grammar which shall be as perfect as possible; and here are two vital ingredients of the universal language.

It is Bacon also that we may regard as the most familiar source for that attitude towards words which was held by inventors of both universal characters and universal languages—the view of verbal ambiguity as a cause of disputes. It is difficult to say when this distrust of words first appeared; certainly it is to be found in England and even before Bacon, as Comenius himself acknowledged in a note on Bright: he refers to the 'praise which TIMOTHY BRIGHT ascribes unto such, as are inventors of brevity, and perspicuity . . . that learners may be eased of all tediousmesse [*sic*] and prolixity, and freed from all ambiguous labyrinths'.[38] Bacon himself did not explicitly recommend the construction of a universal language as a solution to verbal ambiguity, but he certainly emphasized the role of such ambiguity in causing disputes. In that section of the *Advancement of Learning* which deals with the universal character he regrets 'the consumption of all that ever can be said in controversies of religion, which have so much diverted men from other sciences' and elsewhere in the same work he deplores 'the false appearances that are imposed upon us by words'. His attack on the 'Idols of the Market-place' is too well known to need repetition here, but we may note briefly his conviction that 'ill and unfit choice of words wonderfully obstructs the understanding . . . and lead[s] men away into numberless empty controversies'.[39] Bacon made plain the dangers inherent in words; others sought a practical solution. One early attempt was made in a dictionary defining disputed theological terms in which the author, Thomas Wilson, claims that 'words which beare difference between Protestants and Papists, are written downe and cleared in this Book', since 'the right distinguishing of things, the one from the other, when the Nature and due bounds of every word is declared, would prove some preservative against errors'.[40] In his attack on ambiguity he modestly declares: 'I doe herein but breake the Ice'; others, he hoped, would continue his work, and this they did—in other fields too. One such scholar was cited by a language planner whose work was never printed—John Beale, who was working on a character for the Royal Society in the early 1660s. Beale refers to Meric Casaubon, who gives his opinion that 'Accuratam verborum cognitionem non Philologis solum & humaniores literas professis esse necessariam; sed in omnibus & singulis scientiis artibusque percipiendis adeò locum habere, ut in singulis ex illorum ignorantiâ gravissimi interdum & perniciosissimi oriantur errores'; and in this work he considers five major semantic fields where ambiguity may cause disputes—theology, jurisprudence, medicine, philosophy and politics. He discusses such topics as the nomenclature of plants (in the section on medicine) and, in the sphere of politics, the way in which the safety of nations may depend on verbal precision—'ex unius ambiguæ aut obscurioris voculæ variâ interpretatione multorum hominum millium salus pendeat'.[41]

There is little doubt that Bacon's views of verbal ambiguity underlie the work of Wilson and Casaubon, but neither of these connects his distrust of words explicitly with suggestions for a new symbolization, as Wilkins did. Such a connection is first to be found, in a rudimentary form, in the work of shorthand inventors. The seventeenth-century practice of 'brachygraphy' required the writer to précis as he wrote; as Bright himself remarked, 'he tooke himself to his heels' needs to be recorded as 'he fled'.[42] If a single symbol might represent a phrase of many words it is not surprising that rhetorical flourishes became suspect, and we find Thomas Metcalfe, author of one of the most popular books on shorthand in the 1630s and 1640s, introducing his work with the comment: 'As it is the propertie of my professed Art, to comprize many things within the Limits of a narrow circle, so I hold it a point of wisdome, without Circumlocution or idle multiplication of words to expresse a mans intent and meaning.'[43] It is not surprising that Dalgarno himself, in inventing a form of shorthand, noted how 'Rhetoricall flourishes of words doe often obscure best literature' and also 'what strife hath been in the world meerly about words'.[44]

Bacon is frequently cited by all the English language planners, and there is no doubt that his views on semantics must have been well known to them. Yet Bacon still did not demand in completely unequivocal terms the creation of a new language for scientific communication. Is it to be presumed that, after the initial impetus given by Bacon to the construction of 'real characters', the ideal of a universal language developed naturally out of the contemporary cultural background; or can we find any one scholar who made public a demand for such a language, and whose influence on the English linguists can be clearly traced? The enquiry brings us back to the point at which we began—the statement by Mersenne in 1640 that 'facilius esset novam linguam condere'. Father Mersenne was, in fact, the first European scholar to suggest a universal language for the advancement of learning. In November 1629 Descartes sent him a letter suggesting the creation of a language in which words were analogous to things, but already Mersenne had received permission from his Order for the publication of a work on music which comments in some detail on such a language. The licence is dated 23 October 1629, although the *Harmonie Universelle* was not printed until 1636. Mersenne notes first the possibility of using the octave as a universal character, so that 'celuy qui cognoistroit toutes les especes des plantes, des animaux, des mineraux & des pierres, pourroit les exprimer & enseigner toutes les sciences auec toutes sortes d'instrumens de Musique' (p. 41). His scientific interests are beyond question. He then makes a further suggestion under the heading:

> *A sçauoir si l'on peut inuenter la meilleure langue de toutes les possibles.*
> Si l'on pouuoit inuenter vne langue dont les dictions eussent leur signification naturelle, de sorte que tous les hommes entendissent la pensee des autres à la seule prononciation sans en auoir appris la signification . . . cette langue seroit la meilleure de toutes les possibles . . . Mais puis que le son des paroles n'a pas vn tel rapport auec les choses naturelles, morales, & surnaturelles, que leur seule prononciation nous puisse faire comprendre leur nature . . . il faut voir si l'art & l'esprit des hommes peut inuenter la meilleure langue de toutes les possibles; ce qui ne peut arriuer si l'on ne suppose premierement que la meilleure langue est celle qui explique les notions de l'esprit le plus briefuement & le plus clairement (*De la Voix*, p. 65).

Mersenne then considers the problems of constructing a vocabulary. Words should be as short as possible, and must denote classes of object rather than individual items; his comment is worth noting, since it indicates his special interests. One names a single example of 'tous les indiuidus des herbes que l'on appelle *betoine*, *verueine*, *romarin*' by saying '*cette betoine*', etc. (p. 72). It would be desirable to include in the name a reference to all the properties of an object, but he regards this as an impossibility. He searches for an analogy between sounds and things, without much success, although he notes a certain amount of phonetic symbolism, e.g. 'La voyelle *i* signifie les choses tres-minces

& tres-petites' (p. 75). Finally he gives a table for the formation of words, and notes that this 'table generale pourroit seruir pour establir vne langue vniuerselle, qui seroit la meilleure de toutes les possibles, si l'on sçauoit l'ordre des idées que Dieu a de toutes choses' (p. 13). Mersenne's desiderata include, therefore, the essential features of Wilkins's *Essay*—a constructed language in which words are invented so as to be as brief and clear as possible and (though Mersenne considers it to be beyond human ingenuity) to indicate the properties of the object symbolized. Throughout the 1630s Mersenne seems to have kept in mind the possibility of such a language, and discusses it in letters to Peiresc and Gassendi. When sending the former a copy of *Harmonie Universelle* in 1636 he says that he has been considering a language 'que sa seule lecture peut tellement enseigner la Philosophie accomodée a son ordre, qu'on ne peut l'oublier, ou, si on l'oublie, qu'on peut la restablir sans l'ayde d'aulcun'.[45]

Mersenne's views were undoubtedly known throughout Europe, and it has been said of him that he

> is responsible perhaps more than any other single person for the establishment of the intellectual centre of Europe in Paris during the middle third of the seventeenth century. Of prime importance in this connection is his universal correspondence; there is hardly a figure of importance in the learned world who does not appear in the pages of his letters. From all parts of Europe news of the advancement of the sciences came to the convent 'des pères Minimes'.[46]

Among his friends were many Englishmen, including Selden, Hobbes, Digby, Cavendish and Pell; but there are also special links with the language planners.

First, he was in touch with the Hartlib circle, and in direct correspondence for a time in 1647–8 with Hartlib himself, patron of Lodowick and George Dalgarno. It is possible that Mersenne's views on language also reached England via another route—the publications of Renaudot's *Bureau d'Adresse*, which are mentioned in Hartlib's *Ephemerides* for 1639 and are awarded high praise in 1642: 'As for the variety and solidity of the matters and notions contained in them according to the ordinary straine of Philosophy I am almost confident there are no Encyclopaedias in any Nation . . . that can be compared with them.' The *Bureau* was an informal scientific society which had been meeting in Paris in the early 1630's and among the discussions which must have been known to Hartlib and his friends there was one which may well be a reflection of views held by Mersenne (and, of course, expressed by Descartes in the famous letter of November 1629):

> il y a vn ordre dans la nature . . . selon lequel on peut colloquer apres le Createur, les substances creées spirituelles, puis les corporelles . . . particulierement les corporelles selon leur lieu . . . la terre & ses animaux, la mer & ses poissons: les plantes selon leur grandeur, celles qui seront esgales entr'elles selon leurs vertus & autres accidens: faisant le mesme des metaux, mineraux . . . puis on viendra aux categories des accidens, ausquelles on reduira & mettra en leur vray lieu tout ce qui est au monde . . . Il reste donc de trouver aussi vn ordre dans les mots, qui responde à celuy des choses: le premier au premier, & le second au second.[47]

Whether or not such ideas were directly derived from Mersenne, there is no doubt that a universal language was much talked about in Paris in the 1630s and echoes of the discussion were heard in England. (Again there are several references in the *Ephemerides* which imply a knowledge of such linguistic scholarship in France.)

But Mersenne's most direct known link with the Hartlib circle is via his correspondence with Theodore Haak. Haak was one of those who were associated with Comenius on his visit to England in 1641, and who would have had the opportunity of discussing with him Mersenne's views on universal language as well as those expressed in the Bureau d'Adresse. But Haak was also the man who suggested the meetings of scientists which began in London in 1645 and eventually led to the foundation of the Royal Society, and he kept up a correspondence with Mersenne for two separate periods, 1639–40, and in 1647, shortly after the meetings of scientists began. The earlier correspondence seems to have been designed to introduce Mersenne to the 'Pansophic' ideas of Comenius, as well as the scheme for the classification of mathematical knowledge set out by Hartlib's friend John Pell. Mersenne was not especially interested in Comenius's pseudo-scientific ideas based on his striving for religious harmony; he himself was more concerned with the advancement of learning for its own sake, and after suggesting to Haak that Comenius ought to look at Descartes' *Method*, he dismisses the Pansophic work which Haak has sent him in somewhat odd terms: 'ce genre de Livres a coustume de se bien vendre'. But he is extremely interested in Pell's project and makes suggestions for its extension: that 'douze personnes entendus et amis entreprennent de reduire chacun sa douzaine à un juste volume bien clair'.[48] With these words we should compare an entry in the *Ephemerides* for 1651 which records a report by William Petty: 'The Club-men have cantonized or are cantonizing their whole Academie to taske men to several imploiments and amongst others to make Medullas of all Authors in reference to experimental learning.' The Oxford club which succeeded the London one founded by Haak is here carrying out a suggestion made by Mersenne some dozen years before. In the correspondence of 1639–40 preserved among the Hartlib manuscripts Haak and Mersenne exchanged opinions on various aspects of language; Mersenne described the work of Jean le Maire, who had a new method of language teaching with guaranteed results in a limited period, and who had also been working on some form of international communication for twenty years, while Haak reported to Mersenne on the language of Johnston, the Irishman whose work was due to appear in 1640. They also discussed the possibilities of communication with inhabitants of the moon via Le Maire's alphabet, and the shortcomings of brachygraphy. It is in connection with Le Maire that Mersenne remarks in the letter to Comenius that a new language is necessary 'In qua unica esset conjugatio, et quam amissam quispiam philosophus restituere poterit, cujus fundamenta satis ampla jeci in libris harmonicis, quorum copiam Tibi posset aliquis facere in Anglia.'[49] This letter reached Comenius via Haak, who would thus have heard Mersenne's views on the invention of language, even if they were not addressed to him directly.

The second link between Mersenne and the English linguistic reformers is an even closer one. Hartlib's friend William Petty joined the London scientific club in about 1646 and later went to Oxford, where the meetings of the Oxford Philosophical Club were held at his house until he left in 1651.[50] Hartlib reports in 1650 that 'Dr. Petty was studying once how to know the virtues besides the names of all herbes and plants, which Mr. Ward is studying to make universal to all other things.' Hartlib means that Petty was constructing botanical terms which would indicate the properties of the plants they symbolized; he also records that Ward has taken up Petty's work and extended it to other subjects. Ward described his system of technical words in his *Vindiciae Academiarum*, and Wilkins acknowledged in the *Essay* that from Ward he first obtained any clear idea of how to proceed in the formulation of his language. There is thus a link between Petty and Wilkins via Ward. At the end of the entry for 1650 Hartlib notes 'Of this also see Dr. Kinners letters', and he is clearly referring to Kinner's comment in 1647 that he had been considering a botanical character of technical words. Hartlib does not say that Petty is carrying out Kinner's wishes; he is merely referring to other work of the same nature. If we accept that Hartlib is implying a direct borrowing, we still need assume nothing about Petty's religious motives in undertaking the task. Kinner offered a method of scientific nomenclature; Petty may have tried it out. It is Petty's relationship with Marsenne which suggests why Petty did so. Petty had studied medicine and mathematics at Leyden, where he was on friendly terms with John Pell, professor of mathematics at Amsterdam. Pell had been brought into touch with Mersenne in 1639 when the latter had read and admired his *Idea of Mathematicks*, and Pell was also an old friend of a member of Mersenne's circle in Paris, Thomas Hobbes. When Petty moved to Paris in 1644 it is natural that Pell should have given him an introduction to Hobbes, for which Petty sends enthusiastic thanks in a letter of November 1645, which also mentions his frequent conversations with Mersenne. Petty's medical training would have provided him with one subject in which he would have shared a special interest with the French scholar.[51] As Casaubon noted, physicians were particularly concerned with the nomenclature of plants, and this problem was one which Mersenne had in mind in his discussion of a constructed language in *Harmonie Universelle*. But in 1640 Mersenne felt a special need for a universal language for botany. When corresponding with Haak in 1640 he constantly referred to the works of Gabriel Plattes, the agriculturist and botanist; Haak sent him two of them, but unfortunately they were in English and he had to reply: 'Je n'ay peu encore trouver personne pour me traduire les 2. traittés de mr. Plattes.' As Harcourt Brown has noted,[52] Mersenne took a special interest in problems of practical botany, and it is a not unreasonable supposition that he discussed his frustration with Petty in connection with his long-standing interest in a universal language. When Petty started work on his botanical character he may have known of Kinner's suggestions; we know nothing whatsoever about Petty's methods, but it is worth noting that Ward, who was working in association with Petty, refers specifically to the inspiration of mathematical characters and associates his quest with that of Cabbalists and Lullists, whose use of letters of the alphabet as symbols has been noted above. Moreover, we know that Ward's system of symbolization is entirely different from that of Kinner; the only common feature is the use of letter-symbols.[53]

Haak and Petty, members of the London club in which the Royal Society originated, and colleagues of Wilkins both in the club and after 1660 in the Royal Society itself, are shown to have enjoyed a friendship with a scholar who was the first to publish a plea for a universal language which would assist the dissemination of human knowledge; and Mersenne's may well have been the most important single influence on English efforts in this field. But it would be foolish to postulate any one route by which the idea entered the stream of our seventeenth-century culture. During the 1630s the concept was establishing itself in Europe among scholars who were in contact with England via the Hartlib circle. Johannes Bisterfeld, for example, Professor of Philosophy at Weissenberg, wrote to Hartlib in 1638 commenting on Comenius's views on the teaching of Latin as an international language, and asked why instead of using this old language a new vocabulary should not be created 'quorum, ut in omnibus scientiis experior, magna adhuc est necessitas et inopia, vel fingantur, vel saltem, quomodo fingi debeant et possint, accurate ostendatur'.[54] His words were recalled by a friend of Hartlib's when Dalgarno produced in 1657 his first attempt at a character, rather than a language

> the question wch I should make is whether (to vse Bisterfeldes woords in an exerpte you gave me at the time of our first acquaintance) there be a wisdome & reason in the characters of the Radixes . . . soo as that letters in woords, & strokes in characters, & parts of characters, doo truly analogize to elements of things or in things. (Hartlib manuscripts.)

The writer is Cheney Culpeper, who first met Hartlib in 1641, and who may thus in part have influenced Dalgarno to develop his simple 'character' to a philosophical language. Another scholar, whose editor was in close touch with Hartlib, was Campanella, who advocated a 'philosophical grammar' in a text published in 1638, but of which the preface is dated 15 March 1635. There are several references in the *Ephemerides* both to the works of Campanella, the best known of which is the Utopian *City of the Sun*, and to one Adami—and Tobias Adami was a Protestant enthusiast for the Catholic philosopher who edited his works and set up a school using his methods. Campanella writes of the formulation of a new language: 'Si quis nouam linguam philosophicè constituere vellet' he begins, and then describes the necessary steps, such as the construction of names from the nature and properties of objects, the abolition of synonyms and homonyms, and those features of grammar which are most desirable.[55]

Since we find the possibilities of a universal language being discussed by various European scholars in the 1630s, and certain features of it, such as the ordering of concepts and words, being considered even by English scholars like Henry Jacobs, there is no need to look to the manuscript of Comenius's *Via Lucis* as the inspiration of linguistic reformers from Lodowick to Wilkins in their search for a universal philosophical language. We have no proof that any of the linguistic reformers knew of it. Their works give the impression that they are interested in a universal language as one aspect of the dissemination and advancement of international learning; their occasional references to Comenius are mainly to his elementary Latin text-book; and their rare mention of the healing of disputes is part of an attitude towards the difficulties of verbal ambiguity which finds expression in many seventeenth-century English texts. From Johnston to Wilkins, they were living and working in an intellectual milieu from which they could draw all the elements of their linguistic method. Bacon was their master when they criticized language and attempted to find a remedy for its defects, but they found their immediate inspiration in the works of continental scholars of the 1630s who shared their scientific ideals. But it was an English scholar who finally achieved a genuine universal language; it proved unsatisfactory for scientific use, yet the *Essay*, with the work of Lodowick and Dalgarno, remains a monument to an age when educated men, from merchant to bishop, thought, spoke and wrote about language as never before, and possibly as never since.

Notes

1 Cave Beck suggested in his *Universal Character* (London, 1657) that the quest began in the mid-sixteenth century: 'This last Century of years, much hath been the discourse and expectation of learned men, concerning the finding out of an *Universal Character*' (f.A7r.). Theodore Bibliander's *De Ratione communi omnium linguarum* (Tiguri, 1548) contains what is probably one of the earliest discussions of the subject.

2 *The Tongues of Men* (London, 1937), p. 71.

3 Gulielmus Piso, *De Indiæ . . . Re Naturali et Medica* (Amsterdam, 1658), p. 114. Cf. *Essay*, p. 13.

4 Benjamin DeMott, 'The Sources and Development of John Wilkins' Philosophical Language', *JEGP* lvii (1958), p. 11. The suggestion of Comenius's influence was first made by DeMott in 'Comenius and the Real Character in England', *PMLA* 70 (1955), pp. 1068–1081. DeMott has also questioned Wilkins's scientific method, in 'Science versus Mnemonics', *Isis* 48 (1957), pp. 3–12. It is not possible to deal here with DeMott's allegation that Wilkins's approach to semantics was unscientific because he paid too much attention to mnemonic aids, but it should be noted that, in the seventeenth-century context, ease of recall of information was a scientific objective associated with Bacon's regret in the *Advancement of Learning* that memory, as one of the principal parts of the 'custody of knowledge', was but 'weakly enquired of' (*Philosophical Works*, ed. John M. Robertson (London, 1905), p. 120). Bacon also dealt with the problem of memory in a memorandum to Henry

Savile which was not published (in *Resuscitatio*) until 1657, when Wilkins was at work on his language. This text was cited as a source by John Beale, who was constructing a character for the Royal Society in the early 1660s (Sloane MS 4384, ff. 64–116).

[5] Cf. 'On the Sources of John Wilkins' Philosophical Language (1668)', *ES* xl (1959), pp. 208–214. The influence of Comenius is accepted by J. Knowlson, 'The Ideal Languages of Veiras . . .', *JHI* xxiv (1963), p. 273.

[6] An account of Hartlib and his relations with Comenius is given by George H. Turnbull in *Hartlib, Dury and Comenius* (Liverpool, 1947). Hartlib left many manuscripts containing comments on language and language-teaching. These occur especially frequently in his notebook known as the *Ephemerides*, and I am greatly indebted to Mrs. Turnbull and Professor W. Armytage for access to the manuscripts and to the late Professor Turnbull's uncompleted work on the *Ephemerides*.

[7] Cf. Turnbull, op. cit., p. 367. DeMott (1958, p. 4) says that the *Via Lucis* was translated in England; Turnbull states that there is no evidence whatsoever for this belief.

[8] The letter is reproduced in part by DeMott (1958).

[9] The chief projectors of Universal or 'Real' Characters were: William Bedell and his colleague Johnston (unfinished, but some details preserved in the *Ephemerides*); John Wilkins in *Mercury* (London, 1641); Francis Lodowick in *A Common Writing* (London, 1647); George Dalgarno (unpublished, details in Sloane MS 4377, 1657); Cave Beck, *Universal Character* (London, 1657); John Beale (unpublished, details in Sloane MS 4384, early 1660s). The following scholars planned universal philosophical languages: William Petty (a specialised botanical character, *c.* 1647—reference in *Ephemerides* 1650; no details known); Seth Ward (discussed in *Vindiciæ Academiarum* (Oxford, 1654)); Francis Lodowick, *Ground-work . . . for the Framing of a New Perfect Language* (London, 1652); George Dalgarno, *Ars Signorum* (London, 1661); John Wilkins, *Essay* (London, 1668). Henry Edmundson refers in passing to a universal language in his text-book of Latin, *Lingua Linguarum* (London, 1658).

[10] DeMott (1955), p. 1077.

[11] *Jana Amosa Komenského Korrespondence*, ed. A. Patera (Prague, 1892), p. 135.

[12] Ibid., p. 32.

[13] *A Reformation of Schooles* (London, 1642), p. 47.

[14] They are printed in *The Petty Papers* I, ed. Marquis of Lansdowne (London, 1927). Bacon's suggestion appears in the *Advancement of Learning* (*Works*, ed. Robertson, p. 120).

[15] G. Turnbull, *Samuel Hartlib* (London, 1920), p. 12.

[16] Sloane MS 897 (one of Lodowick's notebooks), f. 34v. This description of a 'Reall Caracter' shows a stage between character and language; he envisages a dictionary to enumerate 'things and their affections', but also involving some kind of 'subordination' and a universal grammar.

[17] Sloane MS 4377, f. 145r.

[18] *Vindiciæ Academiarum*, pp. 20–22.

[19] *Didascalocophus* (Oxford, 1680), p. 100, and Introduction, p. 1.

[20] Sloane MS 4377, f. 143r. The sheet refers to a '*Universal Character, and a new Rational Language*'; but it seems to mean his earlier shorthand character, because it mentions the forthcoming publication of testimonials from the Universities. One

such, included at f. 157, is dated May 1658, and is referred to as a 'universal character'. It does not refer at all to the ordering of concepts.

21 'That which first occasioned this Discourse, was the reading of a little Pamphlet, styled *Nuntius inanimatus*.' (f. A4r.)

22 A. Patera, op. cit., p. 77 (8 October 1643).

23 In *Comenius in England* (London, 1932).

24 For Matthew Ricci's *Journals* see *China in the Sixteenth Century*, trans. Louis J. Gallagher (New York, 1953). Wilkins himself cites Ricci, and was no doubt impressed by the claim 'This method of writing by drawing symbols instead of forming letters gives rise to a distinct mode of expression by which one is able, not only with a few phrases but with a few words, to set forth ideas with great clearness, which in our writing would have to be expressed in roundabout circumlocutions and perhaps with far less clarity' (p. 29).

25 In the letter to Mersenne of November 1629 in which Descartes comments on a scheme for a universal language. Cf. *Correspondence du P. Marin Mersenne* II, ed. C. de Waard (Paris, 1937), pp. 323–328.

26 The earlier system is described by William J. Carlton in *Timothe Bright* (London, 1911); the later system is called *Characterie* (London, 1588).

27 This quotation comes from the second edition: Iohannes Alsted *Encyclopædia Vniversa* (Leyden, 1649), I, p. 128; the first edition is dated 1630.

28 Cf. Arthur O. Lovejoy, *The Great Chain of Being* (Cambridge, Mass., 1936).

29 *Linguarum Cognatio* (London, 1639), p. 65. Seth Ward went to Merton in 1649. Jacobs is also mentioned in the *Ephemerides* (1634): 'In short tables hee would bring all the Languages'.

30 Charles Sorel, *La Science Universelle* IV (Paris, 1668), pp. 455–456. There are several references to Sorel's work on language in the Hartlib manuscripts. He composed a universal grammar and alphabet to which reference is made in 1637, and Kinner writes to Hartlib ten years later asking where he can obtain them.

31 Athanasius Kircher, *Œdipus Ægyptiacus* (Rome, 1653) II, 1, p. 228. For Lully's system cf. F. A. Yates, 'The Art of Ramon Lull', *Journal of the Warburg and Courtauld Institutes* xvii (1954), pp. 115–173.

32 Those features of Kinner's system which DeMott (1958, p. 7) sees as influencing Wilkins's method of notation could equally well have been derived from Bright's shorthand practice. In *Characterie* he distinguishes primitives and derivatives, the former denoted by symbols, the latter by points arranged round a character.

33 Letter among the Hartlib manuscripts, 4 September 1640.

34 Details of Wallis's work as a cryptographer are given by John Davys, *Essay on the Art of Decyphering* (London, 1737); and for cryptography and language cf. John Falconer, *Cryptomenysis Patefacta* (London, 1685).

35 *Præcursor Logicus* (Frankfurt, 1654) I, p. 90.

36 Sloane MS 417, f. 180v. (August 1637).

37 *Works*, ed. J. M. Robertson, pp. 523–524.

38 *A Reformation of Schooles*, pp. 48–49.

39 Robertson, op. cit., pp. 167, 119, 264.

40 *A Christian Dictionary* (5th ed., London, 1647), ff. A3v., A2v. The introductory matter is dated 1611.

41 *De Verborum usu* (London, 1647), pp. 20, 155. Beale, Sloane 4384, f. 64r.

42 *Characterie*, f. B6v.

[43] *Short Writing* (6th ed., London, 1646), p. 4.

[44] Sloane MS 4377, f. 145r.

[45] *Œuvres de Descartes*, ed. C. Adam and P. Tannery. *Correspondance* I (Paris, 1897), p. 572. Although the suggestion is not worked out at all, Mersenne is in fact putting forward the idea of the 'technical word', the meaning of which may be deduced from its form.

[46] Harcourt Brown, *Scientific Organizations in Seventeenth Century France* (Baltimore, 1934), p. 32.

[47] *Recueil General des Questions traitées és Conferences du Bureau d'Adresse* (Lyons, 1666) II, pp. 154–155.

[48] Sloane MS 4279, f. 104 (1639); partly translated by Harcourt Brown, op. cit., pp. 45–47.

[49] A. Patera, op. cit., p. 32.

[50] E. Fitzmaurice, *Life of Sir William Petty* (London, 1895), pp. 15, 20–21.

[51] Fitzmaurice, ibid., p. 7.

[52] Harcourt Brown, op. cit., pp. 49–50.

[53] DeMott (1958) gives Kinner's system. In a technical word, the consonant of the first syllable denoted a primary or secondary quality of the plant and the first vowel the degree of that quality. The second syllable denoted the particular attribute (e.g. curative) and the third the plant's provenance. Ward suggested (*Vindiciæ*, p. 21) the limitation of all the 'first & most simple things & notions' to the number of consonants, with their 'modall variations' denoted by vowels and diphthongs. The systems have nothing in common except what could have been derived independently from the Cabbalah or Lullism, or possibly from a text on memory, *Le Magazin des Sciences* of Lambert Schenkelius (Paris, 1623). Schenkelius says that words must be constructed in such a way 'Que l'image de la premiere lettre ou syllable soit mise en son lieu, & pour la seconde & troisiesme, il y aye quelque action, de laquelle la premiere lettre represente la personne qui fait ceste action' (p. 235).

[54] Johannes Kvačala, 'Die pädagogische Reform des Comenius in Deutschland . . .', *Monumenta Germaniae Paedagogica* XXVI (1903), p. 114.

[55] *Philosophiæ Rationalis Partes Quinque* (Paris, 1638), p. 152.

Mon Vowel Systems: A Problem in Phonological Statement

H. L. SHORTO

The suggestion that the phonological facts of many languages might with advantage be stated on a polysystemic rather than on a monosystemic basis, put forward by Professor Firth in an article in 1948,[1] led to some rapid and striking advances, not least in the field of loanword study. Firth observed that for Tamil and Telugu 'it is necessary to assume at least three phonological systems: non-brahman Dravidian, Sanskrito-dravidian, and Sanskritic';[2] for Siamese Miss E.J.A. Henderson wished to posit 'upwards of a dozen' systems and subsystems.[3] The usefulness of such a polysystemic approach is by no means restricted to the problems raised in a language by the occurrence of bodies of imperfectly assimilated loanwords. In Cambodian, for example, words may be distinguished by a complex of features which includes both elements ascribed to 'register' and differences in vowel quality.[4] It is necessary to state separate vowel systems for words on the two registers. A similar situation obtains in Mon, except that the distinguishing complex may further include features affecting the articulation of prevocalic consonantal elements; and not only separate vowel systems but separate consonant systems have to be stated. In this paper I apply polysystemic analysis to a somewhat idiosyncratic problem in the description of the Mon vowel systems: that of oppositions which occur in an extremely limited number of contexts, between elements the distribution of which is in other respects complementary.

The form of the language under discussion is spoken Mon (SM) as exemplified in the usage of U Wāyama (**ləkùn wɛ̀ayəmɛ̀ʔ**), who acted as my research assistant at the School of Oriental and African Studies during 1949–50. U Wāyama was born in Kawkyaik, Kawbein township, Karen State, and is now resident in the Thwezegan Mon monastery, Bahan, Rangoon. The transcription used is that employed in my *Dictionary of Modern Spoken Mon*,[5] supplemented where necessary by phonological transcriptions enclosed between oblique strokes / /.

In the analysis on which this paper is based, the word is one of an ordered series of levels of abstraction from textual material at which patterns are established as a manifold of syntagmatic structures and the paradigmatic systems of commuting terms—in this case sounds—which constitute them. Thus a word **ka** might be referred to a structure CV^R, for which it would be necessary to state a C, a V, and an R system; **k**, **a**, and head register being terms of these three systems respectively. I do not here offer a full analysis of SM word patterns, but give by way of introduction a sufficient outline to set the particular discussion in its context. In order to complete the description of the language there have to be posited, in addition to the primary pattern, a number of secondary patterns of a fragmentary nature; but the present discussion is limited to the primary pattern except where otherwise noted.[6]

Word structures. Words in SM may be either monosyllabic or disyllabic. In disyllabic words the first syllable is unstressed and generally has as its nucleus a short neutral vowel, represented in the transcription by **ə**. This procedure could be justified theoretically as providing an indication of syllabicity, which may itself be distinctive in many types of environment: cf. **kreaŋ** 'eugenia', **kəreaŋ** 'Karen'; **kha** 'spinach', **kəha** 'monastic robe'; **hne** 'rudder', **həne** 'vegetables'; **hla** 'pond', **həla** 'wheel'. In other environments there is no syllabic distinction of this kind: **thah** 'tray'; **kəto** 'ear'. In such cases words are transcribed as monosyllabic or disyllabic on grounds of their phonetic similarity to words of the first group.

An exception to the foregoing is provided by a group of words, including some trisyllables, the first syllable of which is transcribed as **iˀ-**. It might be interpreted phonologically as /yə/; but the group is in any case most conveniently assigned to a secondary pattern, along with words with a first syllable **ə-**, on account of differences in the structural possibilities of the second syllable.

All words have one of two registers. In addition, a monosyllable consists of a consonantal initial, which may be simple or complex; a vocalic nucleus, which may be simple or (at least phonetically) complex; and in some cases a simple consonantal final. A disyllable consists of a simple consonantal initial; a central vowel **ə**; a medial consonant or, infrequently, a consonant complex; a vocalic nucleus; and in some cases a consonantal final.

The paratonal register distinction is broadly similar to that described for Cambodian by Henderson.[7] Its exponents are distributed throughout the articulatory complex but exclude pitch features. Chest register, symbolized by a grave accent placed over the vowel (**kèt**, **həkòa**), is characterized by breathy voice quality in association with a general laxness of the speech organs and a relatively centralized articulation of vowels. The more frequent head register is unmarked in the transcription (**ket**, **həkoa**); it is characterized by clear voice quality, relative tenseness, and peripheral vowel articulation.

Both vowel systems and pre-nuclear consonant systems have to be stated separately for head-register and chest-register words.

The possible structures are illustrated in the following table. The formulation there is, however, pre-phonological in so far as it concerns the nuclear elements, and will be modified in the course of the subsequent discussion.

CV^{R}	**ka** 'tea-kettle'	CVC^{R}	**kaŋ** 'ribs of boat'
CVV^{R}	**kao** 'elder brother'	CVVC^{R}	**paoh** 'tenth month'
CCV^{R}	**kra** 'seal'	CCVC^{R}	**kraŋ** 'byre'
CCVV^{R}	**krao** 'arum'	CCVVC^{R}	**kraoh** 'male'
CəCV^{R}	**həka** 'lay supporter'	CəCVC^{R}	**həkam** 'water-weed'
CəCVV^{R}	**həkao** 'corner'	CəCVVC^{R}	**həkao**ˀ 'self'
CəCCV^{R}	**kəthi** 'rich man'	CəCCVC^{R}	**kəchip** 'seal'
CəCCVV^{R}	**kəchao** 'red ant'	CəCCVVC^{R}	**həprao**ˀ '*Dillenia indica*'

I have found no occurrences referable to the structures CəCCV^{R} or CəCCVVC^{R} among chest-register words.

The total potentialities may be summarized by the formula: (C(ə(C)))CV(V)(C)^{R}.

The vowel systems

'Der Vokalismus des Mon', it has been said with some justice, 'ist äusserst kompliziert'.[8] In fact the possibilities of occurrence of vowels are subject to considerable variation according to the nature of both preceding and following consonants, in addition to the vowel-register correlation already mentioned. The limitations are greatest in respect of the postvocalic consonant, and as a first step towards the statement of the systems I shall proceed by listing possible segments -V(V)(C).

This incidentally helps to clarify a secondary issue, raised by the occurrence of what phonetically are falling diphthongs both with and without a following consonant. A segment such as **-ai** might in theory be analysed either as -VV /ai/ or as -VC /ay/. In practice it does not seem that the distinction between monophthongs and diphthongs is of much phonological importance in SM.[9]

82 segments -V(V)(C) occur in head-register words, as against 55 in chest-register words. We may consider the simpler chest-register series first.

Nucleus + final: chest register

-i	**-iʔ**	**-ih**			**-it**	**-in**	**-ip**	**-im**
-e	**-eʔ**	**-eh**			**-et**	**-en**	**-ep**	**-em**
-ɛa	**-ɛʔ**	**-ɛh**	**-ɛak**	**-ɛaŋ**				
			-ak	**-aŋ**	**-at**	**-an**		
-ɜ	**-ɜʔ**	**-ɜh**	**-ɜk**	**-ɜŋ**	**-ɜt**	**-ɜn**	**-ɜp**	**-ɜm**
-o	**-oʔ**	**-oh**	**-ok**	**-oŋ**	**-ot**	**-on**	**-op**	**-om**
-u	**-uʔ**	**-uh**			**-ut**	**-un**	**-up**	**-um**
-ai			**-aik**	**-aiŋ**				
			-oik	**-oiŋ**				
-ui								
-oa								

The symbols of the transcription have their I.P.A. values except as otherwise noted. Final plosives are unexploded. As was stated above, all vowels in chest-register words are somewhat centralized; **i** and **u** before **h**, and **e** before **ʔ**, **h**, are more centralized and open than in other contexts. **ɛ** is a close variety, slightly diphthongized before **ʔ** and **h** in all but rapid speech; **a** represents a front variety before **t**, **n** and a back variety before **k**, **ŋ**, **i**; **o** is a mid back rounded vowel.

From the table it emerges that (1) the possibilities are identical before any given plosive and the corresponding nasal; (2) they are identical before **ʔ** and **h**, and, if the segments **-ai**, **-ui**, **-oa** are set aside, in the open syllable; (3) two front-closing diphthongs are distinguished in the open syllable (**ai**, **ui**) and before velars (**ai**, **oi**); (4) the same possibilities occur in the contexts listed under (2) and before dentals, except that **ɛ(a)** in the former case corresponds to **a** in the latter.

We shall see that in respect of head-register words, (1) above holds good, and the possibilities are furthermore identical before dentals and labials; statements similar to (2) and (3) can be made, with some minor anomalies in the case corresponding to (2) which are dealt with below; but (4) is inapplicable.

I therefore propose to interpret **-ai, -ui** as -VC, /ay/, /uy/, and **-aik, -aiŋ, -oik, -oiŋ,** in view of the systemic parallelism and degree of phonetic similarity, as /ac/, /uc/, /aɲ/, /uɲ/. **-oa** is also interpreted as -VC, /uɥ/. It may be noted that the sounds transcribed as **k, ŋ** in the segments **-aik,** etc., are a forward variety, the fronting being more marked in the case of the plosive and greatest in **-aik.**

It is then possible to account for vowel occurrences in chest-register words in relation to those of final consonants by positing the following five systems:

(1) in open syllables and before **ʔ, h,** and dentals: **i e ɛ/a ɜ o u**;
(2) before velars: **ɛ a ɜ o**;
(3) before palatals (**y, c, ɲ**): **a u**;
(4) before labials: **i e ɜ o u**; and
(5) before **ɥ**: **u.**

Variation entailed by the nature of the prevocalic consonant is minimal in chest-register words and is restricted to the case where **n** immediately precedes the vowel (as a term of the last C system in any segment (C(ə(C)))C-, e.g. **n-, hn-, kən-**). **a** is not then found before velars nor **ɜ** in other contexts; vowel systems (3) and (5) are unaffected. It is thus necessary to postulate altogether eight contextually differentiated systems to account for vowel occurrences in chest-register words. On the other hand, the sequences initially designated as -V(V)(C) can be reduced to -V(C) in a statement of phonological structure.

Head register. I have in the foregoing indicated the process of analysis as well as stating its result, as a guide to the steps to be taken in elucidating the considerably more complex facts of head-register words. The segments -V(C) which occur in these are as follows.

Nucleus + final: head register

-i	**-iʔ**	**-ih**			**-it**	**-in**	**-ip**	**-im**
-əe	**-əeʔ**	**-əeh**						
-e	**-eʔ**	**-eh**	**-eak**	**-eaŋ**	**-et**	**-en**	**-ep**	**-em**
	-ɛʔ		**-ɛk**	**-ɛŋ**	**-ɛt**	**-ɛn**	**-ɛp**	**-ɛm**
-a	**-aʔ**	**-ah**	**-ak**	**-aŋ**	**-at**	**-an**	**-ap**	**-am**
-ɜ			**-ɜk**	**-ɜŋ**				
-ɒ	**-ɒʔ**	**-ɒh**			**-ɒt**	**-ɒn**	**-ɒp**	**-ɒm**
-ɔ	**-ɔʔ**	**-ɔh**	**-ɔk**	**-ɔŋ**	**-ɔt**	**-ɔn**	**-ɔp**	**-ɔm**
-o			**-ok**	**-oŋ**	**-ot**	**-on**	**-op**	**-om**
-u	**-uʔ**	**-uh**			**-ut**	**-un**	**-up**	**-um**

-ao	**-aoˀ**	**-aoh**		
-ai			**-aik**	**-aiŋ**
			-ɔik	**-ɔiŋ**
-oi			**-oik**	**-oiŋ**
-ui				
-ea				
-oa				

Final plosives are unexploded. **i** and **u** before **h**, and **e** before **ˀ**, **h**, are somewhat centralized and open, approximating to [ɪ], [ɷ], [ȩ]. **ɛ** before dentals and labials is cardinal; before velars it approximates to [æ]; before **ˀ** it represents a short falling diphthong [ɪə]. **a** represents a front variety before dentals and labials, a central variety before **ˀ** and **h**, and a back variety in open syllables and before **k**, **ŋ**, **i**, **o**. **ɒ** is a fairly open unrounded vowel between back and central. **o** before plosives approximates to [ɷ].

It is apparent that, as in chest-register words, the possibilities are identical before any plosive and the corresponding nasal—and before dentals and labials in addition—and the same number of diphthongs moving to a close front position occur in the open syllable (**ai**, **oi**, **ui**) and before velars (**ai**, **ɔi**, **oi**); **ɔe**, with its different closing point and distribution, is dissociated from this series. In order to derive parallel sets of vowels before **ˀ** and **h** and in open syllables, however, it is necessary to exclude a more heterogeneous collection of segments than before: **-ɜ**, **-o**, **-ɛˀ** as well as **-ai**, **-oi**, **-ui**, **-ea**, **-oa**. Even then agreement is lacking between the possibilities in those contexts and those before dentals and labials.

I shall interpret **-ai**, **-oi**, **-ui**; **-aik**, **-ɔik**, **-oik**; **-aiŋ**, **-ɔiŋ**, **-oiŋ** as respectively /ay/, /oy/, /uy/; /ac/, /oc/, /uc/; /aɲ/, /oɲ/, /uɲ/, treating the relative phonetic similarity between the vocalic elements in **-ɔik**, **-ɔiŋ** on the one hand and **-ɔe**, **-ɔeˀ**, **-ɔeh** on the other as coincidental. **-ea**, **-oa** may likewise be interpreted as /iɥ/, /uɥ/. Leaving aside for the moment the problematical contexts of open syllables and those with final **ˀ**, **h**, we can then set up four alternant vowel systems corresponding nearly to systems (2)–(5) in chest-register words:

(*a*) before velars: **e ɛ a ɜ ɔ o**;
(*b*) before palatals: **a o u**;
(*c*) before dentals and labials: **i e ɛ a ɒ ɔ o u**; and
(*d*) before **ɥ**: **i u**.

The greater complexity of these systems compared with those in chest-register words will be noted.[10] At (*a*) a six-term system corresponds to the four-term system (2) above; at (*b*) a three-term system to the two-term system (3); at (*c*) an eight-term system to the six-term system (1) before dentals and the five-term system (4) before labials; and at (*d*) a two-term system to the one-term system (5).

The segments still to be accounted for are:

-i	**-əe**	**-e**		**-a**	**-ɜ**	**-ɒ**	**-ɔ**	**-o**	**-u**	**-ao**
-iˀ	**-əeˀ**	**-eˀ**	**-ɛˀ**	**-aˀ**		**-ɒˀ**	**-ɔˀ**		**-uˀ**	**-aoˀ**
-ih	**-əeh**	**-eh**		**-ah**		**-ɒh**	**-ɔh**		**-uh**	**-aoh**

Of the eleven vowels which are represented in these contexts, four pairs (**i**/**əe**, **ɛ**/**a**, **ɜ**/**ɒ**, **u**/**ao**) have a very limited oppositive value; and the occurrence of the members of each pair can be largely predicated by reference to the prevocalic consonant. This is true also of the vowels **i**/**ɛ** in system (*c*) above; **u**, though it cannot be paired in the same way, has a similarly restricted distribution in that system and before **y**.

The sounds in question are contextually undifferentiated in the following pairs and sets of words: (**i**/**əe**: 3 cases) **hi** 'to float', **hi** 'to glance covertly', **kəmaˀ hi hoŋ**[11] 'golden beetle'/**həe** 'to faint'; **kəniˀ** 'day before yesterday'/**kənəeˀ** 'nipa palm'; **kəli** 'day after tomorrow'/ **kələe** 'wild plum', **yòa kələn kələe** 'dry leprosy'; (**i**/**ɛ**: 1 case) **həmit** 'mosquito', **nəm həmit** '*Zinziber barbatum*'/**hma həmɛt** 'sea'.

(**ɛ**/**a**: 1 case) **cɛˀ** 'to eat', **cɛˀ**, generic particle/**caˀ** 'to be defeated', **caˀ** 'to begin to'.

(**ɜ**/**ɒ**: 1 case) **chɜ** 'to meet'/**chɒ** 'to be fleecy'.

(**u**/**ao**.) There appear to be no restrictions on the distribution of **ao** in open syllables, in which **u** and **ao** are contextually undifferentiated in 5 cases. Before **ˀ**, **h** they are thus undifferentiated in 3 cases: **puh toa** 'index finger', **puh** 'to fillip'/**paoh** 'tenth month'; **nuh** 'pellet-bow'/ **naoh** 'turtle'; **kəmuh** 'bamboo chick', **kəmuh** 'to sprinkle'/**kəmaoh** 'cool'.

In addition **i**, **əe** are opposed in four cases when primary-pattern words are compared with segments of secondary-pattern polysyllables, but there are then further distinctive features attributable to the opposition of patterns as such: cf. e.g. **nəe** 'floor', **nila** 'sapphire', where the vowel in **nəe** is appreciably longer than that in **ni-**.

In stating the distribution of these vowels it is sometimes convenient to speak of a particular sequence as 'normal' and to seek special explanations of the few words which diverge from it, even though the facts may not justify relegating them to a secondary pattern. The distribution of **ɛ**, **a**, which is somewhat aberrant compared with that of the other pairs, may be disposed of first. **-ɛʔ** occurs only following **c**, in the words **cɛʔ** 'to eat',[12] **cɛʔ**, generic particle, **həcɛʔ** 'to feed', **lɛ̀a həcɛʔ** 'to relate'; **-cɛʔ** is also found as a segment of the secondary-pattern words **kitcɛʔ** 'matter', **sətcɛʔ** 'faith, to be faithful'. **-aʔ** follows **c** in structures CVC only, in the two words cited above; and in the secondary-pattern words **pənca**ʔ **kanɔe** 'nut-gall tree', **pəncaʔkao** 'kind of medicinal plant'.

-ɛʔ appears to be the normal sequence following **c**. Of the two primary-pattern exceptions, **caʔ** 'to begin to' is a Burmese loan; while the initial of **caʔ** 'to be defeated' can, by a somewhat elaborate argument, be related to a 'morphophoneme' ky—a conclusion which fits with the restriction of the sequence to CVC structures. (In the dialect of Lopburi, which distinguishes **c** ≠ **ky**, **ch** ≠ **khy** and has few Burmese loans, **ɛ** and **a** are in complementary distribution, the words for 'to eat' and 'to be defeated' being pronounced [**tɕɪəʔ**] and [**ṭaʔ**] respectively.)

(**i**/**ɔe**, **i**/**ɛ**.) **i** occurs in the contexts under discussion following **k**, **c**, **y**, **h** when this is preceded by another consonant, and the glottal consonants **ʔ**, **d**, **b**; and, before **h**, also following **s**. **ɔe**, or before dentals and labials **ɛ**, occurs following **t**, **r**, **l**, the nasals **ŋ**, **ɲ**, **n**, **m**, and—except for **ɔe** before **h**—**s**.[13] Both **i** and **ɔe** or **ɛ** occur following **h** in structures CV(C), **p**, and **w**.

Primary-pattern exceptions to the foregoing are **kəli** 'day after tomorrow'; **pəli** 'to be deceitful'; **həlin** 'to be viscid'; **cìp klip** 'to be subtle'; **kəniʔ** 'day before yesterday'; **həmit** 'mosquito', **nəm həmit** '*Zinziber barbatum*'.

(**ɜ**/**ɒ**.) In the open context **ɜ** occurs following **c**, **y**, **h**, and glottals, **ɒ** following all other consonants except **n**, in respect of which a similar restriction operates to that noted for chest-register words on p. 402: **a** does not occur following it before velars nor **ɜ**, **ɒ** in other contexts. Exceptions are **phyɒ** 'to tickle'; **chɒ** 'to be fleecy'; **phɒ** 'effect'; **klɜ** 'dog'; **pɜ** 'to be surplus'.[14]

(**u**/**ao**.) The distribution of these vowels varies somewhat as between the several contexts under discussion. In the open context **u** occurs following **c**, **h**, and glottals only, while **ao** occurs following all types of consonant. Before **ʔ**, **u** occurs following **h** when this is preceded by another consonant and following glottals; **ao** following all other types of consonant, including **h** in structures CVC, except **c** and **w**. Before **h**, **u** occurs following **k**, **c**, **p**, and glottals, **ao** following **t**, both **u** and

ao following **r** and nasals; there are no relevant instances with pre-vocalic **h**, **s**, **y**, **l**, or **w**. Before dentals, labials, and **y**, **u** occurs only following **k**, **c**, **h**, **y**, **w**, and glottals.

Exceptions involving these vowels are more numerous: **həmuʔ** '*Parashorea stellata*'; **paoh** 'tenth month'; **tut** 'to whistle'; **put** 'base of spine'; **sum krùm** 'camphor tree'; **hmui** 'to be pliant'; **thui hərui** 'to be confused'; **plut** 'to slander'; **pəlup** 'to bring in'; **to pəlui** 'sewing-thread'. All but the first two of these might indeed be accounted for by an extension of the last statement above; but their isolated character, as well as factors now to be discussed, militate against such a solution.

Of the 22 exceptions noted in addition to **caʔ**, 17 are in one way or another suspect. Three (**pəli**, **pɜ**, **həmuʔ**) are loanwords from Burmese and three more (**phɒ**, **paoh**, **put**) from Indo-Aryan languages.[15] Three (**cìp klip**, **sum krùm**, **thui hərui**) exemplify phrasal rhyme; **hmui** does so in its common collocation **hmui həwùi** 'to sway in the wind', which links it with a phonaesthetic series connected with swaying, swinging, rocking: **həwùi**, **ui**, **kui**, **kəhùi**, **dəŋ dui**; since **paoh** occurs most frequently in the collocation **hətaoʔ paoh** 'tenth month', phrasal assonance may play a similar part in its vocalism. **plut** and **pəlup** show the results of analogical levelling; cf. the morphologically related forms **lùt** 'to commit a fault', **lùp** 'to go in', and the unlevelled **plop** 'to introduce'; and so perhaps does **həmit** 'mosquito' if speakers associate it with **kit** 'to bite'; **həmit kit** 'I am being bitten by the mosquitoes' is a frequent collocation. **tut** is an onomatope. **kəniʔ** is probably an arbitrary deformation of **kəneʔ** 'yesterday', and its vocalism may be reflected

(-)C-	-V			-Vʔ		-Vh		-Vt &c.		-Vy
c	**i**	**ɜ**	**u, ao**	**i**		**i**	**u**	**i**	**u**	
(-)Ch	**i**	**ɜ**	**u, ao**	**i**	**u**	**i**		**i**	**u**	**u**
ʔ, d, b	**i**	**ɜ**	**u, ao**	**i**	**u**	**i**	**u**	**i**	**u**	**u**
y	**i**	**ɜ**	**ao**	**i**	**ao**	**i**		**i**	**u**	**u**
k	**i**	**ɒ**	**ao**		**ao**	**i**	**u**	**i**	**u**	**u**
s	**əe**	**ɒ**	**ao**	**əe**	**ao**	**i**		**ɛ**		
r, l	**əe**	**ɒ**	**ao**	**əe**	**ao**		**u, ao**	**ɛ**		
ŋ, ɲ, m	**əe**	**ɒ**	**ao**	**əe**	**ao**	**əe**	**u, ao**	**ɛ**		
n	**əe**		**ao**	**əe**	**ao**		**u, ao**	**ɛ**		
t	**əe**	**ɒ**	**ao**	**əe**	**ao**		**ao**	**ɛ**		
#h	**i, əe**	**ɜ**		**əe**	**ao**			**ɛ**	**u**	**u**
p	**i, əe**	**ɒ**	**ao**	**əe**	**ao**		**u**	**i**		
w	**i**	**ɒ**	**ao**	**əe**				**i, ɛ**	**u**	**u**

in that of **kəli**; the same structural relation obtains between **kənaʔ** 'three days ago' and **kəla** 'in three days' time'. Finally, the initial complex of **chɒ** can be related to a special 'morphophoneme', khy.[16]

These distributions are tabulated at the foot of p. 406.

To state these facts in terms of the alternant systems invoked hitherto would not be impossible, but it would be a lengthy procedure. However, it seems useful in the course of the phonological description to take cognizance of two polar vowel systems found in certain contexts: one including **i, ɜ, u** which follows **c, h** when this is preceded by another consonant, and glottals, and another including **ɔe/ɛ, ɒ, ao** which follows **t**; except before **h** a similar system can be posited following **s, r, l,** and nasals. Systems of intermediate or mixed type are found following **k** and **y**, while the occurrences following **h** in structures CV(C), **p**, and **w** are perhaps best explained in terms of an 'overlap' of systems.[17]

To arrive at parallel sets of vowels in open syllables and before **ʔ** and **h**, even in those contexts where there is no overlap, it is necessary to account for the segments **-o** and, where it is opposed to **-u, -ao.** This might be done by interpreting them as /ow/ and /aw/ respectively, a solution which assumes an overlap not of systems but of patterns—a form **kəsao** might equally be referred to CəCVC /kəsaw/ or CəCV /kəsu/. In the case of this particular form comparison with morphologically related words supports the assumption of bivalence; cf. **kəsao** 'curse', **chao** 'to curse'; **kəsao** 'writing', **chu** 'to write'.[18]

It would then be possible to set up, in the extreme cases, two related sets of vowel systems which more nearly resemble the systems postulated for chest-register words: in open syllables and before **ʔ** and **h**, (i) **i e a ɜ ɔ u**, (ii) **ɔe e a ɒ ɔ ao**; before dentals and labials, (i) **i e a ɒ ɔ o u**, (ii) **e ɛ a ɒ ɔ o**; and before **y**, (i) **a o u**, (ii) **a o.** I do not suggest that it is desirable to dispense with any of these symbols; I wish to draw attention to the functional difference between an opposition such as **i** ≠ **ɔe** and one such as **i** ≠ **e.**

In each of the linked pairs one vowel—**i, ɛ(ʔ), ɜ, u**—bears a close phonetic resemblance to a particular term of the relevant chest-register systems. It is interesting that the four vowels in question are not used in reciting the traditional syllabary; *kī, kit,* for example, are then pronounced **kɔe, kɛt**, although such sequences are not met with in SM or in the ordinary reading pronunciation. Henderson found that in Cambodian a sequence of head-register consonant and chest-register vowel, or vice versa, was the mark of a secondary pattern especially appropriate to loanwords.[19] The superficially similar phenomena in

SM can hardly be given a similar history, but the divergence of vowel qualities in different contexts has a like disruptive effect; and the overlapping following **p** and **w**, with other anomalous occurrences, suggests the filling of *cas vides*, sometimes no doubt by interdialectal borrowing.[20]

The asymmetrical distribution of the SM vowels can only be fully explained by reference to comparative and historical data, such as have been glanced at here and there in the course of this paper. This does not absolve us from assigning it a place in a purely descriptive study, if necessary by reference to considerations of 'oppositive value' or 'functional load'. The invocation of such concepts as 'overlapping' systems and 'partly complementary' distribution, objectionable as they are in many ways, may be justified in the measure in which they enable us to handle the facts of language in all their order and disarray.

Notes

1 'Sounds and prosodies', *TPS* 1948, pp. 127 ff., reprinted in J.R.Firth, *Papers in linguistics* 1934–1951 (Oxford University Press, London, 1957), pp. 121 ff.

2 *Papers in linguistics*, p. 121, n. 1.

3 'The phonology of loanwords in some South-East Asian languages', *TPS* 1951, p. 132, n. 4.

4 Eugénie J.A.Henderson, 'The main features of Cambodian pronunciation', *BSOAS* xiv.1 (1952), pp. 149 ff.

5 Oxford University Press, London, etc., 1962.

6 For 'structure', 'system', cf. R.H.Robins, 'Formal divisions in Sundanese', *TPS* (1953), p. 109, n. 2, and *passim*; and for other terms Shorto, 'Word and syllable patterns in Palaung', *BSOAS* xxiii.3 (1960), pp. 544–545. In this terminology 'primary pattern' corresponds to Henderson's 'primary system' ('The phonology of loanwords', p. 132), 'secondary pattern' to her 'subsystem'.

7 'Cambodian pronunciation', pp. 151–152.

8 Heinz-Jürgen Pinnow, *Versuch einer historischen Lautlehre der Kharia-Sprache* (Harrassowitz, Wiesbaden, 1959), p. 47.

9 In contradistinction, for example, to Palaung, where one set of monophthongs is opposed to another largely diphthongal set of 'ə-vowels': Shorto, 'Word and syllable patterns', pp. 549–552.

10 Whereas in Cambodian the chest-register systems are the more complex: Henderson, 'Cambodian pronunciation', pp. 153–158.

11 The citation in word lists of a polyrhemic phrase implies that a given word occurs only in that phrase, not necessarily that its vocalism can be attributed to the phrasal pattern.

12 It is interesting that the probably cognate Cambodian word **sì** 'to eat' is phonologically aberrant: Henderson, 'The phonology of loanwords', pp. 147–148.

13 Only one instance of **-əeh** was noted: **pəròik kəməeh** 'black pepper'. There may be an effect of phrasal assonance here, as in **hətaoˀ paoh**, infra; the initial **k** is historically irregular and represents a special phrasal development.

[14] U Wāyama recognized **sɜ** as a possible alternative form to **sɒ** 'sheep'. I have recorded **pəyɒ** as a variant of **pəyɜ** 'boundary' from speakers whose dialect did not appreciably differ from his.

[15] The etymologies of these words will be found in Shorto, *Dictionary of Modern SM.*

[16] The Lopburi dialect has [tɕhɜː] 'to meet', [ɕɒ̟ː] 'to be fleecy'; **ɜ** and **ɒ** are probably in complementary distribution.

[17] For **h** in structures CV(C) morphophonemic analysis suggests a similar bivalency to that found for **c** and **ch**. This is borne out by historical grammar, which relates **hi**, etc., to literary Mon (LM) *hī*, etc., **həe**, etc., to LM *sṅī*, etc.

[18] The proposed solution also assumes asymmetry between the registers, since in chest-register words no final **w** was posited. The Lopburi dialect, however, distinguishes, e.g., **mɛ̀a** 'to crouch', **mɛ̀aw** 'to suck'.

[19] 'The phonology of loanwords', p. 147.

[20] Compare the alternative pronunciations of **sɒ** and **pəyɜ** recorded in n. 14 above.

Beginning the Study of Lexis

J. McH. SINCLAIR

It might sound strange to suggest that great difficulties lie in the way of anyone who wants to study the vocabulary of a language. One could point to the great dictionaries and thesauri, the fat concordances and the humbler word-lists, or one could note that the popular accounts of the history of languages are often little more than histories of their vocabulary. Nevertheless, if one wishes to study the 'formal' aspects of vocabulary organization, all sorts of problems lie ahead, problems which are not likely to yield to anything less imposing than a very large computer. The reasons why these problems arise plunge us into the study of lexis.[1]

I am not here going to defend the setting-up of lexis as an independent part of language **form**. That is done in a paper presenting the present approach to lexis by M.A.K. Halliday elsewhere in this volume.[2] I take it for granted that it is desirable and necessary to look at the internal patterns of language from two different, interpenetrating aspects. When we are studying language form, we are concerned to examine the way in which patterns recur, without taking into account other patterns which lie outside language, patterns of social or natural organization. It would be surprising indeed if a great many of these external patterns were not reflected in language, but we try not to inflate this expectation into preconception.

Let us consider three words: *tome*, *paperback* and *cruelty*. The first two share a non-linguistic notional similarity—in an 11-plus test, we would all select *cruelty* as the odd word out. The first two occur in the same paragraph in Roget.[3] But if we consider the chances relative to the total frequency of any given two of them occurring within a short stretch of language, there is little to choose between them. No pair would get better odds than the others. All the **collocations**[4] are unlikely.

This is not to say that the patterns of language form give us no way of pairing the first two against the third; we may well find that *tome* and *paperback*, while showing no special tendency to co-occur, may share collocations with other words which are not associated with *cruelty*, words like *edition*, *bookshop*, *paper*, *print*. If we find such patterns, we satisfy our expectations, but express them in terms of the way in which language is internally organized, without having assumed in the first place that their similarity of reference was *a priori* a similarity reflected in linguistic form.

The two interpenetrating ways of looking at language form are **grammar** and **lexis**. In grammar we look at the patterns of language as if they could be described by a large number of separate choices, each choice being from a small list of possibilities. In each case, the possibilities can be itemized in full, and we can talk of choosing one item *rather than* another. The choice between Active and Passive Voice in the verbal group in English offers a typical example of a grammatical **system.** Every verbal group is either one or the other, and there are only two possible choices.

I used the words *as if* above. Grammar organizes language form in its own terms, and generally ignores any patterns that do not resolve themselves into systems. Items involved are listed, at the end of each piece of grammatical description, as items between which grammar has failed to distinguish.[5] If grammar accounted for the whole of language form, then this situation would not be satisfactory, and the grammarian would have to try to continue, using material which would get more and more intractable to his methods, and getting less and less generality for his efforts.

But running parallel to grammar is lexis, which describes the tendencies of items to collocate with each other. A study of these tendencies ought to tell us facts about languages that cannot be got by grammatical analysis, since such tendencies cannot be expressed in terms of small sets of choices. One lexical item is not chosen *rather than* another, lexical items do not contrast with each other in the same sense as grammatical classes contrast. There are virtually no impossible collocations, but some are much more likely than others.[6] At the present time, lexical statements look very much weaker than statements made using the precise and uncompromising machinery of grammar. There is a much less elaborate framework to lexical descriptions and much less certainty in the statements. Thus *he is taught* contrasts with *he teaches* in one grammatical system, with *he was taught* in another and with *he isn't taught* in another; but we cannot so describe the difference between *teaches*, *learns*, *reads*, *studies*, . . . etc.; what we can say about these is that they often occur close to each other and in the company of items like *history*, *desk*, *class*.

This aspect of the patterning of language has been known for a long time, and occasional references to it are found in description, particularly when the patterns are strong and tending towards the cliché. It is easy enough to hint at it, give a few examples, and move on. It is at present impossible to *prove* even the assertions about lexical patterns that I have made, or to justify calling any of the words quoted **lexical items** (and so suggest that they are identified units of a description) or to say anything at all objective about the lexical structure of a language. Whereas we can collect a few thousand examples of the verbal group and notice what patterns recur, there is no such general lexical category as 'verbal group' turning up several times a sentence, and there is no easy way of collecting a few thousand occurrences of any lexical item. Furthermore, it seems likely that the more common items will be much more difficult to describe than the rare ones.[7]

Consequently the theory of lexis is fairly rudimentary; it may satisfy our intuitions but it has not been shown to be valid and we have yet to see what a comprehensive description of the lexis of a language looks like. The central problem is the circularity in the definition of the basic unit of description, the lexical item.

The theory can readily define a lexical item as follows:

> a formal item (at least one morpheme long) whose pattern of occurrence can be described in terms of a uniquely ordered series of other lexical items occurring in its environment.[8]

The criterion throughout will be that of collocation in a given stretch of text. Unfortunately, the stretch of text is *not* 'given'; we are trying to define the item in terms of its environment and the environment (by implication) in terms of the item. The implied definition of the environment is that it is the extent of text which is relevant in the description of an item.

To make these statements clearer, let us consider the nature of the predictive power of items in a text. In the first place, it seems clear that we shall have to measure the extent of each environment in lexical items, thus dealing another blow to the usefulness of our definition in practice. But if we do not do this, then we must use a unit of measurement (e.g. the orthographic word) from another level of language description, thus violating the autonomy of the level of lexis which we have made a basic part of our theory. Let us look at an example.

it was an auspicious occasion
the occasion on which it was done was not an auspicious one

It is likely that the lexical value of the collocation of *auspicious* and *occasion* is similar in each sentence. The two items are lexically more or less contiguous, and the description of the material intruding in the second sentence will be made at a more delicate stage of analysis.

In the sentence

I posted the letter in the pillar-box

we might expect the items *post*, *letter*, *pillar-box* to predict each other much more than *drop*, *letter*, *puddle* in

I dropped the letter in a puddle.

It seems reasonable to hope that in

he flipped the letter with careless elegance into the pillar-box

we can count an instance of the collocation *letter*, *pillar-box*. But if we find examples like:

the letter in his hand, that strangely anonymous, insignificant monument to his dreadful toils of composition, he posted, with a careless elegance which belied the gnawing terror he felt at the thought of whose cruel hands might open it. Then he continued past the pillar-box into the engulfing night

we might still feel that there was a pattern *post*, *letter*, *pillar-box* but it would be difficult indeed to devise a workable procedure for recognising it. A thread runs through: *letter* - *hand* - *composition* - *post* - *hands* - *open* - *pillar-box* but we cannot build a superstructure on such a slender thread.

We do not have to assume that patterns which we perceive in examining a text and patterns that our techniques allow us to describe are identical. Neither of these may be the same as the most efficient possible account of the lexical structure[9] of the text. The patterns perceived by a trained linguist examining a text are unreliable and usually extremely tentative. Our techniques are perforce based on the capabilities of machines, though the demands made by the machines do not affect the theory.

At this point we must note that the techniques of analysis are extremely crude. The lexical patterns we perceive in examining texts occur over varying extents of text according to the particular circumstances of each example. The existence of a mutual prediction can depend on any or all of

(a) the strength of the predictions of items over each other
(b) the distance apart of the items
(c) the nature of the items which separate them, whether continuing a 'thread' as above, or not
(d) the grammatical organization.

The feature of physical distance apart of two items is one that requires further comment. It is clear that distance ultimately sets the boundary of collocation, although it will be a different distance in different cases. Ought we to argue from this that the proximity of items within a collocation should be assessed? If *post* in a text occurs 100 times just next to *letter* and 100 times with another item in between, do we have a less strong pattern than say, if *pillar-box* occurs 150 times next to *letter* and only 50 times next but one? Often we might feel that there are grounds for distinguishing collocations on this basis, rather than merely noting that both *post* and *pillar-box* occur 200 times in collocation with *letter* and relegating the differing proximities to a less important place. But with some frequent collocations (e.g. *buy* and *cheap*) we might find that they are habitually separated, but we will be reluctant to argue from this that the collocation *buy* + *cheap* is less strong than another that occurred without any interventions. The theory, as far as it goes, gives us no grounds for weighting proximities, and the study of examples tends to deny that items become *steadily* less mutually predicting as the distance between them increases. So we reject, for the moment, the suggestion that degree of proximity within the chosen boundaries of collocation should be considered of primary importance, thus also rejecting a neat but dangerous way of fixing the boundaries of each collocation.

It is also likely that there are cases of two or more items collocating more frequently with each other in certain of their possible sequences. *Buy* and *cheap* might well exemplify this. But as the theory stands at present, the primary structural criterion is that of co-occurrence, in any sequence, with or without intervening material; features such as preferred sequences, or habitual interventions, are secondary in structure. It remains for the facts to confirm or refute this order of priority, and a manual study has been started to collect hints as to the extent to which simple co-occurrence is inaccurate in describing the facts.

We may use the term **node** to refer to an item whose collocations we are studying, and we may then define a **span** as the number of lexical items on each side of a node that we consider relevant to that node. Items in the environment set by the span we will call **collocates.** The extent of the span is at present arbitrary, and depends mainly on practical considerations; at a late stage in the study we will be able to fix the span at the optimum value, but we start with little more than a guess.

What we call **items** are of course not really entitled to the term, since only after looking at the collocations over a long text will we be able to identify what the actual items are. Let us examine the collocations in a short piece of text and introduce some more terms.[10]

/ here that's where we can save money / in what way? / we can't drink. We don't drink and we don't smoke and we spend all our money on clothes / We do spend all our money on clothes / I know, and what an excuse for having to spend our money somehow / I wish I could save mine / It's impossible to save money / that's my lament yes / unless you never go out and are very strong willed / Oh it's not so bad for women, you know, it's / is it not? / us poor blokes that suffer. / It's poor blokes like me that gets persuaded to take some woman to the what d'you call it ball at two guineas a ticket and a quid for drink and a quid for taxis / They're very lucky that can persuade you / They're lucky they can persuade you. I'm in with the wrong set / Well she didn't persuade me. It was someone else / ha / persuaded me to buy a ticket / — / I'm still not sure whether it's the thing to do to accept a quid from the girl towards the ticket / — / I see no reason why not / no not for not if the tickets are two quid / two guineas and she says she'll pay half you think that's reasonable do you? / I'd get the extra shilling off her / Oh you wouldn't / oh medics honestly they're worth every inch of their reputations / if a bloke were taking you to a ball and you offered to pay / I suppose I better offer eh? / no and you offered to pay two half of a ticket you don't think there's anything wrong with the boy to accept it? / half of your own ticket? / no no you offered to pay / but you're not a student (well I have got) you're earning are you / you should be earning / my income is not no larger really than anybody who's on a grant / well I think it would be all right to accept the money / yes I think so 'cos it cost plenty of money in drinks, I mean, I can just say 'well I can get all of the drink' /

We will take the span as 3 lexical items before and after each node, and we will only select fairly obvious lexical items. The first occurrence of *money* embraces the piece (items underlined)

save money / in what way / we can't drink. We don't drink

and the second embraces

drink and we don't smoke and we spend all our money on clothes / I know, and what an excuse

and so on. Very little valuable information can be got from such a small text because we cannot assume that each item is behaving at its most

TOTAL ENVIRONMENT TABLES

Item:	money		pay		ticket	
occurrences	7		4		6	
collocates			offer	5		
(frequency	drink	4				
ordered)	save	4			quid	4
	spend	4				
(2 or more	clothes	3	half	3	accept	3
occurrences)	think	3				
	cost	2	better	2	boy	2
	excuse	2	think	2	guinea	2
	impossible	2	ticket	2	half	2
	know	2			offer	2
	money	2			pay	2
	plenty	2			persuade	2
					reason	2
					see	2
					ticket	2
collocates	accept		ball		ball	
	all right		earn		buy	
(1 only	get		guinea		drink	
occurrence)	go out		have got		girl	
	lament		quid		say	
	say		reasonable		student	
	smoke		say		sure	
	strong willed		student		the thing to do	
	way		suppose		think	
	wish		take		woman	
					wrong	

typical However, to show the processes, let us look at the collocations of *money*, *pay* and *ticket* displayed on p. 416.

Below each item is listed its total environment in the text, so that in this text, with a span of 3 items on either side, *spend* occurs four times as a collocate of *money*, *think* three times, etc. This is in miniature the source data for what we call the **cluster** of a lexical item. The Total Environment Table for an item differs from a cluster in two main respects:

(a) It does not relate the number of occurrences of a collocate to the total frequency of that collocate. Obviously the more frequent an item is, the greater is the chance of it appearing regardless of lexical connections. In the environment for *money*, for example, both *think* and *save* occur, but while this fact accounts for all the occurrences of *save* in the passage, there are two occurrences of *think* which are not in collocation with *money*.

(b) In this example, the lexical items have been isolated. An objective study would consider each morpheme as potentially a lexical item, and so total environment tables would be prepared for what are often called 'grammatical items'. If we are correct in assuming that such items are lexically independent (that is, ultimately they can show no significant cluster since other items appear in their environments in accordance with predictions based on the total frequency of the items in a text), the total environment tables will not show this independence, because they do not relate the total number of occurrences of node and collocate to each other.

To summarize, we measure both the way in which an item predicts the occurrences of others (and get results such as the table on page 416), and also the way in which it is predicted by others. Then we choose the second of these measurements for our statement of the lexical meaning of the item. This statement is called a **cluster** and is derived from the total environment tables.[11]

Firth said (op. cit., page 196) 'One of the meanings of *night* is its collocability with *dark*' and we can go on from there to say that the **formal meaning** of an item A is that it has a strong tendency to occur nearby items B, C, D, less strong with items E, F, slight with G, H, I, and none at all with any other item. And that is exactly what is tabulated in the cluster.

Already we can see how crude the technique of collocation is. There is an enormous amount of **casual collocation**, that is, the span setting has netted a lot of items which are most unlikely to have any predictive power over the node. They may be accidental, reflecting the place, perhaps, where someone breaks into a committee meeting with the coffee; or they may include the magnificent images of some of our greatest poetry. But lexis has a broad mesh in the early stages, looking always for typicality, and rejecting the atypical. The unusual collocations will come into their own only when they have been proved to be unusual, and their degree of unusualness has been measured.

The vital distinction between casual and significant collocation is, as we have seen, made according to the frequency of repetition of the collocates in several occurrences of an item. The more occurrences of an item that we study, the clearer the picture will be; each particular casual collocate will be unlikely to occur again, and though there will be more and more of them the significance of any one of them will steadily decrease. At the same time collocates typical of the item in question will impress their pattern more and more strongly until the pattern is broadly speaking complete and the evidence of further occurrences does not materially alter the pattern.

If $p =$ the total number of occurrences of items in a text, and $f =$ the total number of occurrences of a particular item, then the probability of that item occurring at each item-place in the text is $\frac{f}{p}$. If $s =$ the span setting multiplied by two (since the span measures the number of item-places on *each* side of a node), the probability of our item collocating with each successive node is $\frac{sf}{p}$. Then if we consider a particular node which occurs n times in the text, the probability of our item collocating with this node is $\frac{nsf}{p}$. This figure can then be compared with the actual facts of the text, the actual number of times this collocate occurs with this node. Statistical tests can assess the significance of any discrepancy between the predicted and the actual figures, giving a positive correlation (where the collocate attracts the node to itself), a negative correlation (where the collocate repels the node), or an absence of correlation. The last state of affairs tells us that the items in question are neutral with regard to each other in the text, possibly because they just *are* neutral with regard to each other, or possibly because the text is not long enough to reflect their performance in the language as a whole.

No matter how long a text was chosen, there would be some items that did not occur often enough to be described on the evidence of this text alone, and they could only be studied with reference to items that had been established in the text. In a very long text, these would probably only amount to a few barely-assimilated foreign words, stray technical terms, and, of course, misprints.

We have reached the stage of postulating the arrangement of the clusters of all 'text-described' items, and devising methods of removing the non-significant 'tails' of these clusters. Since our items are only provisionally identified, we must not permanently discard the tails. Subsequent adjustments may well call for part of a tail to be incorporated in the cluster. What sort of adjustments can we make?

To answer this question we must return to the stage where we guessed at the provisional items, and refine our guesswork, relying on the near certainty that the more the occurrence of two items in collocation defies the chance predictions, the nearer we are to a correct identification of them. Our procedures depend on the way in which we guessed in the first place.

(a) We could guess, throughout the text, where each item stopped and the next one started, and mark forms differently where we felt sure that more than one item had the same form (like *quack*$_1$ collocating with *duck*, and *quack*$_2$ collocating with *medicine*). This method ought to yield a good approximation to lexical items, but it is impracticable, since it depends on a plentiful supply of trained editors; and unreliable, since it would hardly be possible to keep track of the millions of subjective decisions that would be introduced at an early stage.

(b) We could rely on the orthographic word (in a transcribed text) as the best approximation. This is, we think, the best unit from the point of view of quick results, but it would require that many words which appeared to vary only on a grammatical axis would be conflated. *Drive*, *drives*, *drove*, *driving* and *driven*, for example. It is a fair guess that it is proper to conflate these forms, but it may not be a correct guess, and we would have to retain the possibility of reconstructing the original form quickly. If it happened, for example, that *-ing* was an essential component of a lexical item, as in

I'm dying to see the show

we would lose a very useful criterion for identifying the item *be dying to*. All we really know about the two parts of *driv/ing* is that the first is lexically important and probably has very little influence in the grammar while the second is operative in the grammar, and probably has little influence in the lexis.[12]

(c) Perhaps the most reliable method, then, would be to split *driving* into its two parts (which we crudely call **morphemes**), being confident that *-ing* is not very important, except when considered in conjunction with other morphemes. At least we could be confident that no lexical item was smaller than the chosen unit, and the remaining problems would be:

(i) detecting multi-morpheme items;
(ii) detecting more than one item with the same **form.**[13]

The method requires a minimum of guesswork, and readily adapts to mechanical editing. If we assume that this method has been adopted, we can now look into the way in which we can make our provisional analysis more accurate. At this stage it becomes obvious that the work will get beyond the capacity of the most dedicated human drudge. Because, if we get evidence to split the form *quack* into $quack_1$ and $quack_2$, then all clusters in which *quack* is a significant collocate will have to be adjusted, the various occurrences of *quack* will have to be identified as one or other of the two possibilities, and the arithmetic will have to be done all over again. Similarly if we get evidence to identify the item *run to seed* we will have to look at each occurrence of *run* and examine its environment, and identify whether or not it is part of the item *run to seed.* There are probably twenty or more items incorporating the form *run,*[14] so the ultimate significance of an occurrence of *run* will look very different from the provisional results. The process of refinement, one must stress, is not one of merely jettisoning collocates because they appear in clusters under false pretences. Since significance is related to the total number of occurrences of an item, the recognition of a fairly rare item like *run to seed* among the nondescript *runs* may bring it into prominence in places where before the vast frequency of *run* had obscured the significance.

Before we go further into the processes of refinement, we had better set out certain assumptions about the nature of polymorphemic lexical items. We shall try to avoid preconceptions, and, particularly, to avoid analogies with other levels of language, particularly grammar.

We fix no upper limit to the size of polymorphemic items. *Take the bull by the horns, don't put all your eggs in one basket,* may well turn out to be best regarded as single lexical items. A polymorphemic item may have its components in any sequence. Though no clear examples of varying sequence have come to light yet, the best model we have for the behaviour of component morphemes in lexical items is collocation, and there is certainly no sequence restriction there.[15] The components of a polymorphemic item may be discontinuous. Oaths can interrupt them almost anywhere, and concoctions like

you must cut your coat, I'm afraid, according to your cloth
he's run utterly to seed
put all his nuclear eggs in the West German basket

do not sound wildly esoteric (and one is remembered from a Sunday newspaper).

As soon as we accept these assumptions, we must face the charge of distorting the facts in order to exclude grammatical considerations, and we must take a closer look at the influence of grammar on lexis. But now we have a framework of lexical theory within which to study whatever influence grammar has.

It is quite true that most of the polymorphemic lexical items that spring to mind are grammatically restricted in some way. Alter the grammar and you no longer have the item. The *seed* in *run to seed* cannot inflect, for example, and *cats* in *raining cats and dogs* cannot remain a constituent of the item if it is made singular. The key point is that such grammatical considerations are not typical of grammar. It is characteristic of a word like *cats* in grammar that there *is* a word *cat* with which it contrasts, not that there is not.

One's attitude to grammar may change a little when it becomes clear that lexis can bear some of the troublesome burdens of description. The ambiguity in a sentence like

I looked over the house

may be explained

(a) by assigning different grammatical analyses to the two meanings; considering *look over* to be the verb when it is also a lexical item, and *look* to be the verb when the *over* is not an essential constituent of a lexical item. The primary analytical cuts would then be, respectively,

I / looked over / the house
I / looked / over the house

It is too early to be sure that lexis and grammar will always correlate so neatly: some results of an investigation of about 600 'phrasal verbs' carried out by Halliday and Dixon suggest that an intuitive answer to the question 'Is this phrasal verb a single lexical item?' correlates very poorly with nineteen other questions, all of which are grammatical.

(b) by forcing lexis and grammar artificially apart, and assigning but one grammatical analysis to the example above, leaving the lexical analysis only to show the ambiguity. This separation would help cases like

(i) It's raining cats and dogs.
(ii) He's training cats and dogs.

Grammatically, one could then say, both occurrences of *cats* are plural; the lack of choice in (i) is a consequence of lexical item componence.

It is important to notice that all the components of a polymorphemic item are equally relevant, no matter what other patterns any of the same forms may have elsewhere. In *run to seed* the *to* is just as much an identifying component of the item as *seed*, even though there may be a (different) lexical item *run* but no item *to*. The sequence is also a component of this item, but the various inflections of *run* probably are not. So with the *-s* of *cats and dogs*, the *and* and the sequence.

Grammar has ranks,[16] and it is possible to talk of items as being 'free' at one rank and 'bound' at another, higher rank. The form *the* as a morpheme is free, that is, it can stand alone as a word. But as a word it is bound, since it cannot stand alone as a nominal group. We must not take this concept over into lexis, since we can detect only one rank in lexis, the item, which must therefore be free.[17] Its components may have the same forms as other free items but there is no way of relating them at the level of lexis. There is no way of relating *cats* as part of *cats and dogs* and *cat* on its own as a free item, except trivially. Lexically the two are no more likely to be related than any other two forms, and since this lack of relationship is the criterion for separating them, the situation is not to be lamented.

These points regarding the componence of lexical items can be used to question a fundamental assumption about the natures of grammar and lexis. Because of the pre-eminence of grammar, one is inclined to think of a text as 'having a grammatical structure' throughout, but only sporadically 'having a lexical structure'. We speak casually about 'fully grammatical items' or 'function words' as if there were items which were entirely irrelevant in the study of lexis. In the early examples in this article this assumption was made for the sake of exposition, but it seems to have no foundation in fact. Every morpheme in a text must be described both grammatically and lexically; against the fact that *boy*, *boys*, *boy's* and *boys'* are likely to be lexically distinguished only at a very delicate stage in the description, if at all, we must set the fact that *boy*, *man*, *youth* are in the same position grammatically. Each successive form in a text is a lexical item or part of one, and there are no gaps where only grammar is to be found. The so-called 'function words' are presumably words which never attain the status of separate lexical items, but neither do *amok*, *hale*, *eke* as words, or the famous *cran* of *cranberry*, *ceive*, of *receive*, etc., or the splendid truncations of Wodehouse, as morphemes.

To conclude the remarks on polymorphemic items, we must anticipate how we will recognize them. Why do we expect that some occurrences of *cold* + *feet* will be singled out for treatment as occurrences of a separate polymorphemic item whereas *cold* + *hands* will not so tempt us? In essence we pick out a polymorphemic item when its cluster cannot be predicted from the clusters of its components. The 'macro-cluster' of *cold* + *hands* will indeed be different from the cluster of *cold* and the cluster of *hand* but it should be predictably different. The common collocates in the two clusters we might expect to be strengthened in significance, and we would be surprised to find any item appearing that did not occur prominently in one of the two original clusters. With *cold* + *feet*, on the other hand (assuming that we have managed to isolate the occurrences of the polymorphemic item[18]), we would expect items like *risky*, *call off* to appear, although in the two original clusters their significance was masked by the numerous collocates relevant to the two words as separate items. Instances of *amok*, *cran*, *umbrage*, etc., will be identified by the feature of 100 per cent prediction of another form. There is, therefore no choice, and so without looking at their clusters we can combine *run* + *amok* and *cran* + *berry*, rearrange the clusters and spans (since we will have counted each as two items before) and try again. So the question of whether the *berry* in *cranberry* is the same morpheme as the *berry* in *raspberry* or just plain *berry* can be easily answered, without recourse to notional contemplation. From a lexical standpoint, if the clusters of *cranberry*, *raspberry* and *berry* are identical then it is the same morpheme *berry*, and if not, it isn't. This follows from the point that the *berry* in *cranberry* has as little choice as the *cran*, and we must follow the fortunes of the two together.

The argument is perhaps worth illustrating with a further example, involving three sentences:

(a) He might come soon.
(b) He strove with all his might.
(c) He strove with all his might and main.

The same form *might* appear in all three sentences, and the problem is how this form relates to one or more than one lexical item. The *might* of sentence (a) is clearly different from the others; whether it is or is not the exponent of a lexical item can be left aside for the moment. The reason for its separation can be expressed lexically, in terms of its differing pattern of collocation from the others.

The form *main* cannot significantly collocate with *strive*, etc., unless *might* is also present, so *main* can only be one component of a polymorphemic lexical item which we can identify as *might and main.* So the question whether the two *mights* of (b) and (c) are lexically the same (they seem notionally the same) depends on whether or not the cluster of *might* is identical to the cluster of *might and main.* We can only hazard a guess as to this at the present time; it seems not unlikely that there may be 'long forms' and 'short forms' of the same item (compare *fed up* and *fed up to the back teeth*).

We will now further discuss the lexicogrammatical features in relation to the second of the two dimensions of refinement on page 420, the detection of two or more items having the same form. Here grammar can again help a lot, but it must not be used in defiance of lexical considerations.

It is true, for example, that grammatical word-class distinctions may parallel lexical distinctions, though a glance at the repetitiveness of dictionaries which give separate entries according to the word-class of an item shows that the parallelism may be carried too far. But we may point to examples like:

mat, noun, collocating with *door, wipe, hall,* etc.
mat, verb, collocating with *hair, jam, thick,* etc.
mat, adj., collocating with *paint, finish, surface,* etc.

where the coincidence of grammatical and lexical boundaries is considerable. In contrast with this we can advance examples like *quack* noted earlier, where the pattern is different:

LEXIS / GRAMMAR	$quack_1$ (duck)	$quack_2$ (medicine)
quack (noun)	x	x
quack (verb)	x	

Here the grammatical and lexical patterns only partly coincide. If we started with the grammatical evidence, treating lexis as a follow-up from grammar, then it is true that some distinction between *quack* (noun) and *quack* (verb) would emerge in collocation. But it would not be as clear or as accurate a distinction as the lexical item distinction which cuts across the grammar. On the other hand, the grammatical information can be used in lexical description. It will emerge clearly that *quack* + *ing* only occurs in *quack*$_1$, for example.

On what grounds do we split *quack* into two or more lexical items? Or the several hundred much more complex cases like *hand*, making new items with *bird*, *in*, *over*, etc., and collocating with *marriage*, *give*, *factory*, *whist*, *horse*, *tall*, *legible*, *big*, *finger*, *fortune*, etc.? Grammar is hardly any help at all, and the distinctions gained by a word-class division make little inroads on the complexity of this form. We are forced to examine the 'internal consistency' of the cluster.

There is no theoretical requirement that collocates of an item must intercollocate but in practice it can be seen that some occurrences of *hand* are collocationally distinct from other occurrences. That is, there will be a group of collocates, e.g. *marriage*, *daughter*, *engagement*, which will occur together frequently as collocates of *hand*, and another group including *whist*, *rummy*, *ace*, *flush* also often together within collocations of *hand*. But the chances of *whist* and *marriage* co-occurring are as poor as those of *archbishop* and *fish*. The only way in which these groups are joined is by co-occurrence with the form *hand* (and possibly other accidental ambiguities, e.g. *card*). The way in which the various groups of items can be separated is to compare each collocation with all the others, drawing together those that are like each other until as clear groupings as possible are obtained. Groupings which separate themselves from each other will suggest different lexical items, while groupings which shade into each other, even though opposite ends do not intercollocate, suggest one item with a wide **range**.

These proposals are extremely tentative, since they are based on the very limited results of studies of small clusters. It is not at all clear what sort of generalizations will emerge which can be applied to a text as a whole, and what use such generalizations will be in determining cases where one's intuition is helpless in deciding whether or not a form should be split. Nor will it be clear, in a monolingual study, what procedures are workable only because of the features of the particular language under study. But let us assume success, and a final, accurate description of the lexical items discernible in a text, in terms of their collocational patterns.

We will then know, or be able to find out:

(a) the total number of items in the cluster;
(b) a measure of the 'internal consistency' of the cluster, which can now be called **range**, that is, the chances of the collocates themselves inter-collocating. The lexical item *vote*, for example, will probably have a wider range, over much the same ground, as *poll*;
(c) the variation in degree of significance between items in a cluster. We may assume that some items are only barely significant, and that others approach the cliché state. Clusters will differ in the range of the significance degree of the collocates;
(d) the distribution of items according to the degree of significance. This allows us to distinguish between clusters where the (c) figures are similar, but where the number of collocates at each degree of significance is different. (c) and (d) together measure the dependence of an item on its collocates.

In all our comments so far, we have taken the text more or less item by item. Pairs of items, perhaps, and clusters relative to a single node item. We have said nothing about the lexical structure of a whole text. Even when we have accumulated a vast number of facts, tiny details and generalized cluster-shapes, the total interrelations between all the items in our text are fragmented in such a way that it will be impossible to make clear statements on the basis of the processes already described. We have been forced by the nature of the material to unravel all the strands at once, without perceiving which are the main lines of the organization. We must move towards a framework of some kind in which each item has as far as possible only one 'address'—its 'best fit' in the lexical structure of the language exemplified in the text. Most of our details will have to be discarded as soon as they have contributed towards underlining the general connections, and we must arrive at a list of what we call the **lexical sets** of a language. A lexical set is a discrete part of an organization of the lexical items of a text where each lexical item appears once only.

There are two assumptions made here. One is that the lexical organization will in fact divide into discrete parts. This is further discussed below. The other is that it will be possible to limit the appearance of an item to once only without undue distortion of its patterns. This is a problem with items like *put* and *thing* which may never show a strong enough tendency to one set rather than another. The idea of a 'setless' item may become a reality.

Although we are many years away from producing definite sets from a sufficiency of actual text, it is worth while discussing tentative procedures within the framework set up for the earlier part of the study. As in so many pieces of research, the very last results may well form the best start to applications of the research. Lexical sets parallel the categories of a thesaurus, but are linguistically arranged, and are the distillation of the massive evidence got, initially, from the study of collocations.

There seem two starting points from which sets can be got; the list of clusters, and the individual attraction of each pair of items. Starting from the clusters we can envisage:

(a) selecting the best list of actual clusters, by correlation of all possible combinations of clusters. Each set would then be the cluster of an item, and could have as a head-item the node of the cluster. There might be several possible lists which satisfied the criterion of maximum differentiation, and some of them might have little value. For example, if it happened that the clusters of *make* and *mandolin* together listed all the items in the text once only, this would be of merely passing interest.

(b) conflating the clusters and producing macro-clusters where two or more clusters share similar patterns (in effect extending the node from one item to more than one, without extending the span). This could be additive, that is the two (or more) clusters would simply be thrown together, inclusive of the items that were unique to each of them; or subtractive, where only the items common to the two clusters would be put together, and the unique items would be rejected, to find a home where they were in fact common to two or more clusters. So we might conflate the clusters of *post* and *letter*; if *write* occurred only with *letter*, and *parcel* only with *post* then the additive procedure would accept them both, while the subtractive procedure would attempt to find a better-fitting place for them.

Alternatively, starting from a huge matrix, where the power of each item over each other item was plotted, the work on Factor Analysis done by Shepard[20] might be applied, adapted to cope with the enormous amount of data. The 'distance' of one item from another might be represented by 1 minus its predictive power (on a scale from 0 to 1) and the position of each item relative to each other item in a multi-dimensional space would be plotted by using the distances as co-ordinates. Shepard's programme seeks to reduce the number of dimensions in the space with the minimum of distortion to the co-ordinates. Each resulting dimension would be a lexical set.

Such a piece of work is further complicated by a feature of lexis that we have only hinted at so far. We are interested in the lexical *meaning* of items as represented by their collocations, and it has already been shown that the number of times two items inter-collocate is not a direct measure of the meaning of either item, which must be based on the total frequency of the two items. The same collocation has a different significance to the items involved. Consider a collocation like:

a good omen.

It is of greater significance to *omen* that it occurs with *good* than it is to *good* that it occurs with *omen*. *Good* occurs so very often that *omen* should not feature large in its cluster, while for *omen*, a few items like *good, bad, propitious* will very frequently collocate. So, paradoxically, the distance between *good* and *omen* is different according to the viewpoint.

It is this feature which allows some morphemes and words to be frequent collocates of other items but never items themselves, and it is the incorporation of this feature which complicates the preparation of clusters, and forces us to describe an item as an 'address list' in the environment of other items rather than according to the patterns that emerge with itself as node.

Whichever method or combination of methods is finally chosen for set description, it is likely that a very large computer will be strained to the utmost to cope with the data. Pilot studies can be done up to the stage of arriving at the clusters of individual items, but there seems no accurate way of simulating the organization into sets.

Many questions have not been faced at all in this article. Of particular importance is the problem of language varieties or **registers**, where items, collocations and clusters may group themselves together according to features of the situation in which utterances are made. *Horse* and *hand* may not collocate significantly at all except in a register where utterances like

my smallest horse is thirteen hands

feature, and the item *hand* exemplified here will probably not emerge at all unless texts from this register are collected. *Vigorous depression* and *dull highlights*[19] may stand as unusual collocations unless found in the registers of meteorology and photography respectively. The additional dimensions of register have been excluded from this discussion; we assume that our text is reasonably homogeneous, and particular stray register collocations will be rejected on a frequency basis. The rigorous description of registers is still a long way off, and it is probably a better approach to make a series of lexical descriptions of different registers and then search for their common elements.

The theory of lexis opens up exciting areas for describing language more accurately and more usefully. The practical problems are immense, and no secret has been made of them here, but the results that they promise are, possibly because of their novelty, no less fascinating than those of any other branch of linguistics.[20,21]

Notes

1 The initial stages of a study of lexis on the lines described in this article have been made possible by a grant from the Ford Foundation to the University of Edinburgh. Most of the linguists there have given help to the study; particular acknowledgement for help in preparation of this article is due to Professor Angus McIntosh of Edinburgh, Professor M.A.K. Halliday and Mr. Robert M.W. Dixon of University College London, and Dr. P.J. Wexler of Manchester.

2 See pp. 148–162; also 'Categories of the Theory of Grammar', *Word* 17.3 (December 1961), pp. 273–277.

3 *Roget's Thesaurus of English Words and Phrases* (London, 1962 edition, Longmans, Green & Co.), paragraph 589.

4 For this and other technical terms, and discussions of lexis on which this article draws heavily, see: J.R. Firth, *Papers in Linguistics* 1934–1951 (London, 1957); M.A.K. Halliday, op. cit.; Angus McIntosh, 'Patterns and Ranges', *Lg* 37.3 (1961); T.F. Mitchell, 'Syntagmatic Relations in Linguistic Analysis', *TPS* 1958.

5 Commonly called **classes.**

6 cp. Angus McIntosh, op. cit., for an extended discussion of this point.

7 cp. pages 425, 427.

[8] Notes on this definition: (a) the term **formal item** is used rather than **stretch of language**, etc., to emphasise that, just as with grammatical items, a lexical item is not uniquely related to a piece of language substance; (b) I make no apology for misusing the term *morpheme* since this article indirectly throws doubt on its status. All I want it to mean is 'a stretch of language which is formally indivisible', and I wish to beg the question of whether it is a unit of grammar, or of lexis, or both, or whether two terms are required, one for grammar and one for lexis.

[9] The use of *structure* here is by analogy from grammar. The analogy may not be a good one, and perhaps a neutral term such as **componence** will be preferred; it is used here to refer to that area of lexical analysis which corresponds to structure in grammar.

[10] The solidus indicates 'new speaker'. The text is from a transcription of an impromptu conversation.

[11] This distinction, which may not be obvious at first, is further discussed on page 428.

[12] This is a general statement. It may happen, with examples like *driving rain*, that the *-ing* is important lexically. There is evidence that it is not always sufficient to consider the grammatical morphemes independently of their grammatical function. The item *quarry* which collocates with *chase*, *corner*, *hunter*, etc. will also collocate frequently with a grammatical class we could call **possessive**. The exponents could be *his*, *their*, *Bill's*, etc., and the lexical description would be more accurate if these varying exponents could be conflated.

[13] A **form**, in this article, is a stretch of language which has not yet been assigned a lexical status. It is relevant to language form but its relevance has not been determined in detail.

[14] e.g. *run up*, *run out of*, *run down*, *runaway*, *runabout*, *run to earth*, *run in*, *run-around*, *overrun*, *run aground*.

[15] If the forms *dirt cheap* and *cheap as dirt* have identical clusters, then they would be regarded as instances of the same lexical item with variable sequence.

[16] cp. Halliday, op. cit., p. 261, note 47.

[17] It may be helpful to think of lexis as concerned with 'degrees of freedom' of items, a concept foreign to grammar, which makes a sharp distinction between free and bound.

[18] There may be in English a tendency to avoid saying 'You've got cold feet' when one is not intending an occurrence of the polymorphemic item. If so, our work will be the easier for it.

[19] These are genuine.

[20] R. N. Shepard 'The Analysis of Proximities', *Psychometrika* 27.2, 3 (1962). I am indebted to Dr. Donald Michie for this reference. A recent unpublished paper by P. Leroy of Rennes 'On the Factor Analysis of Proximities' suggests that the prohibitive computational complexity of an extended Shepard programme may be avoided.

[21] This paper was written at the outset of research in this field, which is now supported by a grant from the Office for Scientific and Technical Information. For a clarification and reformulation of some basic concepts as a result of more recent work see Paul van Buren, 'Preliminary Aspects of Mechanization in Lexis' (1965, mimeographed).

Phonological Formulae for the Verb in Limbu as a Contribution to Tibeto-Burman Comparison

R. K. SPRIGG

Not much systematic comparison of contemporary spoken Tibeto-Burman languages has yet been attempted; but an increasing number of phonological analyses has made clear some of the difficulties with which the comparatist in this field will be faced. One of these difficulties arises out of differences in the phonetic form of particular lexical items in accordance with differences in junction;[1] another, not present in Burmese and Arakanese but a prominent feature of Tibetan and of Limbu, one of the Kiranti languages of eastern Nepal, is that of differences in verb root.[2] The main purpose of this article is to demonstrate from Limbu material that prosodic analysis not only can surmount this second difficulty but does in fact surmount it in such a way as to simplify the task of a comparatist in the Tibeto-Burman field. Whatever success it achieves will go some way towards justifying the hopes placed in this his theory by the late Professor J. R. Firth.[3]

This article has also a subsidiary aim: to examine the extent of those stretches of the continuum, pieces, for which a prosodic statement can usefully be made.

PROSODIC AND PHONEMIC ANALYSES

It is clear from the present dominance of the phoneme theory that the analyses on which future comparison in the Tibeto-Burman field will be based can hardly fail to be most of them phonemic; any advantage that prosodic analysis has to offer must therefore be at the expense of the phoneme theory and of phonemic forms of lexical items.[4] One such advantage is that prosodic analysis can lead to the establishing of a single formula, a lexical-item phonological formula, for each lexical item, and thus bypasses difficulties arising out of a possible multiplicity of phonemic forms for that item reflecting phonetic diversity from one context to another, or a difference of root, or both. By this means the comparatist avoids the problem of having to make a choice from among two or more phonemic forms, and of having to set up a criterion to govern his choice.

That the problem of choice of form is real enough in phonemics-based comparison appears from the verb lexical items of such Limbu words as the following:[5]

TABLE 1

	1.		2.		3.	
i.	**kɛ-jɛp**	/yɛp/	**kɛ-jɛp-piː**	/yɛp/	**jɛb-ɛ**	/yɛp/
ii.	,, **dƶɛp**	/cɛp/	,, **dƶɛp-piː**	/cɛp/	**tȼɛpt-ɛ**	/cɛpt/
iii.	,, **sɛt**	/sɛt/	,, **sɛp-piː**	/sɛp/	**sɛr-ɛ**	/sɛr/
iv.	,, **mɛt**	/mɛt/	,, **mɛp-piː**	/mɛp/	[**mɛtt-ɛ** **mɛt-ɛ**	/mɛtt/ /mɛt/
v.	,, **gɦɛm**	/khɛm/	,, **gɦɛm-biː**	/khɛm/	**khɛps-ɛ**	/khɛps/
vi.	,, **lɛm**	/lɛm/	,, **lɛm-biː**	/lɛm/	**lɛm-ɛ**	/lɛm/[6]
i.	you stand		do you stand		stand up	
ii.	he cuts you		does he cut you		cut it	
iii.	,, kills you		,, ,, kill you		kill it	
iv.	,, speaks to you		,, ,, speak to you		speak to him	
v.	,, listens to you		,, ,, listen to you		listen to him	
vi.	you are lazy		are you lazy		laze about	

The verbs in (ii)–(v) have each more than one phonemic form: (ii) /cɛp/, /cɛpt/; (iii) /sɛt/, /sɛp/, /sɛr/; (iv) /mɛt/, /mɛp/, /mɛtt/; (v) /khɛm/, /khɛps/; the comparatist would be obliged to choose one form in preference to the other or others.[7]

Phonemic analyses commonly give preference to the isolate (or absolute) form, and derive whatever variant phonemic forms there may be from it; or, in the absence of an absolute form, they give preference to those phonemes which are appropriate to open juncture;[8] but in dealing with Limbu the comparatist would be ill-advised to follow them in this: it is in the imperative forms, in which the syllable final is not in the open juncture, that verb lexical items are maximally distinguished. In the examples in Table 1 it will be seen that the verbs that translate *stand* and *cut* (i and ii), that translate *kill* and *speak to* (iii and iv), or *listen to* and *laze* (v and vi), are not distinguished each from the other in open juncture (col. 1); but each member of each of these pairs is distinguished in the imperative form (col. 3) from the other member by syllable-final consonant features. In fact it is the imperative form that is the key to the formal scatter of all regular verbs.[9] If, therefore, one were obliged to choose one phonemic form rather than another, the examples in Table 1, powerfully reinforced by those of Table 2 (p. 437), show that the imperative form is as suitable for comparison as any other, and better than most; but prosodic analysis does not require the comparatist to make such a choice: lexical-item phonological formulae arrived at by prosodic analysis are equally representative of all variant phonetic forms, both those which reflect a difference of root and those which can be treated as co-variants (junction variants and tempo variants) of the same root.

DISYLLABIC PIECES

The prosodic systems of prosodic analysis, as opposed to the phonematic systems, are set up in order to state syntagmatically associated features 'of more than one segment';[10] clearly, then, much turns on the definition of the term segment, or, alternatively, on the extent of a single segment. Where, however, syntagmatically associated features characterize more than one syllable, and therefore cross a syllable boundary, there is general agreement among the adherents of prosodic analysis that more than one segment must be concerned, and that a prosodic statement can therefore properly be made.

Since the type of piece that comprises two or more syllables is least controversial, it is from this type of piece that the first examples to illustrate the prosodic analysis are drawn; more controversial types of piece are considered later (pp. 444–50).

The contribution of prosodic analysis to lexical-item phonological formulae is illustrated in this article mainly from syllable-final features of monosyllabic verbs. The examples at Table 1 (p. 432) have already given some indication of the phonetic diversity of verbs in this respect; a comprehensive series of examples appears at Table 2 (p. 437). The examples in Table 2 are Limbu words each of which contains one of twenty-three verbs, all twenty-three of them of the same prosodic type as regards quantity.

Quantity

Limbu is a quantity language; and every verb can be classified prosodically in terms of a two-term quantity system as either s (so named from *short*) or l (from *long*). The verbs in the examples in Table 1 are s verbs.

The exponents of the two terms s and l are not drawn only from the verb syllable: exponential features can also characterize the negative-particle syllable **mɛ(ː)**, which precedes the verb. The exponents of s and of l, then, can be drawn from a disyllabic as well as from a monosyllabic piece, and can therefore transcend syllable boundaries.

In the particle syllable the exponential features are:

s: long/short vowel duration; same pitch as the verb ¯**mɛ(ː)**
l: short ,, ,, ; lower pitch than the verb _**mɛ**

(for examples see p. 435).

In the majority of examples of this particle syllable in the disyllabic s piece in the available material the vowel duration was in fact short; but the minority of examples in which long duration was observed (about a third of the total) is large enough to be significant. The l piece too was, admittedly, not entirely without examples of long vowel duration; but they were so few that they can fairly be dismissed as accidental.

In the verb syllable the exponency of s and of l is not so easily stated; for the vowel-duration features of certain sub-classes of both s verb and l verb are variable, and have to be related to other features of the following (particle) syllable or to differences in tempo. In detail the exponents are:

s

i. short duration + **i/ɩ ɛ a ɔ ɷ**
ii. [short / long] ,, + constricted voice quality + **i e ɛ a ɔ o u**[11]
iii. long ,, + clear ,, ,, + **ɛ a ɔ u**[12]
iv. ,, ,, + **ˀ p t k m n ŋ**[13]

l

i. long duration + clear voice quality + **i e ɛ a ɔ o u**
ii. short ,, + ,, ,, ,, + **i e**[14]
iii. absence of vowel
iv. ,, ,, ,, , initial palatality (**tɕ/dʑ tj/dj lj**)[14]
v. long duration (ː), of a vowel (ɛː) shared with the following (particle) syllable[15]
vi. other vowel features shared with the following (particle) syllable[16]
vii. where a dental (**t n**) follows, centrality: **iɩ ɔə oə uə**
viii. short duration + syllable-final **ˀ p t k**[13]
ix. short/long duration + syllable-final **m n ŋ**[13]

e.g.

		s
i.	**¯mɛː¯dɦɷ ŋɛnnɛ**	**¯mɛˀ¯ˀɩ ŋɛnnɛ**;
	do not drink it	do not buy it;
ii.	**piːˀmaˀ**	**ɦuˀmaˀ**;
	to give	to teach;
iii.	**ˀaɦaːsuˀ**	**ˀasuːsuˀ**;
	we two share it	we two touch it;
iv.	**piˀˀaˀ**	**tsɷmmaˀ**;
	he gives me	I meet;

		l
i.	**_mɛ¯gɦuːndɛnnɛ**	**_mɛ¯beːgɛnnɛ**;
	do not steal it	do not go;
ii.	**siah**	**_mɛ¯gɦeɛnnɛ**;
	he died	do not quarrel;
iii.	**sjah**	**jah**;
	he died	he descended;
iv.	**tɕɛh**	**tjɛ**
	eat it	come;
v.	**_mɛ¯jɛːnnɛ**;	
	do not descend;	
vi.	(**ɦɛllɛ**) **tsɔːˀ**	**tsaŋː**;
	he eats it	I ate it;
vii.	**kɛˀuət**	(**ɦɛn**) **noən**;
	he calls you	he is ashamed;
viii.	**juːˀaˀ**	**jeːtaˀ**;
	I descend	I laugh;
ix.	**tuː(ŋ)ŋaˀ**	**lɔː(m)maˀ**;
	I stoop	he beats me;

(for further examples of s-piece exponents (i)–(iii) see p. 437, Table 2: (i), 1–18; 19–20, col. 3; (ii), 21–23; (iii), 19–20, cols. 1–2; for exponent (iv) see p. 442).

To summarize, s verbs have either (i) short vowel duration in all contexts (Table 2, 1–18), or (ii) short in most contexts but long in some (19–20), or (iii) in the case of those s verbs which are characterized by constricted voice quality (21–23), either short or long, the short duration being a fast-tempo feature; l verbs, on the other hand, all have clear voice quality, and either (i) long vowel duration in all contexts, or (ii) long in most contexts but short in some, alternating, in fast-tempo utterances, with non-syllabic vocality, or even with complete absence of vowel.

Thus, not all s verbs are invariably characterized by short vowel duration, and not all l verbs by long duration;[17] e.g.

s: i. short:	**təjɷŋː**	**təjɛ**	**kɛdəjuˀ**
	I sewed it	sew it	you sew it
long:	**təːmaˀ**	**ˀadəːsuˀ**	
	to sew	we two sew it	
ii. short:	**ɦassɷŋˀ**	**ɦassɛ**	**kɛɦassuˀ**
	I share it	share it	you share it
long:	**ɦaːmaˀ**	**ˀaɦaːsuˀ**	
	to share	we two share it	
l: i. long:	**siːmaˀ**	**siːˀaˀ**	**siːbiː**
	to die	I die	does he die
cf.	**mɛsiɛnnɛ** **mɛsɛnnɛ**	**sjaŋ**[18]	**siah** **sjah**[18]
	do not die	I died	he died
ii. long:	**juːmaˀ**	**juːˀaˀ**	**ɦɛn juːˀ**
	to descend	I descend	he descends
cf.	**mɛjɛːnnɛ**	**jaŋ**	**ɦɛn jah**
	do not descend	I descended	he descended
iii. long:	**taːmaˀ**	**taːˀaˀ**	**kɛdaː(ˀ)**
	to come	I come	you come
cf.	**mɛdɛnnɛ**	**tjɛh**	**tiah** **tjah**[18]
	do not come	come	he came
iv. long:	**tsaːmaˀ**	**ˀadzaːsuˀ**	
	to eat	we two eat it	
cf.	**mɛdƶɛnnɛ**	**tsaŋˀ**	**ɦɛllɛ tsəː**
	do not eat it	I eat it	he ate it[19]

From a comparison of the two statements of exponency it will be seen that, while most vowels are common to both s-piece verb and l-piece verb, the vowels **ɩ** and **ɷ** are exclusive to the s-piece, and are therefore s-piece criteria. So, too, are the syllable-final consonants **ks**, **ss**, and **md**, and the non-syllabic vowel **j**, while syllable-final **ŋkt**, on the other hand, serves as an l-piece criterion. The remaining syllable-final consonant sequences are part of the exponency of either term, and, since there is an example of each in Table 2 (p. 437), they have not been listed among the exponential features.

Every verb can be prosodically classified as s or as l according as it is exemplifiable in the (disyllabic or monosyllabic) s, or l, piece. The

TABLE 2

	1. interrogative does he — you? does he —? + -piː/-biː		2. indicative he —s us two[20] we two — + -siˀ/-tɕhiˀ[20]		3. imperative — it! —! + -ɛ/-hɛ		4. transln. tr. int.
1	**jɛppiː**	**pp**	**ˀajɛpsiˀ**	**ps**	**jɛbɛ**	**bɛ**	int. stand
2	**kɛdʑɛppiː**	,,	,, **dʑɛpsiˀ**	,,	**tɕɛptɛ**	**ptɛ**	tr. cut
3	,, **lakpiː**	**kp**	,, **laksiˀ**	**ks**	**lagɛ**	**gɛ**	,, lick
4	,, **dɦɔkpiː**	,,	,, **dɦɔksiˀ**	,,	**thɔktɛ**	**ktɛ**	,, fight
5	,, **sɛppiː**	**pp**	,, **sɛ(t)tɕhiˀ**	**(t)tɕh**	**sɛrɛ**	**rɛ**	,, kill
6	,, **mɛppiː**	,,	,, **mɛ(t)tɕhiˀ**	,,	**mɛ(t)tɛ**	**(t)tɛ**	,, tell
7	,, **dɔmbiː**	**mb**	,, **dɔntɕhiˀ**	**ntɕh**	**tɔrɛ**	**rɛ**	,, abuse
8	,, **bɦɛmbiː**	,,	,, **bɦɛntɕhiˀ**	,,	**phɛndɛ**	**ndɛ**	,, untie
9	,, **bɦɔmbiː**	,,	,, **bɦɔntɕhiˀ**	,,	**phɔ(t)tɕhɛ**	**(t)tɕh**	,, employ
10	no suitable form		,, **bɛntshuˀ**	**ntsh**	**pɛntɕhɛ**	**ntɕh**	,, bevel
11	**kɛɦɪŋbiː**	**ŋb**	,, **ɦɪŋsiˀ**	**ŋs**	**ɦɪ(k)khɛ**	**(k)kh**	,, rock
12	,,	,,	,,	,,	**ɦɪŋkhɛ**	**ŋkh**	,, rear
13	**kɛŋbiː**	,,	,, **gɛŋsiˀ**	,,	**kɛŋɛ**	**ŋɛ**	int. fall
14	**kɛdɦɔŋbiː**	,,	,, **dɦɔŋsiˀ**	,,	**thɔksɛ**	**ksɛ**	tr. make fight
15	**lɛmbiː**	**mb**	,, **lɛmsiˀ**	**ms**	**lɛmɛ**	**mɛ**	int. laze
16	**kɛjɛmbiː**	,,	,, **jɛmsiˀ**	,,	**jɛmdɛ**	**mdɛ**	tr. tattoo
17	,, **dɛmbiː**	,,	,, **dɛmsiˀ**	,,	**tɛmsɛ**	**msɛ**	,, seize
18	**ˀimbiː**	,,	,, **ˀimsiˀ**	,,	**ˀipsɛ**	**psɛ**	int. sleep
19	no suitable form		,, **lɛːsuˀ**	**Vːs**	**lɛssɛ**	**ssɛ**	tr. know
20	**waːbiː**	**Vːb**	,, **waːsiˀ**	,,	**wʌjɛ**	**jɛ**	int. be
21	no suitable form		,, **dɔ(ː)ˀsuˀ**	**V(ː)ˀs**	**tɔ(ː)ˀjɛ**	**V(ː)ˀjɛ**	tr. dig
22	**kɛbi(ː)ˀbiː**	**V(ː)ˀb**	,, **bi(ː)ˀsiˀ**	,,	**pi(ː)ˀrɛ**	**V(ː)ˀrɛ**	,, give
23	no suitable form		,, **bɛ(ː)ˀsuˀ**	,,	**pɛ(ː)ˀsɛ**	**V(ː)ˀsɛ**	,, vomit

particle **¯mɛ(ː)/_mɛ** clearly cannot be classified in this way; but its alternative phonetic forms can:

s-piece: **¯mɛ ¯mɛː** l-piece: **_mɛ**

The remaining prosodic and phonematic systems are, for convenience, illustrated solely from s-piece verbs, or, rather, from words that include them; and the examples in Table 2 (p. 437) show some of the phonetic forms of twenty-three s-piece verbs, with one verb to each line. These examples are arranged in three columns, (1) interrogative, (2) indicative, and (3) imperative, with the relevant phonetic features abstracted from each word; the right-hand column (4) contains the classification of the verb as transitive (tr.) or as intransitive (int.), together with a translation meaning. It is on the grammatical classification that the translation of a given example depends. Bracketed features (5–6, 9, 11, 21–23) are not appropriate to fast-tempo utterances.

Interrogative Forms

The alternation of initial voice with voicelessness for the interrogative particle **piː/biː** (col. 1) in association with differences in final feature in the preceding verb syllable qualifies for prosodic treatment under the conditions stated above (p. 433), a syntagmatic association of features extending over a syllable boundary. For these interrogative words two prosodic types of piece, temporarily termed I and II, need to be distinguished; they comprise the verb syllable and the following particle syllable. The exponents of the terms I and II are:

	verb		particle	
I:	final voicelessness	**p k**	initial voicelessness	**p**
II:	„ voice	**m ŋ V**	„ voice	**b**

In the type-I piece the interrogative particle is characterized initially by voicelessness (**p**, 1–6), and in the type-II by voice (**b**, 7–9, 11–18, 20, 22). The verbs of lines 1–6 are appropriate to the type-I piece but not the type-II, and can therefore be classified prosodically as I-piece; the verbs of the remaining lines can be classified correspondingly as II-piece. The Roman numerals I and II could then, at this stage, be used in phonological formulae to express the relationship of the I-piece verb to the disyllabic I piece, and of the II-piece verb to the II.

Indicative Forms

Column 2, however, presents a rather different picture. Here it is an alternation in phonetic features of the dual particle **siˀ/tɕhiˀ** (lines 10,

19, 21, 23, **suˀ/tshuˀ**) in association with a difference in the final features of the preceding verb syllable that provides grounds for prosodic statement. For words such as these a further two prosodic types of piece, temporarily termed A and B, are distinguished; and again the piece comprises verb syllable and following particle syllable.

The exponents of the temporary terms A and B are:

	verb		particle	
A:	final non-alveolarity	**p k ŋ m V**	friction	**s**
			voiced vowel	**i/u**
B:	,, alveolarity/vocalic[21]	**t n V**	voiceless vowel	**h**
		affrication	**tɕ/ts**	

In the type-A piece the dual particle is characterized initially by friction (**s**) and the vowel by full voicing (**i/u**) (1–4, 11–23); in the type-B piece the particle is characterized by partial voicelessness of vowel (**h**, alternatively **i̥/u̥**), while both particle and verb share the affrication feature (**tɕ/ts**) (5–10).

Those verbs which can be contained in the type-A piece (1–4, 11–23) can be prosodically classified as A-piece; the remaining verbs, which are restricted to the type-B (5–10), are classified as B-piece. This second classification overlaps the previous classification of these verbs as I-piece or as II-piece, and, if the two classifications are combined, yields the following four prosodic classes:

IA	IB	IIB	IIA
1–4	5–6	7–10	11–23

A comparison of the phonetic form of each verb lexical item as between columns 1 and 2 shows that type-IA and type-IIA verbs are characterized by the same syllable-final features in either type of piece; but the other two classes of verb differ in phonetic form from one type of piece to the other: final labiality (**p**) is appropriate to the type-IB verb in the type-I piece, but alveolarity (**(t)tɕ**) in the type-B; final labiality (**m**) is also appropriate to the type-IIB verb in the type-II piece, but alveolarity (**ntɕ/nts**) in the type-B.

Imperative Forms

The imperative particle **ɛ/hɛ** alternates in phonetic form between complete voicing (**ɛ**) and partial voicelessness (**hɛ**); and the alternative features can again be associated with phonetic differences in the final of the preceding verb syllable, thus producing a fourth set of syntagmatically associated features extending over syllable boundaries.

The two prosodic types of piece required to account for these associations of features are termed, temporarily, 1 and 2. The exponents of these terms are:

		verb		particle	
1:	i.	final velarity + voice	**g ŋ**, or	voiced	**ɛ**
	ii.	„ non-(alveolarity + affrication)	**b t r d s m V**	vowel	
2:	i.	„ velarity + voicelessness	**k**, or	voiceless	**h**
	ii.	„ alveolarity + affrication	**tɕ/ts**	vowel	

The phonetic form **ɛ** of the imperative particle, with full voicing, is appropriate to the type-1 piece, and the phonetic form **hɛ** (or **ɛ̥ɛ**), with partial voicelessness, to the type-2.

The verbs can again be classified by type of piece just as they were for the three preceding types of disyllabic piece, as 1-piece (1–8, 13–23) or as 2-piece (9–12).

The particle of column 3, **ɛ/hɛ**, unlike those of columns 1 and 2, is vowel-initial, and the matching final features of the preceding verb syllable are, in consequence, different from those appropriate to the verb in the I–II piece (col. 1) or the A–B piece (col. 2) for all except verbs 10, 13, and 15. It is not only, therefore, from the point of view of phonetic variation in the initial of the particle syllable that the three types of piece exemplified in columns 1–3 are important.

The particle **ɛ/hɛ** is not the only one that can be contained in the 1–2 type of piece; there are also the vowel-initial particles **ɛnnɛ/hɛnnɛ** (imperative-negative), **uˀ/huˀ** and **uː/huː** (third-person-object, present and past respectively), **aŋ/haŋ** (first-person-past, intransitive-subject or transitive-object), and **ah/hah** (second/third-person-past, intransitive-subject or transitive-object), all of which can be given the same prosodic classification (1–2 piece) as **ɛ/hɛ**. An exception, the particle **aˀ**, is considered at pages 441–2 below.

In the 1–2 type of piece (col. 3) such final features as the following characterize verbs 1–5:

1, 3: voice + plosion (**b g**), cf. voicelessness + occlusion (**pˈ kˈ**)

2, 4: labiality, or velarity, + occlusion, and dentality + plosion (**pˈt kˈt**), cf. labiality, or velarity, + occlusion (**pˈ kˈ**)

5: voice + flap + alveolarity (**r**), cf. voicelessness + occlusion + labiality or alveolarity (**pˈ tˈ**)

The space available does not allow the variant features of each of the remaining verbs to be stated for this type of piece, and contrasted with the features appropriate to other types of piece; but, since they have been abstracted from each of the examples in Table 2, they can be arrived at without much difficulty.

This third prosodic classification of s verbs, as either type-1 or type-2, overlaps both the preceding classifications, as I-piece or II-piece and as A-piece or B-piece, and, when conjoined, gives the following six classes:

IA1	IB1	IIB1	IIB2	IIA2	IIA1
1–4	5–6	7–8	9–10	11–12	13–23

A six-term prosodic system, to which the name quality system is given, would therefore be adquate for the purpose of dealing with differences in the initial features of the various classes of particle syllable represented in Table 2 by **piː/biː**, **ɕiˀ/tɕhiˀ**, and **ɛ/hɛ** in association with matching differences in the final of the preceding verb. The temporary names used above to designate the six terms (IA1, IB1, IIB1, etc.) could of course be discarded at this point in favour of single-letter names, preferably of some mnemonic value, and therefore probably best based on some characteristic orthographic, or phonetic, feature of each class. It is on this principle that the following six names are given:

IA1	IB1	IIB1	IIB2	IIA2	IIA1
p	t	n	s	ŋ̇	m

Some of the twenty-three verbs of Table 2 show the same set of syllable-final features in all three types of piece (13: **ŋ**; 15: **m**); others show two sets of features (1–4, 10–12, 14, 16–21, e.g. 1: **p/b**; 2: **p/pt**; 3: **k/g**); yet others show three (5–9, e.g. **p/(t)tɕ/r, p/(t)tɕ/(t)t, m/ntɕ/r**). The prosodic statements made thus far, summarized in the six-term quality system, account for that variation in each lexical item; but this need not necessarily mean that the range of syllable-final variant features of each verb is limited to the two sets, or the three, shown in Table 2. On the contrary most of those verbs have additional variant features; and further contexts, both phonetic and grammatical, remain to be accounted for; but it is also true that these additional contexts do not affect the number of terms stated for the quality system above. The six terms are valid for them too.

In the course of stating the exponents of the 1–2 type of piece (Table 2, col. 3), in which the verbs are characterized by final features appropriate to a syntagmatic relationship with a vowel-initial type of particle syllable (**ɛ/hɛ, ɷŋˀ/hɷˀŋ, ah/hah**, etc.), an exception was made of the particle **a?** (first-person-present). Not only does this particle not show the initial voice-voicelessness (**V/h**) alternation that is characteristic of the other vowel-initial particles; the matching final features of the verb syllable are quite different for this particle from those shown in Table 2, column 3. No phonetic reason can be given for this difference in syntagmatically associated features; so the difference must be dealt with at the grammatical level, as a difference of grammatical context, of the first-person-present particle versus the remaining vowel-initial particles.

When colligated with the sub-class of verbal particle of which **a?** is the only member in the available material the verbs of Table 2 are characterized by long duration (cf. also s exponent (iv), p. 434) together with the following features:

1–2	labiality + voicelessness + plosion	**pp**
3–4	velarity + „ + „	**kk**
5–6	dentality + „ + „	**tt**
7–9	„ + (voice +) nasality	**nn**
11–14	velarity + („ +) „	**ŋŋ**
15–18	labiality + („ +) „	**mm**
20, 22	glottality, short vowel duration	**V??**

e.g.

TABLE 3

pp:	1 **jɛppa?** I stand	2 **tɕɛppa?** he cuts me	
kk:	3 **lakka?** it licks me	4 **thɔkka?** he fights me	
tt:	5 **sɛtta?** he kills me	6 **mɛtta?** he tells me	
nn:	7 **tɔnna?** he abuses me	8 **phɛnna?** he unties me	9 **phɔnna?** he employs me
ŋŋ:	11 **fiιŋŋa?** he rocks me	12 **fiιŋŋa?** he rears me	
	13 **kɛŋŋa?** I fall down	14 **thɔŋŋa?** he makes me fight	
mm:	15 **lɛmma?** I laze about	16 **jɛmma?** he tattoos me	
	17 **tɛmma?** he seizes me	18 **?imma?** I sleep	
??:	20 **wa??a ?** I am		22 **pi??a?** he gives me

Thus far the syllable-final variation in s verbs has been related to initial features of the following (particle) syllable *within the word*, i.e. in intraverbal junction (Tables 2–3), to syllable-initial consonance in the particle versus vocality (Table 2, cols. 1–2 versus Table 2, col. 3, and Table 3), and to syllable-initial labiality versus alveolarity in the particle (Table 2, col. 1, **p/b** versus Table 2, col. 2, **s/tɕ/ts**); but it is also possible for the verb to be final in the word. In this type of junction, junction between words (interverbal), verbs 1–18, 20, and 22, there being no examples of the others, are characterized by the same final features as for junction with **aˀ**, but with short duration instead of long, e.g.

TABLE 4

p:	1 **ɦɛn jɛp** he stands	2 **kɛdʑɛp** he cuts you	
k:	3 **kɛlak** it licks you	4 **kɛdɦɔk** he fights you	
t:	5 **kɛsɛt** he kills you	6 **kɛmɛt** he tells you	
n:	7 **kɛdɔn** he abuses you	8 **kɛbɦɛn** he unties you	9 **kɛbɦɔn** he employs you
ŋ:	11 **kɛɦɩŋ** he rocks you	12 **kɛɦɩŋ** he rears you	
	13 **ɦɛn kɛŋ** he falls down	14 **kɛdɦɔŋ** he makes you fight	
m:	15 **ɦɛn lɛm** he lazes about	16 **kɛjɛm** he tattoos you	
	17 **kɛdɛm** he seizes you	18 **ɦɛn ˀim** he sleeps	
ˀ:	20 **ɦɛn waˀ** he is		22 **kɛbiˀ** he gives you

A syntagmatic relationship can be stated for the syllable-final features of each of the word-final verbs in the above examples in association with initial features of the initial syllable of the following word, unless, of course, those verbs happen to be not only word-final but utterance-final as well. The available Limbu material is limited to a study of the verb, and does not therefore include those matching features of the following syllable; for these will generally be initial features of the initial noun of the following sentence.[22]

The interverbal term forms with the intraverbal a (two-term) junction system. The I–II, A–B, and 1–2 disyllable pieces (Table 2) and the disyllabic pieces in **a**ʔ (Table 3) are equally examples of intraverbal junction; they cover most of the different types of intraverbal junction, not all of which can be exemplified here.

The examples of the verb in interverbal junction (Table 4), and the partial statement of the exponency of the interverbal-junction term that accompanies them, complete the series of disyllabic-piece prosodic statements, in which one syllable is linked to another through features extending over syllable boundaries, and, for the interverbal-junction term, over word boundaries too; but there remains the possibility of further prosodic differentiation for verbs in accordance with internal features of the verb syllable, associations of features that extend over segment boundaries within the verb syllable but without crossing syllable boundaries.

INTRASYLLABIC PIECES

At this point one is again faced with the problem of delimiting the segment; but there is general agreement that vowels and consonants belong to different segments, and that where a syntagmatic relationship can be shown between features of a vowel and features of a preceding or a following consonant, a prosodic statement can appropriately be made.

Vowel and Consonant

A syntagmatic relationship of this intrasyllabic type can be shown for duration and voice-quality features of the vowel in each of the twenty-three verbs of Table 2 and either particular post-vocalic consonant features or non-syllabic vowel features, or absence of either. The examples in Table 2, column 2, can be put into one or other of two prosodic classes, temporarily denominated a and b, according as the verb syllable is characterized by:

a: **ɩ/i ɛ a ɔ ω** + short dur. — consonance

b: **i e ɛ a ɔ o u** + [long dur. / short ,, + constricted voice quality] — no consonance

The vowels **ɩ** and **ω** provide a type-a criterion, and **e**, **o**, and **u** a type-b.

The twenty-three verbs could then be prosodically classified again, as type-a (**VC(C)**, 1–18) or as type-b (**Vː**, 19–20; **V(ː)ˀ**, 21–23); but this classification cannot stand without modification for the column 3 examples: in column 3 verbs 19–20 are distinguished from verbs 21–23 by invariably short vowel duration (**ɛ ʌ**), by clear voice quality, and, for 19, by long consonant duration (**ss**), i.e. by **Vss** and **Vj** versus **V(ː)ˀj/r/s**.

Thus, three prosodic types of verb need to be distinguished as a result of syntagmatic associations of features of both vowel and following consonant or consonants or neither in columns 2 and 3 combined:

a: 1–18; b: 19–20; c: 21–23.

At this point mnemonically more suitable letters can be used to name these three types: g (from glottal constriction) instead of c, ḡ (non-g, from non-glottal constriction) instead of b, and c (from clear voice quality) instead of a. g, ḡ, and c will then be the three terms of a voice-quality system statable for an intrasyllabic piece. Every s (quantity) verb can then be classified as g, as ḡ, or as c in terms of this system, just as, before, they were classified in terms of the six-term quality system (p, t, n, s, ŋ, m).

The c voice-quality classification correlates with the p, t, n, s, and ŋ, all of which therefore imply c; but a verb classified as m can be either g, ḡ, or c. g and ḡ both imply m; but m does not imply g or ḡ. The quality and voice-quality systems combined give eight prosodic classes of s verb:

p(c)	t(c)	n(c)	s(c)	ŋ(c)	mc	mḡ	mg
1–4	5–6	7–8	9–10	11–12	13–18	19–20	21–23

g verbs (21–23) can be characterized by a wider range of vowels (**i e ɛ a ɔ o u**) than ḡ verbs or c verbs. ḡ verbs (19–20) are characterized only by **ɛ**, **a**, **ɔ**, and **u**, and c verbs (1–18)by **i/ɩ**, **ɛ**, **a**, **ɔ**, and **ɷ**. Half-closeness (**e o**) is therefore peculiar to g.[23]

The only other intrasyllabic-piece prosodic system that concerns the syllable final of verbs is a two-term system set up for a prosodic sub-class of c (voice quality) verbs (Table 2, 1–18) in order to associate a degree of centrality and openness of vowel (**ɩ**) with syllable-final velar nasality (**ŋ**) and with velar plosion + voicelessness (**(k)k**), e.g. Table 2, 11–12 (**ɩŋ ɩ(k)k**), and **ˀɩŋɛ** buy it, of the same type as **kɛŋɛ** (Table 2, 13), while the other term of the system associates frontness and closeness (**i**) with syllable-final velar plosion + voice (**g**), e.g. **ˀigɛ** twist it, with velar occlusion + voicelessness (**k˥**), e.g. **mɛːdɦik˥tɛnnɛ** do not card (wool), and with non-velarity (**p b m n (t)t**), e.g. **ˀipsɛ** sleep.[24] The former term (**ɩŋ ɩ(k)k**) correlates with the ŋ term of the quality system (p. 441; Table 2, 11–12) and with mc (Table 2, 13), the latter (**ip ib im in i(t)t**) with the p, t, and n terms (Table 2, 1–8), and with mc (14–18).

Consonant and Consonant

The prosodic systems stated for disyllabic pieces (quantity, quality; pp. 433–44) and for intrasyllabic pieces in which a syntagmatic relationship has been shown for a vowel segment and a following consonant (pp. 444–6) has produced the eight prosodic classes of verb distinguished above, p(c), t(c), n(c), etc. Each of these classes contains two or more lexical items that are phonetically distinguished from each other by final consonant features at least in Table 2, column 3, and, in some cases, in columns 1 and 2, and in Tables 3 and 4, as well. The four p(c) verbs (1–4), for example, are distinguished from each other by the final-consonant features **b**, **pt**, **g**, and **kt** in column 3, the two t lexical items (5–6) by **r** versus **(t)t**, and the two n lexical items (7–8) by **r** versus **nd**. This further degree of phonetic differentiation has still to be dealt with, either prosodically or phonematically. Whether the form of statement is prosodic or phonematic depends on whether such sequences of consonants as **pt**, **kt**, **tt**, and **nd**, for example, are attributed to one segment or to two; in other words the analysis of these features again raises the question of the segment and its extent. If, for the sake of argument, such sequences as **pt**, **kt**, **tt**, **nd**, etc., are ascribed each to a single segment, then the four consonants and consonant sequences **b**, **pt**, **g**, and **kt** of p(c) verbs in the 1–2 piece (Table 2, col. 3, 1–4) are all four uni-segmental; in which case no further prosodic statement would be appropriate, and a four-term phonematic system, B, P, G, and K, could be set up for the p(c) class of verb, for example, while, correspondingly, a two-term system, D and T, could be set up for the t verb (Table 2, 5–6), and a two-term, for which the letters D and T might again be used, for the n verb.[25] Any phonetic differences that there are in final consonant between the four p verbs in Table 2, column 3, will then be stated as exponents of B, of P, of G, or of K:

1 B:	labiality + plosion + voice	**b**
2 P:	labiality + occlusion, and dentality + plosion, + voicelessness	**pt**

3 G: velarity + plosion + voice **g**

4 K: velarity + occlusion, and dentality + plosion, + voicelessness **kt**

These are the exponents that are statable for B, P, G, and K in the 1–2 type of piece (Table 2, col. 3), in which the following syllable is vowel-initial (**ɛ/hɛ, ɷŋ/hɷŋ, uˀ/huˀ**, etc., but excluding **aˀ**; pp. 441–2). In all other types of piece, including the **aˀ** vowel-initial type, B is not distinguished in exponency from P, nor G from K; but B and P are together distinguished from both G and K by labiality (**p pp**) as opposed to velarity (**k kk**) (Table 2, cols. 1–2; Tables 3–4).

Similarly, the difference in final consonants between the two t verbs (5 and 6) in Table 2, column 3, would be stated as the exponency of D and T:

5 D: alveolarity + flap + voice **r**

6 T: dentality + plosion + voicelessness + [short duration **t** / long „ **tt**]

Apart from the type of piece exemplified in Table 2, column 3, there is no difference in exponency between these two terms (Table 2, cols. 1–2; Tables 3–4).

Provided that each of the eight prosodic classes of verb distinguished above (p. 445) is further analysed in this way, eight phonematic systems would be set up, one for each of the eight prosodic types:

p	t	n	s	ŋ	mc	mḡ	mg
1–4	5–6	7–8	9–10	11–12	13–18	19–20	21–23
BPGK	DT	DT	DT	GK	ÐKMTSP	SY	YRS

At first sight something of a parallel to this form of statement is afforded by the analysis of the homorganic labial, alveolar, and velar nasal-and-plosive consonant sequences **mb**, **nd**, and **ŋg** in, e.g., *timber*, *tinder*, *finger*, as unitary, i.e., for the purposes of this article, as single segments;[26] but on closer inspection this parallel turns out not to be so very close phonetically to the Limbu final-consonant sequences: only some of the Limbu sequences share with the English examples the feature of common localization: 6, 8, dentality **tt nd**; 9, 10, palato-alveolarity **ttɕ ntɕ**; 11, 12, velarity **kk ŋk**; 19, alveolarity **ss**; the others show a difference in localization between one consonant and the other: 2, 4, 14, 16, 17, 18, **pt kt ks md ms ps.** The difference in localization on the part of nearly half the final-consonant sequences strengthens the case for treating all these final-consonant sequences as two-segment sequences rather than as one-segment. Another argument in favour of distinguishing two segments is the fact that in dental-final sequences (**pt kt tt**, 2, 4, 6; **nd md**, 8, 16) either voice or voicelessness is a feature of the whole sequence. Not only does the alternation of voice with voicelessness as co-articulated features of the final dentality in association with voice or voicelessness respectively as a feature of the preceding consonant suggest that a prosodic statement could profitably be made; but it also presents a striking contrast with the sibilant-final sequences (**ttɕ/tts ntɕ/nts ks ms ps ss**; 9, 10, 14, 17–19) and the velar-final sequences (**kk ŋk**; 11–12), in which only voicelessness is coarticulated with the sibilance or velarity, irrespective of whether the preceding consonant is voiced or voiceless.

Treating the Limbu final-consonant sequences, including **tt**, **kk**, and **ss**, as bi-segmental naturally opens up the possibility of further prosodic statement, of syntagmatic associations of features extending over both segments. One such statement was suggested in the previous paragraph as a means of accounting for the alternation of voice with voicelessness in dental-final syllables (**pt kt tt** versus **nd md**); but it is first necessary to distinguish dental-final verbs from others.

Verbs having two syllable-final consonant segments can be grouped by final feature into (i) dental (**pt kt tt nd md**), (ii) sibilant (**ttɕ/tts ntɕ/nts ks ms ps ss**), and (iii) velar (**kk ŋk**). Dentality, sibilance, and velarity as features of the second of the two segments can then be associated with features of the first segment as follows:

i. dentality (**t/d**):	labiality (**p m**), velarity (**k**), dentality (**t n**)
ii. sibilance (**tɕ/ts s**):	labiality (**p m**), velarity (**k**), palato-alveolarity (**t n**), alveolarity (**s**)
iii. velarity (**k**):	velarity (**k ŋ**)

Translated into systemic terms these three sets of syntagmatic relations extending over the two segments can be ascribed to three terms of a system, the terms being named t (**pt kt tt nd md**), s (**ttɕ/tts ntɕ/nts ks ms ps ss**), and k (**kk ŋk**); these three terms contrast further with the single-final-consonant type of syllable to be seen in 1, 3, 5, 7, 13, 15, 20–23 (**b g r r ŋ m j j r s**), which type gives to the system a fourth term, named z (from zero). Since it has to do with syllable-final features, this four-term prosodic system is named the final system.

The twenty-three verbs of Table 2 are classified in terms of the final system as:

z	t	s	k
1 3 5 7 13 15 20–23	2 4 6 8 16	9–10 14 17–19	11–12

The k term correlates exclusively with the ŋ term of the quality system, and vice versa, the z term with the quality terms p, t, n, and m (the g term of the voice-quality system, 21–23, correlates exclusively with z), and the s final term with the s quality term and the m (mc and mḡ, but not mg).

When the final system (z, t, s, k) is combined with the prosodic systems that have preceded it, the following fourteen prosodic classes of verb emerge:

pz	pt	tz	tt	nz	nt	s(s)	ŋ(k)	mcz	mcs	mct	mḡs	mḡz	mg(z)
1 3	2 4	5	6	7	8	9 10	11 12	13 15	14 17 18	16	19	20	21–23

Two further prosodic systems are statable, one applicable only to t (final) verbs (2 4 6 8 16) and the other only to s (final) verbs. The system set up for t verbs is designed to associate either voice or voicelessness as features of the final segment with voice or voicelessness respectively as a feature of the preceding segment: (i) **nd md** (8 16); (ii) **pt kt tt** (2 4 6). This system will not, however, affect the classification given in the preceding paragraph; for the t verbs with final voice (**-nd -md**) are already in different classes (nt and m(c)t respectively) from the t verbs with final voicelessness (**-pt -kt**, pt; **-tt**, tt).

The further prosodic system to be set up for s verbs is designed to associate affrication (**tɕ**) as a feature of the second segment with dorso-alveolarity (**t n**) as a feature of the first (**ttɕ ntɕ**; 9 10) as opposed to friction (**s**) as a feature of ths second, with velarity, labiality, or alveolarity as a feature of the first (**ks ms ps ss**; 14, 17–19). This system too leaves the fourteen prosodic classes unaffected; for the s verbs in **ttɕ** and **ntɕ** are already in a different class, s(s), from those in **ks**, **ms**, **ps**, and **ss** (mcs, but mḡs for **ss**).

There being no further prosodic systems to state that are relevant to syllable-final features, phonematic analysis can now be carried out where appropriate. For verbs of the prosodic classes tz (5), tt (6), nz (7), nt (8), m(c)t (16), mḡs (19), and mḡz (20), phonematic analysis is not appropriate; for there are no further syllable-final phonetic distinctions; such verbs are already fully distinguished by prosodic classification alone. Phonematic systems can, however, and must be stated for the remaining prosodic types of verb:

pz: P: labiality (**b**) (1); K: velarity (**g**) (3)
pt: P: ,, (**p**) (2); K: ,, (**k**) (4)
s(s): T: voicelessness + occlusion (**t**) (9)[27]
N: voice + nasality (**n**) (10)

ŋ(k):	K:	voicelessness + occlusion (**k**) (11)[27]
	ŋ:	voice + nasality (**ŋ**) (12)
mcz:	M:	labiality (**m**) (13); ŋ: velarity (**ŋ**) (15)
mcs:	K:	velarity + occlusion + voicelessness (**k**) (14)
	P:	labiality + „ + „ (**p**) (18)
	M:	„ + nasality + voice (**m**) (17)
mg(z):	Y:	palatality + non-syllabic vowel + voice (**j**) (21)
	R:	alveolarity + flap + voice (**r**) (22)
	S:	„ + friction + voicelessness (**s**) (23)

These exponents are valid for the 1–2 type of disyllabic piece (Table 2, col. 3), in which the following syllable is vowel-initial. In other types of piece the exponential features of each phonematic unit may or may not be different from those given here, and may or may not be identical with those of the other term or terms of the system. Thus, in the A–B type of disyllabic piece (Table 2, col. 2) the exponents of the units of the pz, pt, and s(s) phonematic systems, for example, are:

pz:	P:	labiality (**p**) (1);	K:	velarity (**k**) (3)
pt:	P:	„ („) (2);	K:	„ („) (4)
s(s):	T:	voice + nasality (**n**) (9)		
	N:	„ + „ („) (10)[28]		

Here, the exponents of Ppz and Kpz (**p, k**) do not differ from those given for these two units in the preceding paragraph (**b, g**; 1–2 piece); but the exponents of Ts (**n**) not only differ in this type of piece from those given in the 1–2 type (**t**) but are here identical with those of N.

Stating the phonematic systems, and the exponents of the terms contained in those systems, for each prosodic type of piece for which a phonematic statement can in fact be made is the final stage of this prosodic analysis, an analysis limited to the syllable-final features of Limbu verbs; but, limited though it is, it is hoped that it will have been sufficient to demonstrate that Firth's phonological theory can offer the comparatist the advantage of working from a single formula for each lexical item summarizing its whole range of phonetic variation, e.g.:

	I–II piece	A–B piece	1–2 piece	a' piece	inter.	formulation
5	**kɛ-sɛp-piː**	**ˀa-sɛ(t)tɕ-hiˀ**	**sɛr-ɛ**	**sɛtt-aˀ**	**kɛ-sɛt**	stz
7	**kɛ-dɔm-biː**	**ˀa-dɔntɕ-hiˀ**	**tɔr-ɛ**	**tɔnn-aˀ**	**kɛ-dɔn**	snz
9	**kɛ-bɦɔm-biː**	**ˀa-bɦɔntɕ-hiˀ**	**phɔ(t)tɕ-hɛ**	**phɔnn-aˀ**	**kɛ-bɦɔn**	sTs(s)

(quantity: s; quality: t, n, s; final: z (s)).

Notes

[1] For this difficulty in Burmese see Richard K. Sprigg, 'Prosodic Analysis, and Phonological Formulae, in Tibeto-Burman Linguistic Comparison', *Linguistic Comparison in South East Asia and the Pacific* (School of Oriental and African Studies, London, 1963), pp. 91–2 and 93–5, and for Tibetan the examples given on pages 136–142 of 'The Tonal System of Tibetan (Lhasa Dialect) and the Nominal Phrase', *BSOAS* xvii (1955), 1, and P. M. Miller, 'The Phonemes of Tibetan (U-Tsang Dialect) with a practical romanized orthography for Tibetan-speaking readers', *Journal of the Asiatic Society* (Calcutta), *Letters* XVII (1951), 3, p. 201: '"n^{y}o" "buy" changes to "n^{y}op" in "n^{y}op̉.čá" "purchases"; "sá" "earth" becomes "sáp̉" in "sáp̉.t^{ə}rá" "map"'; and, further, 'every syllable in Tibetan may be assigned one or other of these [two] tonemes or inherent tones . . .' (p. 200), but 'Final Intonation: . . . Natural tone is often disregarded' (p. 206).

[2] First classified as Tibeto-Burman by E. L. Brandreth ('On the Non-Aryan Languages of India', *JRAS*, New Series x (1878), p. 31) the Kiranti languages were re-classified by Przyłuski as Munda, 'bien que saturées de mots indo-aryens et tibéto-birmans' (*Langues du Monde*, Paris, 1924, p. 400). In the 1952 edition of *Langues du Monde* (p. 558), however, Maspero returned to the earlier classification, which also has the support of Konow and Wolfenden, and of Shafer, who assigns Limbu to the East Himalayish Section of the Bodic Division (Robert Shafer, 'East Himalayish', *BSOAS* xv (1953), 2, pp. 356–357).

Shafer's solution to the problem presented by the Tibetan verb roots is to use the perfect, usually with the omission of postpositions, in his comparisons ('Newari and Sino-Tibetan', *SL* 6 (1952), p. 95). Phonological formulae summarizing all roots of each Tibetan verb are proposed as the solution to it in my 'Prosodic Analysis, and Phonological Formulae' (pp. 79–84).

[3] 'I venture to hope that some of the notions I have suggested may be of value to those discussing laryngals in Indo-European, and even to those engaged on field-work on hitherto unwritten languages' (John R. Firth, 'Sounds and Prosodies', *TPS* 1948, 1949, p. 150). On prosodic analysis compare also his 'A Synopsis of Linguistic Theory', *Studies in Linguistic Analysis* (Blackwell, Oxford, 1957), pp. 15–17, and Robert H. Robins, 'Aspects of Prosodic Analysis', *Proceedings of the University of Durham Philosophical Society*, vol. I, Series B (Arts), 1957, 1, pp. 1–12.

For an application of prosodic analysis to language comparison see Richard K. Sprigg, 'A Comparison of Arakanese and Burmese Based on Phonological Formulae', *Linguistic Comparison in South East Asia and the Pacific* (School of Oriental and African Studies, London, 1963), pp. 109–32.

[4] It is phonemes and phonemic forms, and not, for example, morpho-phonemes (with which the lexical-item phonological formulae of this article clearly have something in common; pp. 433–44), that are the sole basis of Henry J. Hoenigswald's reconstructions in his recent *Language Change and Linguistic Reconstruction* (The University of Chicago Press, Chicago, 1960).

[5] These examples are of the Pantharea dialect, as spoken by Randhoj Nembang, *pujārī*, of Imbung village, Panthar (or Panchthar), Dhankuta District, Nepal; the material from which they are taken was collected during a month's stay in the neighbouring villages of Sartap and Powa during 1956. Randhoj was literate in both Limbu and Nepali, writing the former in the modern form of the so-called Kiranti script ('Limbu Books in the Kiranti Script', *Akten des XXIV. Internationalen*

Orientalisten Kongresses München 1957, Deutsche Morgenländische Gesellschaft, Wiesbaden, 1959, pp. 590–592).

Limbu words can be monosyllabic or polysyllabic; the words in Table 1 comprise members of both verb and particle categories, the verb syllable being separated from the other syllables of the word by hyphens.

6 In the phonetic transcription used here **t**, **d**, and **n** symbolize dorsality and alveolarity when followed, respectively, by **ɕ**, **ʑ**, and **tɕ**, apicality and alveolarity when followed, respectively, by **s**, **z**, and **ts**, and apicality and dentality in all other circumstances; **r** symbolizes an alveolar flap (I.P.A. ɾ); when followed by **ɦ** the symbols **g**, **d**, and **b** indicate lax plosives that were occasionally heard as fully voiced, and identical with the 'voiced aspirates' of Nepali (I.P.A. **gɦ**, **dɦ**, **bɦ**), but more commonly heard as at least partially voiceless (I.P.A. **g̊ɦ**, **d̥ɦ**, **b̥ɦ**); the symbol ˀ is used for constricted (or 'creaky') voice quality; **k**, **g**, and **s** in front-vowel **(i e ɛ)** syllables symbolize some degree of palatalization; **V** symbolizes vowel, and **C** consonant.

7 In the phonemic analysis of these examples **p** and **b**, **tɕ** and **dʑ**, and **kh** and **gɦ** have been treated as allophones of /p/, /c/, and /kh/ respectively; for no lexical distinctions are involved provided that the analysis is restricted to verb forms; but, since in nouns voice + plosion (**g dʑ d b gɦ dɦ bɦ**) is a possible initial combination of features in lexically significant contrast with **k**, **kh**, **tɕ**, **t**, **th**, **p**, **ph**, e.g. **ga** I, cf. **kaˀko(ˀ)wa** [kidney?], **kham** earth, **b**, **dʑ**, and **gɦ** would have to be assigned to different phonemes (/b/, /j/, and /gh/ respectively) from **p**, **tɕ**, and **kh** in an overall transcription. The phonetic forms **jɛb**, **dʑɛp**, and **gɦɛm** (i, ii, v) would then have to be analysed as /yɛb/, /jɛp/, and /ghɛm/, thus further increasing the number of phonemic forms of each of the lexical items concerned.

8 E.g. William Cornyn, 'Outline of Burmese Grammar', *Lg* xx (1944), 4, suppl., p. 9 (25, 28–29); Raven I. McDavid, 'Burmese Phonemics', *SIL* iii (1945), 1, pp. 6 (1), 11 (8.1), 15 (9.2); P. M. Miller, 'The Phonemes of Tibetan', p. 451, n. 1 above.

9 An exemplary feature of Major H.W.R. Senior's *A Vocabulary of the Limbu Language of Eastern Nepal* (Government Monotype Press, Simla, 1908) is that he gives an imperative form of each verb, when known, in addition to the infinitive. Imansingh Chemjong, in his *Limbu-Nepali-English Dictionary* (Nepal Academy, Kathmandu, [2018?] V.S.), gives a past-tense form, which is equally helpful.

10 Robins, 'Aspects', pp. 3–4.

11 Short in fast-tempo utterances.

12 Applicable only to a sub-class of s verb, in disyllabic pieces in which the following (particle) syllable is characterized initially by a consonant (pp. 444–5).

13 Applicable only to a sub-class of verb, when followed by **aˀ** (first-person particle). The alternative short duration in l exponent no. ix is thought to be a fast-tempo feature.

14 Applicable only to a sub-class of l verb in words in which the following particle is vowel-initial, e.g. **ɛ/hɛ** (imperative-affirmative), **ɛnnɛ/hɛnnɛ** (imperative-negative), and, for intransitive verbs, the past particles **aŋ** (first-person) and **ah** (second/third-person). The features stated at (ii) are thought to be slow-tempo.

15 Applicable only to a sub-class of l verb, when colligated with the imperative-negative particle (**ɛnnɛ/hɛnnɛ**).

16 Applicable only to a sub-class of l verb, when colligated with the third-person-object particle (vowel-initial): (i) second/third-person-subject, **uˀ** (present) and **uː** (past); (ii) first-person-subject, **ɷŋˀ** (present) and **ɷŋː** (past).

[17] This is an additional reason for preferring the names s and l for these two phonological terms to *short* and *long*, which are more readily confused with the terminology of the phonetic level. The decisive reason, though, is that letters are suitable for formulae; words are not.

[18] **tj** and **dj** are not possible initials in a phonological syllable, nor is **sj** in a phonological syllable of which the vowel is **a**; though monosyllabic phonetically **sjah**, **sjaŋ**, **-djɛn-**, **tjah**, and **tjɛh** must therefore be examples of two phonological syllables.

[19] The vowels of **tsaŋʾ** and **tsɔː** serve for both verb and particle, the backness and rounding of **tsɔː**, for example, being attributable to the particle (**uː** in other prosodic types of piece) and the half-openness to the verb (alias **tsaː**); there are no forms ***tsaːɷŋʾ** and ***tsaːuː**.

[20] In a few instances (nos. 10, 19, 21, 23) it has been necessary to give words in **-suʾ/-tshuʾ** (we two — it) instead.

[21] The vocalic feature (V) applies only to fast-tempo utterances.

[22] Cf. p. 452, n. 5. Since the time available was so limited, I thought it preferable to make a complete analysis of verb forms rather than incomplete analyses of forms from all grammatical categories.

[23] For l verbs no voice-quality system can be stated; and, apart from a small subclass, they are characterized by the vowel features **iː eː ɛː aː ɔː oː uː** in all types of piece (for examples see pp. 435–6).

[24] This system is not statable for all s (quantity) verbs but only for syllables in which the vowel is front and close (**i**/**ɩ**), i.e. only for s (from *spread*) syllables, so classified from the s term of the four-term initial prosodic system, whose function it is to associate initial-consonant and vowel features. s (initial) syllables are distinguished from the other three types by absence of initial semi-vowel: **je/ɛ/a/ɔ/o/u** and **we/ɛ/a**, but no ***ji/ɩ** or ***wi/ɩ**.

[25] Phonematic units are symbolized by capital letters. Additional exponents of the suggested phonematic units can be found on p. 442 (words in **aʾ**) and on p. 443 (interverbal junction). Ideally it would be better to use different letters for terms in different systems; but the Roman alphabet is insufficient for this.

[26] I owe these examples and the analysis of them to my colleague Mrs. E. M. Whitley.

[27] Nil in fast-tempo utterances.

[28] The exponent shown here for each of the six phonematic units is also valid for it in interverbal junction (p. 443) and, with the addition of long duration, in the **aʾ** type of piece (p. 442).

Numeratives in Uzbek
A Study in Colligation and Collocation

NATALIE WATERSON

The need to establish a separate category of numerative became evident to the writer through the study of collocations in Uzbek[1] when engaged in work on lexicography, and the aim of this paper is to show how the concept of colligation[2] and collocation can be used in grammatical analysis.

On consulting studies in various Turkic languages,[3] it was found that in general, numeratives had only a passing mention under the heading of numerals, as special words used in counting, and had not been formally established as a separate grammatical category. It is intended here to establish the category of numerative in Uzbek as a member of the nominal class by a study of the colligation of the noun with certain other members of the nominal class. This involves some re-examination of the controversial question of nouns and adjectives in Turkic languages.

Because of the large number of words in Turkic languages that are identical in form but different in function,[4] there has been some disagreement among Turcologists as to how far there are separate categories of noun and adjective, the discussion centering more particularly on words like **tɑš**, *stone*, **ɑltin**, *gold*, **temir**, *iron*, **yɑğɑč**, *wood*,[5] which are sometimes referred to as 'material nouns', and on the substantival use of adjectives. These questions have been much discussed by Soviet linguists since 1950 and as far as can be seen from works available since that date, have not yet been satisfactorily settled.[6]

Some linguists consider that **tɑš**, *stone*, in such structures as **tɑš koprik**, *stone bridge*, is an adjective and in structures such as **uning tɑši**, *his stone*, **bu tɑš**, *this stone*, is a noun, i.e. two homonyms, one of which is an adjective, and the other a noun. Cf. **qizil bayrɑq**, *red flag*, where **qizil**, *red*, is an adjective, and **uning bayrɑği**, *his flag*, **bu bayrɑq**, *this flag* where **bayrɑq**, *flag*, is a noun. Others consider that **tɑš**, *stone*, is a noun in both cases, a noun indicating material out of which something is made, which, like an adjective, can qualify another noun without a genitive and possessive.

A brief analysis of the views held by some Soviet scholars is given to illustrate ways in which words in the nominal class have been analysed, with special reference to nouns, adjectives and numerals, as these are the categories required to be studied and compared in a discussion on numeratives. Nouns and adjectives are generally classified by the way they qualify a noun and as the confusion is between noun and adjective, and there is none between noun, adjective, participle and pronoun, participles and pronouns are excluded as not being relevant to the problem under discussion here.

In general, Soviet linguists base their analysis of Turkic languages on syntactic, morphological and semantic criteria. The morphological and syntactic criteria are quite adequate for establishing the different categories in Turkic languages. The addition of semantic criteria only serves to cloud the issue.[7] Some Soviet linguists seem to use the concept of colligation. For instance, in discussions on adjective and noun, the possible combinations of noun with other classes of nominal are considered. This is referred to as **slovosočetanije** which may be translated as 'the combining of words' and is different from **slovosloženije**, the 'compounding of words', i.e. the formation of compounds.

G.D. Sanžejev, writing in 1954 about the problem of noun and adjective,[8] said there were two main schools of thought, (a) those who followed Latin grammar and considered that Altaic languages had the same kind of nouns and adjectives as Indo-European languages and held the view that words like **taš**, *stone*, are both nouns and adjectives, and words like **jaxši**, *good, well*, are both adjectives and adverbs, and (b) those who considered a noun could function as an adjective in a sentence when in a position before another noun and an adjective could function as an adverb in a position before a verb.

Sanžejev quotes A.V. Avrorin's analysis into four classes of nominal instead of the more usual two classes, adjective and noun,[9] i.e. (a) noun substantive, defines other nouns with the possessive suffix, e.g. **partiya komiteti**, *party committee*. (b) noun objective, defines other nouns without any suffixes and represents mostly concrete as opposed to abstract notions, e.g. **taš balta**, *stone axe*, **temir yol**, *railway* (lit. *iron road*). (c) noun adjective, represents the quality of an object, e.g. **yazgi payt**, *summertime*, **yangi yol**, *new road*, but cannot be used to qualify a verb.[10] (d) noun qualitative, defines an object or action, especially of abstract quality, e.g. **jaxši at**, *good horse*, **jaxši yazmaq**, *to write well*. In this analysis (c) and (d) can only be treated as separate classes on the basis of considering words in (d) as having two syntactic functions, viz., qualifying a noun and qualifying a verb. Words belonging to (c) have the function of qualifying a noun only. It seems preferable to group the noun qualifiers in (d) with the noun qualifiers in (c) and have verb qualifiers only in (d). This means that there would be homonyms in two different classes but this is of no consequence. The separation of the verb qualifiers from the noun qualifiers would link up with the rest of the grammatical analysis which requires a verb qualifier class, e.g., forms derived from other classes, e.g. **ozbekča** in **ozbekča gapirmɑq**, *to speak Uzbek*.

No formal criteria are given here for separating (b) and (c) although criteria for such a division have been given by other linguists.[11]

Sanžejev suggests that there is no clear division between (a) and (b) in some Turkic languages, among them Uzbek, and proposes three classes only: (1) noun substantive, e.g. **ɑt**, *horse*, **yaxšilik**, *goodness*, *kindness*. (2) noun adjective, e.g. **yɑzgi**, *summer* (adj.), **kok**, *blue*. This class contains mostly adjectives derived from other classes. (3) noun qualitative, e.g. **yaxši**, *good*, *well*, **arzɑn**, *cheap*, *cheaply*. This is the same as Avrorin's (d). The amalgamation of Avrorin's (a) and (b) classes into one does not seem to be justified on formal grounds[12] and it is significant that Sanžejev omits words like **temir**, *iron*, **tɑš**, *stone*, from his examples.

With regard to the substantival use of adjectives and qualitatives, Sanžejev states[13] that this phenomenon is generally understood as the replacement of a noun by an adjective. He quite rightly points out that an adjective so used does not replace any noun but that it is a characteristic of the class of adjectives and qualitatives to function thus, i.e. with noun substantive suffixes.[14]

A. N. Kononov, in his Turkish grammar,[15] uses morphological, semantic and syntactic criteria to separate the classes of noun and adjective.[16] He states on pp. 61 and 135 that 'material' nouns are linked directly with the noun they qualify without any suffixes. They only qualify objects while other nouns can stand in other grammatical relationships. In other words, his 'material' nouns are a special class of noun. The examples he gives are Turkish **taş**, *stone*, in **taş duvar**, *stone wall*, **cam**, *glass*, in **cam boru**, *glass pipe*. He compares them with what he classes as compounds, e.g. **baş doktor**, *head doctor*, **ana yol**, *main road*, **Orta Doğu**, *Middle East*.[17] His adjective can qualify an object and an action without a change of form, cf. Avrorin's and Sanžejev's qualitative.

Numerals, as is usual in the case of Turkic languages, are classified as members of the noun class.[18] Under the heading of cardinal numbers on p. 165 § 291, there is a sub-heading 'numeratives' followed by a statement that special explanatory words may be inserted between the cardinal number and the noun, and the following list is given, with examples, **baš**, *head* (of animals), **adet**, *object* (of separate items), **tane**, *object* (of small items), **takım**, **kat**, *set*, *pair* (of clothes) **çift**, *pair* (of clothes), **el**, *hand*, *time* (of firing), **dilim**, **parça**, *slice*, *piece* (of measure). What he calls concrete numerals are said to stand in apposition to the corresponding noun, e.g. **uç kilo elma**, *3 kilos of apples*, **iki şişe şarap**, *2 bottles of wine*, **beş kilometre yol**, *road 5 kilometres long*.

In his Uzbek grammar,[19] Kononov again makes use of morphological, semantic and syntactic criteria. Nouns and adjectives are separate categories on the basis of similar criteria to those stated for Turkish.[20] Adjectives qualify nouns without izafet.[21] In a sentence they can be used attributively e.g. **yangi uy**, *new house*, pre-verbally, e.g. **yangi keldi**, *he came again*, and predicatively, e.g. **bu uy yangi**, *this house is new*. He has a separate adverbial class as a pre-nominal or pre-verbal qualifier. Words like **yaxši**, **yangi**, which function adjectivally and adverbially without a change of form, are classed as adjectives. Derived verb qualifiers, i.e. those forms which have a suffix of some kind added to the root of another word class, are classified as adverbs.

Kononov considers that an adjective becomes substantival when it takes any noun suffix, e.g. **yaxši**, (adj.) *good*, **yaxšilar**, (noun) *good things/people*. He lists the ways in which a noun may be qualified, i.e. by (1) adjective, (2) numeral, (3) pronoun, (4) noun, (5) verb forms in **-gan**, etc.

Kononov describes three types of noun qualification:[22]

I. Noun linked to noun without suffixes. In this group are included 'material' nouns, e.g. **temir**, *iron*, **tɑš**, *stone*, etc., and nouns denoting profession, title, nationality, e.g. **temirči Karim**, *blacksmith Karim*, **student Salimov**, *student Salimov*, **leytenant Hakimov**, *lieutenant Hakimov*, **ozbek Žora**, *Uzbek Jora*. Words used to indicate gender[23] which also qualify a noun without any suffixes are included here, e.g. **er**, *man*, **erkak**, *man*, *male*, **xɑtin/ayɑl**, *woman*, **qiz**, *girl*, **urğɑči**, *female*. Examples: **er bɑla**, *boy*, **qiz bɑla**, *girl* (**bɑla**, *child*), **orɑqči (erkak)**, *reaper*, **orɑqči xɑtin/ayɑl**, *woman reaper*, **ayiq (erkak)**, *bear*, **urğɑči ayiq**, *she-bear*.

II. Noun linked to noun with possessive suffix of the noun qualified (**-i**/**-si**). All nouns can function thus as a qualifier with the exception of those in class I, e.g. **šaxmat taxtasi**, *chessboard*, **kitɑb magazini**, *bookshop*.[24]

III. The qualifying noun has the genitive case (**-ning**) and the noun qualified has the third person suffix (**-i**/**-si**), e.g. **bu maktabning oquvčilari**, *pupils of this school*, **dostlarimning biri**, *one of my friends*.

Kononov's type II is like Avrorin's (a) noun substantive, and his type I is like Avrorin's (b) noun objective.

Within the numeral class, Kononov gives examples of numeral qualifying noun: **ikki kitɑb ɑldik**, *we took two books*,[25] **ɑvci tortta ordak ɑtdi**, *the huntsman shot four ducks*, **birinči zvonok**, *first bell*, **kop ɑdamlar**, *many people*, **birneča dostlar**, *several friends*, etc.[26]

He has a sub-class of 'item' numerals which, he says, is formed by (a) the addition of **-ta** to the cardinal numbers, e.g. **ikkita daftar**, *two copybooks*, and (b) the use of special explanatory words, numeratives, between the numeral and noun. He lists those he considers to be the most common, with examples, e.g. **nafar**, *person*, **bɑš**, *head*, **nusha**, *copy*, **tup**, *bush/plant*, **žuft**, *pair*, **tilim**, *piece*, **dɑna**, *thing*. Examples like **bir piala čɑy**, *one glass of tea*, **ikki arava otin**, *two loads of firewood*, **beš metr čit**, *five metres of cotton*, **uč litr sut**, *three litres of milk*, are dealt with separately under cardinal numbers as one of the uses of the nominative case of the noun.

T.I. Grunin[27] has a slightly different analysis. He too uses morphological, syntactic and semantic criteria but considers syntactic criteria to be the most important. Adjectives, he says, can only be established by the analysis of the formal links of the components of a qualifying group. He divides qualifying groups into three types:

(1) Analytic word combination. Here word order is important. The qualifier precedes the qualified. Examples from Turkish, **sarı çiçek**, *yellow flower*, **altın saat**, *gold watch*.

(2) The second type, synthetic, is characterized by the presence of the suffix **-ı** (**-i, -u, -ü, -sı, -si, -su, -sü**) of the qualified. Examples from Turkish **kadın robası**, *woman's dress*, **ekmek fiyati**, *price of bread*.

(3) The third type is characterized by the presence of the genitive suffix **-ın** (**-in, -un, -ün, -nın, -nin, -nun, -nün**) of the qualifier and the possessive suffix **-ı** (**-i, -u, -ü, -sı, -si, -su, -sü**) of the qualified. Examples from Turkish, **kadının robası**, *the woman's dress*. This type he called 'possessive synthetic'.

He groups together Turkish **köylü, inkılâpçi, sarı, kalın, altın, ağaç** as belonging to the analytic type of qualifier, e.g. **köylü hastalar**, *the village* *sick*, **inkılâpçi talebeler**, *revolutionary students*, **sarı çiçek**, *yellow flower*, **kalın kitap,** *thick book*, **altın saat,** *gold watch*, **ağaç teneke,** *wooden box*. The group of qualifier and qualified, he says, can be separated by **bir**, e.g. **sarı bir çiçek,** *a very yellow flower*, **kalın bir kitap**, *a very thick book*, and the order is changed in a predicative construction, e.g. **hastalar köylü**, *the sick are villagers*, **talebeler inkılâpçi**, *the students are revolutionary*, **çiçek sarı**, *the flower is yellow*, **saat altın**, *the watch is a gold one*. Grunin points out in a footnote on p. 61, op. cit., that analytical groups of this type can only be split by **bir** to intensify the quality expressed by the qualifier, and groups like **altın saat**, **ağaç teneke** cannot be so divided because **altın** and **ağaç** express absolute qualities. It would seem preferable to use this indivisibility as a criterion for putting such words in a separate class, as is done by Kononov and others. It is then unnecessary to resort to notional criteria such as absolute or non-absolute qualities.

N. A. Baskakov,[28] has two main types of nominal word combinations:

I. No formal link except word order.
II. Link by suffixes, i.e. genitive and possessive.

Among those belonging to group I are words referring to gender, age, type, nationality, profession, material, and numerals and demonstrative pronouns.[29]

Examples in Karakalpak:

(1) Gender: **ata pıšıq**, *tom cat*, **ana pıšıq**, *female cat*, **erkak at**, *stallion*, **urğašı at**, *mare*, **qız bala**, *girl*, **ul bala**, *boy*.

(2) Age: **žas adam**, *youth*, *young man*, **qarrı kisi**, *old man*, **qarrı šeše,** *old woman*.

(3) Kind, profession: **qaragay ağaš**, *pine tree*, **sazan balıq**, *carp*, **orus adam**, *a Russian*, **temirši adam**, *blacksmith*.

(4) Title: **Aqmet baba**, *grandfather Ahmet*, **Urumbay temirši**, *blacksmith Urumbay*.

(5) Description showing the form of an object, e.g. **pušuq kisi**, *snub-nosed person*, **oraq ay**, *sickle-shaped moon*.

(6) Material: **temir žol**, *railway*, **tas köpir**, *stone bridge*, **altın žüzük**, *gold ring*.

(7) Definition by personal and demonstrative pronouns, e.g. **bu adam**, *this man*, **anav kisi**, *that man*, **sol vaq**, *that time*.

(8) Definition by substantival numerals, e.g. **altav kisi**, *six people*.

Adjectives and numerals also come into this type I group, e.g. **žaqsı adam**, *good man*, **qara köz**, *black eyes*, **birinši kün**, *first day*, **törtinši**

topar, *fourth group*, **bes kisi**, *five people*, **üš topar adam**, *three groups of people.*

Group II has the following possessive combinations: (a) with possessive only, examples in Karakalpak: **köz žası**, *tears*, **tün žarımı**, *midnight*, and (b) with genitive and possessive, **pısıqtıng žüni**, *cat's fur*.

In this work no reference is made to numeratives although **topar** in **üš topar adam** quoted above is an example of one. However, in an earlier work[30] Baskakov has a short paragraph on numeratives. He states that cardinal numbers are sometimes followed by numeratives which are used in listing. These indicate measures of length, weight, volume, and counting by item, person and group. He gives a few examples with sentences to illustrate their use, e.g. **batpan**, *weight of 10 lb.*, **yüyür**, *herd*, **qol**, *detachment*, **top**, *group*. Nouns and adjectives are separate categories, nouns being primarily defined by the presence, in a noun-noun qualifying group, of the third possessive suffix of the noun qualified and the possibility of the genitive in the noun qualifying. Words like **tas**, *stone*, in **tas yüy**, *stone house*, are called attributive nouns by virtue of their similarity to adjectives both semantically and in their method of qualifying a noun.[31] But under the heading of adjectives, lists are given of forms where noun and adjective are not clearly differentiated, e.g. **ağaš**, *wood*, *wooden*, **yümis**, *silver*, *silvery*, **altın**, *gold*, *golden*, **batır**, *hero*, *brave*, **er**, *man*, *manly.*[32]

M.B. Balakajev[33] classes words like **altın**, *gold*, **temir**, *iron* as nouns.[34] Of the relevant colligations, he has (a) noun and noun in the nominative case, e.g. **altın žüzik**, *gold ring*, **žibek oramal**, *silk kerchief*, **temir peš**, *iron stove*, **altın sağat**, *gold watch*, **suv diyirmen**, *watermill*. Here there is no formal link except word order. His second group is (b) adjective and noun, e.g. **biyik tav**, *high mountain*, **žaqsı bala**, *good boy*, **kök aspan**, *blue sky*, **aqıldı qız**, *clever girl*, **köp balalı æyel**, *woman who has many children*. His third group is (c) numeral and noun, e.g. **bes kitap**, *five books*, **bir žüz otiz qoy**, *130 sheep*, **altınšı brigada**, *sixth brigade*, **qırıq toğızınšı mektep**, *49th school.*

With reference to his first group, i.e. noun and noun in the nominative case, Balakajev states that only certain nouns with 'concrete' meaning can be used attributively as qualifiers for nouns, but they cannot be used predicatively. He points out that what appears to be a predicative construction has a different meaning and cannot therefore be interpreted as the predicative form of the corresponding attributive form. Cf. **biyik tav**, *high mountain*, and **tav biyik**, *the mountain is high*, with **köz æynek**, *spectacles* (lit. *eye glass*) but **æynek köz**, *glass eyes*, **qalta**

sağat, *pocket watch* but **sağat qalta**, *watch pocket, pocket for watch.* Balakajev points out that some nouns with 'concrete' meaning can only act as a qualifier if they themselves have a qualitative qualifier, and among his examples are some with a numeral qualifier, e.g. **bir arqa otın**, *one bundle of firewood*, **üš qap astıq**, *three bags of corn*, **bir qaynatım šay**, *measure of tea for one brewing*, **bir üzim nan**, *one slice of bread.* He therefore classes as 'nouns with concrete meaning' what in this paper is classed as numerative, but whereas it is not easy to define 'concrete meaning', it is simple to classify the numerative by its colligation.[35]

Nouns which can function attributively are subdivided by Balakajev into seven groups as follows:[36]

(1) material, e.g. **temir peš**, *iron stove*, **ağaš kürek**, *wooden spade.*
(2) comparative epithet, e.g. **qoy köz**, *sheep's eyes.*
(3) naming object, e.g. **at qora**, *stable*, **kir sabın**, *household soap.*
(4) spatial relationship of objects, e.g. **tav teke**, *mountain goat.*
(5) measure relations, e.g. **bir qora qoy**, *flock of sheep*, **bir uvıs biyday**, *handful of wheat*, **šelek-šelek süt**, *several buckets of milk.*
(6) gender, e.g. **qız bala**, *girl*, **ul bala**, *boy.*
(7) kind, type, e.g. **alma ağaš**, *apple tree*, **nar tüye**, *dromedary.*

Balakajev has no separate category of numerative but group (5) stands out as being different from the rest in that two examples have **bir** preceding the noun qualifiers and the third example has reduplication of the qualifier. **Bir**, according to the Russian translation, seems to be treated here as the indefinite article[37] whereas it would be preferable to treat it as the numeral 'one' as in the examples cited earlier, viz. **bir arqa otın**, *one bundle of firewood*, **üš qap astıq**, *three sacks of corn.*

When considering the colligation numeral and noun, Balakajev states that a numeral relating to a word indicating measure forms a compound qualifying group with it.[38]

Nouns qualifying nouns with izafet are dealt with under word combination with subordinate construction.[39]

In a later work[40] words like **ağaš**, *wood*, **tas**, *stone*, in the groups **ağaš kürek**, *wooden spade*, **tas köpir**, *stone bridge*, are again analysed as nouns. Balakajev here points out that another qualifier cannot be substituted in such a word group nor can the order of the words in the group be changed, and if a further qualifier is added, it qualifies the whole group. This, he says, proves that such nouns (i.e. the qualifiers) do not change into adjectives as some Turcologists think.

It is interesting to see that R. G. Syzdykova, in an article on the numeral in Kazak,[41] seems to feel the need for separating the 'counting by item' from the rest of the numeral class. She says 'the so-called item-numerals (see Kononov's Uzbek Grammar, Moscow–Leningrad, 1960, p. 167) formed for example in Uzbek by the affix **-ta** or by special defining words such as **baš**, **tup**, **tilim**, **dana**, are also found in Kazak (with the exception of **-ta**). However, it is not customary in Kazak linguistics to deal with them as a separate category. Syntactic formations such as **eki tilim nan**, *two pieces of bread*, **bes dana dæpter**, *five* (*items*) *books*, are examined within the framework of cardinal numbers'.

F. G. Isxakov considers that nouns and adjectives can be formally established as separate categories but that under certain conditions adjectives can be used as nouns and nouns can be used as adjectives, this resulting in homonyms belonging to both classes,[42] i.e. for him words like 'gold', 'wood', are noun and adjective homonyms. He emphasizes that Turkic languages have a vast number of homonyms belonging to different grammatical categories.[43] In a later work written with the co-authorship of A. A. Pal'mbax[44] the same definition of noun and adjective is given, i.e. that where a noun is qualified by another noun, it has the possessive suffix, but there is no possessive suffix when the noun is qualified by an adjective. Words like Tuvin **sook**, *cold, frost*, and **daš**, *stone*, are treated as homonyms in two separate categories, e.g. **daš**, *stone*, in **daš bažın**, *stone house*, is an adjective, and in **ulug daš**, *large stone*, a noun. If, however, such words as **daš**, *stone* are treated as adjectives they should be placed in a separate sub-class, because they do not have all the characteristics of adjectives such as for example, **ulug**, i.e. they cannot be used predicatively nor can they be separated from the noun they qualify by the indefinite article.

E. V. Sevortjan states[45] that certain nouns in Azerbaijani, i.e. those referring to material, occupation, space relations, social relationship, gender, habit and a few others, do not require an izafet construction when qualifying another noun. He considers that these words should not be analysed into noun and adjective homonyms on the basis of the absence of izafet because examples of such words may be found linked to a noun with the possessive suffix like a true noun. They should therefore be analysed as nouns. He cites examples from various Turkic languages and points out that some forms of gender indication have suffixes and others do not, e.g. examples in Azerbaijani, **diši žanavar**, *she-wolf*, non-suffixed but **gız ušağı**, *girl* (lit. *girl child*) and **oğlaš ušağı**, *boy* (lit. *boy child*), suffixed, where other Turkic languages have no possessive suffix, e.g. Turkish **kız çocuk**, *girl*, **erkek çocuk**, *boy*, and Nogaj dialects have **qız bala**, *girl*, and **erkek bala**, *boy*. Sevortjan considers that the fact that a gender word requires the possessive suffix of the noun it qualifies in Azerbaijani proves that all the other gender words in Azerbaijani and other Turkic languages are nouns and not adjectives. This is not sound reasoning. His examples merely show that, e.g., the word **gız**, *girl*, when used to indicate gender, belongs to a different class from the word **dišі**, *female*, and belongs to a class different from Turkish **kız** and Nogaj **qız**. He claims too that words representing material out of which something is made are nouns, not adjectives, because although some qualify another noun without izafet, others require izafet, e.g. Uzbek **ipak qurti**, *silkworm*, Azerbaijani **ipæk gurdu**, Turkish **ipekböceği**, Uzbek **paxta zavodi**, *cotton factory*, Azerbaijani **pambıg zavodu**, Turkish **pamuk fabrikası**, Uzbek **paxta ipi**, *cotton thread*, Azerbaijani **pambıg ipliyi**, Turkish **ipek ipliği**. He also draws attention to the use of such words with an adjectival suffix when used attributively and gives some examples. Uzbek **ipakli**, *silk*, Azerbaijani **ipækli**, *silk*, Turkish **ipekli**, *silk*, **pamuklu**, *cotton*. This surely adds support for classing the words for silk and cotton in Uzbek, Azerbaijani and Turkish as nouns, and has no bearing on the grammatical category of any other words in these languages representing material, which function differently, i.e. without izafet. The fact that Turkish **demir yolu**, *railway*, is being preferred to the earlier **demir yol**, and that Uzbek has forms **ziğir mɑyi**, and **ziğir mɑy**, *linseed oil*, Sevortjan considers as proof that **demir** and **ziğir** are nouns not adjectives, but one could also say that this proves the existence of noun and adjective homonyms, with the noun homonym as the form preferred.

Having set up a class of words on the basis of meaning, viz. words which represent material out of which something is made, Sevortjan is obliged to consider all the 'material' words together, e.g. silk, cotton, wood, iron, gold, etc. If, however, the problem is approached syntactically, there is no pressure to class together words which have different functions.

Fahri Kamɑl[46] recognizes separate categories of noun and adjective and treats words like Uzbek **tɑš komir**, *coal*, **temir yol**, *railway* (lit. *iron road*), **kozɑynak**, *glasses* (lit. *eye glass*) as compounds, together with other compounds like **belbɑğ**, *sash* (lit. *waist band*) and **yer yɑnğɑq**, *groundnut* (lit. *ground nut*). This is, perhaps, a more satisfactory way of dealing with these 'material' nouns than in the other works referred to previously because of the recognition that they form one unit with the noun they qualify,[47] but there would seem to be some justification for separating them from the noun they qualify and grouping them in a separate class on the grounds that words like Uzbek **taš**, *stone*, **temir**, *iron*, **yağac**, *wood*, **altin**, *gold*, etc., form compounds with a fairly large number of words whereas there are few compounds with, e.g., **bel** or **yer** as their first element.

Numeratives are mentioned under the heading of cardinal numbers **(sanaq san)**[48] as being used in counting by item or in measures of length. Eleven examples are given: **yuz gektar yer**, *one hundred hectares of land*, **yuz tsentner paxta**, *one hundred tsentners of cotton*, **ming tonna buğday**, *one thousand tons of wheat*, **bir baš uzum**, *one bunch of grapes*, **bir tilim qavun**, *one slice of melon*, **uč dana alma**, *three* (*items*) *apples*, **uč žan aila**, *three* (*souls*) *women*, **bir bağ beda**, *one sheaf of clover*, **bir dana qavun**, *one* (*item*) *melon*, **ikki havuč mayiz**, *two handfuls of raisins*, **bir siqim tuz**, *one pinch of salt*.

The analysis proposed in this paper is based on the colligation[49] qualifier and noun, both qualifier and noun being members of the nominal class. In order to establish the category of numerative, it is necessary to show that it is a separate category from certain other categories in the nominal class, viz. nouns, adjectives and numerals.

The study of the colligation qualifier and noun suggests the subdivision of qualifier into five separate categories as follows:

I. Qualifier = Noun

Here word order is important. The noun acting as qualifier precedes the noun that is qualified and either has (a) no suffix or has (b) the genitive suffix **(-ning)**. The noun that is qualified has the third possessive suffix **(-i/-si)**, e.g. (a) **šahar maktablari**, *city schools*, **temir qanlari**, *iron mines*, **altin zapasi**, *gold reserve*, **anar danalari**, *pomegranate seeds*, **ozbek operasi**, *Uzbek opera*; (b) **bu šaharning maktablari**, *the schools of this city*, **Taškentning qizil maydani**, *Tashkent's Red Square*.

II. Qualifier = Adjective

The noun qualified has no possessive suffix. The adjective can be used attributively, e.g. **qizil gul**, *red flower*, **baland daraxt**, *tall tree*, **yaxši maktab**, *good school*, **sakalli adam**, *bearded man*, **sakalsiz adam**, *beardless man*. The adjective can also be used predicatively, e.g. **gul qizil**, *the flower is red*, **daraxt baland**, *the tree is tall*. The adjective can be separated from the noun by the indefinite article **bir**, e.g. **baland bir daraxt**, *a very tall tree*, cf. **bir baland daraxt**, *a tall tree*.

III. Qualifier = Affix

The noun qualified has no possessive suffix. The affix is used attributively only, i.e. it cannot be used predicatively. Most affixes precede the noun but some follow. The affix forms one unit with the noun and cannot be separated from it, nor can anything come between. Words in this class indicate gender, material, profession, nationality, title. This class is collocationally much more limited than the two previous classes, e.g. words indicating gender can only collocate with words referring to animate objects, words indicating rank, title, nationality and occupation can collocate only with words referring to people.

As previously stated the qualifier and noun form one indivisible unit and could be treated as a compound, such as words of the type **belbağ**, *sash* (lit. *waist band*), **qolqap**, *gloves* (lit. *hand sack*), **asalari**, *honeybee* (lit. *honey bee*). However, the first elements of these latter examples do not occur very commonly as the first element of compounds and cannot really be considered productive. It would therefore be uneconomical to separate them out as affixes. Examples of affixes: **temir karavat**, *iron bedstead*, **altin saat**, *gold watch*, **taš koprik**, *stone bridge*, **oqituvči Tašmat**, *teacher Tashmat*, **qiz bala**, *girl*, **er bala**, *boy*, **arslan (erkak)**, *lion*, **orğači arslan**, *lioness*.

IV. Qualifier = Numeral

The noun qualified has no possessive suffix. The numeral has either (1) the suffix **-inči** or **-ala**, e.g. **ikkinči kitab**, *second book*, **ikkala kitab**, *both books*, or (2) has no suffix and is followed (a) by a numerative, e.g. **onta kitab**, *ten books*, **uč qap un**, *three sacks of flour*, or (b) directly by a noun in a limited number of cases, as shown below.

When used with a numeral, the majority of nouns require the colligation **numeral + numerative + noun.** A study of the collocations of numerals enables one to observe the usage of numeratives. In the speech of my informants, numeratives were generally used with all nouns except those having reference to (a) time and (b) mathematics. They were also omitted in certain cases (c) where the noun had a numerative homonym. Numeratives were often omitted with nouns referring to persons, and were never used with the word **kiši**, *person*. Examples: (a) **ottiz kun**, *30 days*, **ellik beš minut**, *55 minutes*, **on ikki ay**, *12 months*, **beš saat**, *5 hours*, **qirq yil**, *40 years*; (b) **uč čarak**, $\frac{3}{4}$, **ikki butun bešdan uč**, $2\frac{3}{5}$, **sakkiz yaq**, *8 sides*; (c) **toqsan som**, *90 roubles*, **yigirma varaq**, *20 pages*, **alti yuz metr**, *600 metres*.

Similar observations about numerals have been made for Kazak by R. G. Syzdykova.[50] She says that cardinal numbers often combine with the words **žasar**, *age*, **ret**, *time*, **ese**, *time*, **qaytara**, *time*, **türli**, *aspect, form*,

ara and **orta** in the combination **eki arada**, **eki ortada**, *at this time*, also with words referring to periods of time, e.g. **kün**, *day*, **žıl**, *year*, and the names of months, and words relating to weight, length and distance, e.g. **kilometr**, *kilometre*, **kilogramm**, *kilogramme*, **gektar**, *hectare*, **put**, *pound*, **tsentner**, *tsentner*. She says that in these cases the numeral forms a lexical semantic unit with the word.

V. Qualifier = Numerative

The noun qualified has no possessive suffix. The numerative must be preceded by a numeral or else be reduplicated.[51] Numeratives cannot be separated from the numeral by an adjective but an adjective can come between the numerative and the noun, e.g. Uzbek **ikki tup baland ɑlma daraxti**, *two tall appletrees* (**ɑlma daraxti**, *appletree*). A numerative cannot colligate with another numerative. If it seems that a numerative is being qualified by another numerative, a closer examination will reveal that the word qualified should be classified as a homonym in another category, e.g. **učta qɑp**, *three sacks*, where-**ta** is a numerative and **qɑp** is a noun and **uč qɑp un**, *three sacks of flour*, where **qɑp** is a numerative and **un** is a noun. Examples with reduplication: **qɑp-qɑp buğdɑy**, *sacks of wheat*, **gala-gala qušlar**, *flocks of birds*.

Words in the numerative class indicate size, quantity, length, weight and listing by item, and, like affixes, are a more restricted class than nouns and adjectives. Their correct usage, i.e. which numerative to use with which noun, can only be ascertained by the study of their collocations. For instance there are several numeratives which may be translated by the word '*piece*', e.g. **burda, bolak, parča, čaqmɑq** but they do not all have the same collocations, as will be seen from the table given below.

Numerative	Collocations[52]										
burda	—	nɑn	—	—	meva	yer	—	—	—	—	—	—
bolak	gošt	nɑn	qand	—	—	—	kitɑb	sɑvun	čay	—	—	—
parča	gošt	nɑn	qand	qɑğɑz	—	yer	—	—	—	mata	teri	arqɑn
čaqmɑq	—	—	qand	—	—	—	—	—	—	—	—	—

It will be seen that some of these numeratives can collocate with the same nouns, i.e. there is some overlapping but none of them have identical collocations, thus illustrating the importance of the study of collocation for lexicography.[53] For a study of numeratives and their collocations, see pp. 469–471.

It seems that much of the difficulty in establishing members of the nominal class in Turkic languages has arisen because of the large number of words identical in form but different in syntactic function. If such words are put in the same class, the grammar is made needlessly complex. Some examples of homonyms in different classes have already been given and a few more are given below. Some of these homonyms are related in meaning, others are not. In many cases there are noun and numerative homonyms but not in every case.

Examples of homonyms in different classes:

bolak: (1) noun. **bu yerning bir bolagi meniki**, *a part of this land is mine.*
(2) adjective. **bolak uyga kiraylik**, *let's go in another room!*
(3) numerative. **bir bolak nɑn yedim**, *I ate one piece of bread.*

varaq: (1) noun. **bu varaq ozimga lɑzim**, *I need this sheet* (*of paper*).
(2) numerative. **onbeš varaq qɑğɑz**, *15 sheets of paper.*

bɑš: (1) noun. **bɑlaning bɑšini bɑğladim**, *I bandaged up the child's head.*
(2) numerative. **bir bɑš uzum**, *one bunch of grapes.*

ɑltin: (1) affix. **ɑltin sɑat**, *gold watch.*
(2) noun. **ɑltin zapasi**, *gold reserve.*

Sometimes noun and numerative homonyms are completely unrelated in meaning:

qadɑq: (1) numerative. **tort qadɑq ɑlma**, *4 lb. of apples.*
(2) noun. **uning ɑyɑğida qadɑq bɑr**, *he has a corn on his foot.*

Some numeratives have no noun homonyms: **gala,** *flock*; **bir gala qoy,** *one flock of sheep*, **tup**, *plant*; **bir tup daraxt**, *one* (*plant*) *tree.*

Writers of Turkic grammars generally state that adjectives are sometimes used with noun suffixes and thus change into nouns. Such statements lead to the view that there is no clear differentiation between nouns and adjectives. However, as shown earlier, there are sufficient formal criteria to establish nouns and adjectives as separate classes, and in order to keep these classes apart it is necessary to state precisely under what conditions adjectives can be used with noun suffixes and can function as nouns.

A study of the colligation of the adjective in a 'piece' larger than a sentence shows that the colligation **adjective + noun suffix** is part of a larger colligation, viz. **adjective + noun + adjective + noun suffix**, where the colligation **adjective + noun** precedes the colligation **adjective + noun suffix** and where the adjective in both cases is the same lexical item, i.e. in cases where the adjective is used with noun suffixes, there is some previous reference in the text to the adjective in colligation with a noun. A simple example will help to make this clear:

Katta ɑdam keldi. Men kattaning sozini ešitdim, *The great man arrived. I heard the words of the great one.*[54] **Katta** is the adjective in colligation with the noun **ɑdam.** In the next sentence **katta** is used with the genitive case of a noun and is in colligation with another noun **soz. Katta** is collocated with **ɑdam** in the first sentence and this 'meaning' stands as no other collocation has been given for **katta** in the second sentence.

The second example is taken from the Tuvin grammar of Isxakov and Pal'mbax:[55] **stol kırınga kızıl bolgaš kök karandaštar čıtkan, kızıldarın men ap aldım, a kökterin—meeng ežim (ap aldı),** *On the table lay red and blue pencils: I took the red ones, my friend the blue ones.*

In cases where there appears to be an adjective used with noun suffixes but without there being any previous colligation of this 'adjective' with a noun, it would be more satisfactory to analyse it as a noun homonym, e.g. in a text where a new speaker arrives and asks the question **bu yerning kattasi kim?** *who is the manager of this place?*, the word **katta** would be classed as a noun in colligation with the noun **yer.**

A similar problem arises in the analysis of numeratives. The colligations of the numerative have so far been stated as **numeral + numerative + noun**, and **reduplicated numerative + noun**, but cases may be found of the use of numeratives with a noun suffix when a demonstrative pronoun and not a numeral precedes. Such usage is similar to that discussed for adjectives above and is limited to a particular context of situation.[56] The study of a 'piece' larger than the sentence shows that the colligation, **demonstrative pronoun + numerative + noun suffix** is part of a larger colligation, viz. the colligation **numeral + numerative + noun + demonstrative pronoun + numerative + noun suffix**, in the order given, e.g. **menga bir bolak nɑn bering! bu bolakni bering!** *Please give me a/one piece of bread! This piece please!* The context of situation is the speaker and the relevant object (here the bread) in close proximity, the speaker pointing directly at the object. This was the only situation in which the colligation with demonstrative pronoun could be used according to my informants.

It has earlier been stated that some numeratives can have the colligation **reduplicated numerative + noun**, without a numeral preceding, e.g. **qɑp-qɑp buğdɑyimiz bɑr**, *we have sacks and sacks of wheat*, **ular dasta-dasta gul keltirdilar**, *they brought bunches and bunches of flowers*. The possible colligations for numerative are therefore

(1) **numeral + numerative + noun.**
(2) **reduplicated numerative + noun.**
(3) **demonstrative pronoun + numerative + noun suffix**, in a particular context of situation.

Having established the numerative as a separate category of the class of nominal qualifier by the study of colligation, it now remains to complete the description of this category of word by listing all known examples with their collocations, to demonstrate their usage. As pointed out on p. 466, the use of each numerative is limited to the words with which it can collocate and the only way in which the usage can be ascertained is by the study of the collocations of each numerative.

The collocations were supplied by my two informants and are not claimed to be exhaustive but are believed to be representative.[57]

The numeratives collocate most commonly with the numerals 1–5 but some, e.g. those representing length and weight, can collocate with most numbers.

Numerative[58]	**Collocations**
aršin, *measure of length.*	**čit**, *cotton*, **gazlama**, *cloth.*
bɑğ, *sheaf.*	**beda**, *clover*, **buğdɑy**, *wheat*, **piyɑz**, *onion*, **sabzi**, *carrot.*
bɑğlam, *bundle*, *bunch.*	**piyɑz**, *onion*, **rediska**, *radish.*
bɑš, *bunch.*	**uzum**, *grapes.*
burda, *piece.*	**nɑn**, *bread*, **yer**, *ground*, **meva**, *fruit.*
bolak, *piece.*	**nɑn**, *bread*, **kitɑb**, *book*, **qand**, *sugar*, **gošt**, *meat*, **sɑvun**, *soap*, **čɑy**, *tea.*
varaq, *sheet.*	**qɑğɑz**, *paper.*
gaz, *measure of length.*	**čit**, *cotton.*
gala, *flock.*	**quš**, *bird*, **qoy**, *sheep*, **mɑl**, *cattle.*
dasta, *bouquet*, *bunch*, *handful.*	**gul**, *flower*, **ot**, *grass*, **sɑč**, *hair*, **piyɑz**, *onion*, **karta**, *card.*
dɑna, *item*, *thing.*	**sabzi**, *carrot*, **qɑvun**, *melon*, **sɑvun**, *soap*, **mɑl**, *cattle*, **qalam**, *pencil*, **tuxum**, *egg*, **ɑlma**, *apple*, **behi**, *quince.*[59]

žuft, *pair.*	**at**, *horse*, **hokuz**, *ox*, **kavuš**, *shoe*, **qalam**, *pencil*, **kitab**, *book*, **it**, *dog*, **paypaq**, *sock*, *stocking*, **etik**, *boot.*
zuvala, *ball.*	**xamir**, *dough*, **lay**, *mud.*
kalava, *skein*, *hank.*	**ip**, *thread.*
kilogramm, *kilogramme.*	**qand**, *sugar*, **uzum**, *grapes.*
kasa, *cup.*	**vino**, *wine*, **suv**, *water*, **aš**, *soup*, **šorva**, *soup.*
kulča, *piece*, *cake.*	**nan**, *bread*, **savun**, *soap.*
loqma, *mouthful.*[60]	**avqat**, *food*, **sut**, *milk*, **šorva**, *soup*, **suv**, *water.*
metr, *metre* (*measure of length*).	**čit**, *cotton.*
nafar, *person.*	**adam**, *man*, **oquvči**, *student.*
ağiz, *mouthful.*	**gap**, *talk*, **avqat**, *food*, **soz**, *word.*
palla, *half.*	**ašqavaq**, *pumpkin*, **qavun**, *melon*, **alma**, *apple.*
parča, *piece.*	**nan**, *bread*, **qağaz**, *paper*, **gošt**, *meat*, **mata**, *cloth*, **qand**, *sugar*, **yer**, *ground*, **teri**, *leather*, **arqan**, *string.*
piyala, *cup.*	**čay**, *tea.*
som, *rouble.*	**pul**, *money.*
-ta, *item.*	**adam**, *man*, **kitab**, *book*, **barmaq**, *finger.*
tonna, *ton.*	**alma**, *apple.*
tup, *growing plant.*	**daraxt**, *tree*, **gul**, *flower*, **ğoza**, *cotton plant*, **taq**, *grapevine.*
toda, *group*, *flock*, *heap.*	**qağaz**, *paper*, **gağča**, *jackdaw*, **qoy**, *sheep*, **mal**, *cattle*, **kitab**, *book*, **taš**, *stone*, **adam**, *man*, **kiši**, *person*, **xatin**, *woman*, **qiz**, *girl*, **bala**, *boy*, *child*, **žasus**, *spy.*
top, *group*, *heap.*	**adam**, *man*, **xatin**, *woman*, **qiz**, *girl*, **bala**, *boy*, *child*, **mal**, *cattle*, **qoy**, *sheep*, **qağaz**, *paper*, **taš**, *stone.*
toplam, *group*, *collection.*	**sabzi**, *carrot*, **piyaz**, *onion*, **kitab**, *book*, **otin**, *firewood*, **adamlar**, *people.*
čaqmaq, *piece.*	**qand**, *sugar.*
čelak, *bucket.*	**suv**, *water.*
šingil, *bunch.*	**uzum**, *grapes.*
yapraq, *sheet*, *slice.*	**qağaz**, *paper*, **qazi**, *breakfast sausage.*
ğaram, *stack*, *heap*, *rick.*	**otin**, *firewood*, **paxta**, *cotton*, **paxal**, *rice straw*, **kir**, *washing*, **šax**, *branch.*

qavat, *layer, storey.* — **ip**, *thread,* **uy**, *house.*
qadaq, *pound.* — **un**, *flour*, **uzum**, *grapes*, **buğday**, *wheat*, **alma**, *apple*, **sabzi**, *carrot.*
qap, *sack.* — **un**, *flour*, **buğday**, *wheat.*
qulač, *measure of length.* — **arqan**, *string.*
quti, *box, packet.* — **qurt uruği**, *silkworm eggs*, **gugurt**, *matches*, **papiros**, *cigarettes*, **sigaret**, *cigarettes*, **šakar**, *sugar*, **konfet**, *sweets.*
qučaq, *armful.* — **otin**, *firewood*, **beda**, *clover.*
havuč, *handful.* — **mayiz**, *raisins*, **un**, *flour.*
hoplam, *sip, gulp.* — **suv**, *water.*

The wide use of a large number of numeratives in Uzbek made the writer wonder whether numeratives are not in fact more widely used in Turkic languages than is generally acknowledged. A brief check was made with a Turk[61] who was unaware of this usage in his own language, and within one hour, he supplied the writer with the following examples in Turkish: **Bir sarı çiçek**, *a yellow flower*, **bir adet sarı çiçek**, *one in number yellow flower* (e.g. on order list), **bir/iki/üç demet karanfil**, *1/2/3 bunches of carnations*, if more than three bunches, the numerative is changed to suit a larger grouping, e.g. **bir sepet karanfil**, *a basket of carnations* or **iki/üç buket karanfil**, *2/3 bouquets of carnations*. **Bir küme toprak**, *a heap of soil*, **iki öbek çiçek**, *two clumps of flowers*, **öbek-öbek çiçekler**, *clumps of flowers*, **bir demet maydanos**, *a bunch of parsley*, **bir demet dereotu**, *a bunch of dill* (**demet** used with words meaning thin-stalked plants), **bir deste gül**, *a bunch of roses* (poetic only), **iki salkım üzüm**, *two bunches of grapes*, **bir/iki küfe/sepet üzüm**, *a large basket of grapes*, **bir/iki bakraç ayran/süt**, *one/two copper bucket(s) of buttermilk/milk*, **iki metre kumaş**, *two metres of cloth*, **iki yüz baş hayvanı var**, *200 head of cattle*, **iki dilim ekmek/karpuz/elma**, *two slices of bread/melon/apple*, **iki manga asker**, *two squads of soldiers*, **iki takım asker**, *two platoons of soldiers*, **iki bölük asker**, *two companies of soldiers*, **iki tabur asker**, *two battalions of soldiers*, **iki alay asker**, *two regiments of soldiers*, **iki tugay asker**, *two brigades of soldiers*, **iki tümen asker**, *two divisions of soldiers*, **bir kolordu asker**, *one army*, **iki yaprak kâğıt**, *two sheets of paper*, **iki sayfa kâğıt**, *two pages of paper*, **beş sayfa tasik**, *five pages of proofs*, **üç sütün haber**, *three columns of news*, **bir güruh insan**, *a horde of people*, **bir/iki çift okuz/koyun/söz**, *one/two pair oxen, sheep, words*, (*1–18, etc.*) **çile yün**, *1–18, etc., skein(s) of wool*, **bir/iki kâsa yoğurt/ayran**, *one/two cup(s) of yoghurt/buttermilk*, **bir/iki lokma ekmek**, *one/two mouthfuls of* *bread*, **dört parça elbise**, *a suit consisting of four pieces*, **dört parça ekmek**, *four pieces of bread*, **dört parça eşya**, *four separate items*, **bir tutam tuz**, *a pinch of salt*, **bir tutam saç** *a 'pinch' of hair*, **üç tutam çay**, *three pinches of tea*, **bir tüp diş macunu**, *a tube of toothpaste*, **bir tüp harda**, *a tube of mustard*, **1–50 top kumaş/kâğıt**, *1–50 roll(s) of cloth/paper*, **beş hane köy**, *village of five houses*, **beş kat elbise**, *five suits of clothes*, **iki kat camaşir**, *two sets of underwear*, **üç kap yemek**, *three courses* (of a meal), **iki kutu kibrit**, *two boxes of matches*, **üç şişe şarap**, *three bottles of wine*, **iki kalem eşya**, *two items*, **üç tane elma**, *three apples* (as separate items). **Tane** and **adet** were the most commonly used.

It would be interesting to see whether a careful study of such structures in other Turkic languages would reveal a similar wide use of numeratives.

Notes

1 See J.R. Firth, 'A Synopsis of Linguistic Theory, 1930–1955', p. 12. 'The collocational study of selected words in everyday language is doubly rewarding in that it usefully circumscribes the field for further research and indicates problems of grammar.' Also 'Collocations of a given word are statements of the habitual or customary places of that word in collocational order but not in any other contextual order and emphatically not in any grammatical order.' (In *Studies in Linguistic Analysis*, Oxford, 1957.)

2 Colligation is 'the inter-relation of grammatical categories in syntactical structure'. J.R. Firth, op. cit., p. 15.

3 References to these works are made in the course of this paper.

4 For examples see the work referred to in note 43 of this article.

5 Examples throughout are given in Uzbek unless stated otherwise. All examples taken from Turkic languages using the Cyrillic script are given in transliterated form. In many cases identical letters are used in the different languages but this is done for ease of printing and in no way implies identity of pronunciation. Turkish examples are given in the Turkish orthography.

6 Summaries of some analyses made by Soviet linguists are given on pp. 455–464 for readers who are not familiar with these works.

7 For examples of this, see note 14; p. 459 the reference to absolute qualities, and p. 463 the treatment of 'material nouns'.

8 G.D. Sanžejev, 'Spornyje voprosy v izučenii grammatičeskogo stroja uzbekskogo jazyka', in *Voprosy uzbekskogo jazykoznanija* (Tashkent, 1954).

9 Sanžejev, op. cit., pp. 50–51.

10 Sanžejev states, op. cit., p. 51, that **yangi kelmaq** is not possible but A.N. Kononov gives the example **yangi keldi** on p. 146 of his Uzbek grammar, *Grammatika sovremennogo uzbekskogo literaturnogo jazyka* (Moscow–Leningrad, 1960).

11 See A.N. Kononov, Uzbek Grammar, p. 66 and p. 354 § 465.

12 See pp. 457–458 of this article for formal criteria for separating these two classes as given by Kononov.

[13] See Sanžejev, op. cit., pp. 51–52.

[14] His attempt to explain this semantically is not very convincing, viz., that 'substantivized' adjectives and qualitatives represent certain objects and phenomena having certain characteristics, e.g. **čuqur**, meaning '*pit*' and **kok**, meaning '*sky*' but not the actual characteristics, i.e. **čuqur**, '*depth*' and **kok**, '*blueness*'.

[15] A. N. Kononov, *Grammatika sovremennogo turetskogo literaturnogo jazyka* (Moscow–Leningrad, 1956). This is a very comprehensive grammar which is excellent in many ways.

[16] A. N. Kononov, Turkish Grammar, p. 60 § 71. He states that the noun has the following categories, number, gender, definite and indefinite, possessive and case, and that the adjective has none of these. When it acquires one of these categories it becomes substantival.

[17] A. N. Kononov, Turkish Grammar, p. 127 § 210, and p. 135 § 223.

[18] A. N. Kononov, Turkish Grammar, p. 61 § 73.

[19] A. N. Kononov, *Grammatika sovremennogo uzbekskogo literaturnogo jazyka* (Moscow–Leningrad, 1960).

[20] See note 16 of this article.

[21] Izafet is the term used to denote the 'noun qualifying noun' relationship, i.e. the first noun has the genitive or no suffix and the second has the third possessive suffix.

[22] A. N. Kononov, Uzbek Grammar, pp. 354–357 §§ 465–467.

[23] These are described on p. 71, Kononov, Uzbek Grammar.

[24] However, Kononov has **ozbek operasi**, *Uzbek opera*, on p. 355 of his Uzbek grammar, and there are other examples, e.g. **temir qanlari**, *iron mines*, **altin zapasi**, *gold reserve*.

[25] My informants used the form with **-ta** in cases like this, i.e. **ikkita kitab aldik**. Both informants, the late Dr. Ismail Tacibay and Dr. Baymirza Hayit, were from the Ferghana Valley of Uzbekistan.

[26] A. N. Kononov, Uzbek Grammar, p. 353.

[27] T. I. Grunin, 'Imja prilagatel'noe v tjurkskix jazykax (na materialax turetskogo jazyka)', *Voprosy jazykoznanija* 4 (July–August, 1955).

[28] N. A. Baskakov, 'Slovosočetanija v karakalpakskom jazyke', in *Issledovanija po sravnitel'noj grammatike tjurkskix jazykov. III. Sintaksis*, pp. 51–61 (Moscow, 1961).

[29] This is similar to Kononov's first group, see p. 457 of this article.

[30] N. A. Baskakov, *Karakalpakskij jazyk, II, fonetika i morfologija, čast' pervaja* (Moscow, 1952), p. 228.

[31] N. A. Baskakov, op. cit., p. 176.

[32] N. A. Baskakov, op. cit., p. 204.

[33] M. B. Balakajev, *Osnovnyje tipy slovosočetanij v kazaxskom jazyke* (Alma-Ata, 1957).

[34] Examples are in Kazak.

[35] See p. 466 and pp. 468–469 of this article.

[36] Not all his examples are quoted here. For the rest see Balakajev, op. cit., p. 26. Word groups in Uzbek similar to the Kazak examples in nos. (2), (3), (4) and (7) would be treated either as compounds (if indivisible) or as affixes. For 'affix' see pp. 464–465 of this article.

[37] **bir qora qoy**, *stado baranov*, **bir uvis biyday**, *gorst' pšenitsy*.

[38] Balakajev, op. cit., p. 31.

[39] Balakajev, op. cit., p. 35 and p. 39.

[40] Balakajev, *Sovremennyj kazaxskij jazyk, sintaksis* (Alma-Ata, 1959).

[41] R. G. Syzdykova, 'Imja čislitel'noe', in *Sovremennyj kazaxskij jazyk* (Alma-Ata, 1962), p. 216, footnote 107.

[42] See F. G. Isxakov, 'Imja prilagatel'noe', in *Issledovanija po sravnitel'noj grammatike tjurkskix jazykov, II, Morfologija* (Moscow, 1956), p. 144 and p. 155.

[43] See F. G. Isxakov, 'Leksiko-grammatičeskaja klassifikatsija slov ili časti reči', in op. cit., pp. 75–76.

[44] F. G. Isxakov, A. A. Pal'mbax, *Grammatika tuvinskogo jazyka, fonetika i morfologija* (Moscow, 1961), pp. 182–183.

[45] E. V. Sevortjan, 'K probleme častej reči', in *Voprosy grammatičeskogo stroja* (Moscow, 1955), pp. 188–225.

[46] *Hazirgi zaman ozbek tili* (Tashkent, 1957), pp. 340–341 §§ 107–108.

[47] Balakajev also recognized them to be one unit, see p. 461 of this article.

[48] F. Kamɑl, op. cit., p. 361 § 13.

[49] 'Colligation is the interrelation of grammatical categories in syntactical structure', J. R. Firth, 'A Synopsis of Linguistic Theory, 1930–1955', p. 12. Also 'colligation of a grammatical category deals with a mutually expectant order of categories, attention being focused on one category at a time', op. cit., p. 17.

[50] R. G. Syzdykova, 'Imja čislitel'noe', in *Sovremennyj kazaxskij jazyk* (Alma-Ata, 1962), p. 223.

[51] See also p. 468 of this article, for its colligation with demonstrative pronoun.

[52] This was the usage of my two informants.

[53] 'It (the collocational study of selected words) is clearly an essential procedure in descriptive lexicography'. J. R. Firth, 'A Synopsis of Linguistic Theory, 1930–1955', p. 12.

[54] A literal translation is given to simplify the example for those unacquainted with Uzbek.

[55] Isxakov and Pal'mbax, op. cit., p. 179.

[56] 'Context of situation' is another concept that was used as a level of analysis by J. R. Firth. See 'Personality and Language in Society', pp. 182–183, in *Papers in Linguistics* 1934–1951 (London, 1957).

[57] Only those examples given by my informants are listed. They were collected from material which was not supplied specifically for making a collocational study of these numeratives and there are no doubt others, e.g. only two collocations are give for *kilogramm* whereas many other items of grocery and fruit are weighed by the kilogramme.

[58] The numeratives are listed in the Uzbek alphabetical order.

[59] **dɑna** can be used with most nouns relating to countable items but not with nouns referring to people. **dɑna** and **-ta** are probably the most commonly used numeratives.

[60] Collocates only with **bir**, *one*.

[61] Mr. Özcan Başkan studied for a short period at SOAS and acted as my informant for some research in Turkish for a term.

Contextual Analysis and Swift's Little Language of the Journal to Stella

E. M. WHITLEY

The little language—'ourrichar Gangridge' as Swift with evident delight named it—is that mode of private address to Esther Johnson found scattered through the sixty-five letters written to the 'Ladyes of St. Mary's' in Dublin during Swift's stay in London from 1710–13. The letters were first published in two separate lots, incorporated with other correspondence of the period or with other of his works. They were collected together under the title of *Dr. Swift's Journal to Stella* in 1784. The *Journal* in this form has had many editors, and has aroused interest and speculation ever since. There is now a great deal of information about the text itself, and the references to historical and literary persons and events have been almost completely identified and annotated. From the linguistic standpoint the position is less satisfactory, particularly in the treatment of the little language.

Recent editors differ in their attitude to this aspect of their task. Moorhead (1924)[1] was painstaking, though sometimes misguided, in his efforts to establish an exact text. He was wholly unsympathetic to the little language:

> The more attention we pay to this little language, the less important it seems.... Whenever an undeciphered obliterated passage, couched in the little language, was reached by the present transcriber, he found that what had gone before in the same gibberish was an almost unfailing clue to the worthless secret. It is in these passages that you will find this most original writer's most unoriginal remarks: etc.

Hayward (1944)[2] concludes a textual note to extracts from the *Journal* in the Nonesuch Library as follows: 'For the rest, the reader, if he wishes, may exercise his own ingenuity. It is scarcely incumbent upon an editor to explain, even if he could, such very intimate and peculiar nonsense.'

Williams (1948)[3] corrects these points of view in the Oxford edition:

> In the little language of his journal Swift found happiness and refreshment of spirit as he turned from the business and vexations of the day. If we dismiss it as a rather absurd foible on the part of a middle-aged lover writing to a younger woman we fail in understanding.

Yet despite sympathy, which is essential, and despite the fullness of the Oxford commentary on the text and its contents, the puzzles of the little language from a linguistic point of view are no nearer solution. It is clear that specifically linguistic questions must now be asked before linguistic answers can be given.

The *Journal to Stella* provides a restricted language field in which to apply some aspects of Professor Firth's contextual theory of meaning and this is the purpose of this study.[4] In searching the field more hares were started than have yet been tracked down. One thing came as a surprise. Not only were previous doubts of the interpretation of the text strengthened but new doubts were raised of the text itself. They were points of detail but of sufficient linguistic interest to warrant looking at the manuscripts in the British Museum.[5] This gave rise to further queries which are now being investigated. Firm solutions are not possible for all the questions raised, but it seems better to return a 'Don't know' in accord with linguistic probability rather than accept conjecture which is not squarely based on the contextual and formal characteristics of the *Journal.*

The problems fall under two main heads:

1. The nature of the 'mystic letters', 'cyphers', or 'odd combinations of letters' as they have variously been called; their identification with persons; the translation meanings given them by different editors and other related difficulties. I propose to call them 'Monogram' problems, using the term to cover forms such as 'Md' 'FW' and 'ppt' or 'pdfr' equally.

2. The nature of the little language as a whole, its place in the total text and its function. It can be said at once, to keep matters in perspective, that this little language is fragmentary and only a small part of the whole. We are dealing with the last few pieces of a large mosaic and one misplaced piece can affect others without disturbing the main design. Yet this language is an integral part of the pattern; its very intimacy guarantees, as it were, the freedom of expression elsewhere.

The nature of the little language is the main topic of this paper, but all matters of detailed interpretation whether of normal language, of obliterated or clear text, or of the monograms must be considered in the light of contexts of situation[6] which are set up to handle the total text. For the interpretation of the little language itself reference to other levels of analysis must be made. The commentary may require special contextual, colligational, collocational and prosodic statements but they will be partial, *ad hoc* statements as befits the fragmentary nature of the material. The purpose is to illustrate a contextual approach rather than to make an exhaustive analysis of the forms of the little language.

Three phases in the history of the *Journal to Stella* can be singled out, with texts appropriate to each phase:

1. *The Contemporary Phase* (1710–13) with Swift's holographs of Letter 1 and Letters 41–65 (excluding 54) as the text. The originals of Letters 2–40 and Letter 54 have not survived so they are not taken into account for this phase. This is the MS. text.

2. *The First Printing Phase* (1766–68) with two relevant texts:
   (i) Letter 1 and Letters 41–65 inclusive in *Letters by J. Swift and Several of his Friends 1703–40*, edited by John Hawkesworth, 1766. This is the Hawkesworth text.
   (ii) Letters 2–40 inclusive in the *Works Vol. XII*, edited by Deane Swift, 1768. This is the Deane Swift text.

3. *The Modern Phase.* There are many texts between the previous phase and this, but the Oxford text will principally be quoted. The editorial notes to this text reject or accept, correct and largely add to, the contributions of earlier editors.

The texts of the three different phases must be set in three different contexts of situation for their detailed interpretation. The first in point of time and in contextual and linguistic importance is the *Letter Context.* Some of the factors in this context are these:

Letters are passing at regular intervals between Jonathan Swift in London and Esther Johnson (Stella) and her companion Rebecca Dingley in Dublin. The replies from Dublin are lost but are recorded by number in the *Journal.* Swift is very concerned to keep the record straight and acutely anxious to send off his letters so that he will not be owing a reply. Through Swift's comments we can glimpse what was in the Dublin letters. He often replies *seriatim* to a letter open before him. Whether we judge that he is doing so or not will sometimes affect the interpretation put on successive sentences in a letter. For instance it is possible to argue a connection between successive items and draw certain conclusions, or to miss a connection between successive items and so leave a wrong text unchallenged. Examples of this will be found in the final section of this paper.

Abrupt changes of subject are a characteristic of the *Journal* but they give rise to problems of interpretation only when looked at from the standpoint of the later phases. In the Letter Context the persons and events of the text are all known to at least one, sometimes all three, of the principals. For Jonathan, Stella and Mrs. Dingley the letters were unambiguous and needed no footnotes. They knew, in every sense of the phrase, who was who and what was what. The disclosure of their private language was unthinkable during their lifetime, and only hinted at in the First Printing phase; deciphering and translation have come stage by stage during the two hundred years following the death of the principals. Swift did what he could by obliteration to keep the little language secret. Even on this point there are puzzles which will be referred to later.

There are four linguistic styles in the Letter Context which will be named the Court, the Personal, the Little and the Coda styles. The Court style is the fairly formal language used by Swift for political and Court matters. It now has a period flavour and appearance but it must have been close to the colloquial of what we may call Establishment circles of the day. Swift himself calls attention to his use of it: Letter 52 (Sept. 15th 1712), p. 556:

> I am again endeavouring as I was last year to keep People from breaking to pieces, upon a hundred misunderstandings. One cannot withhold them from drawing different ways while the Enemy is watching to destroy both. See how my Stile is altered by living & thinking & talking among these People., instead of my Canal & river walk, and Willows.

There are topics and forms of personal reference special to this style, though there is overlap with other styles. Swift is here talking to himself, or at least for himself, as he makes plain (Letter 43, p. 513): 'What's all this to you; but I must talk of things as they happen in the day whether you know any thing of them or no.' He is keeping a diary which he may want to use later (Letter 7, Oct. 23rd, p. 68) with the knowledge that Stella is interested. Passages of this kind often end with transition questions such as 'What's all this to you' or 'But what care oo for all this'. Swift at first is not sure how they will be received: Letter 5, p. 35:

> I can't tell whether you like these journal letters: I believe they would be dull to me to read them over; but, perhaps, little MD is pleased to know how Presto passes his time in her absence.

These journal letters are marked off in the MSS by successive date numbers at the beginning of each section—a blessing in finding the way about these closely written texts.

The Court style can also be linguistically defined by the absence of 'monograms'. There are shortened forms of various kinds (the Qu—, Ld Treasr. or Ld Tr., etc.) and occasional dashes for expletives (D— for Devil, P—x for Pox) but there are no concealments or mystifications. Obliterations in this style are such as might occur in any handwritten text. Swift does attempt once to use the monogram device in this style, but not very effectively: Letter 62, pp. 644–645:

> let me henceforth call Ld Tr, *eltee*, because possibly my Letters may be opened; pray remember Eltee; you know the Reason, LT and Eltee plonounced the same way . . .
>
> I endeavor to keep a firm friendship between D. Ormd & Eltee. oo know who Eltee is have oo flodot it already?
>
> then I visited Ld Keepr, who was at dinner; but I would not dine with him, but drove to Ld Tr— (Eltee I mean) payd the Coachman, & went in . . .
>
> then went to the Latin play at Westminster School, acted by the Boys & Ld Tr— (Eltee I mean again) honored them with his Presence.[7]

This mixture of the little language with topics of the Court style is not a success and the name Eltee does not outlast this letter. Perhaps Swift was never serious about it, meaning only to let anyone opening his letters know that they had been 'smoakt', to use a favourite word of his. It gives, however, a useful pointer to the reading of other monograms.

The Personal style has a more familiar ring about it and many of the passages could be spoken today with hardly a change, although to the eye the passage below looks dated, with its punctuation and its capital letters for Hot, Shouldr, Lettr, etc. It illustrates recurrent themes in this style as well as three surname forms of reference, which are more frequent here than in the Court style: Letter 50, July 17th 1712, p. 548:

> I am dead here with the Hot weathr, yet I walk every night home, & believe it does me good. but my Shouldr is not yet right, itchings, & scratchings, and small akings. Did I tell you that I have made Ford Gazeteer, with 200ll a year Salary, besides Perquisites. I had a Lettr lately from Parvisol, who says my Canal looks very finely; I long to see it; but no Apples; all blasted again. He tells me there will be a Triennial Visitation in August. I must send Raymd another Proxy. So now I will answr ee Rettle N.33 dated Jun. 17.

The last sentence illustrates the mingling of the little language with the Personal style, even within a single sentence. There are few sustained passages in any one style in the *Journal* and there is no feeling of composition.

The Little style is that of Swift's private fragmentary language which can be interpreted as a mutation of the normal colloquial forms of the Personal style.[8] One type of mutation is by substitution, of which the most common as far as writing goes is *l* for *r*. There are some purely graphic substitutions implying no phonetic change, e.g. 'rite' for 'write' and 'nite' for 'night'. These identify the little language for the eye. The passage below is typical: Letter 50, p. 549:

> So here comes ppt aden with her little watry postcript; o Rold, dlunken Srut drink pdfrs health ten times in a molning; you are a whetter, fais I sup Mds 15 times evly molning in milk porridge. lele's fol oo now, and lele's fol ee Rettle, & evly kind of sing; and now I must say something else.—You hear Secty St John is made Vicount Bullinbrook; . . .

The change of key from the Little to the Court style is achieved through the transition sentence ' and now I must say something else'.

With the exception of 'FW', all the monograms occur in the Personal and Little styles. The occurrence of 'FW' in the body of the text in Letter 43 is uncharacteristic and may be treated as a quotation of the monogram.[9] Though the forms of the little language are to be considered as mutants of the normal colloquial of the Personal style, there are grammatical and other features special to each of these styles. One illustration is the special value in the Personal style of the qualifier 'your' in such phrases as 'your dean', 'your new Bishop', 'your Banker', where it must be stressed, as against the unstressed form in 'your letter', 'your cards', etc. In the first examples the 'your' is not meant for the ladies personally, it signifies 'of Dublin'.[10] The use of this stressed form has a certain teasing value in some of its contexts. The forms 'oo' and 'ee' in the little language have no such connotations. They are mutants of unstressed 'your' or 'you', e.g. 'ee Rettle' or 'oo Rettle' for 'your letter'; 'I'm drad oo rike oo Aplon' for 'I'm glad you like your Apron'.

The *Codas* are part of the little language but are distinct, with styles of their own. There are two kinds—the Nite and the Farewell—distributed differently in the text. One example of each will do: Letter 43 (March 17th 1711–12) 'Nite my two deel sawcy dallars.' Letter 48 (June 17th 1712) 'Farewell deelest lole deelest Md Md Md Md Md FW FW FW Me Me Lele Me lele Me lele Me lele lele lele Me.'

Nite codas occur as end pieces to sections in journal letters, excluding the final section, so that each section begins with a date number and more often than not ends with a Nite coda. The language here is restricted and varies from the single word 'Nite' to six-, seven- or eight-word patterns. The forms can still be interpreted as mutations of normal forms. Apart from the occasional use of 'pdfr' the only monogram occurring in Nite codas in the Oxford text is 'Md'.

Much has been made by earlier editors of the differences in expressions of affection in the Deane Swift text and the later letters. Some have seen in this a sign of waning affection due to the entry of Esther Vanhomrigh (Vanessa) on the scene. The matter is argued in the Oxford Introduction and elsewhere. The only linguistic point that requires to be made is that in such discussions the Nite codas should not be compared with the general little style. It needs more detailed investigation of the Deane Swift text (Letters 2–40) before it can be said with confidence where the little language in it begins and ends. Deane Swift leaves few gaps in his text although in his MSS there were doubtless obliterations. He may have guessed where he could not read. It is doubtful whether the Nite codas can properly be said to have a place in his texts. On a brief examination there appear to be no patterns identical with the Codas of the extant holographs. In an early letter we find: 'Well little monkies mine, I must go write; and so good night.' In the last Deane Swift text (No. 40), which is a journal letter written on fifteen consecutive days, there are only two possible coda-like phrases: Jan. 27th ''Tis very late, so I must go sleep.' Feb. 1st 'You know 'tis late', etc. In the immediately following MS journal letter (No. 41), which Swift began on the same day as he sent off the previous letter, there are fourteen codas on fourteen consecutive days, thirteen of them beginning with the word Nite. There is clearly need to look closely at Deane Swift's treatment of the little language before arguing from it.

One further interesting point about the Nite codas is this. The choice of a short (1–3 words) or long (up to 8 words) Nite coda depended entirely on the space available. The line had to be filled and the coda must not overrun. Swift could not bear to waste space, particularly in the journal letters, and he hated gaps in the end margin. When a sentence was not complete and the next word was too long for the line, he put a flourish of the pen, short or long as required, in the gap. Letter 52, for instance, has twenty-four flourishes in some seventy lines in the MS. Letter 53 has sixteen flourishes in seventy lines. Both of these are long letters written over more than one day but without Nite codas.[11] In the journal letter No. 63 there are twenty codas varying from one to six words. In two cases there is a coda and a flourish. The coda word-counts read: 6 2 2 2 3 2 4 3 3 4 2 2 2 5 3 2 3 2– 4– 1. The Nite codas are parting phrases but they have a further linguistic function in the *Journal* as line-fillers, verbalised flourishes, and this controls their linguistic form. Parting and greeting phrases are ritual phrases and it is unwise to pursue their meaning beyond this. We need not follow Moorhead when he says: 'to add that the accompanying God-bless-you at the close of each day is also mere ritual is not to accuse Swift of any greater hypocrisy than he implicitly confessed when he said: "It is often with religion as it is with love; which by much dissembling, at last grows real."'

The *Farewell Coda* is to be found at the end of letters of all types. Sometimes it is followed by a lengthy postscript (No. 57) or by business documents (No. 64). Only one of Swift's manuscript letters (No. 59) is without a Farewell Coda. Hawkesworth's text (No. 54) ends without one. None of Deane Swift's texts gives a complete formula, but only four of his thirty-nine letters show no sign of a final coda. It seems clear that he omitted the full text because he could not translate it into readable form, as he could for most of the little language.

The coda of Letter 50 (June 17th 1712) is typical of the longer ones: 'Farewell deelest lole deelest Md Md Md Md Md FW FW FW Me Me Lele Me lele Me lele Me lele lele lele Me'. These codas vary in length and frequently overrun the line. They do not share the line-filling function of the Nite codas and they cannot be interpreted simply as a mutation of a normal colloquial text. The longer ones are part in little language and part in code. This code delighted Swift;[12] we can now only conjecture what it means. The first part of the message above may be little language for 'Farewell dearest love dearest';[13] then comes the code sequence of three repeated monograms. The number of the repeats can vary, but the sequence of the monograms, with two exceptions, is always as above. Only the monograms 'Md', 'FW', 'Me' are shown in the Oxford text to occur in the code proper of the Farewell codas.

It is convenient at this point to dismiss the suggestions that 'FW' can mean either 'Farewell' or 'Foolish Wenches'. Swift and Stella knew the meaning of the code, so for whose benefit was the word 'Farewell' given in full at the beginning of the coda? Nor would the meaning 'farewell' make much sense between the other two monograms, however we interpret them. If we look at Swift's use of the word 'wench' we find it once only in the MSS. Letter 53, p. 563: 'he has left . . . the whole to his Heir Male a Popish Priest . . . after him it goes to his chief Wench and Bastard'. Swift might have used the word as an affectionate form of address, though it does not ring true, nor is the adjective 'foolish' a favourite one. The monogram 'FW' had a special importance for Swift but what would be so specially clever about using it as a short form for 'Foolish Wenches'? And if we accept that the monogram 'Md' refers to Stella and Mrs. Dingley, what would be the point of successive monograms 'Md', 'FW' both standing for the two ladies?

The third monogram of the code sequence has been deciphered as 'Me' and it is suggested that this can be interpreted as referring to Mrs. Dingley and be translated 'Madam Elderly'.[14] This seems improbable since Mrs. Dingley is not central in the situation and would not have been singled out. To have called her 'Madam Elderly', however affectionate the tone of voice, would seem, from a woman's point of view, outrageous. Swift may have found Mrs. Dingley irritating but he could not have wanted to hurt her. The translation of this code sequence as it stands at present is unsatisfactory. I believe the text is faulty and the mystery is not only what the monograms mean but how they have been accepted in this form by successive editors who have looked at the holographs. The last line of the facsimile of Letter 1 in the first volume of the Oxford text (opp. p. 4) illustrates the point. The monogram sequence has been deciphered as Md/FW FW/Md Md/Me Me Me. Leaving aside the meaning of the individual monograms I think it is clear that the sequence is X/YYYY/ZZZ. Swift has tried four different ways of constructing the second monogram. None of them, to my eye, bears any resemblance to 'FW'. The question of the monograms and their meaning will be left for detailed treatment elsewhere.

The last point about the text of the Letter Context can only be briefly mentioned. This is the question of the obliteration of the little language and the codas, sometimes with a light scoring through and sometimes with heavy spirals. Some of the letters have escaped censorship. It looks as if Swift might have been reviewing the letters, possibly after Stella's death. The letters could have been tied up in separate packets and he may have left the job uncompleted, or a packet of the letters might have been mislaid. This is conjecture, but the fact is that Letter 1 and Letters 42–52 have no obliterations of the little language; Letters 41, 53, 55 and 59–65 have the little language completely scored through; Letters 56, 57 and 58 have been partially censored.

It must be sufficient now merely to name the two other Contexts of Situation with brief notes on the character of the texts. No attempt will be made to identify those parts of the Deane Swift text which might have been in little language. The texts of the First Printing Phase (1766–68) are still printed as letters along with other correspondence of the period but the interest is now focused on them more as memoirs of an important period in history and politics. The principals of phase 1 are dead long since, but there may be survivors of those mentioned in the letters, or their relatives, to consider. Some events may remain in living memory but most of them have passed into history. Both Hawkesworth and Deane Swift were concerned to present their public with readable texts, annotated where absolutely necessary. Thus the two editors in relation to their audience and their texts become the principal persons in what may be called the Memoir Context. Hawkesworth was embarrassed by the personal and 'little' aspect of Swift's letters and solved the problem by excising most of it. Letter 54, of which the original is lost, survives today in Hawkesworth's version.[15] Deane Swift keeps the personal text and much of what is clearly little language translated into normal forms, thereby giving his texts an intimacy which contrasts with Hawkesworth's 'more polished' text and accords with his relationship to Jonathan. (He was his first cousin once removed.) He gives no indication of whether or where his texts were obliterated and provides only snippets of the little language in the original spelling. There are no gaps in his texts except for the codas. 'Farewel, &c &c' is as much as he gives. We owe to him the identifications of the monograms 'MD', 'DD', 'ppt' and 'pdfr' but nowhere in his texts do we find the monograms 'FW' and 'Me'. The originals of his texts of letters 2–40 are lost.[16]

In the Modern Phase there is no possibility of contact with the persons and events of previous phases. The link is through the work of successive editors. The increasing interest in establishing an accurate text of the MS letters is a distinguishing factor in the final context, which we may call the Document Context. Most of the obliterated passages have now been deciphered, sometimes in face of great difficulty. Each editor had the benefit of what had been previously suggested and footnotes in the Oxford text indicate variant readings. I find one or two restored passages unlikely on linguistic grounds and will refer to them later.

Whether or not the text is easy to read is not the primary concern of editors of this phase. Editorial habits differ, naturally, but on the whole the emphasis is on the accurate representation of the MSS as far as this is possible or desirable, and on ever more detailed annotation of the text for the benefit of scholars. The documentation of people, places and events is almost complete. The questions that the linguist might ask are less often satisfied and the problems of the non-specialist reader are hardly considered.

The change in editorial outlook from Context 2 to Context 3 is clearly marked by the different look of the texts on pages 483–484, where the Deane Swift text changes to the Oxford version of the MSS, and again on pages 569–572 where we have the contrast with Hawkesworth's text. There are forms where I believe the First Printings were right and the Modern texts are wrong, as for instance the forms 'beig', 'charmig' and similar '-ig' for '-ing' forms. Swift never wrote this. He wrote the first downstroke of the *n* followed by a quickly written tailed stroke. The result is often not unlike a rough cursive form of the phonetic symbol for a velar nasal [ŋ]. Swift has not omitted the *n* here in the same way as he omits the *e* in the past suffix '-ed', and the final letter is quite unlike a fully written *g*. Swift uses the same letter shape in the word 'wrong' which has been correctly rendered in the normal way. The worst example of such a misinterpretation is in Letter 56 (Dec. 12, 1712): 'I make few Visits nor go to Levees; My onely debauhig is sitting late when I dine if I like the Company;'. Moorhead gives 'debauhig (? debauching)', but the Oxford text has no comment. Why it should be more difficult to recognize the *ch* in this word than in the word 'richr' it is hard to say. (See the facsimile of Letter 1, last line first word in the Oxford Vol. I.) To leave 'beig', 'charmig' and 'debauhig' in the text without comment is surprising, even granted that they were accurate representations of the MS forms, but in this case we have barbarous forms which were never in the original. These 'adenoidal' -ig forms coming in the middle of normal passages mar the text. The earlier editors have not and could not have made this mistake since their concern was for the reader and they would have rendered the MS forms as it suited them and their public.

Before looking at the little language in detail we can summarize its relation to the total text as follows: it is only a fragment of the whole and for the most part must be considered a mutation of normal Personal style. Some part of the little language is found in all the letters of the Letter Context. The Little style and the related codas are among the criteria for identifying three types of letter. Another criterion is the number of successive days on which the letters were written. Thus we have Short letters, with only one date in the text, with no Nite codas, but with a Farewell coda and often excluding reference to public matters. Long letters are written on more than one day but these days are not consecutive, they have no Nite codas but a fair amount of public information. Journal letters are written on at least fourteen consecutive days, have both Nite and Farewell codas and always use all the linguistic styles. The MS letters are listed below under these three headings. The first column gives the letter number; the second indicates whether the text is clear (C) or obliterated (O) or part obliterated, part clear (O/C); the third the number of days mentioned in the text. Swift marks only Nos. 45 and 46 in his account book as 'short'. The Oxford notes show that the other letters classified here as 'short' were perhaps not written on one day. They were certainly not all posted on the day indicated at the head of the letter. As far as the text itself shows they are one-day letters. None of the letters has an opening formula, nor are they signed.

Short			*Long*			*Journal*		
No.	Text	Days	No.	Text	Days	No.	Text	Days
1	C	1						
						41	O	15
						42	C	15
						43	C	15
						44	C	18
45	C	1						
46	C	1						
47	C	1						
48	C	1						
49	C	1						
			50	C	2			
51	C	1						
			52	C	2			
			53	O	2			
			55	O	4			
			56	O/C	2			
						57	O/C	17
						58	O/C	21
						59	O	20
						60	O	14
						61	O	21
						62	O	18
						63	O	20
64	O	1						
65	O	1						

Deane Swift's texts 2–40 are journal letters without complete codas. They are preceded by a short clear letter and followed by an obliterated journal letter. Letter 54, which is Hawkesworth's, comes between two O texts and may have been obliterated also. This letter has no little language beyond the monograms 'D.D.' and 'Ppt', and no Farewell coda. The only other letter without a Farewell is 59 which records Harrison's death and ends: 'Pray Gd Almighty bless poor Md—adieu—I send this away tonight and am sorry it must go while I am in so much Grief.'

The change from journal to short letter (44–45) is already signalled in 44 (March 29th): 'I am plagued with these Pains in my Shouldr' and in the postscript 'I must purge & clystr after this; and my next Lettr will not be in the old order of Journall till I have done with Physick. An't oo surprised to see the Lettr want half a side.' Short or long letters follow at irregular intervals and journal letters are not resumed until the following December.

What is the function of the little language? First we must consider the situation in which it might have been used prior to the *Journal*. Even if we assume that here we find its first use in writing, which is unlikely since it is used quite naturally in Letter 1 without explanation, there is plenty of evidence in the text to show that this was a spoken language between Swift and Stella. Most of the statements are found in the Deane Swift section of the text but he could not have invented them. Letter 13 p. 154

> ... and all the while I was undressing my self, there was I speaking monkey things in air, just as if MD had been by, and did not recollect myself till I got into bed.

Letter 17 p. 210

> ... Do you know what? when I am writing in our language I make up my mouth just as if I was speaking it. I caught myself at it just now.

Letter 22 p. 261

> ... Do you know that every syllable I write I hold my lips just for all the world as if I were talking in our own little language to MD. Faith, I am very silly; but I can't help if for my life.

Forster's view that Stella and Swift used the little language from the time they met in Sir William Temple's house, when Stella was eight and Swift, Temple's secretary, was twenty-two, seems likely. But the little language is not a child's language. Swift must have initiated it and established its forms. In one of the few little passages in the Deane Swift text we find: 'and zoo must cly Lele and Hele, and Hele aden. Must loo mimitate pdfr, pay? Iss, and so la shall.' Even if the text is not accurate the use of the word 'imitate' is clear. Of course we can only speculate on the origin and use of the little language. Why should Swift or Stella, or Mrs. Dingley, as a third party, have 'left any statement on the question'?[17] This is a secret language and no concern of anyone else. Why did they come to use it? Again we can only speculate along with others.

There is evidence in the *Journal* that Swift was not very happy in the Temple household. Letter 19, pp. 230–231:

> I called at Mr. secretary's, to see what the D— ailed him on Sunday; I made him a very proper speech . . . and one thing I warned him of, Never to appear cold to me, for I would not be treated like a school-boy; that I had felt too much of that in my life already . . .
>
> . . . Why I think what I said to Mr. secretary was right. Don't you remember how I used to be in pain when Sir William Temple would look cold and out of humour for three or four days, and I used to suspect a hundred reasons? I have pluckt up my spirit since then, faith; he spoiled a fine gentleman.

and again, referring to Sir William's nephew: 'I thought I saw Jack Temple and his wife pass by me to-day in their coach; but took no notice of them. I am glad I have wholly shaken off that family.' Swift did not like Lady Giffard, Temple's sister, either. Stella's mother was in her service when Swift was with Sir William at Moor Park and still was at the time of the *Journal*. None of the references to Lady Giffard in the letters is friendly. Perhaps Stella, too, did not always find Moor Park a happy place. In any event her health at this time was poor. Swift may first have used the little language to comfort the child Stella, and himself, when the atmosphere was chilly or when she was not so well. It would then serve to mark the bond of affection between them (Swift had been shown little affection during his childhood) and, being a secret language, would cut them off from the rest of the household. The little language thus becomes the key which unlocks the door to this inner life and effectively locks outsiders out. The use of it in the *Journal* serves this purpose still. Letter 25, p. 303:

> Remember if I am used ill and ungratefully, as I have formerly been, 'tis what I am prepared for, and shall not wonder at it. . . .—Pox of these speculations! They give me the spleen; and that is a disease I was not born to. Let me alone, sirrahs, and be satisfied: I am, as long as MD and Presto are well: Little wealth, And much health, And a life by

stealth: that is all we want; and so farewel, dearest MD; Stella, Dingley, Presto, all together, now and for ever all together. Farewel again and again.

We cannot be sure how much of this Deane Swift text was in little language but it sums up the feelings that the little language was intended to excite. When using it Swift was able to feel himself 'at home' in the secure, loving background which he could not live without. The Vanhomrigh circle was a necessary substitute home for some purposes, but it did not take the place of the 'inner home' with its own private language.

It will be simpler not to discuss point for point what others have written about the 'distortions' of the little language. The material will be analysed in fresh terms without comparison. There is only the written evidence to argue from, but since this is a spoken language it is necessary broadly to infer the phonetic forms.

The problem must be looked at from two angles. Swift was trying to represent on paper a pronunciation which would recall the very tones of his voice to the ladies in Dublin, yet at the same time he had to write forms which the eye could identify immediately. There is the dual aspect of difference from normal and likeness to normal in every little form. With this in mind the changes *r* for *l* and *l* for *r* in the same sentence are seen to complement each other. E.g. I'm drad oo rike oo Aplon (I'm glad you like your apron). Counted as letter substitutions this gives *r*/*l* twice, *l*/*r* and *d*/*g* once each—four substitutions in the same sentence. Taking the whole sentence together this can be regarded primarily as an inversion of the liquids [l, r] with a secondary substitution of the plosives in the initial cluster. Dissimilar clusters of the normal sentence are still dissimilar when inverted; like consonants in the normal sentence remain like when inverted. Final consonants and vowels are unaffected by the inversion.

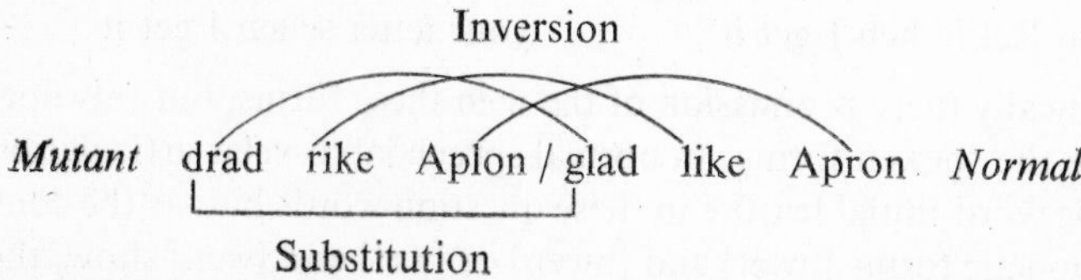

The substitution *d*/*g* in the initial cluster can be considered secondary because elsewhere the form 'grad' is found: I am grad at halt to hear of Ppts good Health (I am glad at heart . . .). The first part of this sentence shows *r*/*l* inversion without substitution while the second part remains normal. Regularity of sound change in specific words cannot be predicted. We must expect variant mutant forms and also abrupt changes from mutant to normal within a single phrase or sentence. Each piece must be taken separately before the kind of mutation can be stated. There are, however, systemic statements of a general nature which can be made.

Nowhere in the text does Swift say what position the mouth was in when he was speaking in this way, but experience of language of this kind and evidence from the forms Swift writes show that the lips must be strongly pursed and the speech in consequence would be markedly labialized. This lip posture is the 'comforting' position used in baby-talk to infants, chiefly by women. It must be of ancient origin and its use is doubtless widespread. It serves two important purposes in that the teeth are covered, and this is a friendly posture in contrast to the teeth-bared position for snarling, and it eliminates shrillness in the voice, which is also a comforting thing. In phonetic terms we can say that labialization coupled with velarization giving a central or back quality to vowel sounds, together probably with lowered pitch and less forceful and precise articulation, all characterized the little language as a whole in contrast to the other styles. If we choose to treat labio-velarization as a phonetic exponent of a prosodic element in the structure of the little language referable, as tonal features would be, to the whole piece, we can mark the prosody as a key signature and study the mutations in a different light. Several examples of the relevance of this prosodic feature—w prosody—to the forms of the little language will now be discussed.

1. Interrogatives 'hat' and 'hen' for 'what' and 'when'.

Mutant	*Normal*
and hat is Md doing now	and what is Md doing now
hat care I, but rove pdfr	what care I, but love pdfr
oo Rettle hen I get it	your letter when I get it

Graphically there is omission of the *w* in these forms, but this does not handle the spoken forms. In normal speech labio-velar articulation is a specific word-initial feature in these question words but, as the contrasting phonetic forms [hwɔt] and [hwen] or [wɔt] and [wen] show, the rest of the word is not necessarily rounded or velarized. In little language labio-velarization is a phonetic characteristic of the whole piece; being diffused it is doubtless less clearly marked at a given point, but it is not omitted in the sense that the letter *w* is omitted from the written forms.

The difference can be expressed by writing the examples under the prosodic key signature:

$$\frac{\text{w}}{\begin{array}{l}\text{hat is}\ldots\\ \text{hat care}\ldots\\ \text{hen I}\ldots\end{array}}$$

The spoken forms must be read [hɔt] and [hœn] with strong lip-rounding. They cannot be [hæt] and [hen] as the spelling might suggest. The omission of *w* is Swift's clue for the eye that the form is in little language. The function of the words as interrogatives prevents their being confused when reading with the nouns *hat* and *hen*. Phonetically they are quite different.

This same prosodic key signature explains Swift's mutant 'sollahs' for 'sirrahs', and the variant oo/ee pronouns where they can be identified with certainty. It is often difficult from the MSS to decide which to write. In fact in the little language it is of no consequence. The use of *ee* would indicate that the initial palatal element of the normal form [ju:] was maintained in the word as a whole, giving a front rounded vowel quality in the mutant form. *ee* cannot be considered a mutant of the plural form [ji:] ye. The variants oo/ee are used for 'you' and 'your' alike. The form 'oor' for 'your' is also found but with no variant.

2. The form 'richar' for 'little' is also explicable in terms of *w* as a word prosody. In normal speech word-initial *r* is labialized and has a dark tamber no matter what the following vowel. Word-initial *l* is clear in tamber and only labialized where the following vowel is rounded. Thus in pronouncing the words 'root' and 'loot' the lip position is rounded throughout. The difference is in the clear tamber and the tip contact for *l* as opposed to the dark tamber and absence of contact for *r*. In pronouncing 'reap' and 'leap' the lip-action is different. There will be initial rounding for 'reap' but not for 'leap'. The dark tamber of the *r* is also very plain before a following front vowel. The substitution of a labio-velarized [ɹ] for [l] in the little language is therefore in harmony with the *w* prosody of the whole.

Similarly we may support by the prosodic evidence the view that the medial *ch* is to be read as an affricate [tʃ] in this word, giving the spoken form [ɹitʃəɹ]. The affricate is labialized in English no matter what the following vowel, unlike the plosives which show a more complicated system. Thus the substitution of [tʃ] for [t] in this word would make prosodic sense. The view that 'richar' is to be read [ɹikəɹ] would take no account of labialization as a word prosody.[18] The phonetic form [ɹikəɹ] might find support in the one instance of the form 'ickle' in the Farewell coda on p. 566. I take this, however, to be a misreading of an obliteration. The MS equally supports the reading 'richar'. The use of the letter *a* in the final syllable of 'richar' is no more than a visual device to differentiate the form from the normal word 'richer', and the form 'richr' is also found. The phonetic form could have a syllabic *r* in this position.

The opposite substitution of *l* for *r*, which is even more common in terms of letter change, might seem to contradict the argument. As has already been shown it necessarily follows that normal *r* forms must be mutant *l* forms and vice versa if we take longer stretches into account and state a mutation by inversion. E.g. O Rold hat a Cruttle (O Lord what a clutter). In other cases this substitution serves to bring a word into the little language: 'you know the Reason, LT and Eltee plonounced the same'.

3. Further *r* substitutions illustrate other phonetic patterns. In medial position in the word 'Madam' *r* is substituted for *d*. This substitution is not found elsewhere. The word 'Madam' belongs almost exclusively to the little style and is frequently collocated with 'Ppt' or 'Dd'. It needs a little form and this is the only possible substitution. It is probable that the phonetic form of this word was [mæɾəm]. It might be inferred that Swift used a flapped *r* in medial position rather than a fricative in his normal speech, which would not be unusual in words like *very, carry*.[19] But the form 'Maram' may merely indicate a lax articulation of this word with momentary contact of the *d*, without any special implication for intervocalic *r* in Swift's normal speech.

In final position *l* is often substituted for *r*, one of the commonest little forms being 'deel' for 'dear'. The complementary ee/ea alternance illustrates again the two sides of the problem. It may indicate that the closer vowel [i:] is substituted for [iə] as being more compatible with final *l*. This would point to a clear *l* in final position, and be evidence of an Irish trait in Swift's pronunciation. Or it might only be a visual device to differentiate 'deel' from the normal word 'deal' with which it has no connection. The forms 'dee' and 'deelest' for 'dear' and 'dearest' also occur. It seems likely that there was a phonetic difference and that [di:], [di:l] and [di:list] replace [diə], [diəɹ] and [diəɹist].

Finally, this one sentence in the little language illustrates most of the *r*/*l* problems: Bed oo paadon Maram, I'm drad oo rike oo Aplon, no harm I hope. (Beg your pardon Madam, I'm glad you like your apron, no harm I hope.) The form 'paadon' contrasts with the normal 'harm'. Is Swift here representing, with a tinge of mockery, an English pronunciation without *r* [pa:dn] for [paɹdn]? This might be further evidence of his Irish accent and of his awareness of it. If not, this is a purely graphic substitution.

It is not possible to take all the mutations in detail but three others are of special interest for different reasons. The examples are italicized:

Letter 41: I assure oo *it im* vely rate now. But *zis* goes to morrow.

Letter 46: I'm angry almost: but I won't tause *see im* a dood dallar in odle *sings, iss* and *so im* DD too.

Letter 42: and oo lost oo money at Cards & dice *ze Givars* device.

it im, see im, so im are mutant forms of *it is, she is* and *so is.* They can be stated as substitutions of *m* for 'voiced *s*' but it is more important to recognize them as simplifications of a verbal system, [aim, si:m] for the more complicated [aim, ʃi:z]. This simplification extends to the past tense 'I wam vely kick' [ai wəm veli kik] for I was very sick [ai wəz veri sik]. There is further evidence in the passage, p. 563: 'I believe I scaped the new feaver . . . because I am not well, but why should Dd scape it pray. *she is mel*thigal oo know and ought to have the Feavr'. The italicized form should be reckoned a mutated verbal form with a final nasal consonant and in speaking it the *m* should be lengthened and form a syllable to link the verb with the adjective. The meaning 'she is a healthy girl' is not affected but the interpretation of the mutation is. It is not a substitution of *m* for *h*, nor a substitution of *m* for *n* after elision of *h* as Moorhead's rendering 'she is an healthy girl' seems to suggest. If this were accepted it would imply that 'healthy' can be classed with words such as 'hotel' or 'historic' which have variant aspirate and non-aspirate forms i.e. *a hotel* [ə houˈtel] or *an hotel* [ən ouˈtel, ən houˈtel]; *a historic* [ə hisˈtərik] or *an historic* [ən isˈtərik, ən hisˈtərik]. Is there any possibility of this? No, Swift has changed key from normal to little in the middle of the phrase. The omission of *h* made difficulties for word division. The phonetic form is more likely to be [ʃi:im̩ ˈelθigæl] than [ʃi: iz ˈmelθigæl].

The mutant forms *zis, sings, ze* and *iss* for 'this', 'things', 'the' and 'yes' illustrate an important principle which is generally observed. Swift respects certain prosodic distinctions of normal forms so that voiceless sounds are substituted for voiceless and voiced for voiced; the distinction between long and short vowels is maintained, the syllabic structure and number of syllables in a word are kept or the absence of a syllable indicated where necessary. He has at the same time to keep within the framework of English spelling. In these examples initial *z* for *th* in *zis* and *ze* indicates a phonetic alternance [z/ð], initial *s* for *th* in *sings* means [s/θ], thus voiced for voiced and voiceless for voiceless. In the final position in *sings* no change is called for since there is no final mutation here. This sibilant will be phonetically a voiceless lenis (or perhaps a partially voiced) alveolar fricative following the voiced nasal [-ŋz̥] in this word; in a word such as 'sticks' the sibilant would be voiceless and fortis following the voiceless plosive [-ks], in accordance with the regular phonetic patterns of English. In the form *iss* meaning 'yes' the doubling of the consonant is necessary to indicate a voiceless fortis sibilant and to differentiate the word in writing from the normal word 'is'. These facts must be taken into account when there are disputed readings of obliterated texts.

The interpretation of the word *Givars* as 'devil's' is certainly right. The suggestion that Swift might have written *givar's* where Deane Swift has *givers* (Letter 5, p. 42) seems also likely. The form is an exceptional one since only *v* remains to connect it with the normal form. It is perhaps a fanciful suggestion but I believe that this word should be read with an affricate [dʒivəɹz] and not a plosive [givəɹz] for two reasons. The vowel of the first syllable seems to suggest an Irish pronunciation and in Dublin affrication of the initial plosive is not unknown [dzivil]. Coupled with labialization [dʒ] would be the expected substitution for [dz]. It seems, too, that the spelling and pronunciation of Givar might owe something to the name Giffard [dʒifəɹd]. The references to Lady Giffard in the *Journal* are far from friendly. Was it a long-standing private joke between Stella and Swift to link the words 'devil' and 'Giffard' in their little language? Elsewhere, when 'devil' is used as an expletive, Swift writes D——. If the notion that Givar was pronounced [dʒivəɹ] is accepted then it provides a substitution [d/dʒ] to match with [t/tʃ] in the word 'richar'. If not, then we have a substitution [g/d] which reverses the [d/g] substitution in 'drad' for 'glad'.

The mutations have not all been accounted for but the examples serve to illustrate the application of certain aspects of prosodic techniques of analysis to the problems of the little language. The further problems of the monograms and codas must be left aside. The concluding examples illustrate the relevance of grammatical and collocational criteria to the interpretation of two obliterated texts, and of contextual criteria to two instances in clear texts.

In Letter 57 the first entry for Christmas Day has been read through heavy obliterations as: 'A melly Tlismas; melli Tlismas, I sd it first. I wish oo a sousand' zoll, with halt and soul.' The Oxford footnote to this (n. 16, p. 588) reads: 'The sentence, heavily scored through, is difficult to decipher. This, which is also Moorhead's reading, seems to be justified. Ryland and Aitken read: "All melly Titmasses—melly Titmasses—I said it first—I wish it a souzand [times] zoth with halt and soul.' If "zoll" be right it probably means "fold"; "halt" stands for "heart".'

There are difficulties in accepting 'zoll' to mean 'fold'. First it introduces a new substitution *z* for *f* instead of the usual initial mutation [z/ð]. The change of voiced from voiceless [z/f] is against the normal pattern. Then we have elision of final *d*. In -ld clusters it is Swift's habit to omit the *l*, giving 'cod' for 'cold'. Finally why should the *l* be doubled, since the vowel is not short nor is there a word 'zol' which might lead to misunderstanding? Four exceptional devices to explain in one word are altogether too many. There is one other compelling reason for rejecting 'fold'. Both the Everyman and Oxford texts agree in putting an apostrophe at the end of 'sousand' and a comma after 'zoll'. What can this apostrophe mean? 'Thousand's fold' is not English. In the MS the apostrophe seems to be placed between the two words and could equally well be taken with the second word to indicate the omission of a syllable at this point. The comma following 'zoll' and the word 'with' between 'zoll' and 'halt' are hard to justify. It also seems that there is a tailed letter to be accounted for before the word 'halt'. With this in mind I propose the reading: I wish oo a sousand, 'zall my halt and soul. (I wish you a thousand, with all my heart and soul.) The word 'with' is justified by the apostrophe to indicate the omission of 'wi-', and by the substitution of *z* for final *th*. There is the same problem of word division as was found with 'melthigal'. The *z* here should be prolonged to constitute a syllable. The word 'my' accounts for the tailed letter. The resulting collocation 'with all my heart and soul' seems more usual than 'with heart and soul' though this in itself is possible. The present reading 'I wish you a thousand' fold, with heart and soul' is not.

The second obliterated passage is 'O poo ppt, lay down ee heads aden; fais I flodive ee'. (Letter 53, p. 563.) This is Moorhead's reading, too. 'Ppt' is never used except to refer to Stella alone, so the meaning 'O poor Stella, lay down your heads again; faith I forgive you' must be nonsense. The word is surely 'hands' not 'heads'. Stella has got her hands raised in supplication, Swift is saying. There seems no difficulty in reading 'hands' from the MS.

Finally, to illustrate the importance of contextualization for the detailed interpretation of the text, there is an instance where the Oxford text has followed the Everyman text in a misreading of Hawkesworth's 1766 text of Letter 54. The entry for Oct. 30th, p. 569, begins:

> The duchess of Ormond found me out to-day, and made me dine with her. Lady Masham is still expecting. She has had a cruel cold. I could not finish my letter last post for the soul of me. Lord Bolingbroke has had my papers these six weeks, and done nothing to them. Is Tisdall yet in the world? I propose writing controversies, to get a name with posterity. The duke of Ormond will not be over these three or four days.

There is no thread connecting items in this passage so there need not be a link between successive sentences. But the sentence 'I propose writing controversies, to get a name with posterity' jars with the rest of the piece. If it is to be taken seriously it is out of place in the middle of a sequence of random items. It is also not typical of Swift's character and literary habits since much of his work was unsigned. Could Hawkesworth have omitted some personal sentences on either side? The Hawkesworth text in fact correctly reads: 'Is Tisdall yet in the world? I suppose writing controversies, to get a name with posterity'. The two sentences go together and Swift is poking fun at Tisdall, not for the first time. In the Oxford Introduction, p. xxxi, we read: 'Tisdall, if a man of some intellectual ability, mistook his gifts in rating himself a leading political pamphleteer, and he seems to have been a tedious character.' A footnote says: 'he published several controversial pamphlets, 1700 to 1715, when, with the Whig supremacy, he found it safer to remain silent.' The contextual meaning of the sentence with 'I propose writing' is wrong and its grammatical structure is different. 'I propose writing' can be taken as a colloquial alternative to 'I propose to write'. The subject is in this sentence. The alternatives to 'I suppose writing' are either the expanded form 'I suppose he is writing' or the colloquial alternatives with the tag phrase 'I suppose' following 'controversies' or at the end of the sentence: 'Writing controversies, I suppose, to get a name with posterity' or 'Writing controversies to get a name with posterity, I suppose.' In either case the subject must be sought in the previous sentence. Whoever first misread Hawkesworth's original text failed to appreciate this fact and subsequent editors (but not Hayward) have continued the mistake.

An example from Letter 26 (July 17, 1711), p. 315, illustrates the reverse of the situation above. Here again we have a passage of unrelated sentences:

> I long for a Wexford letter; but must not think of it yet: your last was finished but three weeks ago. It is d—d news you tell me of Mrs. F—; it makes me love England less a great deal. I know nothing of the trunk being left or taken; so 'tis odd enough, if the things in it were mine; and I think I was told that there were some things for me, that my mother left particularly to me. I am really sorry for —; that scoundrel — will have his estate after his mother's death. Let me know if Mrs. Walls has got her tea:

A footnote reads: 'The allusion may be to Mrs. Fenton, Swift's sister (p. 101, n. 38), for he passes on to speak of "some things in a trunk, which he had not received, although he understood them to have been left him by his mother."' It is not possible with certainty to reject this identification, but the reason given for it is not convincing. Swift is answering points in Stella's letter open before him. Can we be sure that the reference to Mrs. F—— was followed immediately in Stella's letter by mention of the trunk? The two items seem to me to have no connection. There is other evidence in the *Journal* which is against the identification. Wherever else Mrs. Fenton is mentioned her name is given in full with two exceptions. The abbreviation 'Mrs. F.' (p. 357) is used once where the full name has just been mentioned. The other reference said to be to her is to 'poor Jenny', Letter 30, p. 368. The Mrs. F—— of the July 1711 passage seems to have been harshly treated in England. As n. 2 to Letter 30, p. 357, makes clear, Mrs. Fenton did not enter Lady Giffard's service until Sept. 1st, 1711, which is two months later than the passage in question. In Letter 11, p. 136, dated Dec. 1710 Swift writes: 'I had another letter from Mrs. Fenton who says you were with her.' This must mean in Ireland. Was Mrs. Fenton in England some time prior to July 1711? The *Journal* does not say.

What was the purpose here in disguising the identity by writing Mrs. F——? Two other names are omitted in this same passage and we must ask whether this was Swift's doing or whether it was Deane Swift's subsequent editing. It was unusual for Swift to obscure names and if it was he it could only be explained by the fact that he was referring to Stella's letter and did not need to repeat them. If Deane Swift struck them out it would be because he did not wish to give offence by using the full name. Mrs. Fenton, however, died in 1738, thirty years before the publication of these letters by Deane Swift.

An alternative conjecture might be that this Mrs. F—— is Mrs. Filby, Stella's sister Anne, who is otherwise only referred to as 'Stella's sister' (p. 39), 'your Sister' (p. 564) or 'a relation of Ppts whose Affairs she has so at heart' (p. 564). Her husband's name is given—he was a stupid person and Swift was having difficulty in getting him a job—and Swift talks of having 'taken down his name & his Case (not her Case)...' as if Stella were pleading on behalf of her sister (p. 565). If this identification were right it could show that Anne was already married in 1711. This would still not completely explain the footnote on p. 39: 'Anne Johnson, Stella's younger sister by over two years... was baptized 12 Aug. 1683.... She seems to have been unmarried at this time (Oct. 1710), for it is not till the latter part of 1712 that we meet with the name of her husband Filby, for whom Swift was soliciting employment.... Nanny Filby, who entered the service of Lady Giffard, in Aug. 1718, was, presumably, a daughter.' Could so young a child be taken into service? If the name Filby were substituted for Fenton in the July 1711 passage it would be necessary to prove she was married and in England at the time Swift was writing, and also whether she was still alive when Deane Swift printed his text in 1768.

There are other instances which suggest that analysis in contextual terms might offer more satisfying solutions to some remaining puzzles. But the contextual theory of meaning, valuable as it is in its application to details, finds its main justification in its wider uses, because it helps us to understand and to make explicit how, to quote Firth's phrase, 'we use language to live'. Language was Swift's life and some of the facets of that life are revealed to us in this text of many languages—the *Journal to Stella*. It is a fascinating text which still provides problems for the linguist.

Notes

1 Jonathan Swift, *Journal to Stella*, ed. J.K. Moorhead (Everyman's Library No. 757, 1924, reprinted 1948), p. xviii.

2 Jonathan Swift, *Gulliver's Travels and Selected Writings in Prose and Verse*, ed. J. Hayward (Nonesuch Press, Bloomsbury, 1944), p. 857.

3 Jonathan Swift, *Journal to Stella*, ed. Harold Williams, 2 vols. (Clarendon Press, Oxford, 1948), p. lv. All page references in the paper are to this edition.

4 See R.H. Robins, 'John Rupert Firth', *Lg* 37.2 (April–June 1961), which gives a bibliography.

5 Add. MSS 4804.

6 J.R. Firth, 'Personality and Language in Society', *Papers in Linguistics* 1934–1951 (Oxford University Press, 1957), p. 182.

7 This phrase is still used in Court Circulars. It now refers only to the Monarch and the pronoun has a capital letter—'honoured them with His/Her Presence'.

8 Cf. Irvin Ehrenpreis, 'Swift's "Little Language" in the *Journal to Stella*', *Studies in Philology* 45 (1948), pp. 82–83: '. . . those obvious examples of "baby talk" which editors of the *Journal* have agreed in classifying as the little language and which have been satisfactorily translated.' His count of 'fairly regular substitution of certain consonantal sounds for one another' is as follows: 'Each of the following may be found at least the number of times noted in the parentheses: "d" for "th" (2) or for hard "g" (6); "g" for "d" (2) or for 'l" (1); "h" for "w" (1); "k" or "ck" for "t" (4); "l" for "r" (45); "m" for voiced "s" (2); "n" for "m" (2); "r" for "l" (21), for "d" (1), or for "u" (1); "s" for "th" (6); "t" for "th" (1) or for "k", "ck", "ch", or "c" (13); "z" for voiced "th" (7) or for soft "g" (2). These estimates take no account of repetitions of the same specimen; while "deelest" for "dearest" occurs scores of times, it is counted only once. Similarly, words of unclear meaning are left out of the calculations.'

9 Letter 43, p. 510: Ld Treasr has lent the long Lettr I writt him, to Prior, and I can't get Prior to return it; and I want to have it printd, and to make up this Academy for the Improvemt of our Language. Fais we nevr shall improve it as much as FW has done. Sall we? No fais, ourrichar Gangridge. (Faith we never shall improve it as much as FW has done. Shall we? No faith, our little language.) This is the only example of the monogram 'FW' outside the Farewell coda.

10 Oxford, p. 507, n. 48: 'All editors before Moorhead print "the". Swift wrote "yr" because Burton was a Dublin banker.'

11 Oxford, p. 550, n. 13, p. 557, n. 3. Williams calls attention to the exceptional occurrence of a date number half-way through a line in these letters.

12 See n. 9 above.

13 The translation of 'lole' is conjectural, but does not affect the point here. The meaning of this word will be considered along with the monograms in a separate paper.

14 Oxford, p. lvi–lvii: '"MD" or "Md", My dear or My dears, may either be Stella alone or denote both the ladies. "D", or "Dd", is Dingley, and she is sometimes indicated by "Me", which may be Madam Elderly. Swift himself is "Pdfr" pronounced "Podefar" perhaps Poor Dear Foolish Rogue, or a slurred Poor Dear Fellow. "FW" seems to serve both for Farewell and Foolish Wenches.'

15 The Everyman and Oxford versions of this text have a mistake in one sentence. See p. 496.

16 I cannot help feeling that the 'leaf from Swift's "Journal to Stella"' referred to in n. 1, p. *l* of the Oxford Introduction, if it did exist and was genuine, might have been from the missing Letter 54 rather than from Deane Swift's set of letters; he might well have burned his originals, especially if he had guessed freely what was behind an obliterating scrawl.

17 Cf. Ehrenpreis, *Studies in Philology* 45 (1948), p. 80.

18 I must confess that this possibility did not occur to me until I read Ehrenpreis: 'Although there is no example besides "richar" of "ch" replacing "t", there is one of "t" replacing "ch": "Tlismas" for "Christmas". Furthermore, there are two replacements of "t" by "ck" and many replacements of "c" (sounded "k") by "t".'

19 In my own speech *very*, *carry*, *herring* are frequently pronounced with a flapped *r* with no labialization; this pronunciation is only possible for me in monomorphemic words with initial stress and, principally, with front vowels. In the monomorphemic word *story* where the vowel is a back one, and in the dimorphemic words *starry* and *hearing*, I use a fricative with weak lip rounding.